Life after Dictatorship

Life after Dictatorship launches a new research agenda on authoritarian successor parties worldwide. Authoritarian successor parties are parties that emerge from authoritarian regimes, but that operate after a transition to democracy. They are one of the most common but overlooked features of the global democratic landscape. They are major actors in Africa, Asia, Europe, and Latin America, and have been voted back into office in over one-half of all third-wave democracies. This book presents a new set of terms, definitions, and research questions designed to travel across regions, and presents new data on these parties' prevalence and frequent return to power. With chapters from leading Africanists, Asianists, Europeanists, and Latin Americanists, it asks: Why are authoritarian successor parties so common? Why are some more successful than others? And in what ways can they harm – or help – democracy?

James Loxton is Lecturer in Comparative Politics in the Department of Government and International Relations at the University of Sydney. His research interests include authoritarian regimes, democratization, and political parties, with a focus on Latin America. He is the coeditor of *Challenges of Party-Building in Latin America* (Cambridge University Press, 2016).

Scott Mainwaring is the Jorge Paulo Lemann Professor for Brazil Studies at the Harvard Kennedy School. His research interests include political parties and party systems, democratic and authoritarian regimes, and political institutions in Latin America. Among his many books is the award-winning *Democracies and Dictatorships in Latin America: Emergence, Survival, and Fall* (with Aníbal Pérez-Liñán, Cambridge University Press, 2013). He was elected to the American Academy of Arts and Sciences in 2010. His edited book, *Party Systems in Latin America: Institutionalization, Decay, and Collapse*, was published by Cambridge University Press in 2018.

6	The Survival of Authoritarian Successor Parties in Africa: Organizational Legacies or Competitive Landscapes? *Adrienne LeBas*	206
7	The Contrasting Trajectories of Brazil's Two Authoritarian Successor Parties *Timothy J. Power*	229

PART III WHAT ARE THE EFFECTS OF AUTHORITARIAN SUCCESSOR PARTIES ON DEMOCRACY? 255

8	Mexico's PRI: The Resilience of an Authoritarian Successor Party and Its Consequences for Democracy *Gustavo A. Flores-Macías*	257
9	Game for Democracy: Authoritarian Successor Parties in Developmental Asia *Dan Slater and Joseph Wong*	284
10	Reluctant Democrats: Old Regime Conservative Parties in Democracy's First Wave in Europe *Daniel Ziblatt*	314
	Conclusion: Life after Dictatorship *James Loxton*	336

Bibliography	360
Index	398

Contents

List of Figures	page vii
List of Tables	ix
List of Contributors	xi
Preface	xvii
List of Acronyms	xxii

	Introduction: Authoritarian Successor Parties Worldwide *James Loxton*	1
PART I	**WHY DO AUTHORITARIAN SUCCESSOR PARTIES EXIST (AND OFTEN WIN ELECTIONS)?**	51
1	Linkage Strategies of Authoritarian Successor Parties *Herbert Kitschelt and Matthew Singer*	53
2	Authoritarian Successor Parties in South Korea and Taiwan: Authoritarian Inheritance, Organizational Adaptation, and Issue Management *T. J. Cheng and Teh-fu Huang*	84
3	Personalistic Authoritarian Successor Parties in Latin America *James Loxton and Steven Levitsky*	113
PART II	**WHAT EXPLAINS VARIATION IN AUTHORITARIAN SUCCESSOR PARTY PERFORMANCE?**	143
4	Victims of Their Own Success: The Paradoxical Fate of the Communist Successor Parties *Anna Grzymala-Busse*	145
5	Authoritarian Successor Parties in Sub-Saharan Africa: Into the Wilderness and Back Again? *Rachel Beatty Riedl*	175

CAMBRIDGE
UNIVERSITY PRESS

University Printing House, Cambridge CB2 8BS, United Kingdom

One Liberty Plaza, 20th Floor, New York, NY 10006, USA

477 Williamstown Road, Port Melbourne, VIC 3207, Australia

314–321, 3rd Floor, Plot 3, Splendor Forum, Jasola District Centre, New Delhi – 110025, India

79 Anson Road, #06–04/06, Singapore 079906

Cambridge University Press is part of the University of Cambridge.

It furthers the University's mission by disseminating knowledge in the pursuit of education, learning, and research at the highest international levels of excellence.

www.cambridge.org
Information on this title: www.cambridge.org/9781108426671
DOI: 10.1017/9781108560566

© James Loxton and Scott Mainwaring 2018

This publication is in copyright. Subject to statutory exception and to the provisions of relevant collective licensing agreements, no reproduction of any part may take place without the written permission of Cambridge University Press.

First published 2018

Printed in the United States of America by Sheridan Books, Inc.

A catalogue record for this publication is available from the British Library.

Library of Congress Cataloging-in-Publication Data
NAMES: Loxton, James, editor. | Mainwaring, Scott, 1954– editor.
TITLE: Life after dictatorship : authoritarian successor parties worldwide / edited by James Loxton, Scott Mainwaring.
DESCRIPTION: Cambridge, United Kingdom ; New York, NY : Cambridge University Press, 2018. | Includes bibliographical references and index.
IDENTIFIERS: LCCN 2018005016| ISBN 9781108426671 (hbk) | ISBN 9781108445412 (pbk)
SUBJECTS: LCSH: Dominant-party systems – Case studies. | Authoritarianism – Case studies.
CLASSIFICATION: LCC JF2051 .L446 2018 | DDC 324.2/1–dc23
LC record available at https://lccn.loc.gov/2018005016

ISBN 978-1-108-42667-1 Hardback
ISBN 978-1-108-44541-2 Paperback

Cambridge University Press has no responsibility for the persistence or accuracy of URLs for external or third-party internet websites referred to in this publication and does not guarantee that any content on such websites is, or will remain, accurate or appropriate.

Life after Dictatorship

Authoritarian Successor Parties Worldwide

Edited by

JAMES LOXTON
University of Sydney

SCOTT MAINWARING
Harvard University

Figures

I.1	Authoritarian successor parties in third-wave democracies, 1974–2010	page 8
1.1	Use of clientelism by former authoritarian ruling parties	73
2.1a	Presidential elections in South Korea, 1987–2012	87
2.1b	Presidential elections in Taiwan, 1996–2012	87
2.2a	Legislative elections in South Korea, 1988–2012	88
2.2b	Legislative elections in Taiwan, 1992–2012	89
2.3a	Ethnic identity in Taiwan, 1991–2000	91
2.3b	National identity in Taiwan, unification vs. independence, 1996–2003	91
2.4	Changes in party identification in Taiwan, 1992–2017	92
4.1a	Votes for reinvented communist successor parties	156
4.1b	Votes for orthodox communist successor parties	156
4.2a	Communist successor party membership: Polish SLD	167
4.2b	Communist successor party membership: Hungarian MSzP	167
5.1	ASPs in Sub-Saharan Africa: electoral performance by country	180
5.2	Model of the argument	186
5.3	Economic performance of authoritarian incumbent prior to defeat: Benin, Ghana, Senegal, and Zambia	188
5.4	Economic performance of new ruling parties: Ghana, Senegal, and Zambia	188
7.1	Genealogy of the two authoritarian successor parties in Brazil	231
7.2	The authoritarian DNA of Brazil's major parties in the first five democratically elected legislatures	236
7.3	Sympathy for military prerogatives among major Brazilian parties in the first five democratically elected legislatures	237
7.4	Reputational conservatism among Brazil's major parties, 1990–2013	238

7.5	Estimating left–right placement of major Brazilian parties in the first decade of democracy: manifesto method vs. elite surveys	240
7.6	Share of lower house seats won by the two Brazilian authoritarian successor parties, 1986–2014	243
7.7	Share of municipal mayoralties won by the two Brazilian authoritarian successor parties, 1988–2016	244
8.1	PRI performance in Congress, 1979–2015	262
8.2	States, GDP, population, and municipalities governed by the PRI, 1989–2015	265
8.3	Network average prime-time audience share (%)	274
8.4	Party identification in Mexico, 1991–2012	277
9.1	Polity scores by year: Taiwan, South Korea, and Indonesia	292
9.2	Conceding to thrive and moderating to stabilize	295
10.1	Legacy of conservative party strength and 1922 Carlton Club vote	326

Tables

1.1	Typology of clientelistic exchange	page 61
1.2	Characteristics of countries with each type of party	64
1.3	Electoral strength by party type	65
1.4	Parties' organizational traits: extensiveness and social networks	69
1.5	Organizational characteristics of political parties	70
1.6	Average clientelistic score (b15) by party size and former authoritarian ruling party status	74
1.7	Hierarchical model of clientelistic effort	75
1.8	Hierarchical model of different types of clientelistic effort	77
1.9	Levels of programmatic effort by party origin	78
1.10	Hierarchical model of programmatic effort	79
3.1	Prominent personalistic ASPs in Latin America, 1945–2010	117
4.1	Patterns of reinvention and electoral performance	150
4.2	Correlates of votes for all authoritarian successor parties, mixed-effects regression	157
4.3	Correlates of votes for communist successor parties only, mixed-effects regression	161
5.1	Case selection and independent variable measures	189
6.1	Authoritarian successor party outcomes in Sub-Saharan Africa	214
7.1	Authoritarian successor parties in presidential races in Brazil, 1989–2014	245
10.1	Old regime conservative parties in Europe before 1914	317
10.2	Fragmentation of the right in interwar Europe and democratic breakdown	330

Contributors

Editors

James Loxton is Lecturer in Comparative Politics in the Department of Government and International Relations at the University of Sydney. His research interests include authoritarian regimes, democratization, and political parties, with a focus on Latin America. He is the coeditor of *Challenges of Party-Building in Latin America* (Cambridge University Press, 2016), and is currently writing a book on conservative party-building in Latin America. He holds a PhD in Government from Harvard University.

Scott Mainwaring is the Jorge Paulo Lemann Professor for Brazil Studies at the Harvard Kennedy School. His research interests include political parties and party systems, democratic and authoritarian regimes, and political institutions in Latin America. Among his many books is the award-winning *Democracies and Dictatorships in Latin America: Emergence, Survival, and Fall* (with Aníbal Pérez-Liñán, Cambridge University Press, 2013). He was elected to the American Academy of Arts and Sciences in 2010. His edited book, *Party Systems in Latin America: Institutionalization, Decay, and Collapse*, was published by Cambridge University Press in 2018. From 1983 until 2016, he taught at the University of Notre Dame.

Other Contributors

T. J. Cheng is Class of 1935 Professor of Government at the College of William and Mary. He specializes in comparative political economy and East Asian development. Formerly the editor of *American Asian Review* and currently the editor of *Taiwan Journal of Democracy*, he has published numerous journal articles, book chapters, and has coauthored or coedited several volumes. Among his recent publications are "China's Foreign Exchange Reserves" in the *Journal of Post-Keynesian Economics*, *Routledge Handbook on East Asian Democratization*, and *Public Opinion, National Security and Asymmetric Dyads*. He holds a PhD from the University of California, Berkeley.

Gustavo A. Flores-Macías is Associate Professor of Government at Cornell University and the 2017–18 Democracy and Development Fellow at Princeton University. He is the author of *After Neoliberalism? The Left and Economic Reforms in Latin America* (2012), which won the Latin American Studies Association's Tomassini Award. His research on political economy and state capacity has appeared in such journals as *American Political Science Review, Comparative Politics, Journal of Conflict Resolution, Journal of Democracy, Journal of Politics, Peace Review, Political Science Quarterly, Studies in Comparative International Development*, and as chapters in edited volumes. Before academia, he served as Director of Public Affairs in Mexico's Consumer Protection Agency.

Anna Grzymala-Busse is Michelle and Kevin Douglas Professor of Political Science at Stanford University and Senior Fellow at the Freeman Spogli Institute for International Studies. With a research focus on religion and politics, informal politics, and postcommunist state development in Eastern Europe, she has written about the paradoxical comeback of communist successor parties, party competition and its impact on constraining rent-seeking, state theory, and the unintended consequences of European Union enlargement. Her books include *Rebuilding Leviathan: Party Competition and State Exploitation in Post-Communist Democracies* (Cambridge University Press, 2007) and *Nations under God* (2015). She holds a PhD from Harvard University and previously taught at Yale University and the University of Michigan.

Teh-fu Huang is Adjunct Professor of Political Science at the University of Taipei. Previously, he directed the Election Study Center at National Chengchi University and the Center for Public Opinion and Public Policy at the University of Taipei in Taiwan. His research interests include parties and elections, comparative politics, and political economy. He has contributed to a number of publications, including *Democracy and the New International Order in the 21st Century* (1993), *Taiwan's Electoral Politics and Democratic Transition: Riding the Third Wave* (1996), *Consolidating the Third Wave Democracies* (1997), and *Democratization in Taiwan: Implications for China* (1999). He holds a PhD from Northwestern University.

Herbert Kitschelt is George V. Allen Professor of International Relations at Duke University. He specializes in European studies of comparative political parties and elections in established and new democracies, comparative public policy/political economy, and twentieth-century social theory. His work explains the rise of the new radical right parties in Europe and explores the formation of party systems in postcommunist democracies. He has authored and edited numerous articles and books, including *Post-Communist Party Systems: Competition, Representation, and Inter-Party Cooperation* (with Zdenka Mansfeldova, Radoslav Markowski, and Gabor Toka, 1999) and *Patrons or Policies? Patterns of Democratic Accountability and Political Competition* (with Steven Wilkinson, 2007), both from Cambridge University Press. He holds a PhD from the University of Bielefeld.

Adrienne LeBas is Associate Professor of Government in the School of Public Affairs at American University. A specialist in African politics, her areas of interest include social movements, political parties, and democratization. She is the author of *From Protest to Parties: Party-Building and Democratization in Africa* (2011). Her current book project addresses the causes of persistent electoral violence in some new democracies, and other research examines tax compliance and urban development.

Steven Levitsky is David Rockefeller Professor of Latin American Studies and Professor of Government at Harvard University. His research interests include political parties and party-building, authoritarianism and democratization, and weak and informal institutions, with a focus on Latin America. He is the author of *Transforming Labor-Based Parties in Latin America: Argentine Peronism in Comparative Perspective* (Cambridge University Press, 2003); coauthor of *Competitive Authoritarianism: Hybrid Regimes after the Cold War* (Cambridge University Press, 2010) and *How Democracies Die* (2018); and coeditor of *Argentine Democracy: The Politics of Institutional Weakness* (2005), *Informal Institutions and Democracy: Lessons from Latin America* (2006), *The Resurgence of the Left in Latin America* (2011), and *Challenges of Party-Building in Latin America* (Cambridge University Press, 2016). He is currently writing a book (with Lucan Way) on the durability of revolutionary regimes.

Timothy J. Power is Professor of Latin American Politics at the University of Oxford, where he is a fellow of St. Antony's College. He is the author of *The Political Right in Postauthoritarian Brazil: Elites, Institutions, and Democratization* (2000), a study of the "authoritarian diaspora" of pro-military elites in the wake of Brazil's transition to democracy. His most recent book, with Paul Chaisty and Nic Cheeseman, is *Coalitional Presidentialism in Comparative Perspective: Minority Presidents in Multiparty Systems* (2018).

Rachel Beatty Riedl is Associate Professor of Political Science at Northwestern University, where she is a faculty fellow at the Institute for Policy Research and serves on the Executive Committee of the Program of African Studies. The author of the award-winning *Authoritarian Origins of Democratic Party Systems in Africa* (Cambridge University Press, 2014), she studies institutional development in new democracies, local governance and decentralization policy, and authoritarian regime legacies, with a regional focus on Sub-Saharan Africa. She holds a PhD from Princeton University.

Matthew Singer is Associate Professor of Political Science at the University of Connecticut. His research focuses on Latin America. His research interests include public opinion and voting behavior, with an emphasis on how voters seek to hold politicians accountable for their actions. Singer is the coeditor of *The Latin American Voter: Pursuing Representation and Accountability in Challenging Contexts* and the author of articles published in the *Journal of Politics*, *British Journal of Political Studies*, *Comparative Politics*, *Comparative Political Studies*, the *European Journal of Political Research*, and *Electoral Studies*, among other journals. He holds a PhD from Duke University.

Dan Slater is Professor of Political Science and Director of the Weiser Center for Emerging Democracies (WCED) at the University of Michigan. He specializes in the politics and history of democracy and dictatorship, with a regional focus on Southeast Asia. The author of *Ordering Power: Contentious Politics and Authoritarian Leviathans in Southeast Asia* (Cambridge University Press, 2010), he is currently working with Joseph Wong on a book project that explores the phenomenon of "democracy through strength" in Northeast and Southeast Asia. Earlier articles on this project can be found in *Perspectives on Politics*, *South East Asia Research*, and the *Journal of Democracy*. He has also published in journals such as the *American Journal of Political Science*, *American Journal of Sociology*, *Comparative Politics*, *Comparative Political Studies*, *International Organization*, and *World Politics*. He taught at the University of Chicago from 2005, when he received his PhD from Emory University, until 2017.

Joseph Wong is Ralph and Roz Halbert Professor of Innovation at the Munk School of Global Affairs at the University of Toronto, where he is also Canada Research Chair in Health, Democracy and Development and Professor of Political Science. A former director of the Munk School's Asian Institute, Wong focuses his research on poverty and social policy innovation. He is currently collaborating with Dan Slater on a book about Asia's development and democracy. Among his recent publications are *Innovating for the Global South: Towards an Inclusive Innovation Agenda* (coedited, 2014) and *Betting on Biotech: Innovation and the Limits of Asia's Developmental State* (2011). He holds a PhD from the University of Wisconsin–Madison.

Daniel Ziblatt is Professor of Government at Harvard University. His research interests include democratization, state building, comparative politics, and historical political economy, with a particular interest in European political development. He is the author of *Conservative Parties and the Birth of Democracy* (Cambridge University Press, 2017) and *Structuring the State: The Formation of Italy and Germany and the Puzzle of Federalism* (2006).

List of Contributors

He directs the "Politics through Time" Program, a historical geospatial data collection project at Harvard University. Most recently, he is coauthor (with Steven Levitsky) of *How Democracies Die* (2018). He holds a PhD from the University of California, Berkeley.

Preface

In June 1989, Poland held its first relatively free and fair election in decades. Polish voters used the opportunity to deliver a stunning rebuke to the communist regime: the Polish United Workers' Party, the regime's ruling party, suffered a devastating defeat, with Solidarity, the party of the democratic opposition, winning every contested seat in the lower house and all but one in the Senate. In 1990, Solidarity leader Lech Walesa was elected president, the seemingly happy ending of one of the best-known stories of the third wave of democratization.[1] Less well known is what happened next. In 1993, just three years later, voters used their newly acquired democratic rights to return the old communist party (renamed Social Democracy of the Republic of Poland, SdRP) to power, and in 1995, they elected SdRP leader Aleksander Kwaśniewski president in a matchup against democracy hero Walesa.[2]

This is a book about *authoritarian successor parties*, or parties that emerge from authoritarian regimes but that operate after a transition to democracy.[3] In some cases, such as Poland's SdRP or Taiwan's Kuomintang (KMT), they are former "official" parties of authoritarian regimes that continue to exist after a transition to democracy. In others, such as Spain's People's Party (PP) or Tunisia's Nidaa Tounes, they are new parties formed by high-level authoritarian incumbents shortly before or shortly after a transition to democracy. While many people find the existence and frequent electoral success of such parties counterintuitive – why, in a democracy like Poland, would voters support a party with a history like that of the SdRP? – they are extremely common. As the chapters in this volume show, they are prominent actors in virtually every major world region. In fact, as discussed in the Introduction, prominent authoritarian successor parties have emerged in *nearly three-*

---

[1] On the third wave of democratization, see Huntington (1991).
[2] See Grzymala-Busse (2002: 3).   [3] See Loxton (2015).

quarters of all third-wave democracies and were voted back into office in *over one-half* of all third-wave democracies.

This is not the first book about authoritarian successor parties. Indeed, there is a relatively long history of studying such parties, under a variety of different headings. Scholars of postcommunist Europe have produced a substantial body of work on such parties, and smaller bodies of work have also emerged on Latin America, East and Southeast Asia, and Sub-Saharan Africa.[4] These works have generated important insights. In two groundbreaking books on communist successor parties in East Central Europe, for example, Anna Grzymala-Busse (a contributor to this volume) showed how these parties could draw on "usable pasts" from the previous dictatorship to win votes under democracy, and argued that they could help structure party systems and even improve the quality of democracy.[5] In recent years, there has been a new burst of interest in such parties, with scholars such as Rachel Beatty Riedl, Dan Slater, Joseph Wong, and Daniel Ziblatt (all contributors to this volume) producing innovative and important works on related topics.[6] However, existing works did not conceptualize their subjects as a subset of a larger category of authoritarian successor parties, nor did they employ this term.

One of the editors of this volume (James Loxton) has been part of this new wave of scholarship, focusing in his earlier work on authoritarian successor parties of the right in Latin America.[7] In the course of his research, he became increasingly aware of the worldwide nature of this phenomenon. Authoritarian successor parties could be found everywhere from Mexico to Mongolia, Poland to Panama, Spain to South Korea, Taiwan to Tunisia. The literature, though, did not adequately reflect this. Existing works mostly examined these parties in specific regional contexts. They were often not well known to scholars of different regional interests, limiting the accumulation of knowledge. More fundamentally, political scientists – not to mention the general public – were not aware of just how prevalent these parties were, or how common it was for them to be voted back into office. Indeed, we ourselves were stunned at the prevalence and frequent return to power of authoritarian successor parties.

The goal of this book is to generate new knowledge about authoritarian successor parties and to spark a new scholarly conversation about this extremely widespread – but hitherto underappreciated – aspect of the democratization experience. To this end, it brings together chapters by leading Africanists, Asianists, Europeanists, and Latin Americanists, all of whom either have published on authoritarian successor parties previously or possess deep country or regional knowledge that makes them exceptionally qualified to write on specific parties. In contrast to earlier works on this subject, this volume does not focus on a single region. On the contrary, it is

---

[4] For a discussion of existing works, see the Introduction of this volume.
[5] See Grzymala-Busse (2002, 2007).
[6] See Riedl (2014); Slater and Wong (2013); and Ziblatt (2017).   [7] See Loxton (2014a, 2016).

unabashedly cross-regional in scope, with the aim of drawing attention to – and promoting a new research agenda on – authoritarian successor parties worldwide. Authoritarian successor parties require serious cross-regional analysis, concepts that can travel, and theory-building specific to this category. This volume takes up these challenges. No previous volume has adopted a cross-regional perspective, systematically documented the global prevalence of authoritarian successor parties, or developed a common vocabulary and shared set of research questions.

The chapters focus on three broad puzzles. First, *why do authoritarian successor parties exist (and often win elections)?* When ruling parties of authoritarian regimes win unfair elections, this can be explained by the unevenness of the playing field. However, as discussed in the Introduction, a core defining attribute of authoritarian successor parties is that they operate *in democracy*. This means that they cannot rely on fraud, intimidation, or censorship to win elections. Why, then, do they so often perform well at the ballot box? On this issue, the contributors to this volume are largely in agreement: authoritarian successor parties often benefit from *authoritarian inheritance*. They may inherit valuable resources from the previous dictatorship that, paradoxically, help them to thrive under democracy. In their chapter, Herbert Kitschelt and Matthew Singer show that authoritarian successor parties often inherit large organizations and informal networks that facilitate clientelistic party–voter linkages. Analyzing Taiwan and South Korea, T.J. Cheng and Teh-fu Huang explore how parties inherited strong brands based on a history of economic development and national defense; financial resources; and, in the case of Taiwan's KMT, a vast territorial organization. In their chapter on personalistic authoritarian successor parties in Latin America, James Loxton and Steven Levitsky show how parties benefited from reputations based on the achievements of past dictators in areas ranging from public security to social policy.

Second, *why are some authoritarian successor parties more successful than others?* While these parties have been prominent actors in many countries, they have varied considerably in terms of electoral performance and longevity. Here there is less agreement among authors, with chapters exploring a range of possible causes. These include disappointing governing performance (Anna Grzymala-Busse), the nature of the former authoritarian regime (Rachel Beatty Riedl), the competitive landscape (Adrienne LeBas), and loss of access to state resources (Timothy J. Power). The Introduction explores a number of additional possible causes, including the performance of the former authoritarian regime, the nature and timing of the transition to democracy, electoral institutions, and strategies for dealing with the authoritarian past. The range of explanations offered by the chapters suggests that variation in authoritarian successor party performance is multicausal. Given the lack of consensus on the relative importance of these potential causes, this is a ripe topic for future research.

Finally, *what are authoritarian successor parties' effects on democracy?* In his chapter on Mexico, Gustavo A. Flores-Macías finds that the resilience of the Institutional Revolutionary Party (PRI) has been harmful for democracy, with the party linked to subnational authoritarianism, corruption, and human rights abuses. Some of the chapters, however, offer a more sanguine vision. Dan Slater and Joseph Wong argue that Taiwan's KMT, South Korea's Democratic Justice Party (DJP)/Saenuri, and Indonesia's Golkar played an important role in stabilizing new democratic regimes (and before that, in encouraging transitions to democracy). In his chapter on "old regime conservative parties" in Europe, the first wave's equivalent of authoritarian successor parties, Daniel Ziblatt comes to a similar conclusion, suggesting the robustness of this finding. In short, as discussed in the Introduction, authoritarian successor parties' effects on democracy appear to be neither wholly negative nor wholly positive, but rather *double-edged*.

This book has benefited from previous works on authoritarian successor parties, drawing on them liberally and including several of their authors as contributors. That said, it makes a number of original contributions, breaking new ground at the conceptual, theoretical, and empirical levels. Conceptually, it provides a new set of terms, definitions, and operationalizations – in short, a common language – to facilitate a new research agenda on authoritarian successor parties worldwide. It offers a definition of authoritarian successor parties that can travel across regions and develops concepts such as *authoritarian inheritance* and its opposite, *authoritarian baggage*, which we believe provide a useful framework for analysis. Theoretically, its argument about authoritarian inheritance goes beyond existing works by demonstrating the range of resources that parties may inherit from authoritarian regimes; develops new hypotheses to explain variation in party performance; and provides a more systematic and nuanced account of the double-edged effects of authoritarian successor parties on democracy than has existed previously. Finally, the volume makes a significant empirical contribution by bringing together chapters with a geographical scope unprecedented in the history of research on this subject and by providing new data in Appendix I.1 and Appendix I.2 of the Introduction that illustrate, unequivocally, that authoritarian successor parties are not outliers or regional curiosities, but part and parcel of the democratization experience.

* * * *

In the course of bringing this project to fruition, we benefited from the assistance of many individuals and organizations. We are particularly grateful to the Kellogg Institute for International Studies at the University of Notre Dame, which funded and hosted the two-day conference in April 2015 upon which this volume is based. Particular thanks go to Director Paolo Carozza and Managing Director Sharon Schierling for their encouragement and support; Therese Hanlon for organizing the conference; and Nancy Sawyer Thomas,

Elizabeth Rankin, and Karen Clay for generating materials for it. We would also like to thank Kenneth M. Roberts, who first coined the term "authoritarian successor party"[8] and who provided invaluable feedback.

We benefited from the comments and participation of Michael Albertus, Regina Bateson, Fernando Bizzarro, Rodrigo Castro Cornejo, Michael Coppedge, Sarah Zukerman Daly, Robert Dowd, Robert Fishman, Andrew C. Gould, Victoria Tin-bor Hui, Joy Langston, A. James McAdams, and Erin Metz McDonnell.

We thank our editor at Cambridge University Press, Robert Dreesen, for his support and encouragement. Thanks also to two anonymous reviewers for insightful comments and to María Victoria De Negri for assistance in putting the book together.

---

[8] See K. Roberts (2012).

Acronyms

AD	Democratic Action
ADN	Nationalist Democratic Action
AFORD	Alliance for Democracy
AFP	Alliance of the Forces for Progress
ANAP	Motherland Party
ANAPO	National Popular Alliance
AP	Popular Action (Peru)
AP	People's Alliance (Spain)
APC	All People's Congress
APR	Alliance for the Republic
APRA	American Popular Revolutionary Alliance
APRC	Alliance for Patriotic Reorientation and Construction
AREMA	Association for the Rebirth of Madagascar
ARENA	National Renovating Alliance (Brazil)
ARENA	Nationalist Republican Alliance (El Salvador)
ARP	Anti-Revolutionary Party
ASP	authoritarian successor party
AVF	General Electoral League
AWS	Solidarity
BDP	Botswana Democratic Party
BNP	Bangladesh Nationalist Party (Bangladesh)
BNP	Basotho National Party (Lesotho)
BSP	Bulgarian Socialist Party
C90	Change 90
CCM	Chama Cha Mapinduzi
CCN	Nationalist Civic Crusade
CDP	Congress for Democracy and Progress
CEDA	Spanish Confederation of Autonomous Rights
CHU	Christian Historical Union
COPEI	Social Christian Party

List of Acronyms

CPN	National Patriotic Coalition
CTM	Confederation of Mexican Workers
DEM	Democrats
DJP	Democratic Justice Party
DK	Democratic Coalition
DKP	German Conservative Party
DLP	Democratic Liberal Party
DNVP	German National People's Party
DPP	Democratic Progressive Party (Malawi)
DPP	Democratic Progressive Party (Taiwan)
DPS	Democratic Party of Socialists of Montenegro
DRP	Democratic Republican Party
FDN	National Democratic Front
FDP	German Free Democrats
FDSN	Democratic National Salvation Front
Fidesz	Young Democrats
FMLN	Farabundo Martí National Liberation Front
FN	National Front
FNV	Velasquista National Federation
FOBAPRA	Fund for Bank Savings Protection
FP	Popular Force
FRELIMO	Mozambique Liberation Front
FRG	Guatemalan Republican Front
FSLN	Sandinista National Liberation Front
FSN	National Salvation Front
FSTSE	Federation of Unions for Workers Employed by the State
GNP	Grand National Party
HZDS	Movement for a Democratic Slovakia
IFE	National Electoral Institute
ISSSTE	Institute for Social Security and Services for State Workers
JAP	Popular Action Youths
KANU	Kenya African National Union
KBL	Kilusang Bagong Lipunan
KMT	Kuomintang
KPK	Corruption Eradication Commission
KPRF	Communist Party of the Russian Federation
KPU	Communist Party of Ukraine
KSČ	Communist Party of Czechoslovakia
KSČM	Communist Party of Bohemia and Moravia
KSS	Communist Party of Slovakia
LDDP	Democratic Labor Party of Lithuania
LDP	Liberal Democratic Party (Japan)

LDP	Liberal Democratic Party (Kenya)
LKP	Liberty Korea Party
LiD	Left and Democrats
LN	National Lottery
LSDP	Social Democratic Party of Lithuania
MAS	Movement toward Socialism
MC	Citizens' Movement
MCP	Malawi Congress Party
MDB	Brazilian Democratic Movement
MDF	Hungarian Democratic Forum
MDN	National Democratic Movement
MIEP	Hungarian Justice and Life Party
MLSTP	Movement for the Liberation of São Tomé and Príncipe
MMD	Movement for Multiparty Democracy
MNSD	National Movement for the Development of Society
MORENA	National Regeneration Movement
MPC	Popular Christian Movement
MPP	Mongolian People's Party
MPRP	Mongolian People's Revolutionary Party
MSzP	Hungarian Socialist Party
NAC	National Affairs Conference
NAP	New Aspiration Party
NCNP	National Congress for New Politics
NDC	National Democratic Congress
NDP	National Democratic Party
NDRP	New Democratic Republican Party
NHI	National Health Insurance
NLD	National League for Democracy
NM	New Majority
NP	National Party (South Africa)
NP	New Party (Taiwan)
NPP	New Patriotic Party
ODM	Orange Democratic Movement
OPZZ	All-Poland Alliance of Trade Unions
OXDP (also PDPU)	People's Democratic Party of Uzbekistan
PAICV	African Party for the Independence of Cape Verde
PAIGC	African Party for the Independence of Guinea and Cape Verde
PAN	National Action Party
PANAL	New Alliance Party
PAP	Progressive Action Party (Cuba)
PAP	People's Action Party (Singapore)
PARM	Authentic Party of the Mexican Revolution

List of Acronyms

PCB	Brazilian Communist Party
PCC	Communist Party of Cuba
PCdoB	Communist Party of Brazil
PCN	Party of National Conciliation
PCR	Romanian Communist Party
PCRM	Party of Communists of the Republic of Moldova
PCT	Congolese Party of Labor
PD	Democratic Party (Romania)
PD	Democrat Party (Indonesia)
PDC	Christian Democratic Party
PDCI	Democratic Party of Côte d'Ivoire
PDIP	Indonesian Democratic Party of Struggle
PDL	Democratic Liberal Party
PDP	People's Democratic Party
PDS	Social Democratic Party (Brazil)
PDS	Party of Democratic Socialism (Germany)
PDS	Senegalese Democratic Party (Senegal)
PDSR	Party of Social Democracy of Romania
PF	Patriotic Front
PFL	Liberal Front Party (or Party of the Liberal Front)
PFP	People First Party
PiS	Law and Justice
PJ	Justicialista Party (also Peronist Party)
PL	Liberal Party
PLD	Dominican Liberation Party
PLN	National Liberation Party (Costa Rica)
PLN	Nationalist Liberal Party (Nicaragua)
PMDB	Party of the Brazilian Democratic Movement
PNC	People's National Congress
PNR	National Revolutionary Party
PNU	Party of National Unity
PO	Civic Platform
PP	Progressive Party (Brazil)
PP	People's Party (Spain)
PPB	Brazilian Progressive Party
PPD	Party for Democracy (Chile)
PPD	Party for Peace and Democracy (South Korea)
PPI	Italian People's Party
PPR	Reformist Progressive Party
PPS	Popular Socialist Party
PR	Republican Party
PRD	Party of the Democratic Revolution (Mexico)
PRD	Dominican Revolutionary Party (Dominican Republic)

PRD	Democratic Revolutionary Party (Panama)
PRI	Institutional Revolutionary Party
PRM	Greater Romania Party (Romania)
PRM	Party of the Mexican Revolution (Mexico)
PRN	Party of National Reconstruction
PRPB	People's Revolutionary Party of Benin
PRSC	Social Christian Reformist Party
PS	Socialist Party of Albania
PS	Socialist Party of Senegal
PSD	Social Democratic Party (Romania)
PSD	Social Democratic Party (São Tomé and Príncipe)
PSD	Social Democratic Party (Brazil)
PSD	Social Democratic Party (Portugal)
PSDB	Brazilian Social Democracy Party
PSL	Polish Peasants' Party
PSM	Socialist Party of Labor
PSOE	Spanish Socialist Workers' Party
PSOL	Socialism and Freedom Party
PSUV	United Socialist Party of Venezuela
PT	Workers' Party
PTB	Brazilian Labor Party
PUP	Unity and Progress Party
PVEM	Mexican Green Ecologist Party
PZPR	Polish United Workers' Party
RB	Renaissance Party of Benin
RDC	Central African Democratic Rally
RDP	Reunification Democratic Party
RENAMO	Mozambican National Resistance
RN	National Renewal
RPP	Rastriya Prajatantra Party
SBY	Susilo Bambang Yudhoyono
SD	Social Democrats
SDA	Social Democratic Alternative
SDL'	Party of the Democratic Left
SDP	Social Democratic Party of Croatia
SDPL	Social Democracy of Poland
SdRP	Social Democracy of the Republic of Poland
SDSM	Social Democratic Union of Macedonia
SKJ	League of Communists of Yugoslavia
SKS	League of Communists of Serbia
SLD	Democratic Left Alliance
Smer-SD	Direction-Social Democracy
SNSP	National Public Safety System
SNTE	National Union of Education Workers

List of Acronyms

SNTSS	National Union of Social Security Workers
SNU	National Youth League of Sweden
SPD	Social Democratic Party of Germany
SPS	Socialist Party of Serbia
SPU	Socialist Party of Ukraine
STPRM	Union of Oil Workers of the Mexican Republic
SzDSz	Alliance of Free Democrats
TNA	The National Alliance
UCD	Union of the Democratic Center
UD	Democratic Union
UDF	United Democratic Front
UDI	Independent Democratic Union
UDPM	Democratic Union of the Malian People
UMNO	United Malays National Organisation
UNIP	United National Independence Party
UNO	Odriísta National Union
UNP	United National Party
UPRONA	Union for National Progress
URD	Union for Democratic Renewal
USDP	Union Solidarity and Development Party
UW	Freedom Union
ZANU-PF	Zimbabwe African National Union-Patriotic Front
ZKS	League of Communists of Slovenia
ZLSD	United List of Social Democrats

Introduction

Authoritarian Successor Parties Worldwide

James Loxton

A surprising feature of democracy in many countries is that large numbers of people, after gaining the right to choose their leaders through free and fair elections, vote for political parties with deep roots in dictatorship. Since the third wave of democratization, *authoritarian successor parties* (ASPs) have become prominent actors in Africa, Asia, Europe, and Latin America (Loxton 2015). In many countries, former authoritarian ruling parties (e.g., Hungarian Socialist Party, MSzP; Taiwan's Kuomintang, KMT; Mexico's Institutional Revolutionary Party, PRI; African Party for the Independence of Cape Verde, PAICV) and parties founded by high-level authoritarian incumbents shortly before or shortly after a transition to democracy (e.g., Spain's People's Party, PP; Bolivia's Nationalist Democratic Action, ADN; Ghana's National Democratic Congress, NDC; Tunisia's Nidaa Tounes) have been voted back into office. Many of them grew out of regimes responsible for large-scale human rights abuses. Nevertheless, there was life after dictatorship: authoritarian successor parties remained major political actors and were frequently voted back into office.

In this introductory chapter, I provide an overview of the concept of authoritarian successor parties and develop an original framework for analyzing them as a worldwide phenomenon. To this end, I present a new set of terms, definitions, and operationalizations – in short, a common language – to facilitate a new research agenda on this topic and present a number of questions to serve as the basis for this agenda. The chapter is structured as follows. In the first section, I offer a minimalist definition that can travel across regions and thus allow for broad comparative analysis. In the second section, I present new data showing that authoritarian successor parties are one of the most common features of democratization worldwide: they have been prominent actors in nearly three-quarters of all third-wave democracies, and they have been voted back into office in over one-half of all third-wave democracies. In the third section, I ask why they are so widespread and argue that much of this is due to *authoritarian inheritance*: they may inherit valuable resources from authoritarian regimes that, paradoxically, help them to thrive under democracy. In the fourth section, I consider the flip side of the ledger – *authoritarian baggage*, or the liabilities of an authoritarian past – and examine the various strategies that parties can employ to offload this baggage. In the fifth section, I ask why some authoritarian successor parties are more successful than others and outline a number of hypotheses to explain variation in their electoral performance and longevity. Finally, I examine the effects of authoritarian successor parties on democracy and argue that these are *double-edged*. While they can be harmful in a number of ways, they can also have surprisingly salutary effects.

DEFINING AUTHORITARIAN SUCCESSOR PARTIES

Authoritarian successor parties are *parties that emerge from authoritarian regimes, but that operate after a transition to democracy* (Loxton 2015).[1] There are two parts to this definition. First, these are parties that operate *after* a transition to democracy. This means that ruling parties of existing authoritarian regimes are excluded, even if the regime in question holds somewhat competitive elections, as in "competitive authoritarian" (Levitsky and Way 2010) or "electoral authoritarian" (Schedler 2013) regimes. To be sure, many authoritarian successor parties begin their lives as authoritarian ruling parties. However, after democratization, they become – if they survive – authoritarian successor parties. To illustrate, Mexico's PRI was an authoritarian *ruling* party until the country's transition to democracy in 2000; thereafter, it became an authoritarian *successor* party. An important implication of this part of the definition is that to win votes, party leaders cannot rely on the "menu of manipulation" (Schedler 2002) used by electoral authoritarian regimes, such as coercion, fraud, or the massive abuse of state resources. Authoritarian successor parties can, and often do, win large numbers of votes. To be considered authoritarian successor parties, however, they must do so while broadly abiding by the democratic rules of the game.[2]

---

[1] For an earlier use of the term "authoritarian successor party," see K. Roberts (2012). Scholars have used various labels for such parties. In the context of the postcommunist world, they have used terms such as "ex-communist parties" (Ishiyama 1997), "communist successor parties" (Bozóki and Ishiyama 2002; Ishiyama 1999a, 1999b), "post-communist parties" (Kitschelt et al. 1999), and simply "successor parties" (Grzymala-Busse 2002). In other contexts, they have used terms such as "continuist parties" (Haggard and Kaufman 1995), "old regime parties" (Tucker 2006), "formerly hegemonic parties" (Langston 2006a), "former dominant parties" (Friedman and Wong 2008), "ex-authoritarian parties" (Jhee 2008), "formerly authoritarian parties" (Slater and Wong 2013), and "authoritarian legacy parties" (Kitschelt and Kselman 2013).

[2] In practice, it can sometimes be difficult to determine with absolute certainty whether this condition has been met, given borderline cases of democracy and the existence in some countries of what Way (2015) calls "pluralism by default," in which there is oscillation between unstable democracy and competitive authoritarianism. In Appendix I.1 and Appendix I.2, I rely on Geddes, Wright, and Frantz's (2014a) widely used Autocratic Regimes Data Set to score regimes. Other chapters in this volume (e.g., LeBas, and Kitschelt and Singer) use alternative operationalizations.

Second, these are parties that emerge from authoritarian regimes. This can happen in one of two ways, corresponding to two distinct subtypes of authoritarian successor party. The first are *former authoritarian ruling parties*. Many authoritarian regimes in the twentieth century – both civilian and military – used "official" parties as instruments of rule.[3] In some regimes, this involved a formal "one-party" arrangement, in which all parties but the ruling party were legally proscribed; in others, it occurred through a "hegemonic party" system, in which opposition parties existed and theoretically could contest for power, but in which competition was severely constrained.[4] Following transitions to democracy, former authoritarian ruling parties often continued to exist (though they sometimes changed their names), thus becoming authoritarian successor parties. Examples include Hungary's MSzP, Social Democracy of the Republic of Poland (SdRP)/Democratic Left Alliance (SLD), Taiwan's KMT, South Korea's Democratic Justice Party (DJP)/Saenuri, Indonesia's Golkar, Mexico's PRI, Brazil's Social Democratic Party (PDS)/Progressive Party (PP), and many others. (See Appendix I.2 for a complete list of prominent authoritarian successor parties since the third wave.)

The second subtype is *reactive authoritarian successor parties*. As the name suggests, these are parties formed in *reaction* to a transition to democracy. They are new parties created by high-level authoritarian incumbents in anticipation of an imminent transition or by former incumbents shortly after a transition. By high-level incumbents, I mean figures such as heads of state, ministers, and key members of the security apparatus.[5] While such parties have received less scholarly attention than former authoritarian ruling parties, they are widespread. Examples include Spain's PP, founded in 1976 (as the People's Alliance, AP) by former ministers of the Franco regime such as Manuel Fraga; Bolivia's ADN, formed in 1979 by former military dictator Hugo Banzer; the Independent Democratic Union (UDI) in Chile, founded in 1983 by hard-line *Pinochetistas* during a regime crisis that they feared would result in democratization; Ghana's NDC, created in 1992 by dictator Jerry John

---

[3] There is a large literature on the role of parties in authoritarian regimes. See, for example, Brownlee (2007a); Gandhi (2008); Geddes (1999); Levitsky and Way (2012); and Smith (2005).

[4] On the distinction between "hegemonic" and "one-party" arrangements, see Sartori (1976).

[5] In dictatorships that last for long periods of time, much of the population is often implicated in the regime in some way. Even Lech Walesa, one of the heroes of Poland's pro-democracy movement and its first democratic president after the fall of communism, is alleged to have served as an informant for the communist regime in the 1970s. (See Joanna Berendt, "Lech Walesa Faces New Accusations of Communist Collaboration," *The New York Times*, February 18, 2016.) In order to prevent the concept from being stretched to the point of meaningless, the definition therefore excludes parties founded by individuals who held low-level positions in the former authoritarian regime.

Rawlings after being forced to initiate a transition to multiparty elections (and eventually full democracy); and Nidaa Tounes, founded in 2012 by figures such as Beji Caid Essebsi, who held numerous ministerial portfolios in Tunisia's authoritarian regime before it was toppled in the "Arab Spring."

I add three notes about this definition. First, it is located relatively high on Sartori's (1970) "ladder of abstraction." As Sartori noted, this is appropriate for concepts designed to travel across regions, and thus for the purposes of this book. One of the major goals of the book is to launch a conversation about authoritarian successor parties as a worldwide phenomenon. To be sure, this is not the first study of such parties. A substantial body of work exists on authoritarian successor parties in the postcommunist world,[6] and smaller but still significant bodies of work also exist on Latin America,[7] East and Southeast Asia,[8] Sub-Saharan Africa,[9] and other regions.[10] To date, however, most of these works have had a regional focus, with only a handful of

---

[6] On postcommunist Europe, see Bozóki (1997); Bozóki and Ishiyama (2002); Dauderstädt (2005); Evans and Whitefield (1995); Grzymala-Busse (2002, 2006, 2007); Higley, Kullberg, and Pakulski (1996); Ishiyama (1995, 1997, 1998, 1999a, 1999b, 1999c, 2000, 2001a, 2006); Ishiyama and Bozóki (2001); Ishiyama and Shafqat (2000); Kitschelt et al. (1999); Kuzio (2008); Lewis (2001); Mahr and Nagle (1995); Orenstein (1998); Rizova (2008); Tucker (2006); and Waller (1995). See also Ágh (1995); Clark and Praneviciute (2008); Doerschler and Banaszak (2007); Grzymala-Busse (1998); Gwiazda (2008); Haughton (2004); Haughton and Rybar (2008); Hough and Koß (2009); Kimmo (2008); Kirchick (2012); Komar and Živković (2016); Kopeček (2013); Kopeček and Pseja (2008); March (2006); Olsen (2007); Patton (1998, 2011); Phillips (1994); Pop-Eleches (1999, 2008); Racz (1993); Rizova (2012); Rybar and Deegan-Krause (2008); Spirova (2008); Stojarová and Emerson (2010); Thompson (1996); Vuković (2015); Ziblatt (1998a); Zimmer and Haran (2008); and Zubek (1994, 1995).

[7] On Latin America, see K. Roberts (2006, 2016) and Loxton (2014a, 2014b, 2016). See also Abente-Brun (2009); Ackerman (2012); Adrogué (1993); Aibar (2005); Azpuru (2003); Cantanhêde (2001); Copeland (2007); Crenzel (1999); Deming (2013); Flores-Macías (2013); Garrard-Burnett (2010); Harding (2001); Holland (2013); Jetté, Foronda, and López (1997); Joignant and Navia (2003); Klein (2004); Koivumaeki (2010, 2014); Kyle (2016); Langston (2006a, 2017); Levitsky and Zavaleta (2016); Luna (2010, 2014); Martí i Puig (2010, 2013); McCann (2015); Meléndez (2014); Olmeda and Armesto (2013); Ortega Hegg (2007); Peñaranda Bojanic (2004); Pérez (1992); Pollack (1999); Power (2000); Ribeiro (2014); Serra (2013); Sivak (2001); Sosa Villagarcia (2016); Thaler (2017); Turner (2014); and Urrutia (2011a, 2011b).

[8] On East and Southeast Asia, see Hicken and Kuhonta (2011, 2015) and Slater and Wong (2013). See also Cheng (2006); Copper (2013); Kim (2014); Muyard (2008); Park (2010); Suh (2015); and Tomsa (2008, 2012).

[9] On Sub-Saharan Africa, see Ishiyama and Quinn (2006) and Riedl (2014). See also Creevey, Ngomo, and Vengroff (2005); Ibrahim and Souley (1998); Marcus (2001); Marcus and Ratsimbaharison (2005); Meyns (2002); and Whitfield (2009); and chapters in Diamond and Plattner (2010), Doorenspleet and Nijzink (2013, 2014), and Villalón and VonDoepp (2005).

[10] On Southern Europe, see Balfour (2005), Hopkin (1999), López Nieto (1998), and Montero (1987). On South Asia, see Hossain (2004). On the Middle East and North Africa, see Masoud (2011, 2013), Romdhani (2014), and Zederman (2016). On "old regime conservative parties" in late nineteenth- and early twentieth-century Europe, see Ziblatt (2017).

Introduction 5

exceptions.[11] An unfortunate by-product of this is that these works have not always been well known to scholars of different regional interests. This has impeded the accumulation of knowledge and, more fundamentally, resulted in an inadequate appreciation of just how common authoritarian successor parties are. Given the diverse regions covered by the chapters in this volume, and the volume's goal of encouraging cross-regional dialogue, I have therefore opted for a broad definition that can travel across space. Scholars focusing on particular countries or regions may wish to move down the ladder of abstraction and adopt a more detailed definition.[12]

Second, this definition focuses on the *origins* of authoritarian successor parties, and is intentionally agnostic about other important issues, such as how the party positions itself toward the legacy of the former authoritarian regime or the extent to which it draws upon that regime's organizational infrastructure. As the chapters in this volume show, authoritarian successor parties vary considerably on these dimensions. Some embrace the past; others run from it. Some deploy large authoritarian-era organizations to engage in clientelism; others win votes primarily on the basis of ideational factors. For this reason, I treat these as "variable properties" rather than "defining properties."[13] Finally, the concept of authoritarian successor parties is used here to refer to parties that emerge from modern authoritarian regimes in the second and third waves of democratization (that is, from 1945 onward).[14] As Ziblatt's chapter shows, however, an important analogue can be seen in the "old regime conservative parties" of first-wave Europe, which are conceptual cousins of modern-day authoritarian successor parties.

---

[11] See Haggard and Kaufman (1995); Jhee (2008); Loxton (2015); Shafquat (1999); and some chapters in Friedman and Wong (2008).
[12] In her work on East Central Europe, for example, Grzymala-Busse (2002: 14) uses a more detailed definition: "*[S]uccessor parties* are defined as the formal descendants of the communist parties – that is, the main political parties that arose from the ruling communist parties in 1989 and that explicitly claim their successor status." Such a move down the ladder of abstraction has the benefit of greater specificity, or what Sartori (1970) called "intension." However, this comes at the cost of inclusiveness, or what Sartori called "extension." Thus, Grzymala-Busse's (2002) definition includes more information about the parties in which she is interested, but excludes those that did not emerge from communist regimes (and therefore most authoritarian successor parties in Africa, Asia, and Latin America), as well as parties that downplay their authoritarian origins.
[13] According to Gibson (1996: 8), "[defining properties] define the concept; they provide the basis for excluding specific cases from the pool of cases being compared. Variable properties are characteristics associated with the concept, but their absence from a specific case does not provide grounds for removing it from the pool of cases being compared."
[14] On the first, second, and third waves of democratization, see Huntington (1991).

A WORLDWIDE PHENOMENON

How prevalent are authoritarian successor parties? How common is it for them to return to power under democracy? To answer these questions, I put together a list of all countries that democratized during the third wave. Drawing on Geddes, Wright, and Frantz's (2014a) Autocratic Regimes Data Set, I included all countries that they scored as having democratized between 1974 and 2010 (see Appendix I.1 for full list).[15] In order to avoid biasing my sample toward consolidated democracies,[16] I included cases where the new democracy later broke down (and in some cases democratized again). The only cases not included were those where the new democracy broke down so quickly that it was not possible to hold even a single free and fair election after the year of the transition (Armenia, Azerbaijan, Mauritania, Russia, Sudan, and Zambia).[17] Excluding such cases was essential, since a core part of the definition of authoritarian successor parties is that they contest elections under democracy. In total, I counted sixty-five countries that had experienced at least one transition to democracy.

I then examined each of these countries to see if a prominent authoritarian successor party emerged (see Appendix I.1 for the list and Appendix I.2 for details). By "prominent," I meant simply winning 10 percent or more in a single national election after the transition to democracy. A party could be scored as an authoritarian successor party *either* by having served as the ruling party of an authoritarian regime *or* if it was formed by high-level authoritarian incumbents in anticipation of a transition to democracy or by former incumbents shortly after a transition (see Appendix I.1 for detailed coding rules). I made a number of conservative coding decisions. First, I excluded parties that had long histories predating authoritarian rule and later became official parties of authoritarian regimes, but that held that position for less than ten years (e.g., National Party in

---

[15] Some of the chapters in this volume use different operationalizations than the one used here (e.g., LeBas, and Kitschelt and Singer). However, as discussed below, using alternative operationalizations of democracy does not affect the main finding of this section about the prevalence and frequent return to power of authoritarian successor parties.

[16] Looking only at democracies that consolidated would have made it impossible to examine one of the possible effects of authoritarian successor parties discussed later in the chapter: that their return to power may trigger an authoritarian regression.

[17] Burundi could arguably be excluded on these grounds, as well. Although its 2005 elections were considered free and fair by observers, its 2010 elections were marred by violence, fraud allegations, and an opposition boycott. (See Human Rights Watch, "Burundi: Violence, Rights Violations Mar Elections," July 1, 2010, www.hrw.org/news/2010/07/01/burundi-violence-rights-violations-mar-elections.) Following the severely flawed follow-up elections in 2015, Freedom House changed its classification of Burundi from "Partly Free" to "Not Free" (https://freedomhouse.org/report/freedom-world/2015/burundi). Nevertheless, in order to avoid ad hoc coding, I include Burundi in my list of third-wave democracies, since Geddes, Wright, and Frantz (2014a) score it as a democracy from 2006 onward.

Introduction 7

Honduras), on the assumption that their pre-authoritarian pasts were likely to have been the main determinants of their identities and resources. Second, I excluded parties created by former high-level authoritarian incumbents more than one election cycle after the transition to democracy (e.g., Slovakia's Direction-Social Democracy, Smer-SD), on the assumption that their leaders were likely to have developed political identities independent of the former authoritarian regime in the intervening years. Finally, I excluded parties founded by authoritarian incumbents who went into opposition before the transition to democracy (e.g., Mexico's Party of the Democratic Revolution, PRD), on the assumption that their role as champions of democratization was likely to have absolved them of their links to the authoritarian regime in the eyes of voters.[18] While including these three types of parties would have expanded my list considerably, I excluded them in order to avoid conceptual stretching. In total, I counted forty-seven countries that had produced at least one prominent authoritarian successor party.

Finally, I looked at each party to see if it had been democratically voted back into office (see Appendix I.1 for the list and Appendix I.2 for details). For this, I set a high bar: *winning the presidency or prime minister's office in an election after the transition year*. Once again, I made a number of conservative coding decisions. First, I excluded cases where the party had contested democratic elections for a time, and then, after a democratic breakdown, returned to power through nondemocratic means (Burundi, Central African Republic), given the definitional requirement that authoritarian successor parties contest free and fair elections. Second, I excluded one case where the party held the presidency for a single term after the transition, but did not hold it in any subsequent election (Brazil), since it never won power in a direct election or in an election after the transition year.[19] Finally, I excluded two cases where the party held cabinet positions in coalition governments after the transition but never held the top job directly (Indonesia, Slovakia), since in countries with multiparty systems, it may be possible to serve as a junior partner in a governing coalition with only minimal electoral support. Again, while including such cases would have expanded my list, I excluded them in order to avoid stretching the concept. In total, I counted thirty-five countries in which an authoritarian successor party had returned to power democratically.

---

[18] One borderline case that I include is Brazil's Liberal Front Party (PFL)/Democrats (DEM). The PFL/DEM emerged from a breakaway faction of the military regime's official PDS in the lead-up to the 1985 founding election. I score it as an authoritarian successor party for two reasons. First, it was not formally created until after the transition to democracy. Second, under democracy, it became the primary destination for former authoritarian incumbents and held such pro-military positions that, even though the PDS was the former official ruling party, the PFL/DEM was "the true heir" of the regime (Power 2000: 80; also Power, Chapter 7, this volume).

[19] For details, see Power (Chapter 7, this volume).

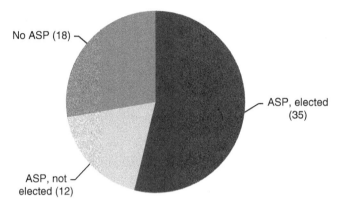

FIGURE I.1 Authoritarian successor parties in third-wave democracies, 1974–2010

In sum, of the sixty-five countries that democratized during the third wave, *forty-seven of them (72 percent) produced prominent authoritarian successor parties, and in a whopping thirty-five countries (54 percent), voters returned these parties to power in democratic elections.*[20]

Notable authoritarian successor parties also emerged in Germany, Cape Verde, São Tomé and Príncipe, Guyana, Suriname, and Tunisia, but were excluded from my count because of small population size;[21] because the party formed after 2010; or, in the case of Germany, because of complications arising from national reunification.[22] In Cape Verde, Suriname, Tunisia, and Guyana, the party was voted back into office. (See table "Other Notable Authoritarian Successor Parties" in Appendix I.2 for details.)

---

[20] This broad finding is robust to changes in the operationalization of democracy. If we use Cheibub, Gandhi, and Vreeland's (2010) Democracy and Dictatorship dataset, we find that seventy-two countries democratized from 1974 to 2008; in fifty-one (71 percent) of these countries, prominent authoritarian successor parties emerged, and in thirty-nine (54 percent), an authoritarian successor party was elected back into office. If we use Freedom House data, we find that forty-four countries made the transition from "Not Free" to "Free" from 1974 to 2015; in thirty (68 percent) of these countries, prominent authoritarian successor parties emerged, and in twenty-three (52 percent), an authoritarian successor party was elected back into office. Data available from the author upon request.

[21] Geddes, Wright, and Frantz (2014a) include in their dataset only countries that had at least 1 million inhabitants as of 2009.

[22] In March 1990, the German Democratic Republic (GDR), or East Germany, held democratic elections, thus ending over four decades of communist rule. Less than a year later, it was absorbed into the Federal Republic of Germany (FRG), or West Germany. Because West Germany had democratized decades earlier during the second wave, and because its population was approximately four times that of East Germany at the time of national reunification, I do not count Germany as a third-wave democracy and thus do not include it in my overall count. However, post-1990 Germany *did* have a prominent authoritarian successor party in the form of the Party of Democratic Socialism (PDS)/The Left, which I discuss in the table "Other Notable Authoritarian Successor Parties" in Appendix I.2.

Introduction

In short, authoritarian successor parties are one of the most common features of the democratization experience – a fact that, to date, has largely been overlooked. They have been prominent actors in nearly *three-quarters* of third-wave democracies, and they have been voted back into office in over *one-half* of third-wave democracies. For better or worse, authoritarian successor parties are a normal part of democracy: it is normal for them to exist, and it is normal for them to return to power.

AUTHORITARIAN INHERITANCE

The widespread existence of authoritarian successor parties – and their frequent success at the ballot box – is puzzling. If the Workers' Party in North Korea or the Communist Party of Cuba "wins" 100 percent of the vote in an uncontested election, this outcome can be dismissed as the product of totalitarian repression. Similarly, if the ruling party of a competitive authoritarian regime, such as Robert Mugabe's Zimbabwe African National Union-Patriotic Front (ZANU-PF) or Malaysia's United Malays National Organisation (UMNO), ekes out an electoral victory, this can be explained by the unevenness of the playing field. However, if a party with roots in dictatorship performs well or is even voted back into office *under free and fair conditions*, that is harder to explain. Yet that is what happens in *most* new democracies. Instead of saying "good riddance" after the fall of dictatorships, voters frequently use their newly acquired democratic rights to vote for parties rooted in regimes that previously ruled them in an undemocratic – and sometimes brutal – manner.

Scholars who have attempted to make sense of this puzzle have found that authoritarian successor parties often succeed under democracy because they inherit valuable resources from the previous authoritarian regime. One of the earliest expressions of this argument can be found in Grzymala-Busse's (2002) seminal study of communist successor parties in East Central Europe. Many of these parties, she argued, benefited from "usable pasts" ("the historical record of party accomplishments to which the elites can point, and the public perceptions of this record") and "portable skills" ("the expertise and administrative experiences gained in the previous regime") (Grzymala-Busse 2002: 5). Particularly in countries such as Poland and Hungary, where authoritarian ruling parties carried out some reforms and engaged with the opposition during the communist period, they entered democracy with reputations for pragmatism and managerial competence, and their cadres possessed many of the skills necessary to thrive in the rough-and-tumble of democratic politics.[23]

---

[23] In his discussion of the "red return," or the return to power of communist successor parties under democracy, Huntington (1996: 8) offers a similar reflection: "[P]erhaps all that the red return signifies is that people who have the political talent to rise to the top in communist systems also have the political talent to rise to the top in democratic systems."

In my own work on authoritarian successor parties of the right in Latin America (Loxton 2014a, 2014b, 2016), and on authoritarian successor parties more broadly (Loxton 2015), I expanded on such findings by developing the concept of *authoritarian inheritance*. Authoritarian inheritance refers to the various resources that authoritarian successor parties may inherit from authoritarian regimes – resources that, paradoxically, can help them to survive, and even thrive, under democracy. Potential forms of authoritarian inheritance go beyond usable pasts and portable skills, and may include (1) a party brand, (2) territorial organization, (3) clientelistic networks, (4) source of party finance, and (5) source of party cohesion.

First, authoritarian successor parties may inherit a *party brand*. "Party brand" is a term used by scholars to denote the ideational component of parties.[24] According to Lupu's (2014, 2016) influential formulation, a party's brand is the image of it that voters develop by observing its behavior over time. Parties with strong brands come to stand for something in the eyes of voters. To the extent that they feel a sense of "comparative fit" between a party's brand and their own views, they become loyal partisans who consistently turn out to vote for it at election time. Brand-building is crucial to party-building. Yet it is not easy to develop a well-known and attractive brand, especially in the face of competition from older parties with already established brands and new parties trying to stake out their own position in the party system.

Authoritarian successor parties may be spared the difficulties of brand-building by simply inheriting a brand from the former dictatorship. While the idea of a popular brand derived from an authoritarian regime may seem counterintuitive, it is undeniable that such regimes sometimes enjoy considerable popular support.[25] In Chile, when citizens were given the opportunity in 1988 to vote in a relatively free and fair plebiscite on whether to extend General Augusto Pinochet's rule for an additional eight years, 44 percent voted in favor. In Mexico, at the time of the transition to democracy in 2000, 38 percent of the population identified as *priístas*, or supporters of the authoritarian ruling party – more than the two main opposition parties combined (Medina Vidal et al. 2010: 68). And in South Korea, surveys have repeatedly shown that its most popular former political leader is Park Chung-hee, the country's military dictator from 1961 to 1979, with 55 percent of those surveyed expressing a favorable opinion of him in 2006 (Suh 2015: 15).

In some cases, popular support for authoritarian regimes is based on "position issues," or the regime's position on the left–right ideological spectrum. Perhaps more common, though, is for such regimes to generate

---

[24] Parts of this section draw on Levitsky, Loxton, and Van Dyck (2016).
[25] In recent years, a significant literature has emerged on this phenomenon of "popular autocrats" (Dimitrov 2009). See, for example, Chang, Chu, and Welsh (2013); Rose and Mishler (2002); Rose, Mishler, and Munro (2006, 2011); Shin and Wells (2005); and Treisman (2011). For more, see Conclusion (Loxton, this volume).

support on the basis of "valence issues," or issues about which virtually all voters share a preference, such as corruption, inflation, economic growth, national defense, and public security.[26] While voters may not wish for an actual return to authoritarianism, they may nevertheless feel nostalgic for aspects of the former regime if it was viewed as a competent steward of the economy, protector of public security, defender of the nation's borders, or opponent of corruption – particularly if the new democracy's performance is seen as disappointing in these areas.[27] If an authoritarian successor party inherits the brand of a popular authoritarian regime, as occurred in the cases of Chile's UDI, Mexico's PRI, or South Korea's DJP/Saenuri, it is born with a ready-made source of votes.

Second, authoritarian successor parties may inherit a *territorial organization*. Parties rarely survive in voters' minds alone. Instead, most successful parties have an organized presence on the ground, whether in the form of formal branch structures, informal patronage-based machines, or allied social movements. These organizations play an indispensable role in disseminating the party's brand and mobilizing voters on election day. As with party brands, building a robust territorial organization is difficult. It is thus no surprise that scholars have found that parties that build upon preexisting mobilizing structures, such as religious associations (Kalyvas 1996) or labor unions (LeBas 2011), are born with an advantage.[28]

Authoritarian successor parties may be spared the hard work of organization-building by inheriting an organization from the former dictatorship. In the case of former authoritarian ruling parties – especially those that operated in regimes that carried out undemocratic elections – a grassroots organization well suited for electoral mobilization may already be in place. After the transition to democracy in Taiwan, for example, the KMT was able to draw on "its immense organizational network at [the] grassroots level," which historically had "penetrated all state apparatuses and major associations in society" (Cheng 2006: 371). Indeed, even after its loss in the 2000 presidential election, "the KMT [was] still the only party with branch offices in every township and urban district, and it remain[ed] the party with the most card-carrying members" (Cheng 2006: 371).

In other cases, it may be necessary to "retrofit" authoritarian-era organizations originally designed for different purposes. El Salvador's Nationalist Republican Alliance (ARENA), for example, was built upon a vast paramilitary organization called the Nationalist Democratic Organization (ORDEN).[29] ORDEN had been created and used by the country's previous

---

[26] On "position issues" and "valence issues," see Stokes (1963).
[27] See Chang, Chu, and Welsh (2013); McCann (2015); and Serra (2013).
[28] As Kalyvas (1996: 41) notes, the reason is straightforward: "Organization building does not come naturally or automatically to political actors. It is a difficult, time-consuming, costly, and often risky enterprise."
[29] The acronym "ORDEN" spells the Spanish word for "order."

military regime for spying and repression, including torture and extrajudicial executions, and is considered a precursor to the infamous death squads of the 1980s. After democratization, however, ORDEN was successfully repurposed into a grassroots, nationwide organization that could be used to mobilize votes for ARENA (Loxton 2014a, 2016).

Third, authoritarian successor parties may inherit *clientelistic networks*. Clientelism, or the selective distribution of material goods in exchange for electoral support, is one of the classic strategies used by parties of all stripes to win votes.[30] For this to be effective, however, it is necessary to have a clientele – that is, a group of individuals locked into a stable relationship of dependency with their patron. The patron must be known and viewed as reliable by his or her clients, and clients must come to expect and depend on payouts from their patron. As with party brands and organizations, constructing a clientele represents a costly and time-consuming effort.

Authoritarian successor parties may be able to avoid this difficulty by simply inheriting clientelistic networks forged under authoritarian rule.[31] Most authoritarian regimes do not hold onto power through coercion alone; instead, they try to build popular support through various means, including the selective distribution of material goods. Authoritarian successor parties that manage to transfer these clientelistic networks to themselves are born with an advantage. For example, the Pinochet dictatorship in Chile sought to build popular support in shantytowns through selectively distributed handouts by military-appointed mayors. Many of these mayors later joined the UDI and brought with them their clientelistic networks, giving the party a strong base among Chile's urban popular sectors.[32] In their chapter (Chapter 1, this volume), Kitschelt and Singer argue that this is common, with authoritarian successor parties – particularly former ruling parties of regimes that lasted for many years – often entering democracy with their clientelistic party–voter linkages intact.

Fourth, authoritarian successor parties may inherit a *source of party finance*. Parties need funds for everything from campaign spending to organizational upkeep. Authoritarian successor parties may be able to avoid the difficulties of fund-raising by inheriting a source of party finance from the former dictatorship. In countries where business was part of the social coalition backing the authoritarian regime, the party may inherit the reputation of being a trustworthy ally and thus enjoy business support under democracy. This was the case with several authoritarian successor parties of the right in Latin America, such as El Salvador's ARENA and Chile's UDI (Loxton 2014a, 2016). Similarly, in South Korea, close ties between business and the military regime

---

[30] See Kitschelt (2000) and Stokes et al. (2013).
[31] For a classic analysis of how patrons are sometimes able to retain their clientelistic networks after a regime transition and subsequently "lend" these to political actors, see Hagopian (1996).
[32] See Klein (2004) and Luna (2010).

allowed the DJP/Saenuri to draw on its "intimate ties to big business groups in order to raise political funds" (Cheng and Huang, Chapter 2, this volume) under democracy. In other cases, the relationship has been even more direct, with the party itself owning businesses. In Taiwan, the KMT "possessed hundreds of real estate properties and business enterprises, making it the richest party on earth and the sixth largest conglomerate in corporate Taiwan," and giving it access to "ample in-house campaign financing" (Cheng 2006: 371).

Finally, and somewhat more speculatively, authoritarian successor parties may inherit a *source of party cohesion*. Party cohesion is the propensity of party leaders and supporters to hang together – especially in the face of crisis. This is the Achilles' heel of new parties, with many collapsing after suffering schisms in their early years. According to Levitsky and Way (2012: 870), one of the most robust sources of party cohesion is a history of "sustained, violent, and ideologically-driven conflict." When party activists have fought in the trenches together, they are more likely to be animated by a sense of mission and esprit de corps. Moreover, such struggles produce high levels of polarization, which exacerbates the "us-versus-them" distinction and raises the cost of defection to opposition parties (LeBas 2011; Chapter 6, this volume). While Levitsky and Way (2012) mainly have in mind revolutionary and anti-colonial struggles, there is good reason to think that counterrevolutionary struggles may have similar effects (Slater and Smith 2016). When authoritarian regimes forged in the fires of such struggles eventually break down, they may bequeath this "us-versus-them" mentality and sense of mission to their partisan successors. This may help to explain why parties such as Taiwan's KMT, El Salvador's ARENA, Chile's UDI, and Cape Verde's PAICV, all of which have histories of violent struggle, have not experienced devastating schisms.

Another potential source of cohesion is a dominant leader. As discussed by Loxton and Levitsky (Chapter 3, this volume), this was the case with several personalistic authoritarian successor parties in Latin America led under democracy by former dictators, such as Hugo Banzer in the case of Bolivia's ADN and Joaquín Balaguer in the case of the Dominican Republic's Social Christian Reformist Party (PRSC). These former dictators/party leaders combined what Van Dyck (2018) calls "external appeal" and "internal dominance," meaning that they were popular with many voters and possessed undisputed authority within their parties. Both can contribute to party cohesion: internal dominance limits conflict, since the leader's word is effectively law, and external appeal discourages defections, since others in the party rely on the leader's coattails to get elected. In the long run, however, this is unlikely to serve as a viable source of cohesion, as seen in the cases of ADN and the PRSC, which both faced major crises after the deaths of their founders.

To conclude, authoritarian successor parties may inherit resources from authoritarian regimes that help them to succeed under democracy. This suggests that, paradoxically, there can be benefits to an authoritarian past for parties operating under democracy. Three caveats are in order. First, there is no guarantee that a party will inherit all – or even any – of the resources discussed in this section. Authoritarian successor parties vary dramatically in the amount and types of authoritarian inheritance that they possess. Several possible reasons are discussed later in the chapter, including the performance of the authoritarian regime and the nature and timing of the transition to democracy. Second, the effects of authoritarian inheritance may diminish over time. For example, if a party's brand is based on its reputation for providing protection against a perceived threat from the past (e.g., communism, foreign invasion), the brand may become less appealing as memories of the threat fade and there is generational turnover in the electorate.[33] Finally, while roots in dictatorship may provide some advantages to authoritarian successor parties, they are hardly an unalloyed good – a topic to which I turn in the next section.

STRATEGIES FOR DEALING WITH THE PAST

If roots in dictatorship can be beneficial to authoritarian successor parties in a number of ways, they can also be a liability. Invariably, much of the electorate will disapprove of the party's origins and thus be unwilling to support it. If the valuable resources bequeathed by an authoritarian regime to its partisan successor can be thought of as *authoritarian inheritance*, the opposite can be thought of as *authoritarian baggage* (Loxton 2015).[34] One source of authoritarian baggage for virtually all dictatorships is human rights violations. If an authoritarian regime has killed, tortured, or imprisoned large numbers of its own citizens, this is likely to haunt any party that emerges from it. Another potential source of authoritarian baggage is a poor performance in key areas such as the economy and national security. As discussed in the next section, while some authoritarian regimes can claim significant policy achievements, others perform disastrously. In extreme cases (e.g., Greece 1967–1974, Argentina 1976–1983), the baggage may be so great that outgoing authoritarian incumbents do not even bother to form a party, since they know that its chances of success

---

[33] This may help to explain why older voters were more likely than younger voters to vote for Park Geun-hye, the daughter of former military dictator Park Chung-hee, in South Korea's 2012 presidential election (Kim 2014).
[34] One way to think about this distinction is in terms of what Hale (2004: 996) calls "starting political capital," which he defines as the "the stock of assets [that parties] possess that might be translated into electoral success." If authoritarian *inheritance* can be thought of as a form of starting political capital, then authoritarian *baggage* is the stock of *liabilities* with which parties are burdened that might impede their electoral success.

would be nil.³⁵ It is more common, however, for authoritarian regimes to produce a mix of inheritance and baggage, with the proportions varying according to a variety of factors (see next section). If they wish to succeed, party leaders must craft strategies for dealing with the past that allow them to minimize the costs of their authoritarian baggage while maximizing the benefits of their authoritarian inheritance. In this section, I discuss four major strategies that authoritarian successor parties have employed: (1) contrition, (2) obfuscation, (3) scapegoating, and (4) embracing the past.

The first strategy is *contrition*. This is the approach that Grzymala-Busse (2002: 6) describes as "symbolically breaking with the past." Communist successor parties in East Central Europe, she argues, were "both handicapped and helped by their past" (Grzymala-Busse 2002: 7). On the one hand, some of them had earned a reputation under communism for managerial competence and pragmatism, which constituted a *usable past*. On the other hand, they were burdened by their historical connection to "regimes widely despised by their own citizens" (Grzymala-Busse 2002: 2), which constituted an *unusable past*. In order to minimize the damage caused by the latter, Grzymala-Busse argues that parties had to engage in public acts of contrition, such as "changing the party's name, program, symbols, and public representatives," and "denouncing [the] former misdoings and crimes" of the former regime (2002: 73, 79). In countries where parties made these symbolic gestures and promoted a new generation of relatively unsullied leaders (e.g., Poland, Hungary), they were able to reinvent themselves and quickly return to office, while in countries where they did not (e.g., Czech Republic), they were less successful.³⁶

A second strategy is *obfuscation*. In this strategy, rather than acknowledging and expressing contrition for the past, the party tries to downplay it. One example is Brazil's Liberal Front Party (PFL), which was founded in 1985 as a breakaway faction of the military regime's official party, the PDS. Under

---

[35] No significant authoritarian successor parties emerged in either country at the national level. However, in Argentina, several such parties emerged at the subnational level, including Republican Force in Tucumán, Chaqueña Action in Chaco, and the Renewal Party of Salta. The existence of these subnational authoritarian successor parties can be explained in terms of authoritarian inheritance. While the 1976–1983 military regime was generally a disaster, military governors in some provinces could point to accomplishments. In Tucumán, for example, where guerrilla insurgents had been stronger than anywhere else in the country, General Antonio Domingo Bussi, military governor from 1976 to 1977, effectively (and brutally) put down the insurrection. Under democracy, Bussi drew on his authoritarian past to bolster his image as a champion of "law and order," and was democratically returned to the governor's mansion in 1995. See Adrogué (1993), Aibar (2005), and Crenzel (1999).

[36] However, as Grzymala-Busse argues in her chapter (Chapter 4, this volume), authoritarian successor parties in Poland and Hungary eventually became "victims of their own success." Having built their brands on the issues of probity and managerial competence, they were harshly punished by voters and largely wiped from the electoral map when they failed to deliver. By contrast, those parties that did not make a clean break with the past, as in the Czech Republic, continued to exist and win a sizeable number of votes as protest parties.

democracy, the PFL became the go-to destination for former authoritarian incumbents and was arguably the "true heir" (Power 2000: 80) of the military regime. However, because its founders had broken with the regime in its final months, it was able to downplay its status as an authoritarian successor party. In 2007, in a particularly unsubtle act of obfuscation, it changed its name to "Democrats" (Power, Chapter 7, this volume).

Another example is El Salvador's ARENA. The party was founded in 1981 by Major Roberto D'Aubuisson, who had been the deputy director of intelligence under military rule and became the public face of El Salvador's notorious death squads in the 1980s. As the country made the transition to competitive elections, he drew on the infrastructure of a vast paramilitary network created by the previous military regime in order to build his new party, as discussed above. Yet, while ARENA members strongly embrace D'Aubuisson's memory, they deny accusations that he engaged in extrajudicial violence and have actively sought to distance the party from the country's former authoritarian regime (Loxton 2014a).

A third strategy is *scapegoating*. This involves distinguishing between a "good" dictator, whom the party embraces, and a "bad" dictator, whom it denounces. Although the party acknowledges the unsavory aspects of the former regime, it blames these entirely on the bad dictator. An example is Panama's Democratic Revolutionary Party (PRD). The PRD was founded in 1979 by military dictator Omar Torrijos to serve as the regime's official ruling party. In 1981, Torrijos died in a plane crash and was replaced by Manuel Noriega, who continued to use it as the regime's official party. After the 1989–1990 US invasion and resulting transition to democracy, the PRD fully embraced the memory of Torrijos, who had earned broad popular support by increasing social spending and winning control of the Panama Canal from the United States (Loxton and Levitsky, Chapter 3, this volume). To this day, the PRD's emblem is an "O" with an "11" inside it – a reference to October 11, 1968, the day of the coup that brought Torrijos to power (García Díez 2001: 570). However, the party categorically denounced Noriega, who had become notorious for his brutality and corruption. Thus, during the 1994 election, the PRD's successful presidential candidate, Ernesto Pérez Balladares, asserted that Torrijos "was a hero, and a great innovator," while claiming that "Noriega was an opportunist, a traitor and a disgrace to the country."[37]

A more recent example is Nidaa Tounes in Tunisia. The party was founded in 2012 by former high-level authoritarian officials after the overthrow of dictator Zine El Abidine Ben Ali during the "Arab Spring." Like the PRD with Noriega, Nidaa Tounes attempted to distance itself from the disgraced Ben Ali, whose 1987–2011 period of rule was known for its corruption and

---

[37] Quoted in Howard W. French, "Panama Journal; Democracy at Work, Under Shadow of Dictators," *The New York Times*, February 21, 1994. For more, see Loxton and Levitsky (Chapter 3, this volume).

Introduction

repressiveness. However, the party embraced the memory of Ben Ali's predecessor, Habib Bourguiba, who ruled for thirty years as Tunisia's first post-independence president, and who many associated with the values of secularism and national independence (Zederman 2016). In order to highlight its connection to "Bourguibism," the party's founder, Beji Caid Essebsi, kicked off his successful presidential campaign in 2014 in front of the mausoleum housing the former dictator's remains.[38]

The final strategy is simply to *embrace the past*. In this strategy, rather than expressing contrition, obfuscating its origins, or scapegoating a disgraced former dictator, the party simply acknowledges and celebrates its authoritarian past.[39] It proclaims, loudly and proudly, the accomplishments of the former regime and highlights the contrast between the supposedly idyllic state of affairs when that regime was in place versus the alleged dysfunctions of the present. In Suriname, this was the strategy of National Democratic Party (NDP) founder Dési Bouterse, who was military dictator from 1980 to 1987 before democratically returning to the presidency in 2010. As *The New York Times* reported, "Rather than playing down his past, Mr. Bouterse has defiantly celebrated it since his election last July by Parliament. He has designated Feb. 25, when he and other soldiers carried out a coup in 1980, as a national holiday, calling it the 'day of liberation and renewal.'"[40]

As Loxton and Levitsky show in their chapter (Chapter 3, this volume), several personalistic authoritarian successor parties in Latin America, such as the Guatemalan Republican Front (FRG) and Bolivia's ADN, have also opted for this strategy. As parties whose identities were intimately linked to a former dictator – and who in most cases continued to be led by that former dictator under democracy – they had little choice but to embrace the past and hope that their authoritarian inheritance would outweigh their authoritarian baggage.[41] More surprising is Grzymala-Busse's finding in her chapter (Chapter 4, this volume) that embracing the past turned out to be an effective strategy in the postcommunist world, as well. While she argued in her 2002 book that breaking with the past was crucial for the success of authoritarian successor parties in Poland and Hungary, the eventual demise of these parties – and the survival of unreconstructed ones like the Communist Party of Bohemia and Moravia (KSČM) in the Czech Republic – has led her to reconsider her earlier argument.

---

[38] See "Tunisia's Presidential Election: In the Shade of Bourguiba," *The Economist*, November 4, 2014.

[39] For a similar argument, see Deming (2013).

[40] See Simon Romero, "Returned to Power, a Leader Celebrates a Checkered Past," *The New York Times*, May 2, 2011.

[41] Such parties may also try to blame regime underlings for misdeeds, as Peru's *Fujimorismo* has done with Vladimiro Montesinos, the intelligence chief of former autocrat Alberto Fujimori (Urrutia 2011a: 113). However, this version of the scapegoating strategy is unlikely to be as effective, as most voters will find it implausible that the autocrat was simply unaware of what was going on.

To conclude, while all authoritarian successor parties are born with authoritarian baggage (some more than others), parties have developed various strategies to deal with that baggage, including contrition, obfuscation, scapegoating, and embracing the past. It may also be possible to employ hybrid strategies. For example, a party might embrace the positive aspects of the former regime (e.g., economic growth, public security), but show contrition for others (e.g., particularly egregious episodes of violence). Another possibility may be to pursue what Luna (2014) calls a "segmented" appeal, whereby a party communicates to one constituency in one way and to other constituencies in different ways. Thus, an authoritarian successor party might enthusiastically embrace the past when talking to its core supporters, but downplay it when speaking to the broader electorate.

An important question for future research is why parties choose one strategy over another. One likely reason is the *amount* of authoritarian baggage: the greater the baggage, the greater the incentive to try to offload it through contrition, obfuscation, or scapegoating rather than simply embrace the past. However, other factors are also likely to affect the constellation of opportunities and constraints facing party strategists. In Panama and Tunisia, for example, scapegoating was only possible because the authoritarian era could be divided into two clearly demarcated periods: the Torrijos and Noriega periods, and the Bourguiba and Ben Ali periods. In the case of personalistic authoritarian successor parties in Latin America, the fact that the former dictator usually continued to lead the party no doubt contributed to the decision to embrace the past, since it is difficult to break with the person at the top of the party ticket.

VARIATION IN AUTHORITARIAN SUCCESSOR PARTY PERFORMANCE

While authoritarian inheritance can help to explain the general prevalence of authoritarian successor parties, it is also clear that there is major variation among these parties on two key dimensions. First, they vary in terms of *electoral performance*. In some cases, they enjoy massive electoral support and are democratically voted back into office (e.g., Ghana's NDC); in others, they win fewer votes and never return to power (e.g., Malawi Congress Party, MCP). Second, they vary in terms of *longevity*. In some cases, they survive for long periods of time (e.g., Panama's PRD); in others, they eventually fizzle out and disappear (e.g., Guatemala's FRG). These two types of variation can be seen cross-nationally (see chapters by Grzymala-Busse, Riedl, LeBas, Slater and Wong, and Loxton and Levitsky), as well as within the same country in cases where more than one authoritarian successor party emerged. In Spain, for example, the PP continues to be one of the country's major parties to this day, while the Union of the Democratic Center (UCD), an important actor in the 1970s and early 1980s, no longer exists.[42] Similarly, as Power shows in his

---

[42] On Spain's UCD, see Hopkin (1999). On the PP, see Balfour (2005).

Introduction 19

chapter (Chapter 7, this volume), Brazil's PFL/DEM was more electorally successful than the PDS/PP for the first two decades of democracy, but the two parties "traded places" in the 2010s.

What accounts for this variation? In the previous section, I discussed an important voluntarist factor: strategies for dealing with the past. Parties that craft effective strategies to offload their authoritarian baggage stand a better chance of succeeding than those that do not. However, scholars have proposed a range of possible factors to explain authoritarian successor party performance, many of them more structural or institutional in nature. In this section, I discuss six possible factors: (1) performance of the authoritarian regime, (2) performance of the new democracy, (3) nature and timing of the transition to democracy, (4) electoral institutions, (5) authoritarian regime type, and (6) the competitive landscape.

The first is *performance of the authoritarian regime*. Authoritarian regimes vary dramatically in terms of how well they govern.[43] At one extreme, regimes in Taiwan and South Korea could claim extraordinary achievements in the areas of economic development and national security (Cheng and Huang, Chapter 2, this volume). In Taiwan, the KMT regime oversaw average GNP growth of 8.8 percent between 1953 and 1986, with the island going from having a GNP per capita similar to Zaire's in the 1960s to that of a developed country in the 1980s (Wade 1990: 38, 35). The experience of South Korea's military regime was similarly impressive.[44] In addition, both could claim to have protected their countries from serious foreign threats (the People's Republic of China and North Korea, respectively). At the other extreme, Greece's military regime of 1967–1974 and Argentina's military regime of 1976–1983 led their countries to defeat in wars against geopolitical archrivals (Turkey and Great Britain, respectively), and in Argentina, the regime oversaw bouts of hyperinflation and negative economic growth (Haggard and Kaufman 1995: 34–35). The closer an authoritarian regime is to the Taiwan/South Korea end of the performance spectrum, the more likely it is to produce an attractive brand;[45] the closer it is to the Greece/Argentina end of the spectrum, the more likely it is to produce only baggage. It is no wonder, then, that the KMT in Taiwan and the DJP/Saenuri in South Korea are among the world's most successful authoritarian successor parties (see chapters by Cheng and Huang, and Slater

---

[43] For an earlier reflection on the effects of authoritarian regime performance (though in this case applied to the issue of democratic consolidation), see O'Donnell (1992: 31–37).

[44] As Kohli (2004: 25) summarizes: "Starting from a war-destroyed, improvised economy in the mid-1950s, South Korea industrialized rapidly and in 1996 joined the 'rich man's club,' the Organization of Cooperation and Development."

[45] According to Slater and Wong (2013: 719), especially important is a "history of successful state-led development," since an "impressive record of transformative accomplishments in the economic realm provides the kind of 'usable past' that aids a formerly authoritarian party seeking 'regeneration' under democracy."

and Wong, this volume), while in Greece and Argentina, outgoing authoritarian incumbents did not even bother to form parties.

In addition to looking at issues such as the economy and national security, it is important to consider what Huntington (1991) calls "negative legitimacy" when assessing an authoritarian regime's performance. Negative legitimacy stems not from what a regime *does*, but from what it is *against*. It is defined in terms of the enemy from which the regime claims to have saved the country, such as "communism," "subversion," and "social turmoil" (Huntington 1991: 49–50). If an authoritarian regime takes power against a backdrop that much of the population perceives as profoundly threatening, it is more likely to enjoy negative legitimacy. This may help to explain the success of parties such as Spain's PP and Chile's UDI. Both grew out of authoritarian regimes that took power in the context of severe polarization (civil war in Spain and the socialist government of Salvador Allende in Chile), which enabled regime officials to make a compelling case that they had "saved" their countries from sinister forces. This, together with strong economic performances,[46] resulted in considerable regime support for both regimes. The fact that some of the major protagonists of the pre-authoritarian crisis period (e.g., Socialist Party in Chile; Spanish Socialist Workers' Party, PSOE) remained powerful actors after the transition to democracy also likely encouraged some former regime supporters to vote for authoritarian successor parties, to serve as bulwarks against a return to the "bad old days."

A second possible cause of variation is the *performance of the new democracy*. Popular perceptions of authoritarian regime performance do not develop in a vacuum. Instead, they are affected by events that occur before and after the period of authoritarian rule. Negative legitimacy, as discussed above, hinges on what occurred *before* the onset of authoritarianism. What occurs *after* the transition to democracy is also likely to color how voters remember the past. The performance of the former authoritarian regime may come to look increasingly good in retrospect if the performance of the new democracy is sufficiently bad.[47]

---

[46] Economic growth under Franco was impressive: "Between 1960 and 1975, only Japan experienced higher rates of economic development than Spain" (Encarnación 2008: 445). The Pinochet regime in Chile likewise enjoyed a relatively strong economic performance, averaging over 6 percent annual growth during the last five years that it was in power (Haggard and Kaufman 1995: 176).

[47] In their analysis of survey data on "authoritarian nostalgia" in democracies such as Mongolia and the Philippines, Chang, Chu, and Park (2007: 78) write, "Many East Asian democracies are still struggling against a haze of nostalgia for authoritarianism, as citizens compare life under democracy with either the growth-oriented authoritarianism of the recent past or with their prosperous nondemocratic neighbors of the present."

In Mexico, for example, the transition to democracy in 2000 was accompanied by a mediocre economic performance and, during the presidency of Felipe Calderón (2006–2012), an explosive drug war that resulted in thousands of deaths (Flores-Macías 2013; Chapter 8, this volume). It is therefore perhaps not surprising that survey data in the lead-up to the 2012 general election showed that 43 percent of the Mexican public believed that conditions had been better under the old PRI regime – a retrospective judgment that almost certainly helps to explain the victory of the PRI's presidential candidate, Enrique Peña Nieto (McCann 2015: 91–92).[48] In the postcommunist world, Tucker (2006) has observed something similar at the subnational level: authoritarian successor parties have tended to enjoy greater support in regions where there were larger numbers of "economic losers" after the transition to democracy, and less support in regions with larger numbers of "economic winners." The upshot is that when new democracies perform poorly in key areas such as public security and the economy, voters are more likely to remember the former authoritarian regime in a positive light – and thus more likely to support parties with roots in that regime.

A third possible cause is the *nature and timing of the transition to democracy*. Democratic transitions are not all alike. In some, authoritarian incumbents exit in good times and largely on their own terms; in others, they exit in disgrace and have little influence on the terms of the transition.[49] When authoritarian regimes end on a high note, they are more likely to be remembered positively by voters and to leave behind electoral institutions favorable to their partisan successors. This was one of the findings of Haggard and Kaufman's (1995: 126–135) classic work on the political economy of democratic transitions. They found that the nature of the transition – specifically, whether it was a "crisis" or a "non-crisis" transition – had an important impact on the performance of authoritarian successor parties (or what they call "continuist parties"). According to their data, regimes that democratized during the third wave under non-crisis conditions – that is, without contracting economies or severe inflation – were more likely to produce viable authoritarian successor parties than those that came to an end in the midst of economic crises.[50]

In their work on "conceding to thrive," Slater and Wong (2013; Chapter 9, this volume) make a similar argument, highlighting the importance of timing for authoritarian successor party performance. In their view, the ideal moment to democratize is during what they call the "bittersweet spot." It is "bitter" because no authoritarian incumbent is likely to consider initiating a transition to democracy without first receiving some ominous warning that the status quo is unsustainable (e.g., declining returns in undemocratic elections, an economic

---

[48] See also Flores-Macías (2013; Chapter 8, this volume) and Serra (2013).
[49] There is a large literature on modes of transition to democracy. See, for example, Hagopian (1990); Karl (1990); and O'Donnell and Schmitter (1986).
[50] For a similar finding, see Jhee (2008).

shock, or an uptick in contentious politics). However, it is "sweet" because if the warning is promptly heeded and democratization conceded before the regime falls into terminal crisis, the authoritarian *ruling* party has a good chance of thriving in the new democracy as an authoritarian *successor* party. They argue that variation in timing helps to explain the differing levels of success of Taiwan's KMT (most successful), Indonesia's Golkar (least successful), and South Korea's DJP/Saenuri (intermediate level of success) under democracy.

A fourth possible cause is *electoral institutions*. Democracies differ in the rules that they use to structure elections, such as the formula for translating votes into parliamentary seats (e.g., proportional vs. first-past-the-post), the weight given to different electoral districts (e.g., equal weight to districts of similar population size vs. greater weight for some districts regardless of population, such as rural districts), and barriers to entry for new parties (high vs. low). As Riedl (2014; Chapter 5, this volume) argues, when authoritarian incumbents remain strong during the transition to democracy, they may be able to impose electoral institutions that favor their partisan successors. In Chile, for example, the Pinochet regime ended in the midst of an economic boom in the late 1980s and was largely able to dictate the terms of the transition. One result was an electoral formula known as the "binomial system," which virtually guaranteed equal representation to the top two tickets in legislative elections, even if the winning ticket outperformed the runner-up by a large margin.[51] Under democracy, this gave the country's two authoritarian successor parties, the UDI and National Renewal (RN), a percentage of seats in Congress that exceeded their share of the vote.[52]

In other cases, authoritarian incumbents have exercised less control during the transition, and their partisan successors have consequently had to operate in the context of less favorable electoral institutions. An example from the second wave is Venezuela, whose dictator, Marcos Pérez Jiménez (1952–1958), fell from power after a mass uprising and fled the country. His followers subsequently formed a party, the Nationalist Civic Crusade (CCN), which won 11 percent of the legislative vote in 1968, with the exiled Pérez Jiménez winning a seat in the Senate. Fearing that Pérez Jiménez might win the upcoming 1973 presidential election, the country's major parties passed a constitutional amendment prohibiting the former dictator from running, which undermined the CCN's main source of appeal and contributed to the party's demise (Martz and Baloyra 1976: 75–82).

Similarly, Guatemala's constitution barred FRG founder Efraín Ríos Montt from running for president during the 1990s while he was at the height of his popularity, on the grounds that he was a former

---

[51] See Siavelis (2008: 203–206). Chile's binomial system was finally replaced in 2015.
[52] However, the effects of the binomial system were not as disproportional as sometimes claimed (Zucco 2007).

dictator.[53] In this case, however, the prohibition did not have the same deleterious effects as it did in the case of Venezuela's CCN: in the 1999 general election, the FRG won the presidency with a different candidate by an overwhelming margin and became the biggest party in Congress. This case suggests that while electoral institutions matter for authoritarian successor party performance, they are probably not the decisive factor. Not only are they largely endogenous to the nature of the transition (a controlled transition is more likely to result in electoral institutions favorable to the authoritarian successor party than is a transition by collapse), but a party with broad popular support may perform well even in the context of unfavorable electoral institutions. Moreover, electoral institutions cannot explain within-country variation, such as why the PFL/DEM enjoyed a stronger electoral performance than the PDS/PP during the first decades of Brazilian democracy, or why Spain's PP managed to outlive the UCD.

A fifth possible cause is *authoritarian regime type*. While all authoritarian regimes share the characteristic of not being democracies, that is where their similarities end. Scholars have developed various typologies to describe these differences. For example, Geddes (1999) distinguishes between "personalist," "military," and "single-party" regimes, and Schedler (2002) distinguishes between "closed authoritarian," "hegemonic electoral authoritarian," and "competitive electoral authoritarian" regimes. Even among authoritarian regimes of the same type, there can still be significant differences. Thus, in her study of military regimes in Latin America, Remmer (1989: 3) distinguishes between "exclusionary" and "inclusionary" regimes, and asserts that the "differences among military regimes are as profound as the differences between dictatorship and democracy." While there is no consensus on this issue, scholars have advanced a number of plausible arguments linking authoritarian regime type to authoritarian successor party performance.[54]

In Africa, Riedl (2014; Chapter 5, this volume) finds that authoritarian regimes that incorporated local "big men" into the ruling coalition, such as the Rawlings regime in Ghana, tended to produce more viable authoritarian successor parties than those that tried to substitute them with new elites, such as the regime of the People's Revolutionary Party of Benin (PRPB). The strategy of incorporation, she argues, resulted in "reservoirs of local elite support" (Riedl 2014: 106) that could be drawn upon to mobilize support for parties such as Ghana's NDC after the transition to democracy. By contrast, the strategy of substitution made these elites into an "arsenal of enemies" (Riedl 2014: 107) who contributed to the collapse of parties like Benin's PRPB.

Two other chapters in this volume make arguments linking the nature of the authoritarian regime to authoritarian successor party performance. In their

---

[53] Ríos Montt was eventually allowed to run for president in 2003. By then, however, his popularity had declined and he lost the election.
[54] See, for example, Jhee (2008).

chapter, Kitschelt and Singer (Chapter 1, this volume) emphasize the importance of authoritarian regime duration. They argue that former ruling parties of authoritarian regimes that lasted for at least ten years tended to inherit large organizations and informal networks that facilitated a clientelistic linkage strategy under democracy. By contrast, parties that emerged from regimes that lasted for fewer than ten years were less likely to inherit these resources, with implications for their chances of success.

In their study of personalistic authoritarian successor parties in Latin America, Loxton and Levitsky (Chapter 3, this volume) focus on a different factor: whether or not the party emerged from a personalistic dictatorship. While a handful of such parties managed to "de-personalize" and survive in the long term (e.g., Peronism in Argentina, the PRD in Panama), most collapsed after the death or retirement of their founding leaders. Thus, while parties that emerge from personalistic dictatorships may win large numbers of votes, they face severe challenges on the dimension of longevity.

A final possible cause is the *competitive landscape*. Party cohesion, as discussed above, is a major determinant of party survival. There are various possible sources of cohesion, including a history of violent struggle (Levitsky and Way 2012) and the presence of a leader whose undisputed leadership and strong coattails discourage defection (Van Dyck 2018). In her chapter, LeBas (Chapter 6, this volume) emphasizes the importance of another potentially important factor: the strength of *opposition parties*. While it was common for former authoritarian ruling parties in Sub-Saharan Africa to experience defection-fueled collapse after the transition to multiparty elections, some managed to avoid this fate. LeBas claims that one major reason that parties such as Ghana's NDC and Sierra Leone's All People's Congress (APC) survived was the existence of strong opposition parties and a polarized competitive landscape. While one might expect that authoritarian successor parties would benefit from a weak or divided opposition, LeBas argues the opposite. By promoting an "us-versus-them" dynamic, strong opposition parties contributed to authoritarian successor party cohesion by increasing partisan identification and raising the cost of defection. The absence of strong opposition parties, she argues, was an important factor in the disintegration of parties such as the Kenya African National Union (KANU) or the PRPB in Benin. Thus, LeBas argues that the performance of authoritarian successor parties depends not just on their own inherited resources but also on the broader competitive environment in which they operate.

To sum up, authoritarian successor parties vary dramatically in terms of electoral performance and longevity. In this section, I have discussed several plausible hypotheses to explain this variation, but this is a topic ripe for further research. It is also amenable to various methodological approaches, including large-N statistical analysis and within-case analysis of countries where more than one authoritarian successor party emerged (e.g., Spain, Brazil, Chile, Romania).

DOUBLE-EDGED EFFECTS ON DEMOCRACY

Authoritarian successor parties are one of the most common features of the global democratic landscape. In the previous sections, I discussed three major questions that such parties raise: Why are they so prevalent? What strategies can they employ to deal with their pasts? And why are some more successful than others? In this final section, I turn to a fourth question: What are their effects on democracy? As parties that emerge from authoritarian regimes – and that in some cases remain openly nostalgic for those regimes – they would seem to be patently harmful. This suspicion, I argue, is well founded. Authoritarian successor parties can (1) hinder processes of transitional justice, (2) prop up vestiges of authoritarianism, and, in extreme cases, (3) trigger an authoritarian regression. However, they can also have surprisingly salutary effects on democracy. Authoritarian successor parties can (4) promote party system institutionalization, (5) incorporate potential "spoilers" into the democratic system, and potentially even (6) encourage new transitions to democracy in other countries. In short, the impact of authoritarian successor parties on democracy appears not to be entirely negative, but rather *double-edged*.

One way that authoritarian successor parties can be harmful to democracy is by *hindering processes of transitional justice*. While it may seem easier to let sleeping dogs lie, scholars such as O'Donnell and Schmitter (1986) argue that it is imperative to hold human rights violators accountable after democratization. While their book is best known for its advocacy of pacts as a means of securing the "vital interests" of key actors such as the military, they also argue that "transitional actors must satisfy not only vital interests but also *vital ideals* – standards of what is decent and just" (O'Donnell and Schmitter 1986: 30; emphasis added). "Some horrors," they write, "are too unspeakable and too fresh to permit actors to ignore them," and thus "the 'least worst' strategy ... is to muster the political and personal courage to impose judgment upon those accused of gross violations of human rights under the previous regime" (O'Donnell and Schmitter 1986: 30).[55] As parties that emerge from regimes that, in many cases, committed large-scale human rights abuses, authoritarian successor parties have strong incentives to block processes of transitional justice. This may be out of normative convictions (i.e., "the military saved the country and thus deserve to be celebrated, not persecuted"), electoral considerations (drawing attention to the unseemly side of the former regime may cost the party votes), or because party leaders themselves could end up in the hot seat in the event of human rights trials.

There are many examples of authoritarian successor parties using their influence to shield human rights violators. In Panama, one of the first acts of

---

[55] In addition to satisfying an ethical imperative, holding human rights trials may help to decrease the probability of human rights violations in the future (Sikkink 2011).

newly elected President Ernesto Pérez Balladares of the PRD after taking office in 1994 – barely four years after the US invasion that toppled Manuel Noriega and installed a democratic regime – was to issue pardons to hundreds of former authoritarian officials for crimes ranging from corruption to murder.[56] In Suriname, after winning the presidency in 2010, NDP leader and former military dictator Dési Bouterse passed an amnesty for himself for the execution of several prominent political opponents during his 1980–1987 dictatorship.[57] In Mexico, the PRI used its strength during the transition to democracy to prevent any serious accountability for abuses committed during its seventy-one-year-long dictatorship (Treviño-Rangel 2012). In the postcommunist world, transitional justice seems to have ebbed and flowed depending on whether or not a communist successor party was in office (González-Enríquez 2001: 245, 247); and when such parties implemented their own transitional justice, these tended to be mild measures introduced preemptively in order to avoid harsher measures later (Nalepa 2010).[58] Finally, in Guatemala, FRG founder Efraín Ríos Montt was able to avoid prosecution for the genocidal violence of his 1982–1983 dictatorship because of the parliamentary immunity that he enjoyed as a congressman. It was not until after the 2011 general election, when the FRG's poor showing caused Ríos Montt to lose his seat, that he was tried and found guilty of genocide by a Guatemalan court.[59]

A second way that authoritarian successor parties can be harmful to democracy is by *propping up vestiges of authoritarianism*. Scholars have become increasingly aware of how authoritarian-era institutions and practices may persist after a transition to democracy.[60] Two kinds of authoritarian vestige are particularly noteworthy. First, outgoing authoritarian incumbents may leave behind *authoritarian enclaves* (Garretón 2003), or undemocratic institutions such as tutelary powers for the military that limit the ability of elected governments to govern.[61] Second, nondemocratic practices may continue at the subnational level following a national-level transition to democracy. In recent years, a growing literature has examined this phenomenon of *subnational authoritarianism*.[62] As parties that emerge from dictatorships, authoritarian successor parties may be motivated by ideology,

---

[56] See Larry Rohter, "Some Familiar Faces Return to Power in Panama," *The New York Times*, February 9, 1995.
[57] See "Suriname Parliament Gives President Bouterse Immunity," *BBC News*, April 5, 2012.
[58] In Nalepa's (2010: 169) words, they needed to "scratch themselves a little bit to avoid a blow."
[59] See Juan Carlos Pérez Salazar, "Ríos Montt: de mandatario a culpable de genocidio," *BBC Mundo*, May 10, 2013. However, this verdict was overturned shortly thereafter by the Constitutional Court on procedural grounds. See Elisabeth Malkin, "Guatemalan Court Overturns Genocide Conviction of Ex-Dictator," *The New York Times*, May 20, 2013.
[60] See, for example, Albertus and Menaldo (2017).
[61] Other terms used to describe such phenomena include "reserved domains" (Valenzuela 1992) and "military prerogatives" (Stepan 1988).
[62] See, for example, Gibson (2012) and Giraudy (2015).

Introduction

self-interest, or a sense of ownership to prop up both kinds of authoritarian vestige.

An example of a party propping up authoritarian enclaves is Chile's UDI. The UDI's founder, Jaime Guzmán, was Pinochet's most important political advisor and one of the architects of the military regime's 1980 constitution. This constitution included a number of undemocratic features, such as appointed senators, tutelary powers for the military, and restrictions on various forms of political activity.[63] After the end of military rule in 1990, elected governments gradually whittled down most of these provisions. The UDI, however, remained a steadfast opponent of constitutional reform, with Guzmán (2008: 186) boasting that the UDI was "virtually the only movement that is not in favor of modifying the Constitution."[64] As Power discusses (Chapter 7, this volume), the PDS/PP and PFL/DEM in Brazil were similarly supportive of authoritarian enclaves, expressing greater support for special prerogatives for the military than any of the country's other major parties.

The PRI in Mexico is an example of an authoritarian successor party propping up pockets of subnational authoritarianism. In 2000, the PRI lost power at the national level, but retained control of a majority of state governments.[65] In some of the states under its control, the party continued to employ the same kinds of dirty tricks that it had previously used at the national level, such as fraud, intimidation of opponents, and the abuse of state resources (Gibson 2012; Giraudy 2015). It was, in part, thanks to these pockets of subnational authoritarianism that the PRI was able to regroup after its 2000 defeat, and, in 2012, catapult back to the presidency (Flores-Macías 2013; Chapter 8, this volume).[66]

Finally, in extreme cases, authoritarian successor parties may *trigger an authoritarian regression if elected back into office*. New democracies are often precarious, and there is good reason to think that the leaders of authoritarian successor parties would make for poor stewards of the new regime. For one, they may lack a normative commitment to democracy. As former authoritarian incumbents, they are likely to have few qualms about authoritarianism. Indeed, they may wish for nothing more than to return to the status quo ante. They may also simply possess greater authoritarian know-how than their competitors. Other parties may also wish to perpetuate themselves in power through less-than-democratic means, but lack skills in the art of authoritarianism (skills that are especially important in electoral authoritarian regimes, where

---

[63] See Siavelis (2008: 191–192).
[64] Guzmán wrote these words in 1987, in the lead-up to the 1988 plebiscite on Pinochet's rule.
[65] Remarkably, the PRI continued to control over half of all state governments in Mexico until 2016, when the number of state governments it controlled fell to 15 of 32 (Flores-Macías, Chapter 8, this volume).
[66] The same occurred in Brazil, with the PFL/DEM governing in an authoritarian manner in some of the country's poor northeastern states, such as Bahia (Durazo Herrmann 2014; Souza 2016).

authoritarian behavior must be balanced with an outward respect for democratic forms).[67]

An example of an authoritarian successor party whose return to power triggered an authoritarian regression is the Dominican Republic's PRSC. In 1978, dictator Joaquín Balaguer was defeated in a presidential election, resulting in Latin America's first third-wave transition to democracy. But in 1986, Balaguer was voted back into office (as the candidate of the PRSC), whereupon he installed a competitive authoritarian regime (Levitsky and Way 2010: 132–137). Another example is the Association for the Rebirth of Madagascar (AREMA), the official party of the dictatorship of Didier Ratsiraka. AREMA lost the founding democratic election of 1993, but Ratsiraka returned to the presidency in 1997. Back in power, he packed the National Election Commission and Constitutional Court, harassed opponents, and engaged in fraud, resulting in a slide into competitive authoritarianism (Levitsky and Way 2010: 276–282; Marcus 2001). A final example is the Sandinista National Liberation Front (FSLN) in Nicaragua, the country's authoritarian ruling party between 1979 and 1990. After FSLN leader Daniel Ortega democratically returned to the presidency in 2007, his government stacked the Supreme Electoral Council, engaged in fraud, and harassed opponents (Martí i Puig 2013; Thaler 2017). In all three cases, then, the return of authoritarian successor parties to power triggered an authoritarian regression.[68]

But while authoritarian successor parties can be harmful to democracy in a number of ways, they can also have surprisingly salutary effects. First, they can *promote party system institutionalization.* In their classic work, Mainwaring and Scully (1995) argue that party system institutionalization is an important determinant of the stability and quality of democracy. Democracy tends to work better when there is stability in interparty competition, parties have relatively deep roots in society, parties are largely accepted as the most legitimate route to power, and party organizations are governed by fairly stable rules and structures. In recent years, various scholars have drawn attention to how authoritarian successor parties can contribute to this outcome.

In East Central Europe, Grzymala-Busse (2007) finds that where communist parties lost power and successfully regenerated, they helped to structure party systems around a "regime divide." This gave voters a clear choice and helped to

---

[67] See Levitsky and Way (2010) and Schedler (2013).
[68] However, it is notable that all three also shared a peculiar characteristic: the person elected president was not only the candidate of an authoritarian successor party (PRSC, AREMA, and FSLN), but also a *former dictator* (Balaguer, Ratsiraka, and Ortega). This raises the possibility that it is not authoritarian successor parties as such that cause democratic breakdown; instead, it may simply be that former dictators tend to act dictatorially. For more on former dictators elected back into office, see Conclusion (Loxton, this volume).

Introduction 29

hold newly elected governments accountable, since "[t]he same elite skills that allowed the communist successors to transform after the communist collapse ma[d]e them able critics and highly competent governors" (Grzymala-Busse 2007: 62). In Asia, Hicken and Kuhonta (2011: 575) argue that "authoritarian, institutionalized parties that are now democratic or maintain some aspects of democracy ... serve as the anchor for emerging democratic, institutionalized party systems."[69] In Latin America, K. Roberts (2006, 2016) and Loxton (2014a, 2016) have both found that authoritarian successor parties helped to anchor the right pole of some of the region's most stable party systems, notably Chile and El Salvador. And in Africa, Riedl (2014; Chapter 5, this volume) finds that there is a correlation between strong authoritarian successor parties and party system institutionalization (though this correlation may be the product of a third factor: the strength of authoritarian incumbents at the time of democratization, and thus their ability to impose favorable electoral institutions).

Second, authoritarian successor parties can help *to incorporate potential "spoilers" into the democratic system*. A challenge for all democracies is to manage what Linz (1978) called the "disloyal opposition." These are actors who question not only the policies of particular democratic governments, but the legitimacy of the democratic regime itself. Following democratization, there is a danger that former authoritarian incumbents and their supporters will become spoilers. One option for preventing this is to incorporate them into the new democratic regime, thereby reducing incentives for disloyal behavior. While this is clearly in tension with the imperative of pursuing transitional justice,[70] it is arguably better for the stability of democracy – if not necessarily for its quality – to have such actors inside the democratic game as players than outside trying to kick over the board. Given their origins, authoritarian successor parties can play a crucial role in incorporating figures from the previous regime. By giving such figures an institutionalized means to make their voices heard – and quite possibly return to power – these parties may help to stabilize new democracies.

---

[69] Hicken and Kuhonta (2011, 2015) examine party systems in both democratic *and* authoritarian regimes. As such, some of the cases that they discuss (e.g., Malaysia's UMNO, Singapore's People's Action Party, PAP) would not qualify as authoritarian successor parties, but instead are ruling parties of existing authoritarian regimes. In a hypothetical democratic future, however, it seems likely that parties such as UMNO and PAP would contribute to party system institutionalization, much as the KMT and DJP/Saenuri have done in democratic Taiwan and South Korea, respectively.

[70] The potentially intractable nature of this dilemma can be seen in O'Donnell and Schmitter's (1986) classic work on transitions from authoritarian rule. On the one hand, they argue for securing the vital interests of the military, which includes "[not] seek[ing] sanctions against military offices for 'excesses' committed under the aegis of the authoritarian regime" (O'Donnell and Schmitter 1986: 40). On the other, they argue that in extreme cases, it is necessary "to muster the political and personal courage to impose judgment upon those accused of gross violations of human rights under the previous regime" (O'Donnell and Schmitter 1986: 30).

In Taiwan, South Korea, and Indonesia, Slater and Wong (Chapter 9, this volume) find that the KMT, DJP/Saenuri, and Golkar, respectively, all helped to stabilize new democratic regimes. By giving former authoritarian elites an influential position in the new regime, authoritarian successor parties made them "game for democracy." In Tunisia, the only case of successful democratization of the Arab Spring, scholars have likewise found that the emergence of Nidaa Tounes was critical for stabilizing the country's young democracy. By sweeping the legislative and presidential elections of 2014, the party made democracy "safe" for figures who might otherwise have felt tempted to subvert the new regime. In Egypt, no equivalent of Nidaa Tounes emerged, which may have contributed to the breakdown of the country's short-lived experiment with democracy by pushing former authoritarian officials and their allies into the disloyal camp.[71] Finally, during Europe's first wave of democratization, Ziblatt (2017; Chapter 10, this volume) finds that "old regime conservative parties" – analogues to modern-day authoritarian successor parties – were a crucial determinant of successful democratization. In countries where strong old regime conservative parties existed, such as Great Britain and Sweden, elites felt less threatened and became "reluctant democrats." In countries where they did not exist, such as Germany and Spain, elites remained enemies of democracy, and it was also more likely that strong radical right parties would later emerge.[72]

Finally, and more speculatively, the existence of authoritarian successor parties may even *encourage new transitions to democracy*. As noted previously, a classic argument in the literature on democratic transitions is that the "vital interests" of powerful actors such as the military must be protected for the transition to be successful.[73] While much of this literature focuses on the importance of pacts for providing such safeguards, authoritarian successor parties can play a similar role by serving as vehicles for former authoritarian incumbents in the new regime, as discussed above. Yet the impact of authoritarian successor parties may not be limited to the stabilization of already existing democracies; they may also help to encourage *new* transitions to democracy by affecting the calculations of authoritarian incumbents. If those incumbents believe that they stand a good chance of remaining influential under democracy, they have less of an incentive to cling to authoritarianism.

---

[71] See Ellis Goldberg, "Arab Transitions and the Old Elite," Monkey Cage, *Washington Post* blog, December 9, 2014; Masoud (2011: 30–32, 2013); and Romdhani (2014).
[72] For earlier arguments about the importance of strong conservative parties for democratic stability, see Di Tella (1971–1972), O'Donnell and Schmitter (1986: 62–63, 67), and Gibson (1996).
[73] See O'Donnell and Schmitter (1986) and Karl (1990).

Slater and Wong make this argument in their work on "conceding to thrive," arguing that authoritarian incumbents may initiate their own transitions to democracy on the belief that *"ruling parties can democratize without losing office"* (2013: 717–718; emphases in original).[74] If they have a high degree of "victory confidence" – that is, confidence in their ability to perform well under democracy as authoritarian successor parties – they may decide to concede democracy as part of a new legitimation strategy. Slater and Wong (2013) argue that such calculations were critical to the decisions to democratize in Taiwan, South Korea, and Indonesia, and that Singapore and Malaysia – and perhaps even China, eventually[75] – are strong candidates for this "democratization through strength" scenario in the future. Not only would parties like the People's Action Party (PAP) in Singapore and UMNO in Malaysia possess a high degree of victory confidence based on their strong records in office, but they could also derive "democratic hope" (Slater and Wong 2013: 730) from the example of their neighbors. In other words, the success of parties like the KMT in Taiwan and the DJP/Saenuri in South Korea could have a *demonstration effect*: seeing that former authoritarian incumbents fared well under democracy elsewhere, current authoritarian incumbents in countries such as Singapore and Malaysia could be inspired to initiate their own transitions.

To conclude, authoritarian successor parties' effects on democracy appear to be double-edged rather than entirely negative. The ratio of benefits to harm, however, is unlikely to be the same across cases. Future research is needed to determine under what circumstances these effects are mainly harmful or mainly salutary.

PLAN OF THE VOLUME

This volume is structured as follows. Part I examines *why authoritarian successor parties exist – and why they often win elections*. Chapter 1, by Herbert Kitschelt and Matthew Singer, examines the linkage strategies of authoritarian successor parties. Kitschelt and Singer demonstrate through a large-N analysis that former ruling parties of authoritarian regimes that

---

[74] Eventually, however, the normal dynamics of democratic alternation take hold and the party is voted out of office. As Przeworski (1991: 10) reminds us, "[d]emocracy is a system in which parties lose elections." While there are several cases of authoritarian successor parties winning one or more consecutive elections after a transition to democracy, there is only one case where the party has *never* lost an election: the Democratic Party of Socialists of Montenegro (DPS) (Komar and Živković 2016; Vuković 2015). However, this unbroken winning spree is almost certainly an artifact of Montenegro's youth: it only became an independent country in 2006 and thus has had very few elections. It is likely that the DPS, like all other authoritarian successor parties, will eventually be voted out of office.

[75] For a similar argument, see Chu (2012).

existed for long periods of time often inherited large organizations and informal networks that facilitated clientelistic party–voter linkages under democracy. Chapter 2, by T.J. Cheng and Teh-fu Huang, examines the extraordinary success of Taiwan's KMT and South Korea's DJP/Saenuri. Cheng and Huang show that these parties benefited from various forms of authoritarian inheritance, such as brands based on strong records of economic development and national security, and that they also skillfully managed issue dynamics. Chapter 3, by James Loxton and Steven Levitsky, examines personalistic authoritarian successor parties in Latin America. Loxton and Levitsky argue that when former personalistic dictators have sufficiently strong records to run on, their parties can win votes without making a clean break from the past, and in some cases can even "de-personalize" and survive in the long term.

Part II explores *why some authoritarian successor parties are more successful than others*. Chapter 4, by Anna Grzymala-Busse, examines why communist successor parties that were initially very successful, such as those in Poland and Hungary, ended up collapsing. Grzymala-Busse shows that while these parties were able to win elections by highlighting their probity and managerial competence, they were later punished by voters when they failed to deliver, becoming "victims of their own success." Chapter 5, by Rachel Beatty Riedl, examines variation in authoritarian successor party performance in Sub-Saharan Africa. Riedl argues that much of this was due to the different organizational strategies of former authoritarian regimes: where those regimes tried to incorporate local powerbrokers, authoritarian successor parties were more likely to remain cohesive after the transition to democracy; where they tried to substitute those brokers with outside officials, parties were more likely to collapse. Chapter 6, by Adrienne LeBas, also examines variation in Sub-Saharan Africa, but emphasizes a different causal factor: the competitive landscape. In countries where strong opposition parties existed, LeBas argues that this paradoxically helped authoritarian successor parties by creating an "us-versus-them" dynamic that promoted party cohesion. Chapter 7, by Timothy J. Power, examines Brazil's two authoritarian successor parties, the PDS/PP and PFL/DEM, and tries to explain why they ended up "trading places" in terms of electoral performance. Power argues that the main reason was access to state resources: the PFL/DEM suffered a decline because it lost access to state resources after 2002, while the PDS/PP retained access and thus remained significant.

Part III considers *the effects of authoritarian successor parties on democracy*. Chapter 8, by Gustavo A. Flores-Macías, discusses the case of the PRI in Mexico. Flores-Macías finds that the PRI's effects on Mexican democracy have been mostly harmful, due to the party's ongoing association with subnational authoritarianism, corruption, and human rights abuses. Chapter 9, by Dan Slater and Joseph Wong, looks at Taiwan's KMT, South Korea's DJP/Saenuri, and Indonesia's Golkar, and offers a more sanguine

Introduction

view. Slater and Wong argue that these parties contributed to democratic stability by providing former authoritarian officials with a vehicle for representation and, in so doing, made them "game for democracy." Chapter 10, by Daniel Ziblatt, looks at the first wave's equivalent of authoritarian successor parties, or what he calls "old regime conservative parties." Similar to Slater and Wong, Ziblatt finds that these parties, when strong, contributed to democratic transition and consolidation by converting old regime elites into "reluctant democrats."

The Conclusion by James Loxton recaps some of the major themes of the book and discusses a number of related topics: popular support for authoritarian regimes, the utility of the "authoritarian inheritance-versus-authoritarian baggage" framework, former dictators voted back into office, "authoritarian diasporas," the future of authoritarian successor parties, and pathways out of dictatorship.

APPENDIX I.1

Authoritarian Successor Parties in the Third Wave of Democracy[i]

Country	Transition to democracy[ii]	Prominent ASP[iii]	ASP returns to power[iv]
Albania	1992–	Yes	Yes
Argentina	1974–1976, 1984–	No[v]	No
Bangladesh	1991–2007, 2009–	Yes	Yes
Benin	1992–	No[vi]	No
Bolivia	1983–	Yes	Yes
Brazil	1986–	Yes	No[vii]
Bulgaria	1991–	Yes	Yes
Burundi	1994–1996, 2006–	No[viii]	No
Central African Republic	1994–2003	Yes	No
Chile	1990–	Yes	Yes
Congo, Republic of	1993–1997	Yes	No[ix]
Croatia	1992–	Yes	Yes
Czech Republic	1993–	Yes	No
Dominican Republic	1979–	Yes	Yes
Ecuador	1980–	No	No
El Salvador	1995–	Yes	Yes
Estonia	1992–	No	No
Georgia	2005–	No	No

(*continued*)

(*continued*)

Country	Transition to democracy[ii]	Prominent ASP[iii]	ASP returns to power[iv]
Ghana	1980–1981, 2001–	Yes	Yes
Greece	1975–	No	No
Guatemala	1996–	Yes	Yes
Guinea-Bissau	2001–2002, 2006–	Yes	Yes
Haiti	1991–1991, 1995–1999, 2007–	No	No
Honduras	1982–	No[x]	No
Hungary	1991–	Yes	Yes
Indonesia	2000–	Yes	No[xi]
Kenya	2003–	No	No
Latvia	1992–	No	No
Lesotho	1994–	Yes	No
Liberia	2006–	No	No
Lithuania	1992–	Yes	Yes
Macedonia	1992–	Yes	Yes
Madagascar	1994–2009	Yes	Yes
Malawi	1995–	Yes	No
Mali	1993–	No	No
Mexico	2001–	Yes	Yes
Moldova	1992–	Yes	Yes
Mongolia	1994–	Yes	Yes
Montenegro	2007–	Yes	Yes
Nepal	1992–2002, 2007–	Yes	Yes
Nicaragua	1991–	Yes	Yes
Niger	1994–1996, 2000–	Yes	Yes
Nigeria	1980–1983, 2000–	No[xii]	No
Pakistan	1989–1999, 2009–	No	No
Panama	1990–	Yes	Yes
Paraguay	1994–	Yes	Yes
Peru	1981–1992, 2002–	Yes	No
Philippines	1987–	Yes	No
Poland	1990–	Yes	Yes
Portugal	1977–	No[xiii]	No
Romania	1991–	Yes	Yes
Senegal	2001–	Yes	No

(*continued*)

Introduction 35

(*continued*)

Country	Transition to democracy[ii]	Prominent ASP[iii]	ASP returns to power[iv]
Serbia	2001–	Yes	Yes
Sierra Leone	1997–1997, 1999–	Yes	Yes
Slovakia	1993–	Yes	No[xiv]
Slovenia	1992–	Yes	Yes
South Africa	1995–	No	No
South Korea	1988–	Yes	Yes
Spain	1978–	Yes	Yes
Sri Lanka	1995–	Yes	Yes
Taiwan	2001–	Yes	Yes
Thailand	1976–1976, 1989–1991, 1993–2006, 2008–	Yes	Yes
Turkey	1984–	Yes	Yes
Ukraine	1992–	Yes	No[xv]
Uruguay	1985–	No	No
TOTAL	65	47	35

i   The following list of third-wave transitions to democracy is drawn from Geddes, Wright, and Frantz's (2014a) Autocratic Regimes Data Set, which covers all countries with at least 1 million inhabitants as of 2009. I include all countries that they score as having democratized between 1974 and 2010, except for those in which the new democracy broke down before even one national election could be held after the year of the transition (Armenia, Azerbaijan, Mauritania, Russia, Sudan, and Zambia). Excluding such cases is essential for the purposes of this volume, since a core part of the definition of authoritarian successor parties is that they contest elections under democracy, and in cases of immediate democratic breakdown, it was not possible for this condition to be met.

ii Following the coding rules used by Geddes, Wright, and Frantz, democracy is operationalized as "a regime in which the executive achieved power through a direct competitive election in which at least ten percent of the total population (equivalent to about 40 percent of the adult male population) was eligible to vote, all major parties were permitted to compete, and neither fraud nor violence determined the election outcome; or indirect election by a body at least 60 percent of which was elected in direct competitive elections" (2014b: 9). Elections are not considered to be competitive "if one or more large party is not allowed to participate; and/or if there are widespread reports of violence, jailing, and/or intimidation of opposition leaders or supporters; and/or if there are credible reports of vote fraud widespread enough to change [the] election outcome (especially if reported by international observers); and/or if the incumbent so dominates political resources and the media that observers do not consider elections fair" (2014b: 6). Although this is a minimalist conceptualization of democracy, it nevertheless excludes regimes in which elections are held regularly but are patently unfair (e.g., Belarus, Mozambique, Singapore). In cases where democracy remained in place as late as 2010, this is indicated with an open-ended "–" after the transition year (though some of these democracies broke down after 2010). In cases where democracy broke down or was interrupted prior to 2010, this is indicated with a year after the "–". Following Geddes, Wright, and Frantz, the date given for the transition to democracy is "the calendar year for the first January 1 in which the [new] regime holds power" (2014b: 1).

iii Authoritarian successor parties are defined as parties that emerge from authoritarian regimes, but that operate after a transition to democracy (Loxton 2015). For the operationalization of transition to democracy, see previous footnote. A party is scored as having emerged from an authoritarian regime if *one* of the following conditions holds:
- It is a former authoritarian ruling party. The party may have been created by authoritarian incumbents for this purpose (e.g., Indonesia's Golkar), or it may have predated the regime, provided that it was created shortly before the onset of authoritarian rule (e.g., Peru's *Fujimorismo*) or was used by the regime as its ruling party for at least ten years (e.g., Paraguay's Colorado Party).
- It was created by high-level authoritarian incumbents in anticipation of a transition to democracy (e.g., Chile's UDI) or by former incumbents shortly after a transition to democracy (e.g., Tunisia's Nidaa Tounes). High-level authoritarian incumbents include heads of state, ministers, and key members of the security apparatus. Parties founded by authoritarian incumbents who defect and go into opposition before the transition to democracy are excluded (e.g., Mexico's PRD), as are parties founded more than one election cycle after the transition year identified by Geddes, Wright, and Frantz (2014a) (e.g., Slovakia's Smer-SD).

A party is scored as "prominent" if it wins 10 percent or more in a single national election *after* the year of the transition to democracy. See Appendix I.2 for details on individual cases.

iv A party is scored as having returned to power if a member of the party occupies the presidency in a presidential system, the prime minister's office in a parliamentary system, or the presidency *or* the prime minister's office in a semi-presidential system. The party member must earn or hold onto this position in an election *after* the year of democratic transition, since founding elections are sometimes less than fully democratic. See Appendix I.2 for details on individual cases.

v As discussed by Loxton and Levitsky (Chapter 3, this volume), Argentina's Justicialista Party (Peronism) qualifies as an authoritarian successor party. However, since it emerged during the second wave of democratization, it is not included in this table.

vi In 1996, former dictator Mathieu Kérékou was democratically returned to the presidency. However, he was elected as an independent, with the former authoritarian ruling party, the PRPB, having collapsed during the transition to democracy.

vii Although PFL/DEM founder José Sarney occupied the presidency from 1985 to 1990, and although the PFL/DEM and PDS/PP both held cabinet positions in multiple governments under democracy, Brazil is not coded as a case of an authoritarian successor party returning to power, since neither party won/retained the presidency in an election after the founding election.

viii Although Burundi's former authoritarian ruling party, the Union for National Progress (UPRONA), returned to power after the 1996 coup, it is not included here, since it never won 10 percent in a national election in 1994–1996 or after 2006.

ix The Congolese Party of Labor (PCT) did return to power after the 1997 civil war, but it did so through violence, and thus is not coded as a case of an authoritarian successor party returning to power democratically.

x Although Honduras' National Party was a partner in the military regime from 1963 to 1971, it is excluded because it long predated military rule and did not serve as the regime's ruling party for at least ten years.

xi Golkar held cabinet positions in multiple governments after Indonesia's transition to democracy. However, because it never won the presidency, it is not coded as a case of an authoritarian successor party returning to power.

xii In Nigeria, the People's Democratic Party (PDP), which was founded in 1998 by Olusegun Obasanjo, military dictator from 1976 to 1979, is excluded because it was formed more than one election cycle after the 1980 transition to democracy. The case of Obasanjo, who was

Introduction 37

democratically elected president in 1999 (as well as the case of Muhammadu Buhari, another former dictator who was democratically elected president in 2015), is discussed in the Conclusion (Loxton, this volume).

xiii Although several of the founders of the Social Democratic Party (PSD) had been members of parliament under Portugal's authoritarian regime, the PSD is not scored as an authoritarian successor party, since none of them had been heads of state, ministers, or high-level members of the security apparatus.

xiv Although the Party of the Democratic Left (SDL') held cabinet positions in a coalition government from 1998 to 2002, it never held the prime minister's office after the transition to democracy. An SDL' splinter party formed in 1999, Smer-SD, did reach the prime minister's office in 2012, and before this, in 2005, the SDL' had merged with Smer-SD. However, because Smer-SD was formed more than one election cycle after the transition to democracy, it does not qualify as an authoritarian successor party.

xv In 1994, Vitaliy Masol, a former prime minister of Ukraine under communism, was appointed prime minister of Ukraine. (See "Choice of New Ukraine Premier Raises Questions about Reform," *The New York Times*, June 17, 1994.) According to Kuzio (2015: 292), Masol was a member of the KPU at the time, which would make this a case of an authoritarian successor party returning to power. Other sources, however, describe Masol as an independent at this time. I err on the side of caution and thus do not include this as a case of an authoritarian successor party returning to power.

APPENDIX I.2

Prominent Authoritarian Successor Parties from the Third Wave[i]

Country	Party	Description[ii]
Albania	Socialist Party of Albania (PS)	Formerly Party of Labor of Albania (PPSh), ruling party under communism. Loses power with transition in 1992, but voted back into office in 1997. Remains one of country's major parties.
Bangladesh	Bangladesh Nationalist Party (BNP)	Founded in 1978 by military dictator Ziaur Rahman ("General Zia"). Loses power after Zia's assassination in 1981 and coup in 1982, but returns to power twice under leadership of widow, Khaleda Zia, after transition in 1991.
Bolivia	Nationalist Democratic Action (ADN)	Founded in 1979 by former military dictator Hugo Banzer after he was overthrown in a coup. One of Bolivia's major parties in 1980s and 1990s, winning the presidency in

(continued)

(*continued*)

Country	Party	Description[ii]
		1997 with Banzer as candidate. Highly personalistic and collapses after Banzer's death in 2002.
Brazil	Social Democratic Party (PDS)/Progressive Party (PP)	Former ruling party of military regime. Following transition to democracy, never wins presidency, but forms part of multiple cabinets. Remains a significant actor.
Brazil	Liberal Front Party (PFL)/Democrats (DEM)	Formed in 1985 by defectors of PDS, ruling party of military regime. Holds presidency from 1985 to 1990 (though not directly elected) and forms part of cabinet until 2002. Enters into decline thereafter.
Bulgaria	Bulgarian Socialist Party (BSP)	Formerly Bulgarian Communist Party (BCP), ruling party under communism. Loses power in 1991 transition, but returns in 1994 and 2005. Remains one of country's major parties.
Central African Republic	Central African Democratic Rally (RDC)	Founded in 1987 by dictator André Kolingba. Loses power in 1993 founding election. Remains major actor during subsequent decade of democracy, but never returns to office.
Chile	Independent Democratic Union (UDI)	Founded in 1983 by former officials of military regime during regime crisis. Wins most votes in all legislative elections since 2001 (except 2017) and forms part of cabinet in 2010–2014 and after 2018, but never wins presidency. Remains one of country's major parties.
Chile	National Renewal (RN)	Founded in 1987 by former officials of military regime and right-leaning democrats. Wins presidency in 2010 and 2017 with Sebastián Piñera as candidate. Remains one of country's major parties.

(*continued*)

Introduction 39

(continued)

Country	Party	Description[ii]
Congo, Republic of	Congolese Party of Labor (PCT)	Former ruling party of one-party regime. Loses power in 1992 founding election, but performs relatively well in 1993 election. Returns to power after 1997 civil war, but not democratically.
Croatia	Social Democratic Party of Croatia (SDP)	Formerly League of Communists of Croatia (SKH), Croatian branch of League of Communists of Yugoslavia (SKJ). Loses power in 1990–1992 secession and transition to democracy, but returns in 2000 and 2011. Remains one of country's major parties.
Czech Republic	Communist Party of Bohemia and Moravia (KSČM)	Formed in 1989 as Czech branch of Communist Party of Czechoslovakia (KSČ), ruling party under communism. Loses power in 1990–1993 secession and transition to democracy. Never returns to power, but remains important actor.
Dominican Republic	Social Christian Reformist Party (PRSC)	Former ruling party of dictator Joaquín Balaguer. Party loses power in 1978 founding election, but wins presidency in 1986 with Balaguer as candidate. Highly personalistic and enters into decline after Balaguer's death in 2002.
El Salvador	Party of National Conciliation (PCN)	Former ruling party of military regime. Loses power in 1979 coup. Never returns to power, but remains relatively important actor during semi-democratic 1980s and after full transition to democracy in 1990s.
El Salvador	Nationalist Republican Alliance (ARENA)	Founded in 1981 by Major Roberto D'Aubuisson, deputy chief of intelligence in pre-1979 military regime and death squad leader in 1980s. Party wins presidency in

(continued)

(continued)

Country	Party	Description[ii]
		semi-democratic 1989 election, and in fully democratic elections in 1994, 1999, and 2004. Remains one of country's major parties.
Ghana	National Democratic Congress (NDC)	Founded by dictator Jerry John Rawlings in 1992 in anticipation of transition to multiparty elections (and eventually full democracy). Loses power in 2000 election, but returns in 2008 and 2012. Remains one of country's major parties.
Guatemala	Guatemalan Republican Front (FRG)	Founded in 1989 by former military dictator Efraín Ríos Montt. Party wins presidency in 1999. Highly personalistic and enters into decline in 2000s as Ríos Montt loses popularity.
Guinea-Bissau	African Party for the Independence of Guinea and Cape Verde (PAIGC)	Former ruling party of one-party regime. Loses power in 1999 coup and 1999–2000 founding election, but returns in 2009, 2012, and 2014. Remains one of country's major parties.
Hungary	Hungarian Socialist Party (MSzP)	Formerly Hungarian Socialist Workers' Party (MSzMP), ruling party under communism. Loses power in 1990 founding election, but returns in 1994 and 2004. Enters into decline in 2010s.
Indonesia	Golkar	Former ruling party of General Suharto's New Order regime. Loses power in 1999 founding election. Forms part of multiple cabinets under democracy, but never returns to presidency.
Lesotho	Basotho National Party (BNP)	Former authoritarian ruling party. Loses power in coup in 1986. Performs well in first few elections after 1994 transition, but never

(continued)

Introduction 41

(continued)

Country	Party	Description[ii]
		returns to office. Enters into decline in late 2000s.
Lithuania	Democratic Labor Party of Lithuania (LDDP)/Social Democratic Party of Lithuania (LSDP)	Formerly Communist Party of Lithuania (LKP), Lithuanian branch of Union of Communist Parties-Communist Party of the Soviet Union (UPC-CPSU). Retains power after 1991–1992 secession and transition to democracy. Loses power in 1996, but returns in 2001 and 2012. Remains one of country's major parties.
Macedonia	Social Democratic Union of Macedonia (SDSM)	Formerly League of Communists of Macedonia (CKM), Macedonian branch of League of Communists of Yugoslavia (SKJ). Retains power after 1990–1992 secession and transition to democracy. Loses power in 1998, but returns in 2002 and 2015. Remains one of country's major parties.
Madagascar	Association for the Rebirth of Madagascar (AREMA)	Former ruling party of dictator Didier Ratsiraka. Loses power in founding election of 1993, but wins presidency in 1996 with Ratsiraka as candidate. Enters into decline in 2000s.
Malawi	Malawi Congress Party (MCP)	Former ruling party of one-party regime. Loses power in founding election of 1994. Never returns to power, but remains one of country's major parties.
Mexico	Institutional Revolutionary Party (PRI)	Former ruling party of hegemonic-party regime. Loses power in 2000 transition, but continues to dominate subnational politics and wins presidency in 2012. Remains one of country's major parties.
Moldova	Party of Communists of the Republic of Moldova (PCRM)	Formerly Moldovan branch of Union of Communist Parties-Communist Party of the Soviet Union (UPC-

(continued)

(continued)

Country	Party	Description[ii]
		CPSU). Loses power in 1991–1992 secession and transition to democracy, but returns in 2001 and 2005. Remains one of country's major parties.
Mongolia	Mongolian People's Revolutionary Party (MPRP)/Mongolian People's Party (MPP)	Former ruling party under communism. Loses presidency in founding election of 1993 and parliament in 1996, but wins presidency in 1997, 2001, and 2005, and parliament in 2000, 2004, 2008, and 2016. Remains one of country's major parties.
Montenegro	Democratic Party of Socialists of Montenegro (DPS)	Formerly League of Communists of Montenegro (SKCG), Montenegrin branch of League of Communists of Yugoslavia (SKJ). Since country's independence in 2006, party has never lost power. Only authoritarian successor party to do so.
Nepal	Rastriya Prajatantra Party (RPP)	Founded in 1990 in anticipation of transition to democracy by officials of monarchical Panchayat regime (e.g., former prime ministers Lokendra Bahadur Chand and Surya Bahadur Thapa). Performs relatively well in 1990s, with both Chand and Thapa returning as prime ministers. Enters into decline in 2000s.
Nicaragua	Sandinista National Liberation Front (FSLN)	Former authoritarian ruling party. Loses power in founding election of 1990, but returns after winning 2006 presidential election with former dictator Daniel Ortega as its candidate. Remains one of country's major parties.
Niger	National Movement for the Development of Society (MNSD)	Founded in 1989 by military regime. Loses power in 1993 founding election. After 1996 coup, wins new founding election in 1999 and also

(continued)

Introduction 43

(*continued*)

Country	Party	Description[ii]
		2004 election. Remains in office until 2010 coup.
Panama	Democratic Revolutionary Party (PRD)	Founded in 1979 by military dictator Omar Torrijos as ruling party, and also used by Manuel Noriega in 1980s. Loses power in 1989–1990 US invasion and transition to democracy, but wins presidency in 1994 and 2004. Remains one of country's major parties.
Paraguay	Colorado Party	Ruling party of authoritarian regime from 1940s onward. Remains in power after 1994 transition, but defeated in 2008. Returns to presidency in 2013. Remains one of country's major parties.
Peru	Popular Force (*Fujimorismo*)[iii]	Ruling party of Alberto Fujimori's 1992–2000 competitive authoritarian regime. Loses power with Fujimori's resignation and transition to democracy. Has not returned to presidency, but remains one of country's major parties.
Philippines	Kilusang Bagong Lipunan (KBL)	Former ruling party of dictator Ferdinand Marcos. Loses power in 1986 transition to democracy. Does poorly in most elections, but wins over 10 percent in 1992 presidential election with Imelda Marcos, former dictator's widow, as candidate. Borderline case for inclusion.
Poland	Social Democracy of the Republic of Poland (SdRP)/ Democratic Left Alliance (SLD)	Formerly Polish United Workers' Party (PZPR), ruling party under communism. Loses power in 1989–1990 founding elections, but returns by winning parliamentary elections in 1993 and 2001, and presidential elections in 1995 and

(*continued*)

44 Introduction

(continued)

Country	Party	Description[ii]
		2000. Enters into decline after 2005.
Poland	Polish Peasants' Party (PSL)	Former satellite party of the PZPR, ruling party under communism. Allied with SdRP/SLD for much of democratic period. Holds prime minister's office in 1992 and 1993–1995. Remains somewhat significant actor.
Romania	National Salvation Front (FSN)/ Democratic National Salvation Front (FDSN)/Party of Social Democracy of Romania (PDSR)/Social Democratic Party (PSD)	Emerges from the Romanian Communist Party (PCR), ruling party under communism. Wins founding election of 1990 and 1992 election. Loses power in 1996, but wins presidency and prime minister's office in 2000. Remains one of country's major parties.
Romania	National Salvation Front (FSN)/ Democratic Party (PD)/Democratic Liberal Party (PDL)	Result of split in the FSN in lead-up to 1992 election. Wins prime minister's office after winning largest number of seats in 2008 election. Remains one of country's major parties.
Senegal	Socialist Party of Senegal (PS)	Former ruling party of one-party regime. Loses power in founding election of 2001. Performs relatively well in 2001 parliamentary election, but then enters into decline.
Serbia	Socialist Party of Serbia (SPS)	Formerly League of Communists of Serbia (SKS), Serbian branch of League of Communists of Yugoslavia (SKJ). Loses power with fall of Slobodan Milošević and founding election of 2000. Holds prime minister's office in 2012–2014 and 2017. Remains one of country's major parties.
Sierra Leone	All People's Congress (APC)	Former ruling party of one-party regime. Loses power in 1992 coup

(continued)

Introduction
(continued)

Country	Party	Description[ii]
		and subsequent civil war. Following 1999 transition, wins presidency in 2007 and 2012. Remains one of country's major parties.
Slovakia	Party of the Democratic Left (SDL')	Formerly Communist Party of Slovakia (KSS), Slovak branch of Communist Party of Czechoslovakia (KSČ). Loses power in 1990–1993 secession and transition to democracy. Never returns to power. In 2005, merges with Smer-SD, splinter party that broke from SDL' in 1999.
Slovenia	United List of Social Democrats (ZLSD)/Social Democrats (SD)	Formerly League of Communists of Slovenia (ZKS), Slovenian branch of League of Communists of Yugoslavia (SKJ). Loses power in 1990–1992 secession and transition to democracy. Forms part of multiple cabinets, and holds prime minister's office in 2008–2012. Remains relatively significant actor.
South Korea	Democratic Justice Party (DJP)/Democratic Liberal Party (DLP)/Grand National Party (GNP)/ Saenuri	Former ruling party of military regime installed by Park Chung-hee. Retains power after 1987–1988 transition to competitive elections. Loses power in 1997, but returns in 2007 and 2012. Remains one of country's major parties.
Spain	Union of the Democratic Center (UCD)	Founded in 1977 by Prime Minister Adolfo Suárez and other officials of Francisco Franco regime. Wins founding election of 1977 and 1979 election, but then collapses in early 1980s.
Spain	People's Alliance (AP)/ People's Party (PP)	Founded in 1976 by former minister Manuel Fraga and other officials of Franco regime. Remains out of office for several years, before

(continued)

(*continued*)

Country	Party	Description[ii]
		winning in 1996, 2000, 2011, 2015, and 2016. Remains one of country's major parties.
Sri Lanka	United National Party (UNP)	Former ruling party of 1978–1994 authoritarian regime. Loses power in 1994 transition, but wins prime minister's office in 2001 and 2015 parliamentary election (though not presidency). Remains one of country's major parties.
Taiwan	Kuomintang (KMT)	Former ruling party of one-party regime. Loses power in 2000 election, but returns in 2008 and 2012. Remains one of country's major parties.
Thailand	New Aspiration Party (NAP)	Founded in 1990 by General Chavalit Yongchaiyudh, former Supreme Commander of Royal Thai Armed Forces during military rule. Wins election in 1996, and Chavalit becomes prime minister. Collapses in 2000s.
Turkey	Motherland Party (ANAP)	Founded in 1983 by Turgut Özal, former deputy prime minister responsible for the economy under military rule. Wins founding election of 1983 and 1987 election; Özal becomes prime minister and later president. Enters into decline in 2000s.
Ukraine	Communist Party of Ukraine (KPU)	Formerly Ukrainian branch of Union of Communist Parties-Communist Party of the Soviet Union (UPC-CPSU). Loses power with collapse of communism and briefly banned. Major actor in 1990s, but does not return to power. Enters into decline in 2000s.
Ukraine	Socialist Party of Ukraine (SPU)	Founded in 1991 by former communist officials such as

(*continued*)

Introduction 47

(continued)

Country	Party	Description[ii]
		Oleksandr Moroz after Communist Party banned. Moroz wins over 10 percent in 1994 and 1999 presidential elections, but otherwise borderline case. Enters into decline in 2000s.

i The main table of this appendix provides information on all authoritarian successor parties that emerged between 1974 and 2010 in countries with at least 1 million inhabitants as of 2009, and which won at least 10 percent of the vote in a national election after the year of transition to democracy. See Appendix I.1 for a full list of democratic transitions.

ii The descriptions in this appendix draw on the following sources. Albania: Bajrovic and Satter (2014). Bangladesh: Hossain (2004). Bolivia: Loxton and Levitsky (this volume). Brazil: Power (this volume). Bulgaria: Spirova (2008). Central African Republic: Mehler (2005). Chile: Loxton (2014a). Republic of Congo: Clark (1997); Englebert and Ron (2004). Croatia: Šedo (2010a). Czech Republic: Grzymala-Busse (2002, this volume). Dominican Republic: Hartlyn (1998); Agosto and Cueto Villamán (2001). El Salvador: Loxton (2014a). Ghana: Riedl (this volume); LeBas (this volume). Guatemala: Loxton and Levitsky (this volume). Guinea-Bissau: Magalhães Ferreira (2004); O'Regan (2015). Hungary: Grzymala-Busse (2002, this volume). Indonesia: Slater and Wong (this volume). Lesotho: Makoa (1996, 2004). Lithuania: Clark and Praneviciute (2008). Macedonia: Šedo (2010b). Madagascar: Marcus (2001); Marcus and Ratsimbaharison (2005). Malawi: Posner (1995); LeBas (this volume). Mexico: Flores-Macías (2013, this volume). Moldova: March (2006). Mongolia: Fish (1998a); Fritz (2008). Montenegro: Vuković (2015); Komar and Živković (2016). Nepal: Baral (1995); Sharma, Stevens, and Weller (2008). Nicaragua: Martí i Puig (2013); Thaler (2017). Niger: Ibrahim and Souley (1998). Panama: Loxton and Levitsky (this volume). Paraguay: Abente-Brun (2009); Turner (2014). Peru: Levitsky and Zavaleta (2016); Loxton and Levitsky (this volume). Philippines: Putzel (1995); Hicken (2015). Poland: Grzymala-Busse (2002, this volume). Romania: Pop-Eleches (2008). Senegal: Riedl, this volume). Serbia: Bochsler (2010). Sierra Leone: Wyrod (2008). Slovakia: Grzymala-Busse (2002, this volume); Haughton (2004); Haughton and Rybar (2008). Slovenia: Fink-Hafner (2006). South Korea: Cheng and Huang (this volume); Slater and Wong (this volume). Spain: Hopkin (1999); Balfour (2005). Sri Lanka: de Silva (1997); DeVotta (2002). Taiwan: Cheng and Huang (this volume); Slater and Wong (this volume). Thailand: McCargo (1997). Turkey: Kalaycioglu (2002); Haggard and Kaufman (1995). Ukraine: Zimmer and Haran (2008); Kuzio (2015). Cape Verde: Meyns (2002). Germany: Patton (2011); Doerschler and Banaszak (2007). Guyana: Singh (2008). São Tomé and Príncipe: Seibert (2006). Suriname: Weyden (2006); Marchand (2014). Tunisia: Wolf (2014); Lefèvre (2015).

iii *Fujimorismo* has gone by several different names over the years, including Change 90, New Majority, Let's Go Neighbor, Peru 2000, Alliance for the Future, Force 2011, and, most recently, Popular Force.

Other Notable Authoritarian Successor Parties[i]

Country	Party	Description
Cape Verde	African Party for the Independence of Cape Verde (PAICV)	Former ruling party of one-party regime. Loses power in founding elections of 1991, but returns in 2001 and 2006. Remains one of country's major parties. Not included in main table because Cape Verde does not meet Geddes, Wright, and Frantz's (2014a) population threshold.
Germany	Party of Democratic Socialism (PDS)/The Left	Formerly Socialist Unity Party of Germany (SED), ruling party of communist German Democratic Republic (GDR). Following transition to democracy in 1990, PDS crosses 10-percent threshold in all federal elections in former GDR, and, after becoming The Left, wins over 10 percent nationally in 2009. Not included in main table because GDR ceases to exist in 1990, and much larger West Germany, which absorbed it, not a third-wave democracy.
Guyana	People's National Congress (PNC)	Former authoritarian ruling party. Loses power in founding election of 1992, but returns in 2015. Not included in main table because Guyana does not meet Geddes, Wright, and Frantz's (2014a) population threshold.
São Tomé and Príncipe	Movement for the Liberation of São Tomé and Príncipe/Social Democratic Party (MLSTP/PSD)	Former ruling party of one-party regime. Loses power in 1991 transition, but remains one of country's major parties. Not included in main table because São Tomé and Príncipe does not meet Geddes, Wright, and Frantz's (2014a) population threshold.

(continued)

(continued)

Country	Party	Description
Suriname	National Democratic Party (NDP)	Founded in 1987 by military dictator Dési Bouterse in anticipation of transition to competitive elections. Party returns to power in 2010 and 2015, and Bouterse becomes president. Not included in main table because Suriname does not meet Geddes, Wright, and Frantz's (2014a) population threshold.
Tunisia	Nidaa Tounes	Founded in 2012 during democratic transition by Beji Caid Essebsi, former official of Habib Bourguiba and Zine El Abidine Ben Ali dictatorships. Wins presidential and parliamentary elections in 2014. Not included in main table because formed after 2010, last year for inclusion in Geddes, Wright, and Frantz (2014a).

i The following authoritarian successor parties are not included in the main table of this appendix or in the list of third-wave democracies in Appendix I.1 because of small population size, date of formation, or other excluding factors (see individual country entries for details). However, I include them in this second table because of their significance in their respective countries.

PART I

WHY DO AUTHORITARIAN SUCCESSOR PARTIES EXIST (AND OFTEN WIN ELECTIONS)?

1

Linkage Strategies of Authoritarian Successor Parties

Herbert Kitschelt and Matthew Singer

Do political parties that are steeped in the personnel, practices, and regime party organization of authoritarian regimes give new democracies a distinctive dynamic of party competition? In this chapter, we examine the linkage strategies of authoritarian successor parties (ASPs), focusing on those parties whose operatives are affiliated with political networks that were rooted in the party governance of durable authoritarian regimes before the advent of the most recent spell of competitive party democracy. Our goal is to explore whether such parties, which correspond to the subtype of authoritarian successor parties called *former authoritarian ruling parties* (FARPs) discussed in the Introduction (Loxton, this volume), develop distinctive citizen–politician linkage profiles in their quest to establish or maintain political hegemony. And, in fact, they do. We find that FARPs mount a greater effort to develop targeted clientelistic appeals to electoral constituencies than other parties. More specifically, FARPs appear to have particular advantages when it comes to cultivating clientelistic transactions with individuals via their extensive preexisting networks that continue from the authoritarian period.

The same advantages do not apply to the other subtype of authoritarian successor parties discussed in the Introduction (Loxton, this volume), namely *reactive authoritarian successor parties* (RASPs). We do not dwell empirically on this contrast later in the chapter, but many RASPs simply lack the strength and continuity of personnel and organization that give FARPs their unique capacity to promote clientelistic partisan linkages into the democratic era.

While FARPs develop a robust and unique effort at clientelistic linkage building, they do not promote particularly high levels of programmatic clarity and cohesion. Nor are they particularly adept at embracing strategies of "linkage differentiation" to deliver both clientelistic and programmatic benefits to distinct constituencies (cf. Kitschelt and Singer 2016). The emergence of programmatic representation seems to reflect the development of state capacity to deliver on policy promises and the emergence of an electorate that cannot be easily mobilized through material inducements, not the kinds of networks that FARPs inherit from the authoritarian period.

We begin with theoretical considerations of what may enable parties to choose among different linkage strategies to attract electoral constituencies. Against this backdrop, the first section develops our conception of FARPs as a subset of the authoritarian successor parties that are the focus of this volume, and hypothesizes about whether and how such parties may have particular advantages in crafting certain electoral linkages. Crucially, we do not believe that all ASPs will have access to these resources. In particular, we do not expect that RASPs founded by former autocrats after the transition will possess the same advantages nor will ASPs that were ruling dictatorial parties for only a short period of time. Finally, we expect that the head start that FARPs enjoy will fade over time as other parties develop their own networks and as generational turnover in party leadership occurs. In the second section, we introduce the data to measure parties' linkage strategies and organizational capabilities. In the third section, we present results for parties' efforts to engage in clientelistic targeted exchanges and in programmatic ones. In the conclusion, we speculate about how the dynamics of FARP linkage building may also make these parties particularly vulnerable to electoral decline.

1.1 GENERAL CONDITIONS FOR THE FORMATION OF CITIZEN–POLITICIAN LINKAGES AND THE UNIQUE ADVANTAGES OF FORMER AUTHORITARIAN RULING PARTIES

Aldrich (1995) argues that parties often manage to master two tasks, but typically after a historical period of trial and error. First, they solve collective action problems for politicians and voters. By pooling resources, politicians use parties to develop brand recognition and economies of scale in reaching out to voters while also reducing voters' costs in comparing alternative vote options and helping them to turn out to the polls. Second, parties may also enable politicians to work out common policy positions in legislatures and campaigns (policy platforms, programs, manifestos, etc.). This allows them to speak on policy in a collective single voice, cutting through the cacophony of individual politicians' diverse preferences and enabling voters to take simple programmatic cues that constitute credible partisan policy signals.

Aldrich's historical work on US party formation illustrates that solving collective action and social choice problems under conditions of electoral competition is no mean feat. It involves heavy investments in time, money, and psychic energy and does not bear fruit overnight. As a first cut, this suggests a model of party careers through *long-term maturation through stages, if not whole life cycles, involving the construction of party organization and citizen linkages*. At the aggregate level, whole party systems may pass through this trajectory in tandem as democracies age and continue

Linkage Strategies of Authoritarian Successor Parties 55

through multiple rounds of party competition.[1] We introduce this model as a foil to highlight how FARPs can shortcut this developmental stage model:

- In *founding democratic elections*, when new parties have no time to make these investments, they and voters will be compelled to rely on simple clues to build linkages such as (1) descriptive representativeness of parties (whether in terms of class, ethnicity, religion, language, gender, or other markers), or (2) the personal charisma and pre-partisan professional and civic achievements of candidates (this is why successful soldiers win presidential office), or (3) the momentary intense salience of a single issue and the valence advantage of a party (or particular candidate) on that issue because of its issue entrepreneurship in the founding election campaigns.
- Next, in subsequent rounds of party competition, as parties begin to *accumulate a track record in the eyes of voters beyond the initial rounds of elections*, citizens may choose among them retrospectively based on (4) their ability to deliver benefits, whether in terms of large-scale collective and club goods (such as improving one's relative and absolute income), or (5) localized, small-group, restricted, and specific pork and constituency service.
- Only if parties go through a *further cumulation of rounds of competition*, however, can they achieve the *organizational investments* that enable them to generate (6) clientelistic linkages and/or (7) programmatic commitments that crystallize their electoral appeals in the competitive game.
- Ultimately, these practices may in turn help them to nurture (8) the *emergence of party identifications* that establish affective bonds between citizens and party alternatives. Whether a running tally of past clientelistic or programmatic services or an emotional bond, party identification results from cumulative partisan histories, crystallized around a record of political action and rhetoric.
- Life cycles sometimes end with the decomposition of party organization, the withering of activists, and the decline of electoral support. The remaining participants eventually have to choose between disbanding the effort and fundamentally reconceiving the party's mission and electorate. This is the process that many agrarian, some religious, and most former communist parties have undergone.

In later rounds of the electoral game, the "primitive" and "early" forms of linkage (candidate personality, descriptive representation, single-issue valence) will not entirely go away, but the more complex forms may additionally become available. And depending on the context, some will even then not entirely kick in. For the purposes of our analysis, it is important to note that clientelistic linkage presupposes organizational capabilities and thus takes time to be established (see Hicken 2011 for an overview). Clientelism, after all, involves

---

[1] For a life cycle interpretation of party-building, see Panebianco (1988: chapter 4).

a double contingency, governed by the temporal sequence of the interaction. Voters may accept benefits, but then defect and not deliver their votes and other commitments to make partisan contributions. Politicians may do likewise: they may accept support, but not deliver benefits. Incorporating partisan supporters into lasting formal party organizations and informal networks lowers the need for costly monitoring and sanctioning voters who might opportunistically defect from clientelistic, contingent exchange. Politicians will substitute heavy-handed enforcement of spot-market contracts that is difficult to engineer, particularly in a contest where the universal vote is effectively secret, by inserting agents in local partisan and social networks who observe citizens, register their gossip, and instill party allegiance by nurturing normative commitments to the party based on frequent interactions.

Because clientelistic exchange requires time to build complex organizational networks, we believe that the influential claim that clientelism is predominantly a linkage practice of "young" democracies (Keefer 2007) does not withstand close scrutiny – or at the very least needs to be qualified. At the aggregate level of comparing entire party systems, there is, if anything, a *curvilinear relationship between democratic stock, understood as the cumulative experience of politicians with democratic party competition, and parties' clientelistic linkage efforts* (Kitschelt and Kselman 2013).

There is one critical condition, however, under which the appearance of clientelism in early stages of democratic partisan competition seems warranted: if former authoritarian ruling parties are present. Political parties that ruled and mobilized regime support during an authoritarian period and then compete after a subsequent democratic transition typically have already made heavy organizational investments in personnel, party infrastructure, and linkages to administrative, economic, and social associational networks, especially in local settings. At least some of these networks and organizational capacities are likely to have survived the transition. As a consequence, these FARPs, unlike RASPs, enjoy a "flying start" into the era of democratic competition and may have capabilities to establish clientelistic linkages. The maturation or life cycle model therefore does not apply to these parties and party systems dominated by them. Our first hypothesis, therefore, states:

H1: *All else equal, former authoritarian ruling parties will display greater clientelistic effort than the average of rival parties not formerly entrenched in the governance of an authoritarian regime.*

However, FARPs are not likely to enjoy a similar advantage when it comes to developing a programmatic profile. First, in many emerging democracies, the conditions for the development of programmatic party competition may not be that promising for any political party. Let us just state a few adverse conditions that tend to undercut programmatic partisan appeals:

- Only in the presence of a sizeable proportion of citizens with elevated education and occupational skills is there a chance for strong programmatic policy demands.[2]
- Even in middle-income countries with strong developmental states,[3] the emergence of high state capacities may promote programmatic party competition and the provision of collective goods (Besley and Persson 2012; Piattoni 2001; Shefter 1977), but this applies only to a certain extent. Politicians in such polities have rapidly growing economic resources at their political discretion and may succumb to the temptation to use them for clientelistic linkage building. Taiwan, South Korea, and Japan were famously developmental states with high state capacity, yet also exhibited entrenched clientelistic parties in order to pay off the losers of rapid economic change. Parties in developmental states therefore sometimes engage in dual clientelistic–programmatic "product diversification" (cf. Díaz-Cayeros, Estévez, and Magaloni 2016; Kitschelt and Singer 2016; Magaloni 2006; and Magaloni, Díaz-Cayeros, and Estévez 2007). When developmental states move closer to the global innovation frontier, their forms of economic governance become inefficient and costly. The crisis of developmental states therefore typically also precipitates a crisis of clientelism.[4] FARPs in middle-income developmental states are thus not predestined to be particularly programmatic.
- Under some conditions, ethnic group divisions may deepen and perpetuate the viability of clientelistic partisan linkages to a certain extent (Kolev and Wang 2010).
- Democratic institutions per se are surprisingly weak determinants of parties' predominant linkage strategies (cf. Kitschelt 2011a; Lyne 2007, 2008). If demand for clientelism is high, parties can counteract the programmatic incentives encouraged, for example, by closed-list proportional representation electoral rules (e.g., Carey and Shugart 1995; Harmel and Janda 1982; Samuels and Shugart 2010) by building compensatory party organizations that sustain clientelism. Conversely, programmatic parties may overcome clientelism-nurturing institutional incentives, as the emergence of programmatic parties in Brazil beginning in the 1990s demonstrates (Hagopian, Gervasoni, and Moraes 2008; Hunter 2010; Samuels 2004).

---

[2] The development paradigm loomed large over the early literature on clientelism in the 1960s and 1970s (see Schmidt, Guasti, Landé, and Scott 1977). More recently, what is disputed are the mechanisms through which development affects linkage strategies (for a review, see Hicken 2011: 209–214; Lyne 2007, 2008).
[3] On the developmental state, see Amsden (1989), Doner, Ritchie, and Slater (2005), Evans (1995), Haggard (1990), Haggard and Kaufman (2008), Johnson (1982), Rodrik (2011), Wade (1990), and Woo-Cumings (1999).
[4] For a development of this argument and empirical evidence, see Greene (2007) and Kitschelt (2007), as well as Kitschelt and Wang (2014), and Kitschelt (2012, 2013).

Second, even in the circumstances where FARPs encounter a receptive context and opportunity structure of state capacities and political-economic development trajectories, they are likely to be in no better a position to devise a program than other more novel democratic parties. In some ways, in fact, FARPs are worse off. Just like other parties, they face the burden of devising a new programmatic formula in an environment for which they were not built. And often enough, FARPs did not subscribe to a clear ideology while serving as pillars of dictatorship. Even where they did, most citizens are likely to have discounted the ideology, as occurred, for example, under communism, where most citizens lived in a state of "preference falsification" in their public lives (Kuran 1987a, 1987b, 1991). Moreover, their past spells of authoritarian dominance may have burdened them with programmatic baggage (and a reputation) that is difficult to unload. Such baggage constitutes a liability and exacerbates FARPs' programmatic challenges. This applies especially to postcommunist parties, in particular to those with a legacy of an inflexible, rigid, doctrinal communism that did not permit any room for divergence.[5]

This generates a second hypothesis:

H2: *All else equal, FARPs in democracies will be no more able to develop a programmatic profile than parties without a legacy of authoritarian governance.*

Indeed, we find no evidence in our empirical analysis of FARPs standing out in terms of programmatic structuration of partisan appeals. We will therefore address the evidence supporting our claim in only a cursory fashion toward the end of the chapter.

Overall, our argument is that FARPs in democratic polities where there are demand- and supply-side incentives for politicians to invest in clientelistic linkages can "jump the queue" postulated by the life cycle model of linkage formation, according to which a full-fledged clientelistic effort becomes viable only after a number of rounds of party competition. From the beginning of democratic multiparty competition on a more or less level playing field, FARPs are spontaneously endowed with the resource- and organization-intensive linkage capabilities that facilitate clientelistic deployment.

In making this argument, we explicitly narrow our focus to a subset of the authoritarian successor parties that are the focus of this volume. In contrast to FARPs, many of the parties included in the other subtype of ASPs discussed in the Introduction (Loxton, this volume) did not play a role in maintaining support for the regime, but instead were created by regime incumbents in anticipation of an imminent transition to democracy or by former regime incumbents shortly thereafter. Since our analytical focus is on the importance of past organizational investment under authoritarianism for parties' later linkage strategies under democracy, we set aside reactive authoritarian successor parties that did not have this explicit authoritarian history.

---

[5] For an overview of these different legacies, see Pop-Eleches (2007).

We further restrict our qualification of authoritarian successor parties with two additional criteria. First, authoritarian ruling parties must have governed and acted as mobilizing agents for an extended period of time in order to entrench themselves and build the organizational residues that might give them an advantage in terms of clientelistic linkage building under democracy. *We propose here a minimum of ten years of authoritarian rule.* Like Svolik (2012: 42–43), we distinguish between the tenure of individual authoritarian leaders and authoritarian ruling coalition spells that may embrace a succession of leaders.

Second, we believe that organizational investments have to be treated as a perishable asset. FARPs may have a head start, but these investments are degraded by continuous turnover of personnel and changing environmental conditions and shocks to the system. Consequently, the passage of time after the end of authoritarianism devalues the usefulness of the erstwhile organizational stock as party structures evolve and as other parties catch up. Eventually, and with a new generation of leaders and middle-level cadres in charge, it becomes difficult to recognize a party as a FARP. We have empirically played with different cutoff points for a party ceasing to be a FARP after the end of dictatorship. In an earlier draft, we employed a less charitable frame of twenty years, but that met resistance by knowledgeable students of FARPs. *We have therefore settled here for a more generous, longer framework of thirty years, a period of tenure achieved or exceeded by few party leaders.* It is fair to say that after a thirty-year window, parties will have gone through an all but complete generational turnover that allows new elites and middle cadres to work through the environmental shocks and stimuli to which the party has been exposed since the end of dictatorship. We therefore cease to code a party as a FARP if its spell of authoritarian rule ended more than thirty years before our point of observation.[6]

In the remainder of this theoretical elaboration of the chapter's empirical argument, let us go one step further in specifying FARPs' advantages in forming clientelistic linkage strategies by disaggregating the concept of clientelism. The organizational advantage of FARPs in projecting clientelistic efforts may be specified more precisely by distinguishing the channels through which clientelism actually occurs. Different techniques of clientelism may address the double contingency and opportunism of the exchange in different ways. Let us distinguish between a "temporal" and a "contractual" dimension along which clientelism can be organized in different ways.

---

[6] Since our data on party organization and linkage strategies are from 2008 to 2009, our cutoff point is 1978, well before the full unfolding of most third-wave transitions to democracy. Again, we do not necessarily see this as a strict cutoff; we believe that legacy advantages will wane over time as parties evolve and either feed these networks or replace them. But for this first cut of the analysis, we needed a rule of thumb and thirty years seemed sufficient to us.

On the *temporal dimension*, the exchange may be limited to a single transaction (vote buying, gifts, and one-off services such as regulatory favors) or mark the opening of inter-temporally extended "relational" transactions (Nichter 2014). Relational clientelism may involve citizens' access to discretionary social benefits (disability insurance, health care, unemployment wage replacement, income subsidies, scholarships, etc.), as well as jobs in the public sector or in companies and nonprofits ("patronage") that are regulated and funded by government agencies, such as procurement contracts to build and run infrastructure. On the *contractual dimension*, parties may target individuals and small groups for clientelistic benefits, or they may rely on external intermediaries, such as owners/managers of large enterprises, community organizers and local intraparty or independent political brokers, or personnel of neighborhood nonprofits as the recipient of benefits,[7] in exchange for the recipients' commitments to make the brokers' constituencies support their partisan benefactor. If parties contract with external intermediaries rather than voters directly, they de facto "delegate" or "contract out" the task of partisan organization building to an external agent, or rely on an external organizational infrastructure that already exists for a different purpose. Thus, the entrepreneur who cajoles his workers into supporting a particular party or candidate does not create the organization for the purpose of electoral coordination. Parties acquire votes from an external contractor "wholesale," whereas in other instances they have to deal "retail" with individual voters and small groups.

In the empirical survey on which this chapter draws, respondents evaluated parties' efforts on five different clientelistic techniques (Table 1.1). The first, gifts and vote buying, is clearly a form of spot-market transaction targeted at individuals and small groups (e.g., families). The second and third, discretionary social benefits and employment patronage, involve relational exchanges, but are also targeted at individuals and small groups ("retail" level). The fourth, material favors through regulatory rulings, is harder to locate. For the most part, these are of a wholesale contractual nature, as they accrue to firms more than to individuals. However, they may be both spot-market or relational. Finally, procurement contracts are clearly in the realm of relational-contractual clientelism.

From the perspective of political parties, the effort the party organization has to make to counteract voter opportunism and defection is greater the more individualized ("retail"), short-term, and single-shot the contract. In other

---

[7] There is now an extensive literature on political brokerage, particularly in Latin American countries, but also elsewhere. See, for example, Auyero (2001), Gay (1994), Stokes, Dunning, Nazareno, and Brusco (2013), Szwarcberg (2012, 2013, 2014), and Weitz-Shapiro (2014). But the concept of brokerage should not be confined to party-affiliated vote consolidators; they should also include independently operating political mobilizers and community-inserted notables. See, for example, Holland and Palmer-Rubin (2015).

TABLE 1.1 *Typology of clientelistic exchange*

		Contracts	
		Retail	Wholesale
Time frame	Single shot	Vote buying (b1)	Regulatory rulings (b5)
	Relational	Social benefits + patronage (b2 + b3)	Procurement contracts (b4)

words, spot-market vote buying exchanges are the most expensive transactions, requiring the most elaborate party organization and suffering the greatest dissipation of resources through the "leakiness" of the clientelistic bucket. The opposite applies across the diagonal, with iterated "wholesale" group transactions, such as procurement grants to company towns. Individually geared relational clientelism (social program benefits, patronage) and wholesale spot-markets (e.g., some regulatory decisions) are somewhere in between.

Given that organizational networks – both within the formal organization of the party as well as the informal networks in the community – are FARPs' main strength in clientelistic linkage building compared to other parties, we would expect them to have the greatest comparative advantage with regard to the deployment of short-term "retail" clientelism, but less with regard to wholesale iterated clientelism. This yields our third hypothesis:

H3: *The FARP advantage through channels of party organization affects specific clientelistic exchanges most. Mediated by their organizational and network capabilities, FARPs are expected to make greater efforts in providing "retail" and "spot-market" clientelistic transactions than other parties.*

Because of their deeper and broader organizational infrastructure, FARPs are more prone to deliver spot-market clientelism (gifts and vote buying), as this requires more organized effort (monitoring, sanctioning of defectors) to counteract the ever-present opportunism of the clients to take the benefit but not deliver their votes. Even so, FARPs are also likely to devote most of their resources to iterative and corporate-wholesale clientelism. But sustaining these practices of relational exchange also involves the construction of rather elaborate social networks of supporters and often enough a quite extensive organizational infrastructure (cf. Kitschelt and Kselman 2014).[8] These may give FARPs an advantage as well.

---

[8] The literature on clientelistic party organization has proliferated, but because of its micro-focus it has been confined to a few highly studied empirical reference cases, such as Argentina (cf. Auyero 2001; Stokes et al. 2013; Szwarcberg 2012, 2013, 2014).

1.1.1 Alternative Explanations

We will control for a range of rival explanations for clientelistic efforts, both at the level of the individual party and that of features of the polity as a whole. Electoral size of party and government incumbency are the obvious mechanisms that may advance a party's capacity to build party organization quickly and thus compensate for the disadvantages of having an authoritarian past. More difficult would be a party age control, as it is obviously collinear with FARP status.

At the level of general features of the polity, we have to control for demand- and supply-side conditions of clientelism. On the demand side, development plays a role, but its relationship to clientelistic partisan linkage efforts is not linear but curvilinear. Middle-income countries show the greatest prowess to promote clientelistic parties (Kitschelt and Kselman 2013). Indeed, middle-income developmental states with a broad scope of economic resources at the disposal of politicians embrace clientelism most vigorously. We also control for democratic experience and its square term that take into account Keefer's (2007) argument about age of democracy and linkage strategy. Finally, we will control for the presence of a level playing field or the democratic openness of political competition, as in the absence thereof FARPs' chances of producing clientelistic and programmatic linkages would be shaped by authoritarian advantages and liabilities.

To summarize, we expect FARPs to shortcut the arduous pathway of organizational investments in clientelistic networks. But we see no theoretical grounds to expect them to promote highly programmatic appeals when compared to their competitors. In a similar vein, even in middle-income countries on a developmental state trajectory, it is unlikely that FARPs will be more vigorous programmatic or differentiated dual-track clientelistic and programmatic linkage builders, at least once we control for electoral size and government participation.

1.2 THE DATA

Most of the theoretically interesting variables and indicators are constructed from the Democratic Accountability and Linkages Project (DALP) and are publicly available online (http://sites.duke.edu/democracylinkage). Before we explain the construction of programmatic and clientelistic partisan linkage efforts, let us briefly discuss our empirical operationalization of FARPs.

1.2.1 Former Authoritarian Ruling Parties

As discussed above, for the purposes of exploring the role of prior investments in party organization on clientelistic and programmatic strategies, we focus on a subset of authoritarian successor parties: former authoritarian ruling parties.

In addition, we constrain our classification of former authoritarian ruling parties by two criteria, namely (1) that they ruled for a minimum of ten years and (2) that the end of that rule predates the point at which we observe parties' linkage strategies by no more than thirty years.

But even with this definition, empirical classification of cases may not be entirely unambiguous. It is in the nature of constructing a dummy variable that some cases appear to be just below or above the coding cutoff point, and reasonable minds may disagree on where to draw the precise line. This challenge concerns the question about which polities should be considered sufficiently democratic to qualify parties as "former" authoritarian ruling parties,[9] as well as the question about which parties in more or less competitive electoral polities have sufficiently strong organizational and personal ties to past authoritarian ruling parties to qualify as FARPs.

These borderline parties are located in Croatia, Lithuania, Slovakia, and Slovenia. The main consideration here is not so much that three of the four candidates for FARP classification display substantially less clientelistic effort than most FARPs in the full set (see Appendix 1.1 for a list of FARP codings). The critical question is their link to the former regime. In the case of Slovakia's Direction-Social Democracy (Smer-SD), the link is the most tenuous, as the party is a personalistic breakaway from the communist successor Party of the Democratic Left (SDL'), which had already strayed far from its authoritarian origins in terms of personnel and organizational reach and had also undergone severe electoral decline. Slightly more plausible cases are the Social Democratic Party of Croatia (SDP), the Social Democrats (SD) in Slovenia, and the Democratic Labor Party of Lithuania (LDDP), which became part of the Social Democratic Party of Lithuania after merging with the Social Democratic Party in 2001. But several considerations weigh against including these parties. Even as regional ruling communist parties in the 1980s, they were increasingly set against the federal ruling parties of the Soviet Union and Yugoslavia, which imposed the will of the dominant titular majorities (Russian, Serbian) on formally affiliated regional parties. These regional parties effectively became strongholds of regional resistance and in that capacity tolerated (if not nurtured) a range of ethnoregional civic associations, many of which later transformed into parties in their own right. This configuration led to the almost complete disappearance of former regional communist party affiliates in some countries (Estonia, Latvia), and to very profound organizational, personnel, and programmatic ruptures with the old regimes and their titular ethnic Russian or Serbian majorities in others. Unlike

---

[9] Thus, we included in our count the somewhat problematic cases of Botswana and Senegal. However, we excluded the clearly authoritarian countries of Angola, Egypt, Malaysia, Morocco, Mozambique, Russia, and Tanzania, even though DALP data are available on parties in all of these polities. The results are similar if Botswana and Senegal are excluded as these cases are not outliers with respect to clientelism (Figure 1.1).

Loxton's coding (Introduction, this volume), we therefore exclude the parties in these four countries from our list of FARPs. However, we have also estimated our statistical calculations with his coding to ensure that the basic pattern of associations is robust and the substantive conclusions are the same.[10]

We identify a total of 25 FARPs in an equal number of countries. FARPs appear in 25 of the 82 democratic polities covered by the DALP (30 percent) and make up 5.2 percent of the 478 parties scored. The specific parties are listed in Appendix 1.1 of this chapter. Comparing this list to Loxton's FARPs, the DALP dataset does not have data on eight of Loxton's cases (Central African Republic, Republic of Congo, Guinea-Bissau, Lesotho, Malawi, Montenegro, Nepal, and Sierra Leone). Moreover, in three instances former authoritarian ruling parties were not entrenched for a sufficiently long time period to qualify for our FARP criterion (Bangladesh, Nicaragua, and Peru).

To isolate the effect of a party's FARP background on clientelistic linkage, we must control for other conditions that affect parties' choice of linkage strategies and that display some at least mild correlation with the presence of FARPs. Clientelism tends to be more prominent in poorer and middle-income countries and among countries with less democratic experience, as measured by Gerring, Bond, Barndt, and Moreno's (2005) index of democratic capital stock. Of course, by restricting our sample to only democracies there is little difference in the contemporary level of democracy in these countries (Table 1.2). While FARPs

TABLE 1.2 *Characteristics of countries with each type of party*

	Per capita GDP	Democracy stock	Average democracy score (polity)
Country has former authoritarian ruling party (N = 25)	9,340 (1,564)	−152 (24)	8.31 (0.24)
Countries without former authoritarian ruling party (N = 56)	18,308 (1,827)	198 (41)	8.13 (0.40)
T-test of equality (df = 79)[(i)]	3.06 ($p < 0.01$)	5.54 ($p < 0.001$)	−0.30 (NS)

Notes: Standard errors in parentheses. (i) Two-tailed t-tests; NS = not significant at conventional levels.

---

[10] The Party of Regions in the Ukraine is also a borderline case. While the party was founded in 1998, it attracted most of the former Communist Party apparatus and politicians following the Orange Revolution, as well as most of the Communist Party's voters (the Communist Party went from 19.9 percent in 2002 to 3.7 percent in 2006). However, because of the indirect linkage to the country's former authoritarian ruling party, we do not code it as a FARP in the analysis that follows. This coding choice does not affect the substantive interpretation of the statistical analysis.

TABLE 1.3 *Electoral strength by party type*

	Average vote in last two elections	In government at the time of the survey?
Former authoritarian ruling party ($N = 25$)	28.5% (3.2)	56%
All other parties ($N = 453$)	13.8% (0.6)	35.5%
T-test of equality ($df = 476$)[i]	5.25 ($p < 0.001$)	2.07 ($p < 0.05$)

Notes: Standard errors in parentheses. (i) Two-tailed t-tests.

tend to be electorally more successful than their domestic competitors (Table 1.3), there is substantial variation in electoral success across FARPs at the time of the DALP survey. Four of them averaged less than 10 percent of the vote in the last two national legislative elections preceding the DALP survey, and only a handful of them command majorities in legislatures.

1.2.2 DALP Coded Variables: Clientelistic and Programmatic Partisan Linkage Efforts and Organizational Scope

The Democratic Accountability and Linkages Project (DALP) is an expert survey-based data collection effort implemented in eighty-eight countries between 2007 and 2008.[11] In most countries, the DALP solicited responses from between ten and thirty political scientists with relevant expertise, along with a handful of journalists covering these processes for national newspapers.[12] The survey focuses on political parties' organization, clientelistic linkage strategies, and programmatic appeals. The unit of observation is the individual party, and summary indices can be created for each party's clientelistic effort and electoral effectiveness, as well as its organizational extensiveness, centralization and emergence in associational networks beyond its organizational boundaries, and the extent of its programmatic structuring and the substantive focus of its policy appeals.

---

[11] As criteria for inclusion in the study, we chose democracies with a minimum of 2 million inhabitants. In this chapter, we exclude some countries in the DALP dataset that have not completed the transition to competitive democracy. The DALP was implemented with support from the World Bank, Duke University, and the Chilean National Research Agency.

[12] We enlarged the sample in India, where a total of seventy-eight respondents completed the survey. However, they were regionally stratified, such that only a core set of approximately national parties were scored by all Indian experts, whereas regional parties were scored only by experts located in different regions. We also recruited a particularly large sample for Nigeria to code regional differences.

We provide here a sketch of critical indicator construction while more information can be found on the project website.

1.2.2.1 *Extensiveness of Party Organization*

Given that our theory looks at the advantage that FARPs have in deploying an organizational infrastructure of mobilization, we first begin by looking at how they differ from comparable parties with regard to their organizational structure. The DALP survey offers several indicators to measure a party's formal or informal organizational extensiveness and network ties. These measures all treat organizational size independently of parties' electoral support. (There is, of course, some correlation between the two. Some parties, however, have strong electoral support, yet minute organizations on the ground.) To generate an estimate of party organization, we focus on what Janda (1980) conceptualizes as a party's geographical extensiveness. It refers to the portion of a country's (inhabited) territory in which a party maintains active contact with the local population. Contact with local populations may be overseen by formal branch offices staffed by supporters and activists who serve as the party's local voice and representatives (variable a1). However, such relations – especially in developing countries and younger democracies – may also be organized through *informal* channels via personal, diffuse connections with local "notables" such as religious leaders, neighborhood captains, labor activists, and merchants.

Thus two questions from the DALP survey's first module tap the extent of a party's formal (a1) and informal (a3) geographical extensiveness. Both are prefaced with a short vignette, and then ask respondents to assess whether parties maintain formal and informal ties in "MOST" of a country's districts, in "SOME" of a country's districts, or in almost "NO" districts.[13] One of them asks about the rough share of a country's local districts in which the party has a presence through offices and staff (a1). The other asks for the rough share of local districts in which the party relies strongly on local intermediaries (a3). Informal and formal extensiveness are correlated at $r = 0.74$, i.e., parties that maintain formal ties to the local population also tend to maintain informal networks, and vice versa.

1.2.2.2 *Clientelistic Effort*

Our main hypotheses focus on the overall levels of clientelism that FARPs use (H1) and the specific forms of clientelism that they will be positioned to emphasize (H3). We test these hypotheses through a series of questions about

---

[13] The survey item on formal extensiveness had response options scaling whether local branches are present in most, some, or none of the localities, and also had an option indicating that parties maintain local branches only during periods of electoral competition. We scale the option that local branches exist only temporarily as being between parties having offices in "none" of the districts and "some" of the districts. This choice has no bearing on subsequent results; other rescaling options yield indices correlated with ours at $r = 0.97$.

the types of material benefits that parties provide. The survey avoids the notion of "clientelism" because of its negative semantic loading and vague connotations, at least among intellectuals. Instead, it asks experts to score parties' use of various transactional practices, as listed in Table 1.1. A quasi-vignette at the opening of the survey section dealing with clientelistic party efforts was meant to prime respondents to follow a specific interpretation of the scoring scale, thus reducing the problem of differential item functioning (DIF). The specific question wordings for the indicators are discussed in Kitschelt (2011b), but high values represent parties making a major effort to secure support by offering each form of goods. A summary indicator additively combines the scores on all five variables to capture total levels of clientelistic effort.

Given that intellectuals assessed the parties, we suspect that there is an upward bias in scoring clientelism across the board in the entire dataset. A problem for comparative analysis, however, will result from this bias only if it affects different parties and countries in distinctive ways. We checked whether experts scored parties for which they indicated less sympathy higher on clientelistic effort, but this relationship surfaced rarely and only in mild form. Construct validity tests suggest that there is only limited (if any) bias resulting from DIF, the use of systematically different anchor points in scoring parties across countries.[14]

1.2.2.3 *Programmatic Appeal*

In the Online Appendix to this chapter, we provide more detail on the construction of the index of parties' programmatic structuration and voter appeal.[15] We follow a thoroughly Downsian spatial conception of programmatic appeals (Downs 1957). To enable voters to discern a party's program and make that program a criterion of choice among competing considerations, the party's appeal must simultaneously meet three standards. First, parties must exhibit a modicum of internal *cohesiveness* in their policy appeals, such that a party's key politicians pretty consistently support identical policy programs that enable experts to agree on the party's policy scores. Second, parties must attribute *salience* to the issue dimensions on which they take relatively cohesive positions. Voters discount partisans' policy pronouncements if they do not see parties making a credible effort to act on their positions. Third, voters can employ these party positions to choose among competitors only if parties support *positional alternatives*.

---

[14] One strategy of construct validation is to relate clientelistic effort to economic development, the most robust predictor of this linkage strategy. Not finding an association between the two would not have cast doubt on the theory of development so much as on the validity of the clientelism measures. The scoring of parties is also generally in line with conventional wisdom, where detailed individual case studies are available.

[15] The web appendix is available at https://sites.duke.edu/democracylinkage/papers/.

We develop a multiplicative term for each issue dimension, combining cohesion (Co) with salience (Sa) and positional differentiation (Po) of a party's program as a singular index score ("CoSalPo"), with each component running from 0 to 1.0, and therefore the whole index also covering the unit range. For each party, we then compute the average CoSalPo score over their four "best," most programmatic policy areas from a larger set of policy areas. Parties cannot score high on the index by being programmatically structured on just one issue (say, immigration). However, they need not be highly programmatic on all issue dimensions scored by experts.[16] For more details, as well as robustness tests and validation, see the Online Appendix and Kitschelt and Freeze (2010).

1.3 ANALYSIS: ORGANIZATIONAL STRUCTURES AND LINKAGE EFFORTS

Let us state up front that with only cross-sectional observational data at hand, our analysis is confined to a "correlational" exercise, where no compelling conclusions can be drawn as to the direction of causality among the observed phenomena. Case study narratives and plausibility considerations about the historical flow of political developments may support some causal interpretations, yet supply no clinching proof. Nevertheless, the quest to establish causality becomes enticing only when the correlation between relevant phenomena has first been established. And that, as we will see, is hard enough to achieve for our chapter.

1.3.1 Former Authoritarian Ruling Parties Have Larger Networks

We have argued that FARPs are potentially able to take advantage of their roots in the previous regime to build more extensive formal and informal infrastructures than parties in similar developmental circumstances. Table 1.4 reveals that FARPs are more likely to have extensive formal networks, connections to informal networks and local notables, and ties with civil society organizations than other parties in our sample.[17] We also include a summary measure of network extensiveness that is based on a factor analysis of these three variables,[18] and we see that FARPs are more likely to have extensive networks

---

[16] In other words, our conception of parties' programmatic appeal does not accommodate a pure valence or (single) issue-ownership model of political party competition.

[17] Raw variables were recoded on a 0–3 (a1), 0–2 (a3), and 0–6 (a8s) scale, with high scores always indicating greater organization and denser network relations. Unfortunately, expert coding instructions for some Latin American countries in DALP were at variance with those in other countries and consequently yield a different a8s count (see the DALP online codebook, p. 21, at http://sites.duke.edu/democracylinkage/files/2014/12/DALP_Codebook_2014-04_01.pdf). All relations hold, regardless of whether countries with divergent a8s coding are included or not. Data on this variable is missing for two parties, the Belgian FN and the Irish Sinn Fein.

[18] This variable ranges in size from −2.78 to 1.68 and has a mean value of 0.

Linkage Strategies of Authoritarian Successor Parties 69

TABLE 1.4 *Parties' organizational traits: extensiveness and social networks*

	Extensiveness of local offices (a1)	Ties to local notables (a3)	Ties to civil society organizations (a8)	Latent variable of network size
Among all parties				
Former authoritarian ruling party (N=25)	2.64 (0.09)	1.58 (0.07)	2.27 (0.20)	0.76 (0.12)
All other parties (N=453)[i]	2.03 (0.03)	1.19 (0.02)	1.97 (0.05)	−0.06 (0.04)
T-test of equality (df=476)[ii]	4.61 ($p<0.001$)	4.38 ($p<0.001$)	1.40 (NS)	4.74 ($p<0.001$)
Among parties that averaged more than 15 percent in the last two elections				
Former authoritarian ruling party (N=19)	2.78 (0.07)	1.68 (0.06)	2.44 (0.21)	0.97 (0.09)
All other parties (N=144)	2.45 (0.4)	1.54 (0.02)	2.21 (0.10)	0.59 (0.05)
T-test of equality (df=161)[ii]	2.95 ($p<0.01$)	1.91 ($p<0.10$)	0.84 (NS)	2.80 ($p<0.01$)

Notes: Standard errors in parentheses. (i) Belgium's National Front and Ireland's Sinn Fein are missing information on the ties to civil society organization and network size variables and so those measures are based on 450 parties. (ii) Two-tailed *t*-tests.

than do other parties. Part of this gap reflects the FARPs' electoral support advantage. However, even if we restrict the sample to parties that averaged at least 15 percent of the vote in the last two elections, we see that the gap between FARPs and other parties remains substantial, even if their number of ties to civil society organizations is not quite significant at conventional levels.

Multivariate analysis confirms these basic descriptive patterns. In Table 1.5, a hierarchical linear model enters each of these three organizational variables with controls for the (logged) level of economic development, democratic experience or "capital stock" using Gerring et al.'s (2005) measure, and level of current democratic competitive openness. For each dependent variable, the first specification includes only national-level controls; the second also includes party-level controls (average electoral support in the two most recent legislative elections[19] and cabinet participation at the time of the survey). Given that the relationship between electoral success and parties' organizational structures is

---

[19] Parties' electoral support is logged because we expect there to be diminishing returns to size. It is then centered to facilitate interpretation.

TABLE 1.5 *Organizational characteristics of political parties*

	Extensiveness of local offices (a1)		Ties to local notables (a3)		Ties to civil society organizations (a8)		Overall network size (latent variable)	
	[1]	[2]	[3]	[4]	[5]	[6]	[7]	[8]
Former authoritarian ruling party	0.549*** (0.120)	0.209* (0.089)	0.382*** (0.091)	0.113° (0.068)	0.358* (0.150)	0.067 (0.132)	0.781*** (0.172)	0.264* (0.124)
Log(average vote in last two elections), centered		0.915*** (0.053)		0.670*** (0.040)		0.737*** (0.079)		1.322*** (0.073)
Party is in government		0.068 (0.043)		0.084** (0.033)		0.165** (0.064)		0.150* (0.060)
Log(GDP)	0.352** (0.129)	0.401** (0.128)	−0.052 (0.070)	−0.033 (0.066)	−0.623*** (0.189)	−0.598** (0.199)	0.134 (0.145)	0.193 (0.143)
Democracy stock	−0.001** (0.000)	−0.001*** (0.000)	0.001 (0.001)	−0.001 (0.001)	0.001 (0.001)	0.001 (0.001)	−0.001 (0.001)	−0.001* (0.001)
Polity democracy score	0.009 (0.021)	−0.004 (0.021)	−0.014 (0.012)	−0.022* (0.011)	0.022 (0.031)	0.015 (0.032)	−0.006 (0.024)	−0.024 (0.023)
Latin American country					−1.470*** (0.154)	−1.507*** (0.161)		
Constant	0.600 (0.453)	0.472 (0.449)	1.522*** (0.247)	1.480*** (0.231)	4.540*** (0.667)	4.428*** (0.701)	−0.512 (0.511)	−0.661 (0.501)

Variance components							
Country level	0.097	0.123	0.013	0.022	0.234	0.292	0.076	0.130
	(0.024)	(0.024)	(0.007)	(0.006)	(0.052)	(0.057)	(0.030)	(0.029)
Party level	0.301	0.154	0.179	0.093	0.461	0.339	0.635	0.307
	(0.021)	(0.011)	(0.013)	(0.007)	(0.033)	(0.024)	(0.045)	(0.022)
N parties	478	478	478	478	476	476	476	476
N countries	81	81	81	81	81	81	81	81
Wald χ^2	36.29***	436.05***	23.63***	418.22***	102.60***	227.35***	24.62***	472.37***

Notes: Hierarchical linear models, standard errors in parentheses; ° $p<0.10$, * $p<0.05$, ** $p<0.01$, *** $p<0.001$.

strongly endogenous, we want to ascertain whether FARP status makes an independent contribution when controlling for those factors. The estimated hierarchical linear model controls for clustering in the errors within country cases while adjusting for the smaller number of degrees of freedom for the country-level variables. We use the same specification in all multivariate analyses in this chapter.

FARPs consistently have larger party networks in all but one specification for civil society associational ties. Interestingly, country-level controls explain little of the organizational variance, even in organizational structure, while party-level controls perform as expected.[20] Net of multilevel controls, FARPs invariably display greater organizational extensiveness, something we expect to position them well in launching clientelistic linkage building.[21] This picture also does not change when the five disputed borderline-FARPs are recoded (Slovakia, Croatia, Slovenia, Lithuania, and Ukraine). In analyses not shown here, we created a dummy for Loxton's (Introduction, this volume) other subset of ASPs, reactive authoritarian successor parties. Some of them do have large networks, especially parties like ARENA in El Salvador that did not draw on a preexisting party but were able to activate other preexisting networks the authoritarian regime had used to manage its rule. Yet these do not have consistently larger organizational networks than equivalent non-ASPs in similar settings. There are so few of these parties that we should take care in interpreting that non-finding. But the results are consistent with our expectations: having an authoritarian legacy before democratization is associated with more extensive networks afterwards.

1.3.2 Former Authoritarian Ruling Parties Expend More Effort on Clientelism

Our next step is to determine whether FARPs also engage in more clientelistic efforts and whether the mechanism through which this practice operates indeed involves the availability of more organizational network capabilities. There is variation across FARPs in how much they rely on clientelism (Figure 1.1). Yet

---

[20] One exception is the additional dummy variable control "Latin American" in columns 5 and 6, Table 1.5. This delivers a distinctive negative impact on the presence of party ties to civil society associations, but does not disturb the relationship between the variables of theoretical interest and parties' organizational features. We had to enter the Latin American control for civil society organizations for a purely technical reason. In most Latin American countries, experts completing the DALP questionnaire could only single out a party's relationship to one set of civil society associations (e.g., labor, business, women), whereas everywhere else experts could indicate multiple ties. This generates a downward bias for the Latin American scores in case of the civil society association variable.

[21] We also checked whether expert sympathies could have biased these results. Do experts unsympathetic to FARPs systematically score them lower and those sympathetic score them higher and does it make a difference for the observed main effects? Whatever traces of bias we find is mild and does not affect the results of interest.

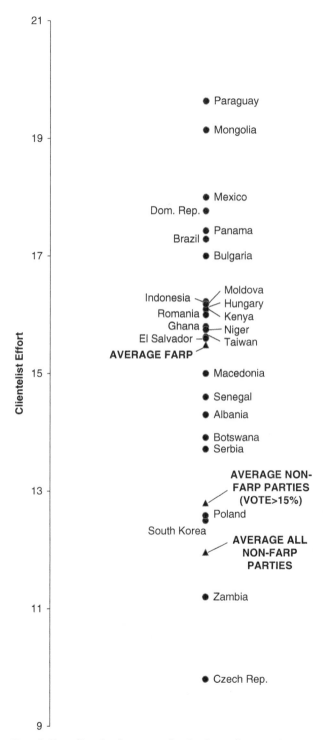

FIGURE 1.1 Use of clientelism by former authoritarian ruling parties

TABLE 1.6 *Average clientelistic score (b15) by party size and former authoritarian ruling party status*

	All parties	Parties whose average vote in last two elections<15%	Parties whose average vote in last two elections>15%
Former authoritarian ruling party	15.49 (SE=0.47, N=25)	14.16 (SE=0.88, N=6)	15.9 (SE=0.52, N=19)
All other parties	11.96 (SE=0.18, N=453)	11.5 (SE=0.21, N=309)	12.8 (SE=0.32, N=144)
T-test of equality[i]	4.62 ($p<0.001$)	1.73 ($p<0.10$)	3.39 ($p<0.001$)

Notes: Standard errors and number of cases in parentheses. (i) Two-tailed t-tests.

the descriptive data confirm that FARPs engage in more clientelistic mobilization than other parties on average, even when we distinguish between electorally more or less successful parties (Table 1.6). In spite of the variation in pursuing clientelism among FARPs, almost all of them make more clientelistic effort than the average non-FARP.

A series of multivariate HLM models suggests that FARP status indeed contributes to a party's clientelistic effort, and that this effort is (1) partially endogenous to the FARPs' outsized (logged) electoral success in the two most recent legislative elections,[22] and also (2) a function of its organizational network size. So organizational capabilities are indeed the mediating factor through which FARPs arrive at greater clientelistic targeting. Hence, when we enter either electoral size or organizational network capabilities as controls (columns 3 and 4 in Table 1.7), the size of the direct effect of a party being a FARP is cut by more than half. When both variables are entered simultaneously (column 5, Table 1.7), that coefficient falls a little further, albeit remaining statistically significant. FARPs may have other factors that make them prone to using clientelism, but much of their reliance on clientelism is a function of their preexisting networks and their success at reentering office. At the national level, the estimations reproduce only the patterns familiar from and analyzed by Kitschelt and Kselman (2013), with the prominent curvilinear effects of GDP and of democratic experience on parties' clientelistic efforts.

[22] In alternative specifications we have used the percentage of the vote received in the most recent election and, if anything, the difference between FARPs and their competitors is larger when this control is used to measure party size. Because there are a couple of parties that received less than 1 percent in the most recent election, we add 1 to the average vote total before logging it to facilitate its interpretation.

TABLE 1.7 *Hierarchical model of clientelistic effort*

	[1]	[2]	[3]	[4]	[5]
Former authoritarian ruling party	2.019*** (0.494)	1.937*** (0.489)	0.981* (0.445)	0.868* (0.420)	0.745 (0.419)
Network size			1.230*** (0.119)		0.497*** (0.157)
Log(average vote in last two elections), centered				2.397*** (0.249)	1.725*** (0.324)
Party is in government				0.801*** (0.201)	0.730*** (0.201)
Log(GDP)		32.633*** (6.992)	38.224*** (7.140)	34.213*** (7.399)	36.114*** (7.283)
Log(GDP)^2		−4.688*** (0.924)	−5.456*** (0.944)	−4.885*** (0.978)	−5.153*** (0.963)
Democracy stock		0.001 (0.001)	0.001 (0.001)	0.001 (0.001)	0.001 (0.001)
Democracy stock^2		−0.001*** (0.001)	−0.001** (0.001)	−0.001*** (0.001)	−0.001*** (0.001)
Polity democracy score		0.119 (0.088)	0.121 (0.090)	0.095 (0.094)	0.104 (0.092)
Constant	12.145*** (0.347)	−42.462*** (13.097)	−52.519*** (13.363)	−45.720*** (13.849)	−49.062*** (13.627)
Variance components					
Country level	8.672 (1.512)	1.688 (0.437)	2.015 (0.455)	2.342 (0.485)	2.237 (0.469)
Party level	4.881 (0.346)	4.937 (0.353)	3.870 (0.277)	3.437 (0.245)	3.390 (0.242)
N parties	478	478	476	478	476
N countries	81	81	81	81	81
Wald χ^2	16.68***	239.2***	334.49***	375.57***	393.63***

Notes: Hierarchical linear models, standard errors in parentheses; ° $p<0.10$, * $p<0.05$, ** $p<0.01$, *** $p<0.001$

With the data used in our regression setup of Table 1.7, we can also again confirm that FARPs, restrictively defined, are different from other authoritarian successor parties, particularly the RASPs, Loxton's (Introduction, this volume) second subtype of ASPs. In additional analyses in the Online Appendix, we have run the models in Table 1.7, adding an additional dummy for being one of the FARPs on Loxton's list that we do not code as FARP. We find no evidence that these parties diverge from other parties in the dataset, even before party- and country-level controls are applied. Authoritarian successor parties that did not play a key role in the authoritarian regime in the relatively recent past and thus did not inherit an advantage in building those networks do not seem to make any special effort when it comes to establishing clientelistic mobilization structures.

1.3.3 Differentiating Between Types of Clientelism

In disaggregating clientelistic exchanges, we hypothesized that former authoritarian ruling parties' network assets should make more of a difference for linkages with high transaction costs, such as single-shot "retail" clientelism (e.g., vote buying or gift giving) rather than relational and/or "wholesale" targeted exchanges. FARPs should have especially few advantages in "wholesale" transactions where parties can contract out the capacity of voter mobilization and monitoring to external agents, such as firms or neighborhood political entrepreneurs (independent brokers). In operational terms, clientelism mediated through procurement contracts or regulatory decisions that accrue to companies and other collectives should be just as attractive a linkage strategy for parties with lesser organizational capabilities and shallower networks as for well-entrenched FARPs.

To explore this question, Table 1.8 replicates the HLM estimations of Table 1.7, column 4, but now without the roundabout consolidated measure of clientelistic effort, combining all forms of targeted exchange in one single category as the dependent variable, but with each of the distinct contractual relations separated as a dependent variable on its own. We then want to compare the coefficients for the FARP dummy across the various clientelistic linkage techniques. What we find is that FARP status indeed makes little difference for targeted procurement (b4) and regulatory decisions (b5), but yields a much larger and robustly significant coefficient for the spot-market, "retail" transactions delivered as material goods (b1). In addition, one of the more often relational "retail" clientelistic techniques, social program benefits (b2), yields a substantively important and statistically significant coefficient. The difference between social program benefits (b2) with significant coefficient and patronage jobs (b3) without may be that, while both are at the retail level, politicians may make social program benefits more easily available on a spot-market basis than patronage jobs.

As we look at why FARPs have less dominance in the wholesale forms of clientelistic exchange, we note that the coefficient for "party in government" as

TABLE 1.8 *Hierarchical model of different types of clientelistic effort*

	Material goods (b1)	Social programs (b2)	Patronage jobs (b3)	Procurement (b4)	Regulatory decisions (b5)
Former authoritarian ruling party	0.272** (0.091)	0.244** (0.091)	0.118 (0.088)	0.085 (0.094)	0.087 (0.084)
Log(vote in last two elections), centered	0.386*** (0.054)	0.451*** (0.054)	0.429*** (0.052)	0.570*** (0.056)	0.495*** (0.050)
Party is in government	0.075° (0.044)	0.121** (0.044)	0.178*** (0.042)	0.215*** (0.045)	0.195*** (0.040)
Log(GDP)	6.314*** (1.718)	6.732*** (1.599)	6.745*** (1.956)	6.011*** (1.791)	7.172*** (1.621)
Log(GDP)^2	−0.966*** (0.227)	−0.942*** (0.211)	−0.979*** (0.258)	−0.865*** (0.237)	−0.975*** (0.214)
Democracy stock	0.001 (0.001)	0.001 (0.001)	0.001 (0.001)	0.001 (0.001)	0.001 (0.001)
Democracy stock^2	−0.001** (0.001)	−0.001** (0.001)	−0.001*** (0.001)	−0.001*** (0.001)	−0.001** (0.001)
Polity democracy score	0.032 (0.022)	0.021 (0.020)	0.049* (0.025)	0.015 (0.023)	−0.022 (0.021)
Constant	−7.446* (3.216)	−9.189** (2.993)	−8.923* (3.659)	−7.544* (3.351)	−10.208*** (3.033)
Variance components					
Country level	0.131 (0.026)	0.109 (0.023)	0.184 (0.034)	0.144 (0.028)	0.119 (0.024)
Party level	0.162 (0.012)	0.163 (0.012)	0.148 (0.011)	0.170 (0.012)	0.136 (0.010)
N parties	478	478	478	478	478
N countries	81	81	81	81	81
Wald χ^2	311.77***	231.58***	270.85***	365.46***	303.99***

Notes: Hierarchical linear models, standard errors in parentheses; ° $p<0.10$, * $p<0.05$, ** $p<0.01$, *** $p<0.001$.

a predictor of clientelistic practice rises from the high transaction cost forms of clientelism (b1, b2) to the low transaction cost forms (b4, b5). So here it is not

FARP status that gives an advantage to a party in crafting clientelistic linkages, but the party's government incumbency, which grants it access to state resources that can be deployed for electoral purposes.

1.3.4 Former Authoritarian Ruling Parties and Programmatic Effort: No Distinctive Results

The data in the previous section confirm that FARPs with established formal and informal networks are better positioned to engage in clientelistic mobilization than parties that lack this legacy. Above we advanced the hypothesis that the same does not apply to programmatic politics. The programmatic policy challenges of a democracy are too different from those of authoritarian rule to give FARPs much of a head start. Indeed, the indicator of programmatic effort constructed from the DALP survey suggests that FARPs do not have any special advantages with regard to programmatic competition. On average, FARPs are less programmatic than other parties (Table 1.9). Yet this may reflect the relatively low levels of development in the kinds of countries where one encounters FARPs frequently. Once that and other confounding factors are controlled for, FARPs are neither more nor less programmatic than other parties of a similar size (Table 1.10). Having an authoritarian legacy to draw upon does not, on average, make parties more programmatic, net of a country's level of development.

Column 3 of Table 1.10 helps to provide some leverage on why FARPs are not necessarily programmatic. We noted that the collective action issues involved in clientelistic mobilization are different than those involved in building a common set of programmatic appeals. Clientelistic mobilization requires a large spatial network of brokers inside the party or across the community who distribute goods and at least indirectly monitor the behavior

TABLE 1.9 *Levels of programmatic effort by party origin*

	Average CoSalPo
Former authoritarian ruling party (*N*=25)	0.244
	(0.027)
All other parties (*N*=453)	0.282
	(0.007)
T-test of equality (*df*=476)[i]	−1.21
	(NS)

Notes: (i) Two-tailed t-tests. NS = not significant.

TABLE 1.10 *Hierarchical model of programmatic effort*

	[1]	[2]	[3]
Former authoritarian ruling party	0.017 (0.017)	0.004 (0.017)	0.001 (0.017)
Log(vote in last two elections), centered		0.031** (0.010)	0.029* (0.014)
Party is in government		0.008 (0.008)	0.007 (0.008)
National leaders control nominations			0.018° (0.009)
Network size			0.000 (0.007)
Log(GDP)	0.204*** (0.034)	0.205*** (0.034)	0.207*** (0.034)
Democracy stock	0.001 (0.001)	0.001 (0.001)	0.001 (0.001)
Polity democracy score	0.001 (0.005)	0.001 (0.005)	−0.001 (0.006)
Constant	−0.548*** (0.118)	−0.554*** (0.117)	−0.569*** (0.118)
Variance components			
Country level	0.009 (0.002)	0.009 (0.002)	0.010 (0.002)
Party level	0.006 (0.000)	0.006 (0.000)	0.006 (0.000)
N parties	478	478	476
N countries	81	81	81
Wald χ^2	78.32***	93.78***	96.20***

Notes: Hierarchical linear models, standard errors in parentheses; ° $p<0.10$, * $p<0.05$, ** $p<0.01$, *** $p<0.001$.

of recipients. Programmatic competition requires building a different set of mechanisms, namely channels within the party through which disputes about policy issues can be resolved and a common message may emerge. This may occur either through party supporters sorting into programmatically cohesive parties that reflect their preferences or party leaders disciplining candidates or factions who would deviate from the party line (cf. Kitschelt and Kselman 2015).

In Model 3 we add a variable that measures one such form of discipline: national-level control of candidate nominations.[23] We also control for the large formal and informal networks that parties can develop using the latent variable measure used in previous analyses. Of these two variables, national party leadership control of nominations is mildly and positively associated with programmatic effort, while large formal and informal networks have no relationship with it. Moreover, in analyses not reported here, we find that FARPs are no more likely to have national-level politicians control nominations than other parties of similar size.[24]

The more general implication is that the networks that we expect FARPs to inherit are useful for solving the collective action issues of distributing resources, but contribute nothing to solving internal coordination around programmatic appeals. This is because party and informal networks did not engage in such activities in many authoritarian states. Some FARPs started out as opposition movements and parties before taking power and expressed a strong commitment to programmatic ideals, such as communism. But many have seen those projects become discredited in the run-up to the transition to democracy. Thus, even FARPs that championed a programmatic agenda under authoritarianism may have incentives to pivot to clientelistic strategies, which their preexisting networks leave them well positioned to pursue. The upshot is that if a FARP wishes to make a programmatic appeal, it has no choice but to engage in the same arduous task of building internal consensus and coordination as any other party.

While FARPs are *more* clientelistic than other parties, they are *not* necessarily less programmatic than their competitors. Many FARPs exist in countries where low levels of development and state capacity restrict popular demand for programmatic competition and thus compete against other parties that also score low on programmatic appeals.

---

[23] Variable A5a: "More generally, the power to select candidates in national legislative elections is always divided between local/municipal party actors, regional/state-level party organizations, and national party leaders. Often one particular level of party organization dominates the selection process, while in other places candidate selection is the outcome of bargaining between the different levels of party organization. Which of the following four options best describes the following parties' balance of power in selecting candidates for national legislative elections? [3] National party leaders control the process of candidate selections. [2] Regional/state-level party organizations control the process of candidate selections. [1] Selection is the outcome of bargaining between different levels. [0] Local/municipal actors control the process of candidate selections."

[24] The purpose of our regression here is only to illustrate the irrelevance of FARP status for programmatic partisan appeals. A more sophisticated analysis of the relationship between organizational centralization and programmatic partisan effort, in fact, yields a more complicated (and theoretically interesting) relationship than a simple linear association (see Kitschelt and Kselman 2015).

1.4 CONCLUSION: THE LIMITS OF THE DEVELOPMENTAL STATE AND THE END OF FORMER AUTHORITARIAN RULING PARTIES' ADVANTAGES?

The most important message of our chapter is that former authoritarian ruling parties have a robust organizational advantage that allows them to build and service more intense clientelistic, targeted voter–politician exchanges than other parties. Whereas parties emerging from opposition to dictatorships have to undertake an often torturous process of investing in party organization, FARPs enjoy a flying start by inheriting a ready-made organizational infrastructure and associational ties to civil society. A number of our results, particularly those indicating the affinity between FARPs and particular types of clientelistic transactions, suggest that it may be both the *quantity* and the *quality* of party organizational structures and associational networks that jointly account for FARPs' advantages in building specific clientelistic linkages.

These historical advantages may be negligible, however, when it comes to the articulation of programmatic appeals. Too often the FARP's existing policy pitch has been discredited and becomes unusable under the changed circumstances of democratic party competition. Moreover, many authoritarian networks were not designed to solve social choice problems by identifying and communicating a common policy program that unites a party's stakeholders. In order to arrive at an electorally distinctive policy pitch, FARPs therefore must undergo lengthy programmatic deliberations, just like any other party.

In the long run, however, the organizational advantages enjoyed by FARPs in the early stages of democratic party competition and their reliance on clientelistic targeting constitute a double-edged sword, especially in middle- and upper-income countries. Under conditions of successful economic growth, the economic governance and allocational mechanisms of a developmental state eventually become counterproductive for further economic advances, as countries approach the global economic innovation frontier. All developmental states with clientelistic citizen–politician linkages tend to privilege economic rentier groups. This is true not just under conditions of import substitution industrialization (ISI) but also under export-oriented industrialization (EOI), which had supposedly solved this problem by beefing up a professionalized and depoliticized state apparatus and by keeping economic interest groups at arm's length. But these forces reassert themselves in politics through clientelistic political parties. And clientelism in developed countries invariably runs into trouble when economic performance slows down and economic crises drain resources away from politicians that need them to feed their support networks (Kitschelt 2007).[25]

The slide into narrow economic special-interest group politics, often with a clientelistic voter rapport, befell FARPs in the 1980s and 1990s under both ISI

---

[25] For further case studies, see Kitschelt (2013).

and EOI regimes. The experience of sudden economic ruptures may serve as a catalyst to reconfigure parties' strategic appeals, however, as the reaction of Korean parties to the financial crisis of 1998 may illustrate (Wang 2013).

The unique affinity of FARPs to clientelistic efforts and their deployment of organizational capabilities in pursuit of that end, however, does not extend to RASPs, the second subtype of authoritarian successor parties discussed by Loxton (Introduction, this volume). In particular, it does not extend to parties that were founded by former authoritarian regime figures, but did not exist under dictatorship, or former regime parties that underwent very profound organizational and personnel renewal.

More generally, clientelistic parties, whether rooted in authoritarian regimes or not, tend to feel the pressure of change and begin to unravel not inevitably when democracy arrives, but only when a deep economic crisis provokes institutional change and a renewal of political linkage strategies. Clear examples include the Liberal Democratic Party (LDP) in Japan, Christian Democracy in Italy, and even the Social Democratic Party and the People's Party in Austria (Kitschelt 2007). Most recently, a similar fate appears to have caught up with initially successful communist successor parties such as the Hungarian Socialist Party (MSzP) and the Polish Democratic Left Alliance (SLD), which were engulfed in scandals due to their coziness with special economic interests.[26]

When economic crises coincide with clientelistic practices of citizen–politician linkage building, they are likely to give rise to waves of corruption scandals, as citizen tolerance for the corruption that often goes hand in hand with clientelism (Singer 2011) suffers without strong economic performance to prop up incumbents' popularity (Carlin, Love, and Martinez-Gallardo 2014; Zechmeister and Zizumbo-Colugna 2013). When no longer delivering the results expected in the past, well-worn operating conventions of clientelistic exchange can be redescribed as scandalous. As the new interpretation begins to resonate with voters, mass media take the lead and amplify the new interpretative frame. The erosion of support for FARPs may give rise to new populist challengers of the economic right or the economic left, who demand more transparency and immediacy of political control.

The one thing that may help FARPs under political pressure is the absence – or quick delegitimation – of whichever populist parties that may have presented themselves as initially plausible alternatives to incumbents. In recent democracies, party systems may not yet have developed a sufficient resilience to absorb and digest the disappearance of a major party without leaving a huge void that may be filled with threats to democracy itself. Yet the reliance of FARPs on clientelism without an alternative programmatic appeal means that they are vulnerable to precisely these types of challenges.

---

[26] On the decline of Hungary's MSzP and Poland's SLD, see Grzymala-Busse (Chapter 4, this volume).

APPENDIX 1.1

List of Former Authoritarian Ruling Parties that Were in Power for 10+ Years and Which Democratized Less than 30 Years Ago

Albania	Socialist Party of Albania (PS)
Botswana	Botswana Democratic Party (BDP)
Brazil	Progressive Party (PP)
Bulgaria	Bulgarian Socialist Party (BSP)
[Croatia	*Social Democratic Party of Croatia (SDP)]* (*)
Czech Rep.	Communist Party of Bohemia and Moravia (KSČM)
Dom. Rep.	Social Christian Reformist Party (PRSC)
El Salvador	National Conciliation Party (PCN)
Ghana	National Democratic Congress (NDC)
Hungary	Hungarian Socialist Party (MSzP)
Indonesia	Golongan Karya (Golkar)
Kenya	Kenya African National Union (KANU)
[Lithuania	*Democratic Labor Party of Lithuania (since 2001 merger, Social Democratic Party of Lithuania]* (*)
Macedonia	Social Democratic Union of Macedonia (SDSM)
Mexico	Institutional Revolutionary Party (PRI)
Moldova	Party of Communists of the Republic of Moldova (PCRM)
Mongolia	Mongolian People's Revolutionary Party (MPRP)
Niger	National Movement for the Development of Society (MNSD)
Panama	Democratic Revolutionary Party (PRD)
Paraguay	Colorado Party
Poland	Democratic Left Alliance (SLD)
Romania	Social Democratic Party (PSD)
Senegal	Socialist Party of Senegal (PS)
Serbia	Socialist Party of Serbia (SPS)
[Slovakia	*[Direction-Social Democracy (Smer-SD)]* (*)
[Slovenia	*Social Democrats (SD)]* (*)
South Korea	Grand National Party (since 2012 Saenuri)
Taiwan	Kuomintang (KMT)
[Ukraine	*Party of Regions]* (*)
Zambia	United National Independence Party (UNIP)

Note: (*) Borderline cases that may not be coded as former authoritarian ruling parties.

2

Authoritarian Successor Parties in South Korea and Taiwan

Authoritarian Inheritance, Organizational Adaptation, and Issue Management

T. J. Cheng and Teh-fu Huang

Democratic transition in South Korea and Taiwan came in the wake of three decades of spectacular economic development, and the expansion of their welfare programs under new democratic regimes came at a time when advanced welfare states in the West were in retreat, offering lessons to be learned. These two new East Asian democracies are also quickly consolidating into liberal democracies, distinct from the electoral democracies of Southeast Asia, where commitment to liberal values has been weak. But the most salient aspect of democratic South Korea and Taiwan for the purpose of this volume is the endurance and spectacular success of their authoritarian successor parties (ASPs), which this chapter seeks to explain.

South Korea's ASP, the Saenuri Party (previously under various names), can be traced back to the Democratic Republican Party (DRP), which was founded in the early 1960s by the leaders of the country's military regime.[1] Taiwan's Kuomintang (KMT, or the Nationalist Party) was the principal political force during the 1911 Republican Revolution in China, the ruling party on the mainland from 1927 until its military defeat by the Chinese Communist Party in 1949 and the ruling party in post-1945 Taiwan.[2] The Saenuri Party and the KMT remained major political players after the advent of democracy in South Korea and Taiwan in the late 1980s. Both parties triumphed in the founding

---

[1] Although the Saenuri Party was officially formed in 2012, it has a long lineage (see Kim 2011). Its immediate predecessor was the Grand National Party (GNP), created in 2007, which itself emerged from the Democratic Liberal Party (DLP). The DLP was the product of a merger of three parties in 1990: the Democratic Justice Party (DJP, the authoritarian ruling party established in 1980 after the coup by Chun Doo-hwan), the Reunification Democratic Party (RDP, the moderate wing of the democratic opposition led by Kim Young-sam), and the New Democratic Republican Party (NDRP, the remnant of the Democratic Republican Party [DRP], founded in 1963 by the country's military ruler, Park Chung-hee, who was assassinated in 1979). In a sense, the DJP was the first face of Korea's ASP, since it dived into electoral competition from the outset of the transition period beginning in 1986.

[2] The official name of Taiwan is still the Republic of China (ROC).

ASPs in South Korea and Taiwan 85

democratic elections and in democratic elections in the early 1990s, then lost two presidential elections, before returning to power for two consecutive terms.[3] Their majority or plurality positions in the legislative arena have remained entrenched. Even at the lowest tide – that is, even when they have lost – their vote share has been significant, never dipping below 33.5 percent for the National Assembly elections in Korea and, with one exception, hovering around 40 percent for various levels of elections in Taiwan. They are arguably the two most successful ASPs in the world.

The existing literature has attributed these two parties' strong electoral performance – as manifested in their ability to remain either the governing party or the principal opposition party – to their embedment in core conservative constituencies. While this explanation is compelling, this chapter argues that two other factors must be taken into account to explain these parties' strong performances. The first is what Loxton (Introduction, this volume) calls "authoritarian inheritance," or the resources they inherited from the previous authoritarian regime. To be sure, they were also burdened with significant amounts of "authoritarian baggage," since they were associated with authoritarian vices such as political exclusion, suppression of opposition, ideological imposition, and other "original sins." However, each inherited significant resources from the old regime that could be leveraged to win votes under democracy, including a party brand based on a strong record of economic development and national security, financial resources, a robust territorial organization (in the case of the KMT), and clientelist networks (in the case of Korea's ASP). The second factor was each party's ability to adapt its organization and reinvent itself in order to remain "in the ring," especially after major electoral defeats. Through party reform and/or realignment, the two ASPs were never dislodged from the leadership position of their respective political camps.

This chapter is divided into five sections. The first section examines the general political landscape in Taiwan and South Korea, tracking the extraordinary electoral success of their ASPs and identifying the social bases of their support. The second section examines the various forms of authoritarian inheritance from which these parties benefited. The third section examines how organizational development and adaptation in both parties prevented them from becoming marginalized by their partisan competitors. The fourth section examines issue dynamics in Taiwan and South Korea's democracies, showing that authoritarian inheritance is not always usable, while authoritarian baggage is not always fatal. Instead, it depends on how issue dynamics are managed by the ASP and its opponents, and how contingent factors make issues more or less salient at a particular moment in time. Finally, the conclusion examines the KMT's devastating defeat in the 2016 general

---

[3] The KMT's 2016 electoral defeat led to political recession, but probably not to the historic dustbin. See the chapter's conclusion for more on this.

election and the poor performance of South Korea's ASP in the 2017 presidential election, and speculates about both parties' political futures.

2.1 THE PERFORMANCE AND CONSTITUENCIES OF SOUTH KOREA AND TAIWAN'S ASPS

The two ASPs in South Korea and Taiwan have enjoyed remarkable success: each has remained either the governing party or the principal opposition party in all elections since the transition to democracy. As this section argues, their ability to remain key players in newly created democratic regimes is best illustrated by three factors: their performances at the ballot box, their grip on national legislatures, and the relative stability of their electoral bases.

South Korea and Taiwan have experienced a number of presidential elections in the approximately three decades since their transitions to democracy. The two ASPs (both of which are at the conservative end of the ideological spectrum) have won a number of electoral victories and have even enjoyed decent performances when they have lost. Of these democratic presidential elections, each party has won four: it retained power for the first two, lost power in the next two, and then regained power in the following two elections (and losing the most recent election, 2016 in Taiwan and 2017 in Korea; see conclusion for details). In the first two elections in which the Korean ASP was defeated, its candidates lost by slim margins: 1.6 percent in 1997 and 2.6 percent in 2002. In both races, a disgruntled conservative wing of the party defected and endorsed the liberal-progressive candidate, which likely contributed to the party's defeat (Kim 2008). In Taiwan, the KMT's electoral defeats were, until 2016, razor-thin: it lost by 2 percent in 2000 (an election in which the party presented two competing tickets) and by 0.22 percent in 2004 (leading to a vigorously contested result). In four elections, the candidates of the ASPs won by comfortable margins, even under very adverse conditions, as when their fellow conservative candidates ran as independents or under the banner of a third party, thereby drawing away votes from the ASPs' bases (see Figures 2.1a and 2.1b).

In addition to performing consistently well at the ballot box, the ASPs and their splinter-group-turned-sister parties (typically much smaller than the ASP itself) in both South Korea and Taiwan have been entrenched in the national legislatures. As shown in Figure 2.2a, out of seven legislative elections in democratic South Korea (which are held every four years rather than every five years, as are presidential elections), the ASP and its like-minded sister parties were outperformed only once (in 2004) by the liberal-progressive parties. During the three decades of South Korea's democracy, the conservative camp was in "pure" opposition for only four years, occupying neither the Blue House (presidency) nor holding sway in the National Assembly. More often than not, the sister parties coalesced around the ASP in the

ASPs in South Korea and Taiwan

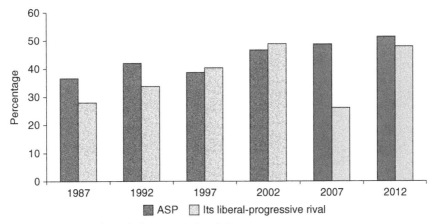

FIGURE 2.1A Presidential elections in South Korea, 1987–2012
Source: Prepared by the authors based on official detailed data published by the National Election Commission of South Korea.

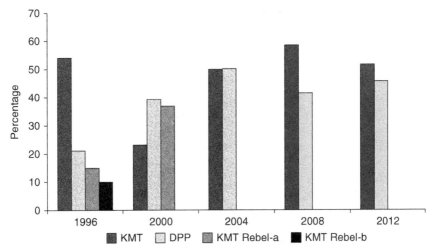

FIGURE 2.1B Presidential elections in Taiwan, 1996–2012
Source: Prepared by the authors based on official detailed data published by the Central Election Commission of Taiwan.

legislative arena, sometimes even reunifying with the ASP. Because it has lacked party discipline (see details below) and an absolute numerical advantage, the Korean ASP has not been able to dominate the legislature to the extent that it did in the authoritarian past. Nevertheless, it has wielded veto power, enabling it to prevent fundamental changes to the political rules of the game, whether in the

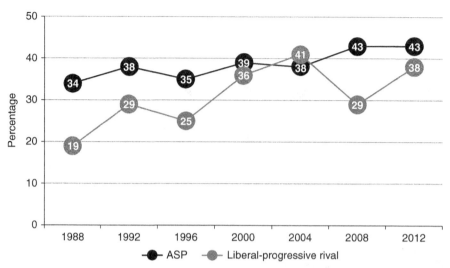

FIGURE 2.2A Legislative elections in South Korea, 1988–2012
Source: Prepared by the authors based on official detailed data published by the National Election Commission of South Korea.

form of constitutional reform or in the form of an electoral formula not to its liking.

The KMT's legislative strength in Taiwan has been, until recently, even more striking than in the case of South Korea. Since 1989, eight legislative elections have been held (every three years initially, and then every four years in order to be concurrent with presidential elections). The first legislative election in 1989 did not take place on a level playing field, as not all seats were open for competition and the KMT's lifelong legislators had not yet been pensioned off. The KMT won the majority of votes and seats in the following six elections. Its main rival, the Democratic Progressive Party (DPP), is at the liberal-progressive end of the ideological spectrum. In the 1990s, the DPP grew in electoral strength and began to eat into the KMT's share of the vote and gain more seats in the legislature, but was not yet a threat to the KMT's majority (see Figure 2.2b). Given its tighter party discipline and more pronounced numerical advantage, the KMT has been able to advance its legislative agenda more forcefully and to modulate democratic reform more adroitly than in the case of South Korea's ASP. There have been significant episodes of intra-party friction within the KMT, and observers have identified a number of instances of tactical alliance-making between KMT legislative elites and the DPP. However, major realignment across party lines has not yet occurred.

In order to explain the electoral success of these two ASPs in the three decades since democratization, the literature highlights their pivotal positions

ASPs in South Korea and Taiwan

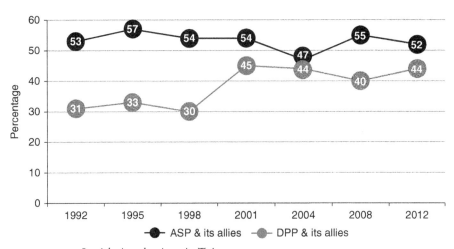

FIGURE 2.2B Legislative elections in Taiwan, 1992–2012
Source: Prepared by the authors based on official detailed data published by the Central Election Commission of Taiwan.

in each polity's political landscape. Regional identity has long been the leading predictor for electoral choice in South Korea, while in Taiwan it has been ethnic-cum-national identity. Conservative political elites in South Korea have been better situated along regional fault lines than their liberal-progressive counterparts, while their counterparts in Taiwan have been better situated along the ethnic or national identity divide than their liberal-progressive counterparts. As long as the ASPs in South Korea and Taiwan can remain the standard bearers of the conservative camp (discussed in the next section), they are likely to continue to exist and remain viable electoral contenders.

The conservative presidential candidates in South Korea have all come from the Southeast region, Yeongnam, and have always captured a high percentage of votes there (typically 60–70 percent). Their liberal-progressive opponents, for their part, have all (with the single exception of 2002) been from the Southwest region, Honan, and have performed extremely well there (typically winning around 90 percent of the vote). Seoul, the national capital populated by people from neighboring areas and other regions, and the Central region, Chungcheong, are inhabited by centrist and undecided voters, and therefore are in a position to tip the balance in elections. This regional bent of electoral politics is rooted in decades of economic development, which benefited the Southeast much more than the Southwest (Ku 2016). These patterns of regional loyalty were reinforced by the merger between the ASP and the moderate wing of the democratic opposition (a critical move discussed below), which was led by someone from the Southeast after the founding election. Political regionalism is biased toward the conservative ASP and against its liberal-progressive rival, for a few reasons. First, the Southeast has around 30 percent of eligible voters, while the Southwest has only about 14 percent (the Central region also has about 14 percent, while Seoul and its environs have about 40 percent). Second, hometown ties and identity are also evident in Seoul, especially among new migrants from the provinces and during the early years of the democratic transition. Third, many political leaders from the Central region were historically associated with the authoritarian regime, thus giving the ASP a small edge in this region.

The principal political divide in authoritarian Taiwan was between liberal democratic forces and the KMT party regime. In 1949, the KMT was essentially a party for mainlanders (who accounted for 13 percent of the population),[4] but by 1986, when Taiwan embarked on its democratic transition, 65 percent of its members were local Taiwanese (Huang 1996). As the democratic transition gained momentum, and with the death of President Chiang Ching-kuo in 1988, the KMT party leadership, which had historically been in the hands of mainlanders, quickly "indigenized." Even before the newly formed opposition party, the DPP, began to frame Taiwan's political cleavage as one based on a sub-ethnic divide between mainlanders and Taiwanese, the KMT leadership had already ceased to be a club mainly for mainlanders, and instead was quickly becoming a joint-stock company of two sub-ethnic groups. While the DPP emerged as a predominantly ethnic Taiwanese party, the KMT was no longer controlled chiefly by mainlanders. When the sub-ethnic cleavage morphed into one of national identity along the fault line of pro-independence versus pro-unification advocates (that is, supporters of turning Taiwan into a de jure independent state vs. backers of unifying Taiwan with mainland China under some formula and within some unspecified but reasonable time frame), the KMT had gradually toned down its former commitment to unification and settled into the midpoint of the spectrum. In other words, it favored the status quo – though without ruling out the possibility of unification, and on some occasions, especially during election years, entertaining the idea of letting Taiwan's future be determined by a majority of Taiwan's residents (Wu 2011).

Thus, until the most recent election in January 2016, the DPP had been locked into a platform favoring Taiwan's independence. It won the support of voters who wanted to secure the dignity of Taiwan's people, were more risk-tolerant, and who identified themselves as purely Taiwanese irrespective of their sub-ethnic backgrounds. The KMT, in turn, which hovered around the center, tended to be supported by voters who were risk-averse and identified themselves as both Taiwanese and Chinese. As Figures 2.3a and

---

[4] In the early 1950s, about 13 percent of Taiwan's population were Chinese who had migrated from the mainland between 1945 and 1949, and 87 percent were "Taiwanese." Of these Taiwanese, 15 percent were Hakka and 70 percent were Minnan (both groups had migrated to Taiwan centuries earlier), and 2 percent were from Micronesia.

ASPs in South Korea and Taiwan

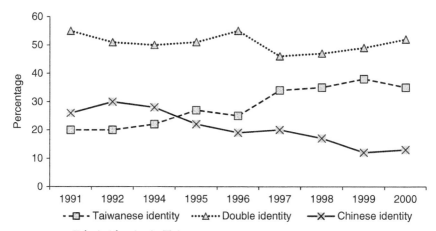

FIGURE 2.3A Ethnic identity in Taiwan, 1991–2000
Source: Prepared by the authors based on official detailed data published by the Central Election Commission of Taiwan.

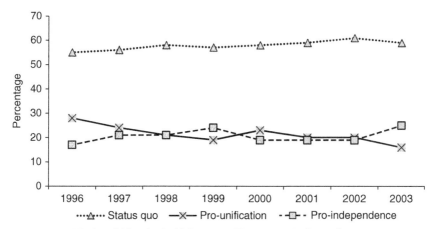

FIGURE 2.3B National identity in Taiwan, unification vs. independence, 1996–2003
Source: Prepared by the authors based on official detailed data published by the Central Election Commission of Taiwan.

2.3b show, the majority of Taiwan's residents have consistently favored preserving the status quo in Taiwan. However, the number of residents identifying themselves as "Taiwanese only" has steadily grown to 40 percent, a trend that is likely to pose a challenge to the KMT. Nevertheless, as Figure 2.4 suggests, until very recently, the KMT and its sister parties have had more party identifiers than the DPP and its sister parties.

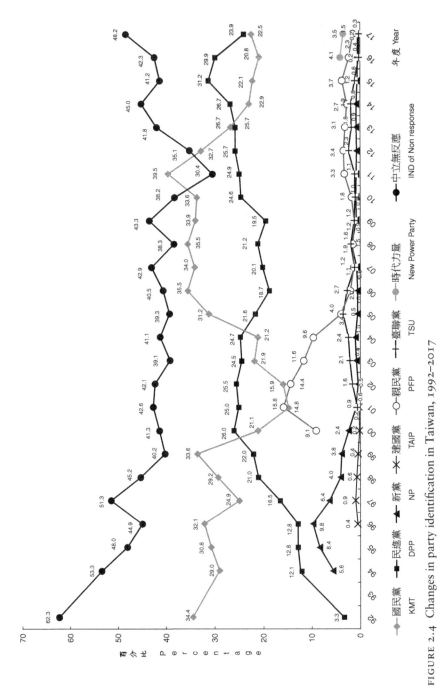

FIGURE 2.4 Changes in party identification in Taiwan, 1992–2017
Source: "Party Preferences Trend Distribution in Taiwan (1992/06~2017/06)," available from: http://esc.nccu.edu.tw/app/news.php?Sn=165 [Accessed September 30, 2017].

2.2 AUTHORITARIAN INHERITANCE

Why were these two ASPs able to perch on their conservative social base and enjoy such impressive electoral support after South Korea and Taiwan's transitions to democracy? One might expect them to have been burdened with immense authoritarian baggage, intuitively associated with authoritarian rule and everything bad about the past. However, they entered the democratic era not just with authoritarian baggage but also with considerable authoritarian inheritance – some tangible, some intangible, but all potentially advantageous in democratic elections.

For one, both ASPs inherited party brands based on strong records of economic development and national security. Both the KMT and South Korea's ASP could take credit for three decades of extraordinary economic growth, which transformed two poor nations into widely admired, newly developed nations. Postwar Taiwan and South Korea were basically agrarian and low-income economies. Thanks to three decades of export-led industrialization under the stewardship of their authoritarian regimes, by the time the two nations began to make the transition to democracy in the second half of the 1980s, they had become the two most stellar economies in the developing world, with per capita incomes approaching OECD levels.[5] In both South Korea and Taiwan, most, if not all, technocrats credited for managing economic development were affiliated with the two ASPs – an association that helped to make credible these parties' claims to be better equipped than the opposition to advance their nations to fully developed status. They also benefited from the conservative nature of the middle class, which had grown as the economy developed, and had arguably become the dominant social forces in both nations. Surveys carried out on the eve of the democratic transition showed that 76.7 percent of people self-identified as belonging to the middle class in South Korea, and 92.8 percent did so in Taiwan (Cheng 1990a). While the middle class had been the driving force for democratic change in South Korea and Taiwan, it also wanted to maintain order and stable change, so as not to put at risk the prosperity that it had begun to enjoy.[6] In Taiwan, after enjoying an initial post-transition boost, the main opposition party needed around two decades to build its electoral support base

---

[5] The fruits of economic development were more broadly shared in Taiwan than in South Korea. In South Korea, the per capita income of the more industrialized Southeast and Central regions was significantly higher than in the less industrialized Southwest region. This meant that the South Korean ASP's economic credentials were more widely recognized in the better-off regions. Gini coefficients in Taiwan were, until recently, typically lower than in South Korea. Per capita income in the Southeast, where most industrialization projects were seated, was already 16 percent more than that of the Southwest in 1965, and that gap had widened to 50 percent by 1985. For regional income disparity in 1986 on the eve of the transition to democracy in South Korea, see Schatzl, Wessell, and Lee (2007: 147).

[6] The bulk of the South Korean middle class was slow to join the democratic movement, but quick to leave it upon signs of radicalization (Cheng 1990a).

to the 30 percent level and had to restrain its nation-building impulses during this time.

In addition to possessing strong credentials on economic development, the ASPs in South Korea and Taiwan could also claim a strong record in the area of national security against the threats of North Korea and China, respectively. Skirmishes and exchanges of fire across the Korean Demilitarized Zone (DMZ), both on land and at sea, have been recurring events since the signing of the 1953 armistice agreement (which is a fragile truce, not a peace treaty). Across the Taiwan Strait, China twice attempted to seize Taiwan's offshore islands (in 1954 and 1958), and in spite of its apparent peace overture in 1981, it could abruptly turn to intimidation, especially on key occasions of Taiwan's democratic processes. For example, it lobbed missiles around Taiwan's harbors during the 1996 presidential election. After the democratic transition, the two ASPs did what their predecessors had done in the past: they modernized defense capabilities and maintained close security ties with the United States. Upon gaining power, their liberal-progressive political rivals tried to advance new approaches to managing national security, but neither worked well enough to replace the two ASPs' policy repertoire. In Taiwan, the DPP's attempt to use a public referendum to assert the island's de jure sovereignty as a way of ensuring national security only invited higher levels of threat from China and strained ties with the United States. In South Korea, the liberal-progressive government's Sunshine Policy of conciliation toward North Korea brought about brief periods of détente, but these were repeatedly shattered by nuclear and conventional provocations from the North. The liberal-progressive government also let South Korea–United States security ties drift, which caused widespread anxiety in society (Oh and Arrington 2007).

In addition to its strong record on economic development and national security, the KMT's brand had a number of other dimensions. Having played a pivotal role in subverting the Qing dynasty and governing during the Republican era on the mainland until 1949, the KMT has taken pride in its nation-building role in modern China. This historical connection made the mainlander community so loyal to the party that its electoral support became nicknamed the "KMT's iron votes." But the KMT's brand was also anchored in the party's co-optation of local elites in the postwar period. Upon its relocation to Taiwan in 1949, the KMT reined in its own factions, which had been rampant during its years on the mainland. It also implemented land reform (which wiped out the socioeconomic bases of the landed elite), institutionalized local elections, and recruited local (that is, indigenous or Taiwanese) elites into its initially mainlander-dominated party-state framework (Cheng 1989). The party was also understood to be a platform upon which local elites could compete electorally in order to gain access to subnational public offices, a process that it assiduously managed so as not to leave any major local faction in the cold for too long. The brand of the KMT thus took on a new dimension: coexistence of local factions based on the mediation and coordination of the party. In due course, this party brand acquired another connotation: cohabitation of sub-ethnic groups in the national leadership ranks. Unlike its main liberal rival, the DPP (a party headed by indigenous elites), the KMT typically displayed an alliance of mainlander and Taiwanese leaders, an equilibrium that emerged from a policy of promoting local elites to the KMT's leadership in pace with Taiwan's democratic transition. Given its various dimensions – economic development, national security, nation-building, political inclusion, and elite accommodation – the KMT brand has largely been an asset at election time. However, when KMT's leaders lose a sense of moderation and balance, emphasizing one particular dimension of the brand at the expense of the others, the party's brand can become a liability and a source of contention. In the wake of the 2016 election debacle, this was precisely the issue facing the KMT, a point that will be discussed in the conclusion.

If a party brand is an intangible asset, territorial organization is a tangible one. Upon arriving in Taiwan, the KMT party regime not only set out to clean up its existing factions and implant party cells in the mainlander-dominant public sector (namely, civil and military services and state-owned enterprises) but also to penetrate and organize Taiwanese society. This was a means both of preventing communist infiltration and running local elections. Local elections proved to be the most effective mechanism for the KMT to develop its territorial organization and take root in Taiwanese society (Cheng and Hsu 2015). In 1949, the KMT was essentially a party for mainlanders, but by 1986, when Taiwan began its transition to democracy, it was already a largely Taiwanese party with 2 million card-carrying members. In each township, the party had (and still has) a local chapter and an office called "the public service station," which, in addition to coordinating nominations and running elections, provided a wide range of public services (e.g., cooking and home economics courses primarily for female voters). Electoral dynamics around the KMT territorial organization also had a transformative impact on the party organization at the center. In due course, the ideologues and their bureaus were overshadowed by the Organization Bureau in charge of candidate selection and electoral campaigns, as well as party cadre recruitment, promotion, and training between elections. On the eve of Taiwan's transition to democracy, the KMT headquarters was less an ideological propaganda machine than an electoral management organization.

In addition to possessing a strong brand and a robust territorial organization, the KMT owned a vast number of enterprises and had access to huge financial resources. Indeed, the KMT was arguably the richest political party on earth.[7]

---

[7] In terms of party-owned assets, Israel's Labor Party – associated with Histadrut, a welfare-minded labor union organization – probably came in a very distant second. It reportedly had 80 buildings and 400 acres of land, which it had to auction off to cover its huge debt (Somfalvi 2007).

Previously hidden from the public eye, the KMT's assets were re-registered under the party's name and valued at more than US$4 billion in 1995, making it the sixth largest business group in Taiwan.[8] The KMT's vast business empire has produced many benefits. First, it is a source of campaign finance. The party has repeatedly used its business proceeds to assist its candidates, especially those who are strong but do not have deep pockets of their own, and those in tight races. Second, the KMT has used it to invest in key local leaders, so as to keep local bases from being eroded and from defecting to the opposition. Third, the KMT has used some of it for public charity and donations to local electoral districts, so as to maintain a favorable image of the party in the eyes of voters. At the same time, these assets have also sometimes created difficulties for the KMT. The origins, functions, and magnitude of these assets have been the subject of considerable controversy, with the liberal-progressive political forces often raising this as a fairness issue, thus putting the KMT on the defensive.[9] With time, these benefits have begun to wear thinner and thinner. Political adversaries astutely framed the KMT's party-owned assets as an equity and transitional justice issue, forcing the KMT to dispose of some of its landholdings, wind down its business operations, and create a trust fund.[10] Thus, not only did the financial value of these assets begin to shrink in the wake of the Asian financial crisis in the late 1990s, but they increasingly became a political liability at election time.[11]

Unlike the KMT, South Korea's ASP did not inherit a robust territorial organization or a huge amount of party-owned assets. However, it did inherit clientelist networks and close ties to big business.[12] Prior to the advent of democracy, South Korea had been a military regime rather than a party-based regime like Taiwan (Cheng 1990b; Im 1987). While its military

---

[8] This ranking is based on an earlier report (Hsu 1992: 144).
[9] Some assets came from confiscated Japanese colonial enterprises, some based on monopolistic franchises. To its critics, the KMT was a rent seeker. To its defenders, KMT enterprises lent support to government industrial policy (Abegaz 2013), and their overseas investment had been used to help to safeguard Taiwan's diplomatic relations. While the party did not always manage its assets well, and a good portion of them were earmarked for party bureaucrats' retirement pensions, many of these assets are probably still profitable and their size is believed to be substantial.
[10] Upon losing the election and political power to the DPP in 2000, the KMT began to dispose of its real estate holdings, selling some and transferring others to governments at all levels (Lin 2014: 28). Attempts to sell other kinds of assets, particularly enterprises and investment portfolios, have met with little success. In 2005, the newly assumed party chairman, Ma Injou, pledged to liquidate them in three years, but again was unable (Lin 2014: 48, 50). More attempts were made afterwards, but again no bidder was found to take them over. One possible reason is that liquidating KMT assets was perceived as a fire sale.
[11] The KMT party assets grew significantly before the period leading up to the 1997–1998 Asian financial crisis, but shrank drastically afterward, largely due to a sharp decline of investment income. By 2015, its earnings from investments were down to 33 percent of their peak (Lin 2014: table II).
[12] On ASPs' inheritance of clientelist networks, see Kitschelt and Singer (Chapter 1, this volume).

leaders established an authoritarian ruling party and periodically carried out grossly unfair elections at the national level, the regime relied mainly on coercion to cope with the democratic movement and never-ending student protests. Relying on coercion, and in no need of running local elections (these were abolished after the military coup of 1961), the regime's leaders had little incentive to build a grassroots party organization. Instead, the ruling party mainly used clientelist ties for recruitment, candidate selection, and campaigning – a modus operandi that the democratic opposition also employed. This clientelist feature remained largely unchanged after the transition to democracy, with all political parties (with the exception of one small progressive party) tending to lack strong programs, card-carrying members, and a grassroots party organization (Hellmann 2011). The clientelist networks that South Korea's ASP inherited are largely concentrated in the Southeast and Central regions of the nation, where most military leaders and their families come from. The clientelist networks of the liberal-progressive forces, far smaller than those of the conservative forces, were (and still are) concentrated in the Southwest.

Unlike the KMT, South Korea's ASP did not possess its own business empire. However, it did inherit close ties to big business, which it could tap for financial resources. This ASP–big business nexus could trace its roots to the developmental authoritarian regime inaugurated by the military coup in 1961. Although the new regime had initially intended to prosecute business tycoons for their illicit wealth, it quickly began to rely on them as agents of industrial development, providing them with credit and monopoly opportunities. This "sword-won" alliance (Cheng 1990b) was not only the bedrock for South Korea's rapid industrialization and export success but also a key component of campaign finance for the military-backed ruling party before and immediately after the transition to democracy in 1986. These chummy relations with big business were not always an unalloyed good for South Korea's ASP, however. As Byung-kook Kim (2008) shows, the ASP–big business nexus could and did become a top agenda for political reform after the transition to democracy. The serial investigations of hidden campaign contributions to ASP elites put the party on the defensive. Moreover, the 1997 Asian financial crisis exposed the corruptive and moral hazard aspects of Korean-style state–business cooperation, and led the liberal-progressive government to rein in big business via enterprise and campaign finance reform. However, connections to big business have nevertheless remained a key element of the party's authoritarian inheritance. Although the law caps business contributions to candidates, it does not abolish them. Moreover, the liberal-progressive camp has also maintained its own (albeit far smaller) pipeline to business, making candidates of this political force the target of corruption investigations, as well. On balance, the association with business groups has been more of an asset than a liability for South Korea's ASP.

2.3 PARTY ORGANIZATIONAL ADAPTATION AND DEVELOPMENT

The survival and endurance of any authoritarian successor party following a transition to democracy requires that it not come to be seen as a spent force or the embodiment of the broken *ancien régime*, but rather accepted as a qualified player in the new political environment. If an ASP is routed or performs poorly in early elections, this may signal that it is not a serious contender, leading potential supporters to abandon it en masse. The ASPs in South Korea and Taiwan were arguably better situated to claim their place in the sun than their counterparts elsewhere. For three decades before democratization, the authoritarian regime in each of these two polities had delivered extraordinary economic progress with a relatively egalitarian income distribution. This gave rise to a sizeable middle class that aspired to democracy and disliked political suppression, but that did not want to put its newfound prosperity at risk. These two ASPs were not only associated with economic development; they also initiated democratic change, thereby helping to offset whatever authoritarian baggage they might have carried with them.[13] Moreover, as discussed above, South Korea's ASP had a very significant regional base, as well as a chance to nurture partisan allegiance among conservatives in other regions, while Taiwan's ASP had been expanding its social base long before the democratic transition. The key challenge for both ASPs lay in whether they could be accepted as the standard-bearers for friendly social bases and avoid being displaced by like-minded parties as leaders of the conservative camp. In order to avoid being displaced, both parties engaged in crucial rounds of organizational development that helped them to adapt to new circumstances and survive in the long term.

There were critical moments when each ASP could have been marginalized, leading to a downward spiral into irrelevance. For South Korea, this critical moment came during the founding election; for Taiwan, it came in the wake of it. The decision of South Korea's authoritarian regime to call for competitive elections in 1987 was a major gamble, as its prestige was low at the time, and its presidential candidate won only 36.6 percent. The combined vote of the two democratic opposition candidates was 56 percent. Had these two opposition candidates and their parties – one moderate (Kim Young-sam), the other more radical (Kim Dae-jung) – maintained a united front as they had in the past (perhaps by working out a formula to run for the presidency sequentially rather than simultaneously), the ruling party could have been defeated in the 1987 founding election. After losing this election, the two democratic opposition leaders could have seized upon a second chance to collaborate in the following election. Such a political alliance might have enabled them to

---

[13] According to Slater and Wong (2013; Chapter 9, this volume), this was one of the core reasons why authoritarian elites in Taiwan and South Korea opted to initiate democratization. They hoped that by being the stewards of democratization, this would contribute to their legitimacy and thus actually help them to remain in power.

relegate the ASP to a distant third position, tar it as the party of the *ancien régime*, define it as a synonym of everything bad about the past, and dethrone it within the conservative camp. The institutional rules for the South Korean presidency (especially the one-term limit for the president and the absence of a vice presidential position) ought to have facilitated such an interparty alliance. In such a hypothetical alliance, the two charismatic opposition leaders – each of whom was equally associated with the fight for democratic change – could have agreed to seek power one after the other rather than try to decide who should be the presidential candidate and who should be the running mate on a joint ticket. Having failed to cooperate during the founding election, the two democratic movement leaders faced mounting pressure from their supporters to collaborate in the next election.

However, before the two main opposition parties were able to explore any collaborative scheme, the ASP in South Korea initiated a merger with the more moderate of the two opposition parties (Reunification Democratic Party, RDP), as well as with a minor conservative party (New Democratic Republic Party, NDRP), a move arguably inspired by the long-lasting pre-1995 Japanese system, which was dominated by one party (Liberal Democratic Party, LDP). This merger included a power-sharing scheme with the leaders of the two recently absorbed parties sequentially bidding for the presidency, as well as the invention of a new name for this new super-sized political force: the Democratic Liberal Party (DLP). This merger with a former democratic opposition party allowed the ASP's leaders to make three claims: (1) that it was the mainstay of the conservative political force, (2) that it was now a co-owner of the movement for democratic reform, and (3) that it was a political force for the future rather than simply a legacy of the authoritarian past. This huge new conservative party easily prevailed in the 1992 presidential election. However, glitches in the arrangements for power-sharing and candidate selection led a major faction to bolt from the party to form a new conservative party and a minor faction to defect to the leading liberal-progressive party. The internal split and defection weakened the enlarged ASP. The result was that the liberal-progressive party won the following two presidential elections (1997 and 2002), while the ASP entered a decade of political recession. But through this merger and acquisition (M&A) and rebranding, the ASP elites and their followers were able to regroup, replenish, and return to power in the third decade after democratization, winning the 2007 and 2012 presidential elections.

It is important to note that the leading liberal party in South Korea has not been immune to centrifugal pressure and fratricide, and has used exactly the same strategy – M&A and rebranding – to safeguard its own leadership position within the liberal camp. In nearly three decades of democracy, this party has staged ten episodes of party realignment within the liberal camp (as frequently as the ASP in the conservative camp) and renamed itself twelve times (the conservative ASP has done so eleven times).

In Taiwan, the challenge to the KMT's position of conservative leadership came much later and from within the party itself, and the strategy used to cope with it differed from that of South Korea. As discussed above, the KMT had incorporated local elites into its leadership stratum well before the 1992 legislative elections (the first time that all seats were up for grabs, and thus Taiwan's founding election). The KMT called for this election with peace of mind, as the opposition was no match in terms of resources, social base, and organizational capacity for voter mobilization.[14] Indeed, the party's goal appears to have been to craft a pre-1995 Japanese-style democratic system, in which one party dominated. But as democracy gained momentum, the opposition grew in strength, internal tension within the KMT leadership surfaced, and the prospect of making the KMT into a dominant party along the lines of Japan's LDP became less and less plausible. By 2000, less than a decade after the beginning of democratization in Taiwan, the KMT almost lost its leadership position within the conservative camp.

Leadership disunity within the KMT, much like in South Korea's ASP, stemmed from disputes over leadership succession, candidate selection, and the pace of democratic reform. Discord within the KMT over the pace of democratic reform had already led a splinter group to form a small conservative party in 1993. More alarming, leadership bifurcation (which began in Taiwan's last indirect presidential election in 1991, deepened in the first direct presidential election in 1996, and escalated in the presidential election in 2000) begot two competing pairs of conservative presidential and vice presidential candidates, which opened the way for the opposition DPP to win the presidency in 2000. In the wake of the 2000 KMT electoral defeat, the first loss for the ASP in eight decades, a charismatic and extraordinarily popular insurgent KMT leader (James Soong) – who won more votes than the official KMT candidate – established a new party (People First Party, PFP) that threatened to dislodge the KMT as leader of the conservative camp.

Instead of turning to pact-making and renaming the party, the KMT's beleaguered leadership opted to expel rebels, launch party reform, and make strenuous efforts to remarket its historical brand name. James Soong, the maverick rebel leader challenging the party center, was expunged from the party, as was a small coterie of party elites allegedly flirting with the DPP during the 2000 election. The option to return to the fold was kept open to those who had been purged, but the barriers to re-entry were set high. Through this party reform, the KMT cleansed itself of inactive or fence-sitting members, as well as those with unsavory records (such as vote buying and befriending organized crime rings); aimed to recruit more young people, women, and other underrepresented groups; and streamlined its bureaucracy. The reform included

---

[14] To use Slater and Wong's (2013; Chapter 9, this volume) terminology, the KMT's abundant "antecedent resources" gave it a high degree of "victory confidence" – that is, its leaders calculated that the party would do well under democratic conditions.

ASPs in South Korea and Taiwan

updated rules for leadership selection and intra-party decision-making. Most notably, it turned the party's Central Committee (CC) into an elective body and made it possible for KMT legislators, most of them Taiwanese with grassroots ties, to become the CC's largest voting bloc. The KMT also introduced direct elections by card-carrying party members for the top leadership. With these reforms, the KMT quickly presented itself to society as a rejuvenated and renovated party. Whether the party really reinvented itself is debatable, but this reform effort prevented most KMT leaders from abandoning ship, kept the party in the driver's seat within the conservative camp, and laid the foundation for its eventual return to the presidency (Cheng 2006).

The KMT reform strategy worked well. The exodus of KMT party *supporters* initially was massive, as suggested by the erosion of KMT party identifiers (see Figure 2.4), but the loss of party *elites* to the newly created PFP was much smaller. Most importantly, the KMT successfully prevented the Taiwanese wing of the party elite (mostly based in the legislature) from defecting to the Taiwanese-dominated DPP – a scenario that, if played out, would have redefined the KMT as a party only for mainlanders and reduced it to a distant third position in the legislature and party system. Moreover, with a much smaller number of legislative seats, the newly created conservative party served as the KMT's junior partner rather than as the party tipping the balance between the KMT and the DPP in the legislature, the main arena for policy deliberation and budgetary allocation. Eventually, the KMT recouped all that it had lost. Elites of the new conservative party rejoined the KMT, while their leader had to settle for second fiddle on the KMT ticket for the next election. The number of KMT party identifiers bounced back to the pre-2000 level. All of these developments contributed to the KMT's strong showing in both the legislative and presidential elections. The second DPP presidency (2004–2008) was plagued with corruption, making it easier for the KMT to market its image of reform and gain even more party identifiers, as Taiwan moved into its third decade of democracy. Other parties in the conservative camp (and, for that matter, in the progressive camp) either became defunct or were totally marginalized.

It is important to note that the KMT's rival, the DPP, has also been obsessed with intra-party reform and polishing its brand rather than with realignment or name changes. Upon its founding in 1986 on the eve of the democratic transition, the DPP adopted a KMT-like organizational structure and a card-carrying membership system. To burnish its reformist brand, the DPP introduced volunteer party workers and institutionalized direct elections for party leaders and a candidate selection process based on polls and primaries. Duopolistic competition in Taiwan quickly led the KMT to adopt these devices and invent new ones, such as welfare benefits for minorities, in order to make itself more electorally competitive.

The deal-making, realignment, and rebranding of South Korea's ASP and the internal reforms and repolishing of the same old brand of the KMT are two different organizational strategies to ensure political longevity after the transition to democracy. Though intrinsically conservative, the South Korean ASP took liberty in inventing new brands, cutting deals, and even engaging in predatory reorganization, mergers and acquisitions. By contrast, its counterpart in Taiwan has persisted in hoisting the same banner and preferred reform to deal-making. Why did these two parties choose to employ such different – though equally successful – organizational strategies? We contend that their different strategic choices were conditioned by the different mixture of authoritarian inheritance and authoritarian baggage in each case, and by the way that each party managed its portfolio of legacies.

First, while the name "KMT" had irreplaceable symbolic value, due to the party's nation-building efforts over eight decades, the original name of South Korea's ASP – the Democratic Justice Party (DJP) – was associated with two coups and one massacre.[15] Sticking to its original name has probably helped the KMT to prevent alienated party members and supporters from exiting the party, and has helped it to distinguish itself from the newer splinter conservative party. The message would seem to be: "We are the direct lineage of the nation-building party; at best, they are simply an offshoot."[16] One telling indicator for the difference between the two ASPs in this aspect is that many leading KMT defectors emphasized their political pedigree and previous association, while those who bolted from South Korea's ASP rarely did.

Second, while both ASPs have patron–client ties or local factions – for South Korea, in the Southeast region, and for Taiwan, in the rural areas – to draw on, Taiwan's KMT has an additional political mobilization tool: its massive territorial organization, which extends to all townships and urban districts. Crafted in the 1950s to run local elections and, in rural areas, to manage local factions, this grassroots organization has been the KMT's long arm in society. Building such an organization is time-consuming and expensive to maintain. Its rival, the DPP, which is fiscally poor and started its party-building effort long after the KMT did so, has field offices only at the county level, not below. In the case of South Korea, the former authoritarian ruling party did not have a strong incentive to build local organizations. Local elections were suspended soon after the 1961 coup, and intimidation and coercion were used to contain the democratic opposition's performance in limited national elections. Creating a strong party was simply not that important for the survival of the military regime. Under democracy, South Korea's ASP opted to make up for its organizational weakness at the local level by drawing on existing clientelist networks belonging to local conservative elites.

---

[15] The first coup by Park Chung-hee inaugurated the military regime in May 1961. The second coup was staged by Chun Doo-hwan in the midst of the chaos following the assassination of Park Chung-hee in 1979. The 1980 massacre, which took place in Gwangju, the capital of Cholla province in the Southwest, brutally suppressed the democratization movement.

[16] See Cheng (2006).

Third, while South Korea's ASP has exploited intimate ties to big business groups in order to raise political funds, Taiwan's ASP has independent financial resources generated from its immense party-owned assets. Established in the authoritarian past, the South Korean ASP's practice of extracting money from business tycoons was typically illicit and non-transparent, and was exposed almost immediately after the country's transition to democracy. As cases of corrupt political contributions were exposed, the infamous ties between ASP leaders and business conglomerates became a campaign issue, tainting the ASP and compelling it to reinvent itself by creating a new party with a new name and a cleaner image. By contrast, political fund-raising has not been a burden for Taiwan's ASP. As the richest party on earth, the KMT has the luxury of using in-house resources to fund party bureaucracy, select quality candidates, run electoral campaigns, maintain party discipline, and reduce cadre defections. Over three decades of democracy, party-owned assets have continued to bridge the gap between the KMT's fund-raising and its campaign spending. The KMT's assets became so instrumental for maintaining its organizational and electoral strength that the DPP eventually decided to make party financing into a top campaign issue, threatening to turn the KMT's business empire – one of the main assets it inherited from the authoritarian regime – into a political liability.

2.4 ISSUE DYNAMICS: MANAGING AUTHORITARIAN INHERITANCE AND BAGGAGE

Winning elections is essential for any party, but especially for an authoritarian successor party. If it has a long losing streak, voters may conclude that it is merely a relic of the authoritarian past rather than a viable actor in the present. Having examined the party structures and organizational adaptation of South Korea and Taiwan's ASPs in the previous two sections, in this section we focus on how the management of issue dynamics can enhance or inhibit an ASP's capacity to compete in the political market.

All told, there have been four main issues for the ASPs in South Korea and Taiwan to manage over the last three decades of democracy: democratic reform, distributive justice, economic revitalization, and the security environment. On the surface, the two ASPs would seem to have the upper hand in the areas of economic revitalization and national security, while their liberal-progressive rivals would seem to have it in the areas of democratic reform and distributive justice. When national security is at stake and economic revitalization is needed, many voters (especially swing voters) are likely to appreciate the ASPs' time-tested ability to cope with the treacherous external environment and deliver economic prosperity. Thus, the ASPs' roots in developmental authoritarian regimes can be expected to generate nostalgia. Other issues, such as democratic reform (righting the wrongs of the past) and distributive justice (taking care of those left behind), would seem to belong to the liberal-progressive parties. These issues tend to remind voters of the two ASPs' authoritarian baggage and, hence, potentially hurt them in elections. However, as seen in the ebbs and flows of politically salient issues in democratic South Korea and Taiwan over the past three decades, issue ownership is neither exclusive nor preordained, and an issue can be disowned, re-owned, or shared. Authoritarian inheritance is not always usable, while authoritarian baggage is not necessarily harmful to the ASP. Instead, their effects are powerfully conditioned by how political actors – both the ASPs and their opponents – manage issue dynamics, as well as how more contingent factors (such as the international context) can increase or decrease the salience of particular issues at a given time.

During the first decade after South Korea's democratic transition, democratic reform was voters' primary concern. Yet, peculiarly, the country's ASP managed to win the first two presidential elections, to the chagrin of its liberal-progressive rivals. The ASP was compelled to call for the founding election in 1987 in order to keep the demonstration–suppression spiral and student–police confrontation from escalating beyond control. But it was a calculated risk that the ASP could afford to take. In the euphoria of a democratic breakthrough, the party had little choice but to embrace the cause of democratic reform, since the public would not have responded to any other issues that the party might have advanced. Highlighting its past economic achievements would not have gained it significant traction. Nor was national security an especially salient issue at that moment, as North Korea was not yet creating trouble, and the democratic opposition parties were not testing the water on that front either. The ASP vaguely endorsed the democratic reform agenda, without providing details or action plans. Instead, it successfully bet on the division rather than on the union of the two democratic opposition forces – Kim Young-sam's more moderate-conservative RDP versus Kim Dae-jung's more liberal-progressive National Congress for New Politics (NCNP). Once validated by the founding election, the ASP government embraced the democratic reform agenda more vigorously than most had anticipated, including the investigation and prosecution of corrupt and human rights-abusing officials (including a former president) from the authoritarian regime, as well as their associates in the state and even private institutions. In an example of what Loxton (Introduction, this volume) calls "contrition" for wrongdoing in the past, such assiduous pursuit of democratic reform allowed the ASP to claim at least co-ownership of the movement of the day. As discussed above, this provided justification for the RDP to merge with the ASP and for a small like-minded party to create a supersized ASP in 1990, the DLP, which dwarfed the liberal-progressive opposition. The expanded and renamed ASP easily won a landslide victory over the liberal opposition in the 1992 election, despite the fact that a splinter conservative group had also fielded a candidate. The ASP's promise of further reform, and its strong record in the area of national security in the context of a looming nuclear crisis suddenly ignited by North Korea, helped the party to win the election.

In the second decade of South Korean democracy, the ASP was driven into the political wildness – at least, temporarily – for two reasons. First, embracing democratic reform helped the new ASP leader (Kim Young-sam), but hurt the party (Kim 2008: 175–176). Given that the unholy trinity of the military, big business, and a large bureaucracy had been the foundation for South Korea's massive and rapid state-led industrialization and economic expansion, democratic reform inevitably involved purges and prosecution of former authoritarian officials and their associates. However, as the democratic reform began to undermine the ASP's conservative base, Kim reversed course. Citing the escalating North Korean nuclear crisis, he suspended the reforms. He then turned his attention to party development, most notably by training a new generation of leaders to replace other senior ASP leaders. Many of these leaders rebelled. One of them defected to the liberal camp and another ran as an independent presidential candidate, helping the liberal party to win the presidency in the 1997 election. Second, not only did the liberal-progressive party, now in power, reclaim ownership of the issue of democratic reform; it also used the 1997 Asian financial crisis to cast doubt on the ASP's achievements in economic development and highlight the issue of distributive justice. The financial crisis hit South Korea particularly hard, exposing the weaknesses of the country's economy (e.g., domination of family-owned conglomerates in nearly all sectors, acute wealth inequality, and business–government collusion). Meanwhile, in addition to expanding the welfare state and pushing for business reform, the liberal-progressive government began to pursue the Sunshine Policy (friendly rather than adversarial) toward North Korea and a more egalitarian security relationship with the United States, thereby offering an alternative approach to national security.

By the end of the second decade of South Korea's democracy, issue dynamics were no longer swinging in the direction of the liberal-progressive party. The liberal-progressive government conflated the issue of democratic reform with that of historical rectification, alienating swing voters and unifying the conservative camp (Kim 2008: 181–183). In addition, during its ten years of political recession, the ASP had not lost its edge on two key issues: national security and economic management. Although these were temporarily discounted during the decade of liberal government, they increased in salience as the 2007 global financial crisis began to unfold, and as the second North Korean nuclear crisis gained momentum. The nuclear crisis reaffirmed the indispensability of the United States to South Korea's national security and the untrustworthiness of North Korea, while the global financial crisis reminded the public that economic revitalization would be an urgent task and that without growth, welfare expansion would be difficult. As soon as the ASP experimented with rule-based party development, allowing the "Bulldozer" Seoul mayor Lee Myungbak (who had a track record of good management, but who lacked factional backing) to run for the presidency in 2007, power rotation back to the conservative camp was pretty much assured. That Lee defeated his liberal opponent by a margin of 2 to 1 fully demonstrated the nostalgia effect that the ASP was able to tap. Five years later, Park Geun-hye, the daughter of the late military dictator, Park Chung-hee (who had been tough on North Korea and who was credited with creating South Korea's economic miracle), was sworn in as president. A study based on pre- and postelection surveys showed that the overwhelming support that Park Geun-hye enjoyed among voters in the gray-hair cohort (a generation that still had vivid memories of South Korea's economic rise under her father's authoritarian rule) was a decisive factor in her victory (Kim 2014).

Issue dynamics in democratic Taiwan have followed similar rhythms, but with distinct spans and a different pattern of "authoritarian inheritance-baggage packaging." The issue of democratic reform also dominated politics in the early years after Taiwan's transition to democracy, as Taiwan continued to experience economic growth with equity. Welfare expansion was essentially a valence issue for all parties and sectors. The 2000 technology bubble-burst seriously affected Taiwan, making economic well-being and vitality into a major concern. Income inequality grew quite noticeably during this decade, although distributive justice became a salient issue only during the third decade of democracy. During the three decades since Taiwan's transition to democracy, democratic reform and economic issues have been blended quite consistently with matters of Taiwan's national security and international status.

Chiang Ching-kuo, leader of the KMT on the eve of the democratic transition, did not have to initiate a transition to democracy – but he did. As a result, the KMT ended up owning more shares of the democratic reform stock than it might have if the party had more obstinately opposed democratization.[17] Due to internal disagreement over specific reform agendas – especially those related to Taiwan's relations with China (association with vs. separation from mainland China) – the KMT, now under the leadership of President Lee Teng-hui, began to bifurcate into two segments. One segment, led by President Lee, was dubbed the "mainstream faction"; the other, consisting of very conservative elders, was dubbed the "non-mainstream faction." Throughout the first decade of democracy, the DPP, the main opposition party, pressed for quick and thorough removal of all authoritarian institutions bearing Chinese trademarks. Its hope was to build a Taiwanese nation-state while simultaneously tackling the issues of democratic reform and Taiwan's international status. The mainstream KMT faction was sympathetic to the DPP's agenda and cause, while the non-mainstream KMT faction opposed them. President Lee accelerated the process of democratic reform (most notably by pensioning off the lifetime legislators and national

---

[17] This is a clear illustration of what Slater and Wong (2013; Chapter 9, this volume) call "conceding to thrive."

representatives, thanks to Taiwan's fiscal surplus), but avoided endorsing the opposition's call for an independent Taiwan or proactively promoting a unified China on Taiwan's terms, the outcome favored by some KMT elders. Its moderate stand on national identity, its progressive stand on democratic reform, and China's intimidation helped the KMT mainstream faction to win a stunning victory in the first direct presidential election in 1996, even though its rival faction also fielded a pair of candidates.

The ascendancy of the mainstream leadership faction within the KMT during the first decade of democratic change came at a price: its deepening alliance with (or its capture by, according to critics) local factions that had grassroots clienteles, owned businesses, allegedly engaged in vote buying, and in some cases had ties to organized crime. As Taiwan entered its second decade of democracy, the DPP emphasized the issue of incomplete democratic reform, focusing on two outstanding issues associated with the KMT: its ownership of a huge business empire (and hence, its immense electoral war chest) and its unsavory local factions, which tarnished the KMT's image as a democratic reformer and painted the party as something that should itself be the target of reform.

The DPP's claim to the issue of democratic reform was not the reason why it dislodged the KMT from the presidency in 2000 and won again in 2004. Instead, the DPP's electoral victory in 2000 was caused by a dispute over the candidate selection process within the KMT and the dividing of party votes between two sets of KMT contestants (a highly contingent outcome, or a case of *fortuna*). The DPP's win in 2004, by contrast, was due more to its management of issue dynamics than to luck. As discussed above, by 2004, the KMT had initiated party reform, adopted candidate selection rules, cleaned up a significant portion of the tainted local factions, and promised to retreat from profit-making businesses. Meanwhile, during the first DPP presidency, maldistribution of income was becoming a major problem (as seen from the growing Gini coefficients), while incidences of corruption by the DPP president's family and confidants began to increase, undermining the party's claim to be the agent of democratic reform. However, by highlighting the issue of Taiwan's international status, championing the need and urgency for new nation-building, defining itself as the party of the future, and resorting to ethnic mobilization, the DPP was able to narrowly defeat the KMT again in the 2004 election. The DPP's vote share increased from 38 percent in 2000 to almost 50 percent in 2004. This indicated that the majority of swing voters had switched sides, and that the "prospect effects" emanating from the DPP's nation-building vision had prevailed over whatever nostalgia effects the KMT could muster by reminding voters of the "good old days" of high growth, egalitarian income distribution, and (supposed) lack of corruption.

Nostalgia effects came to permeate Taiwan's political market once again at the tail end of the second decade of democracy, helping to return the KMT to the presidency in 2008 and 2012. The DPP's push for nation-building angered

Beijing and created anxiety in Washington. This strained Taiwan's relations with both and allowed the KMT to redefine Taiwan's status as a national security issue. But the surge of nostalgia was mainly attributable to the DPP's lackluster economic performance in terms of both growth and income distribution, as well as to the spread of corruption within the DPP government. When KMT candidate Ma Ying-jeou promised to deliver clean politics, economic revival, and cross-Strait stability, swing voters switched sides again (many probably seeing echoes of the late KMT leader, Chiang Ching-kuo).

In the wake of its landslide victory in 2008, the KMT government forged a cross-Strait economic partnership as a means of promoting economic revitalization and pursued a cross-Strait détente, thus laying the ground for another win in 2012. However, the 2012 race was tight, as the DPP was able to redefine cross-Strait economic prosperity as an issue of security and political autonomy. This led many swing voters to worry that economic overdependence on China might jeopardize Taiwan's security and provide China with economic leverage that could erode Taiwan's already shaky political sovereignty. However, a postelection survey showed that in 2012, the majority of voters still saw the KMT, not the DPP, as the party that could best ensure cross-Strait security (Wu and Liao 2015:113). This was an issue that the KMT underscored during the campaign, giving Ma a comfortable margin of victory. In the spirit of doubling down, and in spite of social protest, the KMT government under President Ma assiduously pursued further cross-Strait economic integration. The National Chengchi University annual survey of party identification shows that during this time, swing voters began to abandon the KMT en masse.[18] This trend was confirmed by the KMT's defeat in the November 2014 local elections, and even more dramatically by its crushing defeat in the January 2016 presidential and legislative elections.

2.5 CONCLUSION

During three decades of democracy, South Korea and Taiwan's ASPs have not only survived, but have remained among the principal political actors in each polity. This chapter has argued that their endurance is attributable to the existence of an extensive conservative social base; the various forms of authoritarian inheritance from which each has benefited; their ability to adapt their organizations in order to remain the standard bearers of the conservative camp; and their ability to manage issue dynamics in order to exploit the benefits of their authoritarian inheritance, while offsetting the potentially damaging effects of their authoritarian baggage. A mirror image can be found among their principal opponents on the liberal-progressive end of the ideological spectrum, which have emphasized the ASPs' authoritarian baggage, while

---

[18] See http://esc.nccu.edu.tw/app/news.php?Sn=165 [Accessed September 30, 2017].

ASPs in South Korea and Taiwan

developing policies and expertise designed to neutralize the ASPs' authoritarian inheritance. In both cases, a political party duopoly has emerged, anchored on one side by the ASP and on the other by the major party of the former democratic opposition.[19]

However, at the dawn of the fourth decade of democracy in Taiwan, the KMT suffered a devastating blow in the January 2016 general election. Its presidential candidate was defeated by his chief opponent by a whopping 25 points, a surprisingly huge margin of defeat by its own historical yardstick. What is more, for the first time, the KMT lost its majority in the legislature to the DPP, which won 44 percent of party-list votes, 17 percent more than the KMT. This result completely reversed the pattern displayed in all previous legislative elections, in which the KMT typically won by at least 10 percent. This debacle came in the wake of an already stunning setback in local elections in late 2014, leading many observers to speculate that the party, after three decades of resiliency in democratic Taiwan, might be heading for the dustbin of history.

Undoubtedly, acute intra-party leadership conflict between President Ma and Speaker Wang (a fratricidal conflict that began two years before the 2016 elections), and then between Deputy Speaker Madame Hung and Party Chairman Chu during the party nomination process, was a major cause of the KMT's defeat. Presiding over an economy that was dramatically slowing and registering export contractions eleven months in a row before the election also contributed to the KMT's dismal performance. Yet the KMT had successfully weathered both leadership splits and economic adversity in the past, in part thanks to its authoritarian inheritance. In the 2000 election, for example, the party suffered a severe leadership split, which cost it the presidency in a three-way race. Yet the KMT retained its leading position in the legislature, due to the vast territorial organization and huge war chest that it had inherited from the old regime – neither of which was possessed by its turncoat "sister" party or its liberal-progressive rival. (As discussed above, within a few short years, most defectors had returned to the fold, re-embracing the good old name of the KMT.) With regard to the economy, the KMT was already facing problems by 2012. President Ma's pledge in 2008 to revitalize the economy by meeting the goal of "6-3-3" (6 percent annual growth, a per capita income of US$30,000, and an unemployment rate below 3 percent) was already regarded by many as a broken promise by the time he began to run for reelection in 2012. Nevertheless, he was reelected by a safe margin, and the KMT's grip on the legislature remained firm, thanks in large part to the party's credibility in the area of national security.

---

[19] Thus, both cases provide support for the proposition that ASPs can help promote party system institutionalization by structuring party systems around a "regime divide," with the ASP on one side and the former democratic opposition party on the other (see Loxton, Introduction, this volume).

In the 2016 electoral competition, the KMT party leadership was even more beleaguered than it had been in 2000, and Taiwan's economy had sunk even deeper than in 2012. However, what really led to its unprecedented defeat was not infighting among party leaders or abysmal economic conditions. Instead, it was the alarmingly rapid and simultaneous diminishment of its authoritarian inheritance – its party brand (particularly in the area of national security) and its business empire (which previously had been a valuable source of party funds). This process accelerated during Ma's second terms, following the emergence in 2014 of a student-led protest movement known as the Sunflower Student Movement, which opposed the KMT's management of cross-Strait security conditions and economic ties. The KMT's reputation for economic management was already tainted after Taiwan emerged from the global financial crisis with the most lackluster performance among the East Asian nations. Its efforts to pursue détente and broaden and deepen economic relations with China as a means of enhancing Taiwan's economy and security unintentionally undermined the party's economic and security credentials. To many voters, especially those who strenuously opposed the way that the KMT had short-circuited legislative oversight in order elevate economic ties with China, the high degree of cross-Strait economic integration had made Taiwan overly dependent on China. They also believed that this created a small, privileged constituency in Taiwan that disproportionately benefited from cross-Strait ties, and which would do China's bidding and put its narrow economic interests ahead of the national interest. When the DPP presidential candidate pledged to ignite industrial upgrading projects within Taiwan, diversify Taiwan's economic partnerships, and maintain the political status quo across the Strait, the KMT's economic and security stocks lost much of their value.

The KMT's other authoritarian endowments either became less valuable or turned into liabilities. The party's strong brand had kept it from collapsing following the leadership dissension in 2000 and helped to lure back turncoats a few years later. By contrast, in 2016, the KMT's brand *fueled* intra-party conflict, with each leadership group highlighting a particular aspect of the party's history as the defining feature of its brand – based on its own biased understanding of what the party should really be or be restored to, rather than what it really was or had been. One leadership group openly took pride in the KMT's historic role in building modern China and unequivocally committed itself to forging closer, more intimate ties with China. This group and its supporters mostly resided in urban areas, worked for the state and the security sector, and were mainlanders. They tended to see the KMT's co-optation of local, rural-based, Taiwanese elites as a Faustian bargain: it had not only replenished the leadership ranks of the party but also introduced collusive practices that corrupted it. To grassroots, rural-based KMT elites and their supporters, the KMT brand began to connote exclusion, intolerance, and detachment from society. The KMT brand itself therefore became a source of contention among party elites.

Like its brand, the KMT's business assets also became a liability. In 2016, in the wake of the party's defeat in local elections two years earlier, and facing an uphill battle against a DPP that had been unprecedentedly successful in fundraising (through various means, including social media), the KMT was, for the first time, out-funded by its opponent. One report (unverified but instantly amplified through social media) about the KMT's attempt to sell some of its immense assets in order to finance its campaign converted the KMT's assets into the most salient issue of the day.[20] This led the DPP to promise that it would ask the judicial branch to launch a legal investigation into the KMT's assets – a process that, potentially, could even lead to the nationalization of the KMT's properties. This episode not only gave the KMT pause in using its own assets to fund its election campaign; it also meant that the KMT went from being a party with an unfair financial advantage into a high-profile target for the judicial process.

Finally, like its brand and business assets, the KMT's territorial organization also lost its edge in the 2016 election. Following its landslide victory in the 2014 local elections, the DPP learned to use its incumbency advantages to nurture its own grassroots organization. While the social media-savvy millennial generation that had spearheaded the anti-Ma Sunflower Student Movement in early 2014 was beyond the reach of any party's territorial organization, the DPP was more effective than the KMT in engaging with it in cyberspace, given its long experience of working with social movements. The overall voter turnout rate for the 2016 elections (66 percent) was the lowest in the history of democratic Taiwan. The rate for young voters, though, was the highest, skewing the electoral results in the DPP's favor.

While the KMT is surely in the wilderness as of this writing in 2017, it is probably not heading to the ASP museum just yet, for a few reasons. First, the party's social bases are arguably not as eroded as the discrepancy between its vote and that of the DPP would seem to suggest. While half of the votes that the KMT lost in the 2016 elections (using the 2012 elections as the baseline) went to the DPP, the other half went to smaller conservative parties. Party identification surveys show that in the preceding three years, the KMT's share of party identifiers had dropped precipitously, while the number of independent voters grew dramatically and the number of DPP identifiers remained stable. Second, while the KMT has completely missed the social media-savvy millennial voters, the fact that they are more independent than partisan – and thus not solidified as DPP supporters – means that their votes are up for grabs in the future. As Lin and Su (2015: 137–147) argue, the millennials have typically demanded instant responses from power holders, lending or withdrawing their support based on

---

[20] See http://m.appledaily.com.tw/realtimenews/article/new/20151228/762841/ [Accessed December 30, 2017].

any noble cause. Third, while the KMT has been reduced to the second largest party in the legislature, it remains the standard bearer of the conservative social bases. One of its sister parties (New Party) has long been on the verge of evaporation. The other sister party (People First Party) did well in collecting KMT protest votes, but it lacks organization and resources, and may not survive the retirement of its charismatic but aging leader. The only way for the KMT to lose its leadership position within the conservative camp is through intra-party attrition. To continue to lead the conservative base and eventually attempt to return to power, the KMT will need to prevent implosion and reinvent itself, a task that it is currently undertaking.

In a similar vein, the unexpected loss of power by South Korea's ASP in a special presidential election in May 2017 deserves a postscript. The influence peddling and corruption scandal surrounding President Park Geun-hye – and the massive and sustained protests that followed – led to her impeachment and, subsequently, to Saenuri's stunning electoral defeat (Shin and Moon 2007). In the wake of these events, Saenuri renamed itself the Liberty Korea Party (LKP), and a splinter group formed a smaller conservative party, the Bareun Party. South Korea's ASP (and its smaller affiliate) was abandoned by voters in the Seoul area. These overwhelmingly independent-minded voters had supported Saenuri in the 2012 election, but turned against the party and its smaller affiliate in 2017. Nevertheless, the two parties still garnered close to 30 percent of the vote nationwide, received electoral majorities in their geographic bases, and won just as many legislative seats as the progressive party that now holds the presidency. Thus, this episode does not provide an occasion to write the obituary of South Korea's ASP. On the contrary, it has demonstrated its ability to pass an extraordinary political stress test.

3

Personalistic Authoritarian Successor Parties in Latin America

James Loxton and Steven Levitsky

When Peruvian autocrat Alberto Fujimori fled into exile in Japan in 2000, few observers expected that he or his followers had a political future. Leaked videotapes revealed to the world that Fujimori's government had not only been authoritarian but had also engaged in scandalous levels of corruption and abuse of power (Conaghan 2005). Moreover, Fujimori had been a notoriously personalistic ruler, creating and quickly discarding multiple political parties during his decade in power. The *Fujimorista* movement fragmented and was widely expected to disappear. Seventeen years later, however, *Fujimorismo* was the largest party in Peru. While Alberto Fujimori languished in prison (he was extradited to Peru in 2007, and was tried and found guilty of corruption and human rights abuses), his daughter, Keiko, rebuilt the *Fujimorista* organization, renaming it Popular Force. Keiko Fujimori nearly won the presidency in 2011 and 2016, and Popular Force captured an absolute majority of seats in Congress in 2016.

Fujimorismo is a case of an important, but understudied, type of authoritarian successor party: *personalistic authoritarian successor parties*. While most research on authoritarian successor parties focuses on former ruling parties of institutionalized regimes (see, for example, chapters by Cheng and Huang, Grzymala-Busse, Riedl, LeBas, Flores-Macías, and Slater and Wong, this volume), recent research has shown that authoritarian successor parties may also emerge from very different sorts of dictatorship (Loxton 2014a, 2015). Some, such as the Liberal Front Party (PFL)/Democrats (DEM) in Brazil, are born under military regimes (Power, Chapter 7, this volume). Others, such as *Fujimorismo*, have a more surprising origin still: they emerge from *personalistic dictatorships*, in which power is concentrated in the hands of an individual autocrat. After the transition to democracy, these parties tend to remain inextricably tied to the founding leader, typically running him at the top of the ticket.

Personalistic authoritarian successor parties are surprisingly widespread in Latin America. Indeed, they became prominent actors in a *majority* of Latin American countries – ten out of nineteen countries – between 1945 and 2010 (see Table 3.1). In total, twelve such parties have reached prominence (Panama and Peru each produced two). In five cases, the former autocrat himself was elected back into office (Juan Perón, Getúlio Vargas, José María Velasco Ibarra, Joaquín Balaguer, and Hugo Banzer),[1] and three other parties won the presidency with a different candidate.[2] A few of these parties even managed to "de-personalize" and endure long after the death of their founding leaders: Peronism remains Argentina's largest party more than four decades after Perón's death in 1974; the Democratic Revolutionary Party (PRD) in Panama survived the death of Omar Torrijos in 1981 and remains one of the country's main parties; and the Brazilian Labor Party (PTB) performed well in three election cycles after Vargas' death in 1954. More speculatively, *Fujimorismo* appears likely to outlive Alberto Fujimori, and the United Socialist Party of Venezuela (PSUV), the party of the late Hugo Chávez, would almost certainly survive a democratic transition in Venezuela.

The electoral success of personalistic authoritarian successor parties – and, in a few cases, their long-term survival – is puzzling, for two reasons. First, parties with obvious links to the authoritarian past are generally not expected to perform well under democracy. According to one influential argument, authoritarian successor parties must "break symbolically with the past" in order to thrive under democracy (Grzymala-Busse 2002: 79). However, for parties that are founded and usually led by former dictators, it is difficult to make such a break. Indeed, many of them publicly emphasize their authoritarian roots. Second, personalistic leadership is widely viewed as antithetical to the emergence of durable political organizations. As parties characterized by both personalism and undeniable links to the authoritarian past, then, personalistic authoritarian successor parties should be doubly damned.

In this chapter, we examine the phenomenon of personalistic authoritarian successor parties in Latin America and consider why they often perform well at the ballot box, and in a few cases, "de-personalize." We make two main arguments. First, we argue that such parties' personalism and obvious roots in dictatorship do *not* present major obstacles to a strong electoral performance. Parties may deal with their authoritarian past through a strategy of *scapegoating* or by simply *embracing the past*, and personalism can actually be an asset (at least initially), both as a means of attracting votes and as a source of organizational cohesion. Second, we argue that while personalistic authoritarian successor parties may not face major obstacles in terms of

---

[1] Another case of a dictator being elected back into office is Carlos Ibáñez del Campo, the former Chilean dictator (1927–1931) who democratically returned to the presidency in 1952 (Grugel 1992). However, because Ibáñez did not form his own party, we do not include it here. For more on former dictators elected back into office, see Conclusion (Loxton, this volume).

[2] These are José Antonio Remón Cantera's National Patriotic Coalition (CPN) and Omar Torrijos' Democratic Revolutionary Party (PRD) in Panama, and Efraín Ríos Montt's Guatemalan Republican Front (FRG).

electoral performance, they *do* face serious challenges with respect to longevity. Because so much of their electoral appeal is based on the leader, and because they tend to substitute the leader's personal authority for developed internal party structures, they often face severe crises – and even collapse – when the leader dies or retires. However, we argue that they are more likely to avoid this fate where the founding autocrat is associated with a clear program, set of policies, or constituency, and where the authoritarian regime produces deep societal polarization, as in the cases of Peronism in Argentina and the PRD in Panama.

3.1 INTRODUCING PERSONALISTIC AUTHORITARIAN SUCCESSOR PARTIES

Personalistic authoritarian successor parties are *parties that operate in democratic regimes, but that were founded and initially led by a personalistic dictator (or former dictator)*. Like all authoritarian successor parties, they combine past connections to authoritarianism with present participation in democracy (Introduction, this volume). However, they emerge from a specific kind of authoritarian regime: *personalistic dictatorship*. Barbara Geddes (1999) famously divided authoritarian regimes into three ideal types: single-party, military, and personalist. Whereas in military and single-party regimes, military officers or ruling parties exert significant influence, the distinguishing characteristic of personalist dictatorships is that power is overwhelmingly concentrated in the hands of one leader. As Geddes writes: "Personalist regimes differ from both military and single-party regimes in that access to office and the fruits of office depends much more on the discretion of an individual leader. The leader may be an officer and may have created a party to support himself, but neither the military nor the party exercises independent decision-making power insulated from the whims of the ruler" (1999: 121–122).

Personalistic *dictatorships*, unsurprisingly, tend to beget personalistic *parties*. According to Kostadinova and Levitt (2014: 492), personalistic parties are defined by two main criteria: "the presence of a dominant leader and a party 'organization' that is weakly institutionalized by design." While the leader need not be charismatic,[3] he or she must dominate the party's internal life for it to be personalistic. The leader makes virtually all important decisions, such as "determining the direction and vision of party platforms and campaigns; nominating candidates for elections; deciding on the allocation of organizational resources; and wielding authority over other politicians from his or her party, particularly members of his or her parliamentary caucus" (Kostadinova and Levitt 2014: 500). In addition to dominating the party's internal life, the leader is the party's public face, typically running at the top of the ticket. For example, Hugo Banzer was Nationalist Democratic Action's

---

[3] On "noncharismatic personalism," see Ansell and Fish (1999).

(ADN) presidential candidate in six consecutive elections (1979, 1980, 1985, 1989, 1993, and 1997), and Joaquín Balaguer was the Social Christian Reformist Party's (PRSC) presidential candidate *nine times* between 1966 and 2000. When former dictators are barred from running, presidential candidates are usually surrogates. Thus, Peronism's candidate in 1973, Héctor Cámpora, ran under the slogan "Cámpora to the presidency, Perón to power."[4] Likewise, the Guatemalan Republican Front's (FRG) Alfonso Portillo ran for president in 1995–1996 with the slogan "Portillo to the presidency, Ríos Montt to power."[5] When the founding leader retires or dies, the party leadership often passes to his spouse (e.g., Isabel Martínez de Perón, María Delgado de Odría) or child (e.g., María Eugenia Rojas, Zury Ríos, Keiko Fujimori).

Personalistic authoritarian successor parties have been surprisingly common in Latin America. Using Geddes, Wright, and Frantz's (2014a) Autocratic Regimes Data Set, we identified a total of twenty-four personalistic regimes that existed – and ended – in Latin America between 1945 and 2010.[6] (These cases are listed in Appendix 3.1.) In eighteen of these twenty-four regimes, autocrats or their allies created a party, either during or shortly after the fall of the regime.[7] Of these eighteen parties, fourteen survived the autocrat's fall from power and can thus be described as potential authoritarian successor parties. However, only twelve of them actually competed in democratic elections. These are listed in Table 3.1.[8] All twelve parties won at least 10 percent of the vote in one or more national elections, thereby meeting the criteria for electoral prominence employed in the Introduction (Loxton, this volume). Eight of the twelve parties were elected back into national office (PJ, PTB, FNV, CPN, PRSC, PRD, ADN, FRG), and two others came within a hair's breadth of the presidency (ANAPO, *Fujimorismo*). Four of the twelve parties survived the death of the founder (PJ, PTB, CPN, PRD), which we operationalize as winning above 10 percent in three subsequent elections, though only two have survived to the present (PJ, PRD).[9]

---

[4] Quoted in McGuire (1997: 163).
[5] Quoted in Larry Rohter, "Guatemala Election Becomes Vote on Former Dictator," *The New York Times*, January 7, 1996.
[6] For coding details, see Appendix 3.1.
[7] In the remaining cases, rulers either inherited a party (e.g., Alfredo Stroessner and the Colorado Party in Paraguay; Tiburcio Carías and the National Party in Honduras; and Manuel Noriega and the PRD in Panama) or governed without a party.
[8] We do not include Hugo Chávez's PSUV, since Venezuela remains under authoritarian rule. However, if, as is likely, the PSUV were to survive an eventual transition to democracy, it would qualify as a personalistic authoritarian successor party.
[9] In the case of *Fujimorismo*, the founder (Alberto Fujimori) is still alive. However, as we discuss below, the party seems poised to survive his eventual death.

TABLE 3.1 *Prominent personalistic ASPs in Latin America, 1945–2010*

Country	Party	Founder	Authoritarian regime	Elected back into office?	Survived death of founder?
Argentina	Peronism (now Justicialista Party, PJ)	Juan Perón	1946–1955[10]	Yes	Yes
Bolivia	Nationalist Democratic Action (ADN)	Hugo Banzer	1971–1978	Yes	No
Brazil[11]	Brazilian Labor Party (PTB)	Getúlio Vargas	1930–1945	Yes	Yes
Colombia	National Popular Alliance (ANAPO)	Gustavo Rojas Pinilla	1953–1957	No	No
Dominican Republic	Social Christian Reformist Party (PRSC)	Joaquín Balaguer	1966–1978 1986–1996	Yes	No
Ecuador	Velasquista National Federation (FNV)	José María Velasco Ibarra	1944–1947, 1970–1972	Yes	No
Guatemala	Guatemalan Republican Front (FRG)	Efraín Ríos Montt	1982–1983	Yes	No
Panama	National Patriotic Coalition (CPN)	José Antonio Remón Cantera	1952–1955	Yes	Yes
Panama	Democratic Revolutionary Party (PRD)	Omar Torrijos	1968–1981	Yes	Yes
Peru	Odriísta National Union (UNO)	Manuel Odría	1948–1956	No	No

(*continued*)

[10] Prior to this, Perón was also a high-level official in Argentina's 1943–1946 military regime.
[11] Vargas' dictatorship also gave rise to another political party, the Social Democratic Party (PSD). However, we do not include it in our list of cases, since it was less closely associated with Vargas than the PTB. This could be seen, for example, in the 1950 general election, when the PSD did not support Vargas' presidential candidacy, running its own candidate instead (Levine 1998: 79).

TABLE 3.1 (continued)

Country	Party	Founder	Authoritarian regime	Elected back into office?	Survived death of founder?
Peru	*Fujimorismo* (now Popular Force)	Alberto Fujimori	1992–2000	No	N/A
Venezuela	Nationalist Civic Crusade (CCN)	Marcos Pérez Jiménez	1948–1958	No	No

Despite their obvious personalism, it would be a mistake to view these parties as nothing more than vehicles for individual candidates.[12] Many of them were real parties, with impressive territorial organizations capable of fielding candidates in presidential, legislative, and subnational elections over multiple cycles. This organizational strength was clearest in the cases of Peronism in Argentina and the PRD in Panama, which survived the deaths of their founding leaders and became their countries' most important parties, but it was true of other cases, as well. For example, although the National Popular Alliance (ANAPO) is best known for Gustavo Rojas Pinilla's near-victory in Colombia's 1970 presidential election, it was a well-organized party: "By 1970, at least in the large urban areas, ANAPO had in some ways come to resemble a modern mass party, complete with myriad barrio-level organizations, regular dues and carnets, mass rallies, party training schools, more or less regular party media, a centralized command structure, and strict party discipline" (Dix 1978: 345). Indeed, "[f]or a time it may have been the most effectively organized political movement ever to exist in Colombia" (Dix 1978: 345). Likewise, *Fujimorismo* has displaced APRA as Peru's largest political party (Levitsky 2018; Meléndez 2012, 2014). In short, many personalistic authoritarian successor parties have become among their countries' most important political actors, and several of them have returned to power under democracy.

3.2 DOUBLY DAMNED? PERSONALISM AND AUTHORITARIAN BAGGAGE

The strong performance of so many personalistic authoritarian successor parties in Latin America is puzzling, for two reasons. First, as parties with such obvious roots in dictatorship, they had fewer options available to them for dealing with the past than other authoritarian successor parties. As discussed in

---

[12] On the presidential candidacies of "recycled dictators," see Kyle (2016).

the Introduction (Loxton, this volume), all authoritarian successor parties are born with a mix of *authoritarian inheritance* and *authoritarian baggage*. A crucial part of succeeding under democracy is to find a strategy that allows the party to minimize the costs of its authoritarian baggage, while maximizing the benefits of its authoritarian inheritance. The most obvious strategies are *contrition* and *obfuscation*. With contrition, the party attempts to offload its baggage by making a clean break with the past. As Grzymala-Busse (2002) has shown, this was the strategy pursued to great effect by some parties in East Central Europe, with parties changing their names, abandoning old symbols, and denouncing the abuses of the former regime. With obfuscation, the party attempts to offload its baggage by downplaying its connections to the former regime. As Power discusses in his chapter (Chapter 7, this volume), Brazil's PFL/DEM has attempted such a strategy.

For personalistic authoritarian successor parties, however, neither of these strategies is feasible. The centrality of the former dictator in the party's life and/or identity makes breaking with the past virtually impossible. It is hard to denounce or deny connections to the person at the top of the ticket or who gives the party its formal (e.g., *Odriísta* National Union, *Velasquista* National Federation) or informal name (e.g., *Peronismo, Fujimorismo*). Indeed, connections to the former dictator tend to be these parties' greatest electoral asset. However, two of the other strategies discussed in the Introduction (Loxton, this volume) *are* available to them: *scapegoating* and *embracing the past*. In the former, the party blames the unsavory aspects of the former regime on someone other than the party founder. The best example is Panama's PRD, which embraced the memory of the dictator who founded it, Omar Torrijos, while cutting all ties to the dictator who succeeded him, Manuel Noriega. In the event of a hypothetical transition to democracy in Venezuela, the PSUV would likely pursue a similar strategy, embracing the memory of its popular founder, Hugo Chávez, while blaming his successor, Nicolás Maduro, for the severe economic crisis that came to plague the regime.[13] However, not all parties have a convenient scapegoat, and thus have little choice but to embrace the past. While this would seem a very risky strategy, given that some of the regimes from which these parties emerged committed large-scale human rights abuses (e.g., Ríos Montt dictatorship in Guatemala), it has proven to be surprisingly effective in several cases, as discussed in the following section.[14]

A second reason why the success of personalistic authoritarian successor parties is surprising is that personalism is widely considered to be antithetical to party-building (Mainwaring and Scully 1995; Weyland 1996, 1999). Personalistic leaders rarely invest in party institutions that could limit their power and autonomy, and they frequently discourage the rise of talented new leaders who could potentially challenge their control of the party.[15] In fact,

---

[13] For more on this, see the conclusion of this chapter.
[14] For a similar argument, see Deming (2013). See also Grzymala-Busse (Chapter 4, this volume).
[15] For a similar point, see Panebianco (1988: 67, 147).

many personalistic leaders actively – and repeatedly – undermine their own parties in order to preserve their own power. Perón, for example, dissolved the Labor Party that brought him to power in 1946 and aggressively resisted efforts to build a more institutionalized Peronist party in the 1960s (McGuire 1997). Likewise, Alberto Fujimori abandoned three of his own parties (Change 90, New Majority, and Let's Go Neighbor) during his presidency (1990–2000).[16] According to Keiko Fujimori, her father "didn't believe in parties. Like a good *caudillo*, he doesn't like to cede power. And to build a party organization, you have to cede power."[17] Even in cases where party leaders do not actively sabotage their own parties, personalistic authoritarian successor parties are likely to face a crisis once the leader exits the political stage.[18] Bolivia's ADN, for example, oscillated between 20 and 35 percent of the vote in general elections between 1985 and 1997, with Banzer at the top of the party ticket. In the 2002 general election, however, which took place less than two months after Banzer's death, the party's vote share plummeted to 3.4 percent, before disappearing altogether. Most personalistic authoritarian successor parties in Latin America have suffered a similar fate.

Nevertheless, personalistic leaders may also *contribute* to party-building. In fact, some of the most successful parties in Latin American history have been led by dominant personalities – if not fully personalistic leaders – during their formative years. There are two major ways that such leaders may strengthen new parties. First, they may attract votes. As Samuels and Shugart (2010) have shown, presidential systems compel parties to nominate candidates with broad popular appeal. Without a popular leader at the top of the ticket, new parties are unlikely to be competitive in a presidential democracy. And non-competitive parties rarely endure, with voters and donors throwing their support to other parties with more realistic prospects. In Latin America, party leaders have often played a decisive role in making new parties electorally viable. This has most obviously been the case in populist movements such as Peronism, *Fujimorismo*, and *Chavismo*, but it has been the case in a variety of other kinds of parties, as well.[19]

A second way that personalistic leaders can contribute to party-building is by serving as a source of intra-party cohesion. As Van Dyck (2018) argues, party

---

[16] His fourth, Peru 2000, disappeared after his fall from power.
[17] Steven Levitsky's interview with Keiko Fujimori, Lima, July 25, 2013.
[18] For similar points, see Panebianco (1988: 53, 67) and Kostadinova and Levitt (2014: 500–501).
[19] Even when they were *not* fully personalistic, party leaders have often been crucial for making parties electorally viable. This has been true for some of Latin America's most established parties, such as APRA and Popular Action (AP) in Peru; the National Liberation Party (PLN) in Costa Rica; Democratic Action (AD) and COPEI in Venezuela; and the Dominican Revolutionary Party (PRD) and Dominican Liberation Party (PLD). Party leaders have also been crucial to the electoral viability of newer parties, such as the Nationalist Republican Alliance (ARENA) in El Salvador; Workers' Party (PT) in Brazil; Party of the Democratic Revolution (PRD) in Mexico; and Movement toward Socialism (MAS) in Bolivia.

leaders who combine broad "external appeal" with the electorate and "internal dominance" of the party may help bind new parties together during the critical formative period. Party founders with undisputed internal authority can play a key role in limiting conflict within their parties, since their word is effectively law. As Panebianco (1988: 66) puts it, such leaders can act as a kind of "cement" holding the party's different factions together.[20] Without this cement, parties can enter into crisis. In Bolivia, for example, after Banzer temporarily retired from politics after the 1993 election, ADN descended into bitter factional struggles. This led to calls for Banzer's return, since no one else had the same "capacity to reach agreement" among "the wide and varied array of people" who made up the party (Jetté, Foronda, and López 1997: 56). In many cases, the leader's electoral appeal may also help reduce the likelihood of schism, as the prospect of competing without the leader's coattails discourages other party elites from defecting.

To conclude, undeniable links to a past dictatorship and a high degree of dependence on a party leader create difficulties for personalistic authoritarian successor parties. However, these are not as insurmountable as they might seem. As we show in the sections that follow, scapegoating and embracing the past have proven to be surprisingly effective strategies for winning votes, and the effects of personalism on party-building are double-edged rather than entirely negative. While attachment to a personalistic leader may create obstacles to a party's survival in the longer term, it can also enhance its electoral appeal and internal cohesion during the critical formative period.

3.3 WINNING VOTES BY EMBRACING THE PAST

The idea that embracing the authoritarian past is a viable vote-winning strategy for a party competing in democracy is counterintuitive. In her study of authoritarian successor parties in East Central Europe, Grzymala-Busse (2002) explains why this strategy would appear to be a nonstarter. By the late 1980s, communist regimes were "widely despised by their own citizens" (Grzymala-Busse 2002: 2). Given this "popular hatred," it made sense for authoritarian successor parties to distance themselves from communist symbols, since these "had outlived whatever usefulness and legitimacy they once had" (Grzymala-Busse 2002: 3, 77–79).[21] Another example is the National Party in South Africa. As the ruling party of the undemocratic and explicitly racist Apartheid regime, it left power with exceedingly little legitimacy among the country's nonwhite majority. Given this background, Grzymala-Busse (2002: 276–277) argues that the only way that it could have succeeded

---

[20] Again, this is true even in cases of party leaders who were *not* fully personalistic, such as Víctor Raúl Haya de la Torre in Peru's APRA, Lula in Brazil's PT, Roberto D'Aubuisson in El Salvador's ARENA, and Jaime Guzmán in Chile's Independent Democratic Union (UDI).
[21] In her chapter (Chapter 4, this volume), Grzymala-Busse reconsiders this earlier argument.

under democracy was by thoroughly distancing itself from the past. It failed to do so and collapsed shortly after the transition to democracy.

Yet not all authoritarian regimes are as hated as the communist regimes of East Central Europe or South Africa's Apartheid regime. Indeed, a growing literature on what Dimitrov (2009) calls "popular autocrats" shows that some dictatorships enjoy substantial popular support, especially when they can claim accomplishments in areas such as the economy, national defense, and public security.[22] There is good reason to think that the regimes that gave rise to the twelve parties examined in this chapter enjoyed such support – not necessarily from majorities, but at least from large minorities. Five grew out of what Levitsky and Way (2010) call competitive authoritarian regimes (Peronism, FNV, CPN, PRSC, *Fujimorismo*). While the playing field was tilted against the opposition in these regimes, elections were somewhat competitive, and thus incumbents' victories suggested at least a degree of popular support. Even in cases where dictators came to power through military means, they were not necessarily any more illegitimate than those who preceded and followed them, with three of them (Rojas Pinilla, Banzer, Ríos Montt) coming to power after overthrowing leaders who were themselves authoritarian and three of them being replaced (Banzer, Ríos Montt, Torrijos) by new military rulers.

But even more important than how these leaders entered and exited office was what they did there. As discussed in the Introduction (Loxton, this volume), some dictatorships govern abysmally and thus produce only authoritarian baggage. Others, however, have a more mixed record in office, leaving legacies with both negative and positive dimensions. All of the parties examined in this chapter could claim achievements in areas such as social policy, public security, political stability, or national pride. In some cases, these achievements seemed even more impressive after the transition to democracy, with new democracies plagued by economic crisis, political instability, violent crime, or perceptions of corruption. Thus, while these dictatorships undoubtedly produced authoritarian *baggage*, they also produced considerable authoritarian *inheritance*. Under such circumstances, a strategy of simply embracing the past sometimes proved viable.

One of the best illustrations is Bolivia's ADN. After taking power in a coup in 1971, General Hugo Banzer unleashed a wave of "[v]iolent repression" against "Left party activists, student leaders, labor leaders, church activists, and others" (Malloy and Gamarra 1988: 74–75). This set the stage for seven years (1971–1978) of harsh dictatorship, with widespread torture, political imprisonment, and forced exile, as well as some "disappearances."[23] Yet

---

[22] For more on this, see Conclusion (Loxton, this volume).
[23] See Andres Schipani, "Hidden Cells Reveal Bolivia's Dark Past," *BBC News*, March 5, 2009.

while Banzer was clearly responsible for large-scale human rights violations, he could also claim significant accomplishments. One was political stability. In the year before he took power, Bolivia had experienced "an almost comic series of coups and countercoups," and in the four years after he was overthrown, "there were seven military and two weak civilian governments" (Gamarra and Malloy 1995: 406, 409). Banzer's seven years of rule were, by comparison, an island of relative calm.[24] Second, he presided over an economic boom. Due to a spike in the value of the country's exports and the availability of cheap international credit, Bolivia enjoyed rapid economic growth, which "created popular support for the regime despite its antidemocratic activities" (Klein 2011: 231). Again, the contrast with the period after Banzer was overthrown was stark. When democracy finally took hold in 1982, the country suffered a devastating economic crisis, in which "growth rates were negative, real salaries dramatically deteriorated, and inflation reached 8,000 percent by 1985" (Conaghan, Malloy, and Abugattas 1990: 17). This meant that when Banzer later drew a distinction between, in his words, the "seven years of prosperity [*vacas gordas*]" of his regime and the "seven of leanness [*vacas flacas*]" that followed,[25] there was some truth to it.

Banzer's dominance of ADN and perennial place at the top of the party ticket meant that there was no escape from the past;[26] more to the point, his record as dictator meant there was no *need* to escape from it. In order to capitalize on this past, ADN adopted the Banzer dictatorship's slogan of "Order, Peace, and Work,"[27] and explained that its goal was "to consolidate the seven years of progress" begun during his first period as president.[28] The party made one of its campaign slogans *Banzer vuelve* ("Banzer will return") and ran a series of before-and-after advertisements that explicitly appealed to nostalgia for the Banzer years. One from 1980, for example, shows two images of bread rolls, one smaller than the other, and reads: "Compare. Before, just three years ago, when Banzer governed, this bread cost $bo.50. Now, if you can even find it, this smaller and worse bread costs twice as much. Whose fault is this? Do you want to eat good and cheap bread again? Have faith, because Banzer will return."[29]

---

[24] Indeed, Banzer's seven years in office made him the "longest-serving president since 1871" (Whitehead 1986: 55).

[25] Quoted in Sivak (2001: 247).

[26] From the beginning, ADN was thoroughly personalistic. According to one study, "the party was managed like a business by its owner," and "[a]ny dissent was motive for expulsion or exclusion" (Peñaranda Bojanic 2004: 61).

[27] See Dunkerley (1984: 203) and "Se fundó ADN; La Jefaturiza Hugo Banzer Suárez; Propugna Orden, Paz y Trabajo," *El Diario*, March 25, 1979.

[28] See *Presencia*, March 24, 1979.

[29] See *El Diario*, June 15, 1980. ADN ran similar advertisements about housing, public works, employment, poverty, and shortages of foodstuffs. See issues of *El Diario* from June 22–26, 1979, and May 30-June 20, 1980.

With respect to the repression that occurred under his watch, Banzer showed little remorse, asserting, "We acted with authoritarianism, I admit it. But that was part of a historical moment ... I can't go around on my knees all day apologizing."[30] Besides, he explained, "[t]hose who disappeared were neither little angels nor saints."[31] While such comments no doubt repelled many Bolivians, for others, the slogan *Banzer vuelve* must have sounded like "the rough equivalent of 'Happy days are here again'" (Conaghan, Malloy, and Abugattas 1990: 11). The strategy of embracing the past worked: ADN was one of Bolivia's three main parties for two decades. Between 1985 and 1997, it oscillated between 20 and 35 percent of the vote, and Banzer was democratically voted back into the presidency in 1997.[32] Indeed, ADN held the presidency or was part of a coalition government for all but four years during the 1985–2002 period.

An even more startling example of a personalistic authoritarian successor party winning votes by embracing the past is Efraín Ríos Montt's FRG in Guatemala. Ríos Montt is arguably the worst human rights violator in Latin American history. After taking power through a coup in March 1982, his government unleashed a "scorched earth" campaign of mass slaughter against suspected guerrillas and their supporters.[33] Estimates of the number of people killed during his year and a half as dictator range from 25,000 to 87,000.[34] Most were civilians of various Mayan ethnicities, leading some to describe these events as "the Mayan holocaust" (Garrard-Burnett 2010: 7).[35]

This genocidal killing spree, however, did not turn the entire population against Ríos Montt. In fact, to many Guatemalans he became a "popular hero" (Garrard-Burnett 2010: 9). One reason is that, as the country's first evangelical Protestant president, he won the support of much of Guatemala's large evangelical population (Garrard-Burnett 2010). Another was that he undertook "a well-publicized program against dishonest public officials," preaching about the evils of corruption and urging citizens "to report dishonest government employees" (Handy 1984: 267).[36] Much of Ríos Montt's popularity, however, seems to have stemmed from his effectiveness in violently establishing "law and order." Brutal as it

---

[30] Quoted in "El ex dictador Hugo Banzer, virtual ganador en las elecciones de Bolivia," *El País*, June 2, 1997.
[31] Quoted in Sivak (2001: 40).
[32] Banzer won pluralities in the 1985 and 1997 presidential elections. However, because of the peculiarities of Bolivia's electoral system at the time, he was not elected president in 1985.
[33] For a detailed description of this campaign, see Schirmer (1998).
[34] See Schirmer (1998: 44, 56) and Garrard-Burnett (2010: 6–7).
[35] See also Elisabeth Malkin, "Former Leader of Guatemala Is Guilty of Genocide Against Mayan Group," *The New York Times*, May 10, 2013.
[36] See also Stoll (1990/1991).

was, his regime largely succeeded in decimating the guerrillas, and violence, while "more deadly," was also "more methodical and less chaotic" (Garrard-Burnett 2010: 87) than under previous dictators. This meant that many Guatemalans came to regard Ríos Montt's eighteen months in power as a kind of *"pax riosmonttista"* and credited him "with restoring order and authority" (Garrard-Burnett 2010: 81). In August 1983, he was overthrown in a coup, and in 1985, Guatemala made a rocky transition to competitive elections. High crime rates and persistent corruption, however, made many look back on the Ríos Montt dictatorship with nostalgia. As one focus group participant recalled to the sociologist Angelina Snodgrass Godoy, "[I]n the regime of Ríos Montt, everything was in order. Order. And I liked that." Another agreed, recalling that in those days, "It was a death for a death."[37] Such recollections may help explain Azpuru's (2003) finding that one of the strongest statistical predictors of support for the FRG was fear of crime.

Ríos Montt's record as dictator gave the FRG – created in 1989 – a ready-made electoral appeal. From the beginning, the party was "virtually synonymous with the figure of Ríos Montt," who "'owned' and ruled the FRG as his personal fiefdom" (Sánchez 2008: 138). The FRG embraced Ríos Montt's past: he was referred to as *El General* (Sánchez 2008: 138), and he appeared in his army uniform in campaign advertisements (Stoll 1990/1991: 6–7). The party's emblem was a blue-and-white hand with three raised fingers, the same one that Ríos Montt had used as dictator to symbolize a three-part pledge ("I don't steal, I don't lie, I don't abuse"). During his dictatorship, the hand had been "ubiquitous": in urban areas, "it appeared in all public offices and in full-page ads in the national newspapers," and in rural areas, "it appeared painted on rock, whitewashed on mountainsides ... [and] on signs posted by the army in newly 'pacified' villages" (Garrard-Burnett 2010: 61). Later, the hand became similarly ubiquitous in FRG literature, advertisements, and campaign events.

The FRG also made rhetorical appeals to the past. Citing the problems of corruption and crime, Ríos Montt explained in a 1990 interview: "We eliminated the garbage once and we can do it again."[38] Similarly, in a 1995 interview, he defended his dictatorship, asserting, "I was honest with my country, indifferent to outside pressures ... I found a government that was destroyed, a state that was destroyed, a state that had been looted, a state without law. I put it in order."[39]

---

[37] Quoted in Godoy (2006: 64). See also Tim Weiner, "A Former Ruler's Candidacy Revives Fears in Guatemala," *The New York Times*, November 9, 2003.

[38] Quoted in Trudeau (1993: 145).

[39] Quoted in Tracy Wilkinson, "World Report Profile: Efrain Rios Montt: To the Dismay of Human Rights Activists, the Former Dictator is Now President of Guatemala's Congress, a Position Seen as a Springboard to the Nation's Highest Post," *Los Angeles Times*, February 14, 1995.

This message appealed to many Guatemalans. Although Ríos Montt was constitutionally barred from running for president in 1990, polls indicated that he was by far the most popular candidate, with about one-third of those surveyed backing him (Trudeau 1993: 145). In the second round of the 1999 presidential election, the FRG candidate, Alfonso Portillo, won with a whopping 68.3 percent of the vote.

If Bolivia's ADN and Guatemala's FRG are examples of parties that won votes by *embracing the past*, Panama's PRD is an example of the power of *scapegoating*. The PRD was founded in 1979 by Omar Torrijos, who took power in a coup in 1968 and ruled until his death in a plane crash in 1981. As discussed below, Torrijos could claim significant achievements, notably two treaties with the United States ceding control of the Panama Canal. Under democracy, the PRD enthusiastically embraced Torrijos' memory, featuring him prominently in its literature and regularly commemorating the anniversary of his death (García Díez 2001: 577). The party chose his son, Martín Torrijos, as its presidential candidate in 1999 and 2004 (he won the second time). Martín's campaign theme song was called "Omar lives" (García Díez 2001: 581), and he described his father on the stump as "my hero."[40] The PRD has continued to celebrate even the overtly authoritarian elements of its past. To this day, the party's logo is an "O" with the number "11" written inside it – a reference to October 11, 1968, the date of the coup that brought Torrijos to power (García Díez 2001: 580).[41]

Yet the PRD's ability to capitalize on memories of Torrijos was complicated by the legacy of Torrijos' successor, Manuel Noriega, who took power in 1983 and continued to use the PRD as his own authoritarian ruling party. Given the corruption and brutality of Noriega's rule – and the fact that his action provoked a military invasion by the United States in late 1989 – the PRD has, since the transition to democracy, tried to cut all links to him. In the 1994 election, for example, PRD presidential candidate Ernesto Pérez Balladares called Noriega a "traitor and a disgrace to the country,"[42] who was the worst leader in Panamanian history.[43] He described the Noriega period as an "aberration" and insisted that the post-1989 PRD had "nothing to do with

---

[40] Quoted in Carol J. Williams, "Panama Voters Back Dictator's Son as President," *Los Angeles Times*, May 3, 2004.

[41] Similarly, on October 12, 2014, the PRD posted on Facebook about an event held a day earlier at the party's headquarters – in the Omar Torrijos Room – to celebrate the anniversary of the coup, which, as the general secretary explained, is a "very special day for us." Quoted in Secretaría de Prensa PRD, "PRD recordó el 11 de octubre de 1968" [Facebook status update]. Available from: www.facebook.com/secretariadeprensaprd11/posts/521675364602800 [Accessed July 12, 2016].

[42] Quoted in Howard W. French, "Panama Journal; Democracy at Work, Under Shadow of Dictators," *The New York Times*, February 21, 1994.

[43] Howard W. French, "Businessman Appears to Oust 'Old Guard' In Panama Election," *The New York Times*, May 9, 1994.

Noriega."[44] The PRD's strong electoral performance suggests that this strategy of scapegoating worked. Since the transition to democracy, it has won the largest share of the vote in every legislative election (with the exception of 2014, when it came in second), and it has won the presidency twice: in 1994 (the first democratic election after the US invasion), with the election of Pérez Balladares, and in 2004, with the election of Martín Torrijos.

In Peru, *Fujimorismo* also attempted a variant of the scapegoating strategy. After winning a democratic election in 1990, President Alberto Fujimori carried out a "self-coup" in 1992 and subsequently established a competitive authoritarian regime (Conaghan 2005). Although Fujimori's government was responsible for large-scale corruption and human rights violations, his success in ending hyperinflation and defeating the Shining Path guerrillas generated substantial popular support.[45] The regime collapsed in 2000 after the release of a series of videos detailing massive corruption by his intelligence chief, Vladimiro Montesinos. Fujimori fled the country in disgrace, and later was extradited, convicted, and imprisoned on charges of corruption and human rights violations. Nevertheless, he retained considerable popular support. In a 2006 survey, for example, 48 percent of respondents expressed a positive view of his presidency.[46] In a May 2011 survey, 30 percent of respondents ranked Fujimori as Peru's best president over the last fifty years.[47] And in a 2013 survey, 42 percent of Peruvians described Fujimori's performance as "good" or "very good."[48] This popular support allowed *Fujimorismo* to win votes by "hewing to the past" (Deming 2013). Through 2011, the party continued to be led by prominent members of the Fujimori regime, and Fujimori's daughter, Keiko, was its presidential candidate in 2011 and 2016. During the 2011 campaign, Keiko described her father as "the best president in Peruvian history" and promised to pardon him if elected.[49]

However, like the PRD in Panama, *Fujimorismo* was forced to wrestle with the fact that the Fujimori regime ended in disgrace. It attempted to do this through a scapegoat, Vladimiro Montesinos, whom the party accused of carrying out the regime's worst abuses without Fujimori's knowledge (Urrutia 2011a: 113). Thus, for *Fujimoristas*, "Montesinos did not form part of *Fujimorismo*, but rather was an autonomous entity that had created his own

---

[44] Quoted in Tracy Wilkinson, "Perez Vows New Image for Panama Party," *Los Angeles Times*, 2 September 1994, and "Noriega Party Claims Victory in Panama Race," *Los Angeles Times*, May 9, 1994.
[45] When Fujimori was sworn in for an illegal third term in August 2000, his approval rating stood at 45 percent (Carrión 2006: 126).
[46] Ipsos Apoyo survey, January 2006.   [47] Ipsos Apoyo survey, May 9, 2011.
[48] GfK survey, June 18–19, 2013.
[49] See Mariano Castillo, "Peruvian Candidate Rallies in Shadow of Former Strongman," *CNN*, April 13, 2011. Available from: www.cnn.com/2011/WORLD/americas/04/12/peru.keiko.fujimori/ [Accessed on March 29, 2015]. Moreover, Keiko's 2011 campaign was reportedly directed by her father, with campaign headquarters located just 20 meters from his prison cell. See "Campaña de Keiko Fujimori se dirige desde la Diroes," *La República*, May 18, 2011.

current – '*Montesinismo*' – which was not recognized as belonging to the [*Fujimorista*] legacy" (Urrutia 2011a: 113). The strategy was fairly successful. Under Keiko Fujimori's leadership, *Fujimorismo* reemerged as one of Peru's leading parties (Levitsky 2018; Urrutia 2011a). In 2006, it won 13 percent of the legislative vote, and in 2011, it won 23 percent of the legislative vote and Keiko Fujimori nearly captured the presidency. In 2016, Keiko adopted a strategy of mild contrition, embracing the findings of Peru's Truth and Reconciliation Commission (which implicated her father's government in human rights violations), declaring that she would not have closed Congress as her father had done, and abandoning her pledge to pardon him.[50] She finished first in the first round of the 2016 presidential election, losing the runoff by a mere 0.2 percent, and *Fujimorismo* won an absolute majority in Congress.

3.4 THE CHALLENGE OF DE-PERSONALIZATION

Although personalistic leadership can be an asset to parties during their formative phase, it creates serious obstacles to party longevity. As Table 3.1 shows, there are only four cases of personalistic authoritarian successor parties surviving their founders' deaths, and only two of those have survived to the present day. In seven cases, the party did not survive the death of the leader, and in one case (*Fujimorismo*), the party leader has not yet died. It is no coincidence that relatively few personalistic authoritarian successor parties have endured in the long term. The very contributions that the personalistic leader makes in the short-to-medium term – attracting votes and serving as a source of cohesion – can become liabilities once the leader exits the political stage, for two reasons. First, if the party's electoral performance is dependent on the leader's popularity, the party risks electoral collapse once that leader is no longer at the top of the ticket. Where voters are attached to a particular leader rather than a party brand or program, it can prove difficult to transfer loyalties from the leader to the party when the leader departs (Kostadinova and Levitt 2014: 500–501; also Panebianco 1988: 53, 67, 147). With the disruption of the personalistic linkage, the party's electoral base is suddenly up for grabs, and the result is often dramatic electoral decline.

Second, personalistic parties tend to lack organizational lives of their own. The intra-party power asymmetries generated by the leader's personal capacity to deliver votes endows him with vast discretionary authority (Samuels and Shugart 2010). Party leaders often use that

---

[50] See "Keiko estima garantizar por escrito que no indultará a su padre," *El Comercio*, January 24, 2016, and "Keiko: 'Yo de ninguna manera hubiera cerrado el Congreso,'" *El Comercio*, January 31, 2016.

authority to prevent the creation of party institutions that could constrain them and block the ascent of talented politicians who could challenge them. Personalistic party organizations thus tend to possess weak internal structures dominated by loyalist hacks who lack both independent voter bases and intra-party authority. This is a recipe for crisis following the departure of the leader.

In order to survive in the longer term, personalistic authoritarian successor parties must overcome two major challenges. First, they must *solve the problem of leadership succession.* Because they are prone to collapse in the wake of their founders' death or retirement from politics, finding a viable successor (and ultimately, an institutional mechanism for leadership succession) is critical to their survival. This may be achieved through the far-sighted behavior of the party founder, who uses his authority to promote the rise of a new generation of leaders and then steps aside.[51] Such enlightened leadership is rare, however. Indeed, none of the founders of the twelve parties examined in this chapter made comparable efforts to groom a new generation of leaders.

A more common strategy is hereditary succession. Because personalistic parties tend to lack a strong pool of electorally viable successors (founding leaders' tendency to block the ascent of potential rivals weeds out such politicians) and because succession tends to be fraught with internal conflict, party elites often view a hereditary successor as the best means of preserving the party's electoral base and maintaining unity. As Brownlee (2007b: 597) writes in reference to autocratic regime succession, a hereditary successor "offers a focal point for reducing uncertainty, achieving consensus, and forestalling a power vacuum."[52] Five of the twelve parties examined in this chapter attempted some form of hereditary succession. Perón made his wife, Isabel, his vice-presidential running mate (and thus his successor) in 1973; Odría's wife, María, was the Odriísta National Union's (UNO) candidate for mayor of Lima in 1963, and might have succeeded him as presidential candidate had it not been for the 1968 military coup; ANAPO ran Rojas Pinilla's daughter, María Eugenia, as its presidential candidate in 1974; the FRG attempted to

---

[51] In Ghana, for example, the National Democratic Congress (NDC), which was founded and dominated by dictator Jerry John Rawlings, stepped aside (albeit grudgingly) and supported the rise of new leaders such as John Atta Mills when his final presidential term expired in 2000 (Boafo-Arthur 2003: 228). More recently, Hugo Chávez in Venezuela anointed Nicolás Maduro as his successor shortly before dying of cancer in 2013 (Corrales 2013). Although Chávez's selection of Maduro was motivated by terminal illness, not far-sighted design, and although Maduro was not a skilled leader, the move helped the PSUV avoid a potentially costly leadership crisis.

[52] Hereditary succession is also a common feature of democratic politics, as seen by dynasties such as the Kennedys and Bushes in the United States, the Trudeaus in Canada, and the Nehru/Gandhis in India.

run Ríos Montt's daughter, Zury, as its presidential candidate in 2011;[53] and *Fujimorismo* ran Fujimori's daughter, Keiko, as its presidential candidate in 2011 and 2016.

The case of *Fujimorismo* suggests that in some cases, hereditary succession may provide a generational bridge that helps the party to prepare for a future without the founding leader. Keiko Fujimori, who took over the *Fujimorista* leadership after her father's imprisonment in 2007, was young and politically skilled. Her strong performance as a congressional candidate in 2006 and presidential candidate in 2011 and 2016 rejuvenated the party. *Fujimorismo* expanded its partisan base and began to recruit viable candidates for local and regional office, which gave it an opportunity to institutionalize that few observers had anticipated a decade earlier (Levitsky and Zavaleta 2016: 437–437).

Few hereditary successors, however, prove as effective as Keiko Fujimori. Many lack the political skill or broad appeal of the founding leader; indeed, some of them prove highly incompetent (e.g., Isabel Perón). Moreover, because it reinforces personalistic patterns of authority, hereditary succession may have the effect of simply postponing – or even preempting – the kinds of hard decisions necessary to avoid eventual party collapse. María Eugenia Rojas and Zury Ríos did nothing to forestall the collapse of ANAPO and the FRG, respectively, and although Peronism ultimately survived Perón's death, it did so *in spite of* rather than because of Isabel Perón's incompetent leadership. Two other parties that survived the death of their founders – the PRD in Panama and the PTB in Brazil – did not attempt a hereditary succession.[54] Because the founders of these parties (Torrijos and Vargas, respectively) suffered untimely and unexpected deaths, neither had developed clear plans for succession.

A second – and even more important – element of de-personalization is the development of *durable partisan identities*. To succeed over time, parties need partisans, or individuals who feel an attachment to the party and thus consistently turn out to vote for it. As Lupu (2016) argues, critical to the formation of partisans is the development of a strong party brand. Brands can be rooted in ideology, such as position on the left–right spectrum, or in sociocultural appeals, with parties claiming to represent particular group

---

[53] In 2011, the FRG selected Zury Ríos, who had been an FRG congresswoman for fifteen years, as its presidential candidate. However, she later withdrew from the race. See "Zury Ríos oficializa su retiro como candidata presidencial del FRG," *Prensa Libre*, May 14, 2011.

[54] Although Omar Torrijos' son, Martín, was the PRD's presidential candidate in 1999 and 2004 (he won the second time), this was not a case of hereditary succession. When his father died in 1981, Martín was only eighteen years old. He spent most of the subsequent Noriega period in the United States and did not become involved in PRD politics until he returned to Panama in the early 1990s. Between the time of Omar Torrijos' death and Martín's rise, the PRD had two major – non-hereditary – leaders: Manuel Noriega (dictator from 1983 to 1989) and Ernesto Pérez Balladares (president from 1994 to 1999).

identities (Ostiguy 2009a, 2009b). Personalism tends to inhibit brand development, with voters identifying with the party *leader* rather than with the *party* as such. Thus, for personalistic authoritarian successor parties to survive in the longer term, personal attachments to the founding leader must be transformed into collective identities. In other words, support for an individual must be converted into support for a brand: support for Perón must become support for Pero*nismo*; support for Torrijos must become support for Torrij*ismo*; support for Fujimori must become support for Fujimor*ismo*. Parties that fail to develop such collective identities almost invariably collapse when the leader exits the political stage (e.g., ANAPO, FNV, ADN, PRSC).

Two conditions appear to facilitate the transition from personalistic linkage to party brand. First, autocrats who are associated with a *clear program, set of policies, or constituency* are more likely to leave an enduring partisan legacy. Where authoritarian regimes are associated with major policy changes or achievements that can be linked to a broader programmatic agenda, or where they are viewed as responsible for the incorporation of previously marginal groups, parties will have an easier time transforming their leaders' legacies into a broader program or appeal. This was the case with Perón, who expanded the welfare state and incorporated the working class into national politics, and with Torrijos, who won control of the Panama Canal and carried out a range of social policies designed to improve the lot of the popular sectors. The resulting authoritarian successor parties came to be identified not only with the qualities or performance of a single leader, but rather with a set of policy changes that would ultimately anchor one side of an enduring political cleavage.

A second condition that facilitates the transition from personal attachments to collective partisan identities is *polarization*. As LeBas (2011) and Levitsky, Loxton, and Van Dyck (2016) have argued, intense polarization can help crystallize collective identities. Polarization and (often violent) conflict may foster collective identities, or "groupness," by strengthening "us–them" distinctions and generating perceptions of a "linked fate" among activists (LeBas 2011: 44, 46). Thus, intense conflict between an autocrat's supporters and opponents – particularly when it involves mass mobilization and violence – can generate an enduring political cleavage and new partisan identities. This is most obviously the case with populist autocrats such as Perón in Argentina, Torrijos in Panama, Fujimori in Peru, and Chávez in Venezuela, all of whom mobilized the poor with explicitly anti-elite appeals and consequently polarized societies between populist and anti-populist forces. Amid such polarization, populist autocrats – and, crucially, the parties that emerge from their regimes – come to represent broader political movements. When such movements engage in large-scale mobilization in defense of their leader, and when members of the movement are persecuted after the leader's exit from power (e.g., Peronism), partisan identities tend to harden, making it even more likely that a strong party brand will emerge and endure beyond the founding leader.

To conclude, while personalistic authoritarian successor parties face serious obstacles to longevity, these obstacles are not insurmountable. In some cases, these parties can "de-personalize." While most personalistic authoritarian successor parties die with their leaders, a few have managed to survive in the long term. In the two case studies that follow, we examine the two most striking examples of personalistic authoritarian successor party survival: Peronism in Argentina and the PRD in Panama. In both cases, the parties became associated with clear brands, polarization contributed to the hardening of collective partisan identities, and the parties managed to survive for decades as their countries' most important political actors.

3.5 PERONISM IN ARGENTINA

Peronism is the most successful case of a personalistic authoritarian successor party that de-personalized and survived over the long term. In its origins, Peronism was both authoritarian and personalistic. Juan Perón first ascended to power as part of a 1943 military coup, and it was as labor secretary in the resulting dictatorship that he launched his initial populist appeal (Collier and Collier 1991: 337–338). Although Perón was democratically elected president in 1946, he quickly established a competitive authoritarian regime. The Supreme Court was purged and packed with loyalists (Helmke 2005: 64), many opposition politicians were imprisoned or forced into exile, and leading opposition newspapers were either expropriated or bullied into self-censorship (Page 1983: 209–229). Perón's reelection in 1951 was marred by intimidation and fraud (Page 1983: 252–253; Rock 1985: 305). The regime was also thoroughly personalistic (McGuire 1997: 54–66). The party that brought Perón to the presidency, the Labor Party, was dissolved shortly after he took office and replaced by the Peronist Party, a "monolithic entity controlled strictly by Perón" (McGuire 1997: 61–62). The new party's leaders were handpicked by Perón and his inner circle, and its statutes forbade local branches from displaying any photographs other than those of Perón and his wife, Evita (Ciria 1983: 169).

Despite this personalism, Perón's redistributive social policies and effective populist appeals linked Peronism to a broader programmatic agenda and a well-defined working- and lower-class constituency (James 1988; Torre 1990). The Perón government extended worker and union rights, expanded social welfare policies, and employed highly inclusionary and socially egalitarian rhetoric (Collier and Collier 1991: 337–343; Torre 1990). As a result, the working class "made unprecedented gains in wealth, power and social status" (McGuire 1997: 76). Real wages increased by nearly 60 percent between 1946 and 1949, social security coverage more than tripled between 1946 and 1951, and the number of workers covered by health insurance increased markedly (Collier and Collier 1991: 341; McGuire 1997: 53). These material gains, together with a dramatic expansion of unionization

Personalistic ASPs in Latin America

and a discourse that championed workers' rights and attacked established social hierarchies, helped to crystallize strong Peronist identities among the working and lower classes (James 1988).

Perón's overthrow in a military coup in 1955 posed a major challenge. The Peronist Party, which had been thoroughly dependent on Perón, disintegrated after his downfall and exile, throwing Peronism into disarray (James 1988: 43–54; McGuire 1997: 78). Because the Peronist Party leadership had been packed with loyalist hacks, the movement was effectively left leaderless (McGuire 1997: 78).

Yet Peronism survived Perón's eighteen-year exile, due, in part, to the strength of Peronist identities among the working and lower classes. Though forged during Perón's first presidency, these identities were reinforced by the intense polarization that emerged in the aftermath of his overthrow. The military's repressive efforts to eradicate the Peronist "cancer" triggered the 1956–1957 "Resistance," during which clandestine Peronist mobilization strengthened the movement's organization, subculture, and identities (James 1988: 72–100). Peronism also benefited from its strong ties to the labor movement. The unions, which remained overwhelmingly Peronist, provided a refuge and organizational base while Perón was in exile and his party banned, helping to ensure Peronism's survival on the ground (James 1988: 43–87; McGuire 1997: 82–84).

Peronism took root despite Perón's disruptive efforts to control it from exile. The emergence of a new generation of Peronist union and provincial leaders in the 1960s led to efforts to build a "Peronism without Perón," with the aim of reentering the electoral arena (McGuire 1997: 80–150). Although Perón ultimately defeated these efforts, he could only do so by encouraging the activities of other independent Peronist organizations – including leftist groups such as the Montonero guerrillas – to counterbalance them (McGuire 1997: 161). The result was a new generation of Peronist cadres, many of whom developed considerable political experience and skill.

In 1973, Perón returned to Argentina and was elected president once again, with his new wife, Isabel, as his vice president. Perón's death in 1974, however, posed another major test for Peronism. The presidency passed to Isabel, who proved to be incompetent, and in 1976, her crisis-ridden government was toppled by yet another military coup (Di Tella 1983). Banned and repressed during the 1976–1983 military dictatorship, Peronism again fell into disarray. But once again, the movement could fall back on the unions as a source of organization and leadership (Levitsky 2003: 92–94). As Isabel Perón settled into retirement in Spain, union leaders established themselves as Perón's true successors, leading the Peronist Justicialista Party (PJ) into the 1983 democratic transition.

The PJ has been extraordinarily successful since 1983, winning the presidency five times under three different leaders – Carlos Menem, Néstor Kirchner, and Cristina Fernández de Kirchner. Never once during this period did the party fall below 30 percent of the national vote. This enduring success is attributable, in part, to the PJ's successful de-personalization: during the 1980s and 1990s, the party developed a powerful territorial organization and new mechanisms of leadership selection – most notably, primary elections – to replace the old charismatic patterns of authority (Levitsky 2003). But the PJ's success was also rooted in the persistence of a powerful Peronist identity and party brand (Ostiguy 2009b), which was reinforced over the years by various waves of repression. Although the PJ remained amorphous on the traditional left–right dimension, its continued celebration of Perón and Evita and widespread use of slogans and symbols from the Perón era reinforced partisan identities. Party offices down to the neighborhood level unfailingly display images of Perón and Evita, and Peronists continue to celebrate October 17 ("Loyalty Day"), which marks the mass protests in 1945 that liberated Perón from jail (after falling out with his former military allies) and launched his first presidential candidacy. Indeed, more than four decades after Perón's death, even as the PJ has clearly taken on a life of its own, it is still widely known as "Peronism."

3.6 THE PRD IN PANAMA

A second case of successful de-personalization is Panama's Democratic Revolutionary Party (PRD). The PRD emerged from the personalistic dictatorship of Omar Torrijos, the head of the National Guard (the country's military) and dictator from 1968 until 1981. After participating in a coup in October 1968, Torrijos neutralized his main rivals in the National Guard and established de facto "one-man rule" (Ropp 1982: ix). He maintained absolute control over the military and made all important political and policy decisions (Harding 2001: 72–87; Ropp 1982: 43, 75). Between 1972 and 1978, Torrijos held the constitutional title of Maximum Leader of the Panamanian Revolution, which gave him "dictatorial powers" and allowed him "to administer the state at whim" (Harding 2001: 94).

In 1978, Torrijos announced plans for political liberalization. In anticipation of a return to multiparty elections, he created the PRD, which he hoped would evolve into a national version of Mexico's Institutional Revolutionary Party (PRI).[55] Unlike the PRI, however, the PRD was highly personalistic. Described as "Omar's party" (Ford González 2009: 10), it revolved "around the ideas and personality of General Omar Torrijos Herrera" (García Díez 2001: 574). Its first general secretary was Torrijos' cousin (Ropp 1982: 81), and "Torrijos frequently found himself in the position of having to intervene in the functioning of the party to suppress conflict and rebellion" (Harding 2001: 151). To this day, the PRD's main "mechanism of cohesion" is rooted in "the cult of the founding leader" (García Díez 2001: 584). Given the PRD's

---

[55] See García Díez (2001: 574–575) and Harding (2001: 144–149).

Personalistic ASPs in Latin America 135

personalistic nature, some observers doubted whether it would survive Torrijos' death in a plane crash in 1981.[56]

Yet the PRD did not disappear. Initially, it survived because Torrijos' successors – notably, Manuel Noriega, Panama's dictator from 1983 until 1989 – decided to continue to use it as the country's "official" party. The PRD was "intimately linked" to the National Guard from its inception, and these links became even closer after Torrijos' death (García Díez 2001: 577–578). As one PRD leader stated matter-of-factly, "[The PRD] is the party of the National Guard."[57] These ties to the state help explain Pérez's (2000: 131) later finding that the PRD was the only party in Panama with a significant organization, including "deep roots within the public bureaucracy" and "organizational structures at the neighborhood and individual union levels."

However, the PRD's ties to the military also became a liability in the post-Torrijos era. Noriega's rule was notorious for its brutality, corruption, links to drug trafficking, and erratic foreign policy, particularly with regard to the United States (Guevara Mann 1996: 158–188). Although Noriega tried to present himself as the inheritor of Torrijos' legacy, he was far less popular than his predecessor.[58] In the 1989 presidential race, quick counts indicated that Noriega's puppet candidate had lost by a 3-to-1 margin, prompting the regime to annul the election (Scranton 1995: 70). Panama–US relations deteriorated to such a degree that the United States launched a military invasion in December 1989, toppling Noriega and installing a democratic regime.[59] Given that military defeat is often fatal for authoritarian regimes (O'Donnell and Schmitter 1986: 17–18), this might have been expected to leave the PRD with a crippling amount of authoritarian baggage.

Yet the PRD immediately rebounded, returning to power in 1994 and remaining Panama's most important party under democracy. Much of the PRD's success was rooted in collective memories of Torrijos' policies and achievements. A clear case of "military populism" (Guevara Mann 1996: 114–131) and "inclusionary" military rule (Pérez 2011: 49), Torrijos' regime adopted an anti-oligarchic discourse and sought "to incorporate the lower classes into the political processes [*sic*] as had never before been possible" (Harding 2001: 64).[60] To this end, Torrijos wrote a new socialist-oriented constitution, initiated a sweeping land reform program, oversaw a fivefold increase in union membership, and brought about significant gains in health and education (Harding 2001: 64, 94–97, 135).

---

[56] See, for example, Alan Riding, "Panama's Military Tries to Pick Up Torrijos Reins," *The New York Times*, August 26, 1981, and "Panama Military Close to Direct Rule," *The New York Times*, August 5, 1982.
[57] Quoted in Harding (2001: 158).
[58] See Stephen Kinzer, "Torrijos's Legacy Lingers in Panama," *The New York Times*, August 2, 1987, and "Resucitando al General," *El País*, August 5, 1987.
[59] On the US invasion and subsequent transition, see Harding (2001: 155–179).
[60] See also Ropp (1982: 55–62, 66–71).

Torrijos also adopted a markedly nationalist profile, particularly with respect to the biggest issue in Panamanian political life: the status of the Panama Canal.[61] The 1903 Panama Canal Treaty had granted the US control of the canal and surrounding area "in perpetuity,"[62] depriving Panama of control of the engine of its economy and offending national pride. Torrijos made gaining control of the canal the centerpiece of his agenda. In 1977, Panama and the United States signed two treaties ceding control of the canal to Panama in 1999. The treaties proved "wildly popular in Panama" and were approved by two-thirds of the electorate in a plebiscite in October 1977 (Maurer and Yu 2011: 327, 265). By securing control of the canal, Torrijos resolved the country's thorniest political issue, and, in the eyes of many Panamanians, secured his place in the pantheon of national heroes.

Torrijos' achievements facilitated the creation of a political identity – *Torrijismo* – that became bigger than the man himself. At its core, *Torrijismo* stood for "the recuperation of sovereignty, popular participation, and social justice" (García Díez 2001: 578). As Torrijos' party, the PRD was the natural inheritor of this *Torrijista* brand, becoming the "party of the defense of sovereignty and nationalism" (Ford González 2009: 21). Thus, once it shed its ties to Noriega (as discussed above in the section on scapegoating), the PRD could present itself, in the words of its victorious 1994 presidential candidate, as the country's "populist alternative."[63]

The PRD's survival was also facilitated by polarization. Although it distanced itself from Noriega after the 1989–1990 invasion, it was nevertheless attacked for its ties to his rule (Harding 2001: 187). Hundreds of former regime officials were investigated, charged, and imprisoned during the early 1990s – a process that many PRD leaders saw as a politically inspired witch hunt.[64] After winning the presidency in 1994, Pérez Balladares pardoned hundreds of former officials on the basis that "they were victims of political persecution" – a move that was strongly opposed by non-*Torrijista* parties.[65] He also awarded back pay to former members of the Dignity Battalions, "groups of thugs that had served [as] Noriega's paramilitary enforcers during the last years of his regime" (Harding 2001: 190). This polarization, while not as intense as the Peronism/anti-Peronism divide, reinforced "us–them" distinctions and may have helped the party to remain cohesive under democracy.

In sum, like Peronism in Argentina, Panama's PRD is a case of a personalistic authoritarian successor party that successfully de-personalized. Founded by a personalistic dictator, Omar Torrijos, the PRD became associated with the

---

[61] See Harding (2001: 94–136). [62] See Harding (2001: 27–28).
[63] Ernesto Pérez Balladares, quoted in Scranton (1995: 76). See also Harding (2001: 188) and Pérez (2000: 139–140).
[64] The creation of a truth commission in 2000 by President Mireya Moscoso, a longtime rival, was particularly polarizing (Pérez 2011: 121).
[65] See Larry Rohter, "Some Familiar Faces Return to Power in Panama," *The New York Times*, February 9, 1995, and "Panama Amnesty Plan for Abuses Draws Fire," *The New York Times*, May 14, 1996.

popular brand of *Torrijismo*, and, as of this writing in 2018 – thirty-seven years after the death of its founder – it remains one of Panama's major parties.

3.7 CONCLUSION

In this chapter, we have examined the surprisingly strong electoral performance – and, in a few cases, long-term survival – of personalistic authoritarian successor parties in Latin America. Unlike most of the parties examined in this volume, these do not emerge from party-based authoritarian regimes, but rather from personalistic regimes in which power is overwhelmingly concentrated in the hands of an individual. Such regimes would appear exceptionally unlikely to produce viable parties. Yet personalistic authoritarian successor parties have been prominent actors in a majority of Latin American countries since World War II, been voted back into office on multiple occasions, and in a few cases even managed to survive their founders' deaths.

The chapter has advanced three main arguments. First, it argued that authoritarian successor parties can sometimes achieve electoral success without making a clean break with the past. Provided that they have sufficiently strong records to run on, they may win large numbers of votes through the strategy of scapegoating (e.g., PRD in Panama) or by simply embracing the past (e.g., ADN in Bolivia, FRG in Guatemala). Second, it argued that the effects of personalism on party-building are double-edged rather than entirely negative. While personalistic parties often face a severe crisis after the leader's death or retirement, such leaders can also be a source of votes and internal party cohesion – crucial elements of party-building, especially during the formative phase. Finally, it argued that although longevity is the great weakness of personalistic authoritarian successor parties, under certain conditions they can "de-personalize." Such an outcome is most likely to occur where personalistic leaders are associated with a clear program, set of policies, or constituency, and where their rule triggers intense polarization, as in the cases of Peronism in Argentina and the PRD in Panama.

These two cases may not be the last, however. One strong candidate for long-term success is *Fujimorismo* in Peru. Both of the conditions that we have identified as favoring the emergence of durable partisan identities are at least partially present in this case. First, Fujimori's success in defeating the Shining Path guerrillas in the 1990s has enabled *Fujimorismo* to brand itself as Peru's "law and order" party. This brand proved especially useful during the 2000s, when rising crime rates put security issues at the top of the public agenda.[66]

---

[66] Surveys found that a solid majority of Peruvians approved of Alberto Fujimori's *mano dura* (iron fist) policies of the 1990s, crediting them with having ended terrorism and restoring order. See "Informe Especial Sobre el Fujimorismo," GfK Perú, March 2017, p. 24. Available from: www.gfk.com/fileadmin/user_upload/country_one_pager/PE/documents/GfK_Opinio__n_Marzo_2017__Fujimorismo3.pdf.

In 2016, for example, *Fujiumorismo* performed especially well along the northern coast, where crime rates and perceptions of insecurity were among the highest in the country.[67] Second, *Fujimorismo* generated significant polarization and conflict. Fujimori's fall from power ushered in what *Fujimoristas* describe as an "era of persecution," during which they were treated as pariahs.[68] More than 200 *Fujimorista* former officials were prosecuted for corruption and/or human rights violations (Urrutia 2011a: 102), and in 2002, three leading *Fujimorista* legislators, including former President of Congress Martha Chávez, were expelled from Congress. Finally, although Fujimori's trial and conviction in 2007 were viewed as legitimate by the international community, *Fujimoristas* saw this as political persecution.[69] This reinforced *Fujimorista* identities and strengthened the party's internal cohesion (Navarro 2011; Urrutia 2011a, 2011b).[70] As of 2018, *Fujimorismo* is, by far, the biggest party in Peru. And although it continues to be dominated by Keiko Fujimori, the party appears to be developing a brand and organization capable of transcending her and her father's political careers.

A second possible candidate is Venezuela's PSUV. Although Venezuela is currently an authoritarian regime, in a hypothetical democratic future, the PSUV is likely to emerge as a strong authoritarian successor party – despite the death of its founding leader, Hugo Chávez, in 2013. While the disastrous performance of the government of Nicolás Maduro has clearly cost the party support, the baggage this has generated could be offset by scapegoating Maduro, much as Panama's PRD scapegoated Noriega.[71] And the PSUV, even more than *Fujimorismo*, seems to possess the two main ingredients for the creation of durable partisan identities. First, like Peronism, it is associated with popular redistributive policies and has developed a strong brand, particularly among the poor. Second, again like Peronism, the *Chavista* regime has generated intense – and at times violent – polarization and conflict. Our theory suggests, therefore, that the PSUV would stand a good chance of remaining a durable electoral force if Venezuela were to democratize.

To conclude, if this volume demonstrates that authoritarian officials can remain influential after a transition to democracy through authoritarian successor parties, this chapter has shown this to be true in even the least likely of cases: personalistic dictatorships. Neither conspicuous links to the authoritarian past nor personalistic leadership have prevented parties born

---

[67] For crime rates by region, see Instituto de Defensa Legal (2015). [68] See Urrutia (2011a).
[69] Steven Levitsky's interviews with Jorge Morelli, Lima, June 18, 2011; Martha Moyano, Lima, May 6, 2011; and Santiago Fujimori, Lima, March 24, 2011. See also Navarro (2011: 53–54) and Urrutia (2011a).
[70] As one *Fujimorista* put it, "There is no better glue for a political movement than a feeling of injustice... We were like Christians in Rome" (Steven Levitsky's interview with Jorge Morelli, Lima, June 18, 2011).
[71] See James Loxton and Javier Corrales, "Venezuelans Are Still Demonstrating. What Happens Next for the Dictatorship of Nicolás Maduro?" Monkey Cage, *Washington Post* blog, April 20, 2017.

Personalistic ASPs in Latin America

from such regimes from becoming major electoral players in Latin America. It appears that under some circumstances, personalism and obvious dictatorial roots can contribute to, rather than inhibit, party success.

APPENDIX 3.1

Personalistic Regimes and Personalistic ASPs in Latin America, 1945–2010[a]

Country	Regime	Party created?	Initial survival?[b]	Electoral prominence under democracy?[c]
Argentina	Juan Perón (1946–1955)	Yes: Peronism/ Justicialista Party	Yes	Yes
Bolivia	René Barrientos (1965–1969)	Yes: Popular Christian Movement (MPC)	Yes	No
Bolivia	Hugo Banzer (1971–1978)	Yes: Nationalist Democratic Action (ADN)	Yes	Yes
Brazil	Getúlio Vargas (1930–1945)	Yes: Brazilian Labor Party (PTB)	Yes	Yes
Colombia	Gustavo Rojas Pinilla (1953–1957)	Yes: National Popular Alliance (ANAPO)	Yes	Yes
Cuba	Fulgencio Batista (1952–1959)	Yes: Progressive Action Party (PAP)	No	-
Dominican Republic	Rafael Trujillo (1930–1961)	Yes: Dominican Party	No	-
Dominican Republic	Joaquín Balaguer (1966–1978)	Yes: Social Christian Reformist Party (PRSC)	Yes	Yes
Ecuador	José María Velasco Ibarra (1944–1947; 1970–1972)	Yes: Velasquista National Federation (FNV)	Yes	Yes
El Salvador	Salvador Castaneda Castro (1945–1948)	No (Inherited)	-	-
Guatemala	Carlos Castillo Armas (1954–1957)	Yes: National Democratic Movement (MDN)	Yes	No
Guatemala	Miguel Ydígoras Fuentes (1958–1963)	No (inherited)	-	-

(continued)

(continued)

Country	Regime	Party created?	Initial survival?[b]	Electoral prominence under democracy?[c]
Guatemala	Efraín Ríos Montt (1982–1983)	Yes: Guatemalan Republican Front (FRG)	Yes	Yes
Honduras	Tiburcio Carías (1933–1949)	No (inherited)	-	-
Honduras	Julio Lozano (1954–1956)	Yes: National Union Party	No	-
Nicaragua	Anastasio/Luis/ Anastasio Somoza (1937–1979)	Yes: Nationalist Liberal Party (PLN)	No	-
Panama	José Antonio Remón Cantera (1952–1955)	Yes: National Patriotic Coalition (CPN)	Yes	Yes
Panama	Omar Torrijos (1968–1981)	Yes: Democratic Revolutionary Party (PRD)	Yes	Yes
Panama	Manuel Noriega (1983–1989)	No (inherited)	-	-
Paraguay	Higinio Morínigo (1940–1948)	No	-	-
Paraguay	Alfredo Stroessner (1955–1989)	No (inherited)	-	-
Peru	Manuel Odría (1948–1956)	Yes: Odriísta National Union (UNO)	Yes	Yes
Peru	Alberto Fujimori (1992–2000)	Yes: *Fujimorismo*/ Popular Force	Yes	Yes
Venezuela	Marcos Pérez Jiménez (1948–1958)	Yes: Nationalist Civic Crusade (CCN)	Yes	Yes

[a] This list includes all regimes classified as personalist or hybrid-personalist by Geddes, Wright, and Frantz (2014a), except for Chile (1973–1989), which we classify as a military regime because Pinochet's power was checked by other heads of the armed forces; Costa Rica (1949), which was a transitional regime; and Panama (1949–1951), because President Arnulfo Arias did not control the security forces. We also exclude the cases of Cuba under Fidel Castro and Venezuela under Hugo Chávez because those regimes have not ended. We add the cases of Getúlio Vargas in Brazil, which ended in 1945, and Guatemala under Efraín Ríos Montt (1982–1983), which Geddes, Wright, and Franz (2014a) classify as a military regime. Finally, whereas Geddes, Wright, and Franz (2014a) treat Honduras (1933–1956) as a single regime, we break it into separate regimes, since the country was governed by two distinct personalistic regimes during this period.

[b] Parties are scored as cases of "initial survival" if they continued to exist after the end of the personalistic regime and we find evidence of their intent to compete in democratic elections in the future. However, they need not actually compete in democratic elections to be scored in this way (e.g., if a new, long-lasting authoritarian regime immediately takes hold and the party does not survive until eventual democratization).

[c] Following Introduction (Loxton, this volume), we operationalize electoral prominence as winning at least 10 percent of the vote in one or more national elections after the transition to democracy.

PART II

WHAT EXPLAINS VARIATION IN AUTHORITARIAN SUCCESSOR PARTY PERFORMANCE?

4

Victims of Their Own Success

The Paradoxical Fate of the Communist Successor Parties

Anna Grzymala-Busse

The fate of the communist successor parties in the postcommunist democracies of East Central Europe is paradoxical: the same factors that allowed these parties to gain widespread electoral support, win elections, and govern in the short term then led to their long-term demise. A reputation for managerial competence and internal cohesion made it possible for these parties to succeed initially – and then led to their eventual collapse, as these parties could not meet the standards that they themselves had set.

Initially, after the collapse of the communist regimes in 1989, several of the successors to the authoritarian ruling parties,[1] such as those in Poland, Hungary, Lithuania, and Slovenia, radically reinvented their organizations, ideologies, and strategies to become successful moderate democrats, celebrated for their managerial expertise, democratic commitments, and political savvy. The impact of this transformation was enormous: the exit and reinvention of the ruling communist parties was a prerequisite for, and an integral part of, the consolidation of democracy, economic reform, and the stabilization of party competition (Darden and Grzymala-Busse 2006; Fish 1998b; see also Slater and Wong, Chapter 9, this volume).

Yet fate has not been kind to these parties: the successor parties that reinvented themselves in the wake of the communist collapse in 1989–1991 eventually became victims of their own success and were swept from power. Much like the KMT in Taiwan, these parties won office on the basis of perceived managerial competence (Cheng and Huang, Chapter 2, this volume). Their successful transformation convinced voters to hold the successors to a high standard of competence and probity. Yet unlike the KMT, this was a standard

---

[1] This chapter focuses on communist successor parties, a subset of the broader universe of authoritarian successor parties examined in this volume. Communist successor parties are the legal and organizational heirs of former authoritarian ruling parties in communist regimes. Like other authoritarian successor parties, these parties operate after a transition to democracy and are led by former authoritarian elites.

that few communist successor parties could consistently fulfill. Meanwhile, winning office meant more competition for power and resources *within* the parties, and internal party conflict. Several parties simply collapsed under these pressures.

By contrast, communist successor parties that obstinately did not transform into moderate democrats after the communist collapse – either staying in power without internal change or becoming protest parties with few ostensible democratic commitments – have shown remarkable staying power, surviving and retaining voters at higher rates than their "reinvented" counterparts. While these "orthodox" successor parties were very different from the personalistic authoritarian successor parties in Latin America discussed by Loxton and Levitsky (Chapter 3, this volume), they share with them a common fate of persistence without making a complete break with the past.

Two implications for the study of authoritarian successor parties follow. First, reinvention is not a prerequisite for continued survival under democracy. Second, those parties that do reinvent themselves, and that successfully offer managerial competence as their competitive advantage, can then face especially harsh punishment from voters if they fail to deliver. The bitter irony is that the same communist successor parties that helped to build democracy by participating in and supporting free electoral competition ultimately fell victim to those same electoral forces. As a result, the reinvention of communist successor parties is strongly associated with successful democratization – but not with these parties' long-term success or even survival.

Below, I first examine the communist successor parties in East Central Europe and their patterns of reinvention and electoral success. I show how reinvention benefits authoritarian successor parties in general, but not in the postcommunist cases. I then argue that the same factors that initially led the parties to succeed – a reputation for managerial expertise and strong party organizations – made them electorally vulnerable over time.

4.1 THE COMMUNIST SUCCESSOR PARTIES AND THEIR REINVENTION

Communist successor parties are the formal descendants of the old communist ruling parties, having inherited their legal standing, organizations, elites, and members. When communist rule collapsed in 1989–1991, whether due to internal pressure or external shocks, these parties could radically transform, cling to autocratic orthodoxy, or simply disappear altogether. These strategies of survival and transformation have been well documented (e.g., Bozóki and Ishiyama 2002; Friedman and Wong 2008; Ishiyama 1995, 2001b; Mahr and Nagle 1995; Pop-Eleches 1999; Orenstein 1998; Waller 1995; Ziblatt 1998b).

Both these parties' strategies of adaptation and the levels of their electoral success vary a great deal.[2] Several communist successor parties reinvented themselves[3] and eventually reentered government, this time as freely elected and often wildly popular democratic parties. They are among the most dramatic examples of the reinvention of former authoritarian ruling parties after the collapse of their rule. Among the biggest success stories were the Polish and Hungarian communist successor parties. Along with their counterparts in Slovakia, Slovenia, and Lithuania, these parties transformed immediately and radically after the collapse of communist rule in 1989, becoming centrist social democratic parties. Other parties transformed later, especially those which maintained control during the collapse and enjoyed early electoral success as relatively orthodox formations, as in Bulgaria after the party's electoral defeat in 1997 (see Spirova 2008) or in Romania after 1996 (see Pop-Eleches 2008).

A second group of parties did not transform their organizations or ideology and continued to espouse orthodox authoritarian ideals, counting on a loyal if unhappy electorate. Examples of such parties emerged in the Czech Republic, East Germany, and Slovakia, where it survived alongside a reinvented communist successor party.[4] Some parties, notably in the nondemocratic republics of the former Soviet Union, remained unchanged in name, ideology, or organization.[5] A few either continued to rule (e.g., the Mongolian People's Revolutionary Party, until its electoral loss in 1996 and its ideological transformation by 2000), or even more impressively, returned

---

[2] The vote for communist successor parties ranges from 0 to 69 percent, with a mean of 20 percent and a standard deviation of 16.6. The Slovak and Serbian parties declined steadily over time. Similarly, support peaked early and never recovered for parties in Bulgaria and Lithuania. Votes for the Polish, Slovenian, and Hungarian parties peaked in the early 2000s, only to drop off subsequently. In Albania, Croatia, and Romania, three cases of delayed democratization, we see a rough U-shaped pattern, with initial support dropping, but then recovering.

[3] Reinvention consists of a change in name and symbols, a (credible) transformation of programs and ideology, and reorganization (to eliminate brakes on further transformation, such as orthodox factions or members). The aim is long-term access to governmental power – the capacity to successfully compete for and enter democratic government. To gain office in a parliamentary, proportional-representation system, a party needed to build *programmatic responsiveness* (the correlation between party programs and public concerns, and a focus on public issues rather than on internal party concerns), *popular support for the party* (both votes and public acceptance), and *parliamentary acceptance* (inclusion in coalitions, committees, and in the parliamentary leadership).

[4] Slovakia's main communist successor party, the Slovak Party of the Democratic Left (Strana Demokratickej L'avici, SDL'), is not to be confused with the much smaller Communist Party of Slovakia (Komunistická strana Slovenska, KSS), an orthodox formation founded in 1992. The KSS received 6.5 percent of the vote in 2002, its one time in parliament.

[5] Most became shell parties in nondemocratic regimes (as in Belarus, Ukraine, Russia, and Georgia).

to power in free elections with no great transformation in stances or organization (e.g., the Communist Party of Moldova, PCRM, in the 2001 free elections).[6]

Why did these parties follow such different paths? As I have argued in earlier work (see Grzymala-Busse 2002), the differences in the political resources of the new successor party elites determined the strategies of regeneration. These resources consisted of both elite "portable skills" (the expertise and experiences gained in the previous regime by the mid-level party elites) and the parties' "usable pasts" (the broader historical record of state–society relations and the subsequent references that could resonate with the public). The old communist elites were completely discredited and were either forced out or chose to leave. The natural replacement for these *ancien régime* "dinosaurs" were the ambitious mid-level communist party elites – the government ministers, regional party leaders, and party bureaucrats. Those new party leaders who had the portable skills to do so rapidly and effectively broke with the past and streamlined party organizations. They then relied on broad programmatic appeals rather than on narrow, member-centered ones, and enforced moderation and discipline in the party's public behavior. The more usable the party's past – the more it could point to a favorable record of carrying out reforms and engagement with the opposition under communism – the more credible these efforts were to both the electorate and other parties.

To win over voters and potential coalition partners, the parties relied on both their claims to managerial expertise and their organizational transformation. In effect running on a valence issue, they could claim that they were as committed to democracy and economic reform as their competitors, but would implement these reforms with greater skill and efficiency, and with fewer negative side effects. They pointed to the organizational transformations as a signal both of the new elites' consolidation of power and of a credible commitment to their post-1989 upholding of democracy, pluralism, and progress. Casting off the ballast of auxiliary organizations (e.g., women's and youth organizations), territorial units, and much of their elderly and ideologically orthodox membership further allowed the ambitious new party leaders to radically transform party ideology, appeals, and electoral/parliamentary strategies.

---

[6] Luke March (2005) argues that the Party of Communists of the Republic of Moldova (PCRM) remained avowedly communist, but also increasingly turned to a more opportunistic stance, in which it emphasized a commitment to communism while rejecting "dogmatism" and embracing "reformed socialism" in the early 2000s. Delegalized after 1991, it returned in 1994 to increasing electoral support. In the 2005 elections, the party ran on an explicitly anti-Russian, pro-EU stance, advocating growth of private firms, tax cuts, and welfare state expenditures (Ishiyama 2008: 156–157).

4.2 THE INITIAL SUCCESS OF THE COMMUNIST SUCCESSOR PARTIES

To examine the effects of these party transformations – both in the short term and in the long term – I turn to the four cases I analyzed in earlier work (Grzymala-Busse 2002). These illustrate the three types of party trajectories after 1989: from minimal reinvention (Czech KSČM), to change on some dimensions but not on others (Slovak SDL'), to full reinvention (Polish SdRP/SLD, Hungarian MSzP) (see Table 4.1). Since all four were forced to exit from power in 1989, they represent the "most difficult" cases for reinvention – parties that could not simply retain power and entrench themselves, but had to convince voters and competitors alike.

The Czech successor party, the Communist Party of Bohemia and Moravia (Komunistická Strana Čech a Moravy, KSČM), largely failed to transform itself. After 1989, it did not dissolve its organization nor did it denounce its past symbols, name, or ideology. It was numerically the largest successor party, with about 160,000 members and around 6,000 local organizations (in a nation of 10 million).[7] The party consistently issued narrow appeals and focused far more of its programs on its own history and organization than other Czech parties did. Its programs did not address the public's chief concerns (the one shared emphasis was the provision of competent managers, but the wider public saw the KSČM as the party least likely to provide them). Its supporters were dominated by the elderly and the disaffected.[8] Its electoral support ranged from 10 to 18 percent, with occasional spikes.[9] At the same time, the party's image was very polarizing – among voters, it was the most controversial party in the Czech Republic.[10] Despite its numerical gains, the party did not gain access to office. It was excluded a priori from electoral or governmental coalitions. Its representatives were marginalized in parliament, where the party was denied parliamentary leadership positions and parity in representation in the committees. Nor were its policy proposals taken seriously.

Though ostensibly part of the same ossified federation,[11] the Slovak Party of the Democratic Left (Strana Demokratickej L'avici, SDL') took a different path

---

[7] Under communism, the party had 1,250,000 members and 25,000 local party organizations.

[8] Young, unemployed males tended to vote for the Republicans, an extremist right-wing party.

[9] RFE/RL Newsline, Vol. 3, No. 183, Part II, September 20, 1999. In a 1999 poll, KSČM support peaked at 20 percent. One explanation pointed to the implosion of the Republicans, the other extremist alternative. As one commentator noted, around 25 percent of the Czech electorate has voted for extremist parties since 1989, and with the collapse of the Republicans in 1998, the communists may simply be taking over that protest electorate (Pavel Saradin, *Lidové Noviny*, July 31, 1999, 10).

[10] Throughout the post-1989 period, it was the party seen as *least* likely to ensure democracy and competent governance, scoring even below the extremist right-wing Republicans. After the transition, fifty-five percent of the Czech adult population did not want the party in parliament, the highest such percentage received by any party (STEM Poll, May 26, 1992, *Mlada Fronta Dnes*).

[11] Officially, the Communist Party of Czechoslovakia (KSC) was organized along federal lines after 1968. In practice, there was the Communist Party of Slovakia and the Communist Party of Czechoslovakia. A Communist Party for the Czech Republic was not deemed necessary, and the Slovak party was fully subordinate to the Prague center.

TABLE 4.1 *Patterns of reinvention and electoral performance*

Country	Party	Reinvention?	Peak vote (%)	Collapse?	Coalitions and governance?
Czech republic	KSČM	No	18.5 (2002)	No	No: Excluded a priori from all governmental coalitions
Slovakia	SDL'	Yes, but not fully credible	14.7 (1998)	Yes (1999–2000)	Yes: Two governmental coalitions, briefly in 1994 and 1998–2002
Poland	SdRP/SLD	Yes	41 (2001)	Yes (2002–2004)	Yes: Two governmental coalitions in 1993–1997 and 2001–2005
Hungary	MSzP	Yes	43 (2006)	Yes (2007–2009)	Yes: Three governmental coalitions with the SzDSz, 1994–1998, 2002–2006, 2006–2009, and one minority government, 2009–2010

after 1989, transforming itself on some dimensions. In 1990, the SDL's new leaders forced party members to reregister. Party membership dropped from 450,000 to 40,000, and the number of organizations dropped from 12,500 to 2,000. In a nation of 5 million, this meant that the membership rate was half of the Czech successor's rate. In its programmatic development, the SDL' faced accusations of political inconsistency and programmatic ambiguity. While the party consistently focused on important public issues, its stances on economic reform, administrative transformation, the Hungarian minority question, and Slovakia's NATO and EU membership have shifted back and forth over the years, leading to charges of "fishtailing" and opportunism. While the public saw the economy and managerial competence as two of the most important policy issues, the party changed its views on the former and was unable to fully address the latter.

That said, the SDL' was widely accepted as a party committed to upholding democracy in Slovakia, even if it was not perceived as the most administratively

Paradoxical Fate of the Communist Successor Parties 151

competent. It received 13.8 percent of the vote in 1990 and 14 percent in 1992. However, its "Common Choice Coalition" (Spoločná Vol'ba) lost the 1994 election badly. Instead of the expected 25 percent of the vote, the coalition barely received 10 percent. In the September 1998 elections, SDL' rebounded with 14.7 percent of the vote, coming in third place. The party was widely accepted not only by the electorate but also by its parliamentary competitors. It achieved parity between its seats in parliament and the percentage of committee representation and chairs.[12] It also had a relatively easy time forming coalitions. In March 1994, the SDL' contributed to the downfall of the government of Vladimir Mečiar and his Movement for a Democratic Slovakia (HZDS) by refusing to support the government. The SDL' entered a short-lived governing coalition with the Christian Democrats, presiding over renewed privatization efforts and political reforms. In the 1998–2002 government, the party received nine out of twenty ministries in its coalition government with the Christian Democrats.

The Polish communist successor party, the Social Democracy of Poland (Socjaldemokracja Rzeczpospolitej Polskiej [SdRP] and then Sojusz Lewicy Demokratycznej [SLD] after 1999),[13] arose from the Polish United Workers' Party. This former authoritarian ruling party dissolved itself in January 1990, dropping to 60,000 members and 2,500 organizations.[14] In a nation of 36 million, this meant that the new membership rate was a tenth of the Czech successor party's rate, or a fifth of that of the Slovak party. In its programs, the SdRP focused on public policy from the start, rarely mentioning internal party concerns. It responded to voters' concerns, calling for continuing economic and political reform, but with greater administrative and managerial competence. It appealed to a broad constituency with catchall appeals, and its voters were increasingly better-educated and better-off than average (Grzymala-Busse 2002).

While the party lost every seat it could in the semi-free elections in 1989, it gained support thereafter. In the 1991 elections, the party formed the Democratic Left coalition (SLD), which also consisted of OPZZ, the communist-era official trade union, and other communist-era social organizations.[15] The SLD received 12.0 percent of the vote, coming in second place to the Democratic Union (UD), the main party emerging out of Solidarity

---

[12] The one exception was 1994–1998, when the HZDS took over all committees.
[13] The party changed its name to the Alliance of the Democratic Left (Sojusz Lewicy Demokratycznej, SLD), but this change did not reflect any organizational or programmatic transformations.
[14] This was down from 2,100,000 members and 75,000 organizations in 1988.
[15] Sixty-one out of the 171 seats held by the SLD in 1993–1997 represented the OPZZ. In April 1999, the party and the union coalition transformed itself into a party, also called the SLD. This move was in compliance with the new law on parties in 1997, which stipulated that only parties and their coalitions could run in elections. The leadership of the new party was dominated by the SdRP elites.

after 1989. In 1993, the SLD won over 20 percent of the vote and formed a governing coalition. In 1997, the party actually *gained* voters in absolute numbers in 1997, but lost to the Electoral Action Solidarity (AWS) coalition, a grouping of post-Solidarity political parties and movements.[16] Finally, it returned to power with the 2001 elections, having gained over 40 percent of the vote. In addition to its broad support, the party was seen as the most professional and competent of Polish parties.[17] In parliament, on the other hand, the party initially faced more isolation.

While in power, the party formed the first governing coalition in Poland to last its full term, from 1993 to 1997, and continued the reforms of its predecessors.[18] However, since parties from the former opposition (including those closest to the SdRP ideologically) refused to ally with this communist successor party, the SdRP had no choice but to form a coalition with the successor to the communist-era satellite Peasants' Party (PSL) in 1993. The party's candidate, Aleksander Kwaśniewski, also won the 1995 and 2000 presidential elections. Its governing coalition in 2001–2005 was similarly durable.

Finally, Hungary's communist successor party, the Hungarian Socialist Party (Magyar Szocialista Párt, MSzP), appeared to have the greatest success in reinventing itself. The former authoritarian ruling party from which it emerged dissolved in October 1989, and its membership and local organizations dropped to 40,000 and 2,500, respectively.[19] In its programmatic appeals, the party's claims of managerial competence and administrative effectiveness appealed to broad constituencies, and a sizeable portion of its electorate was made up of white-collar managers and well-educated professionals. The MSzP spent little time justifying its own internal policies in its programs and instead focused on public policy. Its focus was on maintaining social stability and a welfare safety net, two issues that especially resonated with the Hungarian electorate.

In the 1990 elections, the party came in fifth, with 8.5 percent of the vote and thirty-three seats. However, from the start it was seen as an extremely competent party by a plurality of the electorate.[20] As various rifts appeared within the ruling Hungarian Democratic Forum (MDF),[21] such competence

---

[16] AWS leaders repeatedly commented that if the postcommunist forces had succeeded with a disciplined coalition, forming a similar one was the only chance for post-Solidarity forces to regain power.

[17] The SdRP's perceived competence was the item most liked about the party throughout the post-1989 period, and it was seen as the party most likely to provide competent managers and ensure democratic stability.

[18] By contrast, there were five separate governments in the four years from 1989 to 1993.

[19] This corresponds to roughly a quarter of the Czech membership rate or half that of the Slovak party. The communist levels, in 1988, stood at 870,000 members and 25,400 organizations.

[20] After 1989, the party was seen as consistently the most able to provide competent managers, ensure democracy, and maintain stability, even while in government.

[21] These included the rise of an extreme nationalist faction led by István Csurka, government squabbling, minor scandals, and the death of József Antall, the popular prime minister, in December 1993.

was seen as an antidote to the prevailing political turbulence. The 1994 elections resulted in a first place finish for the MSzP, with 33 percent of the vote and 54 percent of parliamentary seats.[22] The party continued to be seen as committed to democracy and effective at governing, even as it lost the 1998 election, with 32.3 percent of the vote, to the Young Democrats (Fidesz). In 2002 and 2006, it roared back into government with enormous popular support: 42 percent in 2002 and 43 percent in 2006.

Unlike Poland's communist successor party, the MSzP was never marginalized in parliament, enjoying consistent and effective representation in parliamentary committees from the beginning. The MSzP repeatedly formed a coalition with the Alliance of Free Democrats (SzDSz), a party that had arisen from the pre-1989 opposition to the communist regime.[23] Such coalitions were largely unthinkable for the former opposition in Poland or in the Czech Republic.

4.3 THE PARADOX OF VICTORY?

Yet despite these auspicious starts – particularly in Poland and Hungary – the paradox is that the more reinvented and successful parties in the short term failed in the long term and disappeared into the margins of politics. These parties did not just lose votes. They also lost party organizations and elites, as fractious elites left to form new (and often more successful) parties. This collapse of party organizations and the defection of elites are signals of a lack of internal commitment to and faith in the party, and thus even more damaging to parties than poor (and reversible) electoral outcomes. By contrast, the party that failed to reinvent itself, the KSČM, continues to lumber along, seemingly a durable fixture of Czech politics (insofar as any aspect of postcommunist party competition can be said to be stable).

The first "victim" was the Slovak SDL': after its foray into government in 1994–1998, it received close to 15 percent of the vote in 1998, only to fizzle to 1.4 percent of the vote in 2002 and subsequently disappear from Slovak politics. Instead, a disgruntled younger SDL' activist, Robert Fico,[24] broke away to found the populist-left SMER ("Direction") in 1999, a party that then won the 2006 and 2010 elections and has governed since then. Another splinter, the Social Democratic Alternative (SDA), founded by former chair Peter Weiss,

---

[22] While the MSzP initially had no contact with the trade unions, most of which were undergoing a massive crisis in 1989–1990, an alliance developed from 1991 onward with the MSzOSz, the main trade union organization. Six unionists stood as MSzP candidates, and union leader Sandor Nagy was given the second place on the party's electoral list in 1994.

[23] Of the twelve ministerial cabinet posts, the MSzP took nine, while the SzDSz took three: culture and public education; internal affairs; and the ministry of transport, telecommunications, and water management.

[24] Fico was the one party leader out of eight not to receive an executive or legislative position in the 1998 coalition, despite receiving the highest number of preference votes (Rybar and Deegan-Krause 2008: 502).

emerged in 2002. It rejected the SDL's shift to a more statist position, but gained 1.8 percent in the 2002 elections. By 2004, both the rump SDL' and the SDA had dissolved and fused with SMER.

Poland's communist successor party had an even more spectacular collapse. Within three years of gaining 41 percent in the 2001 elections, the SLD was relegated to the margins of Polish parliamentary and electoral politics by 2004. In the 2005 parliamentary elections, it received roughly a fourth of its 2001 support (11 percent, down from 41 percent). Two years later, in 2007, it no longer ran as an independent party, but as part of the Left and Democrats (Lewica i Demokraci, LiD) coalition and received 13 percent of the vote. The coalition dissolved within a year, and in the next parliamentary elections in 2011, it ran alone again, obtaining less than 9 percent of the vote.

In Hungary, similarly, the MSzP went from a position of enormous strength, obtaining 43 percent of the vote and 49 percent of seats in 2006, to rapidly crumbling under allegations of deception, mismanagement, and even outright fraud shortly after the 2006 elections. The proximate cause of the collapse was Prime Minister Ferenc Gyurcsány's confidential speech to MSzP parliamentarians in May 2006, in which he admitted that the state of the economy was far worse than had been publicly known, and in fact that the party leadership had lied throughout the 2006 electoral campaign in order to secure victory:

> There is not much choice. There is not, because we have screwed it up. Not a little but a lot. No European country has screwed up as much as we have. It can be explained. We have obviously lied throughout the past 18 to 24 months. It was perfectly clear that what we were saying was not true. We are beyond the country's possibilities to such an extent that we could not conceive earlier that a joint government of the Hungarian Socialist Party and the liberals would ever do. And in the meantime, by the way, we did not do anything for four years. Nothing ... Instead, we lied, morning, noon, and night.[25]

Needless to say, once the tapes leaked a few months later, a political bomb exploded – quite literally – as furious Hungarians took to the streets, with canisters of tear gas, rubber bullets, and Molotov cocktails flying across the cobblestones of Budapest and other cities. Gyurcsány won a vote of confidence and was reelected as MSzP chairman, but resigned in March 2009 in the wake of continuous criticism and the inability to address the economic crisis unfolding in Hungary. The party lost half of its supporters in the European Parliament elections of 2009 and suffered even more in the 2010 Hungarian parliamentary elections. MSzP's support halved, from 43 percent in 2006 to 19 percent in 2010, paving the way for another victory for Fidesz – and its subsequent entrenchment in power through several legal maneuvers that institutionalized its supremacy. For its part, the MSzP fragmented in parliament after the 2010 elections, with Gyurcsány himself leaving to found a new party, the Democratic

---

[25] English translation available from: http://news.bbc.co.uk/2/hi/europe/5359546.stm [Accessed June 3, 2015].

Coalition (Demokratikus Koalíció, DK), in October 2011. The party did even worse in the 2014 parliamentary elections, running as part of a coalition, and in the 2014 European Parliament elections won only 10 percent of the vote, its lowest showing since 1990.

4.4 BROADER PATTERNS

In short, the parties that adapted the most to democracy (and that were very successful as a result) were also the ones to fail most spectacularly over the longer run. They were not unique: others included the Slovenian Social Democrats (SD/ZLSD), who went from being the indispensable party of government (from 1992 to 2004) and obtaining a record 30.5 percent of the vote in 2008 to receiving 10.5 percent in 2011 and 6 percent in 2014; and the Lithuanian Social Democrats (LDDP), who went from being the first major reinvented party success in 1992, with 43 percent of the vote, to fragmenting and merging with the Socialist Party of Lithuania (LSP) to form the Social Democrats in 2001.

It appears that communist successor parties do not profit in the long run from the costly and exhausting process of reinvention. Indeed, both orthodox and reinvented communist successor parties received roughly the same average percentage of the vote over the years and across countries: 19.4 for orthodox parties and 20.6 for reinvented parties, both with standard deviations of 15.2. Here, some of the more orthodox parties, such as those in the Czech Republic or Germany, received lower levels of electoral support – but this support was relatively stable over time (especially for the Czech party, which had a mean vote of 13 percent and a standard deviation of 2.8, against 6.6 percent for the German party and a standard deviation of 3.8). The unreconstructed communist successor party in Moldova, for its part, enjoyed an average 42 percent support in democratic elections, with a standard deviation of 7.7.

Thus, communist successor party reinvention appears to lead to short- to medium-term electoral success – but is little guarantee of long-term electoral support. Votes for reinvented and orthodox successor parties in free elections followed two different trajectories. Figures 4.1a and 4.1b show the fates of communist successor parties in free elections after 1989.[26] As these figures

---

[26] The postcommunist observations are 129 free election years. The threshold for counting an election as free was a score of 6 or higher on the *democracy* variable from Polity IV (on a 0–10 scale) for that year. The countries included are Albania (1992 and after), Armenia (1991–1994 and 1998–2002), Bulgaria, Croatia (after 2000), the Czech Republic, Estonia, Germany, Georgia (1995–1999 and 2004–2014), Hungary, Latvia, Lithuania, Mongolia (after 1992), Moldova, Poland, Romania (after 1996), Russia (2000–2006), Serbia (after 2003), Slovakia, Slovenia, and Ukraine (1991–2013). Azerbaijan, Kazakhstan, Tajikistan, Turkmenistan, and Uzbekistan are excluded (none of these countries ever received a score over 3), as is Belarus, since it crossed the threshold score only in 1991–1994, when no elections were held. Bosnia is excluded because it did not receive a Polity IV score. See Appendix 4.2 for a full list of included parties. Since observations consist of country years and cluster by country, I use a mixed-effects

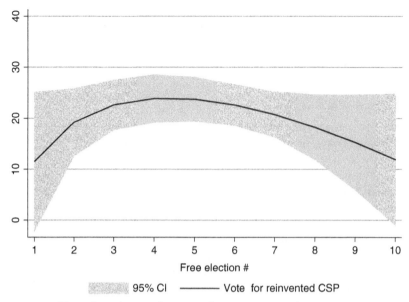

FIGURE 4.1A Votes for reinvented communist successor parties

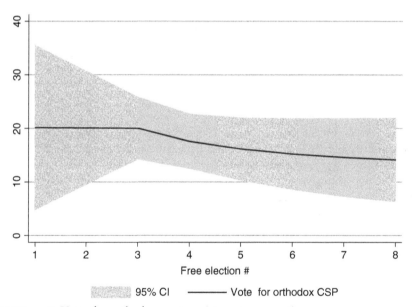

FIGURE 4.1B Votes for orthodox communist successor parties

model with both fixed and random effects to examine the impact of reinvention on electoral success over time. See the very clear exposition of hierarchical linear models in Steenbergen and Jones (2002). The general form is $y = X\beta + Zu + \varepsilon$, where X is an $n \times p$ covariate matrix for fixed effects β and Z is the $n \times q$ covariate matrix for the random effects u. ε is the $n \times 1$ vector of errors, assumed to be multivariate normal with mean 0 and variance matrix $\sigma_t^2 R$.

Paradoxical Fate of the Communist Successor Parties

show, the vote for *orthodox* communist parties dropped from the first to the second free election and then plateaued. By contrast, the average support for the *reinvented* communist parties doubled in the second to fifth election cycles (roughly the mid-1990s to mid-2000s) and then plummeted. In short, reinvention seems to have boosted votes earlier on, but brought no electoral benefits in the longer run. The reinvented parties shone more brightly for a time – but then burned out. By contrast, the orthodox parties never enjoyed the spectacular success of the reinvented parties, but they were able to survive in the long term.

TABLE 4.2 *Correlates of votes for all authoritarian successor parties, mixed-effects regression*

	1	2	3
Reinvention	1.736*	2.112**	2.273**
	(1.02)	(1.02)	(1.08)
	[0.09]	[0.04]	[0.03]
Democracy	−0.858**	−0.963***	−0.625*
	(0.34)	(0.34)	(0.36)
	[0.01]	[0.00]	[0.08]
Postcomm		−11.652***	−12.528***
		(4.28)	(4.33)
		[0.01]	[0.00]
Log GDP			−2.915*
			(1.54)
			[0.06]
Constant	27.033***	33.207***	62.149***
	(3.04)	(3.68)	(16.18)
	[0.00]	[0.00]	[0.00]
sd country mean	15.243***	14.176***	1.265
	(1.65)	(1.55)	(1.49)
	[0.00]	[0.00]	[0.84]
sd residual	11.232***	11.226***	10.256***
	(0.45)	(0.45)	(0.45)
	[0.00]	[0.00]	[0.00]
Obs	360	360	335

* $p<0.10$, ** $p<0.05$, *** $p<0.01$

The low return to investment on reinvention is all the more bitter since for *other* authoritarian successor parties, reinvention seems to *bolster* electoral success. My preliminary research on a broader set of authoritarian successor parties (not presented here) suggests that *in general*, reinvention is positively correlated to electoral support. Economic and democratic development has a negative impact, suggesting that these parties tend to do better in poorer and less democratic countries, perhaps exploiting voter anxieties and lack of pluralism.

By contrast, for communist successor parties, party reinvention is very weakly associated with electoral success, if at all, as Table 4.2 shows.[27] Neither democracy nor economic performance (a proxy for the economic insecurity that could have led to electoral support for the parties; see Tucker 2006) appears to matter much on average, but neither does the transformation of the parties themselves. These results are disheartening for would-be communist party reformers. Organizational, symbolic, and programmatic reinvention is costly and arduous – and yet it has little electoral payoff over the long run. Instead, the impact of party reinvention is very uncertain and unstable: not only do the coefficients change direction, but the high p values suggest we are quite likely to see these coefficients even when the null hypothesis of no effect (of reinvention on votes) holds.

In short, for communist successors, there is little electoral benefit to reinvention over time. Indeed, some of the biggest transformers of the 1990s, as we have seen, paid the highest electoral and organizational price in the 2000s.

4.5 EXPLANATIONS

What is responsible for this reversal of fortune? Why weren't reinvented communist successor parties able to capitalize on and reap long-term benefits from their reinvention? Why was reinvention not rewarded, in other words? By contrast, why did the more orthodox parties such as the KSČM continue as durable electoral actors, with their orthodox ideology, protest politics, and no chance of gaining either government positions or widespread acceptance?

The literature suggests three possible explanations for these parties' collapse. First, it may be that the communist successor parties fell victim to *the anti-incumbent bias* that pervades politics in the region (Pop-Eleches 2010). Communist successor parties that succeeded in winning elections and forming stable governments were punished just like other governing parties. Here, the successors are no different from other incumbents punished by the electorate. Voters experimented with one set of incumbents after another, and the communist successors paid the price both of the high expectations raised by their managerial expertise and of voter disappointment in *any* party's ability to

---

[27] See Appendix 4.1 for the list of variables and coding criteria used.

deliver to the electorate. By contrast, the more orthodox communist successor parties that did not reinvent themselves as radically or as fully, such as the Czech KSČM or the German Linke ("The Left," formerly the Party of Democratic Socialism, PDS), have not governed (and in fact, have been excluded a priori from governing coalitions) – and therefore cannot fall prey to voter behavior that punishes participation in governance.

If we examine the rates of punishment for incumbents, the communist successor incumbents lose 18.6 percent of their voters after governing, while other parties lose 14.7 percent. However, this difference appears to be driven by the spectacular collapse of the communist successor parties after *several* terms in office, not by an anti-incumbent bias that should punish all governing parties after *one* term. Polish voters actually rewarded the communist successor party in 1997 after its first stint in government: the SLD *increased* its vote share by over a third in 1997 (moving from 20 percent of the vote in 1993 to 27 percent in 1997). Voters only punished the party in 2005 after its *second* governing coalition: the party went from 41 percent of the vote in 2001 to 11 percent in 2005.[28] All other Polish governing parties lost votes after their stints in office: the Freedom Union (Unia Wolności, UW) lost 14 percent of its support after 1991–1993, Solidarity (Akcja Wyborcza Solidarność, AWS) lost a whopping 83 percent after 1997–2001, and the Civic Platform (Platforma Obywatelska, PO) lost 5 percent after 2007–2011. In short, Poland's communist successor party gained more votes than any other governing party in the country (in 1997) – and was also more severely punished than any other (in 2005).

Nor did the Hungarian voters punish the communist successors after its first two governing coalitions. The MSzP did not lose its share of the vote after either its 1994–1998 or 2002–2006 governing coalition, but it lost 56 percent of its vote in the 2010 elections, after the disastrous 2006–2010 governing coalition. The Hungarian communist successor party lost more than any other party had before, but also had the most stable vote share up until that point. Other governing parties lost 53 percent of their vote share (the MDF after 1990–1994), or in the case of Fidesz, gained 40 percent from 1998 to 2002, only to lose 13 percent in 2014 after its 2010–2014 term as the governing party. In short, if incumbency tends to hurt governing parties, it harmed the communist successor parties only after repeated terms in office. Similarly, the LDDP in Lithuania was the senior governing party in 1992–1996 (with 44 percent of the vote) and again from 2001 to 2004 (with 31 percent of the vote), only to merge with the Lithuanian Social Democratic Party (LSDP) in 2001 and reenter government in 2006–2008 and again in 2012–present as part of the LSDP (even if the new party received a far smaller share of the vote).

Thus, while other governing parties were punished after their first stint in government, voters initially appeared more forgiving of the communist

---

[28] Law and Justice (Prawo i Sprawiedliwość, PiS) was the only party other than the SLD to gain vote share after governing, moving from 27 percent of the total vote in 2005 to 32 percent in 2007.

successor parties, and only punished them after their *second* or *third* terms in government. (And, of course, parties that never entered government, such as the KSČM, could not be, and thus were not, punished.) This relationship holds even when we examine economic shocks: GDP growth is related to party system volatility, but very weakly (and negatively) to the vote for communist successor parties.[29]

Second, electoral success has been closely associated with *strong party organizations*, as measured by the number of members as a share of the electorate, the number of party branches, and participation in local elections (Tavits 2013). In this account, such organizational strength roots political parties in civil society and allows them to steadily increase their electoral support. By building loyal electorates and entrenching preferences, organizational strength insures parties against electoral failure. One implication here is that organizational collapse *precedes* electoral failure: without these societal roots, parties are unable to weather crises or seek alternative offices on the local or regional levels.

Yet there are two reasons to doubt that this account applies in explaining the failure of the communist successor parties. First, these parties streamlined their organizations and reduced memberships precisely so that they could reinvent themselves and win elections in the first place. Second, changes in membership appear to be at best a symptom of party failure, rather than its cause. For example, the Polish party actually more than *doubled* its membership in the four years before its collapse (going from roughly 60,000 members to close to 150,000 by 2002).[30] The Hungarian successor party held steady throughout the 1990s at around 40,000 members. It dropped to the low 30,000s in 1999–2001, but then regained steadily up to 41,000. It was only in 2007–2008, *after* the scandals that rocked the party and its government, that its membership declined to around 33,000–36,000 (Tavits 2013; van Biezen, Mair, and Poguntke 2012). Meanwhile, the Czech KSČM's elderly membership declined from 200,000 in the 1990s to 140,000 in 1999, to less than 80,000 in 2008. Nevertheless, its electoral performance held steady. In short, at least in these cases, increasing membership is not a guarantee of electoral success – and decreasing membership is not a death knell for the party. Not surprisingly, then, as Table 4.3 suggests, there is no relationship between the number of communist successor party members and their electoral success.

Third, the communist successor parties' sudden collapse may be attributable to *brand dilution*. Such blurring of party reputations is the result of adopting positions inconsistent with ideological traditions, inconsistent choice of coalition partners, and internal party conflict (Lupu 2014, 2016). Ideological coherence and consistency are critical to parties in new democracies (Hanson 2010). Conversely, parties that turn their back on their former ideals and

---

[29] Regression results available from author.
[30] I am grateful to Margit Tavits for much of this data.

TABLE 4.3 *Correlates of votes for communist successor parties only, mixed-effects regression*

	3	4	5
Reinvention	0.089	−3.206	8.933
	(1.27)	(4.19)	(5.69)
	[0.94]	[0.44]	[0.12]
Party membership		0.000	0.000***
		(0.00)	(0.00)
		[0.54]	[0.00]
Democracy			−0.530
			(2.07)
			[0.80]
Log GDP			5.453
			(7.25)
			[0.45]
Constant	19.061***	30.184**	−64.789
	(3.05)	(11.79)	(77.16)
	[0.00]	[0.01]	[0.40]
sd country mean	10.827***	9.743***	7.549***
	(1.94)	(3.42)	(2.68)
	[0.00]	[0.00]	[0.00]
sd residual	12.311***	10.181***	8.153***
	(0.74)	(1.53)	(1.52)
	[0.00]	[0.00]	[0.00]
Obs	168	31	21

* $p<0.10$, ** $p<0.05$, *** $p<0.01$

become indistinguishable from other parties are unusually susceptible to electoral collapses when voters also judge them to perform poorly in office (Lupu 2014, 2016). What follows appears to be a sudden abandonment of the party by the voters during a crisis, but is in fact the culmination of a long process of attrition and brand dilution.

Yet it is not clear that this explanation applies in this context. First, both the Polish SLD and the Hungarian MSzP had consistent and coherent ideological positions prior to their collapse, as the clear alternatives to the post-Solidarity forces and to Fidesz, respectively. Both were the parties of managerial expertise and moderate democratic politics. Their main attraction to the electorate was their perceived competence and unity in purpose, which presented a stark contrast to the messy democratic politics of the 1990s. They did not change their ideology over time – at least, no more than other parties that formed the consensus around the necessity of economic reform in the early 1990s or the entry of their countries into the European Union in 2004. Importantly, all left parties in postcommunist countries tended to adhere to fiscal austerity and tighter budgets, as analyses of political, budgetary, and economic data from the 1990–2004 period suggest (Tavits and Letki 2009: 561).

The communist successor parties in Poland and in Hungary, where party downfall was the most spectacular, were still the most credible representatives of a catchall center-left in the early 2000s. *Other* parties, if anything, tried to approximate their centrist appeal. For example, in Poland, one of the keys to the eventual success of Civic Platform was its increasing centrism in 2003–2005. For its part, the Hungarian party system increasingly *polarized* over the course of the late 1990s and early 2000s (Enyedi 2006). In other words, if this explanation holds for the communist successor cases, we should see both an abandonment of former ideals and a lack of differentiation with other parties – but there is little evidence of either one of these over time.

Nor do we see coalition arrangements that somehow departed from precedent. The Polish successor party's only coalition partner was the postcommunist Peasants' Party, and the Hungarian successor party's coalition partner was the Alliance of Free Democrats (the SzDSz, which ended its strategic alliance with the MSzP in 2008 – and promptly collapsed, both in the 2009 European Parliament elections and in the 2010 parliamentary elections). There were no strange alliances or peculiar ideological twists, then, that could have diluted the communist successor parties' brands. What we do observe are internal party conflicts, but they did not consistently occur before the parties' electoral collapse, as the "brand dilution" explanation would suggest.

In short, we need to account for three separate lacunae. First, why did the electoral punishment of the incumbents come so late but so viciously? Second, why did the streamlined and centralized party organizations, which had been the basis for party cohesion and effective campaigning up until that point, fail to insulate the parties against subsequent electoral vicissitudes? Finally, if ideological dilution or inconsistent coalitions were not the problem, then on what bases did voters punish the communist successor parties?

One answer to these questions lies in the transformation and reinvention that made these parties so successful in the first place. First, they emphasized their expertise, efficiency, and managerial competence – an unusually demanding set of standards to fulfill, and one that would prove difficult to sustain. These standards were all the more difficult to uphold because of the temptations of office, which were made more accessible by electoral success and reelection.

This was less a case of ideological convergence over time or brand dilution than a failure to fulfill the standards for managerial competence and ideological unity that they had set for themselves, and which underlay their reputation. Communist successor parties were punished so severely because so much more was expected of them, and they were punished more severely after the second or third term in office because they had failed to live up to their initial success in implementing reforms. In essence, the communist successor parties had hoisted themselves on their own petards: the high standards of managerial competence that had made them so attractive in the first place eventually came back to bite them.

Second, these parties' electoral success ironically undermined their organizational cohesion. Organizational streamlining and leadership centralization initially contributed to their electoral success. Party elites led disciplined and cohesive organizations that could nimbly respond to changing electoral environments or new policy challenges. That same centralization, however, meant that elites competed fiercely over leadership positions. This competition in turn led to both fragmentation (as frustrated and stifled elites left the party and founded new parties) and organizational decay (as elites tried to find new ways to build competitive strength, including by transferring resources to regional elites to gain a regional power base). In turn, this fragmentation and party capture by regional leaders undermined the parties' reputation for cohesion and competence.

Electoral success intensified this internal competition, both by making the prize of leadership all the more valuable and by giving incumbent parties access to more material and administrative resources, such as tenders and contracts, new administrative offices, and positions on candidate lists for new local offices. The availability of these resources in turn increased internal party competition over their distribution and use, especially at the local and regional levels. In the process, internal unity and centralization gave way to internecine conflict. Such conflict both further damaged the parties' reputations and created internal organizational fissures that precluded an agile and convincing response to the crises of confidence in the parties. As new scandals emerged, party elites could not credibly answer accusations of corruption and incompetence – which in turn lowered voter support and led party members and elites alike to leave in disgust. In short, the organizational change that had initially bred electoral success led to internal conflict, abuse of resources, and competition that undermined the very claims that had made the parties electorally viable. These rifts undermined *both* the organizations *and* the parties' claims of competence. In short, the same adaptive strategies that led to the parties' successful reinvention led to their electoral success – and eventually, and paradoxically, to their downfall.

By contrast, the parties that did not reinvent themselves, such as the Czech KSČM, did not enter office, and thus did not have to worry about either its temptations or the new organizational pressures that this would create. They never claimed managerial expertise or competence as their advantage and were thus not judged by this yardstick. Similarly, parties that reinvented their appeals in the 1990s, but neither transformed their organizations nor claimed managerial expertise, tended to survive with higher rates of support. The Romanian Social Democratic Party (PSD), after the disastrous 1996 elections that prompted a belated and limited transformation, continued to obtain around 33–37 percent of the vote. The Bulgarian Socialist Party (BSP) lost half of its support in 1997, which had previously been above 40 percent, then proceeded to oscillate between around 30 percent while in government and over 20 percent while in opposition. These communist successor parties were elected not on the basis of their reinvention or their claims of competence, but largely, thanks to weak competition, on unorthodox cleavages dominated by unresolved debates about the fundamental direction of the country and a set of formal institutions and informal economic ties that favored their continued election into office.

How, then, did the reinvented communist successor parties become victims of their own success? In the cases of the Slovak, Hungarian, and Polish parties, the combination of high standards and changes in party organizations both ensured their success in the 1990s and led to their failure in the 2000s. Within the Slovak SDL', the party's collective leadership and its commitment to economic reforms led to an exacerbation of internal tensions. The party's collective leadership entailed extensive compromises among national leaders and among the regional backers of these various wings in the name of public unity. Party membership was never particularly a priority for the party, dropping down from over 40,000 in 1990 to around 24,000 after 1994. A bigger problem was the propensity for internal contention and elite rifts. Multiple party reformists at the helm of the party, such as Peter Weiss, Brigita Schmögnerová, or Milan Ftáčnik, signaled the commitment of the SDL' to democratic and market reforms in the 1990s. They were countermanded by the more leftist and populist leaders such as Pavel Koncoš or Jozef Migaš by the mid-1990s. Worse yet, the party's most popular leader, Robert Fico, was the only one not awarded a high-ranking position in the 1998–2002 government, a decision that led directly to the party's collapse.

The party's reputation for commitment to reforms became even more of a vulnerability once it entered the 1998–2002 governing coalition. The Christian Democratic Party, the senior coalition partner, appointed Schmögnerová as minister of finance, and she became the face of the new (and unpopular) austerity reforms. Koncoš and Migaš openly criticized these policies as part of their quest for the party leadership. Even as the Christian Democratic prime minister defended Schmögnerová, these SDL' colleagues called for her dismissal (Haughton 2004: 186). At the same time, the party organization did not remain quiescent, and in fact many regional party heads took sides in the conflict against Schmögnerová. In 2001, the party congress elected a new chair: Pavel Koncoš. He tried to remove party reformers and instill a vote of no confidence in the SDL's own government – moves that prompted former party leader Peter Weiss and his allies to leave the party and found the Social Democratic Alternative in 2002.

The fatal blow had already been dealt, however, with the departure of the embittered Robert Fico, who left the SDL' in 1999 to form a new party, SMER, in protest of his exclusion from government. One of the most popular SDL' leaders, Fico set out to build a party that was very different from SDL' in its organization, if not in its initial programmatic commitments. Fico ran a very tightly centralized SMER, single-handedly shaping election programs, party decisions, and approving electoral lists (Orogváni 2006; Rybar and Deegan-Krause 2008: 505). SMER also limited the number of regional organizations and subordinated them to the party center (i.e., Fico himself). Party membership expanded between 2002 and 2005, but several measures prevented the dilution of power within the party: leaders of parties who merged with SMER were not encouraged to enter, and applicants were not guaranteed party membership. SMER absorbed the SDA and SDL' itself in 2005, and went on to enter the 2006–2010 coalition and win in 2010, 2012, and 2016, forming a single-party government. In short, SMER avoided the problems that had befallen the SDL': both the collective leadership and the commitment to reforms. Instead, the key to its success was a single, very popular leader and a more vague populist program whose appeal was its critique of austerity and harsh economic solutions.

In Poland, the communist successor party's reputation for competence and expertise was not only a difficult standard to sustain; the party's organizational structure also wound up undermining its claims of competence and able administration. If in the early 1990s, the simple quest for survival and vindication subordinated regional ambitions to the party leadership, by the end of the decade, its electoral success, its growing acceptance by other parties, and its steady position in both public opinion polls and government institutions meant growing claims by regional party leaders, who now saw themselves as increasingly important to the party's success.

The party leadership promoted these regional leaders (known as "barons") in the late 1990s. They were critical to Leszek Miller's consolidation of power within the party in 1999, and they were charged with ensuring the party's continued electoral success in the regions. The exchange was nearly feudal: the barons provided the center with funding and votes, and the center gave them near-autonomy in the regions. There, the barons played several critical roles: they served as parliamentarians; determined the candidate lists at the regional level; gained control over the extra-budgetary funds and quasi-governmental organizations; and became active participants of supervisory boards of semi-privatized enterprises.[31]

---

[31] Their regional bases of power included Poznań (Krystyna Łybacka), Silesia (Andrzej Szarawarski), Lublin (Grzegorz Kurczuk), or Płock (Andrzej Piłat).

The result was that a group of regional activists became entrenched at the regional level and gained power bases that were distinct from – and often in conflict with – the party's central leadership. Partly because the regional barons were also parliamentarians and government officials, they had enormous access to state resources and power over their distribution. The barons' financial dealings were often as shady as they were lucrative, undermining the party's image as a competent and honest manager.[32] The party subsequently became enmeshed in both highly public internal squabbles and regional corruption scandals – thus failing to live up to the criteria for coherence and competence that it had earlier set. Some of the conflicts of interest bordered on the farcical. For example, the self-enriching financial dealings and absolutist style of Andrzej Pęczak, the Łódź baron and SLD parliamentarian, finally became too much for his party colleagues in 2002. The party leadership wanted him to account for his finances and business ties. However, because he was also the informal accountant for the party, he would have been in a position to absolve himself.[33]

The crescendo of scandals within the party was only matched by the more public controversies, which repeatedly showed the SLD to be a party unable to withstand the temptations of power. Party elites used their vast policymaking authority and resources for their private benefit. The early 2000s also saw the so-called "Orlengate," in which Miller and other party officials stood accused of meddling in the internal affairs of an oil company by having its CEO detained before an important deal, and "Rywingate," in which the party stood accused of influence peddling in an important media law that would have benefited powerful media concerns. The equation for many voters was simple: a party elected into office on claims of superior expertise and competence turned out to be just as, if not more, susceptible to the temptations of office.

At the same time, over the course of 1998–2002, the ranks of party members doubled to over 120,000, as ambitious would-be politicians sought the SLD's nomination for office.[34] As Figures 4.2a and 4.2b show, party membership exploded after the 1997 elections, as new party members jockeyed for positions on local electoral lists, the mainstay of the barons' power and a lucrative source of state resources in their own right. In the 2002 local

---

[32] By contrast, factionalism within the Institutional Revolutionary Party (PRI) in Mexico based on regional economic differences prevented the national party from "aggregating interests and articulating a coherent national agenda" (Estévez, Díaz-Cayeros, and Magaloni 2008: 43). However, instead of harming the party, this factionalism allowed it to survive after its 2000 electoral defeat by entrenching the PRI in regional strongholds. The difference was that in Mexico, fiscal decentralization gave the governors considerable local support, while in Poland, fiscal and political centralization meant no such local bastions of voter loyalty. For more on the PRI, see Flores-Macías (Chapter 8, this volume).

[33] *Polityka* 29, July 20, 2002, pp. 28–30.

[34] Many of these were former members of the old communist ruling party, who remained politically inactive for the 1990s, only to opportunistically return to the party in order to gain access to government (*Polityka*, 50, December 14, 2002).

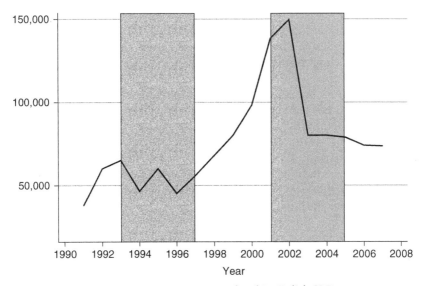

FIGURE 4.2A Communist successor party membership: Polish SLD

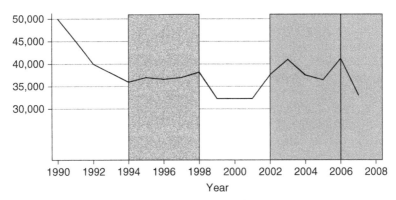

FIGURE 4.2B Communist successor party membership: Hungarian MSzP
Notes: Vertical lines indicate elections. Gray areas indicate when the party was in government.

elections, over 57,000 of them sought local offices – of which there were now 47,000, down from 62,000 in 1998 as a result of administrative reforms (Janicki 2002; Paradowska 2002). The run-up to this election saw the greatest internal struggle and conflict, which the national party office was unable to quell and which regional barons had little interest in resolving.[35] The result was

---

[35] *Polityka* 17, April 24, 2004.

that over the course of 2000–2002, the party increasingly lost the cohesion and discipline that had served it so well in the 1990s.

Miller recognized the damage that the corruption scandals and the barons' autonomy were doing to the party. He began to clean house and remove the barons in 2000–2001, but the party's reputation was already sullied and its ability to call on its managerial experience and expertise greatly diminished. Miller eventually pushed through a new party statute that prohibited party leaders from concurrently holding high national office in 2003. But by this point, the barons' fusion of party and elected office positions had done considerable damage, both by making it impossible for Miller and the central party office to enact discipline, and by damaging the party's reputation. Further, the loyal but nondescript members that they had promoted into office now made it difficult for the party to present itself as dynamic, united, or competent. By early 2004, when a new leader, Krzysztof Janik, assumed power, not only had new party fragments started to break away in parliament (such as the Socjaldemokracja Polska [SDPL], founded in March 2004, followed by Lewica i Demokraci [LiD] in 2006), but Janik declared the party ready to allow internal factions, further undermining the image of the SLD as a centralized and ideologically disciplined party.

Finally, the Hungarian communist successor party had also failed to live up to the very standards of honesty and expertise that it had set in earlier campaigns, thanks to its very electoral success, and was unable to counter the accusations that followed. The MSzP had anchored the "responsible left" wing of the political spectrum since 1990. It had a clear profile of center-left policies and managerial competence, against the more nationalist and conservative Fidesz-MDF wing, and the xenophobic right wing of MIEP or Jobbik. Right and left alternated in power from 1990 onward, and after 1998, the key trend appeared to be a *further* polarization between the MSzP, on the one hand, and Fidesz-MPP, on the other (Fowler 2003: 801). Neither Fidesz nor the MSzP moved to the center.

The party won the 1994 elections with the slogan "Let competence govern the country!" setting a high bar for its subsequent performance. Economic competence was a key factor in the party's 2002 electoral victory as well, both with the election of Péter Medgyessy in 2002 and the "self-presentation of the 'expert government' of Gordon Bajnai in 2009–10" (Bíró-Nagy 2013: 2). The party's ideological profile was clear; its reputation, however, became increasingly muddied. Corruption scandals, such as the Tocsik scandal in 1996, had already emerged. Even before the economic crisis hit in 2008–2009, the MSzP government was accused of mishandling the economy. Over the course of 2002–2006, the MSzP under Medgyessy had increased Hungary's debt burden by 23 billion USD, for a total of over 60 billion USD, a figure that was repeatedly brought up as a sign of the party's financial mismanagement. The economy was in steady decline, and the GDP plummeted close to 7 percent in 2009. Not only were there several scandals involving party officials and various party funding schemes (Grzymala-Busse 2007),[36] but politicians who provided especially lucrative services to the party could be rewarded with places on the national list, giving them seats without a direct popular vote and granting them parliamentary immunity in the process.

The leaked Gyurcsány tape became the proximate cause of the party's downfall. Gyurcsány refused to resign or to hold early elections, and his administration's handling of the protests that followed after his speech was leaked only added fuel to the fire. Gyurcsány's strategy after the 2006 fiasco was to endure austerity as rapidly and radically as possible, within the first two years of his administration, and then regain popularity as the economy recovered.[37] These measures failed, and instead what followed were the political defeats of reforms in health and education (the 2008 "social referendum" initiated by Fidesz revoked fees on medical visits and tuition), a heavy defeat in the 2009 European Parliament elections, and several corruption scandals that erupted after 2008 (Bíró-Nagy 2013: 4). Gyurcsány finally resigned in March 2009, both from the office of prime minister and as chair of the party. By this point, the party's support had dropped to 18 percent, while the opposition Fidesz had gained 60 percent support.

The party's organizational strategies did not help it to weather the storm. Much as in Poland, the party's electoral success led to an organizational expansion and a new reassertion of authority by regional elites. The MSzP in the 1990s had extensive branch organizations, especially relative to the number of members.[38] These regional party leaders, as in Poland, had considerable power: they set candidate lists,[39] nominated local officials, and acted as gatekeepers. The number of branch offices increased considerably after each electoral victory: it doubled to over 400 offices after 1994, grew to 983 after the

---

[36] In a more recent example, Deputy Chairman Gabor Simon resigned in January 2014 after failing to declare close to 800,000 euros in an Austrian bank account. Simon was unable to account for the source of the funds, and it was widely assumed that he was holding the money for the MSzP itself. See "MSZP Deputy Chairman Gabor Simon Caught Red Handed," *The Budapest Beacon*, February 5, 2014 (available from: http://budapestbeacon.com/politics/mszp-deputy-chairman-gabor-simon-caught-red-handed), and Richard Field, "Janos Zuschlag Tells All: Confessions of a MSZP Scapegoat or Turncoat?" *The Budapest Beacon*, March 8, 2014 (available from: http://budapestbeacon.com/politics/janos-zuschlag-tells-all-confessions-of-a-mszp-scapegoat-or-turncoat/5718) [Accessed March 25, 2016].

[37] *Polityka*, 31, 2006, pp. 49–50. He decreased the number of ministries from 15 to 12 and reduced the layers of vice-executive staffing within the government. He also proposed a reduction of parliamentary seats from 386 to 298 in 2006.

[38] In 1995, the MSzP had roughly 36,000 members and 172 local and regional offices. This was nearly twice as many as the next biggest party in Hungary, the SzDSz, which had 32,000 members but only eighty branch offices (Toole 2003: 107).

[39] County party lists were also a safe haven for party regional leaders, until the 2011 Fidesz election law eliminated the county party lists in favor of single-member constituencies and national party lists.

party won the 2002 elections, and reached over 1,100 after the party's 2006 win.[40]

As in Poland, electoral success produced runaway local organizations and leaders that eventually belied national-level efforts to project an image of cohesion, competence, and probity. These regional leaders and party activists were critical to MSzP's electoral victories, but they became a double-edged sword. For one thing, they complicated and delayed the choice of candidates for high-ranking positions. For example, Péter Medgyessy only emerged as the 2002 MSzP prime ministerial candidate in 2001, allowing Viktor Órban to emerge as a more powerful competitor (Fowler 2003: 802). These regional leaders also staged a rebellion in 2004 at the extraordinary congress of the party, electing Gyurcsány as the candidate for prime minister, rather than supporting Medgyessy, the party leadership's preferred candidate. Gyurcsány sought to strengthen local party organizations when he became chair in 2007 (Tavits 2013: 187), emulating both the SLD in Poland and the MSzP's main domestic rival, Fidesz.

MSzP leaders struggled with centralizing authority both in the leadership and over the regional offices, much as their Polish and Slovak counterparts had done. Party leader and prime minister were two separate positions, with the exception of 1994–1998 (Gyula Horn) and 2007–2009 (Gyurcsány). Within the party, several contenders for power arose in the 2000s, including Katalin Szili (the parliamentary speaker, a socialist, and a self-avowed Christian), Imre Szekeres (minister of defense), Péter Kiss (chief of staff), and Ildikó Lendvai (parliamentary faction leader). Lendvai herself became party chair, but resigned in 2010 after the party's disastrous electoral result. Szili left in 2010 to form the Movement for the Alliance for the Future. By October 2011, Gyurcsány himself left to form the Democratic Coalition.[41] Both the increasingly autonomous and empowered set of regional leaders, and the newly open struggle for power at the top meant that it was difficult for the party to articulate a response to the widespread disappointment with the MSzP that followed the 2006 scandal – or for the party to regain the faith of the voters.

In short, reinvented communist parties became victims of their own success, in that they set the high standards of competence and probity that few parties could possibly fulfill. Moreover, their electoral success gave rise to internal

---

[40] These numbers increased again, to 1,110 in 2007, following the party's victory in the 2006 elections. I am grateful to Margit Tavits for this data.
[41] The new party leader as of 2010, Attila Mesterhazy, sought to centralize and reinvigorate the party. He turned away from Gyurcsány's liberal policies and instead promoted labor rights, social mobility, and social justice. He also changed the party statutes to increase the power of the party leadership: as of November 2011, it was compulsory to collect signatures of at least 10 percent of members at the national or county level to become a presidential candidate or county leader (Bíró-Nagy 2013: 3). Since the previous three prime ministers (Medgyessy, Gyurcsány, and Bajnai) had all come from private business or played political advisory roles, this was seen as a big change.

challengers, who had their own bases of power and who asserted their independence and countermanded the decisions of party leaders – and without a loyal and cohesive organization, it became even harder to respond quickly and effectively to policy challenges.

4.6 CONCLUSION

The postcommunist democracies of East Central Europe saw two paradoxes: the first was that authoritarian ruling parties that were widely denounced for their incompetence and poor management could quickly become successful democrats, celebrated for their managerial expertise, democratic commitments, and political savvy. A slew of analyses, including my own (see Grzymala-Busse 2002), examined the *causes* of this reinvention and the ways in which these parties' portable elite skills and usable pasts allowed them to project an image of competence, probity, and credibility.

Yet the *consequences* of this reinvention remained largely unexplored. And here, the second paradox was that this very electoral success would, in the long run, destroy these parties' image of competence and their internal cohesion, as party elites succumbed to the temptations of office and to competition for resources. Their sudden fall in confidence resembles the dynamics of "brand dilution" (Lupu 2014, 2016). However, it was not the result of inconsistent coalition partners or a blurring of ideological lines, but of self-created crises. The downfall of the reinvented communist successor parties goes beyond the anti-incumbent bias that pervades the region: these were parties that *did* succeed in gaining the confidence of voters and getting reelected. Nor could the parties' organizations save them, since they themselves became part of the problem. In short, the very drivers of party reinvention and subsequent electoral success identified in earlier work – a reputation for competence and organizational transformation – now led to their downfall. These consequences were very much unintended by the parties' elites. They were also unanticipated by my own earlier analyses, which stopped at the point of these parties' initial electoral success, without predicting the longer-term feedback effects.

The irony was that these communist successor parties established the high standards by which they would be judged. These standards could not be met – all the more so because electoral success had led to the expansion of organizations and funding that made regional challenges and corrupt financial deals almost inevitable. By winning elections and entering government, these parties were unable to uphold their reputation as expert managers, a problem that was exacerbated by the fact that their electoral success made them less cohesive and disciplined. They paid an unusually heavy price, because they failed the very standards that they had set for themselves. The parties thus became victims of their own success.

APPENDIX 4.1

Coding and Selection Criteria

The postcommunist subset analyzed here includes only those election years when the Polity IV democracy score was 6 or higher, eliminating some postcommunist cases entirely (e.g., Azerbaijan, Kazakhstan, Tajikistan, and Turkmenistan) and many elections held in 1990. These restrictions reduce the number of observations to 129.

The full data set consists of country years from 1945 to 2014 for seventy-eight countries in Europe, Latin America, North America, and Asia, for a total of 5,460 observations.

The data includes indicators for party behavior (their exit, reinvention, and electoral participation), political competition (volatility, fragmentation, electoral institutions, and electoral outcomes), and quality of democracy (democratic rights and freedoms, the degree of pluralist competition, and opposition rights).

> **Authoritarian Successor Parties** in this analysis are the formal successors to the previous autocratic rulers. Parties that subsequently change their names or enter coalitions are coded as one successor. (For example, the successor to the Polish United Workers' Party [PZPR] was initially called the SdRP. This party was part of an alliance called the SLD, which became a party called the SLD in 1999. Both the SdRP and SLD are counted as a single successor to the PZPR.) Fifty-four such parties are included in the data set. These parties include both the formal legal successors to these parties (as in East Central Europe) and parties that were founded during or after the collapse of autocratic rule by authoritarian elites (see Loxton, Introduction, this volume). A full list is available from the author.
>
> **Reinvention** is currently coded along a three-point scale, with a point each for (a) a change in the party's name (to no longer include a reference to the previous authoritarian regime), (b) programmatic/ideological change (in its programmatic publications or electoral campaign, the party had to formally denounce previous authoritarian methods and announce its support for democratic competition), and (c) organizational transformation (any of the following: formal dissolution and refounding, reregistering members, changing the number of local and regional organizations, and cutting or developing ties to auxiliary organizations such as trade unions). A country-year score reflects score for 6 or more months that year. Data from Keesing's Record of World Events and World News Archive.
>
> **Democracy:** *Democ* (institutionalized democracy, 0–10 scale) and *Parcomp* (political competition/competitiveness of participation, 0–5 scale) variables from Marshall, Gurr, and Jaggers (2014).

Paradoxical Fate of the Communist Successor Parties 173

Log GDP: Annual reporting from the World Bank Development Indicators (World Bank 2014).
Proportional and Presidential: Coding of electoral and parliamentary institutions from Bormann and Golder (2013).
Party Membership: Data from Tavits (2013) and Grzymala-Busse (2002).
Vote: Votes obtained by authoritarian successor party *or* the electoral coalition in which it ran if individual party data is unavailable. Data from Nordsieck (2017) for Europe and from Brancati (2017).

Other measures in the data set include the duration of authoritarian rule, parliamentary fragmentation, electoral volatility measured both as the entrance of new electoral parties and as vote-switching among established parties (based on Tucker and Powell 2014), the effective number of electoral and parliamentary parties, turnover, and openness of competition (the number of seats gained by parties that have not been represented in parliament before).

APPENDIX 4.2

List of Communist Successor Parties

- Albania: Socialist Party of Albania (Partia Socialiste e Shqipërisë)
- Armenia: Democratic Party (Hayastani Demokratakan Kusaktsutyun)
- Bulgaria: Bulgarian Socialist Party (Bulgarska sotsialisticheska partiya)
- Croatia: Social Democratic Party (Socijaldemokratska partija Hrvatske)
- Czech Republic: Communist Party of Bohemia and Moravia (Komunistická strana Čech a Moravy)
- Georgia: Communist Party of Georgia (Sakartvelos Komunisturi Partia; earlier Socialist Labor Party)
- Germany (East): The Left (Die Linke; earlier Socialist Unity Party – Party of Democratic Socialism [Sozialistische Einheitspartei – Partei des Demokratischen Sozialismus], Party of Democratic Socialism [Partei des Demokratischen Sozialismus] and The Left Party [Linkspartei])
- Hungary: Hungarian Socialist Party (Magyar Szocialista Párt)
- Latvia: Latvian Socialist Party (Latvijas Sociālistiskā partija; earlier Equality Party)
- Lithuania: Social Democratic Party (Lietuvos socialdemokratų partija; earlier Democratic Labour Party of Lithuania [Lietuvos demokratinė darbo partija, LDDP] and A. Brazauskas' Social Democratic Coalition)
- Macedonia: Social Democratic Union of Macedonia (Socijaldemokratski sojuz na Makedonija, SDSM; earlier League of Communists of Macedonia: Party for Democratic Changes)
- Moldova: Party of Communists of the Republic of Moldova (Partidul Comuniștilor din Republica Moldova)

- Mongolia: Mongolian People's Party (Mongol Ardiin Nam; earlier Mongolian People's Revolutionary Party [Mongol Ardyn Khuvsgalt Nam])
- Poland: Democratic Left Alliance (Sojusz Lewicy Demkratycznej; earlier Social Democracy of the Republic of Poland [Socjaldemokracja Rzeczypospolitej Polskiej])
- Romania:
  - Social Democratic Party (Partidul Social Democrat; earlier National Salvation Front [Frontul Salvării Naţionale, FSN], Democratic National Salvation Front [Frontul Democrat al Salvării Naţionale, FDSN], Party of Social Democracy of Romania [Partidul Democraţiei Sociale in România, PDSR])
  - Democratic Liberal Party (earlier National Salvation Front [Frontul Salvării Naţionale, FSN], United Social Democrats, Democratic Party [Partidul Democrat, PD])
  - Socialist Party of Labor (PSM)
  - Greater Romania Party (PRM)
- Russia: Communist Party of the Russian Federation (Kommunisticheskaya Partiya Rossiyskoy Federatsii, KPRF; earlier Russian Communist Party)
- Serbia: Socialist Party of Serbia (Socijalistička partija Srbije)
- Slovakia: Party of the Democratic Left (Strana demokratickej ľavice)
- Slovenia: Social Democrats (Socialni demokrati; earlier United List of Social Democrats [Združena lista socialnih demokratov, ZLSD])
- Ukraine: Communist Party of Ukraine (Komunistychna Partiya Ukrayiny)

Not included in analysis:

- Belarus: Communist Party of Belarus (Kommunisticheskaya Partiya Belarusi)
- Bosnia: Social Democratic Party of Bosnia and Herzegovina (Socijaldemokratska Partija Bosne i Hercegovine)
- Kazakhstan: Communist Party of Kazakhstan (Kazakstan Kommunistik Khalik Partia)
- Kyrgyzstan: Communist Party of Kyrgyzstan (Kommunisticheskaya Partiya Kirgizstana)
- Tajikistan: Communist Party of Tajikistan (Hizbi Komunistii Tojikiston)
- Turkmenistan: Democratic Party (Türkmenistanyň Demokratik partiýasy)
- Uzbekistan: People's Democratic Party of Uzbekistan (O'zbekistan Xalq Demokratik Partiyasi, OXDP or PDPU)

5

Authoritarian Successor Parties in Sub-Saharan Africa

Into the Wilderness and Back Again?

Rachel Beatty Riedl

The empirical record in Sub-Saharan Africa provides a wealth of variation in former authoritarian ruling parties' fates. Many have disappeared completely, wiped out of existence through violent upheavals, coups, and other extra-institutional changes of government, or by democratization processes that left these parties in the dustbins of history. Others survived the transition from the single-party era of the 1970s and 1980s to the period of multiparty elections beginning in the 1990s, but in the context of competitive authoritarian regimes (Levitsky and Way 2010). Finally, in some countries, they survived the transition to democracy and continued to contest elections, thus becoming authoritarian successor parties (ASPs). Eleven countries in Sub-Saharan Africa have ASPs today,[1] and of these, six have returned to executive power.[2] When and why are former authoritarian ruling parties able to survive – and in a handful of cases, thrive – under democracy? Given the relative rarity of this outcome and its importance in developing stable democratic regimes with well-institutionalized party systems (Riedl 2014), this empirical puzzle is of great theoretical interest.

One might expect that a number of factors would affect the ability of a former authoritarian ruling party to transform successfully and compete in a new democratic regime, such as the economic performance of the old regime; the financial and organizational resources amassed by the party during the authoritarian period; the economic performance of the new democratic regime; or ideological positioning. None of these factors, however, appear to be particularly important in Sub-Saharan Africa. Authoritarian *ruling* parties attempting to make the transition to authoritarian *successor* parties have been

---

[1] These are Cape Verde, Ghana, Guinea-Bissau, Kenya, Malawi, Namibia, Niger, São Tomé and Príncipe, Senegal, Sierra Leone, and Zambia.
[2] These are the African Party for the Independence of Cape Verde (PAICV), Ghana's National Democratic Congress (NDC), Guinea-Bissau's African Party for the Independence of Guinea and Cape Verde (PAIGC), the Association for the Rebirth of Madagascar (AREMA), Niger's National Movement for the Development of Society (MNSD), and Sierra Leone's All People's Congress (APC).

little constrained by their policy and performance past. Nor has the accumulation of resources in the past been a deciding factor, given that most party resources came directly from the fusion with the state (Zolberg 1966) and since material accumulation was often personalized rather than organizational (see LeBas, Chapter 6, this volume). Further, economic conditions do not seem to have encouraged either increased nostalgia for or distrust of the former authoritarian ruling party.

Instead, this chapter argues that authoritarian successor parties' eventual regeneration and electoral success is contingent upon their ability to keep political elites and local social brokers within the party fold and limit defections. Whether or not ASPs can keep these brokers on board in the new era of democratic competition is in turn largely based on how the party ruled during the authoritarian era: did it create strong clientelistic linkages with local social brokers (such as chiefs and religious leaders at the community level) that incorporated these brokers *into* the party (Riedl 2014)? Where the authoritarian ruling party used state-sponsored clientelism to build partisan identity and loyalty, it could establish social rootedness that could endure beyond a temporary loss of power for the ASP decades later. Local brokers *became* the party, and their regions became party strongholds.

In addition to authoritarian legacies of specific forms of clientelism, newly crafted electoral institutions affect ASPs' ability to limit defections by regulating the process of new party formation and party-switching. Finally, the historical and autonomous sources of cohesion of the new ruling party – that is, the former democratic opposition party that takes power after the transition to democracy – can assist ASP survival by limiting defection. Where the new ruling party is cohesive, it is less willing to accept defections from the ASP. As LeBas (Chapter 6, this volume) suggests with reference to the "competitive landscape," I argue that opposition cohesion facilitates a polarized party system and a defined incumbent–opposition cleavage, which limits party-switching and systemic volatility overall. On both sides of the cleavage, internal cohesion is a double-edged sword: it assists party survival by hardening partisan boundaries and limiting defection while inadvertently fostering the opposition's cohesion as well. In sum, these three key factors – authoritarian inheritance, electoral institutions, and new ruling party cohesion – can facilitate the very difficult pathway to ASP success by determining social support for the party and minimizing pressures for party fragmentation, defection, and proliferation.

Although, in theory, an authoritarian ruling party could become an authoritarian successor party without losing power (provided that a transition to democracy had occurred),[3] in practice, all ASPs in Africa have lost power

---

[3] As Slater and Wong (2013: 717–718) put it, "[Authoritarian] *ruling parties can democratize without losing office.* For authoritarian parties, democratization entails the concession to *hold* free and fair elections, but not necessarily to *lose* them. Hence they can maintain incumbency without maintaining authoritarianism." Most eventually lose power, however. As Loxton

(which in fact triggered the transition to democracy in this volume's definition). Prior to the 1990s, most African countries were formally one-party regimes. With the end of the Cold War and a wave of political and economic changes across Africa, multiparty competition was introduced in nearly every country, which resulted in a range of new democracies *and* competitive authoritarian regimes (Young 2012). The cases where we can identify an authoritarian successor party are those in which the authoritarian incumbent lost power in democratic elections, democracy (or semi-democracy) was maintained over successive elections,[4] and the former authoritarian ruling party remained a viable competitor in the new regime.

Suddenly finding themselves out of power – that is, in the opposition – these ASPs had to wrestle with the obstacles faced by all opposition parties. Opposition parties in Sub-Saharan Africa are particularly disadvantaged because of the twin historical legacies of centralized executive power and party–state fusion that inordinately benefits the incumbent (van de Walle 2003). As in many developing democracies, being "in the wilderness" of opposition makes it exceptionally difficult to sustain clientelistic networks of voter support. Without the financial resources of the state and officeholders to fund party activities and candidates, opposition parties often struggle to mobilize followers.

Authoritarian successor parties' success, therefore, hinges on their ability to mitigate and overcome the challenges intrinsic to *all* opposition parties in Africa. However, as this chapter argues, ASPs are often in a *better* position than other types of opposition parties to rise to the challenge because they can build upon their authoritarian inheritance. In particular, they sometimes inherit a transferrable bank of clientelistic networks, which they can use to mobilize for successful electoral competition (see Kitschelt and Singer, Chapter 1, this volume). Where these clientelistic networks of the past fostered not only a flow of resources but also developed partisan loyalty by *incorporating* local social brokers into the party's official hierarchy, the partisan affiliation endured even after the party lost its connection to the state's coffers. By contrast, where the regime tried to bypass and *substitute* these local power brokers with its own

---

discusses in the Conclusion (this volume), the only case of an ASP that has never lost power is the Democratic Party of Socialists of Montenegro (DPS). This is likely a product of its short history; Montenegro has only been an independent country since 2006.

[4] These are countries that meet the minimalist definition of democratic transition proposed by Geddes, Wright, and Frantz (2014a) and applied by Loxton in the Introduction of this volume. Critically, this set of countries excludes competitive authoritarian regimes (Levitsky and Way 2010), where authoritarian ruling parties from the single-party era often maintained power despite the introduction of multiparty elections. In addition to those identified in this volume, I add Cape Verde and São Tomé and Príncipe (excluded from Geddes, Wright, and Frantz's data set due to their small population size), as well as Zambia (excluded for a supposed reversion to authoritarianism prior to the second multiparty election; I include it here because of the general similarity of its regime to other countries scored as democratic during this period).

party or state representatives, the party tended to suffer defections of these brokers – and therefore lose clientelistic networks – after the transition to democracy.

5.1 AUTHORITARIAN SUCCESSOR PARTIES: WITHER OR THRIVE?

There is great variation in the performance of ASPs across Sub-Saharan Africa. Some have been very successful. Ghana's National Democratic Congress (NDC) is one of the most successful ASPs in the world. It has retained continuity on many core dimensions of the party, including its organization, leadership, clientelistic networks, and voter base. Although it lost power in 2000, it was able to leverage its authoritarian inheritance to return to power in 2008 after eight years in opposition (and again in 2012). Although the NDC lost the 2016 presidential election, its strong performance nevertheless demonstrated the party's strength throughout the national territory. The party has also been able to evolve beyond the linkage to a single charismatic individual, party founder and former president Jerry John Rawlings.[5] In short, the NDC has demonstrated both remarkable durability and internal evolution. Other successful ASPs include Sierra Leone's All People's Party (APC), Guinea-Bissau's African Party for the Independence of Guinea and Cape Verde (PAIGC), the Movement for the Liberation of São Tomé and Príncipe (MLSTP), and the African Party for the Independence of Cape Verde (PAICV). Ghana's NDC, Sierra Leone's APC, Guinea-Bissau's PAIGC, and Cape Verde's PAICV have all returned to executive power after spending time in the opposition, while São Tomé and Príncipe's MLSTP regained an absolute majority of legislative seats in 1998 (though not the presidency).[6]

This success stands in marked contrast to the fate of most other former authoritarian ruling parties in Sub-Saharan Africa. Several such parties did not manage to survive the transition to democracy. In Benin and Mali, authoritarian ruling parties were wiped out during the transition to multiparty competition, never to be reconstituted.[7] Others attempted the

---

[5] In this respect, it is similar to parties such as Peronism in Argentina and the Democratic Revolutionary Party (PRD) in Panama, which also managed to transcend their founding leaders (see Loxton and Levitsky, Chapter 3, this volume).

[6] In 2011, the former presidential candidate of São Tomé and Príncipe's MLSTP won, but by running as an independent, and the party's future is uncertain. Madagascar's authoritarian successor party, the Association for the Rebirth of Madagascar (AREMA), returned to power in 1996, but has since declined precipitously and no longer has parliamentary representation.

[7] In Benin, the authoritarian ruling party (the People's Revolutionary Party of Benin, PRPB) collapsed during the transition to democracy. However, the former dictator, Mathieu Kérékou, achieved the astounding feat of returning to power as an independent candidate, with a new political platform and a new religion. Indeed, he sacrificed the PRPB in order to salvage his own reinvention (Banegas 2003). For more on former dictators who are democratically elected back into office, see Conclusion (Loxton, this volume).

transition to multipartism and participated in initial democratic elections, only to fade away with time. Examples include the United National Independence Party (UNIP) in Zambia, the National Party in South Africa, and the Kenya African National Union (KANU). Finally, a few ASPs have continued to exist and retained a stable and significant voter base, but have not been able to return to national power. Examples include the Socialist Party (PS) in Senegal and the Malawi Congress Party (MCP).[8]

These different trajectories represent the full range of possible outcomes in Africa. At one end of the spectrum, former authoritarian parties lose power, go "into the wilderness" as opposition parties, maintain and regenerate popular support, and later return to executive power (e.g., Ghana's NDC). At the other end of the spectrum, authoritarian ruling parties are wiped out during the transition from single-party rule, either through "national conferences" that claim sovereign power, military transitions that dissolve the party, or sweeping losses in the founding multiparty elections (e.g., Benin's PRPB). In the middle of the spectrum are ASPs that survive their initial defeat, but remain relatively marginal players in the new democratic regime (e.g., Senegal's PS). These outcomes can be seen in Figure 5.1, which shows ASPs' performances in elections after their loss of power, including the founding election in which this occurred. ASPs that have crossed the 50 percent threshold to attain a majority of legislative seats sit above the dashed line. Mali and Benin are represented only by dots at 0 percent in the founding elections, to represent visually their disappearance. The remaining parties managed to maintain themselves in electoral competition, but have not returned to power.

Unlike ASPs in some parts of the world, ASPs in Sub-Saharan Africa have largely been free of policy constraints. Even where they were associated with particular agendas at some point in the past, much of this was easily shed and reinvented. Policy programs have therefore not been the determinative factor in ASP success on the continent. Instead, maintaining cohesion and limiting defection in a polarized incumbent–opposition party cleavage has been critical for ASP success. In her chapter in this volume (Chapter 6), LeBas also suggests the importance of the competitive landscape; this chapter identifies the mechanisms of authoritarian inheritance, electoral institutions, and new ruling party cohesion that shape the extent of polarization in the competitive landscape.

The ease with which party elites can leave their current party and form or join another party is the biggest threat to ASP success. Certain electoral institutions and the cohesion of the new ruling party limit the viability of new party formation or party-switching (*"transhumance,"* as it is known in the francophone countries). This facilitates ASP survival in the next regime context both by keeping its elites within the party and by limiting the size of

---

[8] Authoritarian successor parties in Niger and Madagascar have temporarily returned to power, but the role of intermittent coups and political instability in their return makes their trajectories substantially different from the above cases.

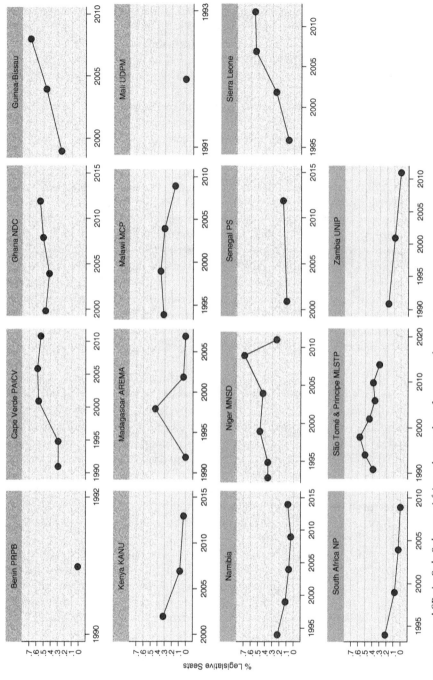

FIGURE 5.1 ASPs in Sub-Saharan Africa: electoral performance by country

the party playing field, thereby helping the ASP to remain as the main opposition player. Where party proliferation and party-switching are frequent (and incentivized by the rules of the game and/or new parties' internal structures), the ASP will have more difficulty keeping its most important members in the party fold and maintaining its prominence of place in the electoral playing field. For example, in democratic Zambia during the late 1990s and early 2000s, independent candidacies were permitted and the cohesion of the new ruling party that took power after democratization was extremely low. This made it viable for high-ranking officials from the new ruling party to break away in the run-up to elections and contest the presidency as independents (or with newly formed, loose movements surrounding a candidate). This phenomenon of breakaway candidacies likewise detracted from the ASP's survival since it could also lose its elites to the same strategy, and because it caused voters to turn their attention to upstart independents.

5.1.1 Difficulty of Being in the Opposition

The success of some African ASPs is surprising. Once ASPs lose office and go into opposition, they confront the incredibly difficult situation faced by all opposition parties in Sub-Saharan Africa. Once out of power – "in the wilderness," so to speak – parties suffer from a lack of financial resources and frequent party-switching by members and officeholders. This is because power in Africa is extremely centralized (van de Walle 2003). This centralization, combined with a history of party–state fusion, means that the party in power benefits from tremendous incumbency advantages. It has largely unbridled authority to set its preferred agenda, fill the bureaucracy with stalwarts, distribute public resources to supporters, and use state resources to its own benefit.[9] Voters, politicians, and constituencies in opposition are frequently targeted for exclusion, even in basic public goods distribution (Franck and Rainer 2012). Opposition parties must rely upon private resources for support, which is particularly challenging in countries where much of the economy is tied to the state and/or dependent upon political favor for regulation and licensing (Arriola 2012). This means that opposition parties often must rely on the salaries and funds of their members of parliament, and the resources of would-be candidates, to fund party operations (Ichino and Nathan 2013).

Extreme centralization of power and party–state legacies also mean that there are major incentives for coattail voting and party-switching.[10] Neither

---

[9] On the history of party–state fusion, see Zolberg (1966). On the weakness of legislative opposition, see Barkan (2009).

[10] Coattail voting here refers to the tendency for a popular presidential candidate to attract votes for other candidates of the same party in an election. In Sub-Saharan Africa, the pressures to align party votes from the executive to the legislative to the local level are high in order to streamline resource distribution through the party and the state once elected.

voters nor individual politicians want to find themselves in the opposition and devoid of state resources. As such, citizens often vote for local and parliamentary candidates to correspond with the executive's party with the calculation that this will facilitate a better flow of resources to their constituency. This logic explains why divided governments in Africa are extremely rare. Politicians may also switch parties following an alternation in the executive.[11] Therefore, we see frequent instances of party-switching as well as grand coalitions that include almost all parties in the executive's majority, leaving few parties in the formal opposition.[12] These strategies further weaken opposition parties, making it difficult for voters to differentiate the opposition from the incumbent, weakening their financial and organizational bases, and draining members and officeholders from their core.

5.1.2 Potential for ASP Success

Given the obstacles that opposition parties in Africa face, authoritarian successor parties find it difficult to survive in the wilderness of opposition. Yet, while ASPs must grapple with the challenges of opposition, they sometimes possess certain advantages that other opposition parties lack. Specifically, they may be the beneficiaries of *authoritarian inheritance*, such as material resources, political experience and formation, clientelistic networks, and a past record of governance, which they can draw upon to sustain themselves while in opposition (see Loxton, Chapter 1, this volume; Grzymala-Busse 2002 and Chapter 5, this volume; Kitschelt and Singer, Chapter 2, this volume). Authoritarian inheritance, however, is not automatic. For African ASPs, it is largely based on the party's built-up stock of loyalty and partisan identity among internal party elites and local social brokers supporting the party over the prior decades when patronage was flowing from the party–state. Developing strong local brokers during the authoritarian era entailed preferential treatment of regions with such hierarchical leadership (Koter 2013); language and development policy that reify brokers' position and power within the community; state aid flowing directly to village headmen and territorial chiefs; civil service jobs; and educational opportunities. As LeBas (Chapter 6, this volume) suggests in the case of Malawi, this created "loyal MCP cadres in the multiparty period." Where the authoritarian ruling party was sufficiently embedded, the fate of local brokers became aligned with that of the party, fostering an enduring identity.

---

[11] The frequency of this, of course, depends to some degree on electoral rules regarding party-switching and maintaining one's office, which will be discussed in greater detail later in the chapter.

[12] See Slater and Simmons (2013). See also Lupu and Riedl (2013) for a further discussion of strategic party calculations under conditions of political uncertainty.

ASPs in Sub-Saharan Africa 183

The particular inheritance from the authoritarian period is the first key variable in explaining variation in authoritarian successor party success in the democratic period (Grzymala-Busse 2002; Hicken and Kuhonta 2011; Riedl 2014). ASPs need to maintain internal elite cohesion and stable links to their voting base once they are in the opposition.[13] Building on Riedl (2014), this chapter argues that they are much more likely to be able to do this where they earlier pursued strategies of broad-based social *incorporation* of rural brokers during the authoritarian period. This strategy was not simply one of clientelistic distribution; it was also one of bringing local authorities into the party hierarchy to make them part of the enduring organization. It resulted in lasting linkages of support between local leaders and political elites in the authoritarian ruling party. To be sure, there were defections when these parties lost power during the transition to democracy; all parties that go into the opposition tend to lose some support. However, those that had pursued the alternative strategy of state-sponsored *substitution* – that is, introducing state and party agents into the local social hierarchy to replace local leaders and establish the party's predominance – were much more prone to massive and ongoing defections of their voting base and party officials. By contrast, building strong clientelistic and party organizational linkages with local social brokers made them less autonomous and brought their social authority into the party's inheritance.[14] Indeed, after these parties lost power, they relied upon the material and social resources of the local brokers to maintain their clientelistic network, often through positions as MPs, as governors, or as civil servants. This provided a superior basis for maintaining social support and clientelistic networks in the long term, and thus increased the likelihood of the former authoritarian ruling party surviving as an authoritarian successor party after the transition to democracy.

A second factor that may give authoritarian successor parties an advantage over other types of opposition parties is that they might have had a direct hand in shaping electoral institutions. The significant electoral institutions that contribute to ASP success are those that encourage cohesion within both the ASP and the new ruling party. Beneficial electoral institutions include those that make it more difficult for candidates to switch parties (such as limits on floor

---

[13] Maintaining party elites is critical for ASP success and endurance. This is because most party activities and clientelistic networks are funded by the party elite, through their salaries as members of parliament while in the opposition and through their businesses (often established during the authoritarian era).

[14] LeBas (Chapter 6, this volume) suggests that a decentralized patronage structure based on individuals makes parties more prone to defection after defeat. However, these authoritarian strategies used patronage *and* party positions to make local social elites and the party synonymous. The result was party structures that were fortified by local authority rather than opposed by it.

crossing in parliament);[15] those that reinforce an opposition-versus-incumbent dynamic rather than encouraging large coalition bandwagoning (as some electoral systems do); those that make it more difficult for new parties to form (such as organizational and territorial requirements that create high barriers for entry); and rules that govern coalition formation and alliances (regulations on when and how electoral and parliamentary alliances can be formed). All of these can help to structure party competition and reinforce party system institutionalization, which can help the ASP to survive in the long term (Riedl 2014).

The third factor is the cohesion of the new ruling party (that is, the party of the former democratic opposition that takes power after the transition to democracy). While this affects all new opposition parties' chances of success, ASPs are particularly threatened by elite defections to the new ruling party. Where the new ruling party is particularly cohesive and well organized internally, it is more difficult for members of the ASP to defect to the new ruling party, which limits ASP elite defections significantly.[16] Where the new ruling party's cohesion helps to structure the electoral playing field into an incumbent-versus-opposition dynamic (as opposed to ruling parties that accept all existing parties into a large governing coalition), this helps to maintain the utility and cohesion of the ASP itself. As the new ruling party takes power, its own historical process of formation, particular characteristics, and social base contribute to the nature of the new party system. Where the new ruling party is more cohesive, this limits systemic volatility, party members' ease of movement across party lines, and frequently shifting coalitions. Further, where the new ruling party is more cohesive, it is generally constructed without members of the former authoritarian ruling party. Here again, earlier authoritarian strategies may shape the cohesion of the new ruling party; however, the new ruling party may also have independent sources of cohesion (LeBas 2011; Levitsky and Way 2012).

In sum, the biggest threat to ASP endurance and success is the defection of both internal party elites and local brokers who command their own loyal followings in the electorate. This means that maintaining the

---

[15] Many of the new democracies in Sub-Saharan Africa have anti-defection clauses in their constitutions (twenty-four countries), which require elected officials to give up their parliamentary seat if they officially change parties (Janda 2009; Nikolenyi 2011). In highly stable party systems, such as Ghana, this keeps party members on one side of the aisle or the other, and contributes to the internal cohesion and durability of the ASP. In more volatile party systems, where parties can move in and out of coalitions supporting the executive, shifting is likely to increase in the run-up to elections as candidates assess the different parties' chances.

[16] Constitutional restrictions against elected officials switching parties are similar in most countries across the continent (Janda 2009). However, the level of implementation (whether an elected official must immediately give up his or her seat and face a by-election if he or she chooses to change party affiliation) varies, as does the level of welcome given by the new ruling party to former members of the authoritarian successor party.

ASPs in Sub-Saharan Africa

adherence of party elites and local brokers is of paramount importance. This allows voters to be mobilized, material resources and organization to endure, and parties to reconstitute themselves. Authoritarian inheritance, electoral institutions, and the character of the new ruling party all contribute to the ASP's cohesion, and thus its ability to retain internal political elites and local brokers.

5.1.3 ASP Success over Time

These three variables – authoritarian inheritance, electoral institutions, and new ruling party cohesion – are tightly interwoven at the moment of the transition to multiparty elections, as the authoritarian ruling party's legacy of power accumulation impacts its ability to select electoral rules and party registration requirements. Paradoxically, when the authoritarian ruling party is strong enough to initially resist full democratization and remain in power during a competitive authoritarian spell, this can actually help to strengthen the cohesion and organization of the democratic opposition. In such circumstances, if the opposition is to have any hope of winning elections and pushing for full democratization, it has to be organized, cohesive, and socially connected. By contrast, where authoritarian ruling parties are immediately swept out of office with the onset of multiparty elections, opposition parties are generally mass-based, heterogeneous movements, able to push down the door of authoritarian rule only because the door is rotten, not because the opposition itself is strong. To be sure, the cohesion of the opposition (which later becomes the new ruling party after the transition to democracy) is the result of several factors, some of them specific to the party in question (e.g., historic and ideational sources of cohesion). However, the dominance of the authoritarian ruling party during a competitive authoritarian spell can serve as a focal point that creates incentives for the opposition to cohere and build a multiethnic, nationally organized political party (Riedl 2014). In short, both the nature of the new ruling party and a country's electoral institutions are shaped by the former authoritarian ruling party (Figure 5.2).

Over time, the linkage between these three variables is likely to fade, as the nature of the new ruling party and the electoral rules take on a life of their own in the newly competitive environment. Authoritarian inheritance continues to affect the ASP's ability to maintain social support while in opposition. However, the character of the new ruling party has its own foundations that can begin to shape its cohesion and organization, and it may also choose to modify the electoral rules. Thus, the effect of authoritarian inheritance on the new party system and electoral rules is likely to diminish over time – though it continues to have an impact on the durability of social support for the ASP.

Because electoral institutions are themselves adapted by political parties, the new ruling party may opt to change the institutions created by the former authoritarian ruling party. This contributes to new party dynamics over time. Parties adapt their strategies to the electoral system and party registration

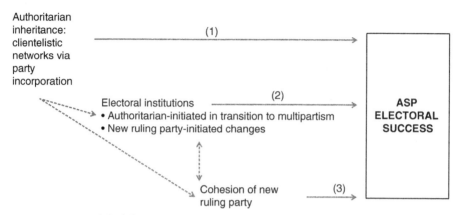

FIGURE 5.2 Model of the argument

requirements of the moment, but they also seek to transform the institutional setting that translates their strategies into outcomes (Benoit 2004; Tsebelis 1990). Therefore, where there is short-term congruence between the interests of the ruling party and the existing electoral rules, there is the potential for institutional continuity. But due to the prevalence of supermajorities in the legislature and executive centralization in Africa (Barkan 2008), when there is incongruence between the electoral institutions and the perceived short-term interests of the new ruling party, these rules can change.

Interestingly, rule changes often have long-term unintended consequences for the strength and cohesion of the ASP and/or the new ruling party that implements the rule change (O'Neill 2003). At the end of periods of competitive authoritarianism, when authoritarian ruling parties are concerned about their future electoral prospects, they have tended to enact reforms that (1) further advantage their proportion of votes to seats in the legislature and (2) attempt to fragment the growing opposition by lowering barriers to party registration. These steps serve the short-term objectives of the party, but they may have long-term negative repercussions in terms of party fragmentation, splits, and proliferation – the biggest threats to ASP success.

The cohesion of the new ruling party is important because where it has independent and enduring sources of unity, it can limit party proliferation and fragmentation. This, in turn, can help sustain the viability of the ASP and limit defections to the new ruling party. If the new ruling party lacks cohesion, it is more likely to suffer ongoing defections to newer opposition parties, which also tend to bleed support from the ASP. If the party system is volatile and inchoate, this creates frequent opportunities for party-switching and lessens the value of the incumbent/opposition divide. Just as isomorphic pressures during the competitive authoritarian period can contribute to the cohesion of the democratic opposition, once that opposition wins power (becoming the new ruling party), its own character, origins, resources, and sources of historical unity can help to create a stable pole in the party system around which competition is organized. This organizing force helps to sustain the ASP, whereas continual splits from the new ruling party to form even newer parties will increase volatility and make ASP endurance more difficult.

5.1.4 The Insignificance of Economic Performance

Neither the performance record of the former authoritarian ruling party nor that of the new ruling party has a significant impact on the likelihood of the ASP returning to power.[17] While economic development is a valence issue of great importance, the lack of overall policy debate in Africa about the management of the economy is related to a greater concern over the distribution of resources and public services (Bleck and van de Walle 2013). These resources and public services can come from a variety of sources, such as MP constituency development funds, official development assistance or other forms of international aid, NGOs and religious associations, and the like. Therefore, while constituents assess the performance of presidential and legislative candidates, they do so in an environment that generally lacks polarized debate on macroeconomic policy and clear indicators of local development.[18]

Thus, an authoritarian ruling party's performance in office does not necessarily indicate whether it is likely to survive as an ASP. Indeed, there is no obvious pattern between the economic performance of the authoritarian regime and ASP success. Many of the African countries that democratized had middling to poor economic performance in the 1980s: in some of these countries, the authoritarian ruling party was completely dissolved during the transition to democracy (e.g., Benin, Mali), whereas in others, a viable ASP emerged. South Africa's level of GDP per capita was well above the rest of the continent, but the National Party's performance declined precipitously throughout the 1990s. Ghana's economic performance in the 1980s was marginally improving, and it led the continent in implementing neoliberal reforms, which increased the flow of development aid but also required short-term adjustments for constituents (Herbst 1993). The NDC went on to enjoy great success as an ASP. However, Kenya's equivalent productivity gains during the 1980s did not result in a strong performance as an ASP, nor did Senegal's economic decline pose the biggest obstacle to the Socialist Party's return to power (see Figure 5.3).

The economic performance of the new ruling party after the transition to democracy also does not appear to have had a significant impact on whether the

---

[17] See van de Walle (2001) for a broader view of African political economy and why this continues to be the case.
[18] However, in countries facing threats to national integrity, constituents may assess party performance based on the provision of security.

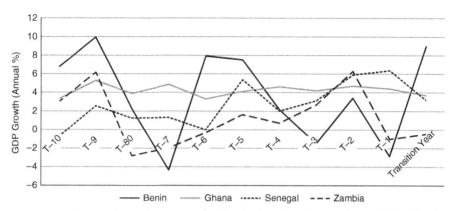

FIGURE 5.3 Economic performance of authoritarian incumbent prior to defeat: Benin, Ghana, Senegal, and Zambia

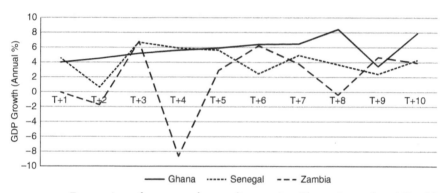

FIGURE 5.4 Economic performance of new ruling parties: Ghana, Senegal, and Zambia

ASP returned to power. Even where the new ruling party was eventually voted out of office, it was not necessarily due to nostalgia for the better economic times of the past. In fact, these new ruling parties were often replaced not by the ASP, but by even newer opposition parties (as in Zambia and Kenya). And in Cape Verde, despite the new ruling party's stellar economic performance, the PAICV was still voted back into office in 2001 (See Figure 5.4).

In the following sections, I examine the trajectories of ASPs in Ghana, Senegal, Zambia, and Benin. These four cases represent the full spectrum of success and failure of ASPs in Africa (Table 5.1).[19] In Ghana, the most successful case, the NDC maintained broad-based social support after going

---

[19] Strategies of incorporation and substitution are coded according to interview data in the four cases with local social brokers active throughout the authoritarian period (n=261), as well as primary documents of party strategy for mobilizing grassroots support and authority (Riedl 2014).

TABLE 5.1 *Case selection and independent variable measures*

Country	ASP name	(1) Authoritarian legacy of social rootedness	(2) Electoral institutions	(3) Cohesion of new ruling party	ASP electoral success
Ghana	NDC	High: Incorporation	Authoritarian party selected: SMD; high barriers to party registration; administrative decentralization	High: historical, organizational, and ideological cohesion	High: regained exec. power and leg. majority
Senegal	PS	High: Incorporation	Authoritarian party selected: mixed electoral system adjusted to advantage incumbent; decreased barriers to party registration over time; deliberate attempts to fragment opposition through coalition legalization	Low: 2000 transition catalyzed by coalition of main opposition party and two authoritarian elite defection parties, lacked durable unity	Mid/low: remains significant member of governing and oppos. coalitions; ~10 percent national support; mayor of capital city
Zambia	UNIP	Low: Substitution	Authoritarian party selected: low barriers to party registration; SMD system insufficient to limit national party proliferation	Low: heterogeneous "movement" of disparate interests; lacked territorial and procedural org.	Low: gradually lost support to other oppos. parties; no longer exists
Benin	PRPB	Low: Substitution	Transitional national conference selected: low barriers to party registration; incomplete national parties can submit candidates for PR list in multimember constituencies	Low: independent candidate created personalist party for legislative coalition bandwagoning	Fail: dissolved prior to founding multiparty elections and never reconstituted

into opposition in 2000 and was returned to power in 2008 (and again in 2012). In Senegal, a less successful case, the PS experienced internal elite splintering, but continued to exist, thanks to deeply rooted social linkages. In Zambia, an even less successful case, UNIP's unstable social base allowed the floodgates to open in the democratic transition period, with local brokers and party elites defecting en masse. Finally, in Benin, a case of total failure, the PRPB suffered a full-blown collapse during the transition to democracy. In each of these case studies, I describe whether the former authoritarian ruling party had followed a strategy of incorporation or substitution during the authoritarian period, and how this affected their ability to succeed as ASPs in the democratic period. These cases demonstrate the enduring impact of authoritarian inheritance on parties' ability to make the leap from authoritarian *ruling* parties to authoritarian *successor* parties.

5.2 GHANA'S SUCCESSFUL ASP: A PARTY'S CONTINUITY IN TRANSFORMATION

The authoritarian ruling party in Ghana, the National Democratic Congress (NDC), successfully transitioned to an ASP in 2000 and regained executive power in 2008 (and again in 2012, but lost narrowly in 2016). The main reason it could do this was because it enjoyed the stable support of local brokers forged throughout the national territory during the authoritarian period – both the single-party period beginning in 1981 and the competitive authoritarian period from 1992 to 2000 (Owusu 1996). Given the continuing importance of chieftancy in Ghana, the NDC decided to incorporate local elites into the party and mobilize their followers as supporters of the party (Pryce and Oidtmann 2014). The grassroots national territorial strategy of early party-building mapped out this strategy of incorporation (Directives Principles of State Policy PNDCL 42). The strong linkages were the key to mobilizing support for the NDC, as the party sought grassroots incorporation to provide "a social base as a foundation for their rule" (Gyimah-Boadi 1993: 109). The NDC further appointed chiefs to high-ranking ministerial positions and created a vast number of new local-level administrators in the new decentralization agenda (Ayee 2004; Ninsin and Drah 1987).

The NDC controlled the transition from one-party rule to multipartism with great success, transforming itself and remaining in power during the 1992–2000 period of competitive authoritarianism (Levitsky and Way 2010). During this period, the NDC further entrenched itself at the local level through targeted public service projects (Briggs 2012), and local governance reforms designed to incorporate local brokers into the machinery of state administration. Many of these positions – decentralized administration and civil service – did not simply disappear when the NDC lost power for the first time in 2000 and provided the party a stable core of supporters and continued salaries and resources for local-level patrons.

Given the way the party had previously ruled, the NDC was well positioned to keep its brokers on board, limiting defections and maintaining social support through the established networks. After the NDC lost the 2000 election and went into opposition, its local brokers remained loyal to the party. They supported it by carrying out activities and maintaining offices in each constituency, and the party continued to enjoy the support of just under 50 percent of the electorate. The presence of NDC personnel (the local brokers who were integrated into the party base) actively meeting with citizens and responding to community issues at the party's headquarters maintained the party's visibility and relevance to local voters. Because these local leaders had been integrated into the party as officials in prior decades, they continued to animate the party's activities and represent the party in the eyes of their followers.

The NDC also linked its party leaders and local brokers through an extensive decentralization agenda in the late 1980s and throughout the 1990s, to create a system of local government based on nonpartisan elected district assemblies. These district assemblies further incorporated key local notables into the party and provided them positions of administrative responsibility that would continue after the NDC lost power. Their nonpartisan basis meant that they could be retained even if the NDC lost power at the national level (Riedl and Dickovick 2014). These local linkages were an enduring source of support for the party, as well as channels of material and administrative resources that helped it to retain its clientelistic networks while in opposition.

In addition to enjoying the continued support of local brokers, the NDC was helped by its privileged position in the shaping of new electoral institutions. The NDC's goal was to make it more difficult for new opposition parties to form. In doing so, it minimized party proliferation; enhanced the opposition's territorial reach, internal organization, and cohesion; and created institutional incentives for the NDC to maintain its own cohesion, as well. In the transition to multipartism (though not yet full democracy), the NDC enacted electoral rules that it believed would help it to maintain its territorial organization and the loyalty of local brokers. There were three key electoral rules: eligibility rules for party formation (which created high barriers to entry for new parties, and thus made it less likely that NDC officials would defect and try to form their own parties), single-member district plurality electoral system, and a decentralization agenda. This decentralization agenda installed loyal local brokers as party agents into the state bureaucracy and as nonpartisan elected officials, thus providing a persistent source of material and administrative support to party loyalists at the local level. These initiatives were taken at the end of single-party rule in 1992, entrenched during the eight years of competitive authoritarianism (1992–2010), and provided a durable foundation for ASP maintenance and a return to power in 2008 (and reelection in 2012). The NDC resisted the opportunity to change the electoral system at the end of the competitive authoritarian period, an instinct that helped maintain the shape of the party system and the cohesion of the NDC over the longer term. This was likely because they expected to win under the rules that were in place; however, an unintended consequence was that these rules helped the NDC to remain united while in opposition and eventually to return to power.

Authoritarian-era controls on party formation shaped electoral institutions as well as the nature of the opposition New Patriotic Party (NPP). The NDC maintained the authoritarian legal code and instruments of state repression throughout the party formation process and founding multiparty elections in 1992. The government maintained a ban on party formation throughout most of the period when the new electoral rules were being crafted, in an attempt to maintain its own prerogatives. The Political Parties Law of 1992 (PNDCL 281) imposed very demanding requirements for party formation, including full territorial organization and founding member representation in every district (160 in total). This kept the majority of NDC elites within the party, as they would have had difficulty starting their own nascent parties (Ninsin and Drah 1991; Oquaye 2004). Over time, these early control measures actually helped to facilitate the cohesion of the NPP, particularly after the party's victory and ascent to power in 2000.

While the single-member district plurality rules did not *cause* NPP or NDC cohesion, they helped to reinforce it over time, by decreasing the incentives of party officials within both parties to split and form new parties. At times, both the NDC and NPP have faced internal succession battles and factionalization; during these moments, the electoral rules and tight competition of the two-party system helped prevent factions from splitting off (Bob-Milliar 2012).

Finally, the cohesion of the new ruling party, the NPP, was a significant factor in fostering a dualistic, polarized, incumbent–opposition cleavage, which contributed to ASP success over the longer term. The new ruling party's ideological and historical sources of party unity limited defections and party-switching from the NDC to the new government. The NPP was able to defeat the NDC in 2000 due to a combination of factors: sustained party organization building and national penetration (which were necessitated by the competitive authoritarian regime), an ethnic core of support in the Asante region, and a particular base of historic cohesion and resources supplied by a business elite (Ayee 2009). Moreover, the NPP's unique connection to an independence-era movement helped it to sustain its networks even during decades of authoritarianism, as affiliated members would regroup at important social events, such as the funerals of key founding leaders.

This level of elite cohesion helped maintain a dyadic competition between the NPP and the NDC, making it difficult for any NDC opportunists to jump ship to the new ruling party. There were no broad power-sharing arrangements or grand coalitions that would allow NDC members to join the new ruling

ASPs in Sub-Saharan Africa 193

party. And because the NPP had been staunch in its opposition while the NDC was in power during the competitive authoritarian era, the NDC was compelled to play the same role. Serving as a clear and identifiable opposition may starve an authoritarian successor party of much-needed resources, but it also positions it for an electoral return in future rounds of competition. A vocal critic of the NPP government, the NDC took its role in opposition seriously and set itself up for a return to the executive. This was made possible by the NPP's high level of cohesion, its lack of grand coalition strategy, and the dyadic competition that it created. The cohesion of the new ruling party and overall lack of party system fluidity, as well as the electoral institutions previously crafted by the NDC, intensified this continuity in party social support throughout the country and helped the ASP to return to power.

5.3 SENEGAL'S ASP: ENDURANCE AND DECLINE THROUGH ELITE DIVISIONS

Senegal's ASP, the Socialist Party (PS), remains an electoral contender today because of the strength of its linkages with traditional leaders across the countryside dating back to electoral mobilization in the pre-independence era. However, the party's support has dramatically declined since its loss of power in 2000. This is due to PS elites, who – making use of changes to the electoral system that the PS itself initiated when in power to fragment the opposition – have defected from the party to form new parties.

Given the ASP's middling but enduring performance in Senegal, the core factor contributing to success was the authoritarian inheritance that contributed a solid bank of loyal brokers for a significant period. Changes in the electoral rules over time and defections within the new ruling party limited its cohesion, and therefore hurt the ASP's ability to harden partisan boundaries and limit defection over the longer term.

The PS took power at independence in 1960 and ruled until its electoral defeat in 2000. Over the decades, the PS has had a number of different incarnations: nationalist independence party in a competitive, multiparty context; authoritarian ruling party in a single-party regime; authoritarian ruling party in a competitive authoritarian regime following the introduction of multipartism in the early 1980s; and an ASP since 2000.

During its years as an authoritarian ruling party, the PS (like the NDC in Ghana) pursued a national territorial strategy of broad-based incorporation and was able to garner the support of the rural masses through an alliance with the country's powerful and autonomous Islamic brotherhood leadership and traditional chiefdoms (Villalón 2006). This strategy created an authoritarian inheritance for the democratic period, by building partisan loyalty and clientelistic networks across the national territory. The religious organization of the country offered the PS the option of partnering with Islamic marabout leaders who had significant spiritual and patronage influence over the majority of peasants in rural areas, and who could direct their loyalties to the ruling party (Fatton 1987).[20] The PS built strong links with the marabouts and traditional leaders to assure the regime's hegemonic position, forming a tripartite relationship between chiefs, "saints," and the state (Diop and Diouf 2002a; Mbodji 1991). This incorporation strategy covered the geographic expanse of the country, integrating heterogeneous identity groups of tribe and religious sect, and earning significant support for the authoritarian regime from local elites who had influence over the majority of the population (Diop and Diouf 2002b).

When the PS eventually lost power in 2000, it was not because of a defection of local brokers from the party or mass rejection, but because of elite splits within the party at the top over the issue of succession (Resnick 2013). The defecting elites formed their own parties and took with them a portion of the clientelistic networks that the PS had previously cultivated. This split affected the cohesion of the new ruling party, the Senegalese Democratic Party (PDS), a coalition from the outset.

Despite losing power in 2000, many local brokers remained loyal to the PS, even given the incentives and opportunity to defect to the new ruling coalition. The enduring loyalty of these local brokers helped the PS to maintain a core base of support across the national territory (approximately 12–15 percent of the electorate). This buoyed the PS while in the wilderness and allowed it to survive under democracy. These ties were maintained because the local brokers had been successfully integrated into core party operations during previous decades, attaining positions of influence both within the party and in local government or the civil service. These local brokers then reciprocated support for the PS while the party was in opposition, providing material support to the party to maintain its clientelistic networks, funding rudimentary party activities at the local level, and mobilizing electoral support for the PS among the masses.

Electoral rules played an important role in first contributing to ASP survival by encouraging cohesion, and then limiting the ASP's success, by facilitating party-switching and overall fragmentation. Starting in 1976, the PS ended single-party rule, legalized "limited multipartism," and determined two acceptable opposition parties that would be allowed to register and compete. This set in motion a highly structured incumbent–opposition dynamic that gave cohesion to both sides and advantaged the authoritarian incumbent (Hartmann 2010; Kanté 1994). In 1978, the country held multiparty presidential and legislative elections, with two opposition parties hand-selected by the newly competitive authoritarian regime. By 1981, the PS decided to allow unlimited multipartism (Law No. 81–16 "*portant revision constitutionelle*") and began its long-term strategy of seeking to divide and fragment the opposition. This law

---

[20] Marabouts are religious leaders and Quranic scholars, often organized in elaborate hierarchies, who actively guide the lives of followers.

also established the mixed electoral system, to overrepresent the PS in the translation from votes to legislative seats (Vengroff and Creevey 1997). The system stipulated that sixty seats in the National Assembly would be allocated by proportional representation through a national party list, and sixty seats would be allocated through plurality vote in multimember constituencies (1–7 seats), in which the party that won a plurality at the department level would be allocated all seats in the constituency. This combination led to a natural advantage for the PS, which had a national territorial organization and could coordinate party lists in each constituency. It disadvantaged opposition parties, which had difficulty coordinating with one another, but also gave them a modicum of representation through the national PR list. The electoral reform of 1981 shifted the barriers to party formation from high to medium: its explicit goal was to encourage party fragmentation while also maintaining some restrictions to benefit the ruling party.[21]

In 1992, following rising social pressure for more political liberalization and succession battles, the PS opted to pursue further electoral reform. These reforms were designed to achieve short-term electoral advantages for the PS, but they ultimately sowed the seeds for both its loss of power in 2000 and its difficulties maintaining cohesion as an opposition party thereafter. Most critically, the 1992 electoral code authorized coalitions of parties to compete in elections, which was a major change and one that facilitated a vast proliferation of parties over the long term. Because the mixed electoral system required a united front to defeat the ruling PS, permitting electoral coalitions significantly changed the strategic value of forming a minority party. It allowed the opposition parties to maintain their individual leadership, but to coalesce temporarily in order to defeat the ruling party. The electoral reform also permitted independent candidacies and a host of reforms to increase the transparency and autonomy of the electoral process.

The elite defections leading up to and following the loss of power in 2000 were facilitated by critical changes that the PS had made to electoral institutions during the prior decades of competitive authoritarianism. During this prolonged period of PS domination, the opposition was beginning to develop strength as an alternative to the PS. The PS initiated electoral reform in 1981 and 1992 as short-term maneuvers designed to fragment the opposition and maintain a temporary electoral advantage. The long-term result was increasing volatility in the party system, the proliferation of new parties, and a slow slide of defections from the PS that greatly weakened the party.

---

[21] First, it required that parties competing for legislative seats have complete electoral lists, which disqualified small and emerging parties with popular leaders in many districts. Second, the election of candidates had to be governed by the party's list, which advantaged the stronger and better organized PS and limited the appeal of some popular and effective individual opposition candidates. Finally, it prohibited coalitions among parties, making the prospects for opposition victory even more unlikely (Hayward and Grovogui 1987).

When the PS was defeated in 2000 by an opposition coalition headed by the main opposition party, the PDS, the minority partners were important ex-PS elites who had splintered off to form their own parties: the Alliance of the Forces for Progress (AFP) and the Union for Democratic Renewal (URD). These two parties placed third and fourth, respectively, in the first round of the 2000 presidential elections and then threw their support to the PDS candidate in the second round. They then presented a coalition list ("Sopi," the Wolof word for "Change") for the 2001 legislative elections, given that the PDS was not able to win a majority of seats on its own. The legislative election was scheduled to follow the presidential election in order to increase the possibility for coattail voting for the newly elected coalition. The 1992 electoral reforms that allowed coalition lists therefore contributed to the eventual defeat of the PS, and thus its transition from an authoritarian ruling party to an authoritarian successor party.

In the longer term, the 1992 electoral reform set the stage for increased party system volatility and decreased party cohesion. Parties across the spectrum had less incentive to invest in territorial organization, as they could now easily make temporary coalitions to cover all constituencies. The mixed electoral system's overrepresentation for the ruling party encouraged coattail voting and reduced opposition viability. For both the new ruling party and the ASP (in opposition from 2000 onward), it became difficult to maintain internal cohesion and preserve its clientelistic networks.[22] Thus, for the PS as an authoritarian successor party, these changes to the country's electoral institutions decreased the utility of its authoritarian inheritance over time, as local brokers were torn between their loyalty to the party as a whole and their loyalty to a particular party patron every time one split off to form a new party in the pursuit of power.

In addition to the electoral rules, the cohesion of the new ruling party (which, in Senegal, began as the opposition party under authoritarian rule) shapes the competitive landscape in critical ways for ASP survival. The cohesion of the new ruling parties – the PDS after 2000 and then the Alliance for the Republic (APR) after 2012 – was also dramatically undermined by the successive electoral institutional changes. The weak cohesion of the PDS was highly detrimental to ASP success because the PDS (and later the APR) welcomed defections from the former authoritarian ruling party *and* was extremely vulnerable to ongoing defections from within. The personalized nature of the PDS meant that it lacked the cohesion and social rootedness that kept much of the PS elite within the party fold. The PDS had built its support over prior decades largely among the urban opposition camp, particularly among students and laborers. These were the natural constituencies available to it, as the PS had already incorporated

---

[22] This was also evident in key splits from the new ruling party, the PDS (such as Idrissa Seck's Rewmi party and Macky Sall's Alliance for the Republic, APR), and increased the likelihood of future alternation. This occurred in 2012, when Macky Sall won the presidency and his coalition APR/Benno Bokk Yakaar won the legislative elections.

rural voters into the party. The PDS, therefore, had a more limited social base from the outset. In order to overcome this challenge, it joined forces with some elite defectors from the PS. These PS defectors brought with them their local brokers, which contributed to the PDS's victory in the 2000 election. Thus, while the PDS had built a national infrastructure, its national majority was always contingent upon partnerships with other influential party leaders (defectors from the PS). This coalitional base of the new ruling elite contributed to a shifting competitive landscape, in which party elites across the board were not constrained from creating their own parties and linking up to the ruling party of the moment in order to attain the perquisites of power. As a result, the longer it spent in the wilderness, the harder it became for the PS to remain cohesive and prevent the defection of key party leaders.

As the new ruling party, the PDS also endeavored to lure aspiring politicians into its fold. However, internal factionalism made it difficult for the PDS to assign each new member a place within the party organization. New members and those acquired from other parties were assigned to ad hoc designations within the party in parallel to the official party structure, in order to avoid a complete revision of the party's leadership structure (Dahou and Foucher 2004). Furthermore, the PDS was a more personalist party (built around Abdoulaye Wade, its founder and Senegal's president from 2000 to 2012) that sought to minimize investment in party organization in order to position his son for internal succession. The PDS suffered from this leadership and began hemorrhaging party elites in the succession debates that ensued, who split off to form their own parties. These shifting affiliations further complicated the PS's position as the main party of opposition. As key party elites split off from the ruling PDS, they took up the mantle of opposition in preparation for the presidential and legislative elections of 2012. The PS ran its own candidate for president, but after placing fourth in the first round, it joined an alliance with the new opposition leader (Macky Sall of the APR) in the second round, in the hope of becoming part of a new ruling majority (Sall won the 2012 election). The PS also competed in the following legislative elections as part of this alliance. In sum, lack of cohesion within the new ruling party, the PDS, damaged the PS's viability and its status as Senegal's main opposition party. Party proliferation and shifting coalitions have limited the ASP's ability to maintain its local brokers over time, and thus reduced its electoral success.

5.4 ZAMBIA'S ASP: FAILED REGENERATION

In Zambia, a case of protracted ASP dissolution, the United National Independence Party (UNIP) was thwarted in its attempt at electoral resuscitation by the lack of durable, entrenched ties with local brokers across the countryside. UNIP ruled from independence in 1964 until 1991, lost power in the 1991 founding election, and then attempted an electoral comeback.[23] However, it lacked the necessary authoritarian inheritance of a loyal social base that it could mobilize for electoral support after going into opposition and dwindled into irrelevance.

Whereas the NDC in Ghana and the PS in Senegal had pursued a strategy of broad-based incorporation of traditional elites during the era of single-party rule, UNIP generally pursued a strategy of substitution in an effort to minimize the power of sectional leaders (rather than empower and ally with them, as in the incorporation strategy), which caused disenchantment and defections (Scott 1980). UNIP, the party that led Zambia to independence, focused on a modern economic base of urban and industrialized workers as its main constituency for support. It built a strong, centralized labor union, concentrating its power into a single federation and securing funding through mandatory affiliation of all laborers (whose union dues were automatically deducted from their pay) (Banda 1997). This strategy greatly increased the power of the union leadership – yet ironically created the infrastructure, organization, and resource base that would eventually contribute to the emergence of an unusually strong democratic opposition movement (LeBas 2011). The union's large membership, national leadership experience, and control over the state's key export commodity (copper) provided a foundation that, over time, became a challenge to the government (Bates 1971; Mwanakatwe 1994; Simutanyi and Mate 2006). UNIP's effort to create its own support base temporarily brought urban economic interests into a relationship with the party. However, the economic problems that began in 1975 with the slump of copper prices, balance of payment inequities through the 1980s, and major structural adjustment reforms in the late 1980s and early 1990s gradually pushed these groups to defect and left the regime without enduring allies of local brokers throughout the national territory (Burdette 1988; Gulhati 1989; Simmance 1973). By pursuing union nationalization and privileging manufacturing and large businesses over farming and small businesses, UNIP inadvertently supported the growth of groups that would eventually become key agents of the opposition rather than bulwarks of the status quo.

UNIP's authoritarian inheritance was built on the premise of replacing social authorities at the local level with state-appointed party agents. The party had a substantial territorial infrastructure, but was not socially rooted by including chiefs and other local authorities into the party and linking their fortunes. Similar to the urban labor union movement, the party organization and its affiliated structures substituted for building strong linkages within society.[24]

---

[23] The party was founded in 1959 in the run-up to independence and won a commanding victory in the pre-independence elections of 1964. UNIP instituted single-party rule in 1973 and retained single-party elections until the introduction of multiparty elections in 1991 – losing the founding election. Thus, UNIP never ruled in a competitive authoritarian regime, as Ghana's NDC and Senegal's PS did during the 1990s.

[24] The era of single-party rule in Zambia (the Second Republic of 1973–1991) favored the principle of party supremacy. UNIP's Central Committee took precedence over any parliamentary or governmental decisions, and the president of the party appointed all senior party and

While it temporarily provided material resources to fund the party's organization locally, it lacked sustainability because it did not build enduring local social support.

The electoral institutions crafted during the lead-up to multiparty elections facilitated the incredibly fluid nature of the entire party system, which UNIP initially thought would benefit it in the founding multiparty elections, but which hurt its cohesion and durability over time.[25] In the initial proposal for a transition to multiparty competition, UNIP calculated that it would do best to set very low requirements for political party registration. The new opposition movement, the Movement for Multiparty Democracy (MMD), was widely viewed as a transitional grouping attempting to dislodge the incumbent and lacking in cohesion (Posner 2005: 187). UNIP was conscious that it faced an electoral challenge and calculated that instituting very low requirements for party registration would encourage the opposition's immediate fragmentation into many smaller entities. UNIP also believed that by taking steps to proactively implement democratic reforms, it could further splinter the growing but rather incoherent opposition movement (Mwanakatwe 2003). UNIP believed the "MMD would divide quickly once political party registration was legalized, as it was not sustainable as a coherent entity in anything other than an oppositional call for change" (Mwanakatwe 1994: 207). The MMD was a product of the broad-based movement for democratic transition that brought together many different perspectives, interest groups, and representatives. Early party conferences were made up of a heterogeneous mix of business elites, labor, academics, ideological democrats, disenchanted youth, and early defectors from UNIP itself. UNIP therefore had an incentive to institute low barriers to entry for new parties, in order to encourage the disintegration of the MMD into multiple parties.

The MMD was aware of its internal differences, and thus sought to change the proposed electoral institutions and limit multipartism to three parties in order to shore up its own membership base and contribute to cohesion by limiting future defections to form new parties. However, UNIP still controlled the legislature as the single party, and thus implemented the low barriers to entry for new parties as a tool to encourage party fragmentation and

---

government officials. UNIP's Central Committee appointed party agents to organize the affairs of the party at the local level, imposing them upon the local communities' authority structure, and carefully managed the selection process of candidates at the local and national levels to minimize emerging factions and ensure loyalty to the party elite (Bratton 1992).

[25] As UNIP approached the transition to multipartism in 1990–1991, it retained formal decision-making control over the terms of the new electoral system through its single-party legislature (as in Senegal). However, it was pushed to implement reforms and systems well beyond its preferences (initially, to maintain single-party rule) because of the rising protests and mobilization of the nascent opposition. Political elites and local brokers alike migrated rapidly to the new, unwieldy, and heterogeneous Movement for Multiparty Democracy (MMD), which influenced UNIP strategy throughout the transition period.

proliferation. Had the MMD been able to implement its preferred rules to enhance cohesion, UNIP may, paradoxically, have survived as a formidable electoral challenger. Instead, this institutional crafting of low barriers to party formation contributed significantly to UNIP's unraveling over the long run by facilitating party proliferation and fragmentation.

The MMD won the founding multiparty elections in 1991 and ushered in a new era of democratic competition – and due to its overwhelming majority, also had the ability to change the electoral rules going forward. UNIP won 16 percent of legislative seats in this election. This demonstrated that it had maintained some of its base of support through the local party infrastructure built up through decades of state resources and investment. However, UNIP's support base continued to dwindle, since party elites lacked a social foundation for mobilizing support. The MMD implemented new eligibility rules specifically designed to limit the potential of UNIP to return to power. Relying on its overwhelming majority in the National Assembly, the MMD pushed through a constitutional amendment in 1996 that made only second-generation Zambians eligible for the office of president. This legislation was specifically designed to bar former president and UNIP candidate Kenneth Kaunda from running in the 1996 election. As a result, UNIP boycotted the 1996 presidential and legislative elections, further weakening its representative and material base.

Following UNIP's boycott, in the 2001 elections, the party won a mere 8.6 percent of legislative representation. In 2006, UNIP joined an opposition coalition in which it was a junior partner. In 2011, its presidential candidate (Kenneth Kaunda's son, Tilyenji Kaunda) won only 0.39 percent of the vote, and the party failed to win even a single legislative seat in the National Assembly. Despite property holdings and decades of party-state distribution, UNIP's clientelistic networks proved to be neither enduring nor sustainable in opposition. Unlike in Ghana and Senegal, local brokers had not been incorporated into the party's inner folds and were, therefore, free to form opportunistic alliances after the introduction of multiparty elections.

The new ruling party's lack of internal cohesion also posed a problem for UNIP to survive and regenerate as an ASP. The MMD had been united in its opposition to the UNIP regime enough to stick together for the founding multiparty elections in 1991. However, once it had won those elections and took power, it rapidly began to disintegrate (Larmer 2009). The MMD's diverse social base of former UNIP elites, businessmen, and union leaders, as well as democratic activists and intellectuals, laid the groundwork for early disagreements over democratic principles and leadership squabbles, which led to an ongoing trickle of defections from the party. In addition to lacking cohesion, the MMD did not possess a party organization built up over time and across the national territory. The temporary coalition of elites and interests that came together to form the MMD gave way to continual fragmentation and the formation of new parties. UNIP party officials followed suit, forming new entities either on their own or in partnership with MMD defectors. Because of the electoral institutions, each new defector from the MMD could easily form his own new party: all that was needed was to furnish a few documents listing the names of the party's leaders and pay an administrative fee. Therefore, instead of defecting elites returning to UNIP to forge a stronger opposition and bolster it as an ASP, party proliferation continued and exacerbated splits within all parties.

Despite a single-member district plurality electoral system, the number of parties at the national level remained high, with five to eight parties represented in the legislature throughout the 2000s. And the shifting landscape of parties changed rapidly as new splits created new parties and older parties faded away (Momba 2005). Indeed, the party that defeated the MMD in 2011, the Patriotic Front, was created through a defection of a former minister and high-ranking MMD official. Because the electoral system for president requires only a plurality victory in a single-round contest, successful candidates have needed only to garner a minimal coalition. This contributes to the fluid and volatile nature of the party system because it has not forced strategic coordination among the main opposition players to unite in a broad-based party. For example, the opposition's continual fragmentation allowed the MMD to remain in power with only 29 percent of the vote in 2001 and just over 40 percent in 2006 and 2008. This inchoate party system undermined UNIP's chances of remaining cohesive and enduring over time, with loyalists and internal elites gradually trickling away to join a host of new party start-ups. Over successive elections, key splits from the MMD resulted in the formation of new opposition parties, which displaced UNIP's role in the system and gradually led to its demise.

5.5 BENIN'S LACK OF ASP: AUTHORITARIAN DISINTEGRATION

Benin's authoritarian ruling party, the People's Revolutionary Party of Benin (PRPB), never contested a multiparty election, and thus never had the chance to become an authoritarian successor party. Instead, it was displaced from power in 1990 in the run-up to multiparty elections by a broad mix of civil society representatives holding a "national conference" to discuss proposed political reforms. The national conference declared itself sovereign, and the PRPB dissolved in the face of swelling opposition to its continued rule. The PRPB's lack of social support can be attributed to its earlier policies of state substitution during the late 1970s and 1980s, in which the party deliberately tried to neutralize the strength of the traditional chiefdoms in an attempt to consolidate its own rule. This led to the disintegration of the monarchy and left the regime without socially rooted partners – the types of partners that in Ghana (and, to a lesser extent, Senegal) laid the basis for the emergence of a strong ASP. The regime attempted (ultimately unsuccessfully) to completely overturn existing political, economic, and social structures, and substitute them with the control of the authoritarian ruling party (Banegas

2003).[26] The PRPB effectively neutralized the organizational capabilities of the traditional kingdoms, which had been the basis for sociopolitical mobilization in prior decades, and launched a highly repressive anti-feudal campaign against influential spiritual leaders (Bako-Arifari 1998; Bierschenk and de Sardan 1998; Magnusson 2001).

The PRPB's attempt to dismantle the traditional kingdoms and religious leaders required them to substitute one type of broker for another. To this end, the party instituted state agents at the local level who were meant to oversee party-led national development and distribute goods; this was meant to provide clientelistic co-optation. This strategy made the regime highly reliant on its continued ability to provide material benefits. The substitution strategy sought to install party–state agents and activities in the districts to mobilize the population, yet ultimately it could not substitute for the deep loyalty of society to traditional authorities. Despite significant party activities and related organs in the districts, the PRPB could not capture the loyalty of peasants or replace the social fabric that it was trying to thwart (Banegas 2003). So long as the PRPB was the sole legal authority, the party-regime reigned supreme; however, with the prospect of democratization, local elites rapidly rejected it and the party fell like a house of cards. The PRPB was dissolved during the transition to multipartism in 1990, lost control over the process for implementing new rules and state agents, and did not survive as an authoritarian successor party.

The new electoral rules selected by the national conference did not foster an environment ripe for ASP survival. Benin's emergent opposition forces favored extremely lax party registration requirements, to ensure that all new forces would be able to form and participate in founding multiparty elections (Dossou 2000). This assured that officials from the *ancien régime* could easily form new parties, join other movements, and avoid being tarnished by their association with the defunct PRPB (Ossou 1993). The former party elites of the PRPB quickly reinvented themselves. Indeed, even the former autocrat and PRPB founder, Mathieu Kérékou, was reelected as an independent in 1996 and 2001 (Houngnikpo and Decalo 2013).[27] Given this institutional context, association with the PRPB was more of a liability than an asset for participants in the old regime, and they rapidly abandoned it in favor of membership in new parties.

Further, the new ruling party (the Renaissance Party of Benin, RB) that replaced the PRPB and came to power in the founding legislative elections of

---

[26] The PRPB was founded in 1975 by then-ruling General Mathieu Kérékou. A new constitution in 1975 made it the sole legal party in the country, until it was displaced in the democratizing national conference in 1990.

[27] Kérékou was nicknamed the "chameleon" for his return to the presidency as a reinvented candidate. He had a new religion (evangelical), ideology (denouncing Marxism-Leninism and returning as a "democrat"), and political affiliation (independent), and barely mentioned his past economic policies or state management.

1991 lacked cohesion and contributed to the ongoing volatility and shape-shifting of the party system. Following the national conference, an independent candidate, Nicéphore Soglo, won the 1991 presidential elections and created the RB as a bandwagon party of supporters following his victory to organize for future legislative elections (Creevey, Ngomo, and Vengroff 2005). The RB was largely open to people of all stripes, leaving little incentive for a strong opposition party to develop. In the run-up to the next elections in 1996, independent candidates followed the same model, splintering off to form individualized machines that could easily be reattached to whichever faction won executive power. While these factors were not responsible for the demise of the PRPB, they contributed to a context in which it was highly unlikely that the PRPB would successfully regenerate as an ASP.

* * * *

These four cases represent the full range of ASP outcomes in Africa: from ASP success and a return to power in Ghana, to a middling performance in Senegal, to gradual dissolution in Zambia, to rapid evisceration in Benin. As this chapter has argued, these different levels of success were not due to these parties' economic management or past records in office. Political parties and their candidates were able to reinvent themselves in terms of policy positions as necessary. Instead, ASP success was the result of different authoritarian legacies: in those cases where the previous authoritarian regime had pursued a strategy of *incorporation* (Ghana, Senegal), the ASP was able to hold onto local brokers and maintain crucial clientelistic networks. In those cases where it had pursued a strategy of *substitution* (Zambia, Benin), it suffered mass defections of local leaders following the introduction of multiparty elections. Over time, the weight of this authoritarian legacy decreased in importance. However, the array of electoral institutions and the cohesion of the new ruling party – both of which were themselves partially a product of the authoritarian past – continued to play a crucial role in determining ASPs' fates, shaping the incentives of party elites to remain loyal or defect.

5.6 CONCLUSION

Given the challenges that all opposition parties in Sub-Saharan Africa confront, ASPs face a very difficult situation after losing power and going "into the wilderness." Those that cannot rapidly establish themselves as the main opposition party are likely to fade away, with their ability to keep party elites and local brokers in the party fold declining the longer they are in opposition. This chapter suggests that the biggest threat to ASP success – and thus their ability to "come back" from the wilderness – is twofold: the defection of party elites, and the departure of local brokers and their clientelistic networks. By contrast, the performance of the old regime appears to be relatively unimportant, as does ideology, since lack of policy debates makes it easy for parties to form coalitions and for individuals to switch parties based on calculations about which party is up and which is down at any given moment. Even party finances seem to be of secondary importance. A party with a large territorial organization and physical infrastructure – as with UNIP in Zambia – can quickly find itself with empty buildings if its members and candidates defect. Instead, this chapter has argued that the most important factors determining an ASP's ability to survive after going into opposition are the ability to maintain party cohesion and sustain clientelistic networks.

One of the implications of this chapter is that the success of ASPs is, to a large extent, dependent upon the nature of the previous authoritarian regime. Whether the ASP can rely upon stable support from local brokers throughout the countryside – one of the crucial differences between successful cases like Ghana's NDC and failed cases like Benin's PRPB – depends on whether the previous authoritarian regime pursued a strategy of *incorporation* of local brokers or a strategy of *substitution*. This chapter has argued that the former was more likely to result in stable support for the ASP from local brokers, while the latter was more likely to result in mass defections. This in turn had an impact on elite cohesion, since party elites were more likely to abandon the party if local brokers abandoned it and, in the process, diminished the party's electoral prospects.

Additionally, this chapter has argued that electoral institutions matter greatly in shaping incentives for new party formation, party-switching, independent candidacies, coalition formation, and electoral strategies. Where electoral rules limit the possibilities for new party formation and create incentives for national territorial coverage and internal party cohesion, ASPs are more likely to keep their elites and followers within the party fold over the long run. These various factors are tightly interwoven at the outset of the democratic transition, given that strong authoritarian ruling parties are more likely to be in a position to craft electoral rules to their liking. Over time, however, these different elements could diverge, since the new ruling party that came to power after the transition had the ability to craft new rules that it believed to be in its favor.

Overall, ASP dynamics in Sub-Saharan Africa suggest that the fate of individual parties cannot be studied atemporally or in isolation from the competitive environment. History matters and so do a party's opponents. The factors emphasized in this chapter reinforce one another: a socially embedded authoritarian ruling party may inadvertently foster the emergence of a more cohesive, territorially organized opposition party that is capable of eventually winning power. This new ruling party, in turn, can contribute to the systemic conditions that help to maintain the ASP's relevance as an opposition party, as well as barriers to party-switching and more generalized defections. These parties alternate in their control over the electoral rules, given the prevalence of legislative supermajorities. However, once in a competitive environment, rule changes meant to weaken the opposition can come back to haunt these parties if they ever return to the wilderness. Once in the wilderness of opposition, it is exceptionally difficult to return to power or even maintain a party in Africa, given the centralization of power and resources in the executive. However, while all opposition parties face serious challenges, ASPs with a strong background of social incorporation may be the ones most likely to overcome these challenges and become viable democratic players.

6

The Survival of Authoritarian Successor Parties in Africa
Organizational Legacies or Competitive Landscapes?

Adrienne LeBas

During the 1990s, multiparty elections were held in most African countries that had previously been single-party or military regimes. Unlike their counterparts in Latin America, Southern Europe, or Eastern Europe, African transitions to multiparty rule rarely involved the forced removal or discrediting of former authoritarian elites. Instead, former authoritarian leaders and their parties contested and often won founding multiparty elections (Bratton and van de Walle 1997; van de Walle 2003). Managed transitions allowed authoritarian ruling parties to hold onto the advantages of incumbency, such as control over patronage and the media. These would seem to be ideal contexts for the scenario that Slater and Wong (2013; Chapter 9, this volume) call "conceding to thrive," in which authoritarian *ruling* parties voluntarily initiate a transition to democracy on the calculation that they will continue to perform strongly in the new regime as authoritarian *successor* parties. Yet this outcome remains strikingly rare in Sub-Saharan Africa, perhaps applying to Ghana alone. Despite several factors that would seem to favor their continued survival under democracy, many former authoritarian ruling parties in Africa collapsed soon after losing power, while others lost power but managed to survive and institutionalize as authoritarian successor parties (ASPs). Those that survived and became viable ASPs did not always possess stronger organizations or brands than those that failed. The variation in ASP survival in Africa is, therefore, puzzling.

In terms of overall political outcomes, authoritarian ruling parties in Sub-Saharan Africa have taken one of three pathways since multiparty elections were widely instituted in the region in the early 1990s. First, many presided over transitions to multiparty elections without losing power, leading to the consolidation of hybrid or "competitive authoritarian" regimes (Levitsky and Way 2010). Many of the authoritarian ruling parties with the strongest organizational structures and ideological brands fall into this category. Notably, these parties have generally resisted further political opening, even in cases where their continued electoral dominance was likely, as in Ethiopia,

Tanzania, and Uganda. Second, several former authoritarian ruling parties lost power to rivals after a transition to democracy and either did not survive or attracted very few votes. Most of these parties entered into decline due to the defection of large numbers of party candidates and structures to opposition parties, which often began prior to the initial electoral defeat. Finally, there is a set of countries in which former authoritarian ruling parties lost power yet managed to adapt to their new contexts, becoming successful authoritarian successor parties. These parties have remained viable electoral challengers, and some regained parliamentary majorities and control over the executive in subsequent elections. This chapter focuses on the second and third paths. If we focus our attention on these two paths, we find substantial variation in the level of success among former authoritarian ruling parties following electoral defeat.

This chapter argues that the primary factor that explains authoritarian successor party survival or demise in Sub-Saharan Africa is the degree to which parties suffered the large-scale defection of political elites, including past holders of political office. Of the former authoritarian ruling parties that entered into steep decline after the loss of power, almost all suffered one or more waves of elite defections. Many defectors won office on rival party tickets, suggesting that voters' anti-incumbent bias was not as absolute as aggregate electoral returns might suggest. It was difficult, however, for former authoritarian ruling parties to recover organizationally from the loss of high-quality candidates and the networks and constituencies that these candidates took with them. By contrast, authoritarian successor parties were more likely to survive and institutionalize if they had suffered less extensive or more geographically delimited elite defections. In these situations, ASPs retained the "portable skills" (Grzymala-Busse 2002) of their long-serving officeholders and party staff, and they suffered less erosion of their ties to mass constituencies. Given the organizational weakness of most authoritarian ruling parties in Africa, candidates' personal and clientelistic networks were often crucial for maintaining communication with local brokers and constituencies after democratization.

How, then, to explain severe versus limited defections? This chapter argues that two factors were especially important in constraining the tendency toward defection-fueled organizational collapse. First, successful ASPs often benefited from patronage structures that had, historically, been more strongly linked to the *party* than to *individual politicians*. By contrast, where parties had more decentralized patronage and party structures, individual candidates had greater confidence that they could defect from the party while retaining the support of their constituencies.[1] This lowered the expected cost of defection for politicians with

---

[1] This did not necessarily strengthen the fortunes of opposition parties, as these candidates' more individualized control over patronage networks made them attractive targets for co-optation (van de Walle 2003). Alliances among defectors, where they occur, often prove short-lived (Arriola 2012).

stronger networks and resources. If enough of these individuals defected, others were likely to follow suit, triggering a "defection cascade" from which parties were unlikely to recover. This is a point of disagreement between my chapter and Riedl's chapter in this volume (Chapter 5), in which she argues that greater authoritarian ruling party reliance on local power brokers (or "social rootedness") led to less defection-prone ASPs in the long run. Instead, I argue that this pattern of authoritarian party-building typically created regional elites with weaker party ties and more readily transferrable assets, as in the case of Kenya. Furthermore, some of the strongest ASPs in the region – such as those in Guinea-Bissau and Cape Verde – followed the alternative, more penetrative authoritarian party-building path.

Second, and perhaps more importantly, ASP survival was more likely where the broader *competitive landscape* increased the costs and the uncertainty associated with elite defection. Stronger and more cohesive rivals – and higher levels of party-based polarization – boosted the cohesion of former authoritarian ruling parties and facilitated their survival after electoral defeat. Where party-based polarization was high, defectors were more likely to be punished by voters, and these politicians' past associations with the authoritarian ruling party were more likely to preclude their co-optation and access to patronage under a new government. In the following pages, I build on my past work on polarization, which argues that strategies pursued by both incumbents and rivals can "craft" a strong and relatively impermeable partisan divide (LeBas 2006, 2011). This chapter therefore provides an explanation for *why* some parties are able to maintain their cohesion and prevent defections across multiple electoral cycles, a factor also identified by Riedl (Chapter 5, this volume) as an important characteristic of successful ASPs in Africa.

The following pages will detail this logic via the examination of cases of both success and failure, focusing especially on the experiences of ASPs in Ghana, Kenya, and Malawi. The next section discusses the distinct qualities of African authoritarian ruling parties, focusing especially on the relatively limited authoritarian inheritance that many of these parties brought to the multiparty period. The subsequent section provides an overview of ASP outcomes in the twenty-two African cases that *either* (a) are ranked as "free" by Freedom House *or* (b) are ranked as "partly free" but have experienced the removal of an authoritarian ruling party from power via multiparty elections. Subsequent sections offer a sustained comparison of ASP success in Ghana and failure in Kenya, followed by a discussion of an intermediate case in Malawi, where the ASP survived but has not enjoyed as much success as Ghana's ASP. The conclusion reflects on why greater attention to the competitive environment in which ASPs operate would enrich our understanding of these parties' emergence and performance.

6.1 AUTHORITARIAN SUCCESSOR PARTY SURVIVAL IN AFRICA

Scholarship on authoritarian successor parties has often stressed factors internal to these parties in order to explain their organizational durability and electoral viability after removal from power. Thus, authoritarian successor party survival is more likely where parties inherit a set of resources or an "authoritarian inheritance" that favors party survival (Loxton, Introduction, this volume). These resources may include disciplined cadres with "portable skills" (Grzymala-Busse 2002); a party "brand" or record of past achievements that stabilizes voter loyalties;[2] and a territorial organization that allows party leaders to easily communicate with voters and grassroots activists. In addition to formal party structures, authoritarian successor parties may inherit clientelistic networks that allow them to retain key brokers and constituencies after a transition to democracy (Kitschelt and Singer, Chapter 1, this volume). The decisions and actions taken by parties during the transition to democracy may also be consequential for ASP survival. According to Grzymala-Busse's (2002) classic argument, ASPs are more competitive if they break symbolically with the past, perhaps even to the extent of changing the party name or denouncing abuses committed during the authoritarian period. They are more likely to do this – and more likely to thrive in other ways – if party leaders quickly create centralized party organizations to control candidate selection and ensure a coherent party message.[3]

Largely missing from the literature on authoritarian successor parties has been attention to how competitive landscapes can shape party outcomes. Though an individual party's resources and strategic choices are important, these may be substantially affected by the strength and cohesion of their electoral rivals. The broader literature on party development and authoritarianism has often drawn attention to these kinds of relational processes in explaining the strength and durability of ruling parties *during* authoritarian rule. For instance, Slater (2010) argues that early competition and the existence of strong, credible rivals encourages elites to make institutional investments that lead to strong and durable authoritarian ruling parties and states.[4] Greene (2007) argues that an authoritarian ruling party's control over patronage resources not only provides it with significant electoral advantages but can also perpetuate its dominance by creating highly ideological "niche" opposition parties that have little hope of attracting mainstream voters. Others suggest that violent conflict can build stronger and more cohesive party organizations (Levitsky and Way 2012), and my own past work argues that

---

[2] On party brands, see Lupu (2014).
[3] To some extent, the capacity of the party to undertake these changes during the transition can also be seen as a form of authoritarian inheritance. Where parties lacked "elite assets," something that was itself partially determined by internal party practices under authoritarianism, they were less likely to successfully centralize the party (Grzymala-Busse 2002: 75–77).
[4] See also Smith (2005).

polarization increases party cohesion and strengthens voter loyalties to parties, even when those parties lack access to power and patronage (LeBas 2011). There are good reasons to believe that relational mechanisms may play a role in explaining the variable cohesion and appeal of authoritarian successor parties as well.

This chapter draws on both these bodies of literature to address variation in authoritarian successor party survival. In terms of causal weight, however, the chapter argues that authoritarian inheritance plays a more marginal role in explaining successor party survival in Sub-Saharan Africa than it may in other regions. There is general agreement in the literature that African party organizations are, with few exceptions, exceptionally weak in comparison to their counterparts in other regions.[5] Instead of campaigning on the basis of ideology or policies, authoritarian ruling parties in Africa have tended to be inclusive or all-encompassing coalitions from their formation (Rothchild and Foley 1988; Schmidt 2005; Zolberg 1966). Some of the nationalist movements did initially invest in building grassroots structures and strong cross-ethnic partisan identities; by the 1970s, however, party structures and elite–mass links had substantially eroded or disappeared (Barkan and Okumu 1978; Bratton 1980; Collier 1982; Kasfir 1974). Even in single-party regimes that continued to hold elections during the authoritarian period, ruling parties did not invest in popular mobilization or programmatic appeals and instead depended on ethnic coalition-building as the primary means of maintaining power (Arriola 2012; van de Walle 2003). Thus, when political liberalization began in the 1990s, few authoritarian ruling parties possessed strong organizational resources.[6] Nor could incumbents run on their track records. Authoritarian ruling parties in Africa were driven toward political liberalization by severe economic crisis and attendant waves of mass protest (Bratton and van de Walle 1997).[7] The one significant exception in this respect is Ghana, where sustained economic growth in the late 1980s provided authoritarian incumbents with a positive track record on which to run in multiparty elections in 1992 and 1996.

Most authoritarian ruling parties in Africa therefore entered the transition period without the large territorial organizations and "usable pasts" (Grzymala-Busse 2002) that assisted ASP survival elsewhere. They did, however, inherit extensive clientelistic networks that had been used to

---

[5] For an extensive discussion of this point, see LeBas (2011: chapter 2).
[6] As mentioned above, those that did were able to resist the turn to democracy and are therefore beyond the scope of this chapter. Levitsky and Way (2012) note that the strong party organizations forged by violent conflict have all been able to sustain authoritarian or competitive authoritarian regimes despite several rounds of multiparty elections (e.g., Zimbabwe, Mozambique, Ethiopia).
[7] Of the sixteen countries that held what Bratton and van de Walle (1997) consider democratic elections by December 1994, eleven had experienced large-scale political protests between 1988 and 1992.

maintain ruling coalitions during the authoritarian period. Riedl (2014), for instance, argues that differences in the strategies used by authoritarian ruling parties to build these networks determined the scale of defection from these parties during the transition period. Where parties incorporated important local elites into party structures, she argues, they were more stable; where they instead deposed these elites and established top-down party control, authoritarian ruling parties were fragile and prone to large-scale defection during the transition.

This argument, however, overstates the advantages of this kind of decentralized patronage structure for preserving authoritarian *successor* parties after electoral defeat, when they lose access to patronage resources. The way that clientelism is organized in Africa tends to increase the likelihood of defection-fueled party collapse following a defeat rather than reduce it. In other regions, strong party control over clientelistic networks has helped to stabilize authoritarian successor party organizations and preserve their electoral support among poor voters. In Latin America, Western Europe, and the United States, clientelism relied on grassroots party activists and block-level operatives who mobilized voters and ensured that the votes-for-patronage quid pro quo actually obtained (Auyero 2007; Stokes 2005). These individuals were strong partisans, and the defection of these networks to rival parties was unlikely. In Africa, on the other hand, decentralized clientelistic networks shift power away from party organizations and party cadres toward brokers at the local level. These brokers typically derive their power from preexisting sources of social authority that are independent of party, notably ethnicity.[8] These individuals' own networks effectively substituted for party structures, creating authoritarian ruling parties that had weak constituency ties. Where brokers' fates were tied to the party, or where they saw defection as risky for their own political survival, then the socially embedded nature of these clientelistic networks could help authoritarian ruling parties make the transition to successful ASPs. Where the party loyalty of these brokers faltered, however, ASPs struggled to survive.

Second, ASPs were more likely to survive in competitive landscapes that increased voters' loyalties to parties and made defection a riskier proposition for brokers and for individual candidates. Where the competitive landscape was polarized or built around a clear "us-versus-them" political cleavage, parties were less likely to face the defection of their brokers and the fragmentation of their base constituencies (LeBas 2006, 2011). This cohesion-boosting process could occur in response to a single strong rival, as in Ghana and Sierra Leone, or interactions among multiple parties could work to build solidarity within the ASP's core constituency, as in Malawi. Where the competitive landscape did not create barriers to defection and did not reinforce party loyalty, brokers could

---

[8] For the most cogent examination of the interplay between this form of clientelism and party weakness, see van de Walle (2007).

form new parties in hopes of maximizing their individual patronage share when a new ruling coalition was created. The result was the fluid and fragmented party systems of Benin, Kenya, Senegal, and Zambia, where not only ASPs but parties of all kinds have struggled to institutionalize.

Before turning to the analysis of cases, it is important to underline the centrality of *defection* – and the relatively low cost that it imposes on candidates in some countries – in shaping party outcomes in Sub-Saharan Africa. As suggested above, authoritarian regimes typically held together fractious ruling coalitions through a reliance on brokers with their own sources of legitimacy, and the parties discussed here did not use programmatic appeals or strong party organization to build direct links with voters. Because of the length of authoritarian rule, the weak and unmoored character of civil society, and the small size of the middle class, nearly all political contenders have emerged from this class of societally embedded brokers. Put differently, the majority of those contesting office – including leaders of opposition parties (especially in the first rounds of multiparty elections) – have roots in the former authoritarian ruling party.[9] There were exceptions: strong opposition parties in Burkina Faso, Ghana, Senegal, and Sierra Leone have been led by outsiders and drew on political traditions and loyalties dating back to earlier periods of multiparty rule. The norm, however, is defection and the creation of what Power (2000; Chapter 7, this volume) calls an "authoritarian diaspora" spanning several parties.[10] Thus, the opposition party that removed the African Party for the Independence of Cape Verde (PAICV) from power in 1991 was launched by Carlos Veiga, who had served as a PAICV attorney-general and an MP during the authoritarian period. Similarly, Miguel Trovoada, who won founding elections in 1991 in São Tomé and Príncipe on an opposition ticket, had been one of the founders of the former authoritarian ruling party and a prime minister during the authoritarian period. Similar patterns obtain in Benin, Kenya, Liberia, Malawi, and Zambia, and multiple rounds of multiparty elections have only gradually thinned the ranks of power-holders with ties to the authoritarian past. Sub-Saharan Africa is hardly alone in this phenomenon, though it does complicate how we define authoritarian successor parties. As Power (Chapter 7, this volume) points out, the decline of Brazil's authoritarian successor parties existed alongside "an impressive degree of political survival by the authoritarian elite as a whole." This has been the case in much of Sub-Saharan Africa as well. This is why understanding how some African ASPs were able to escape from this trap can yield important new insights about ASP survival in systems with much weaker party organizations and more fragmented party systems.

---

[9] Chabal and Daloz (1999) identify the centrality of these "recycled elites" as a core reason that democratization in Africa has not resulted in increased accountability.

[10] For more on "authoritarian diasporas," see Conclusion (Loxton, this volume).

6.2 AUTHORITARIAN SUCCESSOR PARTY OUTCOMES IN SUB-SAHARAN AFRICA

In order to be defined as authoritarian successor parties, parties must operate in a political environment that allows for the possibility of electoral turnover (Loxton, Introduction, this volume). Elections in these regimes are determined to be generally free and fair, and incumbents do not possess undue advantages or influence over electoral results. In Sub-Saharan Africa, the Freedom House "fully free" designation as of 2017 applied to only nine countries,[11] though former authoritarian ruling parties had been defeated electorally in a further thirteen African countries that were coded as "partly free" by Freedom House.[12]

This chapter deals with variation in authoritarian successor party survival in countries that meet one of the following two conditions: (a) rated as a full democracy by Freedom House; *or* (b) "partly free" regimes in which former authoritarian ruling parties have been defeated at the ballot box. In this chapter, therefore, the universe of cases in which ASPs can emerge is operationalized somewhat differently – and more expansively – than by Loxton in the Introduction of this volume. There is good reason to investigate the survival of ASPs in countries that fall short of full democracy but have experienced turnover at the ballot box. Unlike authoritarian ruling parties that remain in power, those that suffer an electoral defeat – and thus go into opposition – no longer have access to the "menu of manipulation" characteristic of hybrid regimes (Schedler 2002; also Levitsky and Way 2010). These parties are therefore victims – rather than beneficiaries – of the flaws in these partly free systems. As in the case of other opposition parties, the cards are stacked against the success of ASPs in partly free systems, yet in Africa we find successful ASPs both in these systems and in full democracies.

Of the multiparty electoral regimes in Sub-Saharan Africa, twenty-two are either scored as "free" by Freedom House or are scored as "partly free" *and* have experienced an electoral turnover. The "free" category includes two countries that have no history of authoritarian rule, Mauritius and Namibia. These countries, by definition, cannot produce an ASP. Botswana has also been excluded from the universe of cases: though it was semi-authoritarian for at least part of its post-independence history, its ruling party has never lost power, again removing the possibility of it producing an ASP. According to my operationalization, then, there were a total of nineteen countries in Sub-Saharan Africa where an ASP could have emerged (see Table 6.1). These

---

[11] The nine countries meeting Freedom House "free" status in 2017 were Benin, Botswana, Cape Verde, Ghana, Mauritius, Namibia, São Tomé and Príncipe, Senegal, and South Africa.
[12] The thirteen countries meeting the "partly free + electoral turnover" standard for inclusion in the universe of cases are Burkina Faso, Burundi, Côte d'Ivoire, Guinea, Kenya, Lesotho, Liberia, Madagascar, Malawi, Mali, Sierra Leone, and Zambia. In Nigeria, founding elections in 1999 did not include any party that was linked to the previous authoritarian regime.

Table 6.1 Authoritarian successor party outcomes in Sub-Saharan Africa

	ASP candidate	ASP outcome	Multiparty election year	ARP removed from power	ASP regains power	Country ranked as "free"	2017 Freedom House score	ARP/ASP% of presidential vote (1990 to present) 1st	2nd	3rd	Last	ARP/ASP% of parliamentary vote (1990 to present) 1st	2nd	3rd	Last
Benin	PRPB	demise	1991	1991	.	1991	2,2,F	.	.	.	.	.	1.2	.	.
Burkina Faso	CDP	unclear	1992	2014(i)	.	.	4,3,PF	87.5	80.35	80.15	barred	72.9	91	49.5	13.2
Burundi	UPRONA	near-demise	1993	1993	.	.	7,6,NF	32.86	8.4	2.14	.	21.89	7.2	6.25	2.49
Cape Verde	PAICV	strong	1991	1991	2001	1991	1,1,F	26.7	uncon tested	46.5	32.7	33.6	29.8	49.5	52.7
Côte d'Ivoire	PDCI	strong	1990	1999	.	.	4,4,PF	81.7	96.2	.	25.2	71.7	64.9	41.8[iii]	29.83
Ghana	NDC	strong	1992	2000	2008	2000	1,2,F	58.4	57.4	44.5	47.9	94.5	66.5	46	49.63
Guinea	PUP (also CDG)	demise(s)	1993	2008	.	.	5,5,PF	51.7	56.1	95.3	0.95	53.9[3]	61.6	0.43	.
Kenya	KANU	near-demise	1991	2002	.	.	4,4,PF	36.4	40.1	31.3	.	29.3	38.4	28.1	6.73
Lesotho	BNP	near-demise	1993	1993	.	2002	3,3,PF	no direct presidential election				22.7	24.5	22.4	4.31
Liberia	.	none	1997	1980	.	.	3,4,PF	.	.	.	.	.	.	.	.
Madagascar	AREMA	unclear	1992	1993	1997	.	3,4,PF	28.6	36.6	40.6	.	.	24.7	1.9[3]	.
Malawi	MCP	strong	1994	1994	.	1994	3,3,PF	33.4	45.2	28.2	27.8	33.7	33.8	23.4	17.4
Mali	UDPM	none	1992	1991	.	1992	5,4,PF	.	.	.	.	.	.	.	.
Nigeria	.	none	1999	.	.	.	3,5,PF	.	.	.	.	.	.	.	.
São Tomé	MLSTP/	strong	1991	1991	.	1991	2,2,F	47.3	40	38.8	4.1	42.5	50.6	39.6	32.8

& Príncipe	PSD									17.4	winning coalition
Senegal	PS	in decline	1960	2002	2,2,F	58.4	50.2	41.3	11.3	56.5	50.2	17.4	
Sierra Leone	APC	strong	2002	2013	3,3,PF	5.1	22.4	44.34	58.7	5.7	19.8	40.7	53.7
South Africa	NP	demise	1994	1994	2,2,F	no direct presidential election				20.4	6.9	1.65	.
Zambia	UNIP	demise	1991	1991-2	4,4,PF	24.2	.	10.1	0.4	24.7	0.03	10.7	0.69

Notes: (i) The former authoritarian ruling party in Burkina Faso was forced from power in October 2014, and its leader, former president Blaise Compaoré, was sent into exile in Togo. Several of the party's ministers and candidates were barred by the new Constitutional Court from contesting the October 2015 elections, which were subsequently postponed. However, the party remained well organized and announced that it would support a presidential candidate approved by the court and would replace those parliamentary candidates who had been barred (RFI, "Le CDP soutiendra un des candidats en lice," October 21, 2015). Following elections in November 2015, the CDP holds 14 percent of the parliamentary seats as of September 2017.

(ii) The December 1999 coup against President Henri Bédié in Côte d'Ivoire was an extra-constitutional transfer of power. Bédié and several other candidates were barred by the military government from standing in the October 2000 elections to restore civilian rule, and the PDCI boycotted the election.

(iii) Raw parliamentary votes are not available in Côte d'Ivoire, so this figure represents the parliamentary seat share.

nineteen cases experienced different sorts of transitions. In South Africa, the break with the authoritarian past was especially transformative. In twelve other cases, democratic progress has occurred via "liberalizing electoral outcomes" (Howard and Roessler 2006), in which authoritarian ruling parties were voted out of office in elections that they contested. And in six cases, these parties were removed extra-constitutionally, but were then defeated in subsequent elections as well.[13] Most of the "partly free" cases experienced substantial improvements in democracy ratings immediately after electoral turnover, sometimes even including a temporary jump to fully "free" status. However, new ruling parties also inherited unreformed institutions that centralized power, and authoritarian practices often resurfaced – though now at the expense of ASPs.

Table 6.1 shows the variation in ASP outcomes in these countries.[14] In addition to ASP outcomes, the table includes 2017 Freedom House scores and ASP electoral performance in parliamentary and presidential elections since 1990. In a handful of cases, for various reasons, former authoritarian ruling parties did not survive into the multiparty period. In Mali, the military government's refusal to concede to democratic reform resulted in large-scale popular protest, a coup, the dissolution of the former ruling party, and a founding election in 1992. In that election, the vote was split between the pro-democracy movement-party and a revival of the party that won Mali's first post-independence elections and ruled from 1960 to 1968. In Liberia, the best candidate for an authoritarian successor party would have been the True Whig Party, which presided over an exceptionally long period of party dominance from 1878 to 1980, when it was overthrown in a coup. Though a revival of the party did participate in the 2005 legislative elections, brutal military rule and civil war in the intervening years had destroyed the party's structures, and the two parties should be viewed as separate entities. In Nigeria, the military rulers of the 1980s and 1990s did not form parties.

The remaining cases show wide variation in outcomes. One of the more prominent explanations for ASP success is *authoritarian inheritance*. Thus, we might expect successful ASPs to be those that were able to draw on resources and reputations built during long and stable periods of single-party or party-dominant rule. In Sub-Saharan Africa, length or stability of rule does not seem to be strongly correlated with ASP survival. Some of the most successful and well-institutionalized authoritarian successor parties, such as those in Malawi, Cape Verde, and São Tomé and Príncipe, did emerge from long periods of single-party rule. On the other hand, several long-ruling parties disintegrated

---

[13] In Burkina Faso, Côte d'Ivoire, Liberia, Mali, and Sierra Leone, authoritarian ruling parties were removed extra-constitutionally, but they were then defeated in subsequent elections as well. In Nigeria, the military regime of President Sani Abacha did not create a party, and no military officers from the Abacha regime contested elections.

[14] Though Niger is coded as partly free and has experienced the electoral removal of its former authoritarian ruling party, it is excluded from my sample due to multiple military coups and other interruptions of constitutional rule since founding multiparty elections in 1993.

soon after the transition to multiparty elections was announced. Benin and Zambia are the best examples of this. Further, some of the region's most robust ASPs did not benefit from long or particularly successful periods of authoritarian rule. Both the National Democratic Congress (NDC) in Ghana and the All People's Congress (APC) in Sierra Leone were fairly weakly institutionalized. The NDC was launched only months before the 1992 multiparty elections, and Ghana's post-independence period had been previously characterized by numerous military coups and high levels of political instability. In Sierra Leone, the APC was overthrown in a military coup in 1992, and the ensuing civil war destroyed the party's fairly weak structures and removed most of the traditional chiefs on which it had also relied (Fanthorpe 2006; Kandeh 2003).

Another factor that does not seem to be tightly correlated with ASP success or failure is the degree to which authoritarian ruling parties were able to "manage" the transition to multiparty elections (Riedl 2014). One might argue, for instance, that retaining power in founding elections might give the party a chance to adapt, change its internal party governance, and lessen its reliance on state institutions prior to the loss of patronage resources. This would then favor its survival as a viable competitor after an eventual defeat. As I will detail further below, the NDC in Ghana was able to use its two terms in power after the transition to multiparty elections to build the organizational and reputational resources that it may have lacked at the time of the first multiparty elections in 1992. Yet this "delayed transition" route to ASP survival does not seem typical. Parties that were able to fend off rivals in successive multiparty elections, such as Senegal's Socialist Party (PS) or the Kenya African National Union (KANU), do not seem to be "immunized" against authoritarian successor party decline. In Senegal, the PS – which retained party dominance in multiparty elections from 1964 to 2000 – survives but is clearly in sharp decline (Kelly 2014). Furthermore, some of the region's more vibrant ASPs lost power in founding elections but were subsequently reelected, as in Sierra Leone and Madagascar.[15]

One factor that *is* associated with authoritarian successor party demise is party system fragmentation. Even in African countries practicing proportional representation, electoral systems are strongly majoritarian. Where votes are split across several parties, it becomes easier for parliamentary and even presidential candidates to win elections with fewer votes, reducing the importance of parties as vote aggregators and making defection more attractive. The majority of cases of ASP demise occurred in countries beset by

---

[15] In Madagascar, the Association for the Rebirth of Madagascar (AREMA) lost power in the 1992–1993 presidential elections by a substantial margin but regained power in 1997. Prior to AREMA leader Didier Ratsiraka's forced exile in 2002, which has thrown the fate of the party into question, the party had achieved full control over national and local elected offices (Marcus and Ratsimbaharison 2005).

high levels of party system fragmentation. In Benin, the authoritarian ruling party lost founding elections in 1991, due in large part to extensive elite defection.[16] Very high levels of party volatility and fragmentation continued throughout the 1990s. In the 1995 elections, of the fifteen parties that received more than 2 percent of the vote, most had not existed in 1991, and no party received more than 14.2 percent of the vote. In Zambia, after the founding elections of 1991 that removed the ruling United National Independence Party (UNIP) from power, the party struggled to establish a foothold in the country's increasingly fragmented competitive landscape. In the 1995 parliamentary elections, the most popular opposition party won only 35 percent of the total opposition vote, and independent nonparty candidates won a further 25 percent of the opposition vote.[17] By 2001, the last election in which UNIP won more than 1 percent of the parliamentary vote, Zambia had an effective number of electoral parties – a measure of vote fragmentation – above five, while most countries with a first-past-the-post system like Zambia's have values closer to two. The fragmentation of Lesotho's party system also tracks closely to the decline of the Basotho National Party (BNP), the country's authoritarian successor party. The BNP lost the founding election in 1992, but remained competitive in several subsequent elections. In 2006, a split in the new ruling party led to a much more fragmented competitive landscape for the BNP, and the 2011 elections were characterized by very high levels of volatility. Over 40 percent of votes cast went to newly formed parties or to independent candidates, and the BNP's share of the vote fell from over 20 percent of the vote to roughly 4 percent.

The reverse dynamic can be seen in countries where ASPs survived. These countries had lower levels of party system fragmentation, as well as lower levels of opposition vote fragmentation in founding elections. Thus, the authoritarian ruling party in Cape Verde (PAICV) was defeated in 1992 by a party that captured 82 percent of the total opposition vote, and that rival party has continued to capture 80–90 percent of the non-PAICV vote. More permissive electoral rules in São Tomé and Príncipe led to higher levels of overall parliamentary vote fragmentation, but elections have been consistently organized around a single pro- and anti-ASP cleavage. In both Ghana and Sierra Leone, stable two-party systems have emerged, and third parties have little traction in wooing away voters. In both these countries, the two main parties have together captured 80 percent of the vote or more in the past two election cycles. Defections from these parties are rare. Though both Ghana and

---

[16] Relying on a survey of 261 local elites in several parts of Benin, Riedl estimates that about 80 percent of local elites defected from the People's Revolutionary Party (PRPB) to the opposition prior to the 1991 elections (2014: 119–120).

[17] The authoritarian successor party, UNIP, boycotted these elections, but the opposition remained similarly fragmented in the 2001 elections, with UNIP winning roughly 10 percent of the overall parliamentary vote.

Sierra Leone have salient ethnic cleavages, which drive party system fragmentation elsewhere in Africa, the two main parties in each country have been successful in building partisan brands that span ethnic divides. Voting in Sierra Leone has a strong ethno-regional character, but its ASP was returned to power in the 2007 elections with cross-ethnic support.[18] Similarly, in Ghana, both its ASP and the party's major competitor have multiethnic support bases that shift across election cycles (Morrison and Hong 2006).

It is possible that party system fragmentation is associated with ASPs that lack inherited organizational and material resources. Riedl (2014), for instance, argues for a kind of institutional isomorphism: stronger and more defection-resistant authoritarian ruling parties produce less fragmented party systems. But most African authoritarian successor parties inherit organizational and reputational resources that, although sometimes significant, do not create sufficiently strong barriers to elite defection on their own. Senegal is a case in point. Riedl identifies Senegal's PS as a strong and deeply rooted party organization at the time of its electoral defeat in 2000, which she argues limited defections and resulted in a more disciplined party system. However, Senegal has experienced a very rapid deinstitutionalization of its party system in the 2000s, and elections are now structured around very volatile supermajorities (Kelly 2014; Resnick 2013).[19] Absent a central cleavage to discipline party competition and increase the salience of party-based identities, individual party candidates have an incentive to engage in strategic defection (e.g., van de Walle 2003). As I will show below, the rewards of remaining with an ASP are uncertain and the costs of defection are low for individual candidates – unless party-based polarization increases those costs.

I now turn to three cases that vary in the character of the transition to multiparty rule, the actions of authoritarian ruling parties during those transitions, and subsequent ASP outcomes. These cases testify to the complexity of explaining ASP survival. Together, however, they suggest that ASP survival is more likely where the cost or uncertainty associated with elite defection is higher. Where decentralized patronage structures were associated with individual politicians rather than with the authoritarian ruling party, as in Kenya, defection was a dominant strategy. In Ghana and Malawi, authoritarian ruling parties entered the transition period with slightly greater control over a subset of their candidates and local brokers. The most important factor in these two countries, however, was the disciplining effect of the polarized

---

[18] Nor have any parties in Sierra Leone attempted to use patronage to swing elections: ethnically diverse constituencies do not differ substantially from their more homogenous counterparts in terms of access to public goods (Glennerster, Miguel, and Rothenberg 2013).

[19] Among the casualties of the 2012 elections were several former PS "barons," who formed their own parties. Other PS cadres retained their seats after choosing to remain with the PS in the coalition it backed in the presidential election (Kelly 2013).

competitive landscape, which limited the number of defections and therefore helped these parties to institutionalize as authoritarian successor parties.

6.3 VARIATION IN ASP OUTCOMES IN GHANA AND KENYA

The routes to authoritarian ruling party defeat in Ghana and Kenya were different, though both can be characterized as "managed transitions." Under significant pressure from civil society and international donors, political reforms began in the early 1990s. Both parties took steps to limit uncertainty, manage the degree of political opening, and ensure their own victory in founding multiparty elections. Both countries therefore remained competitive authoritarian regimes throughout the 1990s. In Ghana, incumbent President Jerry John Rawlings and his party packed a constitutional review commission with supporters and used state resources to sway the 1992 presidential election in their own favor. In Kenya, founding multiparty elections were held quite soon after a constitutional amendment removed the legal ban on opposition parties, but the ruling party used state-sponsored violence to undermine and fragment the opposition vote in the 1992 presidential and parliamentary elections. In both countries, opposition parties cried foul. The Ghanaian opposition, which had together won about 50 percent of the presidential vote on November 3, 1992, boycotted the parliamentary elections that were held one month later. The Kenyan opposition held a majority in parliament after the elections, which they used to form a parliamentary select committee to investigate the violence, but divisions within the opposition undermined its efficacy throughout the 1990s.

Both the National Democratic Congress (NDC) in Ghana and the Kenya African National Union (KANU) would retain power until removed in the third round of multiparty elections in 2000 and 2002, respectively. There were stark differences in the opposition parties that won power in these elections. In Kenya, an encompassing – albeit temporary – opposition alliance swept KANU from power, and many of that opposition alliance's key officers and brokers were former KANU members of parliament and ministers. This opposition alliance had not built a strong brand prior to the election, and it was united by little more than voters' desire for "change." In Ghana, by contrast, the opposition New Patriotic Party (NPP) was a revival of an earlier opposition party that had narrowly lost a series of multiparty elections in Ghana before the 1981 coup that brought Jerry John Rawlings, leader of the NDC, to power. It was able to draw on deeply rooted partisan loyalties that had survived the authoritarian interlude, and its leadership and parliamentary contingent had not served in the Rawlings regime. In the 1996 elections, prior to turnover, the NPP won over 70 percent of the total opposition vote. In Kenya, on the other hand, the largest opposition party won only about one-third of all votes cast for the opposition in the country's second presidential and parliamentary elections in 1997.

After their electoral defeats, the NDC and KANU – now authoritarian successor parties – took different paths. KANU politicians and local brokers continued to defect to new parties, further fueling fragmentation and volatility in the party system. In the 2007 elections, KANU's share of the parliamentary vote plummeted from the 28 percent it had received in 2002 to just 6 percent, which translated into one seat in parliament. By the time Uhuru Kenyatta – KANU's 2002 presidential candidate – successfully ran for president in 2013, he did so on a different party ticket. KANU still had some national reach in 2013: it ran parliamentary candidates in 75 of Kenya's 210 new constituencies.[20] But the party is clearly in decline. It currently holds 7 percent of seats in parliament, and its votes are concentrated in a small number of constituencies.

The contrast with the NDC in Ghana is dramatic. The NDC was decisively defeated in the presidential election in 2000, winning only 43 percent of the vote in the second round. However, parliamentary elections were much closer, with the NDC winning 41 percent of the parliamentary vote to the NPP's 45 percent and capturing only seven fewer seats than the NPP. The NDC remained a much stronger voice in parliament after its defeat than KANU did. In 2004, the NDC again won roughly 40 percent of the parliamentary vote to the NPP's 52 percent. Third parties and independent candidates remained a marginal presence in subsequent elections, winning no more than 6 percent of the parliamentary vote and less than 3 percent of the presidential vote. The NDC served as the primary opposition party to the new NPP government and did not suffer large-scale defections like those of KANU. In the general elections of 2008, the NDC managed to recapture both the presidency and control of parliament in the closest elections in Ghana's history. Nearly all of the votes cast were for either the authoritarian successor party, the NDC, or its main rival, the NPP.[21]

There were some differences in the choices and strategies made by these two parties at the time of transition. Unlike KANU, which clearly demonstrated its non-democratic credentials by using violence and fraud to remain in office, the NDC signaled a willingness to comply with democratic norms. The party was launched just prior to the 1992 multiparty elections, but it was widely understood that the NDC was the organizational equivalent of President Rawlings' similarly named Provisional National Defence Council (PNDC), which had ruled Ghana since the 1981 coup. The NDC inherited the organization and clientelistic networks built by the PNDC under authoritarianism (Riedl 2014: 110–112, 137–142). It also ran Rawlings, the former military dictator, as its presidential candidate in 1992 and 1996, until term limits required his replacement in 2000. Despite this continuity with the

---

[20] Notably, thirty-five of these seventy-five candidates won less than 2 percent of the vote in their constituencies, and another thirteen of the seventy-five won less than 5 percent.

[21] The two parties together won 97 percent of the vote in the first round of the presidential election, and nearly 90 percent of the parliamentary vote.

authoritarian period, the NDC did demonstrate some degree of a break with the past: it swapped out "defence" in favor of "democratic" in the party name; it allowed opposition parties access to media and television; and it did little to repress or prevent open election campaigning by other parties.[22] Echoing the pragmatism of successful authoritarian successor parties in Slovakia and Poland (Grzymala-Busse 2002), Ghana's NDC also abandoned many elements of its leftist ideology and embraced economic liberalization prior to the first elections.[23] KANU, on the other hand, did very little of this kind of work in any of the elections of the 1990s and 2000s. Moreover, its ability to claim democratic credentials or positive accomplishments after electoral defeat was significantly constrained by the party's sponsoring of large-scale electoral violence throughout the 1990s.

In terms of territorial organization and party control over clientelistic networks, the distinction between the two parties is less stark than some might assert. Because comparative work on African political parties largely atrophied between the 1960s and the second decade of the 2000s, it is often difficult to ascertain the material resources and organizational penetration of former authoritarian ruling parties in Africa.[24] Nor is it clear how to assess the strength of authoritarian ruling party organization independent of outcomes. Because KANU fragmented and lost much of its support over the 1990s, it is typically assumed that it was a weaker party, perhaps with less grassroots penetration or fewer structures than its counterpart in Ghana.[25] Though Kenya's second president, Daniel arap Moi, had introduced direct party structures that are somewhat suggestive of Riedl's (2014) "substitution strategy,"[26] KANU relied on power brokers both before and after the institution of multiparty elections at the regional level. These brokers, who held key ministerial portfolios during the authoritarian period, were able to

---

[22] The 1992 elections were considered flawed by academic observers. Election quality improved over subsequent election cycles, but others have pointed to the enduringly patrimonial quality of Ghanaian elections (Lindberg 2003; also Ichino and Nathan 2012).

[23] The NDC's break with the past was not as extreme as in Hungary, for instance, where the former communist ruling party formally apologized for past human rights abuses (Grzymala-Busse 2002: 113–114). It was only in 2002, following an electoral turnover, that a human rights commission in Ghana was empowered to investigate abuses, including politically motivated murders, committed during the PNDC regime. Even at this stage, the party opposed the work of the commission, attacking it as politicized and aimed at discrediting the NDC (Alidu 2010: 156–158, 163–165).

[24] The first reliable public opinion surveys began only in 1999 in a small number of countries, several years after the transition to multiparty rule. Kenya's first Afrobarometer survey was carried out in 2003, eight months after KANU's first electoral loss.

[25] Despite this widespread assumption, in my own fieldwork in the late 2000s, informants often fondly recalled constituency-level KANU party offices with full-time staff, and they contrasted the absent, unaccountable, and evanescent nature of contemporary parties with what they viewed as the strong and more accountable party structures of the "KANU days."

[26] See Widner (1992).

The Survival of ASPs in Africa

draw on traditional loyalties – especially those associated with ethnicity – that were independent of the party. This is the same decentralized party-building strategy that Riedl (2014: 134–142) argues prevented elite defections in Ghana. In addition to the creation of new party-dominated institutions at the local level, Rawlings relied heavily on alliances with societally rooted local brokers, who then played important roles in the NDC's control over the democratic transition and its mobilization of voters (Riedl 2014: 134–142).

Differences in organizational form or party strength are not credible explanations for the two ASPs' different levels of success. But, to some extent, the NDC in Ghana may have been able to reduce the extent of elite defections by reforming the party's internal governance. In the early 1990s, both the NDC and KANU were heavily personalized, and they lacked internal party cultures that would favor meritocratic advancement and open selection of party leadership. Between 1992 and 2000, for instance, Rawlings selected all party candidates and officeholders himself (Elischer 2008: 188). It was only after the NDC's defeat in 2000 that the party constitution was amended, allowing for the beginnings of internal party democracy. Party primaries were only instituted in 2004 by the NDC and the NPP in Ghana, and it is unclear whether there had previously been significant scope for intra-party mobility or other practices that would foster the retention of high-quality candidates. Within KANU, the opaque and top-down selection of candidates repeatedly generated disputes and produced party splinters, both before and after the party's electoral defeat in 2002.

But where the two cases differ most markedly is in terms of the level of party-based polarization both before and after the removal of authoritarian ruling parties from office. As suggested above, the NDC and the NPP in Ghana had built themselves atop existing party traditions and used strategies and rhetoric that reinforced their two "brands," thereby dissuading new party entrants. The competitive landscape established during founding elections reinforced internal party system cohesion in Ghana, while the lack of a single strong opposition movement in Kenya generated few constraints on defections from KANU. Powerful KANU MPs left the party in the 1990s, either in hopes of winning the presidency on their own or in order to extract a larger share of clientelistic spoils from the ruling party. Because polarization had not established the clear "us-them" distinctions that drive voters to punish defectors, these individuals tended to be reelected on their own minor party tickets. The incentives for defection did not shift after the electoral turnover of 2002, and Kenya's strikingly fluid competitive landscape made the institutionalization of all parties – including KANU – much more difficult. Though ethnicity is highly salient for vote choice in Kenya, this does not indicate high levels of political polarization in the sense used here. Instead, elite alliances are incredibly fluid in Kenya, and politicians periodically defect from one party coalition to join former adversaries on the other side of the ethnic divide. For instance, President Uhuru Kenyatta and Deputy President William Ruto – who were known as the "alliance of the accused" during the

2013 elections – were indicted by the International Criminal Court for their involvement in organizing the 2007–2008 political violence *against each other's* ethnic communities.

By contrast, a polarized competitive landscape in Ghana has reinforced the internal cohesion and voter loyalties of both the ASP and its main rival. Starting in 1992, the NDC and the rival NPP drew on separate political traditions that reached back to Ghana's independence period, yielding a solidarity-boosting degree of partisan polarization in early election rounds (Riedl 2014: 181–182; Whitfield 2009). In the context of a strong and united opposition party, defection from the NDC to a smaller third party would have likely resulted in electoral loss, allowing the NDC to retain its candidates and its patronage networks. Over multiple election rounds, the divide between the NDC and the NPP has developed ideological dimensions, with the NDC hewing closer to its traditional leftist or more anti-business orientation (Elischer 2008: 190–191). Though there is an ethno-regional dimension to the parties' bases of support, there are areas of the country where the two parties are highly competitive and must attract swing voters in order to win (Morrison and Hong 2006). In contrast to Kenya, where ethnicity plays a role in party system fragmentation, Ghana's two parties' core vote blocks are differentiated less by ethnicity than by other factors, such as the urban–rural divide and level of education, while swing voters tend to be more sensitive to party performance in office (Lindberg and Morrison 2005). Put simply, Ghana has a nationalized party system with low levels of electoral volatility, the polar opposite of Kenya. This competitive two-party system has produced greater solidarity within each party and limited defection from the ASP after its electoral defeat in 2000. In Ghana, party-based polarization therefore contributed to ASP survival and to its ability to recapture power in 2008.

In the remaining pages, I turn to Malawi, an interesting case since party system fragmentation has occurred alongside ASP survival. Malawi's ASP had some advantages that were internal to the party, notably a strong grassroots presence in one area of the country and a popular former leader. The polarizing rhetoric used by other parties, however, also reinforced the cohesion of the party and its primary constituency.

6.4 ASP SURVIVAL AMID FRAGMENTATION IN MALAWI

The transition to multiparty rule in Malawi has parallels with transitions in Ghana and Kenya. As in those countries, the ruling Malawi Congress Party (MCP) faced vibrant civil society mobilization in support of multiparty democracy. In 1994, President Kamuzu Hastings Banda allowed for a referendum on multiparty rule. Multiparty elections were subsequently held in May 1994. Unlike KANU and the NDC, the MCP was soundly defeated, and it received roughly 34 percent of both the presidential and parliamentary vote. Prior to this election, the MCP suffered a wave of defections of sitting MPs and former ministers, who took their own local support networks with them.[27] At the time of the 1994 elections, four former secretaries-general of the MCP served on opposition party executives. In 1994, the non-MCP vote was split between two main opposition parties, the United Democratic Front (UDF) and the Alliance for Democracy (AFORD). The UDF won about 47 percent of both the presidential and parliamentary votes, and it retained power until 2008, when President Bingu wa Mutharika left the UDF and was reelected to the presidency on a new party's ticket.

Nevertheless, from 1994 to the present, the MCP has retained its organizational cohesion and the cohesion of its core electoral constituency in Central Region, where 90 percent of residents are ethnically Chewa. Over the four election cycles from 1999 to 2014, the MCP consistently retained about 30 percent of the popular presidential vote and the largest opposition parliamentary contingent. In 2009, its share of the National Assembly fell to 13.4 percent of seats, but it rebounded in 2014 and held 25 percent of parliamentary seats after the 2014 elections, only three fewer MPs than the ruling Democratic Progressive Party.

The MCP has been able to retain its party cohesion and competitiveness despite an incredible fragmentation of Malawi's party landscape, which is a single-member district, first-past-the-post electoral system. In the third multiparty elections in 2004, independent parliamentary candidates won a remarkable 25 percent of the vote (or 34 percent of the total opposition vote) and captured 21 percent of the seats in parliament. In these elections, the MCP lost about 10 percent of its voting constituency, yet it retained a stable 30 percent of parliamentary seats, nearly all of which were within Central Region. Other parties suffered more substantially: the UDF's 47 percent vote share in 1999 declined to only 26 percent in 2004, though it won the presidency, and its ninety-three seats in parliament dropped to forty-nine. Malawi's third largest party, the Alliance for Democracy (AFORD), suffered a still more substantial reduction in vote and party seat share, losing twenty-three of its parliamentary seats and 76 percent of the votes it had received in the 1999 elections. In this fragmented context, the MCP was left with the largest share of parliamentary seats in 2004, leading to feverish rounds of negotiation by the UDF, which eventually assembled a working majority in parliament (Rakner et al. 2007). Since 2004, Malawi's party system has not substantially reconsolidated: in addition to splits within the MCP's major competitor, the UDF, independent parliamentary candidates continued to do well in the 2014 parliamentary elections, winning 30 percent of the popular vote and 27 percent of seats in the National Assembly. In addition to the MCP's loss of access to

---

[27] This is van Donge's (1995: 241) argument for the discrepancies between the referendum vote in Central Region and the eventual 1994 MCP vote share. There was a tremendous amount of leadership circulation across the three main parties in other regions as well.

patronage, the fragmentation of the party system would seem to militate against authoritarian successor party survival and institutionalization.

How, then, do we explain the MCP's relative success? The MCP may have entered the transition period in a slightly stronger position organizationally than other African parties, yet organizational inheritance does not seem to have played the determinative role in the party's survival. Like ruling parties in Ghana and Kenya, patronage was central to the MCP's mobilization during the authoritarian period. Though the MCP was fashioned as a top-down instrument of control and surveillance (McCracken 1998), the party also relied substantially on decentralized patronage structures that were similar in form to those in Ghana and Kenya (Lwanda 2006). It does not seem that the party had strong branch structures, and the monitoring and control characteristic of the Banda regime was largely due to the Malawi Young Pioneers, who were forcibly disbanded and disarmed by the military during the transition (Chirambo 2004). Furthermore, the post of secretary-general – responsible for grassroots party organization and campaign coordination – had been vacant from 1982 until shortly before the 1994 elections. It seems unlikely that the MCP's organizational structures were strong enough on their own to prevent defection-fueled party collapse, especially after the party's loss of power in 1994.

Defections did occur. Several members of the MCP executive defected to establish splinter parties targeted at the Chewa vote (Rakner et al. 2007). Yet voting patterns in Central Region have remained more stable than those in other regions, which have been more heavily affected by vote fragmentation and the rise of independent candidates. Partly, this is due to the MCP's ability to capitalize on its association with the authoritarian rule of Hastings Kamuzu Banda, a legacy that is controversial elsewhere in the country but still viewed positively by Banda's Chewa coethnics. The preferential language policy of the Banda regime had created systematic favoritism toward the Chewa for civil service jobs and educational opportunities for several decades (Kamwenda 1997). Development policy after independence consistently favored Central Region, and state aid flowed directly to village headmen and territorial chiefs, who continued to serve as loyal MCP cadres in the multiparty period (Kaspin 1995). Finally, the Banda regime – while reliant on patronage – was also a strikingly ideational regime: the philosophy of "Kamuzuism" (from Banda's first name, Kamuzu) constructed Banda as a father and presented the promotion of the Chichewa language as a means of creating a unified nation. Although the views of Malawians were sharply divided on this legacy, his popularity was sufficient in 1994 that some candidates threw badges bearing his portrait into the crowd at rallies (van Donge 1995: 244).

The MCP was able to leverage the strong brand that Banda had built, but it also benefited from a competitive landscape that divided voters on the question of Banda's legacy and regional power. Both these issues tended to polarize voters along the divide between the MCP and one of its major party rivals, the UDF, which acceded to the presidency in 1994. Though many UDF candidates steered clear of expressing direct criticism of Banda, others urged voters to say "no to another educated Banda," i.e., a Chewa (Lwanda 2006: 537). After the UDF's victory, it began to strip Banda's name from public buildings and roads, and it renamed some of these landmarks after prominent victims of Banda's repression (Chirambo 2004: 549–550). The state also began to investigate both Banda and MCP leader John Tembo for past human rights violations, though the process began to flag as UDF politicians who had served in high-level MCP positions came under scrutiny. The position of Malawi's third major party, the northern-based AFORD, was less dogmatic on Banda. Prior to the 1994 elections, AFORD refused to join the UDF in an opposition alliance, and it instead moved closer to the MCP. This became a formal opposition alliance after the UDF's victory, and van Donge (1995: 255) notes that Banda "occupies a central place in the official photograph" of the shadow cabinet. It is difficult to know the extent to which this single issue accounts for the continued cohesion of the MCP's core voters, even after Banda's death, but the party splinters formed out of the MCP attracted many fewer of the party's core voters than was the case for the breakaways of other Malawian parties. The MCP retains about two-thirds of its 1994 vote base: voters who identify as Chewa are more likely to express a partisan affiliation to the MCP, and they are the Malawian voters who are least likely to be swayed by performance evaluations (Ferree and Horowitz 2010). The strongly partisan character of Chewa voters, itself possibly a response to the UDF's targeting of Banda's legacy, has stabilized the MCP as an authoritarian successor party and deterred candidate defections, despite the fragmentation of Malawi's other parties. Though party-based polarization looks different in Malawi than in strong two-party systems like those in Ghana and Sierra Leone, it seems to have bolstered the internal cohesion of its ASP in similar fashion.

6.5 CONCLUSION

Authoritarian ruling parties in Sub-Saharan Africa rarely entered the transition period with the strong brands, party-controlled clientelistic networks, or territorial organizations that others have identified as determinants of authoritarian successor party survival. In order to explain survival despite these general disadvantages, this chapter has argued for the importance of two factors that constrain the main threat to ASP survival: defection-fueled organizational collapse. First, some ASPs inherited patronage structures that were more closely associated with the *party* than with *individual party brokers*. Though the decentralized patronage structures characteristic of African authoritarian ruling parties tended to increase the likelihood of defection, greater party control over patronage structures could reduce these tendencies. Second, more successful authoritarian successor parties benefited from *competitive landscapes* that established barriers to candidate defection.

A cohesive rival party can create a sense of threat, which causes ASPs' core constituents to "rally around the flag" and reject politicians who attempt to form party splinters.

In terms of factors that have been neglected in the analysis above, the most important remaining question is the role of charismatic leadership in strengthening authoritarian successor parties in Sub-Saharan Africa. As Loxton and Levitsky (Chapter 3, this volume) point out, the personal appeal of charismatic party leaders can compensate for some parties' organizational disadvantages. In Latin America, personalistic authoritarian successor parties have been fairly common, and a handful (notably the Peronist Party in Argentina) have been able to survive the death of the party leader. Given the organizational weaknesses of many African authoritarian ruling parties, it may be that personalism plays a similar role in stabilizing ASPs immediately after defeat. Malawi seems to be an obvious candidate for this pathway, as loyalty to former president Hastings Banda appears to have played a role in structuring inter-party competition after the MCP's defeat. In Ghana, Rawlings remained a crucial figure after the transition to multiparty rule, though his personal charisma seems less important for explaining the NDC's success than the factors emphasized above.

Another factor worthy of greater examination is the impact of rules about the registration of parties and independent candidates, which Riedl emphasizes in her chapter (Chapter 5, this volume). In Malawi, the proliferation of independent candidates has contributed to significant party system fragmentation, which made it more difficult for the MCP to engineer an electoral turnover that would bring it back to power. In Kenya, KANU increased its vote share in the county-level and National Assembly elections in the most recent election in 2017, following a 2016 change to the Political Parties Act that created new obstacles for smaller parties and independent candidates.

The case analysis in this chapter suggests the importance of another factor that researchers may wish to examine in the future: the role of critical junctures or foundational moments associated with authoritarian regime formation in shaping party systems *after* the return to multiparty rule. In both Ghana and Sierra Leone, major opposition parties were revivals of parties that had been formed in the post-independence period of open politics and then banned after the onset of authoritarian rule. The competitive two-party systems that have emerged in both countries, organized around political debates reaching back into the pre-authoritarian period, are fairly rare on the continent. History may therefore play an important role in explaining when and where we are likely to see the emergence of the kind of competitive landscapes that favor ASP survival.

7

The Contrasting Trajectories of Brazil's Two Authoritarian Successor Parties

Timothy J. Power

On March 15, 2015, Brazil completed three decades of uninterrupted civilian rule. Both Brazil's military-authoritarian regime (1964–1985) and its protracted withdrawal from power (1974–1985) were closely observed by scholars of democratization, making the Brazilian case one of the best documented in the comparative politics literature.[1] Scholars emphasized several distinguishing features of the Brazilian case. One was the unusual institutional format of the authoritarian regime, in which Brazilian military elites – in contrast to their counterparts in Argentina, Chile, and Uruguay – chose to retain a political party system and a functioning legislature, although these institutions were severely emasculated and controlled.[2] A second feature was regime performance, characterized by superior economic growth and a relatively low level of physical repression when compared to the other bureaucratic-authoritarian regimes of the Southern Cone. A third feature was the mode of transition to democracy, which was initiated from within the authoritarian regime itself and proceeded via a relatively slow and negotiated process of "transition through transaction" until regime change accelerated in 1983–1984 (Share and Mainwaring 1986).

Taken together, these three factors were unusually favorable to the civilian elites who had supported military rule in the 1960s and 1970s. Authoritarian elites inherited a large and well-oiled political party structure, which was first known as the National Renovating Alliance (ARENA) from 1966 to 1979 and as the Social Democratic Party (PDS)

---

[1] I would like to thank Cesar Zucco Jr. for his collaboration on the Brazilian Legislative Surveys and Octavio Amorim Neto for sharing his cabinet portfolio data. I am grateful to Fernando Bizzarro, Frances Hagopian, James Loxton, Rafael Madeira, Scott Mainwaring, and Cesar Zucco Jr. for comments on an earlier draft of this chapter.

[2] From 1966 to 1979, only two parties were allowed to operate: ARENA (National Renovating Alliance), the regime's official party, and MDB (Brazilian Democratic Movement), the state-sanctioned opposition party. For analysis of this "artificial" two-party system, see Kinzo (1988).

thereafter.[3] Veterans of ARENA/PDS could point to the military's record of socioeconomic modernization, which presided over the "Brazilian Miracle" of 1968–1973 and upgraded many of the productive and infrastructural pillars of the Brazilian economy. These elites were not eliminated or marginalized by the circumstances of the transition to democracy. In fact, the endgame of the transition in 1984–1985 featured a partial merging of the authoritarian alliance with the democratizing alliance, a phenomenon that Guillermo O'Donnell (1992: 31) famously described as a coalition of "all for all."

O'Donnell's evocative term refers to a very specific set of political actions in 1984–1985. Dismayed by the military's backing of a discredited civilian candidate (Paulo Maluf of the PDS) in the indirect presidential election of January 1985, a group of PDS notables calling themselves the "Liberal Front" dramatically abandoned their party at the last moment. The Liberal Front shifted its loyalty to the centrist opposition candidate, Tancredo Neves of the Party of the Brazilian Democratic Movement (PMDB), to whom they supplied José Sarney as a vice presidential running mate (Sarney had been party president of the PDS as recently as June 1984). The "Democratic Alliance" of the PMDB and the newly formalized Party of the Liberal Front (PFL) propelled the Neves–Sarney ticket to an easy victory and formed the founding coalition government of 1985–1990. The upshot of the final fluid moments of the transition is that for the past thirty years, democratic Brazil has had not one but two authoritarian successor parties – the first claiming direct patrilineal descent from the ARENA/PDS party organization founded in 1966 and the second evolving from the defection of the Liberal Front in 1984. The "family tree" is outlined in Figure 7.1. In the remainder of this chapter, I will somewhat awkwardly refer to these two parties as the PDS/PP and PFL/DEM, respectively, concatenating their labels as of 1985 and 2015.[4]

The PDS/PP and the PFL/DEM sit well in dialogue with some of the concepts and definitions outlined by James Loxton in the Introduction of this volume. They indisputably meet Loxton's definition of authoritarian successor parties (ASPs) as "parties that emerge from authoritarian regimes, but that operate after a transition to democracy." ARENA, the forerunner of PDS/PP that existed in the military's enforced two-party system between 1966 and 1979, was centered on civilian notables who had endorsed the military coup of 1964 and who were largely recruited from the two main right-of-center parties that existed in

---

[3] The ruling party in Brazil abandoned the ARENA name in 1979. In 1981, the same acronym was adopted by El Salvador's Nationalist Republican Alliance, a successful right-wing party that held the presidency of that country from 1989 to 2009.

[4] The PDS merged with the small Christian Democratic Party in 1993 to become the Reformist Progressive Party, or PPR. In 1995, the PPR absorbed two additional minor parties and changed its name to the Brazilian Progressive Party (PPB). In 2003, the party renamed itself as the Progressive Party (PP). Notably, both of these name changes occurred in the first year of presidents (Fernando Henrique Cardoso and Luiz Inácio Lula da Silva, respectively) that the party had opposed electorally but then intended to support in Congress. The PFL kept the same name from 1985 to 2007, when it became known simply as "Democrats" (DEM).

Contrasting Trajectories of Brazil's Two ASPs

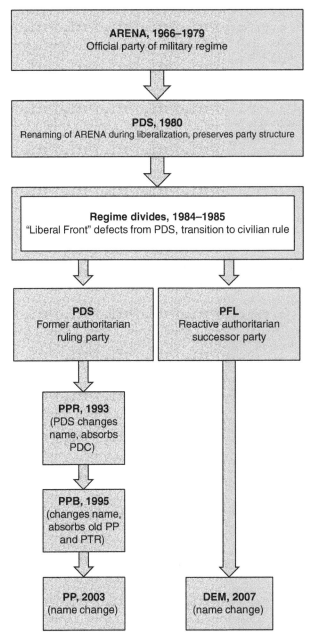

FIGURE 7.1 Genealogy of the two authoritarian successor parties in Brazil

Brazil's second-wave democracy between 1946 and 1964. The Liberal Front of 1984–1985 was drawn from the most senior ranks of the PDS: it included state governors, federal cabinet members, and even the sitting vice president of Brazil at the time, Aureliano Chaves. Moreover, the PDS/PP and the PFL/DEM correspond almost perfectly to the two main subtypes of authoritarian successor party as proposed by Loxton. The PDS/PP is a *former authoritarian ruling party*: it held virtually every major executive post in Brazil from 1966 until the liberalizing elections of 1982. The PFL/DEM is the quintessential *reactive authoritarian successor party*, having been formed by high-level regime insiders in the final moments of military rule. The outcome of the transition led to a departure of the PDS/PP from national power in 1985, whereas the PFL/DEM was a key player in every Brazilian government for the next seventeen years.

The presence in Brazil of *two* authoritarian successor parties,[5] one from each major subtype, provides us with an attractive opportunity to address two questions central to this volume: (1) What explains the success of authoritarian successor parties? and (2) Why are some ASPs more successful than others? These questions lend themselves well to an intranational comparative study that exploits within-case variation across party organizations. Given that both PDS/PP and PFL/DEM have a common ancestor (the ARENA party structure from the heyday of authoritarian rule)[6] and given that some of the key contextual factors affecting the parties (regime legacy, political culture, and institutional rules) are constants for Brazil, we can rule out some of the presumed causes of ASP trajectories across the many parties and political systems explored in the present volume. After all, sharing a good deal of their DNA and being raised in the same "household," PDS/PP and PFL/DEM approximate the status of fraternal twins. Holding some key environmental factors constant, we can assume that a good deal of the observed variation on our outcomes of interest – Loxton's two questions above (see Loxton, Introduction, this volume) – should logically be due to agency, leadership, and strategies of two rival parties operating within the same opportunity structure.

In this chapter, I advance an account of the contrasting trajectories of the PDS/PP and the PFL/DEM. For approximately the first twenty years of democracy, the reactive PFL/DEM had a distinct advantage over its

---

[5] Several other Brazilian parties founded in the 1980s have one or more characteristics of ASPs, but fall short of the definition used in this volume. The most prominent of these is the Party of National Reconstruction (PRN) created by Fernando Collor de Mello as a vehicle for his successful presidential bid in 1989. Collor was a former member of ARENA and PDS and had been the appointed mayor of Maceió, the capital of Alagoas. However, at the time of the democratic transition he was still only a freshman backbencher in Congress and thus could not be described as a *high-level* incumbent of the military regime (although his father, Arnon de Mello, would have qualified). For precisely the same reason, I do not consider the Christian Democratic Party (PDC, founded by Siqueira Campos) and the Liberal Party (PL, founded by Álvaro Valle) as meeting the operational definition of ASPs.

[6] ARENA (1966–1979) will not be discussed in this chapter. Unfortunately, ARENA is quite possibly the least studied major party in Brazilian history. The only published monograph on the party is the archival history by Grinberg (2009). A valuable unpublished source in English is the dissertation by Margaret Sarles (Jenks 1979). For a review of the literature on parties under the military regime, see Carvalho (2008).

Contrasting Trajectories of Brazil's Two ASPs

"continuist" rival the PDS/PP, but that advantage was lost when Brazil shifted left under the Workers' Party (PT) after 2003. I explain the initial advantage of the PFL/DEM with reference to the circumstances of the 1984–1985 transition, the party's impressive ability to transact with all of the first four postauthoritarian presidents, and the congruence between the party's ideology and the zenith of neoliberalism in the 1990s. I explain the recent decline of the PFL/DEM with reference to its exclusion from national power after the victory of the most ideologically distant major party, the PT, in 2002; its highly centralized organizational structure, which deprived subnational factions of the ability to adapt to the long cycle of PT government from 2003 to 2016, especially in the Northeast; and the gradual surrender of its function as a professionalized "support party" (*partido de sustentação*) to a centrist rival, the PMDB. With regard to the critical function of selling governability to presidents, the PFL/DEM's main rival was not the PDS/PP, but rather the decentralized, catchall PMDB – ironically the only other Brazilian party dating from the authoritarian era, when it was the sole legal party opposing military rule. Thus, the PFL/DEM was outflanked on the right by the PDS/PP, which rapidly reached accommodation with the PT-led coalition after 2003, and was displaced as a clientelistic support party by the PMDB, whose more flexible and less ideological approach allowed it to navigate the transition from the government of Fernando Henrique Cardoso of the Brazilian Social Democracy Party (PSDB) (1995–2002) to that of Luiz Inácio Lula da Silva of the PT (2003–2010) much more efficiently. The erosion of the once-mighty PFL/DEM is therefore only weakly related to authoritarian-era cleavages in Brazilian politics: rather, the party's decline is situational and contingent, related more strongly to changes within other major actors such as the PT and PMDB, and to sociodemographic changes in the party's former heartland in the Northeast. This demonstrates that the advantages that accrue to reactive authoritarian successor parties do not last forever: the PFL/DEM was favored by the "big bang" of the transition to democracy and later by Cardoso-era reformism, but the breakthrough election of the PT in 2002 undermined both of these advantages.

This chapter proceeds in four main sections. In the first section, I sketch the key similarities and differences between Brazil's two ASPs. In the second, I document how the PFL/DEM first gained and later squandered its dominance over the other main authoritarian successor party, the PDS/PP. In the third section, I reflect on how a combination of foundational factors, organizational features, and a changing macropolitical opportunity structure came together to reverse the initial balance of power between the two parties. A fourth section concludes.

7.1 THE AUTHORITARIAN DIASPORA AND THE TWO SUCCESSOR PARTIES

Brazil is not the only Latin American democracy to have more than one authoritarian successor party. Chile is the other outstanding example, where the National Renewal (RN) and Independent Democratic Union (UDI) parties continue to embody ideological and regime-change cleavages that emerged among civilian backers of dictator Augusto Pinochet in the late 1980s. In Chile, very few members of the authoritarian and democratizing coalitions "crossed the aisle" to the other camp, and the postauthoritarian party destinations of incumbent elites were mostly restricted to these two prominent right-wing parties. The Brazilian case, by contrast, was messier. While it is correct to identify two ASPs in Brazil, it is also important to note that many ex-authoritarian elites opted to join other parties as well. The diversity of this "authoritarian diaspora" (Power 2000) was evident as early as the founding legislative election of 1986, in which ex-*arenistas* were elected to Congress by no fewer than seven different political parties. While former incumbent elites of the authoritarian regime made up 89 percent of the PDS delegation and 75 percent of the PFL delegation to the National Constituent Assembly of 1987–1988, they also figured prominently in the smaller Liberal Party (PL), Labor Party (PTB), and Christian Democratic Party (PDC). Even more impressive was their stealthy colonization of the then-hegemonic PMDB, the main opposition party under military rule: fully 71 of the 305 PMDB representatives to the Constituent Assembly (some 23 percent of the party caucus) had been members of ARENA or PDS prior to the democratic transition (Power 2000: 98–99). Such a degree of *transfuguismo* (party swapping) would be unthinkable in the Chilean party system.

As Loxton notes in the Conclusion (this volume), the dispersion of an authoritarian cohort across several parties is not unique to Brazil; it is also visible in Sub-Saharan Africa (LeBas, Chapter 6, this volume) and in postcommunist Europe. Yet the highly mobile, diasporic character of the Brazilian authoritarian elite is nonetheless impressive in comparative perspective. The fluid nature of the Brazilian party system in the 1980s empowered authoritarian elites with several right-of-center options for party affiliation, and it was remarkably easy (and common) to migrate even to the party most closely associated with the triumph of political democracy, the PMDB. Not surprisingly, the immediate dispersion of the ARENA/PDS cohort obfuscated authoritarian identities and muted the salience of a "regime cleavage" in the early elections under democracy – again in sharp contrast to the Chilean case. The only clear "loser" in the landmark elections to the Constituent Assembly was the continuist PDS, which saw its legislative delegation shrink to only thirty-seven members (an 80 percent reduction compared to four years earlier). Yet one hundred other PDS veterans were elected to the Constituent Assembly by the PFL and seventy-one more by the

PMDB. Putting it simply, the Brazilian transition is characterized by (1) a drastic reduction in the size of the former authoritarian ruling *party* combined with (2) an impressive degree of political survival by the authoritarian *elite* as a whole.

Therefore, when we engage in comparison of PDS/PP and PFL/DEM as formal political organizations, we are sharply underestimating the size and influence of the ex-authoritarian cohort in the early years of Brazilian democracy. That being said, the PDS/PP and the PFL/DEM are undeniably authoritarian successor parties and as such are comparable units. Figure 7.2 illustrates that these two parties have a far higher degree of "authoritarian DNA" than any of Brazil's other major parties.[7]

The experience of the National Constituent Assembly showed the two parties to be relatively similar on a number of dimensions. Both parties strived to preserve certain institutional characteristics of the defunct military regime, including a strong presidency with decree authority, a legislature with weak autonomy, and low levels of direct popular participation in politics. The parties openly supported the maintenance of a presidential system and a full five-year term for the transitional president, José Sarney (Tancredo Neves of the PMDB, who died before he could take office, had promised to serve only four years).[8] The parties opposed democratizing reforms such as citizen introduction of bills in Congress (which eventually passed) or the institution of recall elections for elected executives (which was defeated). Following in the steps of their parent party, ARENA, both PDS/PP and PFL/DEM were also strongly supportive of the preservation of military prerogatives in the new constitution (Stepan 1988), including the constitutional right of the armed forces to intervene in politics so as to "guarantee internal order." Efforts such as these lend support to the hypothesis presented by Loxton (Introduction, this volume) that ASPs may use their power and influence to preserve authoritarian enclaves in new democracies.

---

[7] Figure 7.2 uses a high standard for operationalizing authoritarian experience: I focus only on membership in ARENA between 1966 and 1979. This criterion is meaningful because party affiliation was a stark, binary choice at the time: there was only one other legal political party, the Brazilian Democratic Movement or MDB (Kinzo 1988). The MDB was the officially sanctioned opposition party to military rule and was the forerunner of the centrist, catchall Party of the Brazilian Democratic Movement (PMDB, 1980–present). Including legislators whose connection to the authoritarian regime was limited to membership to the post-1980 PDS (in the transitional multiparty system of 1980–1985) would constitute a lower standard for authoritarian allegiance, because by then the regime was already committed to advanced liberalization.

[8] Neves, the architect of the "Democratic Alliance" between the PMDB and the PFL, won the indirect presidential election of January 1985 but died before he could take office. His vice presidential running mate, José Sarney, was the PFL representative on the ticket, but the military-imposed constitution in effect at the time required him to join the PMDB for legal reasons. Sarney was thus never formally reckoned a PFL president, even though he exerted strong influence over the party during his presidency (1985–1990) and for many years thereafter. He served as a PMDB senator from Amapá from 1990 to 2014 while continuing to dominate the PFL/DEM in his home state, Maranhão.

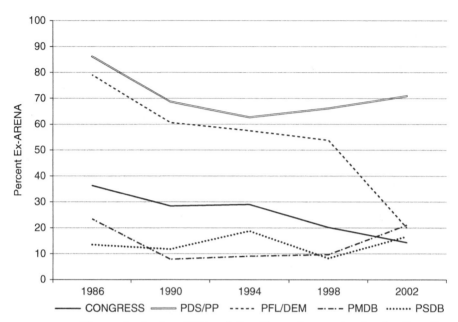

FIGURE 7.2 The authoritarian DNA of Brazil's major parties in the first five democratically elected legislatures

Notes: Lines show percentages of federal legislators declaring in anonymous surveys that they were affiliated to ARENA between 1966 and 1979. The PT is not shown as it had no such members. The solid black line is the average for Congress as a whole.

Source: Power and Zucco (2014).

In Brazil, strong ASP sympathy for the military continued throughout the 1990s and beyond, even as democratic reformers such as Fernando Henrique Cardoso sought to bring the military under civilian control (Cardoso finally succeeded in creating a unified, civilian-led Ministry of Defense in 1999, fourteen years after the democratic transition). Figure 7.3, which uses data from the Brazilian Legislative Surveys (Power and Zucco 2014), traces support for military prerogatives among Brazil's major parties during the first two decades of democracy. The continuist PDS/PP is revealed as the most consistent supporter of the armed forces.

These congruities are unsurprising. The PDS/PP and the PFL/DEM were the two main conservative parties in the first twenty-five years of Brazilian democracy, and they descended from the ARENA/PDS, a unified party organization for eighteen years prior to the transition: therefore we should expect the parties to be broadly similar. Yet what is more interesting here are some of the key differences between the continuist PDS/PP and the reactive PFL/DEM. I now focus briefly on five such differences: ideology, territorial distribution, the sociological profile of party elites, internal organization, and

Contrasting Trajectories of Brazil's Two ASPs

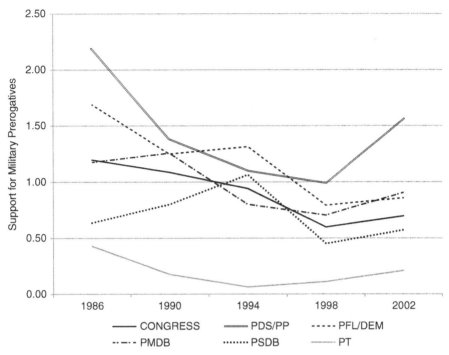

FIGURE 7.3 Sympathy for military prerogatives among major Brazilian parties in the first five democratically elected legislatures
Notes: Y-axis is an additive index of three binary variables measuring preservation of authoritarian-era military prerogatives. These are BLS questions on support for the military's right to intervene to guarantee internal order (Constitution of 1988, Art. 142); support for a single Ministry of Defense rather than separate military ministries; and support for appointing a civilian as the minister of defense. In each case, the pro-military position is scored as 1, so the index runs from 0 to 3. The solid black line is the average for Congress as a whole.
Source: Power and Zucco (2014).

coalitional flexibility. (The reader should keep in mind that given the overall semblance of the parties, these are *relative* differences – of degree, not kind.)

The main ideological difference between PDS/PP and PFL/DEM is not spatial distance but rather in the relative importance accorded to ideology by party elites. The Brazilian Legislative Surveys (BLS, see Power and Zucco 2014) provide twenty-three years of time-series data on the left–right placement of major parties by legislative elites,[9] and we can observe in Figure 7.4 that,

---

[9] The BLS uses a survey questionnaire that has been applied in each parliament since Brazil's return to democracy. Between Wave 1 (1990) and Wave 7 (2013), the BLS received 1,145 survey responses from 890 different legislators. The data are publicly archived at https://dataverse.harvard.edu/dataverse/bls.

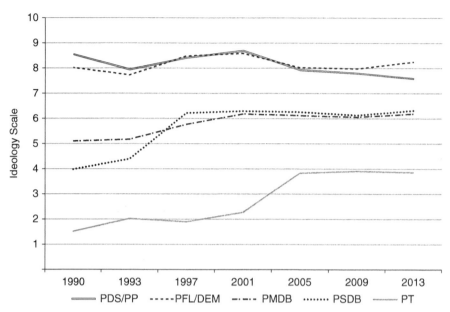

FIGURE 7.4 Reputational conservatism among Brazil's major parties, 1990–2013
Note: Parties are placed (by nonmembers only) on an ideological scale where 1 is left and 10 is right.
Source: Power and Zucco (2014).

reputationally speaking, the differences between the parties are minor indeed. In 1990, the PFL/DEM was seen as slightly to the left of the PDS/PP, no doubt due to its recent defection from the pro-military camp. Yet by 2013 we see an inversion of these perceptions, probably due to the DEM's vociferous opposition to the leftist Workers' Party (PT) and to the PP's loyal support of the two PT presidents, Luiz Inácio Lula da Silva (2003–2010) and Dilma Rousseff (2011–2016). The spatial distances are negligible, but this obscures a key qualitative difference between the two parties: the greater use of ideology for party branding in the case of the PFL/DEM.

From the late 1980s and continuing through the 1990s, the PFL/DEM attempted to reinvent itself as a modern "liberal" party akin to the German Free Democrats (Freie Demokratische Partei, or FDP). The FDP's Friedrich Naumann Foundation helped to create a Brazilian counterpart, the Instituto Tancredo Neves (ITN), whose president was always a member of the PFL/DEM Executive Committee (Tarouco 1999: chapter 5). The ITN promoted research, publications, and events in an effort to formalize the PFL/DEM's "liberalism" in both senses, political (support for the new democratic regime) and economic (support for individualism, free markets, and a smaller Brazilian state). Denise Paiva's excellent study of the PFL (2002) argues that these self-conscious initiatives to define an ideological space were motivated by the party's need to brand itself differently from the PDS in the mid-1980s. Corbellini (2005) claims that these efforts were also intended to position the PFL/DEM as a "modern" party, aligned with ideological principles that were gaining in international legitimacy in the 1980s and 1990s. Such a re-branding would lend "substance" to the party, helping it to overcome its reputation as a clientelistic machine centered in Brazil's Northeastern hinterland. While not all sectors of the PFL/DEM were interested in this elaborate ideological repackaging, the notables who dominated the party's centralized national executive clearly took it seriously (Paiva 2002: 63–65).

The PDS/PP, by contrast, clung to the ideological obfuscation strategy that had characterized it since 1979, when the official party of a conservative military dictatorship chose a name evoking inclusionary social democracy (Partido Democrático Social). This was an early example of "right flight" (Power 2000), in which conservative parties and politicians go to great lengths to avoid any association with right-wing ideology. Although reluctance to self-identify as conservative is a familiar facet of elite political culture in Brazil (Power and Zucco 2009; Zucco and Power 2012), the PDS/PP carried this to an extreme, adopting programs and manifestos that appeared far more progressive than the party ever really was.[10] The difference between the public legitimation strategies of the PDS/PP and the PFL/DEM is clearly visible in Figure 7.5, which compares the left–right positions of major parties in the 1990s using the BLS elite perceptual data and the content-analysis methodology of the Manifesto Research Group (Tarouco and Madeira 2013).[11] While the content of the manifestos of most major parties is well predicted by their left–right reputation among elites, the manifesto of the PDS/PP is remarkably distant from the regression line, being closer to that of the PT than to the openly neoliberal program of the PFL.

As for territorial penetration, there are notable differences between the parties dating back to the division of the PDS in 1984. In that year, the PDS nominee for president was Paulo Maluf, the former governor of São Paulo, a highly industrialized state in the Center-South that at the time was responsible for over 36 percent of GDP. Meanwhile, the anti-*malufista* faction of the PDS was largely based around the party's governors in the Northeast, all elected in 1982, whose rebellion against the outcome of the nominating convention gave rise to the Liberal Front (Lavareda 1985). This schism led to lasting differences in the electoral bases of the PDS/PP and the PFL/DEM, with the former performing relatively better in the more modernized regions of Brazil and the latter inheriting the lion's share of the old Northeastern base of the PDS. For example, in 1986, the

---

[10] As early 1980s wags would have it, the PDS was neither social, nor democratic, nor a party. This was actually a revival of an old 1950s joke about the cadre party of Getúlio Vargas, which had an almost identical name.
[11] For an extension of this method to conservative parties in Brazil, Chile, and Uruguay, see Babireski (2013).

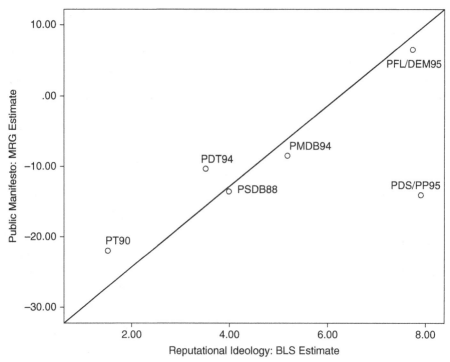

FIGURE 7.5 Estimating left–right placement of major Brazilian parties in the first decade of democracy: manifesto method vs. elite surveys

Notes: Y-axis estimates party ideology using coding scheme of the Manifestos Research Group, as replicated for Brazil by Tarouco and Madeira (2013), and case labels denote manifesto years. X-axis is reputational ideology, using the BLS estimate from the survey (1990 or 1993) closest in time to the manifesto release (Power and Zucco 2014). On both axes, higher values represent more conservative or rightist positions.

PFL drew 37 percent of its national legislative vote total from the Northeast alone, compared to only 17 percent from the much more populous Center-South. In the 1998 legislative elections, the PFL/DEM won 20.5 percent of the seats in the Chamber of Deputies nationally, but 31.1 percent of the Northeastern seats; the equivalent figures for the PDS/PP were 11.7 percent and 4.6 percent. In the South, however, the PFL/DEM won only 13 percent of the Chamber seats compared to the PDS/PP's 18.1 percent; in the Southeast (São Paulo, Rio de Janeiro, Minas Gerais, and Espírito Santo), the parties were tied with 14.5 percent of the seats each. Therefore, some thirteen years after the transition to democracy, the PFL/DEM was still dominating the continuist PDS/PP by a factor of nearly 7:1 in the Northeast, but losing to the PDS/PP in the industrialized states of the South and Southeast – a lingering echo of the "rebellion of the governors" in 1984. Paiva concludes that the PFL/DEM was indeed the "party of the Northeast" as recently as 2000 (2002: 70–82).[12] This excessive dependence on the impoverished Northeastern region was to prove the party's Achilles' heel when the PT launched a series of successful pro-poor policies beginning in 2003 (Borges 2011; Hunter and Power 2007; Montero 2012).

Turning to the sociological profile of party elites, for many years Leôncio Martins Rodrigues (2002, 2014) has been collecting data on the occupational backgrounds of federal legislators. He finds that the two ASPs are broadly similar in their sociodemographic profiles. While he does not report tests of statistical significance, his studies point to two moderate differences between the PDS/PP and the PFL/DEM. First, while both parties are dominated by business elites (65–70 percent of each caucus), federal deputies elected by the PDS/PP appear slightly more likely to be drawn from urban and industrial sectors, and PFL/DEM legislators are slightly more likely to come from the rural sector. This is consistent with the regional differences described above. Second, PFL/DEM deputies are more likely to have roots in the public sector. This is no doubt an outcome of the party's long presence in federal government (1985–2002) and of its domination of most Northeastern state governments prior to the Lula years. For example, in both Maranhão and Bahia, the political machines of José Sarney and Antônio Carlos Magalhães, respectively, elected every governor between 1990 and 2006.[13]

Beyond ideology, regional bases, and recruitment to politics, a fourth difference between the PDS/PP and the PFL/DEM relates to the internal organization of the two parties. Here the contrast is more stark. Comparative analysis of party statutes suggests that the PFL/DEM is the more organizationally centralized of the two parties, with a far greater role for its National Executive Committee than is the case of the PDS/PP (Paiva 2002; Ribeiro 2013). The ability of the PFL/DEM national executive to intervene in subnational party units is very high: among major parties, the only comparison is with the highly disciplined PT. (In Brazil, national-level party interventions typically occur either to veto a state-level party candidacy or to enforce national guidelines about acceptable electoral coalition partners.) Moreover, prior to the party's "refounding" in 2007

---

[12] Illiterates were enfranchised by a constitutional amendment in May 1985, at a time when adult illiteracy in Northeastern states ranged from 35 to 45 percent (compared to a regional average of about 16 percent today). Bruce and Rocha (2014) are the first to show empirically that PFL elites in the Northeast mobilized strategically to register these new voters between 1985 and 1988, thus solidifying their local machines in the early years of democracy.

[13] Both Sarney and Magalhães had been PDS governors of their states during military rule, and both defected from the PDS between 1984 and 1986. Although Sarney was forced by electoral legislation to join the PMDB, the first national convention of the PFL (April 1986) elected Sarney as the "patron" of the party (Tarouco 1999: 70). Magalhães was the powerful minister of communications in the Sarney government before returning to the Bahia governorship in 1990 and then to the Senate until his death in 2007.

(which involved a name change and a generational transfer in the national leadership), the PFL/DEM was marked by extraordinary continuity of membership (R. Ribeiro 2014). In the first twenty years of democracy, the national executive was dominated by many of the same luminaries who had founded the Liberal Front in 1984: Jorge Bornhausen, Marco Maciel, Guilherme Palmeira, Saulo Queiroz, and members of the Sarney (Maranhão) and Magalhães (Bahia) machines. This was decidedly not the case in the PDS/PP, whose leadership has changed hands on numerous occasions, at times due to the absorption of smaller parties (Almeida 2004).

A fifth and final difference between the PDS/PP and the PFL/DEM concerns the parties' participation in national governments. Under Brazil's system of coalitional presidentialism,[14] the nominal party of the president normally has less than 20 percent of lower house seats, and presidents typically build oversized, heterogeneous coalitions in order to pass legislation in Congress (Power 2010; Raile, Pereira, and Power 2011). Octavio Amorim Neto (personal communication) has identified thirty-three distinct cabinet coalitions between 1985 and 2014, some seventeen of which formed prior to the PT's breakthrough victory in 2002 and sixteen of which existed under presidents Lula and Dilma. In the period of center-right dominance in Brazil (1985–2002), the PDS/PP was present in eight of the seventeen cabinets, while the PFL/DEM was in sixteen out of seventeen (it quit the Cardoso government nine months before his term ended). Yet in the period of PT hegemony beginning in 2003, the PDS/PP was present in thirteen of sixteen cabinets and the PFL/DEM in *zero*. No PFL/DEM politician participated in national government between March 2002 and August 2016, when right-leaning Michel Temer (PMDB) assumed the presidency after the impeachment of Dilma (PT).

Therefore, the historic "left turn" in Brazil in 2002 impacted one authoritarian successor party much more than the other. Despite its origins in a military regime that jailed Lula and tortured Dilma, the postauthoritarian PDS/PP evolved into a pragmatic, clientelistic "party for rent" that was able to find ways to offer political support to PT presidents until 2016. The same could not be achieved by the PFL/DEM, despite the fact that its ideological distance from the PT has always been very similar to that of the PDS/PP. The PFL/DEM's more vocal, programmatic, neoliberal stance and its strong identification with the reformist Cardoso administration (1995–2002) led it to a position of firm opposition to the PT-led governments between 2003 and 2016. Given that the core PFL/DEM leadership supported every president, military or civilian, between March 1964 and March 2002, this new opposition status was highly uncomfortable for the party (Ribeiro 2014).

---

[14] On the concept of "coalitional presidentialism," see Power (2010).

7.2 TRADING PLACES? THE PDS/PP OVERTAKES THE PFL/DEM

One of the most important trends in the Brazilian party system over the past decade has been the rapid erosion of the PFL/DEM. For the first twenty years of political democracy, the PFL/DEM was by far the larger and more influential of the two ASPs. However, the two parties had traded places by the end of Lula's second term in 2010, a point at which the PDS/PP was firmly ensconced in national government and the PFL/DEM had already spent years in the political wilderness. The 2008 municipal elections were the first in which the PDS/PP captured more mayoralties than the PFL/DEM (a feat repeated in 2012), and the October 2014 congressional elections were the first in which the PDS/PP won a greater share of Chamber seats than its rival (see Figures 7.6 and 7.7). What explains this role reversal? In this section, I explore the reasons for the PFL/DEM's impressive decline.

One hypothesis would be that the PFL/DEM has failed to field viable presidential candidates. Yet this is a problem affecting *both* authoritarian successor parties, and in any case a failure to recruit competitive presidential candidates is not fatal to Brazilian parties. Under the system of coalitional presidentialism in place over the past twenty years, the number of formateur parties has been small: two, to be exact (the PSDB and PT). Yet parties that are not presidentially competitive have three other options: (1) enter national government as support parties, (2) win executive offices at the subnational level (governorships and important mayoralties), or (3) occupy a position of marginality without access to federal or subnational resources. Only two parties, the PMDB and PFL, have succeeded in combining the first two strategies for lengthy periods:

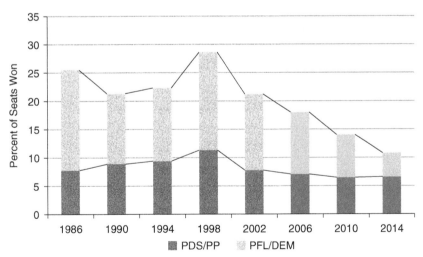

FIGURE 7.6 Share of lower house seats won by the two Brazilian authoritarian successor parties, 1986–2014
Source: Tribunal Superior Eleitoral.

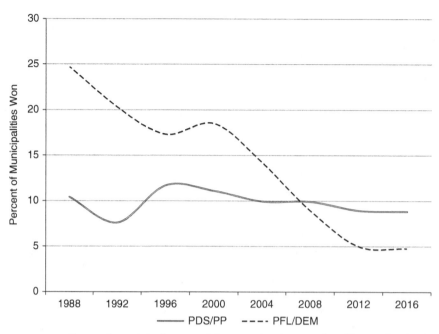

FIGURE 7.7 Share of municipal mayoralties won by the two Brazilian authoritarian successor parties, 1988–2016
Source: Tribunal Superior Eleitoral.

these were highly nationalized support parties that controlled important state governments and had large, pivotal delegations in Congress. Several smaller center-right parties, including the PDS/PP, PTB, and PL/PR,[15] have banked on the first strategy of serving as "parties for rent" in Brasília. These parties moved more or less effortlessly from the Cardoso to the Lula coalitions. The third option – remaining out of coalitional politics altogether – is perhaps the most risky in Brazilian politics and has generally been restricted to a handful of small ideological parties (the Socialism and Freedom Party or PSOL is the best current example). Of the many parties that have occupied this purgatorial space, only the PT has ever succeeded in breaking out of it, largely by having a viable presidential candidate.[16]

Table 7.1 compares the experiences of the two authoritarian successor parties in direct presidential elections, which resumed in 1989. In the first direct presidential

---

[15] The Liberal Party (PL) merged with the Party for Reconstruction of the National Order (PRONA) to form the Republican Party (PR) in 2006.
[16] One could argue that the Communist Party of Brazil (PCdoB) did so as well. But this occurred only because the party had established itself as a satellite of the PT and rode the coattails of the PT's national breakthrough in 2002. The PCdoB split from the historic Moscow-line Brazilian Communist Party (PCB) in 1962 and has backed the PT since the late 1980s.

TABLE 7.1 *Authoritarian successor parties in presidential races in Brazil, 1989–2014*

Election	PDS/PP	PFL/DEM
1989	Nominates Paulo Maluf, who finishes in 5th place with 8.6 percent	Nominates Aureliano Chaves, who finishes in 9th place with 0.86 percent
1994	Nominates Espiridião Amin, who finishes in 6th place with 2.8 percent	Supplies VP candidate Marco Maciel on winning ticket of FH Cardoso (PSDB)
1998	Officially backs reelection bid of FH Cardoso (PSDB), who wins in first round	Supplies VP candidate Marco Maciel on winning ticket of FH Cardoso (PSDB)
2002	Abstains from national race, neutral; focuses on gubernatorial contests	Declines to endorse Cardoso's candidate, José Serra (PSDB); informally backs Serra in runoff, who loses to Lula (PT)
2006	Formally supports reelection of Lula (PT) in both rounds	Supplies VP candidate José Jorge on losing ticket of Geraldo Alckmin (PSDB)
2010	Informally supports Dilma (PT) in first round; formal support in runoff	Supplies VP candidate Índio da Costa on losing ticket of José Serra (PSDB)
2014	Formally supports Dilma (PT) in both rounds	Supports Aécio Neves (PSDB), who loses to Dilma (PT)

Sources: Tribunal Superior Eleitoral and journalistic accounts.

election, the performance of the PFL nominee, Aureliano Chaves (who had been the civilian PDS vice president in the last military government), was beyond dismal: Chaves received less than 1 percent of the popular vote, a reflection of the party's identification with the hugely unpopular Sarney government at the time. Chaves was the first and last PFL/DEM candidate for president. The PDS candidate Paulo Maluf took a respectable 8.6 percent in the 1989 contest, reflecting his party's distance from the federal government and his electoral base in the state of São Paulo, home to 22 percent of the electorate. The PDS attempted the presidency on one further occasion five years later, nominating Santa Catarina governor Espiridião Amin, who received 3 percent of the vote. Since then, neither of the two ASPs has had serious presidential ambitions.[17] The PFL's successful alliance

---

[17] The PFL's Roseana Sarney, the daughter of former president José Sarney, was a promising pre-candidate in late 2001 and early 2002, performing strongly in the polls. However, she was forced to drop out of the race in March when the Federal Police seized large amounts of unexplained dollars in her husband's business. The PFL had no other viable name and abstained from the

with the PSDB in the 1994 and 1998 presidential elections gave the PFL the vice presidency for eight years with Marco Maciel, a founder of the party; the party again supplied running mates to the PSDB nominees in 2006 (Geraldo Alckmin) and 2010 (José Serra), both of whom were defeated by the PT. The electoral potency of the PFL/DEM was so diminished by 2014 that the PSDB candidate Aécio Neves took the unusual step of selecting a running mate from his own party, even though the DEM was formally part of his electoral coalition.

The PFL/DEM, then, was never a presidential contender.[18] However, in the two decades when it was one of the four major parties in Brazilian politics, the PFL/DEM had two outstanding resources: its reliable presence in national government (until 2002) and its domination of Northeastern state and local governments (until roughly 2006). Both of these advantages have now been lost. The reasons for this have to do with the arrival of the PT in national power, but also with the ability of a rival party, the PMDB, to take over the PFL's earlier role as a reliable coalition partner for presidents.

On the first factor, presence in national government, from 1985 to 2002 it was commonplace to refer to the PFL/DEM as a highly professionalized "party of power." The party was one of two key coalition partners in the Sarney administration (1985–1990), helped stabilize and prolong the Collor presidency (1990–1992), offered critical support to the interim president Itamar Franco (1992–1994), and played a major role throughout Cardoso's two terms (1995–2002). The irrepressible *governismo* – i.e., an almost automatic alignment with the government of the day – of the PFL/DEM was the main theme running through most academic treatments of the party (e.g., Mainwaring, Meneguello, and Power 2000; Marcelino, Braga, and Domingos 2009; Paiva 2002; Tarouco 1999).[19] Typical of this perspective was the title of Corbellini's (2005) doctoral thesis on the PFL: "Power as a Vocation." Among ASPs in Latin America, the PFL

---

presidential contest. The party also declined to endorse the government candidate, José Serra of the PSDB, whom it suspected of encouraging the Federal Police raid.

[18] To be fair, this is a glaring weakness of the PMDB as well, and to a certain extent applies to thirty-two of Brazil's thirty-four parties: only the PSDB and PT were consistent presidential contenders between 1994 and 2014. Explaining the weakness of other parties in presidential elections would come down to explaining the emergence of the PSDB–PT duopoly, a debate that is beyond the scope of this chapter (for some hypotheses, see Limongi and Cortez [2010] and Mainwaring, Power, and Bizzarro [2018]). However, the failure of the ASPs to contend for the presidency seems mostly unrelated to regime legacies, given that no major presidential candidate since 1989 has staked a campaign on a defense of the military regime, nor has any plausible candidate been severely handicapped by links to the authoritarian past. For example, in the founding election of 1989, ARENA/PDS veteran Fernando Collor won 30.5 percent of the first-round valid votes; adding the votes of his former co-partisans in the race (Paulo Maluf, Guilherme Afif, Aureliano Chaves, and Affonso Camargo) would bring the ex-ARENA/PDS total to 45.6 percent.

[19] The classic contribution by Victor Nunes Leal, *Coronelismo, Enxada e Voto* (1949), characterizes *governismo* as the "exaggeratedly pro-government character of state and federal representation" in Brazil (Leal 1977: 131).

was perhaps the outstanding example of a "reactive" authoritarian successor party being created in an effort to hang on to national power, and the strategy paid off well in the years from Sarney to Cardoso. Defining the PFL/DEM as a professional "support party" (*partido de sustentação*) was correct in this period, but such a depiction carried with it an implicit hypothesis: that exclusion from national power would irreparably harm the party.

Recent research by Ricardo Ribeiro (2014) tests and confirms this hypothesis. The departure of the PFL from national government in 2002 deprived it of the resources that it had traditionally channeled to voters, to party cadres, and to subnational governments controlled by the party. Its strong antipathy to the PT left it unable to reach an accommodation with the Lula government, something that was rather quickly achieved by the other authoritarian successor party, the PDS/PP. After the PFL/DEM went into opposition, the party leadership was unable to stem defections of elected politicians who preferred to be in parties aligned with the Lula government. In 2002, the PFL elected eighty-four federal deputies, second only to the PT, but some thirty-nine of these deputies abandoned the party over the next four years – with thirty-five of them moving into progovernment parties (Ribeiro 2014: 17–20). The rapid erosion of the party's fortunes led to a major effort at re-branding in 2007, when the party instigated a rapid generational turnover within the national executive committee and decided to change the party's name and acronym as well.[20] The eventual choice of name was simply Democratas (DEM). According to Ricardo Ribeiro, in 2006 political consultant Antonio Lavareda used focus groups to help the PFL settle on a new brand name. Focus group research led not only to the abandonment of the word "party" (eternally unpopular with voters) but also to the adoption of a descriptor ("Democrats") that was intended to put as much distance as possible between the party and the legacy of the military regime (Ribeiro 2014: 12, 31). However, the effort to remake the party's image has had very little to show for it to date: the party's fortunes have continued to erode, as Figures 7.6 and 7.7 demonstrate.

The hypothesis that the PFL/DEM began its decline when it lost federal power is overwhelmingly supported by the available evidence. Yet its coalition partner, the PSDB, also left national government in 2002 without similarly catastrophic consequences. This is largely because the PSDB could retreat into powerful subnational units with significant resources, namely industrialized states such as São Paulo and Minas Gerais, where it controlled state governorships throughout the PT years. (From 2010 to 2014, for example, PSDB notables governed states containing 47 percent of the national population and over 55 percent of GDP.) The redistributive policies of the Lula government dramatically reduced poverty and inequality throughout Brazil, yet

---

[20] Yet the generational change preserved many of the same surnames from the prior leadership of the party: Paulo Bornhausen, Rodrigo Maia, Fábio Souto, and Antônio Carlos Magalhães Neto were all sons or grandsons of earlier PFL luminaries.

these policies had their weakest electoral payoffs in the more socioeconomically modernized states (Hunter and Power 2007; Power 2016; Zucco 2008). But the effect of these pro-poor policies was truly dramatic in the Northeast, the traditional stronghold of the PFL/DEM. A fascinating new avenue of research on the electoral sociology of the Northeast (e.g., Borges 2011; Montero 2012) has shown how federally directed social policies in the Lula–Dilma years weakened traditional clientelistic networks and undermined local oligarchies throughout the region. The result was growing pluralism and competitiveness, leading to breakthrough victories of the left in key Northeastern states, notably in 2006 in Bahia, Maranhão, and Pernambuco. In 2010, left-leaning coalitions including the PT and excluding the DEM won the state governments of Bahia, Ceará, Pernambuco, Piauí, and Sergipe. The repercussions of pluralization have been felt in other elections as well: in the 2014 legislative contests, the DEM elected only twenty-two deputies throughout Brazil, and only nine of these came from the Northeast (Bahia was the only state to elect more than one).

Overall, the PFL/DEM fell victim to a double whammy: it first lost federal power in 2002, and then only a few years later succumbed to a rapid electoral realignment in its traditional electoral strongholds. But there is also another important macropolitical trend here, which has been the consolidation of the PMDB as Brazil's major *partido de sustentação* since early 2004, when it first joined the Lula government. The functional role played by the PMDB in the Lula–Dilma years – occupying key federal ministries, providing a large bloc of votes in Congress, mobilizing support for the federal government throughout the national territory, and even supplying a vice president – was virtually *identical* to the role played by the PFL/DEM in the Cardoso years. The PMDB is now the longest-surviving "party of power" and successfully transacted with both the Cardoso and Lula coalitions, something the PFL/DEM was unable to do.[21]

Meanwhile, the direct descendant of ARENA, today's PP, began supporting the Lula government in 2003 and entered the federal cabinet in 2005. The relationship between the PP and the PT presidents has been laden with controversy: the PP's role as a "party for rent" has been responsible for two of the largest corruption episodes in recent Brazilian history. Party leaders Pedro Henry, Pedro Corrêa, and the late José Janene figured prominently in the *mensalão* scandal of 2005, in which aides to Lula paid monthly stipends to at least eighteen deputies (mostly in the clientelistic parties of the center-right) in return for support on key legislation.[22] Despite the disproportionate involvement

---

[21] The PMDB's value to the PT was so high that, at the urging of the outgoing Lula, the PMDB party president Michel Temer was rewarded with the vice presidential nomination in Dilma's successful presidential runs in 2010 and 2014. This proved a fatal error, as Temer later conspired with opposition forces to secure Dilma's impeachment and his own accession to the presidency in 2016.

[22] Corrêa, a six-term deputy first elected by ARENA in 1978, was expelled from Congress in 2006; Henry resigned his seat to avoid the same fate; and Janene was absolved by his peers in a controversial secret vote. Henry was later arrested, tried, and convicted of receiving R$4 million in support for the PP via an off-the-books campaign finance scheme. A medical

of the PP in the scandal, Lula maintained the party in the cabinet and in the coalition assembled for his reelection bid in 2006. In the 2014–2016 Petrobras scandal, the PP again accounted for thirty-one of the forty-nine politicians who were investigated by the public prosecutor for intermediating corporate bribes.[23] Whether this scandal will mortally wound the PP remains unclear: the party clearly survived the *mensalão* scandal intact, as well as the perpetual controversy surrounding party leader Paulo Maluf.[24] Yet as the fourth largest Brazilian party in terms of *filiados* (card-carrying members), the party remains valuable to presidents. With 1.4 million members in 2017, the PP is approximately the same size as the PSDB, and about 40 percent larger than the once-proud DEM.

At the federal level, both ASPs benefited from the impeachment and conviction of Dilma Rousseff in 2016. In Dilma's ill-fated second term, the PP controlled the influential Ministry of Regional Integration, responsible for public works and one of the best-placed ministries for dispensing political patronage. While the DEM worked tirelessly to engineer Dilma's ouster for illegal accounting procedures in 2015–2016, the PP stayed in the PT-led cabinet until the very end, leaving the government only on April 12, 2016. Four weeks later, the Chamber of Deputies approved articles of impeachment against Dilma, and she was forced to turn over the government to her disloyal vice president, Michel Temer (PMDB), who became acting president on May 12. Temer immediately invited the PP to return to government and rewarded the party with two powerhouse ministries, Health and Agriculture. He also brought the DEM into the cabinet for the first time in fourteen years, awarding it the Ministry of Education, which the party had controlled almost continuously in the 1980s and 1990s.[25] Long sundered by their different responses to the rise of the PT, the two ASPs were finally reunited in the Temer cabinet – easily the most conservative government in a generation.[26]

doctor, he is serving his prison sentence by working in a public hospital. On the *mensalão*, see Taylor (2017).

[23] There is a connection between the two scandals: Janene, who died in 2010, originally secured posts in Petrobras for several corrupt *diretores* (second-tier department heads). These *diretores* then colluded with contractors to overcharge Petrobras for services rendered, with some of the surplus going to political parties for illegal campaign financing.

[24] Maluf, long wanted in the United States for fraud and money laundering, has been on an Interpol arrest list since early 2010. In May 2017, at age 85, he was finally convicted in Brazil's highest criminal court for money laundering and sentenced to nearly eight years in prison.

[25] Only two months after Temer took office, the speaker of the Chamber of Deputies, Eduardo Cunha – the principal PMDB conspirator against Dilma Rousseff – was forced to resign due to corruption charges (he was later arrested, convicted, and sentenced to fifteen years in prison). The snap election to replace the speaker was won by Rodrigo Maia of the DEM, who became the party's highest-serving public official since 2002. Maia, a forty-six-year-old moderate from the modernizing wing of the party, was reelected to the speakership in 2017. With the vice presidency of Brazil vacant under Temer, Maia became first in the line of succession.

[26] In the first electoral test after Dilma's ouster, the PT was massively reduced in size by the contests for 5,568 mayors in October 2016. The party went from electing 638 mayors in 2012

7.3 CONCLUSIONS: THE BRAZILIAN ASPS IN COMPARATIVE PERSPECTIVE

To understand the trajectories of Brazil's two authoritarian successor parties, we need to return to the contextual variables cited at the beginning of this chapter. The Brazilian military regime of 1964–1985 did not eliminate political parties or Congress. Physical repression and human rights violations were relatively low in comparative perspective. The economic performance of the regime was solid, and significant advances were made in infrastructure and state capacity. Liberalization and subnational elections ensured that political pluralism existed prior to national regime change. The military returned to the barracks with a comparatively high level of public legitimacy. A two-way amnesty meant that conflicts arising from transitional justice were off the agenda. A generation of professional politicians that had supported military rule was able to navigate the transition mostly unscathed: in comparative perspective, postauthoritarian Brazil had an extraordinarily high level of continuity in personnel and practices.

Due to these important contextual factors, the existence of a "regime cleavage" (i.e., authoritarians vs. democrats) was strongly attenuated in Brazil, and the democratic transition did not produce sharply defined "winners" and "losers" as in many other cases of democratization during the third wave. What this context means for the study of ASPs in Brazil is that we should put a bit less emphasis on "authoritarian" and on "successor," and quite a lot more on "parties." The PDS/PP and PFL/DEM were never antisystem parties under democracy. Although both parties defended the outgoing military regime in an abstract sense, they by no means defined themselves exclusively by its legacy, nor were they vocal apologists for all of its policies and practices. The two parties certainly benefited from the privileged position held by the parent party, ARENA/PDS, under military rule. But in converting the political and electoral resources of ARENA into successor parties, ex-authoritarian elites behaved much like other Brazilian politicians. For these elites, the transferability of authoritarian-era skills and strategies to a democratic system was rather high, mainly because Brazil maintained the trappings of electoral and legislative politics under military rule. The founders of PDS/PP and PFL/DEM engaged in ordinary political practices – clientelism, patronage, running local campaigns, supporting executives in Congress – before the democratic transition, and they did so again after the democratic transition. They were successors to a nondemocratic regime, but in many ways they could also be understood as traditional Brazilian party politicians.

(11.5 percent) to only 254 mayors in 2016 (4.6 percent). However, as Figure 7.7 illustrates, neither ASP – including the DEM, which loudly spearheaded opposition to the PT for thirteen years – benefited from the PT's subnational collapse. The DEM continued its slow decline, dropping from 278 to 266 mayors. Although Michel Temer retained the party in his coalition, the DEM's value to presidents had eroded sharply compared to the Cardoso era of the 1990s.

This perspective helps narrow the answers to two of the overarching comparative questions addressed by this volume. In Brazil, the best answer to "What explains the success of authoritarian successor parties?" is probably "access to state resources," meaning continuation of a foothold in national government. The best answer to "Why are some authoritarian successor parties more successful than others?" is, once again, probably "access to state resources." The same reason explains why the PFL/DEM was the dominant ASP in 1985–2002 and why the PDS/PP supplanted it in the Lula–Dilma years. The PFL/DEM's initial advantage was due to its creation as an opportunistic "reactive" party: it defected to the opposition camp in 1984–1985, ensuring a major role for itself in the first postauthoritarian presidency and "flipping" nine state governments in the Northeast from the PDS to the new PFL. This initial advantage turned into a more lasting role as a *partido de sustentação*, which took on a more ideological air when the PFL/DEM strongly supported the Cardoso-era neoliberal reforms in the 1990s. Strongly identified with the Cardoso experiment and ideologically very distant from the PT, the PFL/DEM could no longer continue in its role as a "support party" after the victory of Lula in 2002. But the PDS/PP, by now a smaller, less ideological "party for rent" with a less distinguished leadership, was able to reach a rapid understanding with the PT and join a left-dominated coalition. The party's ideological flexibility was on display again in 2016 when it quit the PT government and entered the right-leaning Temer cabinet only a month later.

As a reactive authoritarian successor party looking to build an identity as quickly as possible, the PFL/DEM adopted a centralized governing structure that committed party notables (although not always the rank and file) to a position of "modern liberalism," one that came to policy fruition in the 1990s. This moved the party away from the extreme pragmatism and opportunism that had characterized its birth. Thus the party quickly encountered the traditional tension between pragmatism ("our party should support *all* governments") and ideology ("our party can only support *some* governments"). The PDS/PP, the other authoritarian successor party, clearly resolved this tension in favor of the former option. The PMDB, the PFL/DEM's major rival as a national catchall support party, also unambiguously chose pragmatism. But the PFL/DEM leadership opted for a more programmatic stance: it sided with the post-Cardoso PSDB in its strong opposition to PT governments after 2002. Unlike the PSDB, it could not retreat easily to its traditional electoral strongholds, because at the same time these Northeastern states were undergoing an electoral transformation as a consequence of the PT's national project of social inclusion. The PFL/DEM had no way to prevent the migration of rational Northeastern politicians into parties aligned with the federal government, and this caused a sharp erosion of the PFL/DEM's once-powerful regional machines.

In retrospect, the regional dependency of the PFL/DEM on the Northeast can now be identified as the Achilles' heel of the party. Yet in the first fifteen years of

Brazilian democracy, few observers perceived this, and even fewer (if any) would have guessed that the party that would eventually debilitate the PFL/DEM in this most "traditional" region of Brazil would be the PT. In the conception of the Northeastern elites of the 1980s, the leftist PT was viewed as a minor, remote São Paulo party based largely on labor unions and intellectuals. Yet after 2003, the PT used its control of the presidency and particularly the Ministry of Social Development to pursue transformative pro-poor policies in the hinterland, dislodging oligarchies with surprising ease in the span of two electoral cycles. The PT's signature conditional cash transfer program, Bolsa Família, served as a political eviction notice for the PFL/DEM.

The trajectories of the PFL/DEM and the PDS/PP would be difficult to comprehend in the other major Latin American case with two ASPs, Chile. First, the division between the Chilean UDI and RN originated in differences between "hard-liners" and "soft-liners" that emerged well before the transition to democracy (the coalescence of an openly hard-line civilian faction was apparent as early as 1983, when Jaime Guzmán founded the UDI). No such cleavage was readily visible in the Brazilian PDS, whose internal split was explained better by opportunism than by ideology or defense of the military regime. Moreover, the main drivers of intra-PDS conflict (the debates over possible direct elections for 1985 and the nomination of Paulo Maluf in the indirect election that eventually took place) occurred extremely late in the game, within the final year of military rule. Second, Chile's unitary system discourages the formation of regionalized political parties by subnational elites, as was the case with Brazil's PFL in the mid-1980s. Third, although both Brazil and Chile have permanent minority presidentialism, necessitating coalition government at all times, interparty alliances are far more ideologically consistent in Chile. A coalition between the Chilean Socialist Party and the rightist UDI is unthinkable, whereas in Brazil the analogous alliance (the PT with the PDS/PP) was seen as unremarkable throughout the Lula–Dilma years. This difference is undoubtedly owed to historically higher levels of programmatic party structuration in Chile and also to the binomial electoral system used between 1989 and 2013, which encouraged stable interparty alliances (Siavelis 2006).

Yet the sharp contrast between Brazil and Chile is also related to the relative shallowness of the "regime cleavage" in Brazil, as well as to the timing and sequencing of the respective democratic transitions. Pre-coup party identification remained strong throughout Chilean authoritarianism, but was mostly irrelevant in Brazil by the late 1980s; and even Brazil's new post-coup party loyalties (ARENA vs. MDB, in the 1966–1979 two-party system) were heavily diluted by the muddled circumstances of the transition to democracy (i.e., O'Donnell's coalition of "all for all"). Given a weaker regime cleavage and the presence of robust federalism – which permits incongruent, cross-cutting alliances at all levels of government – one could say that in Brazilian coalitional politics, "anything goes." Moreover, although both the Chilean and Brazilian military regimes could point to policy successes, thus potentially equipping their

ASPs with a "usable past," the timing of their economic booms relative to their democratic transitions could hardly have been more different. The last six years of the Chilean dictatorship (1984–1989) boasted an average GDP growth rate of 7.5 percent per annum; even though General Augusto Pinochet had presided over two earlier downturns, these could be partly forgotten given that the regime ended on an economic high note (with an incredible 10.6 percent growth rate in 1989). By contrast, the final six years of the Brazilian regime (1979–1984, corresponding closely to the presidency of General João Figueiredo) were an economic bust: these years had an average growth rate of 2.5 percent (a third of the rate achieved by the first four military presidents prior to Figueiredo). A major contraction of –2.9 percent occurred in 1983, with inflation approaching 200 percent annually, and the prolonged stagflation led to massive popular protests in favor of direct elections. Although boasting some important policy successes in comparative and historical perspective, the Brazilian military regime ended with a whimper, making it much more difficult for Brazil's ASPs to make a seamless transition to defenders of the *ancien régime* than it was for their Chilean counterparts.

To conclude, some thirty years after the transition endgame of 1984–1985, the contrasting trajectories of Brazil's two ASPs seem only weakly related to regime legacies. The relatively low salience of a postauthoritarian regime cleavage in Brazil, combined with three decades of democratic experience, caused the parties to diverge mainly for reasons of "ordinary politics." The key differences in the long-term trajectories of the two parties are explained by their access to federal resources, by their ability to pivot between rival coalitions, and by the vulnerability of their electoral bases to incursion by other rival parties. It is revealing that DEM politicians in a changing Northeast responded by simply switching to other parties. This last factor echoes the discussion of Africa by Adrienne LeBas in her chapter (Chapter 6, this volume): where party systems are fluid and barriers to defection are low, ASPs have struggled to institutionalize.

If there is a comparative lesson to be drawn here, it concerns the strategic horizons of reactive authoritarian successor parties. While the PFL's opportunistic defection from the military regime gave it the pole position among Brazilian conservative parties in 1985, the advantages of such a maneuver cannot last forever. In the end, they can be undermined by more traditional predictors of party survival such as political recruitment, sociological change, alliance strategies, and access to the state.

PART III

WHAT ARE THE EFFECTS OF AUTHORITARIAN
SUCCESSOR PARTIES ON DEMOCRACY?

8

Mexico's PRI

The Resilience of an Authoritarian Successor Party and Its Consequences for Democracy

Gustavo A. Flores-Macías

Between 1929 and 2000, Mexico was an authoritarian regime.[1] During this time, elections were held regularly, but because of fraud, coercion, and the massive abuse of state resources, the Institutional Revolutionary Party (PRI) won virtually every election. It held onto the presidency until 2000, Congress until 1997, and did not even lose a gubernatorial election until 1989. While the regime preferred to co-opt its opponents, it could also engage in harsh repression, as when it massacred hundreds of university students in 1968. The formula was effective: the regime survived for seventy-one years, making it one of the most durable authoritarian regimes ever and leading the Peruvian novelist Mario Vargas Llosa to describe it as "the perfect dictatorship." By 2000, however, the regime came to an end when the PRI lost the presidency. Mexico became a democracy, and the PRI made the transition from authoritarian *ruling* party to authoritarian *successor* party. Yet the PRI did not disappear. It continued to be the largest party in Congress and in the states, and it was voted back into the presidency in 2012. This electoral performance has made the PRI one of the world's most resilient authoritarian successor parties. What explains its resilience?

The chapter is divided into four main sections. The first one introduces the authoritarian regime of which the PRI was a central part, presents an overview of the democratic transition, and shows the PRI's electoral performance over time. The second provides an explanation for the resilience of the PRI since the transition, emphasizing three main factors: the party's continuous control over state resources at the subnational level; the democratic governments' failure to alter the nature of state–society relations that supported the authoritarian regime; and the mediocre performance of other parties in office after 2000.

---

[1] I am grateful to Candelaria Garay, Frances Hagopian, Chappell Lawson, James Loxton, Scott Mainwaring, Kevin Middlebrook, Mariano Sánchez-Talanquer, and the participants at Harvard's DRCLAS Tuesday Seminar for thoughtful feedback. All errors are my own.

The third section discusses how the PRI's resilience has undermined the quality of Mexico's democracy. The fourth section concludes.

8.1 MEXICO'S PRI

The PRI was the heir to the winning factions of the Mexican Revolution – a bloody, ten-year civil conflict that began in 1910. Although the conflict started as a pro-democracy movement – motivated by the constant reelection of dictator Porfirio Díaz – along the way the adoption of progressive social policies on behalf of workers and peasants became a central part of the revolutionary governments' program. In 1929, after stepping down as president, Plutarco Elías Calles (1924–1928) founded the National Revolutionary Party (PNR) in an attempt to pacify and bring together different revolutionary factions. Organized according to a territorial structure, the PNR became an umbrella for the different revolutionary strongmen to advance their political goals peacefully. As a way to undermine the power of Calles, who was angling to maintain control over the presidency even after the end of his term in what became known as "El Maximato," President Lázaro Cárdenas (1934–1940) restructured the party in 1938. Cárdenas changed the name to the Party of the Mexican Revolution (PRM) and reorganized it along corporatist lines. Rather than state-led organizations, the party's structure would rest on four main occupation-related sectors: workers, peasants, popular (commercial and professional), and military. Eight years later, President Manuel Ávila Camacho (1940–1946) would give the party its current name, the Institutional Revolutionary Party (PRI), as the party launched the candidacy of Miguel Alemán Valdés in the 1946 presidential election. The election of Alemán Valdés (1946–1952) marked the end of the military presidents (previous presidents had all participated militarily in the Mexican Revolution) and the beginning of a civilian tradition within the party.

The regime that emerged out of the Mexican Revolution enjoyed strong legitimacy among a broad cross-section of society for decades and had four key characteristics: it was authoritarian, hyper-presidentialist, corporatist, and nationalist. First, it was authoritarian because, although elections were held at regular intervals and multiple parties were allowed to participate, the cards were heavily stacked against the opposition to deny it electoral victories (Greene 2007; Levitsky and Way 2010: 149–161; Magaloni 2006). The government manipulated electoral outcomes (Schedler 2002). Opposition leaders were arrested, harassed, or killed. The media was either bought off or harassed into submission by the government.

The government also maintained several small "satellite" parties, such as the Authentic Party of the Mexican Revolution (PARM) and the Popular Socialist Party (PPS), whose share of the vote was always minimal, but which provided a dose of legitimacy to the electoral process by giving the illusion of a multiparty democracy. The only real opposition party was the National Action Party

(PAN), a conservative Catholic party founded in 1939 (Loaeza 1999). However, the PAN never received more than 17 percent of the vote prior to the beginning of the transition in the 1990s.

A no-reelection principle guaranteed elite turnover and granted the authoritarian regime a façade of liberal democracy that was instrumental in isolating opposition groups and maintaining legitimacy abroad (Lawson 2000: 270). However, unlike most of the military regimes that prevailed in Latin America during the twentieth century, the PRI's authoritarianism was based more on co-optation than open repression.

Second, throughout most of the twentieth century, power was highly concentrated in the presidency to the point where the president was often referred to as *Tlatoani* – a reference to the powerful rulers of the Aztec empire in precolonial times. Not only did presidents control elections, but they had de facto control over all policy spheres, and a rubber-stamp Congress ensured that the president's legislative initiatives would always pass. Because of the constitutional prohibition on reelection, presidents could not stay in power beyond a single six-year term. However, an informal institution known as the *dedazo* (choosing with the finger) allowed the president to handpick his own successor (Langston 2006b). The president could also handpick candidates for all elected offices (including executives and legislators at all levels of government), as well as the party's leadership and justices throughout the judicial system. If the president changed his mind, he could remove government officials, both elected and unelected, at will (González Oropeza 1983).

Third, corporatism was the currency of state–society relations. The PRI organized its membership along sectoral lines. Labor and peasant organizations provided mass support for the party for decades. This was critical for the long-term stability of the regime. Because unions and peasants supported the PRI, there was no social base for the left, and because of the PRI's cozy relations with business, there was also no basis for the emergence of a strong conservative party. The PRI became an all-encompassing centrist party, with room for all groups of society, as long as they became formally affiliated with one of the party's corporatist sectors.

Fourth, having emerged out of a social revolution, the PRI followed economic nationalism for most of the twentieth century – until the mid-1980s, when governments adopted market-oriented policies. The PRI generally favored domestic industry in exchange for resources and compliance from business groups (Alba Vega 2006). This marriage resulted in stable economic growth and an attractive investment climate. Whenever the government needed to adopt austerity measures, unions and peasant organizations generally went along.[2] This cooperation laid the foundations for a long period of economic growth during the 1950s and 1960s known as

---

[2] Labor's support for austerity was not automatic, however, and real bargaining often took place between the government and labor. For an analysis of state–labor relations, see Middlebrook (1995).

"Mexico's Stabilizing Development." During this period Mexico's economy expanded at a rate of 6 percent annually – the fastest growth in Latin America – and inflation was among the lowest in the region. This sustained economic expansion provided the government with both legitimacy and resources to co-opt dissidents. Eventually, however, the regime became, as Lawson (2000: 270) puts it, a "gigantic, pork-barreling political machine, soaking the bulk of the population and selectively rewarding its leaders and adherents."

Overall, this was an "authoritarian regime with pretty features":[3] it was a civilian regime that held regular elections, enjoyed revolutionary legitimacy, co-opted the country's main interest groups, and performed relatively well economically until the 1982 debt crisis. For these reasons, the regime was remarkably stable and the PRI went virtually unchallenged for seventy-one years, winning eleven consecutive presidential elections.

8.1.1 Mexico's Democratic Transition

Although the PRI governments had been effective in political and economic terms, two major factors eventually contributed to the erosion of the regime (Lawson 2000). On the one hand, its economic success led to the emergence of social sectors whose interests were different from those of the main beneficiaries of PRI rule, especially small and medium business groups and middle-class professionals (González 2008: 21). These sectors were also less easily manipulated than the peasants and blue-collar workers that had constituted the foundation of the PRI's electoral support in the early and mid twentieth century. On the other hand, the series of economic crises in the 1980s and 1990s – including Mexico's default on its foreign debt in 1982 and the so-called "Peso Crisis" of 1994 – plunged the country into severe recessions and undermined the regime's legitimacy. The nationalist model of import substitution industrialization that had worked well for most of the twentieth century ran out of steam due to corruption, lack of competitiveness, and a bloated, ineffective state. The crisis strained the government's ability to distribute spoils in the form of subsidies, patronage, and pork.

The PRI governments of the 1980s and 1990s embraced market-oriented measures to address these crises. As a result of both an ideological shift and the new economic reality, slowly but surely the regime began to shed some of the sectors that had formed its support coalition, including labor, peasant organizations, bureaucrats, and even some business sectors. The ideological shift prompted a schism with the nationalist wing of the party in 1987. This led to the formation of a broad coalition of parties under the label of the National Democratic Front (FDN), led by Cuauhtémoc Cárdenas, the son of former PRI president Lázaro Cárdenas. The FDN, which would become the Party of the Democratic Revolution (PRD) in 1989, lost to the PRI candidate Carlos Salinas

---

[3] I owe this phrase to Steven Levitsky.

de Gortari (1988–1994) in the most contested presidential election in decades amid widespread allegations of fraud. The fraud allegations triggered nationwide mass protests, which shook the regime for weeks and dealt a harsh blow to its legitimacy.

With the regime's legitimacy severely compromised, Salinas reached an agreement with the leadership of the PAN to gain recognition of his government in exchange for electoral concessions. The year after the presidential election, the PRI government began to gradually and selectively recognize PAN victories in a few gubernatorial elections. In 1989, for the first time, the government recognized a PAN victory in the governor's race in the northern state of Baja California. Over the next few years, the PAN won a handful of other governorships.

Responding to social pressure, in 1990 the government created a new authority to oversee elections, the Federal Electoral Institute (IFE). The IFE became a respected institution, and additional reforms in 1993 and 1994 contributed to making elections cleaner. Although the PRI continued to dominate media access, the 1994 presidential election was deemed cleaner than any in Mexico's modern history (Magaloni 2005: 123).

Shortly after the election of PRI candidate Ernesto Zedillo (1994–2000) in 1994, the Peso Crisis further contributed to the regime's legitimacy crisis. If one justification for the lack of democracy had been economic prosperity, that pillar of the regime had crumbled. With mounting social pressure, in 1996 the government engaged in additional electoral reforms, including the granting of autonomy to the IFE and the Federal Electoral Tribunal, whose members would now have to be elected by a two-thirds majority (González 2015).

In the 1997 legislative elections, the first under the autonomous electoral authority, the PRI lost its majority in Congress for the first time, and Cuauhtémoc Cárdenas was elected mayor of Mexico City. Many analysts consider this year the turning point in Mexico's democratic transition (Magaloni 2005: 122). In 2000, the PRI was voted out of the presidency. In an election broadly recognized as free and fair, PAN candidate Vicente Fox (2000–2006), a former Coca-Cola executive, defeated PRI candidate Francisco Labastida, ending seventy-one years of hegemonic party rule and marking the beginning of a twelve-year period of PAN governments.

The turnover at the national level capped Mexico's long march toward democracy. Since the fraudulent election of 1988, several important changes had taken place, including the emergence of a more independent media, the emergence of a multi-party system, the erosion of hyper-presidentialism, and the decentralization and fragmentation of power. Not only had Congress and the courts become more independent, but state governments had also emerged as important political actors.

8.1.2 The PRI after the Transition

Although the PRI *regime* came to an end in 2000, the PRI as a *party* did not disappear. On the contrary, the PRI made a relatively smooth transition from authoritarian ruling party to authoritarian successor party. It not only managed to survive democratization, but remained a powerful political force. As Figure 8.1 shows, the PRI continued to dominate Congress, dipping below 40 percent of seats only briefly (three years for the lower house and six years for the Senate). While this was far from the two-thirds majorities that the PRI used to enjoy, it allowed the party to pass bills requiring a simple majority because of coalitions it forged with small parties that depended on its coattails for survival, such as the Mexican Green Ecologist Party (PVEM) and the New Alliance Party (PANAL). Finally, in 2012, after spending just twelve years out of power, the PRI was elected back to the presidency. Its candidate, Enrique Peña Nieto, the telegenic young PRI governor of Mexico State, won a 38 percent plurality. Although a shadow of the overwhelming victories that the PRI used to win under authoritarianism, this share of the vote was enough to beat the 32 and 26 percent garnered by the PRD and PAN candidates, respectively.

Figure 8.1 also shows that the PRI's electoral fortunes have declined considerably since 1985. The decline in share of the vote and seats was especially steep during the transition to democracy in the 1990s, but has plateaued since the PRI lost the presidency in 2000. Nevertheless, the PRI's

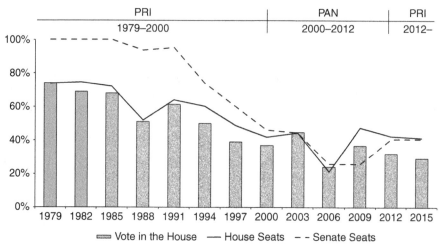

FIGURE 8.1 PRI performance in congress, 1979–2015

Note: Bars and lines are expressed as a share of total seats and total valid votes.
Source: INE (2016).

ability to remain a major player in Mexican politics and return to the presidency so quickly is remarkable. How did a party so negatively associated with authoritarian practices, electoral fraud, and economic mishandling manage to outperform its rivals in a democratic context?

8.2 EXPLAINING THE PRI'S RESILIENCE

In the remainder of the chapter, I highlight three main factors that explain the PRI's resilience in the aftermath of the transition: the PRI's control over government resources at the subnational level, the post-2000 democratic governments' failure to dismantle key institutions inherited from the authoritarian regime, and voters' dissatisfaction with the mediocre performance of the PRI's competitors.

8.2.1 Continuing Control over Subnational Government Resources

The first factor was the PRI's continuing ability to leverage government resources for electoral ends. The PAN's victory in the 2000 election removed the PRI from the presidency, but only partially undermined the PRI's ability to leverage resources at the state and local levels. Although the party's loss of the presidency was a major setback, the more decentralized nature of the political system that emerged after the transition proved to be favorable toward the PRI.

One of the consequences of the transition was the end of the hyper-presidentialist system, in which the president controlled everything from his own successor to the fate of elected government officials at all levels (Greene 2007). Before 2000, incumbency advantages were significant because of the PRI's control over most governments at all levels, the country's large public sector, and the lack of independent local electoral authorities to prevent the diversion of public resources – both human and material – for electoral use (Díaz Jiménez 2014: 24; Greene 2007).

The system that emerged after the transition saw a steady strengthening of state and local governments in Mexico's federal system. This was due to a number of factors, including opposition parties' efforts to empower state and local offices as a means of counterbalancing the power of the president, fiscal reforms that channeled oil surpluses to state and local coffers, and electoral reforms that curbed the informal prerogatives of the president. Concern over the PRI presidents' absolutist past and the PAN's historical commitment to the principle of subsidiarity – devolution of government responsibilities to local communities – further contributed to this trend between 2000 and 2012. Whereas fiscal decentralization reforms adopted in 1997 and 1999 under President Ernesto Zedillo (1994–2000) were an important step in transferring a majority of fiscal revenue toward the states and municipalities (Díaz-Cayeros 2006; Merino 2001: 150), additional reforms in 2003 and 2007 – which set rules for the distribution of oil revenue – further strengthened the fiscal positions of subnational units. Currently, for every peso collected, the federal government keeps only 33 cents (Giraudy 2015: 67).

Additionally, the fragmentation of the political system has made it harder for presidents to govern (Béjar Alagazi 2014), which has made governors increasingly important (Do Vale 2016; Hernández-Rodríguez 2003). In fact, studies suggest that gubernatorial coattails are now more important than presidential coattails in elections (Magar 2012), and that governors are increasingly influential in terms of congressional voting behavior (Cantú and Desposato 2012; Rosas and Langston 2011).

To be sure, the PAN and the PRD have made substantial progress in winning state and local elections. State governments have been particularly valuable because they concentrate important resources in their public budgets. States receive about two-thirds of the yearly federal budget, have bureaucracies of their own to dole out patronage positions, select companies for government procurement and infrastructure contracts, and provide visibility to elected officials through public relations budgets and daily official activities.

However, this devolution of power to the state level has benefited the PRI more than other parties. This is because, until 2016, *the PRI never held less than half of all state governments* – despite losing power at the national level in 2000.[4] Figure 8.2 illustrates the PRI's control of state governments since 1989. Between 1989, when the PRI recognized the PAN's victory in Baja California, and 1997, when it lost control of the lower house of Congress, the PRI allowed for a very gradual turnover in state governments. During this period, the PAN never controlled more than 10 percent of the thirty-two state governor races.[5] Between 1997 and 2002, the PRI's control of state governments declined significantly, to the point where it only controlled seventeen of thirty-two states.[6] Between 2002 and 2015, however, the PRI's position stabilized, with the PRI's control oscillating between sixteen and twenty states, or 50 and 63 percent of the total.[7]

In short, with the exception of the sudden decline between 1997 and 2002, due to changes in the electoral rules promoting transparency, the PRI has enjoyed a sizable and fairly stable resource base at the subnational level. Not only did it control between half and two-thirds of all states between 2000 and 2016, but in nine states (28 percent of the total),[8] it had never lost a gubernatorial election

---

[4] In 2016, the number of PRI-led state governments dipped to slightly less than half, or fifteen out of thirty-two.
[5] This includes the Federal District, now Mexico City.
[6] During this period, the PRD won the Mexico City government, and the PAN won the government of the northern industrial state of Nuevo León. This gave the opposition control of the two wealthiest jurisdictions.
[7] Since 2002, the PAN and PRD also maintained a roughly constant trend, although other parties have begun to win state elections, such as the Citizens' Movement (MC) in Oaxaca in 2010 and the PVEM in Chiapas in 2012.
[8] These are Campeche, Coahuila, Colima, Durango, Hidalgo, the State of Mexico, Quintana Roo, Tamaulipas, and Veracruz.

Mexico's PRI

FIGURE 8.2 States, GDP, population, and municipalities governed by the PRI, 1989–2015
Notes: Number of states corresponds to the left axis. Percentages correspond to the right axis.
Source: INE (2016) and INEGI (2017).

before 2016.[9] These states represent about a third of Mexico's population and GDP. If we take into account the states where the PRI had been out of the governor's mansion for one term only (e.g., Chihuahua, Nayarit, Nuevo León [until 2015], Puebla, San Luis Potosí, Tabasco, Yucatán), the PRI commanded state government resources with little or no interruption in sixteen of thirty-two states. As Figure 8.2 shows, at no point before 2016 did the PRI govern over less than half of the country's population and GDP, even after losing the Federal District (Mexico City), which represents almost a fifth of the country's GDP, to the PRD in 1997.

Figure 8.2 shows that the PRI also maintained control over roughly the same proportion of municipal governments. Control over sizable resources at the municipal level has similarly contributed to the PRI's ability to dole out patronage and maintain clientelistic networks. The uninterrupted availability of resources at the subnational level has allowed the PRI to maintain a territorial organization unrivaled by the country's other political parties.

---

[9] In 2016, the PRI lost in the states of Durango, Quintana Roo, Tamaulipas, and Veracruz.

In short, the PRI's control of subnational governments is one of the major reasons why it has managed to thrive under democracy as an authoritarian successor party. This is consistent with Timothy Power's argument (Chapter 7, this volume) about the importance of access to state resources for the rise and fall of the Liberal Front Party (PFL)/Democrats (DEM) in Brazil. Both of these cases suggest the importance of a form of authoritarian inheritance underemphasized by Loxton in the Introduction (this volume): continuing access to state resources, particularly at the subnational level.

8.2.2 Democratic Governments' Failure to Dismantle Key Institutions Inherited from the Authoritarian Regime

A second factor that helped the PRI was the failure of post-2000 governments to alter the nature of relations between the state and some of the social sectors that had served as pillars of the old regime. The two PAN governments of Vicente Fox (2000–2006) and Felipe Calderón (2006–2012) failed to dismantle key institutions upon which the PRI had built decades of electoral dominance. These included corporatism and crony capitalist relations with business, especially with regard to the media.[10] The failure to dismantle these institutions was the result of both the inability and unwillingness of the two PAN governments. Many important changes, especially those requiring a modification of the Constitution, required a two-thirds majority in Congress, which the PAN did not have. However, in areas of executive authority, where the PAN could have acted on its own, the PAN administrations sometimes deemed it politically advantageous to preserve the status quo inherited from the old regime and thus did not carry out transformations of the existing institutional framework.

8.2.3 Unions

An important pillar of the old PRI regime was corporatist relations between the state and labor unions. Unions were instrumental as a mechanism of control and co-optation. Control over unions allowed the PRI to adopt policies that at times contradicted workers' interests, provided mobilizational muscle for the regime, and translated into electoral support. In exchange, PRI governments gave prerogatives to union leaders, including patronage positions in the government bureaucracy and legislative positions at all levels (Cook 1996, 2007; Murillo 2001). The Confederation of Mexican Workers (CTM), for example, dominated labor representation from the 1940s onwards and guaranteed large numbers of supporters at political rallies and millions of

---

[10] Although the media is often considered "the fourth estate," in Mexico it is also a highly concentrated, influential, and profitable business. See, for example, Lawson (2002).

votes on election day.[11] Its leader for more than five decades, Fidel Velázquez, was a PRI senator on two occasions and remained one of the party's most influential members until his death in 1997.[12]

Although the strength of unions declined during the period of economic and democratic transition in the 1980s and 1990s, they remained an important political ally for the regime. Structural reforms – especially the privatization of state-owned enterprises and the interruption of subsidies and other benefits to state employees – affected unions' ability to distribute jobs and grant prerogatives (Madrid 2003; Murillo 2001). The process of democratization also contributed to weakening unions. With the opening of spaces for the opposition, the legislative seats and other government positions historically available to union leaders decreased.

However, although unions were weaker by the time the PAN won the presidency than during their heyday of the 1960s and 1970s, they still represented a force to be reckoned with (Bensusán and Middlebrook 2013: 18). By 2000, unionized workers still accounted for about 10 percent of the working-age population, or about 4 million people. By 2012, when the PRI returned to the presidency, an estimated 8.8 percent belonged to unions, or about 4.3 million people (Bensusán and Middlebrook 2013: 54; Castañeda and Aguilar Camín 2009). Because of the size of their membership, organizational capacity, and resources, unions could mobilize popular support during campaigns, contribute money and activists, and drum up votes for the PRI through the use of both sticks (e.g., threat of dismissal) and carrots (e.g., salary bonuses).

When the PRI lost the presidency in 2000, there were great expectations that the PAN government would democratize and bring transparency to government–labor relations, as this had been one of Fox's campaign promises. Instead, the PAN administrations shied away from reforming the old corporatist structures and making them accountable. They did little to upend the highly restrictive mechanisms of control regarding the formation and recognition of unions, wage negotiations, collective bargaining, and the right to strike. Additionally, they proved unwilling or unable to pursue high-level corruption cases involving a number of unions.[13] The few corruption investigations pursued by the administration tended to end without significant legal consequences for those involved.

In part, the lack of change was due to concerns over the stability of the young democracy. After all, when Fox promised during his campaign to democratize

---

[11] By the late 1970s, about 16.3 percent (3.5 million people) of the working-age population was unionized (Bensusán and Middlebrook 2013: 54).
[12] Fidel Velázquez is remembered for the phrase *"el que se mueve no sale en la foto"* (literally, "if you move you won't appear in the picture"), meaning that one had to show obedience toward the PRI to succeed professionally.
[13] Pastor and Wise (2005) have characterized Fox's six-year presidential term as the "lost sexenio."

unions, the CTM threatened to call for a general strike if he were elected. But Fox's inaction was also the product of convenience, since the status quo was compatible with the PAN's economic program. In line with the economic policies that the PRI had been pursuing since the 1980s, the PAN's economic policies sought to keep labor costs down to remain competitive internationally.[14] Fox realized that in order to maintain control over unions and curb demands for improved wages and living conditions, he would need to depend on the same union leaders that he had so vehemently vowed to change before 2000 (Bensusán and Middlebrook 2013: 49).

Rather than making internal life democratic or promoting the independence of unions, the PAN administrations engaged in selective confrontation, undermining unions – even those with democratically elected leaders, such as the mining union and the electricians' union – when they interfered with business interests (Bensusán and Middlebrook 2013: 27). They also turned a blind eye to accusations of fraud, such as those over commissioned union representatives who collected a check without working (Cuenca 2010; Tuckman 2011). In return, many unions did not oppose the PAN's economic liberalization policies. In the end, the PAN administrations not only preserved the corporatist framework for government–labor relations that had existed under the authoritarian regime, but even replaced their former criticism of union leaders with praise and incorporated them into important positions in the federal government, giving them access to resources, patronage, and the ability to set policy.

The examples of Mexico's teachers' union, the National Union of Education Workers (SNTE), and the oil workers' union, the Union of Oil Workers of the Mexican Republic (STPRM), illustrate how the preservation of inherited corporatist structures contributed to the PRI's electoral success – as a source of both clientelism and financial resources. Since its foundation in 1943, the SNTE has held a grip over education workers as the only officially sanctioned teachers' union. As the largest union in Latin America, it has enjoyed considerable political influence and prerogatives, including legislative seats, influential positions in the executive branch at all levels of government, and resources (Cook 1996).

The PAN administrations embraced the SNTE and allowed it to thrive after 2000. They incorporated union leaders into important positions in the federal government, including the directors of the agency that administers health care and social security for federal employees (ISSSTE), the National Lottery (LN), and the executive secretariat of the National Public Safety System (SNSP). President Calderón (2006–2012) even appointed the son-in-law of Elba Esther Gordillo – the head of the union – to serve as the Deputy Secretary for Primary Education in the Ministry of Education (Aguayo and Serdán 2009; Bensusán and Middlebrook 2013: 82). Similarly, rather than looking into the

---

[14] Indeed, real minimum wages continued to decrease during the PAN administrations.

large personal fortune amassed by Gordillo, Fox turned a blind eye and Calderón struck an electoral alliance with her. This may have allowed the PAN to edge out the PRD in 2006, but the failure to make unions more accountable and transparent left intact an important source of resources and cadres for the PRI.

The thriving of the SNTE after 2000 provided a lifeline for PRI governments at the local level, allowing them to maintain their prerogatives in exchange for mobilizing votes. Cantú (2009) provides an account of the influence of the SNTE on local governments. Estimating the SNTE's mobilization capacity at about 1.2 million teachers, and based on a study by the transparency-promoting NGO Alianza Cívica,[15] he lists union leaders' mechanisms of control as follows: discretionary control over tenured lines (*plazas*), bonuses, awards, and other incentives – including preferential credit, medical services, retirement benefits, legal protection, and geographic relocation. This is due, in part, to the union's success in embedding its leaders into education-related government positions, including the secretaries of education in eleven of the thirty-two state governments, more than fifty deputy secretaries at the state level, hundreds of mid-level bureaucrats in states' education departments, and 100 percent of inspectors and supervisors of school zones and directors of schools across the country (Cantú 2009).

The SNTE's ability to leverage these resources for clientelistic purposes after the transition has been well documented. The government treasury deposits 1 percent of teachers' wages into the SNTE's central account, and the leadership then distributes it to the regional offices on a discretionary basis (Raphael 2007: 107). Conservative estimates put the union's financial resources at US$6.5 billion per year (Aguayo and Serdán 2009; Bensusán and Tapia 2011: 26). Raphael (2007: 245) also documents the SNTE's use of hundreds of millions of dollars from discretionary government resources toward the fund for the teachers' housing program Vivienda Magisterial. Additionally, an estimated 16,000 members of the SNTE are commissioned to local governments and receive additional salary and prerogatives from these governments. In theory, this is because they are liaisons between governments and the SNTE. In reality, however, many are on the payroll without ever showing up for work.

Control over these clientelistic networks has been a significant electoral asset for the PRI. The SNTE mobilizes not only teachers but also parents via those teachers. Because of the power they have over children, teachers often have parents participate in pyramid schemes, in which every teacher commits to securing ten votes and parents in turn must do the same (Avilés 2012; Cantú 2009; Larreguy, Montiel, and Querubín 2016).

---

[15] For similar estimates, see Bensusán and Tapia (2011: 25), although the Ministry of Education is opaque about this number as well as the union's total resources.

In 2005, the SNTE officially created a political arm in the form of the New Alliance Party (PANAL). This gave the SNTE access not only to public funds for electoral campaigns but also to the voter registration lists with voters' pictures. It is now able to maintain a legally sanctioned presence at the polling stations on election day. Although ballots are secret, the ability to monitor turnout based on the voter registry with pictures – which all parties receive – and the presence of a well-identified union affiliate as party representative at the polling station play important roles in exercising pressure to turn out and vote for a particular candidate (Mercado Gasca 2013; Raphael 2007). Although PANAL has not always supported the PRI for the presidency – it supported the PAN's Calderón in 2006 – it tends to support the PRI candidates at the local level (Paoli Bolio 2012). It threw its weight behind Peña Nieto's candidacy in 2012 and has provided – along with the PVEM – the votes in Congress necessary for the PRI to govern with a simple majority.

The case of the oil workers' union of Mexico's state-owned petroleum company, Pemex, also illustrates how unions have remained electorally instrumental for the PRI. As part of Latin America's second largest company based on revenue, the union has channeled financial resources toward the PRI's coffers. In what became known as the "Pemexgate" scandal, for instance, the union was caught funneling almost US$50 million illegally into the PRI's 2000 campaign coffers. Although the funds benefited the PRI presidential candidate's campaign, union leaders were absolved and the PRI got off with a fine. The PRI rewarded these same union leaders (Carlos Romero Deschamps, the head of the union, and Ricardo Aldana, the treasurer) with seats in both houses of Congress through the party lists. The offices of senator and congressman, respectively, provided them with immunity from prosecution.

Although the electoral authority fined the PRI for the Pemexgate scandal, the punishment for electoral offenses came after the damage was done, i.e., after the resources funneled illegally out of Pemex had already helped the party's candidates perform well in the elections. The party may be fined ex post, but its candidates' victories are rarely reversed. With the union leaders solidly in the PRI's camp, and Pemex classifying millions of dollars funneled toward the union's coffers as "donations," the oil workers' union has been an important source of resources.

Other cases of illegal use of resources at the local level are well documented, as well. For example, in Tabasco, a state continually governed by the PRI until 2013, leaders of the regional office of the oil workers' union were able to avoid charges of illegally channeling hundreds of millions of dollars of Pemex funds toward the PRI campaigns due to the immunity from prosecution granted by the PRI's nomination of them to the local legislature through the party lists (Vázquez Rosas 2012: 29). These practices are not uncommon in other unions, such as the National Union of Social Security Workers (SNTSS) or the Federation of Unions for Workers Employed by the State (FSTSE), which also receive millions of dollars every year in opaque and discretionary funding, and have been historically aligned with the PRI.

In addition to benefiting the PRI electorally at the local level, the corporatist infrastructure became instrumental again for the return of the PRI to the presidency. In 2012, the PRI benefited from the fact that the old system of government control of unions remained largely untouched. For example, the SNTE supported Peña Nieto, the PRI presidential candidate, and contributed to his electoral victory (Larreguy et al. 2016).[16] Not surprisingly, Peña Nieto has pursued measures to preserve the old system of control, such as putting Elba Esther Gordillo, the leader of the SNTE who explored alliances with other parties, in jail (the charge was amassing a fortune she could not justify with her salary) in order to elicit unconditional discipline from the teachers' union, which is once again aligned with the PRI.[17]

8.2.4 Business Sectors

Under the old PRI regime, many of Mexico's main business conglomerates emerged not out of market competition but out of crony capitalism, i.e., preferential treatment resulting from political connections (Alba Vega 2006). The PRI governments organized business sectors into business associations (Schneider 2002), and loyalty to the regime had its benefits: alignment with the PRI resulted in business opportunities and legal advantages. Those against the regime faced various forms of harassment.

During the 1950s and 1960s, Mexico's period of stabilizing development – the period of high growth rates and low inflation – benefited business through a model of import substitution industrialization. This model relied on domestic markets for growth and heavy state involvement in the economy. It shielded domestic industries from external competition and provided subsidies and preferential credit. It also made many business sectors dependent on the government and generated a high concentration of business ownership. Many companies emerged and survived because of government prerogatives and corruption. Licenses and concessions were given to PRI politicians as a reward for loyalty.

Whereas the period of structural reforms in the 1980s and 1990s reduced the degree of state intervention in the economy, the privatization of state-owned enterprises presented another opportunity for cronyism. Many state-owned

---

[16] Aguayo and Serdán (2009) estimate the number of votes that the SNTE commands at around 1 million.

[17] This strategy of selective jailing of union leaders early in the presidency to make clear who is in charge is not new. Carlos Salinas (1988–1994), for example, imprisoned Joaquín Hernández Galicia, "La Quina," the head of the Pemex union, not for corruption, but for illegal possession of weapons at home. La Quina had opposed the liberalization policies of the PRI governments at the time and was suspected of having provided votes to the leftist opposition candidate, Cuauhtémoc Cárdenas, in 1988.

companies were sold below market value to party loyalists who did not necessarily have a successful business record or proven financial means to purchase the company. During this period, major companies, such as Telmex, TV Azteca, and other media concessions, were turned over to the private sector, not following an economic logic, but often a political one (Fernández Jilberto and Hogenboom 2007: 145).

The reprivatization of the banking industry after its nationalization in 1982 is illustrative. The government sold state-owned banks to individuals without experience in the sector, but with political connections to the PRI. For example, Ángel Isidoro Rodríguez, "El Divino," whose father loaned the buses from his transportation company to PRI candidates and was an important donor to the party in the late 1980s, was rewarded with service contracts from Pemex and the ability to open a stock brokerage firm, Mexival (González Amador 1998). He later purchased Banpaís, one of the country's state-owned banks, and was eventually accused – along with others in similar situations, such as Jorge Lankenau (Banca Confía) and Carlos Cabal Peniche (Banca Cremi and Banca Unión) – of lending money to themselves with no collateral for the loan, which helped precipitate the collapse of Mexico's banking sector in 1995. The government eventually bailed out the banks through the Fund for Bank Savings Protection (FOBAPRA) at the cost of a whopping $65 billion to society (De la Garza 1998). Earlier, however, some of the bad loans had been channeled to the PRI coffers to finance Ernesto Zedillo's 1994 presidential campaign (González Amador 2004).

The high concentration of business ownership did not change with the democratic transition. As Castañeda and Aguilar Camín (2009) argue, Mexico is a country where a handful of corporate empires enjoy almost total control over entire industries: the degree of concentration in the telephone sector is 81.4 percent, mobile phones 74 percent, TV audience 68 percent, cement 49 percent, retail 54 percent, and corn flour 93 percent. Many of the country's main holding companies are family-owned rather than having a corporate structure.

To be sure, with the electoral reforms of the 1990s and the increase in political competition, many businesspeople began to openly support other parties (Schneider 2002). The PAN's economic policies, in particular, were ideologically compatible with the demands of parts of the business sector. The PRD, in turn, with its more statist and pro-labor platform, appealed to businesspeople with nationalist views or who benefited from protectionist policies. However, the PAN governments generally balked at leveling the playing field for business and undermining the power of groups that owed their wealth to the PRI. The links between the PRI and business groups were not transformed between 2000 and 2012. Instead, business groups have remained very involved in the party's campaigns and policy making (Alba Vega 2006).

The influence of the two national television networks is a case in point. For decades prior to the transition to democracy, mass media openly served the interests of the PRI and was instrumental in helping it hold on to power. Most media outlets depended on government advertising and subsidies (Huerta-Wong and Gómez García 2013; Rodríguez Castañeda 1993). Concessions were given to PRI loyalists, and Emilio Azcárraga Milmo, the owner of the main media conglomerate, Televisa, even declared himself – publicly and unabashedly – a "soldier" of the PRI.

Between 1972 and 1993, Televisa was the only privately owned TV consortium, operating three national channels (2, 5, and 9) and a metropolitan (4) one.[18] The PRI and Televisa forged a symbiotic relationship during these years: Televisa not only refrained from criticizing government policies but also provided the kind of overwhelmingly positive coverage often associated with state-owned media. Opposition parties were ignored or vilified, whereas the PRI candidates were treated with admiration and enthusiasm (Hughes and Lawson 2004: 85).

In exchange, Televisa received a range of special prerogatives that allowed Azcárraga Milmo to become one of the wealthiest people in Latin America. These included the unchecked proliferation of concessions that expanded profits (Trejo 1988), subsidized access to communications infrastructure, preferential tax treatment, and protection from commercial competition (Hughes and Lawson 2004: 85). The favorable terms for business allowed Televisa to invest in different sectors of the media industry. They also enabled it to integrate vertically across segments of the TV business, from content production to distribution, becoming the largest media company in Spanish-speaking television (Huerta-Wong and Gómez García 2013: 121).

In 1993, the government privatized the state-owned network Imevisión, which became TV Azteca. As Figure 8.3 shows, although the privatization introduced competition and reduced somewhat Televisa's overwhelming share of the audience, from about 90 to 70 percent, the TV industry has remained highly concentrated in the hands of the two networks, and TV Azteca's coverage has resembled that of Televisa.[19] Televisa has remained the dominant player, with close to 70 percent, and TV Azteca's share has remained steady at about 30 percent since the transition (Huerta-Wong and Gómez García 2013: 122).

Democratization has not brought the dramatic change in media coverage many expected. The two networks that owed their concessions to the PRI governments concentrate 95 percent of all TV stations, 99 percent of all advertising, and 98 percent of total audience (CIDE and COFETEL 2011: 10). Both Televisa and TV Azteca continue to play an important role in

---

[18] During this time, the only other option was the state-owned Channel 13 – with three channels (7, 13, and 22) – beginning in 1982.
[19] Television concentration in Mexico is considerably greater than in Argentina, Brazil, and Chile, not to mention other OECD countries (CIDE and COFETEL 2011).

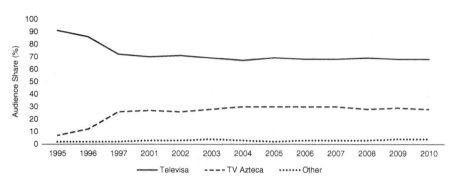

FIGURE 8.3 Network average prime-time audience share (%)
Source: Reproduced from Figure 1 in Huerta-Wong and Gómez García (2013: 122).

making or breaking candidates as a result of their industry dominance and selective coverage.

To be sure, the degree of media bias in favor of the PRI has decreased considerably since the transition to democracy. Most importantly, electoral reforms were instrumental in distributing airtime more evenly across parties. The death of Emilio Azcárraga Milmo in 1997 also contributed to a change in coverage, since his son and new owner, Emilio Azcárraga Jean, saw himself more as a businessperson than a partisan. Additionally, the creation of TV Azteca helped to introduce competition-oriented incentives.

However, considerable partisan biases have remained in the media (Lawson 2008). For example, based on a sample of programs monitored by the IFE for the 2000 presidential election, Hughes and Lawson (2004: 87) find that the PRI received as much coverage as all of the opposition combined. Coverage for the PAN was much lower than was warranted based on opinion polls before the election and the actual electoral results.[20] Hughes and Lawson (2004) also find that media bias has been especially pronounced in local stations. In Tabasco, Channel 9, a private local channel, was reportedly founded by the family of a state governor in 1979 and then sold to a businessperson who "speaks openly of his willingness to use his media empire to support politicians he favors" (Hughes and Lawson 2004: 92). During the presidential race in 2000, the PRI received about 72 percent of all electoral coverage in the state, and bias against the opposition was mandated from the top: Channel 9 journalists were not allowed to give any coverage to the PRD or those associated with it, because "the government's advertising purchases were enough to cover the payroll and thus justified favorable coverage" (Hughes and Lawson 2004: 93). In Baja California, in spite of 11 years of continued

---

[20] The PAN-led Alliance for Change received 24 percent of the coverage, but 42 percent of the vote for president. By contrast, the PRI received 42 percent of coverage, but 36 percent of the vote.

PAN governments at the state level by 2000, coverage by Channel 66 – part of a family-owned network of concessions granted in 1979 and 1993 – also favored the PRI, due to early partisan affinities and economic incentives, all under the guise of "journalistic norms of fairness and balance" (Hughes and Lawson 2004: 94).

Whereas the IFE's oversight of media coverage in national electoral processes has helped to curb these practices,[21] there has been considerable variation in the quality and integrity of the electoral authorities at the state level. In states where the PRI has never lost control of the government, electoral authorities have been much less vigilant about uneven access to the media and campaign finance irregularities. Indeed, Hughes and Lawson (2004) find that a significant predictor of media coverage is not previous electoral results, but whether a PRI governor was in office. Further, even if the electoral authority's oversight at the national level has reduced the room for overt bias in terms of airtime, there continues to be evidence of partisan bias in terms of content. Examples include investigative reports that suggest the PRI paid Televisa for favorable coverage (Tuckman 2012) and studies pointing to the systematically negative portrayal of civil society groups opposed to the PRI, such as the student movement #Yosoy132 (Ruiz 2015).

In short, many of the players who benefited from the authoritarian PRI regime, and who continue to have a stake in maintaining the party in office, are still significant power brokers. The transition produced alternation in the presidency beginning in 2000, but important pillars of the previous authoritarian regime remain in place. Key actors who supported the PRI before the transition are still in positions of power, and the party continues to reward them. These include not only union and business leaders but also judges who are supposed to serve as impartial arbiters in a democracy. Examples abound at the subnational level, in particular, such as the case of Jalisco's Supreme Court Justice Leonel Sandoval Figueroa. He was caught on tape encouraging government employees to violate electoral laws and reassuring them that the state's Electoral Tribunal, Electoral Institute, and governor – who happened to be his son – would provide cover for their wrongdoings and protect them. Indeed, many of the inherited clientelistic and patronage networks have been kept alive with resources from state governments, and through the collusion of certain business sectors and unions.[22] As several authors have suggested (Cornelius 2002; Do Vale 2016; Gibson 2012; Snyder 1999), democratization has been highly uneven across Mexico, and there is evidence that many institutions and practices left over from the old regime persist in the form of "subnational authoritarianism."

---

[21] In 2014, the IFE became the National Electoral Institute.
[22] For work on the decline of vote buying effectiveness for the PRI, see Cornelius (2000).

8.2.5 Mediocre Performance of Other Parties in Government

The third factor is related to the lackluster performance of other parties in office and their inability to organize against the PRI. This mediocre performance has contributed to the fragmentation of the party system that emerged during the transition and has ultimately benefited the PRI. Contrary to the pre-democratization notion that the PRI held the monopoly over corrupt or incompetent practices, government officials from the other parties have engaged in their fair share of corruption and incompetence (Giraudy 2015: 42; Serra 2013: 140), which has affected their electoral prospects.

Rather than breaking with the mediocre economic performance of the PRI governments since the 1980s, economic growth during the PAN administrations was similarly modest – an average of about 0.7 percent per capita per year (World Bank 2016). This mediocre economic performance during the twelve years in which the right-of-center PAN held the presidency prompted voters to search for an alternative. Although the Fox and Calderón administrations kept inflation under control and avoided financial crises of the sort that had plagued Mexico in the 1980s and 1990s, they proved unable to meet the high expectations generated by the transition to democracy in 2000.

Beyond the economy, Fox was largely seen as a weak and ineffective president, and Calderón presided over a sharp escalation of violence after 2006. Whereas violent crime had been steadily declining for decades – with the homicide rate reaching as low as 8.4 per 100,000 people in 2007 – during Calderón's term the rate tripled to 24 and more than 60,000 homicides were recorded (INEGI 2016). Kidnappings and extortion also increased steadily. This gruesome violence left many voters longing for the relative peace of the old PRI regime. As Romero, Magaloni, and Díaz-Cayeros (2016) have shown, public safety has been an important factor influencing Mexican voters.

The disenchantment with the PAN and PRD has come at all levels of government. The PAN faced corruption scandals with former governor of Sonora Guillermo Padrés (2009–2015), who was accused of receiving US$ 3.3 million from companies awarded state government contracts (De Córdoba 2015). Among the most prominent PRD corruption scandals are videos taken during Andrés Manuel López Obrador's administration as mayor of Mexico City (2000–2005). In one, the leader of the PRD's local legislators is shown taking swaths of cash from a businessperson, and in another, the city's finance minister is shown gambling amounts of money he could not justify in Las Vegas. The governorship of Juan Sabines Guerrero (PRD) in the state of Chiapas resulted in exorbitant debt and embezzlement charges against members of his administration. Also, PRD congressperson Julio César Godoy Toscano is wanted for ties to organized crime and remains at large.

Scholars have found that retrospective voting has been prevalent in Mexico since elections became competitive (Domínguez and McCann 1996; Klesner

1993; Magaloni 2006; McCann 2015; Singer 2009). This is an important factor for explaining disenchantment with the PAN, given the high expectations generated by the transition. Retrospective voting has provided an opportunity for PRI candidates to win elections in places where the opposition has not performed well in office. This has occurred at all levels, including the presidency. As McCann (2015: 88) has found, by the time of the 2012 election, 40 percent of survey respondents "believed that times were indeed better when a single party was in control, and Peña Nieto and the PRI benefited from this judgment."

To be sure, the PRI has not been immune to scandals related to corruption and incompetence. However, the fact that the PRI's preexisting baseline of support was higher has allowed it to weather these scandals better than the other parties. Given that the PRI emerged from the transition with a larger electoral base than the PAN and PRD, the disenchantment has been more consequential for these two parties. Whereas 40 percent of respondents longed for a return to the PRI years, those who disagreed were split roughly equally between the PAN and the PRD (McCann 2015: 96).

As Figure 8.4 shows, self-reported identification with the three main political parties has generally decreased over time, with almost half of respondents identifying as independents. Identification with the PRI has experienced the greatest decline – but it was also much greater than that for the other parties to

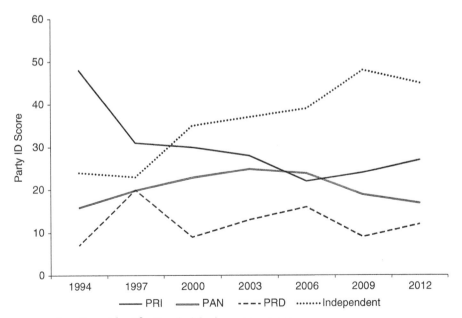

FIGURE 8.4 Party identification in Mexico, 1991–2012
Source: Moreno (2015).

begin with. Party ID has generally declined somewhat for the PAN and remained flat for the PRD, but their base of supporters remains smaller than that of the PRI. It is important to note that levels of party ID are likely lower because the figure reflects self-reported responses only of those who agreed to participate in the surveys. Further, party ID fluctuates considerably between election and nonelection years, and only about 16 percent of voters have effective party ID regardless of campaign effects (Greene 2015). Therefore, Figure 8.4 should be taken as an indication of general trends and relative strength rather than a reflection of actual levels of party ID in Mexican society, which are likely lower.

While lackluster governmental performance since democratization has taken a toll on party ID and vote shares across parties, this has made it especially difficult for the PAN and the PRD to establish a meaningful presence in states where they have not enjoyed traditional sources of support. Because of resource asymmetries, repression, and other barriers to institutional development in the early stages of the transition (Greene 2007), Mexico did not see the emergence of a straightforward national three-party system. Instead, two subnational two-party systems emerged: a PRI-PAN system in the north and a PRI-PRD system in the south (Baker 2009; Klesner 2005: 109).

This electoral geography has generated incentives for parties to prioritize the allocation of limited resources toward strengthening electorally competitive areas instead of trying to make inroads into new states where the cost of establishing a presence would be high (Díaz Jiménez 2014: 18; Harbers 2014). The consequence for national elections is that the PAN and the PRD enjoy limited, regional bases of core supporters for their campaigns. This means they are forced to rely more than the PRI on independents, who are less likely to support the party by donating their time canvassing, participating in get-out-the-vote operations, contributing financial resources, or even showing up to vote on election day. To the extent that the PAN and PRD have to rely more on votes from independents, they have to dedicate more resources toward courting them and fielding campaigns relying on fewer core partisan supporters.

The challenges of mediocre performance and regional fragmentation are compounded by the inability of the PAN and the PRD to form cohesive electoral alternatives (Flores-Macías 2016). The PRI has benefited from a major schism within the left and infighting within the right. A casualty of the Pact for Mexico (an agreement signed by the PRI, the PAN, and the PRD to advance a common set of structural reforms early in Peña Nieto's presidency), the left is now formally divided between those who favor working with the government to shape policy (the PRD) and those who reject any form of collaboration and broke away to form a new party (the National Regeneration Movement, MORENA).[23] Neither is likely to muster enough support to win the

---

[23] MORENA was created by Andrés Manuel López Obrador, the PRD's presidential candidate in 2006 and 2012.

presidency on its own, but the mistrust between them will make it difficult for them to form electoral coalitions in the future.

While the PAN has not suffered a formal fracture, it has had its fair share of infighting among different factions of the party. At times, party notables have called on the population to vote against the party's own candidate. For example, former president Fox explicitly called on voters not to support Josefina Vásquez Mota, the PAN's presidential candidate in 2012, but to vote instead for the PRI's candidate, Peña Nieto. Several groups within the party have also questioned the integrity and transparency of internal elections, and the leadership's inability to explain the sudden appearance of thousands of supporters in the lists on which internal party elections rely. These rifts have created headwinds for the PAN's electoral performance.

In short, retrospective voting on the opposition's mediocre performance and its inability to form cohesive alternatives have allowed the PRI to maintain or recapture executive offices at the state and national levels. However, although the PRI returned to the presidency in 2012, it has not been immune to the decline in voter identification with the largest political parties. However, the PRI's high starting point has allowed it to perform better in the face of declining party ID than other parties. In order to offset this decline, the PRI has increasingly relied on junior partners in electoral coalitions, such as the PVEM and PANAL, which have benefited from voters' discontent with the major parties.

8.3 IMPLICATIONS FOR DEMOCRACY

What are the consequences of the PRI's resilience for Mexico's democracy? In the Introduction of this volume, Loxton argues that authoritarian successor parties' effects on democracy are double-edged. On the negative side, they may trigger an authoritarian regression, prop up vestiges of authoritarianism, or hinder processes of transitional justice. On the positive side, they may contribute to the stability of democracy by promoting party system institutionalization, incorporating potential spoilers into the new democracy (see chapters by Slater and Wong, and Ziblatt), and even offer a model that encourages transitions to democracy elsewhere. In this section, I consider the purported benefits of authoritarian successor parties and find little evidence of these benefits in the case of Mexico. However, I *do* find considerable evidence of the PRI's harmful effects.

First, on the positive side, the resilience of the PRI in the electoral arena might have contributed to democratic governability. Although it is difficult to establish a counterfactual, it is conceivable that the PRI might have helped to incorporate potential spoilers into the democratic system. Given that important sectors of society had benefited from the old regime's prerogatives, some groups might have opted to destabilize the new regime in the absence of a party to represent them. Further, it can also be argued that the party's wealth of experienced politicians with skills at reaching agreements and finding common ground – what Grzymala-Busse (2002) calls "portable skills" – meant that it was not necessary to reinvent the wheel of governing after the transition. After all, today's PRI stalwarts are the heirs of the post-revolutionary project that built modern Mexico. In addition, whatever the flaws of the PRI, its survival made it possible for broad sectors of society that sympathized with its proposals to be represented in government.

However, if the resilience of the PRI has contributed to democracy in this fashion, that contribution has been much less straightforward than in some of the other cases examined in this volume. Rather than significantly lowering the "cost of toleration" among elites, as occurred with "old regime conservative parties" in first-wave Europe (Ziblatt, Chapter 10, this volume)[24] or "stabilizing democracy" (Slater and Wong, Chapter 9, this volume), as with parties such as the KMT in Taiwan, it is not clear that the PRI was really needed to carry out these functions. Many of the PRI's policy proposals have been quite similar to those of the PAN from the 1980s onward, especially with respect to economic reforms. While a collapse of the PRI might have presented governability challenges, parts of the business community would have most likely found adequate representation through the PAN (Alba Vega 2006), and the military never showed any intention of breaking with the constitutional order in the event of an opposition victory (Camp 2005). If the PRI had collapsed, some voters might have found themselves without representation, but party ID for the PRI had already declined considerably by 2000. In short, it is unclear whether governability was really at stake in the aftermath of the transition – and thus whether the PRI was really necessary for democratic stability.

Second, it is not clear whether the resilience of the PRI has contributed much to party system institutionalization. It is conceivable that the party system could have collapsed had the PRI disbanded, leading to turmoil. After all, party systems are much more difficult to institutionalize than to decay (Mainwaring 2018; Roberts 2015). Additionally, the PRI, as a centrist party, may have served as a bridge between the right-of-center PAN and the left-of-center PRD, bringing some moderation to the system. However, compared to the baseline at the time of the transition in 2000, it is not clear that the PRI has really contributed to party system institutionalization in the sense of promoting the routinization of democratic practices, developing roots in society, or preventing volatility (Mainwaring and Scully 1995). Instead, the PRI has embraced shady practices, its party ID has declined, and its share of the vote has decreased. It is a distinct possibility that, in the absence of the PRI, an institutionalized party system would have emerged regardless, anchored on the center-left by the PRD and the center-right by the PAN.

---

[24] According to Ziblatt (Chapter 10, this volume), "old regime conservative parties" were the first wave's equivalent of authoritarian successor parties.

Finally, the PRI's resilience might have encouraged new transitions to democracy by having a demonstration effect. While the Mexican transition came late compared to most in the region, it could, conceivably, still serve this purpose in the future. However, given deteriorating attitudes about the country's democracy, it is unlikely to serve as an inspiration for other countries. According to Latinobarómetro (2016), Mexicans' views of the quality of their country's democracy were the region's lowest in 2015. Whereas 37 percent of Latin American respondents said that they felt somewhat or very satisfied with the quality of democracy in their own country, only 19 percent of Mexicans shared this view. Similarly, confidence in the country's future, while far from robust to begin with, has dropped even lower since the PRI returned to the presidency in 2012. In 2013, slightly more than a quarter (27 percent) of respondents felt confident that Mexico was moving in the right direction. Two years later, that share had dipped to less than a fifth (18 percent). The 2015 Latin American mean was 32 percent. Further, according to different surveys since the transition, more than half of Mexican respondents do not believe that the country's elections are clean – one of the worst rates in Latin America (Díaz Domínguez 2015; Ramos 2009).

In short, there is little evidence that the PRI has had a positive impact on Mexico's democracy. However, there is considerable evidence that the PRI has been *harmful* in various ways. One way is by propping up pockets of subnational authoritarianism. There seems to be something to Cornelius' (1999: 12) prediction that the fragmentation of the old PRI regime would lead to "a crazy quilt of increasingly competitive, pluralistic political spaces ... juxtaposed with hardened authoritarian enclaves." In a very real sense, Mexico is a case of an incomplete transition to democracy: there has been significant progress at the national level, but progress has been uneven at the subnational level (Gibson 2012; Giraudy 2015; Snyder 1999). Mexico's political actors operate at both the national and subnational levels, and as power shifted away from the president and toward state governments, the persistence of competitive authoritarian practices at the subnational level became increasingly apparent.

In addition to authoritarian practices at the subnational level, the resilience of the PRI has supported the continuation of the kinds of corrupt practices associated with the old days. During the PRI's two terms without the presidency (2000–2012), several PRI governors and other party notables continued to be associated with many of the practices that pro-democracy actors had hoped would disappear with the 2000 transition. For example, two former governors of the state of Tamaulipas – Tomás Yarrington (1999–2005) and Eugenio Hernández Flores (2005–2011) – are wanted for money laundering and drug trafficking at the time of this writing. Former governor of the state of Coahuila, Humberto Moreira (2005–2011), whose borrowing sent the state into a debt crisis, is accused of embezzlement and document falsification. The governor of Puebla, Mario Marín Torres (2005–2011), was caught on tape negotiating the incarceration and sexual abuse of a journalist who was pursuing an embarrassing story. Former representative and now senator Emilio Gamboa Patrón was caught on tape peddling his influence to gambling interests in 2006.

As these examples suggest, corruption in the PRI after the transition has not been a matter of a few isolated incidents, nor has it failed to reach the highest echelons of the party. While these practices are by no means the exclusive domain of the PRI, the party has a record of protecting those facing charges of embezzlement and influence peddling (Flores-Macías 2013). After his term as governor of Coahuila, for example, Humberto Moreira became the president of the PRI. Oil workers' union leader Carlos Romero Deschamps became a senator and Emilio Gamboa Patrón is the leader of the PRI in the Senate. Rather than distancing itself from politicians who engage in dubious practices, the PRI has sheltered and even promoted such figures, rewarding them with congressional seats and legal immunity.

After the return of the PRI to the presidency in 2012, there is evidence that the government not only failed to rein in corruption across the bureaucracy, but that the president's inner circle itself was unable to lead by example. Rather than improving oversight, the Peña Nieto administration has been engulfed in a series of high-profile corruption scandals, which have involved the first lady and the finance minister, among others. These have remained unresolved and have tainted the credibility of the "new PRI" – the seemingly renovated party that had put behind the corrupt and undemocratic practices of the past – in the eyes of much of the population. This complicity in shielding corrupt officials from prosecution, though not identical, is analogous to other cases of authoritarian successor parties that have used their clout to impede processes of transitional justice.

Finally, although the country has made progress in terms of media pluralism and civic engagement, it has suffered important setbacks regarding freedom of the press and human rights (Flores-Macías 2016). The harassment of journalists critical of the government continues, as with the high-profile case of several MVS reporters forced to resign after breaking the story about potential conflict of interests involving the president's wife and a government contractor in 2014.[25] Especially worrisome are the murders of journalists critical of the government, such as the gruesome murder of a photojournalist who had fled the state of Veracruz to seek refuge in Mexico City. Additionally, since the return of the PRI to the presidency in 2012, it appears that human rights violations have worsened. In a scathing report, Human Rights Watch (2017: 427) claimed that torture is now "widely practiced in Mexico to obtain forced confessions and extract information."

This does not mean that Mexico will return to the kind of full-blown authoritarianism practiced by the PRI during the twentieth century, when coercion and co-optation ruled the day and elections were stolen in broad daylight. Meaningful checks and balances have emerged since, including an

---

[25] MVS is a Mexican media conglomerate.

independent electoral authority, a legislature that serves as a counterweight to the executive branch, a more independent judiciary, and a freer press. But if the record of the "new PRI" is any indication, the party is unlikely to contribute to Mexico's further democratization.

8.4 CONCLUSION

The PRI is undoubtedly one of the most electorally successful authoritarian successor parties in the world. It returned to the presidency after only two terms out of office, has remained a powerful force in Congress, has dominated politics at the subnational level, and commands the support of a sizable share of the electorate. To be sure, the electoral performance of the PRI has declined over time and continues to erode. This decline has not been smooth; instead, the electoral fortunes of the PRI have ebbed and flowed in a generalized downward trend. Nevertheless, seventeen years after Mexico's transition to democracy, the PRI remains a powerful electoral force.

As the Introduction (Loxton, this volume) argues, what is remarkable about authoritarian successor parties is their ability to perform well *under free and fair conditions*. The Mexican case has been mixed in this regard, however. On the one hand, part of the PRI's success is likely due to its inheritance of a strong party brand.[26] The PRI is the heir to the Mexican Revolution's ideals and successes. Much like in the cases of Taiwan and South Korea (Cheng and Huang, Chapter 2, this volume), past PRI governments were responsible for many of the accomplishments that built modern Mexico, including the incorporation of the popular sectors into politics, sustained economic growth and development, and political stability. Although this legacy is less meaningful among the generations that came of age after the 1982 debt crisis, it has nevertheless bestowed the party with a recognizable brand (albeit one that has experienced considerable dilution over time) and other resources that have helped make its electoral performance impressive in comparative perspective.

On the other hand, part of the PRI's strong electoral performance has been the product of undemocratic practices that, despite important progress made since 2000, have continued, especially at the subnational level. Clientelistic networks and vote buying have helped secure votes for the party. Media bias has given its candidates an edge in campaigns. Misappropriation of government funds has provided a source of party finance. Other parties have also employed such practices, and their own shortcomings in government have undermined their electoral support. However, the PRI's privileged position at the time of the transition – due to its control of significant subnational government resources, corporatist relations, and crony capitalist ties to business – has resulted in a greater electoral payoff and has been crucial for this authoritarian successor party's resilience.

[26] On party brands, see Lupu (2016).

9

Game for Democracy

Authoritarian Successor Parties in Developmental Asia

Dan Slater and Joseph Wong

Democracy arises for various reasons and in various ways. In this chapter we focus attention on the latter point, exploring the consequences of a particular way in which democracy can come about: *democracy through strength* (Slater and Wong 2013). This has been the most common democratization trajectory in the region we define and discuss below as "developmental Asia."[1] Rather than asking why some powerful authoritarian regimes strategically concede democratic reforms while others do not,[2] we focus strictly here on those cases that have pursued this strategy and the downstream consequences of their democratic concessions. In the spirit of this volume, we examine three cases of democracy through strength where "authoritarian successor parties" (Loxton 2015) have played a leading role, both in bringing democracy about and in shaping democracy's course: Taiwan, South Korea (hereafter Korea), and Indonesia.

We commence our analysis with three interrelated findings. First, in all three cases we explore here, the authoritarian ruling parties that initiated political transformation not only survived into the democratic era but continued to thrive as authoritarian successor parties, albeit to different degrees.[3] Second, authoritarian successor parties have generally furthered the stabilization of

---

[1] Our term "developmental Asia" transcends the classic Northeast–Southeast Asian divide and refers to countries that broadly followed Japan's state-led and export-driven growth model during and after the Cold War. Hence Northeast and Southeast Asian cases that have never followed this general model (e.g., the Philippines, North Korea, Mongolia, Laos, Brunei, and Timor-Leste) are not part of developmental Asia by our definition.

[2] In our wider book project, we do consider cases where strong authoritarian regimes have yet to pursue a strategy of democracy through strength (i.e., China, Singapore, Malaysia, Hong Kong, Cambodia, and Vietnam). For some preliminary consideration of such negative cases (or "candidate cases," as we prefer to call them), see Slater and Wong (2013: 729–730) on China, and Slater (2012) on Malaysia and Singapore.

[3] For a similar assessment of the Korean and Taiwanese cases, see Cheng and Huang (Chapter 2, this volume).

democracy during its critical first two decades, rather than act as democratic spoilers, as commonly feared.[4] And third, democratic stability has not meant an absence of democratic substance,[5] as suggested by the generally robust and buoyant Polity scores Taiwan, Korea, and Indonesia exhibited during their first fifteen years as democracies. In sum, developmental Asia's authoritarian successor parties present us with a pattern of democratic *success* for all three parties in question, and a picture of *stability and substance* for all three democracies in question.

To make sense of these outcomes, we begin by stressing the essential point that authoritarian ruling parties in Taiwan (Kuomintang, or KMT), South Korea (Democratic Justice Party, or DJP), and Indonesia (Golkar) initiated democratic transition from positions of *considerable but unequal strength*. The KMT proved to be the strongest party in the aftermath of democratic transition, followed by Korea's DJP, while Golkar brought up the rear. This pattern was highly predictable, we argue, since successful authoritarian successor parties do not simply fall from the sky. This spectrum of democratic success is primarily a product of "authoritarian inheritance" (Loxton, Introduction, this volume), as all three authoritarian parties conceded democracy with impressive institutional and coalitional strengths in hand – though to varying degrees. In other words, developmental Asia's authoritarian successor parties reflect a *spectrum of success* under democracy that mirrors the *spectrum of strength* they exhibited under authoritarianism.

A central implication of this chapter, therefore, is that authoritarian strengths can be assessed and compared *before* democratization to project how successful an authoritarian successor party is likely to be *after* democratization. And if political scientists can assess the promising prospects for strong authoritarian ruling parties to thrive under democracy as authoritarian successor parties, so of course can the parties themselves. To the extent that authoritarian leaders can foresee a successful democratic future for themselves, it makes a democratization strategy less risky and more rational – and hence more likely (Loxton, Introduction, this volume).[6]

Our explanation for these parties' varying levels of success may be deeply structural and historical. But to explain how authoritarian successor parties *stabilize* democracy, we place more stress on proximate

---

[4] We do not deny that democracy through strength has had "double-edged effects" on democratic quality (Loxton, Introduction, this volume). Indeed, we pay substantial attention to these downsides in other venues, especially in the case of Indonesia, which predictably displays the deepest democratic deficits among our three cases. Rather than using this chapter to detail the many positive and negative consequences of authoritarian successor parties and weighing them against each other, we focus on explaining their salutary effects on democratic stability.

[5] For a conceptualization of democratic substance as comprising inclusion and constraints, see Slater (2013).

[6] Authoritarian strength paradoxically lessens both the dangers and the urgency of democratization (Slater 2012, 2014a; Slater and Wong 2013).

factors. Specifically, *these parties moderated their political and economic positions rather than locking in and exploiting their greatest political and economic advantages from the authoritarian past.*[7] More than any other, this strategic choice to moderate determines whether authoritarian successor parties stabilize democracy or, alternatively, become a force for backsliding. If they fail to moderate their policies and refuse to accept democratic constraints, they will most likely polarize and destabilize democracy. This pattern is not exclusive to authoritarian successor parties, since any incumbent party will destabilize democracy whenever it runs roughshod over democracy's institutional constraints (Slater 2013). But when authoritarian successor parties fail to adhere to the rules of the democratic game, historical memories of authoritarian abuse make polarization especially acute. Failing to moderate not only undermines democratic stability; it risks the party's democratic reputation and threatens its electoral success. This makes it important for authoritarian successor parties to show restraint and embrace democratic principles if they are not only *to succeed* under democracy but *to stabilize* democracy through their continued leadership of a reformed political system.

Considering the thematic focus of this volume, it is worth underscoring the centrality of authoritarian successor parties specifically – and not just *ancien régime* elites more generally,[8] or alternative sets of elites such as military officers, the super-wealthy, or leading opposition parties – to democratic transition and stabilization. This institutional focus on a specific type of party helps clarify why our causal argument is not tautological. Our argument is not simply that democratic concession and moderation generally facilitate democratic transition and stabilization. It is that concession and moderation *by authoritarian successor parties specifically* is especially likely to bring the democracy-through-strength scenario to full fruition. As in all of the chapters of this volume, these parties are the pivotal players in our analysis – and potentially productive players at that, in ways that existing theory has failed to appreciate.[9]

Our chapter also echoes other chapters in this volume (see, especially, Chapter 10 by Ziblatt) by presenting a surprisingly sanguine vision of authoritarian successor parties' potential contributions to democratic stabilization. Yet the standards we propose for such parties to fulfill this

---

[7] Moderation is a strategy for winning in the future rather than what Loxton (Introduction, this volume) calls "strategies for dealing with the past." Hence forward-looking moderation can be combined with those backward-looking strategies – contrition, obfuscation, scapegoating, and embracing the past – in multiple ways.

[8] For more on other vehicles that the broader "authoritarian diaspora" can use to remain influential under democracy, such as independent candidacies and the colonization of non-authoritarian successor parties, see Conclusion (Loxton, this volume).

[9] Like all the chapters in this book, in other words, ours is not only making an argument about how and why but about *whom*.

positive role are extremely demanding.[10] Stabilizing democracy requires that parties fully adapt to democracy and not simply preserve the same behaviors that stabilized authoritarianism. Even when they "hew to the past" in many of their developmentally oriented and capitalism-friendly economic policies, authoritarian successor parties must decisively "break from the past" in the political realm by publicly eschewing authoritarian practices.[11] In addition, we argue that improving distributive policies will help stabilize democracy by giving the general public a clear stake in democratic politics.

We thus part company with research portraying such transitions as shallow exercises in authoritarian continuity rather than meaningful democratic breakthroughs. By conceding democracy through strength, Taiwan's KMT, Korea's DJP, and Indonesia's Golkar were not so much "gaming democracy" (Albertus and Menaldo 2014) as becoming *game for democracy*. Nor do we adhere to conventional arguments that democratic stability can only be attained by sacrificing democratic substance (e.g., Aspinall 2010; Mietzner 2015). To be sure, all three of these young democracies (like all old democracies) exhibit shortcomings in democratic quality, especially Indonesia. But *it is not these shortcomings that explain democratic stability*. To the contrary, we argue that it is only because these democracies have been relatively substantive – especially in political terms but also in economic terms – that they have been as stable as they have. Democratic shortfalls do not stabilize democracy as much as they threaten it.

Authoritarian successor parties did not build up democratic substance and stability in a spirit of self-sacrifice but of self-confidence. It is fundamental to our argument that democratic elections do not necessarily usher in a quick defeat for authoritarian successor parties. The *prospect* of uninterrupted early electoral successes is essential if authoritarian ruling parties are to accept the risks that accompany democracy's intrinsic uncertainties. The *experience* of continued success under democracy as authoritarian successor parties should then encourage party leaders and their societal allies to accept and even embrace democracy over time.[12]

Yet it is also fundamental to our argument that if these parties are to stabilize democracy over the long haul, they must eventually "learn to lose" (Friedman and Wong 2008). This means learning that whatever setbacks parties suffer in elections are neither permanent nor complete, and that losing is always

---

[10] We completely agree with other chapters in the volume (especially Flores-Macías' chapter on Mexico) that when authoritarian successor parties fail to seriously moderate and credibly reform themselves, they act as a drag on democratic deepening. As Loxton (Introduction, this volume) points out, authoritarian successor parties must deal with their authoritarian baggage if they are to play a positive role after democratization.

[11] The major work on whether and how dictatorships "break from the past" is Grzymala-Busse (2002). On how authoritarian successor parties can sometimes regain popularity by "hewing to the past," see Deming (2013).

[12] We are grateful to James Loxton and Scott Mainwaring for suggesting much of this language.

accompanied by assurances that parties can compete – and remain highly competitive – in future democratic contests. In Taiwan, Korea, and Indonesia, authoritarian successor parties have accepted electoral defeats whenever they have suffered them. In so doing they prioritized the perpetuation of the democracy they had first helped to forge, and not just their own relative position within it.

9.1 MOVING FROM STRENGTH TO STRENGTH

Authoritarian regimes do not have to collapse for democratization to occur (Riedl 2014; Slater and Wong 2013). In fact, their leaders do not necessarily even have to exit office. Democratization changes the regime *type*, but may not change the regime's leading *players*. When authoritarian elites fundamentally alter the rules of the game, permitting free and fair competition for office and ceasing to tilt the playing field systematically in their own favor, democratization can rightly be said to have occurred – and not only in a minimalist, proceduralist, electoralist sense. In our view, emptying political prisons, removing draconian controls on speech and media, establishing an independent and impartial election commission, and allowing parties and civil society organizations to form without interference or coercion amount to the end of authoritarianism and the birth of democracy, not just procedurally but substantively understood.[13]

Yet the death of authoritarianism need not mean the political demise – or even demotion – of its leaders. This is especially true for authoritarian regimes built upon powerful ruling parties. For authoritarian party elites, democratization entails the concession to *hold* free and fair elections, but not necessarily to *lose* them. Hence they can maintain incumbency without maintaining authoritarianism. What Przeworski (1991) called the "institutionalized uncertainty" of democracy may mean eschewing certain victory, but it does not necessarily mean accepting defeat. Democratization can thus be incentive-compatible for authoritarian ruling parties with promising prospects to remain in office under democratic conditions. Ruling parties are only likely to embark on this democratization path, however, when they possess substantial antecedent resources and marked relative strength vis-à-vis the opposition. These accrued absolute and relative strengths underpin ruling parties' *victory confidence* (i.e., their expectation of winning democratic elections) and *stability confidence* (i.e., their expectation that political stability will be preserved under democratic conditions).

In a nutshell, *democratic concessions become more palatable to ruling parties as they gain confidence that democratic competition will bring neither*

---

[13] For an argument that contemporary comparativists now commonly adhere to a substantive standard for democracy, making the timeworn "procedural-substantive" distinction irrelevant, see Slater (2013: 734).

their own electoral demise nor political instability. This is an important corrective to the democratization conventional wisdom. The decision to concede does not require an imminent threat of a violent overthrow (Acemoglu and Robinson 2006). On the contrary, a conceding-to-thrive strategy requires sufficient antecedent strength to engender confidence that democratization will mean neither a withdrawal from office nor political instability. Although democratic concessions are typically triggered by ominous signals of incipient regime decline – emanating from the electoral, economic, geopolitical, or contentious arenas (Slater and Wong 2013) – one should not confuse the strength of those rising challenges with any intrinsic and lasting weakness within the ruling party itself. Institutionally weak ruling parties cannot concede with confidence; strong ruling parties that are being strongly challenged can.

But where do ruling parties' antecedent strengths come from, and how do they enhance victory confidence and stability confidence? We argue that the most important antecedent resource a dominant party can possess is a long-term connection to a highly capable state apparatus, e.g., the successful "developmental states" of Asia,[14] which have helped produce unrivalled rates of economic growth. As Cheng and Huang (Chapter 2, this volume) note, the developmental state provided authoritarian successor parties in Taiwan and Korea a tremendously useful "brand" that could be mobilized for electoral purposes. Nonetheless, despite a common developmental heritage, these Asian party-states are highly diverse, as we have explored at length elsewhere (Slater 2010; Wong 2011). Among the three cases we consider here, state capacity has historically been especially impressive in Taiwan and Korea, and substantially less so – but far from unimpressive (Mietzner 2015; Smith 2007) – in Indonesia. Party domination has been more pronounced in Taiwan than in Korea, where the military also played a central role in authoritarian rule, or in Indonesia, where not just the military but a highly personalist ruler typically overpowered the ruling party apparatus. Yet even if Indonesia and Korea were not party-*dominated* like Taiwan, they had both effectively become party-*led* regimes by the time decisive democratic concessions were made. Party leaders and not military leaders were best positioned to choose the course of concession and to design new democratic rules, substantially leveling the playing field and breaking decisively with the repressive practices of the authoritarian past.

A history of successful state-led development enhances the victory confidence and stability confidence of party decision-makers in a variety of ways. An impressive record of transformative accomplishments in the economic realm provides the kind of "usable past" that aids an authoritarian successor

---

[14] In East Asia, the term "developmental state" connotes some degree of developmental success as well as developmental orientation. Scholars of other regions might define states that tried but failed to generate rapid and sustained industrial growth as developmental states (e.g., Kohli 2004 on India and Nigeria), but East Asianists generally would not.

party seeking "regeneration" under democracy (Grzymala-Busse 2002). Decades of state-led industrialization and poverty reduction tend to incubate a vibrant middle class with moderate and even conservative political leanings, still valuing development even while rejecting authoritarianism. Such citizens are less susceptible to the electoral and contentious appeals of radical dissenters who lack an established record of fostering developmental success. And to the extent that democratization creates pressure for increased welfare spending, parties are more capable of increasing distribution without sparking macroeconomic instability when they have access to the robust fiscal apparatuses and accrued public savings of developmental states (Haggard and Kaufman 2008; Wong 2004). Indeed, when ruling parties in developmental states lead democratic reform during relatively good economic times (Haggard and Kaufman 1995), they can overcome the greatest threat to their popularity and legitimacy – namely, their authoritarian character.

While state power lies at the heart of stability confidence, the institutional and coalitional strength of the authoritarian ruling party is the most critical component in victory confidence. Like state power, party power is built over time. Four dimensions are of particular importance. First, dominant parties will have higher victory confidence for postauthoritarian elections when they have developed cross-cutting constituencies (e.g., cross-class, cross-ethnic, and cross-region). Second, party strength is enhanced to the extent that the party has constructed a territorially encompassing infrastructure of local branches and cells. Third, parties will have higher victory confidence when they have cultivated experienced electoral candidates. And fourth, party leaders can more confidently embark on democratic reforms when they enjoy strong coalitional ties to prominent elites outside the formal party apparatus (e.g., in the military, bureaucracy, and business community).

Neither authoritarian ruling parties nor authoritarian successor parties exist in a coalitional vacuum. The strength of broader political ties among ruling elites and between ruling elites and their social constituencies shapes victory confidence and stability confidence as much as the formal institutional properties of the ruling party itself. Even in the strong party cases we discuss here, authoritarian successor parties have at times split, changed names, and seen new parties formed by former party members outperform the successor party itself after democratization. Even Taiwan's KMT, the strongest authoritarian successor party examined in this chapter, was split by a splinter faction in the early days of democracy, resulting in the 1993 creation of the New Party (see Cheng and Huang, Chapter 2, this volume). But to the degree that voters continued to elect allies and descendants of the old ruling party with ideological visions that were consistent with those of the successor party, the calculated gamble of democracy-through-strength was still paying off, if not quite as handsomely or straightforwardly as in cases where authoritarian ruling parties became victorious authoritarian successor parties without any interruption. Even when new leaders and splinter parties emerge through democratic elections, the policies they follow and coalitions they build often look familiar and comfortable to former authoritarian elites and to voters.

We do not expect authoritarian regimes to democratize simply because they are strong. As we detail elsewhere, such reforms are only likely to arise during what we call a historical "bittersweet spot" (Slater and Wong 2013). This is when ruling parties perceive their prospects for stable domination under authoritarian conditions are definitively declining, but they retain enough strength and support to fare quite well in democratic elections. For present purposes, however, we set aside this causal argument to make the critical points that: (1) strong authoritarian regimes may indeed democratize strategically to rejuvenate themselves; (2) the democracies which arise through this process can, indeed, become normal and meaningful democracies in a substantive sense over time; and (3) authoritarian ruling parties can become authoritarian successor parties by moving from strength to strength. In other words, democracy *through* strength becomes democracy *with* strength for formerly authoritarian elites. In our cases, the very perception and expectation that democracy and stability could go hand in hand are what make democratic concessions strategically palatable to ruling elites in the first place.

9.2 STABILIZATION THROUGH MODERATION

While democratic *success* was primarily a matter of historical inheritance for authoritarian successor parties in developmental Asia, democratic *stability* demanded that formerly authoritarian elites prove willing and able to moderate their political stances and economic programs. In our cases, moderate authoritarian successor parties have generally served as stabilizers rather than spoilers of democracy, even during moments when their democratic commitments were put to the sternest tests. Electoral setbacks have not produced democratic tailspins.

Before detailing how democratic stability came about in our three developmental Asian cases, however, we should say a few words about what we mean by democratic stability and offer preliminary evidence that Taiwan, Korea, and Indonesia are not only stable democracies but also substantive ones. Democratic stability is related but not reducible to democratic consolidation and democratic quality. Its achievement lies in the avoidance of volatility and polarization over fundamental questions surrounding the legitimate nature of the democratic regime. Simply put, stabilizing democracy means mitigating the risks of democratic backsliding and reversal. For instance, a democracy in which major players are calling for a rollback of civil rights, greater control of the press and civic expression, or the disqualification of peaceful competitors from the electoral arena enjoys less democratic stability than one where such questions are effectively settled. Indeed, *the "democratic" side of the concept is as vital as the "stability" part.* Incumbent governments cannot, for instance, leverage their free-and-fair electoral mandate to justify renewed repression of organized opposition or crackdowns on democratic dissent or to run roughshod over democratic institutions such as courts and anticorruption commissions. In other words, democracy cannot be considered stable unless it remains substantive.

Figure 9.1 demonstrates that Taiwan, Korea, and Indonesia have all become stable and substantive democracies. They also show that Taiwan's democratic performance has generally led the pack while Indonesia's has lagged; Korea is the intermediate case. The three countries' Polity scores suggest that democratic transitions were quite substantive and have been sustained in all three cases. Taiwan surpassed the standard +6 threshold by 1992 and continued its stepwise democratic improvement to a full +10 by 2006, where it has remained ever since. Similarly, if slightly less impressively, Korea reached +6 status by 1990 and its current +8 score by 2000. Last and (predictably) least, Indonesia transitioned from a closed authoritarian regime at −7 to a minimalist democracy at +6 in 1999. As in Taiwan and Korea, Indonesia's democracy deepened rather than backsliding over the course of democracy's crucial first decade, nudging up to a +8 score by 2004 and holding steady there, at least in aggregate terms.

How can we explain the fact that Taiwan, Korea, and Indonesia all managed to stabilize as substantive democracies, even while former authoritarian ruling parties continued to thrive? The case studies to follow provide a sense of the historical process through which this outcome came about. The key argument, theoretically speaking, is that the political and economic *moderation* pursued

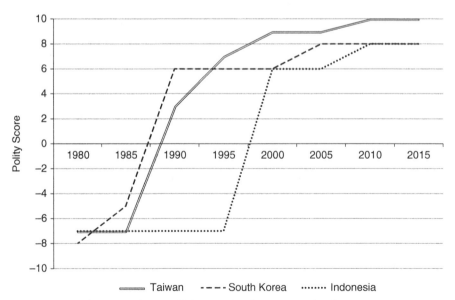

FIGURE 9.1 Polity scores by year: Taiwan, South Korea, and Indonesia

ASPs in Developmental Asia 293

by all three countries' authoritarian successor parties contributed to democratic stability.[15] The overarching reason is straightforward: moderation helps authoritarian successor parties *broaden their winning coalition*, contributing both to their own electoral success and to the stabilization of democratic competition in turn.

We operationalize moderation in three ways. First, the seeds of political moderation can be witnessed in the *initial democratic concession*, which requires moderation in the power appetites of authoritarian elites. Authoritarian domination can never eliminate political uncertainty (Schedler 2013), but the leeway rulers enjoy under authoritarianism is generally of a different magnitude than they can hope to attain under democracy (Albertus 2015). Thus, democracy through strength does not require the total elimination of authoritarian rulers' power appetites, since they very well may continue to hold office, both at the national and subnational levels, after winning free and fair elections. However, without some moderation in those appetites – by which we mean the initial concession of free and fair elections that entail at least the possibility of losing power – democracy through strength cannot commence, much less consummate in full-blown regime change. Fortunately for authoritarian successor parties, this initial act of moderation tends to attract new supporters who had opposed the party for its authoritarian abuses, expanding the winning coalition in the process. This was evident in all three of the cases examined in this chapter.

Second, we insist that moderation continue with *ongoing democratic restraint*. The initial moderation of power appetites at the time of transition is sustained through an ongoing, open commitment to democratic principles and rejection of authoritarian practices. This does not mean an altruistic disinterest on the part of the authoritarian successor party in holding power. What it requires instead is a persistent "ownership" of the democratic system, such that the upholding of democracy and the course of democratic reform are prioritized alongside the party's obvious concern with retaining political office and maximizing its share of the political pie. Potential opponents of democracy inside the authoritarian successor parties lose ground and recede in determining the party's – and hence democracy's – future.

Voters will typically cast an especially skeptical eye on the democratic commitments of authoritarian successor parties – and justifiably so. Alarm bells will sound not only once an outright abuse of power or imposition of authoritarian controls has arisen, but any time the authoritarian successor party appears to act in narrowly self-interested and self-aggrandizing fashion. Democratic voters understandably tend to set an especially high bar for

---

[15] None of these parties behaved as monolithic unitary actors throughout the concession and moderation processes, as our case studies should make clear. Yet they were much more successful at overcoming internal factionalism and pursuing coherent party-rebuilding strategies than one would expect from accounts equating democratic transition with authoritarian collapse.

authoritarian successor parties. To avoid destabilizing polarization and the reopening of old wounds from the *ancien régime* era, such parties must show a level of democratic restraint, moderation, and a propensity to reform that surpasses a mere commitment not to relapse into authoritarian rule.

Third and finally, moderation means *changing the party's economic practices* as well as discarding its authoritarian practices. As Cheng and Huang detail in their chapter (Chapter 2, this volume), issue dynamics and issue ownership are critical in hastening the transformation – or moderation, in our cases – of authoritarian successor parties. This transformation can be much less dramatic but no less significant for stabilizing democracy. Even while maintaining the developmental ethos of the authoritarian era, authoritarian successor parties in our Asian cases had to moderate their economic platforms to stabilize democracy. Most importantly, moderation requires that distributive policies, such as welfare policies, become more generous, inclusive, and even mildly redistributive under democracy's electoral pressures (Wong 2004). Authoritarian regimes in developmental Asia were not necessarily opposed to providing subsidies and other benefits to popular sectors, including valued public goods such as land reform and universal primary education (Doner, Ritchie, and Slater 2005). But no Asian country became a bona fide OECD-style welfare state, even after reaching an OECD-like GDP per capita, before becoming a democracy. In Taiwan, Korea, and Indonesia, the shift from purely growth-oriented developmental states toward what we call "distributive-developmental states" occurred either under the tutelage of or with the active support of authoritarian successor parties. Such economic moderation helped limit electoral losses for the former authoritarian ruling party, and even attracted new supporters among those social constituencies who were receiving newly expanded government benefits.

Democratic moderation exhibits a positive feedback effect on democratic success. We expect political and economic moderation to contribute to the initial electoral success of the authoritarian successor party, broadening its winning coalition and giving it the necessary confidence to stay the democratic course whenever it experiences electoral setbacks. Authoritarian successor parties have restrained their power appetites and remained committed to democracy during times of relative weakness because they possessed confidence in their capacity to rebound from whatever setback they had suffered. Economic moderation ensured them a broad – indeed a broadening – constituency of political support. Authoritarian successor parties in Taiwan, Korea, and Indonesia were thus confident that they could enjoy success again.[16]

---

[16] Our arguments here are centered, however, on the critical decade following democratization. Once these new democracies had navigated three or four electoral cycles, their role in democratic stabilization would become less pivotal as more typical democratic rhythms and dynamics took hold.

ASPs in Developmental Asia

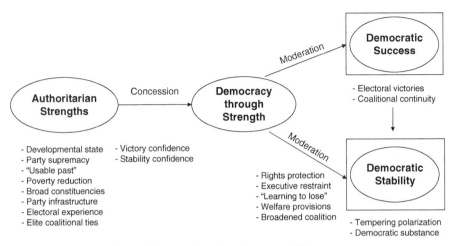

FIGURE 9.2 Conceding to thrive and moderating to stabilize

In sum, developmental Asia has not merely seen authoritarian *ruling* parties transform into authoritarian *successor* parties. It has also seen *conservative* authoritarian parties evolve into *moderate* democratic parties.[17] Choosing to moderate cements former authoritarian ruling parties' commitment to democratic practices. It also contributes to the parties' democratic success, which encourages authoritarian successor parties to stay in the democratic game, even when confronted with electoral setbacks. Moderation thus contributes to democratic stability both directly, by preventing outright authoritarian backsliding and retrenchment, and indirectly, through the continued success and ongoing confidence of the authoritarian successor party.

These arguments are summarized graphically in Figure 9.2. Authoritarian strengths such as a developmental state and established party apparatus help incentivize democratic concessions by giving incumbents both victory confidence and stability confidence. This is the democracy-through-strength scenario. If the authoritarian successor party then pursues a path of political and economic moderation, democratic stability is our hypothesized result. Less deterministically but no less importantly, moderation also contributes to the party's lasting electoral success. This reinforces its victory confidence and hence

---

[17] By "conservative," we mean that developmental Asia's authoritarian successor parties were pro-capitalist, pro-American, and generally suspicious of mass mobilization and major downward economic redistribution. In this context, moderation simply means becoming less conservative. (By contrast, for leftist and populist parties, it requires being less leftist and populist, for instance by finding creative ways to embrace the market and make peace with business elites without totally betraying leftist principles.) Moderation seeks to broaden an existing coalition, not entirely swap one group of supporters for another.

its commitment to the democratic game, even in moments of relative weakness or electoral stress.

9.2.1 Taiwan

The Kuomintang (KMT) fled to Taiwan during the late 1940s, when it lost the Chinese civil war to the Communist Party led by Mao Zedong. Initially intent on retaking the mainland, the KMT established what it thought was going to be a temporary regime on Taiwan. Nonetheless, the KMT failed to maintain its hold on power in China and it was not going to allow that to happen in Taiwan. The party underwent a reorganization campaign in the early 1950s, modeling itself as a strong Leninist party with a cellular structure aimed at penetrating all levels of society. The KMT initiated a mass mobilization campaign, increasing party membership drastically during its early years on the island. The ruling party also institutionalized a developmental state, featuring a capable, meritocratic, and "clean" bureaucracy. From the 1960s onwards, the developmental state not only engineered an economic plan that grew the Taiwanese economy by nearly 10 percent per year but also initiated an industrial upgrading program, such that by the late 1980s Taiwan was an integral part of the global trading system and a high-tech industrial economy.

By the 1970s, when China normalized relations with the United States and Taiwan's government (technically the Republic of China) lost its seat at the United Nations, it had become clear to President Chiang Kai-shek that the KMT's initial plan to retake the mainland was unlikely. The KMT, in an effort to generate political legitimacy on the island, thus set out to rule Taiwan as an indigenous party rather than a mainlander-based émigré regime. To that end, the ruling KMT gradually introduced limited elections at the local level. Opposition parties continued to be banned under Martial Law, which had been imposed in 1947. But independent – that is, non-KMT – candidates were permitted to contest elections. During the 1970s and 1980s, the KMT also initiated a process of "Taiwanization," recruiting into the party and the state leadership ethnically Taiwanese citizens who had previously been excluded. Though the party was transitioning from what Edwin Winckler (1984) refers to as "hard" to "soft" authoritarianism, the regime nonetheless dominated the political scene, often relying on brutally harsh measures to suppress any burgeoning opposition movement. On the eve of Taiwan's transition to democracy, the KMT regime continued to violently put down opposition activists, including through the assassination of anti-regime activists. The KMT regime, even though it had softened by the 1980s, remained a brutal dictatorship with an uncontested hold on political power.

Taiwan's transition to democracy began during the mid-1980s when members of the *tangwai* (literally translated to be "outside the ruling party") social movement announced the formation of the Democratic Progressive Party (DPP) in September of 1986. By then the KMT was led by Chiang Ching-Kuo, the son of former president Chiang Kai-shek, and most Taiwan watchers at the time expected the KMT to quash the DPP. But the unexpected happened. Chiang Ching-Kuo allowed the DPP to form, and in 1987 the regime lifted Martial Law. A few years later, in 1989, the KMT passed a civic organizations law and partial legislative elections were held, in which for the first time non-KMT candidates contested national elections as an opposition party.

As expected, the opposition DPP ran on an anti-authoritarianism platform, demanding broad and sweeping political and economic reforms. The DPP also hoped to tap into voters' ethnic loyalties by portraying the KMT as an outsider, mainland-based party. The KMT, meanwhile, leveraged its postwar economic leadership in not only engineering Taiwan's industrial development but also its commitment to ensuring an egalitarian distribution of income through early land reform and a full-employment strategy. Taiwan is noted for achieving a high degree of growth with equity, with nearly 10 percent growth per year and a Gini coefficient of around 0.3. The party also ran on its commitment to political reform. By permitting the formation of the DPP in 1986, signaling its willingness to contest future elections, the KMT was able to credibly claim its pivotal role in Taiwan's gradual democratic development. Simply put, the KMT inherited tremendous strengths from the authoritarian period, which it effectively translated into electoral success in the dawning democratic era.

Chiang Ching-Kuo did not believe democratizing Taiwan would result in the KMT's defeat. He had many reasons to be confident that the KMT would thrive in democracy and that a political transition managed by the party would not lead to political and economic instability. The 1989 elections reaffirmed the KMT's popularity, despite its authoritarian heritage. Though opposition candidates won more seats than ever before, the KMT won a dominant legislative majority. As Linda Chao and Ramon Myers note, "In many authoritarian regimes that moved toward democracy since the 1970s, voters had frequently rejected the old ruling parties, but not in Taiwan. Despite decades of iron rule, a decisive majority continued to support the old ruling party" (1998: 173). To reiterate: from the point of view of the KMT, conceding democracy did not mean conceding defeat.

The KMT's initial concessions for reform – allowing the formation of the DPP, lifting Martial Law in 1987, contesting the 1989 supplementary elections, and the announcement of full legislative elections in 1992 – were in many ways unexpected precisely because the KMT regime, at the time, was very strong. Unlike in cases of democratic transition through weakness, the KMT regime was not on its political deathbed. There were few proximate pressures for the authoritarian regime to concede political reform. After all, the economy at the time was performing well. The regime's Taiwanization strategy rooted the party inside Taiwan, gradually shedding the KMT's outsider image among Taiwanese. And perhaps most importantly, the KMT retained a brutal security apparatus that could effectively repress any opposition. However, as we have argued elsewhere (Slater and Wong 2013), the KMT chose to concede democracy in large measure because it enjoyed overwhelming strength. The party could have maintained its authoritarian grip on Taiwan, but in the face of longer-term uncertainty, the KMT chose to initiate democratic concessions with the confident expectation that it would continue to dominate under democratic rules of the game (Hu 1993). As Bruce Dickson reasons, the "KMT leaders decided that refusing to adapt to a changed environment was a greater threat than setting and enforcing the terms and pace of political change" (1997: 213). President Chiang himself proclaimed that "the times are changing" (quoted in Moody 1992: 92). Simply put, conceding democracy was not an admission of the KMT's impending defeat; rather, the party was poised to thrive in democracy.

The KMT is the best example of democracy through strength. On the spectrum of antecedent strengths, the KMT was the strongest party-state-regime among our three cases. The party's economic credentials were unequivocal; its political concessions during the mid-1980s were decisive; and its electoral performance in the 1989 supplementary elections reflected its popularity. But while the KMT enjoyed overwhelming confidence to initiate democratic concessions, the party also demonstrated ongoing democratic restraint in the form of subsequent political reforms. As we argue throughout this chapter, democratic stabilization requires not only the authoritarian regime's initial political concessions but also continued efforts to moderate the successor party through *ongoing democratic restraint*.

Chiang died in 1988 and his successor, Lee Teng-Hui, continued to reform Taiwan's political system, deepening the democratic rules of the game. President Lee convened the National Affairs Conference (NAC) in 1990. The NAC allowed Lee to marginalize those within the party who resisted further democratization. In the run-up to the Conference, the KMT split into the reform-minded "mainstream" faction, led by Lee, and the "non-mainstream" faction, comprised of the so-called hard-liners who opposed reform.[18] Lee formed a tacit reform-alliance between the KMT's mainstream faction and the opposition DPP.[19] The opposition, suspicious of the KMT, was initially hesitant to participate in the conference. But as the DPP leadership became increasingly convinced that the mainstream KMT faction sought a stable democracy, the opposition joined the NAC. Together the DPP and mainstream faction of the KMT established a political reform agenda for the conference. The 1990 NAC drew up a blueprint for further democratic reform in Taiwan, putting in place key

---

[18] The factional split within the KMT did not result in what Cheng and Huang see to be party reorganization, but Lee Teng-Hui's efforts to marginalize the more conservative, standpatter hard-line faction gave the impression of what Cheng and Huang (Chapter 2, this volume) characterize as a "re-polish" for the ruling party.

[19] Contra O'Donnell and Schmitter (1986) and others who argue that elite splits between hard-liners and soft-liners prompt democratic transitions, such splits in Taiwan were a *consequence* rather than a *cause* of democratic concessions. Democracy through strength commenced in Taiwan when the KMT was highly unified, not divided.

reforms such as the direct election of the president; constitutional reform; a timeline for the eventual elimination of the National Assembly and Provincial Assembly; and the phasing out of other vestiges of the mainland-era Republic of China institutions (Chao and Myers 1998). The NAC, under the KMT's leadership, deepened Taiwan's democracy, reinforcing democratic restraint and making democratic backsliding less likely.

Commitment to political reform, we argue, is not enough to ensure either democratic stability or democratic success for authoritarian successor parties. *The KMT also needed to maintain, and even broaden, its winning coalition of electoral support.* The party fared well during Taiwan's early elections, though it also learned that as a historically conservative party, it needed to put into place a moderate and inclusive economic reform agenda. Retrospectively, the KMT appealed to voters by highlighting the developmental state's record of growth with equity. But going forward, the democratically elected KMT government sought to broaden its electoral appeal through generous yet fiscally sustainable redistributive social and economic policies. During the 1990s, for instance, the KMT initiated major social welfare reforms, such as expanding the benefits of labor insurance and old-age income security, as well as implementing new workplace and employment protections. In 1988, the KMT announced the creation of a universal National Health Insurance (NHI) scheme to be implemented by 1995. In addition to expanding health-care coverage to all citizens, the NHI was the first national program to recognize and enroll nonformal, self-employed workers, who make up the largest portion of Taiwan's labor market (Peng and Wong 2008; Wong 2004).

Democratic transition in Taiwan forced the KMT to respond to electoral demands to win support; the party could no longer rely on authoritarian practices of suppressing dissent to stay in power. The rules of the game had changed, and the KMT needed to adapt, both by exercising democratic restraint and by broadening its popular appeal. Political and economic moderation translated into early electoral success for the authoritarian successor party. In the 1992 legislative election, Taiwan's first full and free electoral contest, the KMT polled 53 percent of the vote and won 63 percent of the seats. The DPP, meanwhile, polled 31 percent of the vote and took just over 30 percent of the legislative seats. In 1993, the KMT splintered, as the remnants of the non-mainstream, mainlander-dominated faction of the KMT formed the New Party. The KMT thus won a smaller majority in the 1995 legislative election with 52 percent of the seats. However, the so-called Pan-Blue camp (the combination of the KMT and New Party), with the KMT as the coalition leader, accounted for 65 percent of the legislative assembly, more than the KMT had gained on its own in 1992. In other words, the slight dip in KMT support in 1995 did not translate into a decline in support of the authoritarian successors but rather continuity of electoral support for the KMT's old guard. In Taiwan's first direct election for the presidency in 1996, the KMT ticket of incumbent Lee Teng-Hui and Lien Chan won handily with 54 percent of the vote, while the DPP candidate Peng Ming-Min polled just 21 percent of the ballots cast.

With each electoral victory, it appeared the KMT's gamble to concede democracy in the first place was paying off. Though Chiang initiated the democratic transition moment and his successor Lee deepened the course of democratic reform, the KMT not only survived democratization but thrived and continued to dominate politically. The combination of the party's antecedent strengths and its efforts to moderate through its political and economic reform agendas ensured the KMT's democratic success as well as its pivotal role as a democratic stabilizer rather than spoiler. The party's success ensured it had no interest in democratic backsliding.

However, the KMT's hold on power, in the end, was not absolute, since genuine democracy equals institutionalized uncertainty. The party faced a serious test of its commitment to democracy in 2000 when the opposition DPP candidate Chen Shui-bian narrowly won the presidency with just 39 percent of the vote, and again in 2004 when he was reelected by a razor-thin margin. If there was ever a time when the KMT might have been expected to let go of its democratic restraint and become a democratic spoiler, it was after successive defeats in the 2000 and 2004 presidential elections. In this respect, these two elections marked a significant turning point in Taiwan's democratic development, since they were not only the first time the opposition had won executive office, but more strikingly, the first time the KMT had lost *any* election. Many worried the KMT, reeling in its defeat, might close ranks, stall or roll back democratic reforms, and return the former ruling party to its authoritarian roots (Friedman and Wong 2008).

The party regrouped, however, and did not become a democratic spoiler. After the 2004 defeat, the KMT selected Ma Ying-Jeou to lead the party, a "clean" politician from a new generation and with broad electoral appeal. To recast the KMT's image, the party moved its headquarters from its former lavish compound to a much more modest location. The KMT leadership also pushed several reforms to make the party more internally democratic (Cheng 2008; Wong 2008). The KMT benefited from a disastrous second term for the DPP president, which was marred by corruption and dissension within the DPP's rank and file. Ma won the presidency with 58 percent of the vote in 2008 and the KMT retained its legislative majority, winning both again in 2012. It is true that the DPP then won the 2016 elections in a landslide, costing the KMT not only the presidency but also, for the first time ever, its legislative majority. Yet, despite earlier fears that the KMT might derail Taiwan's democracy in the wake of electoral defeat, the party is widely expected to stay the democratic course. Thirty years after the KMT initiated the process of political reform, there are no longer grounds for considering it anything other than a normal democratic party competing in a fully democratic two-party system.

9.2.2 Korea

Korea experimented with democracy in the immediate postwar period, though the political instability wrought by the Korean War, rampant corruption, and sluggish economic development doomed the democratic regime. Syngman Rhee's presidency ended in April 1960 when students mobilized and forced him to resign. Military rule followed soon thereafter, when in 1961 General Park Chung-hee led a coup overthrowing the government before assuming the presidency in 1962. Though the army was always in the wings, Park led and governed through the Democratic Republican Party (DRP). Korea's opposition was tolerated by the Park regime, but a massive seat bonus and directly appointed seats by the president ensured that the DRP remained dominant in the National Assembly. During the 1960s, President Park institutionalized Korea's developmental state, concentrating power within the presidency and the leadership ranks of the state bureaucracy. His regime grew the economy, preparing Korea for a major industrial push in the 1970s. Faced with growing opposition, however, Park imposed the highly repressive Yushin Constitution in 1972, which stamped out any political opposition to the government. From 1972 to 1979, the DRP controlled nearly all of the legislative seats and Park's hold on the presidency was uncontested.

General Chun Doo-Hwan succeeded Park in 1979 after Park was assassinated. Initially, Chun was thought to be a democratic reformer and the transition from Park to Chun was seen to represent a potential democratic opening. In May of 1980, however, Chun imposed Martial Law and ordered the military to brutally put down the Gwangju Democracy Movement. He subsequently abolished all political parties, although he restored the DRP, renaming it the Democratic Justice Party (DJP). Chun handily won the deeply authoritarian 1981 presidential election with over 90 percent of the vote.

Chun's early years in power did not go smoothly, however. The Korean economy had grown at nearly 10 percent per year since the 1970s and undergone a significant industrial transformation, but by the early 1980s, it confronted increasing competition from other economies, rising levels of inequality, and a mini-debt crisis. An oppositional civil society was fomenting as well. In the wake of the 1980 Gwangju Massacre, the *minjung* movement coalesced different segments of Korean society against the authoritarian DJP regime. The confrontation between the *minjung* democracy movement and the authoritarian regime came to a head in the summer of 1987. President Chun failed to deliver on constitutional reform, as he had promised earlier, and civil society actors mobilized to demand political change (Croissant 2002).

The *minjung* movement was a broad-based coalition of social movements, comprising middle-class activists, workers, church leaders, liberal intellectuals, and students. Politically, *minjung* activists were inspired by dissident leaders such as Kim Dae-Jung and Kim Young-Sam, who had joined forces in the 1985 National Assembly elections and won nearly 30 percent of the popular vote, even though the ruling party maintained a legislative majority due to the malapportionment of seats which favored the DJP. Economically, the *minjung* movement sought a more inclusive model of development (Lee 2007). Although the Korean government, like Taiwan's, promoted a full-employment strategy to mitigate income inequality, it pursued a heavy industry program beginning in the 1970s that exacerbated income disparities (Haggard 1990). In response to the *minjung* protests, Chun's anointed successor, General Roh Tae-Woo, unexpectedly conceded a democratic opening when he announced in June of 1987 that direct presidential elections would be held later that year, followed by National Assembly elections in the spring of 1988. Roh's decision effectively set Korea on a new course of political reform. As Tun-Jen Cheng and Eun-Mee Kim put it, "Roh's concession was an alternative to the imposition of martial law, an alternative to the hard-liner Chun" (1994: 135).

The introduction of fully contested elections in 1987 and 1988 put the ruling party at some risk: whereas under authoritarian rule, the DJP had been virtually assured its hold on power, democratic contests introduced electoral uncertainty into the Korean political system. Moreover, the authoritarian regime in Korea conceded democracy from a position of considerably less strength than the KMT did in Taiwan. The regime, when it initially conceded reforms toward democracy, confronted a much more organized opposition, both in the streets and within the formal political arena. Unlike in Taiwan, where the DPP, when it formed in 1986, was an untested opposition party to the still-dominant KMT, opposition parties led by Kim Dae-Jung and Kim Young-Sam were already well entrenched with a solid electoral base, as evidenced by their popularity in 1985. The KMT also did not confront a civil society expressly mobilized against the regime, as the Korean government faced during the early and mid-1980s. Nonetheless, the Roh regime, even in the summer of 1987, enjoyed a fair degree of confidence that by conceding democratic reform, the party would still thrive politically and potentially even emerge victorious under democracy; indeed, the prospects for democratic rejuvenation were more appealing than standing pat against Korea's increasingly militant opposition.

What was the basis of this confidence? Like in Taiwan, the Korean authoritarian regime was able to draw on its record of economic leadership. At one time an economic laggard – poorer than many African countries – Korea had become an industrial power. It was slated to host the Olympics in 1988. Korea was on its way to becoming a member of the OECD, the second Asian economy to be admitted to the "club of rich nations." The DJP and its conservative predecessors under Park and Chun claimed credit for Korea's postwar development and stressed that it was the party that could best manage the economy. The party also enjoyed deep ties with Korea's business establishment. Thus, Roh, when he conceded democratic elections, was relatively sure that the DJP would poll well among middle-class voters and gain support from industry, as these conservative constituencies had benefited mightily from Korea's postwar developmental state. He was hence fairly confident that the DJP would win at least one-third of the popular vote in democratic elections, which would ensure that the DJP continued to have a central political role. Like the KMT in Taiwan, the DJP was a dominant party which inherited considerable strengths from its authoritarian past.

A more proximate source of confidence for Roh came from the divided political opposition. Roh gambled in advance of the founding presidential election that rivals Kim Young-Sam and Kim Dae-Jung would split the opposition vote. Although the two Kims ran on a single ticket in 1985, it was well known that their relationship was chilly and that they drew electoral support from their regional power bases. If the two Kims split the opposition vote, as Roh expected, then the DJP could win outright and remain dominant; if they put their differences aside, it was more likely that the DJP would be defeated, but it would certainly not be sidelined entirely. Either way, it would continue to be a key player in the democratic game as an authoritarian successor party. Roh's bet paid off as Kim Dae-Jung and Kim Young-Sam ran separate presidential campaigns, splitting the opposition vote and allowing Roh to win the 1987 presidential election with just over one-third of the vote. The DJP subsequently gained the largest seat share in the 1988 Assembly elections, as the two Kims' parties again split the opposition's electoral support. The DJP won 34 percent of the Assembly's seats, while Kim Young-Sam's Reunification Democratic Party (RDP) took 24 percent and Kim Dae-Jung's Party for Peace and Democracy (PPD) won 19 percent. A fourth party, the right-wing National Democratic Republican Party (NDRP), led by former intelligence chief Kim Jong-Pil, took 16 percent of the Assembly seats.

Roh had initiated democracy in Korea, though like the process in Taiwan, the former authoritarian ruling party, the DJP, remained in a position of relative dominance. But as we argue in this chapter, a concession by the authoritarian regime for reform does not guarantee that the authoritarian successor party will continue to exercise democratic restraint; there needs to be evidence of such restraint beyond the initial concession to democratic elections if the party is to be a democratic stabilizer. We see such evidence in democratizing Korea. To add to his political reform credentials – to demonstrate democratic restraint – Roh quickly distanced himself from the previous Chun regime. For instance, the DJP defused concerns about the military's role in democratic Korea by immediately putting the generals and the army's rank and file under civilian control. As early as 1987, Roh began to prosecute military officials accused of political interference, thus strengthening the hand of the ruling party vis-à-vis the military. The DJP also negotiated new electoral rules, which in many respects leveled the playing field for the opposition. In the run-up to the 1988 National Assembly elections, the DJP compromised with the opposition parties by adopting a single-member district system, even though its preference was to maintain the multi-member scheme, which would have delivered the DJP a massive seat bonus. In the 1988 election, as before, the DJP won around one-third of the popular vote, but unlike in the past, the ruling party only took a plurality of the Assembly seats rather than an outright majority.

By conceding a democratic opening in the summer of 1987 and by imposing democratic restraints on the party soon thereafter, Roh could credibly portray the DJP as a party of political reform. Nonetheless, the DJP's shaky electoral support in both the 1987 presidential and 1988 Assembly elections made clear that the near-term electoral payoff that came with initiating democratic reform was unlikely to sustain the DJP's electoral support over the long term. The *minjung* activists, after all, not only demanded regime change but also economic reform. The DJP responded. In an effort to broaden the DJP's electoral base, the government quickly put into place major social and economic policies that cut across voters' regional loyalties and appealed to working-class and middle-class voters. In 1988, for instance, the DJP government announced plans for a national pensions program. That same year, the government created a universal medical insurance program for the countryside, incorporating for the first time self-employed workers into the coverage schemes. The following year, in 1989, the DJP government universalized medical insurance for urban workers, again including self-employed workers for the first time in any government-managed and subsidized social welfare program (Wong 2004). In Korea, as in Taiwan, the authoritarian successor party responded to electoral pressures by broadening its electoral appeal and coalition of support. Like the KMT in Taiwan, the DJP pursued a strategy of political and economic moderation. In both cases, this facilitated democratic stability by ensuring that the authoritarian successor parties stayed in the democratic game.

This is not to say that the commitment of Korea's authoritarian successor party to democracy was never in doubt. Worries arose in 1990 when Roh formed a "grand conservative coalition" with the merger of the DJP, Kim Young-Sam's RDP, and Kim Jong-Pil's NDRP. The new coalition party, the Democratic Liberal Party (DLP), was modeled after the electorally dominant Liberal Democratic Party (LDP) in Japan. As a result of the merger, the newly formed DLP assumed control of nearly three-quarters of the National Assembly's seats, as well as the Roh presidency. Essentially overnight, the DJP was transformed from being the governing party into a thoroughly dominant party. Opposition leader Kim Dae-Jung, the odd man out of the merger, criticized the formation of the conservative coalition party as a "coup d'état against democracy," conjuring fears about past coups in pre-democratic Korea. For many, the party merger represented a power grab by conservative elites, and the formation of the DLP in 1990 looked very much like a potential democratic spoiler.

Backsliding did not, however, come to pass. In 1992, former opposition leader and dissident Kim Young-Sam became the leader of the DLP. Kim's first order of business was to turn on his predecessors Chun Doo-Hwan and Roh Tae-Woo, when he ordered investigations into corruption charges against the two soon after his inauguration. Midway through this presidential term, both Chun and Roh were found guilty on a variety of charges, including their roles in various human rights violations during the authoritarian period, and both were given harsh prison sentences.[20] In an effort to highlight his democratic bona fides by distancing the DLP from its military and authoritarian past, Kim, the ruling party's first-ever civilian leader, won the 1992 presidential election with 42 percent of the vote, a considerable increase over Roh's 1987 showing, but still short of a majority. The DLP won 39 percent of the National Assembly seats in the 1992 legislative elections, a slight gain over the DJP's showing in 1988, but well below the nearly three-quarters of the Assembly the DLP controlled after the 1990 merger. To be sure, despite concerns about the overwhelming dominance of the conservative party, the opposition led by Kim Dae-Jung fared better in elections after the formation of the DLP. Kim's PPD increased its share of Assembly seats quite dramatically, from 19 percent in 1988 to 29 percent in 1992. In this regard, the 1990 DLP merger, rather than portend a return to a more authoritarian style of political dominance, actually fomented a bipolar – and hence more stable – party system, in which essentially the same two major parties, though with name changes, have consistently vied for national power.

Korea's democracy seemed to be in some potential peril a second time during the 1997 Asian Financial Crisis (Steinberg 1998). The Korean economy was hit particularly hard. Firms went bankrupt; unemployment, inequality, and poverty rose; banks failed and the financial system was on the brink; the conglomerate firms that had been the backbone of Korea's industries had to be restructured; and Korea required an IMF bailout to meet its liquidity shortfall. Panic ensued and fears about the long-term impact of the crisis on Korea's economy and democracy emerged. Nostalgia for the Park regime and the "golden age" of authoritarian leadership and economic growth began to surface as well.

Yet democracy in Korea remained stable. Indeed, rather than seeing the conservatives consolidate power in order to manage the economic crisis, Korea experienced a transfer of power. Perennial opposition leader Kim Dae-Jung was elected to the presidency in 1997, winning 40 percent of the vote and narrowly beating conservative leader Lee Hoi-Chang. The authoritarian successor party – now called the Grand National Party (GNP) – found itself in opposition for the first time. But rather than become a democratic spoiler, the party adhered to the democratic rules of the game, accepting the 1997 election results. This was because it expected to rebound. As it turned out, the GNP's time in opposition was longer than it had initially anticipated. The GNP failed to win the presidency again in 2002, this time losing to Roh Moo-Hyun.

---

[20] The DLP, more emphatically than Taiwan's KMT, chose to manage its authoritarian baggage aggressively, reflecting Loxton's (Introduction, this volume) notion of "contrition" when dealing with an authoritarian successor party's "unusable past."

The fact that Korea's authoritarian successor party was not badly defeated in either the 1997 or 2002 presidential contests was critical to keeping it in the democratic game. The GNP's candidate Lee lost to Kim Dae-Jung in 1997 by just 1 percent of the popular vote. In the 2002 election, Lee was again defeated by a very small margin, just two percentage points. Meanwhile, the party maintained a strong presence in the National Assembly throughout the 1990s and 2000s, controlling between 34 percent and 44 percent of the seats. In fact, with the exception of the 1996 legislative election, the party always held the largest share (a plurality) of Assembly seats. The GNP was down but definitely not out. Although it lost consecutive elections in 1997 and 2002, the party remained powerful and popular among its core electoral base, which ensured that it stayed the democratic course and prevented it from becoming a democratic spoiler. Like the KMT in Taiwan, Korea's GNP was forced to learn to lose. And also similar to the KMT, the party learned that losing – especially losing by very slight margins – did not preclude the party *from winning again* (Kim 2008), which it did in 2007. GNP candidate Lee Myung-Bak won the presidency in 2007 with 49 percent of the vote, and his successor Park Geun-hye – the daughter of former dictator Park Chung-hee – won 52 percent in the 2012 presidential contest, the first time a democratically elected president won an outright majority.

9.2.3 Indonesia

Indonesia under the authoritarian "New Order" regime led by General Suharto (1966–1998) was never a full-blown developmental state like Taiwan or Korea (Doner, Ritchie, and Slater 2005). Nevertheless, its social and economic accomplishments were substantial, despite being accompanied by widespread corruption and, at times, sweeping brutality and even mass killings. After seizing power from the chronically ineffectual and rapidly radicalizing regime of Indonesia's founding father, Sukarno, the Suharto regime muscularly transformed one of Asia's worst economic basket cases into one of its relative success stories. Poverty levels were dramatically reduced; self-sufficiency in rice was swiftly achieved; and growth rates propelled Indonesia from low-income to middle-income status by the 1980s. Most importantly, the regime's decisive resolution of severe elite conflict – in large measure through coercion, but also through co-optation – brought a kind of stability and order to Indonesia that had been sorely lacking since gaining independence through a violent revolution against the Dutch in 1949.

The New Order was built upon the military, but not the military alone. As in Korea, military rule was buttressed by strengthened civilian institutions, most notably the ruling party, Golkar. By the early 1970s, the Suharto regime had reintroduced elections, which Golkar always won in landslides through the same mixture of intimidation and blandishments that defined the New Order more generally. Although Suharto gradually personalized politics and substantially narrowed his support coalition over time (Slater 2010), his regime was still characterized by regular elections as well as a workable party–state apparatus by the time the Asian Financial Crisis struck in 1997.

The Suharto regime came down with a mighty crash in May 1998. But the party-bureaucratic-military alliance that had backed him for over three decades enjoyed a surprisingly soft landing when democracy was introduced under the leadership of Suharto's successor, President B.J. Habibie, in 1999. At the heart of this soft landing was Indonesia's authoritarian successor party, Golkar. Forged in the early 1970s as an amalgam of military officers, civil servants, and supportive sectoral organizations, Suharto's old electoral vehicle placed a solid second in the 1999 parliamentary elections, securing 22.5 percent of the national vote and 26.0 percent of parliamentary seats.

To be sure, this was a colossal decline from Golkar's golden days of authoritarian hegemony, when stage-managed quinquennial elections consistently delivered the official party over 60 percent of the national vote. In this respect, Golkar was the least electorally successful of the three authoritarian successor parties examined in this chapter. Nevertheless, the party still managed to play the kingmaker role in the indirect parliamentary selection of Indonesia's president in late 1999 (Slater 2004). In the process, it secured seven cabinet positions for itself, as well as six for its longstanding allies in the military, which itself still held 7.6 percent of all parliamentary seats by appointment. Meanwhile, the opposition party that had won a plurality in the free and fair parliamentary election – Megawati Sukarnoputri's Indonesian Democratic Party of Struggle (PDIP), with over 33 percent of the national vote – captured only five portfolios, or fewer than either Golkar or the military. Indonesia's inaugural democratic elections thus did not replace Golkar and the military in government. Instead, it brought a diverse assortment of opposition parties into a new powersharing arrangement with the party and military institutions that had previously backstopped Suharto's New Order.

Golkar's electoral viability was not a merely transitional phenomenon. While falling far short of the electoral performance exhibited by authoritarian successor parties in Taiwan and Korea, Golkar remained popular enough to hold its own in the electoral arena. Although its raw parliamentary vote share slid slightly from 22.5 percent in 1999 to 21.6 percent in 2004, this was good enough to garner a first-place result, given the weakening support for all other major parties as well. Once again, Golkar parlayed solid electoral support into outsized power in the political executive. One of the party's leading figures, Jusuf Kalla, captured the vice presidency on the ticket of retired general Susilo Bambang Yudhoyono (SBY) and then captured the leadership of Golkar in turn. From 2004 to 2009, just like from 1999 to 2004, *Golkar held more cabinet seats than any other party*, including the Democrat Party (PD), the party of the newly and directly elected president, SBY. In addition, Golkar consistently captured the largest number of executive positions at the subnational level in Indonesia's newly decentralized polity in this period – and predictably so, given that President Habibie's original embrace of democratic reforms was largely prompted by his recognition that Golkar enjoyed a massive infrastructural grassroots advantage across Indonesia's sprawling archipelago. Hence *for a full decade after Indonesia's democratic transition, its authoritarian successor party remained its most powerful political party*. Recognizing that party politics was in safely non-radical hands, Indonesia's military gave up its appointed seats in parliament by 2004 with nary a whimper.

Golkar's continuing leadership did not rest on any exceptional mass popularity, but in its unrivaled elite networks and alliances. The party may be relatively good at elections, but it is extremely good at postelectoral bargaining. By taking the lead in crafting a system of "party cartelization" and "promiscuous powersharing" (Slater 2004, 2014b), Golkar assured itself unbroken representation in the presidential cabinet. It also ensured that politics would not take on a polarized *ancien régime*-versus-opposition cast. Much like in Korea, democratization through strength in Indonesia divided the multiple opposition parties – some nationalist, some Islamist – that had emerged from their shared struggle to topple Suharto's authoritarian New Order. Whereas dictatorship had temporarily unified Golkar's opponents during Suharto's final days, democracy lastingly divided them. It would also bring them into Golkar-guided powersharing schemes.

To be sure, Golkar's fortunes declined further in the 2009 and 2014 elections and in the coalitional negotiations that followed them. The party's national parliamentary vote share shrunk to 14.5 percent in 2009 and held steady at 14.7 percent in 2014. Golkar has thus lost approximately a third of its national vote share since the inaugural democratic elections in 1999. Golkar also temporarily lost its hold on the vice presidency in 2009, as party leader Jusuf Kalla challenged SBY and was crushed by the popular incumbent. However, as in 2004, Golkar's decision to oppose SBY in the 2009 presidential election did not mean outright exclusion from executive office, as the party still secured three cabinet seats. Still, this was only half as many as SBY's own party, the PD, controlled. Considering that the PD easily outpaced Golkar in the 2009 parliamentary race, 20.9 percent to 14.5 percent in votes and 26.4 percent to 18.9 percent in seats, it seemed that Golkar had finally been demoted to Indonesia's second-most powerful party by 2009. Yet the PD's electoral implosion amid multiple corruption scandals in the 2014 elections meant that Golkar could once again plausibly claim to be Indonesia's most powerful party. And under the weak presidency of PDIP member Joko Widodo (2014–), the most powerful man in the country is arguably Jusuf Kalla, the former Golkar leader who returned to the vice presidency as Widodo's running mate.

The bottom line is that, thanks in large part to its prowess at powersharing in a multiparty system, *Golkar never had to go into opposition* during the 1999–2014 period. This was despite generating weaker electoral returns than either the KMT in Taiwan or the DJP in Korea. Golkar may have conceded *democracy*, as well as its unchallenged *dominance* of Indonesia's party system. But it has still never been forced to concede outright *defeat*. It continued to thrive, moving from authoritarian strength to democratic strength.

Electoral success and stability have been accompanied by renewed economic success and stability. It is hard to overstate the devastation that the Indonesian economy suffered in the Asian Financial Crisis of 1998–1999. It is also critical to recall that the very depths of the crisis in Indonesia were a direct product of authoritarian politics and a major impetus for democratic reform. Suharto had grown increasingly unpredictable and had made no viable plans for his own presidential succession. Economic downturn thus translated into political panic. The return of democracy brought renewed predictability to the rhythms of regime politics and economic policy. As in Korea, ongoing protests did not threaten to topple the post-Suharto leadership in violent fashion, but they did raise the specter of continued instability if authoritarianism was not definitively replaced with democracy. For all the instability and uncertainty that accompanied Suharto's removal from office, free and fair national elections promised to help restore stability rather than further undermine it. This was especially true because no radical leftist parties were credible contestants for elected office – itself a lasting legacy of how Suharto's New Order regime had managed and, at times, massacred its leftist rivals. By the early 2000s, Indonesia had returned to its familiar trajectory of strong growth driven by foreign direct investment, natural resource exploitation, and light manufacturing exports.

Yet the political and economic continuities from the Suharto era were far from total. In both the political and economic realm, *moderation* was the order of the day – indeed, of the entire decade following democratic transition. Starting with the decisive democratic reforms introduced by President Habibie in 1998–1999, Golkar remained officially committed to the process of regime transition. Golkar's central role in devising a battery of constitutional reforms between 1999 and 2002 showed that the party had no intention of either being left behind in the democratic era or moving backward to the authoritarian era (Crouch 2010). In fact, Golkar played a leading role in certain reforms, such as the introduction of direct executive elections in 2004, where its recalcitrance would have raised fears about a lack of commitment to continued democratization. Party leaders also backed off on their initial support for a first-past-the-post (FPTP) electoral system, acknowledging that the rule change would disproportionately benefit Golkar and hence betray the party's newfound commitment to a level playing field (Horowitz 2013). Similarly, the party did not stand in the way of the creation of a surprisingly powerful anti-corruption commission (the KPK), despite the fact that Golkar politicos have always been among its major targets. As with the democratization experiences in Taiwan and Korea, the authoritarian successor party in Indonesia has shown ongoing democratic restraint beyond its initial reform concessions during the late 1990s.

On the economic side, Golkar has remained the most identifiably pro-business major party in Indonesia. But its programmatic differences with other leading parties are minimal, given how decades-long rule by a developmental state have produced a developmental electorate. Along with the parties with which it consistently shares power, Golkar has supported improvements in the minimum wage, as well as expanded national healthcare provision (Aspinall 2014; Ford and Caraway 2014). Hence in Indonesia as in Taiwan and Korea, the breakneck developmentalism of authoritarian times has moderated into more generous distributive-developmentalism in democratic times.

It is thus hard to avoid the conclusion that Golkar served more as a *stabilizer* than a *spoiler* during Indonesia's crucial first decade of democracy. Yet the continuing leadership role of formerly authoritarian elites has had higher costs for democracy in Indonesia than in Korea or Taiwan. Again, this is a predictable consequence of the weaker position from which Golkar conceded democracy. The paradox is that this relative weakness pressed Golkar to find an alternative strategy for thriving under democracy. Unable to contemplate capturing electoral majorities, Golkar has kept its stronghold in national politics through crafting postelectoral coalitions. Unlike the KMT and DJP, Golkar did not exactly need to "learn to lose." Electoral setbacks came quickly on the heels of President Habibie's big-bang democratic concessions, and Golkar was forced to countenance its loss of both the presidency and the top position in parliament within barely a year of Suharto's resignation. Indeed, the rapidity of Golkar's initial electoral setbacks was precisely a result of its relative weakness vis-à-vis the KMT and DJP in terms of antecedent resources, which prevented Golkar from managing democratic transition entirely on its own terms. Political moderation was thus closer to an instant imperative than a slow-moving lesson learned as we see with the KMT and DLP. What Golkar has learned since democratization is not so much how to lose outright, as how to win leading positions of power even as voters are increasingly rejecting it at the ballot box. It has been Golkar's mastery of backdoor negotiating, and not any growing skill at public electioneering, that best explains its successful acclimation to the rough-and-tumble of democratic competition. Golkar has long been at the epicenter of an elitist brand of "collusive democracy" that has compromised democratic quality in a manner that has no parallel in either Taiwan or Korea. In both 2004 and 2009, voter turnout declined precipitously from its 1999 peak. Vote shares for all five leading parties – Golkar and the four major parties that had been sharing power with it – declined steadily as well. To some degree, this signaled dealignment from the Golkar-centered post-1999 party system (Slater 2014b). Yet it also exemplified the staying power of holdover elites with roots in the Suharto era. When Golkar's performance slipped, President SBY's PD picked up much of the slack, winning the parliamentary elections outright in 2009. The specter of an ex-Suharto ally prevailing through a new party vehicle inspired imitations. Two additional retired generals and a wealthy

ASPs in Developmental Asia

businessman, all of whom had been top contenders for the Golkar chairmanship in 2004, formed three additional parties who gained back the vote share Golkar had been losing. Whereas Golkar alone had won 22.4 percent of the national vote in 1999, by 2014 the vote share for all five parties led by Golkar-based and military-rooted elites (including Suharto's former son-in-law, Prabowo Subianto) had more than doubled, to 48.7 percent of all votes in national parliamentary elections.[21]

In sum, Golkar has lost its dominance since conceding democracy over fifteen years ago. But Indonesia's party system remains dominated by parties with deep roots in the New Order era and more proximate roots to the post-democratization version of Golkar itself. The military has given up its seats in the national parliament, but remains politically untouchable in most other respects. To the degree that new social forces have found entry into national politics, it has not shifted Indonesian politics in any radical new directions, either politically or economically. It is these relative weaknesses in democratic quality, we argue, that best explain why Indonesian democracy showed growing signs of stagnation by the 2010s (Mietzner 2012). But consider the counterfactual: if Golkar had not embraced democratic reforms and participated in Indonesia's more general shift toward distributive yet frugal welfare policies, the risk of ongoing instability and polarization would have been far higher. Golkar proved strong enough to moderate itself and to moderate Indonesian politics in turn. The upshot has been a democracy of less strength and robustness than in Taiwan or Korea, but of greater stability and predictability than democracies arising from purer military regimes in Thailand and (if democracy indeed continues to take root) in Myanmar. Remarkably, Indonesia has become, and currently remains, the strongest democracy in a region where democracy has just experienced a very difficult decade.

9.3 CONCLUSION

Democratic processes transcend democratic elections. The decade following newly competitive elections is as fateful for democracy's prospects as the decade preceding them. This is because stable democracy, like initial democratic concessions themselves, requires ongoing compromise. Having opened the floodgates of democratic competition, authoritarian successor parties in Taiwan, South Korea, and Indonesia confronted continuing popular and partisan pressure to deepen democratic reform and realize democracy's "level playing field" (Levitsky and Way 2010). As controversies inevitably

---

[21] In this respect, Indonesia's "authoritarian diaspora" goes beyond its authoritarian successor party, as in Brazil (Power 2000; Chapter 7, this volume) and some Sub-Saharan African countries (LeBas, Chapter 6, this volume). Among this "diaspora," only Prabowo has posed a serious specter of authoritarian populism threatening Indonesia's democratic survival. For more on "authoritarian diasporas," see Conclusion (Loxton, this volume).

erupted over constitutional reforms, electoral rules, and questions of transitional justice, these parties were forced to walk a fine line. On the one hand, repelling all pressure for further political reforms risked squandering the legitimacy payoff that they had gained from conceding democratic elections in the first place; they had to compromise in order to thrive in democracy. On the other hand, they needed to keep building upon their antecedent strengths if they wished to remain the most pivotal actors in defining the new democracy's trajectory. Elite choices to make difficult political compromises during pivotal movements proved critical in maintaining holdover parties' antecedent advantages.

The democratization of conservative authoritarian regimes generally means rising expectations and demands that economic inclusion should accompany political inclusion. In democracy, ruling parties need to *win support without suppressing dissent*, an important modification of how parties stay in power. Thus, regarding questions of economic reform, as with ongoing controversies over political reform, authoritarian successor parties are similarly forced to walk a fine line. They cannot entirely abandon the developmental models that had made their countries much wealthier and on which they had long staked their claim to legitimacy. Yet they also could not ignore the swelling popular clamor to share the benefits of development more widely. The upshot across the three cases discussed in this chapter was the imperative of economic moderation to complement political moderation. The developmental states from authoritarian times transformed into developmental-distributive states in democratic times (Wong 2004).

If authoritarian successor parties are to stabilize politics during the uncertain days of democratic transition, moderation is critical. Forging a moderate political and economic reform agenda reveals and indeed affirms the parties' commitments to democracy. Moderation also broadens their appeal and contributes to their electoral success. In this respect, while authoritarian *ruling* parties may choose to democratize from a position of strength with the expectation that they will thrive to some degree in democracy, authoritarian *successor* parties are more likely to stay in the democratic game when success is no longer an expectation or mere possibility, but a realized fact. In all of our cases, the former authoritarian ruling party, despite various electoral setbacks after the democratic transition, stabilized democracy by choosing a moderate path for reform, and because they enjoyed electoral success under democracy. *Just as democracy through strength is incentive-compatible for authoritarian ruling parties, democratic moderation is incentive-compatible for authoritarian successor parties.*

This suggests that democratic stability and democratic substance can coexist in a relationship of harmony rather than tension. The claim that new democracies must effectively "sell their soul" to authoritarian holdovers if they are to avoid authoritarian reversals is common both in the theoretical literature and in the best case-study literature on Indonesia, in particular.

From this perspective, the only way to have a stable democracy is by ensuring that outgoing authoritarian elites are treated gently, even if that means forgoing economic distribution, eschewing transitional justice, and tolerating an ongoing absence of civilian control over the military. Although we agree that outgoing authoritarians often accept democratization because they maintain a leading role in shaping it, this does not mean that the new democracies lack substance. Nor does it mean that whatever stability they enjoy is better explained by democracy's shortcomings than by its strengths. Democracy in Taiwan, Korea, and Indonesia is only as stable as it is because authoritarian successor parties moderated as much as they did.

By helping to stabilize democracy in the short run, authoritarian successor parties help "normalize" democracy in the longer run. The three democracies we have been analyzing here have matured to the point that they exhibit syndromes that afflict democracies throughout the world, rather than syndromes specific to democracies with authoritarian successor parties. Taiwan's KMT was defeated in the 2016 presidential and Legislative Yuan elections, as voters punished Ma's government for its mismanagement of Cross-Strait relations and Taiwan's recent economic slowdown. The KMT now faces the challenge of rebuilding its electoral base. Korea's Saenuri (formerly the DJP/DLP/GNP) has possibly slipped into a cycle of dynastic politics: its successful candidate for president in 2012 was Park Geun-hye, the daughter of former dictator Park Chung-hee, and she campaigned by harkening back to a golden age of rapid economic growth.[22] Indonesian democracy battles new forms of corruption and religious extremism that are being fed by electoral politics more than by any Golkar-centered legacies, while Golkar itself struggles to navigate an unprecedented factional split. But these challenges do not portend the death of democracy in these three countries; rather, they are a part of the normal rhythms of otherwise healthy and competitive democracies. In other words, Taiwan, Korea, and Indonesia look quite typical for democracies at their respective levels of economic development. By helping to stabilize democracy through the first three or four elections after democratization, authoritarian successor parties have helped their countries become full, if still flawed, members of the global democratic community.

---

[22] Park Geun-hye was president of Korea from 2013 until 2017, when she was impeached.

10

Reluctant Democrats

Old Regime Conservative Parties in Democracy's First Wave in Europe

Daniel Ziblatt

Europe's first wave of democracy (1830–1933), like all subsequent democratic expansions, represented the collision of democratic forces and nondemocratic incumbents.[1] In this first wave, the nondemocratic incumbents were what historian Arno Mayer (1981) has called Europe's "old regime" – a nexus of landed elites, bureaucratic and military officials, and defenders of monarchy and establishment church institutions. They certainly took on distinctive constellations in different national contexts. Yet, what can one say generally about how these collective political actors survive and shape democratization?

To date, our theories of democratization – especially in its historical emergence in Western Europe – have been silent on this question, typically focusing on democracy's protagonists. These accounts usually emphasize some combination of the bourgeoisie, liberal political parties, social democrats, and organized labor. Europe's old regime elites, if mentioned at all, are cast primarily in a blocking role, accommodating to democracy only if sufficiently challenged. This chapter's core claim is that Europe's democratization is less usefully thought of as a singular overturning of an existing social order and more as a process in which Europe's *old regime conservative parties* – that era's analogue of authoritarian successor parties – actively shaped the process of democratization.[2] Since the often wealthy and always politically powerful elites of nondemocratic regimes tend to resist moves toward democratization, and also have the power to disrupt democracy once in place, understanding how they organize politically is critical for understanding whether transitions to democracy occur and also whether new democratic regimes consolidate. No matter the level of socioeconomic development of a society or the formal constitutional structure of the state, the ability of old regime elites to forge a well-endowed, tightly coupled old regime

---

[1] On the first wave of democracy, see Huntington (1991).
[2] This is the thesis of my book *Conservative Parties and the Birth of Democracy*. See Ziblatt (2017). Many of the insights in this chapter draw on the book.

Old Regime Conservative Parties in Europe

conservative party – a party that represents their interests in the new regime – turns out to be an essential factor in the historical emergence of democracy in Europe.[3] When upper-class groups associated with any pre-democratic or nondemocratic *ancien régime* are able to overcome the enormous collective action problems of forging political parties, democracy emerges in a more settled fashion; when they cannot, democracy emerges, if at all, in a deeply unsettled way.

By successfully recasting themselves in the face of deep political change and effectively representing the interests of the opponents of democracy, old regime conservative parties in the first wave in some instances had positive effects on democratization via two mechanisms. First, if old regime elites had access to strong party organizations, this lowered the "costs of toleration" by helping to protect their core interests and identity, thereby making democratic competition less threatening.[4] Second, strong party organizations provided party leaders with "distancing capacity." This allowed them to sideline their own hard-line right-wing allies, who, if they gained access to leadership positions, were more likely to mobilize against democratic transitions and who in weak parties derailed processes of democratic consolidation.[5]

Certainly, many factors shaped the historical process of democratization in Europe. This chapter's aim is not to supplant existing accounts but rather to *supplement* them by filling, in a way that is consistent with other chapters in this volume (see, in particular, Chapter 9 by Slater and Wong), what has been a black hole in the literature: the particular impact of old regime conservative parties, the first wave's equivalent of authoritarian successor parties, on the process of democratization. The chapter's aim is to highlight the contributions of old regime conservative parties to democratization, not to assert that other factors did not matter. The chapter begins by outlining some of the conceptual issues involved with my argument, particularly the parallels between old regime conservative parties and authoritarian successor parties. Second, the chapter presents two motivating case studies – Britain and Germany between 1884 and 1933 – and analyzes how they illustrate the argument. The chapter concludes by analyzing how the argument works across a broader sample of European countries in democracy's first wave and reflects on implications of argument for this volume's broader agenda.

10.1 OLD REGIME CONSERVATIVE PARTIES: THE FIRST WAVE'S AUTHORITARIAN SUCCESSOR PARTIES

The historical rise of democracy in Europe in the so-called "first wave" from 1832 to 1933 was distinctive, though perhaps not unique, insofar as at least

---

[3] For a similar argument in the context of Latin America, see Di Tella (1971–1972) and Gibson (1996).
[4] The concept of "costs of toleration" draws on Dahl (1971).
[5] The concept of "distancing capacity" draws on Bermeo (2003).

three major societal cleavages came to a head nearly simultaneously with the inauguration of major democratic reforms: church–state conflicts over the role of religion in public life;[6] urban–rural conflict between free-trading cities and protectionist agriculture;[7] and the class dispute over income distribution.[8] The historical conjuncture of these three macro-processes with democratization meant that the church–state divide, the urban–rural divide, and the class divide left particularly strong imprints on the different national European trajectories of democratization.[9]

Less fully appreciated is that one type of political party in this emerging party landscape, members of what Klaus von Beyme (1984) has identified as the Conservative party *familles spirituelles*, were quite explicitly defenders of the old regime and pre-democratic forms of politics in Europe. As the chief partisan defenders of nondemocratic regimes, they loosely resembled some present-day authoritarian ruling parties, particularly those operating in electoral authoritarian regimes. Those parties that continued to exist after democratization can therefore be considered the predecessors of modern-day authoritarian successor parties. Their "family resemblance" is visible on three critical dimensions. First, despite their diversity in 1848 prior to democratization, the "partisan carriers" of old regime interests, like authoritarian successor parties today, represented societal groups at the peak of power, prestige, and wealth. Typically, they represented upper-class elites (usually but not always landed elites), who formed the bulwark of these nondemocratic regimes precisely because of their wealth and allegiance to traditional social and political institutions, such as monarchies and establishment religious institutions.[10] Second, these parties not only relied on but also benefited from their overlapping interests and identification with established nondemocratic institutions, ranging from monarchical and military to religious and bureaucratic institutions. Like the allies of any nondemocratic incumbent, election manipulation, patronage, and other informal strategies of staying in power disproportionately benefited old regime conservative parties.[11] Finally, when they survived democratization, these parties had the potential to have similar consequences as contemporary authoritarian successor parties.

Despite these similarities, old regime conservative parties from the first wave differed from modern authoritarian successor parties in two critical ways. First, in no instance did they have a monopoly on political power like authoritarian ruling parties in modern-day single-party regimes.[12]

---

[6] See Gould (1999) and Kalyvas (1996). [7] See Gourevitch (1986).
[8] See Acemoglu and Robinson (2006). [9] See Lipset and Rokkan (1967).
[10] In some exceptional contexts (e.g., Denmark and the Netherlands), the core constituency of conservatism also included an urban upper-class elite. See Ziblatt (2017: 36) and Boer (2008).
[11] For a case study, see Ziblatt (2008).
[12] For an important account of modern single-party regimes and their consequences on democratization, see Smith (2005).

Instead, these were parties that existed alongside other parties, but represented the interests of the highest-level occupants of the pre-democratic regime.[13] Second, old regime conservative parties typically did not rely on revolutionary foundations, mass mobilization, and ideological intensity to generate loyalty. In fact, in most cases, they began, if anything, as counterrevolutionary elite parties that, like modern-day patrimonial parties, survived by delivering targeted benefits to their allies.[14] Table 10.1 provides a summary of the names and dates of founding (and, sometimes, refounding) of major old regime conservative parties in the largest countries of Western Europe.

Democratization was a challenge to the societal groups that these parties represented – holders of wealth, and particularly holders of landed wealth – for

TABLE 10.1 *Old regime conservative parties in Europe before 1914*

Country	Party	Founded
Great Britain	British Conservative Party	1834
Demark	Højre	1848/1881
Germany	Deutsche Konservative Partei	1848/1876
Portugal	Partido Regenerador	1851
Belgium	Union Constitutionnelle et Conservatrice	1852
Belgium	Parti Catholique Belge	1878
Spain	Partido Conservador	1876
Netherlands	Anti-Revolutionaire Partij	1879
France	Action Libérale	1901
France	Alliance Démocratique	1901
France	Fédération Républicaine	1903
Sweden	Allmänna Valmansförbundet	1904
Italy[15]	NA	NA

---

[13] It is worth noting that in some of these regimes, the parties in question attained nearly hegemonic status. In Portugal, for example, the Partido Regenerador won 85 percent of the vote at points in the nineteenth century. In Britain, the Conservative Party ruled for nearly twenty uninterrupted years until 1906, a period that British historians call the age of "Conservative hegemony."

[14] For a discussion of these distinctions, see Levitsky and Way (2012). On the role of counter-revolution in creating and sustaining some contemporary authoritarian regimes, see Slater and Smith (2016).

[15] Italy did not possess a self-identified conservative political party, despite significant efforts after 1897 by future prime minister Sidney Sonnino and others. See Sarti (1990).

both socioeconomic and political reasons.[16] First, suffrage expansion brought with it a very real "threat" of expropriation for Europe's elites, particularly its landed elites.[17] As the future Lord Salisbury, one influential landed elite who genuinely feared that his class would be expropriated, put it,

> The struggle between the English constitution on the one hand and the democratic forces that are labouring to subvert it on the other, is in reality, when reduced to its simplest terms and stated in its most prosaic form, a struggle between those who have, to keep what they have got, and those who have not, to get it. (*Quarterly Review*, April 1860)

An expansion of the right to vote and an increase in the power of parliaments meant that the concentrated wealth of landed elites would come under assault.[18] But the emerging outlines of electoral contestation threatened more than just the socioeconomic order. It also threatened the political order, which rested on a particular moral economy in which political elites, whether local officials, elite bureaucrats, high-level clergy, military officials, or conservative parliamentary politicians themselves, did not depend on "agitators" and "political organization" (the hallmarks of democracy from their view) to gain power. Instead, they relied on a familiar, informal, and localized world in which their status and power as "natural authorities," in the words of Prussian Junker Helmut von Gerlach (1925), predominated.

Thus, the new age of political egalitarianism and mass politics was a challenge with two faces: a well-documented socioeconomic challenge to economic elites (especially the interests of landed elites, as holders of concentrated and immobile assets) and a less fully appreciated political challenge to an older form of politics in which extended and deep networks of informal authority trumped political organization. In both instances, the old order was under assault and faced the threat of eclipse. Facing mass democratization, old regime conservative parties could be used to diminish the threat of democratization to upper-class elites. However, a prerequisite of this was that in Europe's political development, these parties needed to consolidate into a single, viable, *organized* conservative party before mass democratization came. The sources of conservative party-building in Europe, which were rooted in different national patterns, are a subject I explore elsewhere.[19] However, a great divergence in Europe's first wave of democratization existed between those countries where strong old regime

---

[16] See Przeworski (1991).

[17] See, for example, Acemoglu and Robinson (2006). For an alternative view, see Ansell and Samuels (2014).

[18] With democratization, the very terms of landlord–tenant relations came under public assault, as reformers from Ireland to eastern Prussia vilified landed elites. The reformers, armed with new agricultural census data in the 1880s that exposed the extent of landholding concentrations and inspired by a new critique of the "unearned increment," demanded altering the basic structure of agrarian life. This included calls for fair rents, fixed tenures, and free sale of land.

[19] See Ziblatt (2017).

Old Regime Conservative Parties in Europe

conservative parties emerged early, helping democratization emerge in a settled way, and those countries where conservatives remained fractured, resulting in long-run unsettled pattern of democratization.

10.2 TWO ILLUSTRATIVE CASES: REVISITING GERMAN AND BRITISH PATHS OF DEMOCRATIZATION

How exactly did Europe's old regime conservative parties shape democratization? Although Europe's conservative parties have often correctly been regarded as opponents of democracy, their impact in some instances helped secure democracy, much like modern-day authoritarian successor parties.[20] A way of understanding the importance of the first wave's equivalent of authoritarian successor parties – old regime conservative parties – on democratization is to return to a well-studied and familiar couplet, but through a distinctive analytical lens: Germany and Britain between 1884 and 1933.

These two countries from the late nineteenth century into the twentieth century have often been held up as cases of "successful" and "failed" democratization.[21] Yet, as recent work by political and economic historians has made clear, the two shared some striking similarities on key dimensions that would seem to have made them *both* promising cases for democratization. Only Britain, however, began to democratize before 1914 and remained democratic through the interwar years, while Germany's path was much more unhinged.

10.2.1 Similar Societies, Divergent Polities

What are the similarities that make these two cases such a useful comparison? First, for scholars who emphasize socioeconomic modernization as a driver of democratization, by 1890, Germany and Britain (unlike the southern or eastern edges of Europe) were both at the forefront of the industrial revolution in terms of total GDP, GDP per capita, size of the manufacturing sector, and industrial output.[22] Germany, like Britain, was now a "capital abundant" economy, in which democratizing coalitions between middle-class liberal parties and labor or socialist parties ought to have been dominant.[23] Indeed, societal movements pushing for democratic reform were strong in Germany. Similarly, while analysts ranging from Barrington Moore (1966) to Ben Ansell and David Samuels (2014) have emphasized the importance of a rising middle class, revisionist accounts have made clear that the German middle class was much

---

[20] On the role of authoritarian successor parties in stabilizing some contemporary democracies, see Slater and Wong (Chapter 9, this volume).
[21] They are presented as paradigmatic illustrations in classic works in the field, including Luebbert (1991) and Rueschemeyer, Stephens, and Stephens (1992).
[22] See data in Mitchell (2003). [23] See Rogowski (1989). See also Garst (1998).

stronger, both economically and politically, than traditional accounts have assumed.[24] Yet, democratic reform was not forthcoming. In short, the structure of the political regime was not simply a mirror of the economy.

Others have highlighted the importance not of the "bourgeoisie" but of the working class as democracy's "torchbearers."[25] Again, the German case, when compared to Britain, appears anomalous: in the first decades of the 1900s, the Social Democratic Party of Germany (SPD) was the most successful and powerful such party in the world, as was its labor movement. Germany's SPD, itself a consistent advocate of democratic reforms, received a greater share of votes in Germany's national parliament than any other political party in Germany and than any other social democratic party in Europe. Furthermore, its dense underlying social networks and organizations made it a formidable force for democracy.[26] In the important first decade of the twentieth century, Germany, on an annual basis, typically experienced a greater number of strikes per capita than any other country in Europe.[27] Some might suspect that the very intensity of labor unrest only frightened Germany's conservatives to block democratization. This argument, however, runs counter to the expectations of Rueschemeyer, Stephens, and Stephens (1992). Moreover, it is worth noting that in the only other country that experienced similar levels of strike activity in the same period – Sweden between 1907 and 1909 – elites, and in particular Arvid Lindman's Conservative Party, responded not by blocking but rather by adopting and implementing universal male suffrage.[28] In Britain, the labor movement had historically been tamer, yet its mobilization in pre-1914 led to significant democratic reforms. In Germany, by contrast, economic modernization and intense demands for democratization went unanswered.

Similarly, in the post-1918 years, when democracy swept across all of Western Europe, in Germany, unlike Britain, this came bolstered by a remarkable cross-class Liberal-Social Democratic-Catholic party alliance (Catholic Center Party, Social Democrats, and Left Liberals). This was the so-called "Weimar" coalition that came into power in the first postwar elections and remained dominant into the early 1920s. For those who think that the first democratic election sets the terms, in path-dependent fashion, of a post-transition polity, the fact that a thoroughly democratic governing coalition set the terms of the Weimar regime ought to have set it on a democratic course.

What went wrong? Why, in comparison to Britain, was democratic change so hard to build in Germany before 1914, and why was it so fragile after 1918? Some argue that Germany's stalled democratization before 1914 and its fragility after 1918 was rooted in the economic power of the premodern

---

[24] See Blackbourn and Eley (1984).
[25] See Eley (2002) and Rueschemeyer, Stephens, and Stephens (1992).   [26] See Eley (2002).
[27] See strike data in Mitchell (2003).   [28] See Lewin (1988).

landed elites.[29] Such a perspective is useful in directing our attention not only to those "demanding" democracy but also to occupants and societal allies of the old regime who might either concede or block democratic change. However, the idea that concentrated landed wealth was itself the chief barrier to democracy is challenged by the fact that the average size of agricultural holdings, agricultural census data show, was far greater in Britain than in Germany in the nineteenth century; and tenant farming, rather than owner-occupied farms, was more common in Britain than in Germany.[30] Further, historian David Cannadine (1999) makes clear that the social and political power of landed elites in Britain endured into the twentieth century. This, then, is the puzzle: the chief *political party* representing landed elites in Britain, the British Conservative Party, made its peace with democracy, while its equivalent in Germany, the German Conservative Party (DKP), despite operating in a very similar economy, remained resistant to democracy and could not contain a backlash of the far right after 1918.[31]

10.2.2 Before 1918: Democratic Transition in Britain and Germany

Before 1918, European democratization was incremental, gradual, and partial. In neither Germany nor Britain was there a full democratic transition before 1918 as a result of enduring but different institutional limits in both cases.[32] But democratic reform, even if partial, did occur in both cases, and it is here that we begin to see the independent impact of political party organization of old regime interests – *old regime conservative parties* – in shaping democratization. Before 1914, for example, Britain's Conservative Party, for a variety of reasons explored elsewhere, developed the two key attributes of a hierarchical mass party: (1) professional leadership in control of the party and (2) a national network of local associations. This was in contrast to the German Conservative Party (Deutsche Konservative Partei, DKP), which differed along both dimensions.[33] The sources of this long-run development are explored elsewhere,[34] but their consequences were substantial and can be elaborated here.

---

[29] See Gerschenkron (1948); Rueschemeyer, Stephens, and Stephens (1992); and Ziblatt (2008).
[30] See Ziblatt (2017).
[31] To clarify, *both* the British Conservative Party *and* its chief rival, the Whig Party, represented socioeconomic elites and landed wealth in Britain's pre-democratic oligarchic political system. However, the Conservative Party counts as that political system's "old regime conservative party" for two reasons. First, the most systematic estimates indicate that from the 1830s until at least the 1880s, the Conservative Party (even when combined with its Unionist allies after the 1880s) was more closely associated with landed wealth (rather than industrial and commercial wealth) than the Whig Party (and its Liberal successor), as indicated by the professional and demographic background of MPs. Second, unlike the Whig Party, which was the party of "reform," the Conservative Party defined itself as a defender of the pre-democratic "old regime." See Ziblatt (2017).
[32] See discussion in Ziblatt (2006).   [33] See Panebianco (1988) and Ziblatt (2017).
[34] See Ziblatt (2017).

This was already visible in the early years before a fuller democratic transition in 1918 in both Britain and Germany. First, we see this in Britain's tentative steps toward democracy in the Third Reform Act of 1884, which enfranchised a larger portion of the electorate than any other suffrage reform in the nineteenth century.[35] The British Conservative Party, despite initially opposing the Liberal Party's initiative to grant rural workers the right to vote, actually thrived in the wake of its passage, *governing for the next twenty years with only one brief interruption.* This was a classic illustration of what Slater and Wong (2013) call "conceding to thrive." After the passage of the Corn Laws in 1846, the Conservative Party, a party primarily of rural landowners, became divided over protectionism and remained far from power. However, between the 1860s and the 1880s, the Conservative Party, relying on its own increasingly elaborate network of party agents, as well as cross-class social clubs like the Primrose League, organized in the constituencies. It became the defender of the establishment Anglican Church, Empire, and Queen, and a critic of Irish Home Rule, thus broadening its appeal to suburban and middle-class voters.[36] From 1884 onwards, the party, now calling itself the Unionist Party, in alliance with Liberal Unionists, and in a creative move of cross-cutting electoral maneuvering, transformed itself into the party of property, church, and empire. Party organization was the precondition of this ability to maneuver into this cross-cutting electoral space. And, in this sense, the resulting age of British "conservative hegemony" was in no small part an outgrowth of the party's preexisting organizational prowess.[37]

By contrast, Germany's DKP became increasingly resistant to even much more modest suffrage reforms in Prussia, viewing them, in the words of one DKP leader, as "an attack against the basic laws of nature."[38] The DKP, though starting like the British Conservative Party as a narrow defender of rural interests, failed to develop the organizational infrastructure that would allow it to survive democratic reform. Unlike the British Conservative Party, which could appeal to a homogenously Anglican middle class in order to build a mass organization, the DKP was hemmed in by the confessional divides between Protestants and Catholics that fractured German middle-class society. Even facing an expanded suffrage, no party organization emerged. And without party organization in the last third of the nineteenth century, the aristocratic party of the 1850s had become a right-wing reactionary one by the turn of the century. In 1910 and 1912, for example, the DKP became even more right-wing than the King himself, blocking the King's proposals to make the highly inegalitarian voting system that was weighted by tax contributions less inequitable.[39] An analysis of Members of Parliament (MPs) voting on two

---

[35] See Hayes (1982).   [36] See Ziblatt (2017).   [37] See, for example, M. Roberts (2006).
[38] Quoted in Ziblatt (2017: 242).
[39] See Ziblatt (2008). For concrete evidence that "electoral incentives" shaped MP votes on these bills, see Ziblatt (2017).

critical votes in 1910 and 1912 makes plain that it was electoral self-interest and electoral weakness that made politicians vote *against* this democratic reform: the more an MP expected to lose with a change to the electoral system, the greater the probability that he would vote against it.[40] In the midst of World War I, the reactionary General Ludendorff put the increasingly feverish view of German conservatism on display. Weighing the costs of ending the war against the costs of abandoning the inegalitarian voting system that had been in place since 1848 (the so-called three-class voting system), he wrote, "With the equal franchise we cannot live ... I would rather an end with terror than a terror without end ... it would be worse than a lost war."[41] German Conservative Party leaders found themselves, because of their own enduring weakness, in the grips of a reactionary and radical right-wing spiral. This prevented even the modest democratic reforms that the British Conservative Party, also dominated at the top by landed elites in the twentieth century, easily embraced. In the case of Germany, without party organization to protect itself, the "costs of toleration" were simply too high for the German Conservative Party, while for the British Conservative Party, these had been substantially lowered.

10.2.3 After 1918: Democratic Consolidation in Britain and Germany

Even more direct evidence is visible after 1918, when full-blown regime change swept Western Europe. After 1918, the German Conservative Party regrouped as part of a broader "party of the right," the German National People's Party (DNVP). As parties that made the transition from nondemocratic to democratic rule, both the DNVP and the British Conservative Party were first-wave equivalents of authoritarian successor parties.[42] For new democracies in both countries, a common theme emerges: a robust pre-democratic legacy of party organization aided democratic consolidation in Britain, while a weak legacy of party organization had the opposite effect in Germany.

We can first focus on Britain. After the passage of universal male and limited female suffrage came in 1918, two of the main thresholds of democratization in this era – expansion of the franchise and parliamentary dominance – were now crossed, but one remained: Would groups that had previously been systematically excluded (e.g., the Labour Party) finally be allowed access to the executive?[43] This question, in the case of Britain after 1918, rested de facto in the hands of the British Conservative Party. Specifically, it pivoted on whether or not the party decided to continue its collusive wartime governing coalition with Lloyd George's wing of the Liberal Party, becoming a permanent governing coalition that would prevent Labour from gaining executive office

---

[40] See Ziblatt (2017).   [41] Quoted in Goemans (2000: 179).   [42] See Ohnezeit (2011).
[43] On the idea that there are three thresholds, see Rokkan (1999).

despite its growing electoral strength.[44] This was a decision that would shape the possibility of democratic consolidation in Britain. On the one hand, de facto exclusion of a growing working-class party through the anticompetitive collusion of two establishment parties was in itself inherently undemocratic and would have led to a political monopoly that diminished the quality of British democracy. On the other hand, such a move also would have radicalized the Labour Party, which some contemporaries feared would destabilize the new political order. For example, the future Conservative Party prime minister, Stanley Baldwin, was no less critical of the Labour Party than those in favor of continuing the coalition with Lloyd George's Liberals. However, he feared that permanently excluding Labour from power would backfire by pushing the party away from constitutional politics, thus leading to precisely the outcome that such a strategy was intended to avoid. As his close ally and future party chairman, J. C. C. Davidson, put it in correspondence in 1922, "To deprive Labour of their constitutional right – is the first step down the road to revolution."[45]

How did events unfold? In the run-up to the November 1922 general election, the Conservative Party backbench increasingly put pressure on their leaders to have the party run on its own, thus ending the party's eight-year-old alliance with the Liberal Party. Conservative Party leaders sought the coalition nonetheless.[46] But in a secret meeting of all sitting Conservative Party MPs on the morning of October 19, 1922, at London's Carlton Club, 185 MPs voted against their party leaders' plans to continue the wartime coalition with the Liberals, while a total of 85 MPs wanted the coalition with the Liberals to continue.[47]

This showdown was a turning point in interwar British politics. By breaking the coalition, the Conservative Party was allowing the possibility that Labour would gain executive office. And, indeed, the election ultimately resulted in a Labour government within two years for the first time in British history, led by Ramsey MacDonald. What determined whether Conservative MPs embraced this strategy? Ironically, it was a *legacy of Conservative Party organizational strength* that unintentionally contributed to the toleration of Labour and shaped the postwar structure of British politics. Sitting MPs from districts where the Conservative Party had historically been dominant before 1914 were most likely to support a break with the Liberal coalition; those from districts where the Conservative Party had a legacy of organizational weakness voted for a continuation of the collusive coalition. In short, despite its opposition to the Labour Party, the strength (and self-confidence) of this old regime conservative party actually *facilitated* democratization.

---

[44] On the politics of collusion and "promiscuous power-sharing" in the very different contexts of contemporary Bolivia and Indonesia, see Slater and Simmons (2013).
[45] Quoted in Davidson (1969: 189). [46] See Kinnear (1973).
[47] For a firsthand account of this event, see Davidson (1969: 100–133).

Evidence for this proposition comes from an unusual historical source. Though the vote at the Carlton Club was secret at the time, party chairman J. C. C. Davidson's memoirs provide a complete list of how all sitting MPs voted on the crucial day.[48] We can assess the proposition that the Conservative Party's robust prewar legacy of organizational prowess was associated with postwar support for Conservative Party independence by using F. S. W. Craig's (1976) historical election data. From this we can calculate the share of seats that the Conservative Party won in each sitting MP's district in the previous three elections prior to the war. Were supporters of independence (i.e., non-coalition) from historically dominant conservative districts?

I estimate a simple logit model in which each sitting Conservative Party MP's vote in the 1922 Carlton Club is the dependent variable, coded as either "yes" (for coalition) or "no" (against coalition). The main independent variable is average share of votes for the Conservative Party in the MP's district in the last three prewar general elections (1906, January 1910, and December 1910), which ranges from 0 to 1. One control variable is also included: the percentage of a constituency population that is Anglican (based on census data estimates), since as I show in other work, defense of the establishment Anglican Church was a key appeal for British conservatism.[49]

To illustrate the findings, Figure 10.1 graphs the predicted probability of voting for independence and the end of coalition based on the historical dominance of the Conservative Party in a district. We see that the greater the historical dominance, the greater the probability of an MP supporting Baldwin's vision of an independent Conservative Party – which in effect allowed for the rise of the first Labour government in British history in 1924.

To be clear, the rejection of collusion to block Labour accession was self-interested and not premised on a broad-minded concern about the lack of accountability that typically accompanies collusive methods of powersharing.[50] Instead, the rejection efforts were driven by a web of MPs from safe seats and party operatives, including Conservative Party agents and constituency association members, who resented accommodating Liberals in

---

[48] See Davidson (1969).
[49] See Ziblatt (2017). See also Wald (1983). Data on religious profile of districts in 1922 draw on Kinnear (1968). Data in Figure 10.1 draw on a bivariate logit equation with the following results:

internal_vote	Coef.	Std. Err.	z	P>|z|	[95% Conf. Interval]
conserv_dom	.6050742	.329414	1.84	0.066	-.0405654 1.250714
_cons	.4767675	.199274	2.39	0.017	.0861976 .8673375

[50] See Slater and Simmons (2013).

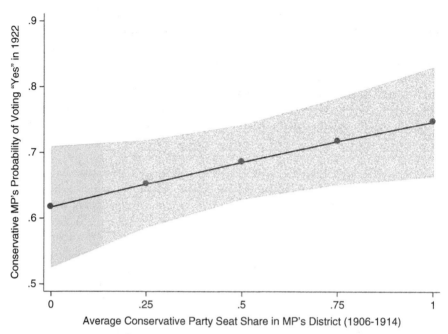

FIGURE 10.1 Legacy of conservative party strength and 1922 Carlton Club vote

their constituencies and confidently thought that the most effective response to the rise of Labour was an independent and united Conservative Party that might actually win elections.[51] Again, party strength unintentionally democratized British politics. Further bolstering this assertion is the fact that the day before the Carlton Club vote, a Conservative candidate won a high-profile and much discussed three-cornered (Labour, Liberal, Conservative) by-election at Newport. This reinforced the view of the Conservative Party Central Office's chief organizer, Leigh Maclachlan, who informed party leaders in October 1922 that "if the Conservatives stood against all comers, they would get a clear majority."[52]

While Labour gained office twice over the next ten years (1923 and 1929), in the resulting unstable three-party system of Labour, Liberals, and Conservatives, it was the Conservative Party along with a growing Labour Party that was organizationally prepared to thrive. Because the Conservatives abandoned coalition with the Liberal Party, and as the Labour Party became the chief new party on the scene, the Conservatives' position became increasingly dominant. But in the meantime, a monopolistic collusion of two parties with

[51] See McKibbin (2010: 40).   [52] Cited in Sanders (1984: 190).

roots in the pre-democratic regime had been broken and Britain was on a steady path of democratic consolidation.

A very different scenario unfolded in Germany after 1918. Here the new political regime came into being at the impetus of a major military defeat at the end of World War I. Domestically, however, the push for democracy was aided by the genuinely democratically minded supermajority coalition of Liberals, Catholics, and Social Democrats (with more than 60 percent of the vote in the founding election). Historians typically divide Weimar's history into three periods: the founding years of instability (1918–1924); the "golden age" of stability (1924–1928), in which the political regime seemed to take root; and the period of decomposition (1928–1933), which led to complete democratic breakdown. The three periods are revealing of the dynamics underpinning the regime. In the first years (1918–1924), as the regime was being built, the renamed and revamped successor organization for the various strands of German conservatism, the DNVP, struggled to do well electorally.[53] It was also during this period that a major coup attempt occurred, carried out by disgruntled officers with links to the DNVP.[54] Beginning in 1924, however, a group of traditional aristocratic and bureaucratic conservatives, described by historians as "Tory-Konservativen" (literally, "Tory Conservatives"), took the reins of this old regime conservative party, campaigned for office and became the single biggest non-socialist party in the German parliament.[55] Political leaders such as Kuno von Westarp conceived of their party as the major right-wing alternative to the Social Democratic Party seeking to form governments and to influence policy.[56] While certain key elements looked nostalgically on the monarchy and in principle rejected the legitimacy of the regime as a whole, party leaders de facto accepted it by participating in two governments in these years. And, with these potential "spoilers" now in government, the regime became more stable. Consistent with this chapter's argument, it was when the former opponents of the regime were electorally viable that the regime was most stable, with fewer government collapses and no coup attempts or major assassinations of government officials in this period.[57]

This apparent stability itself collapsed, however, when the DNVP faced its first major electoral defeat in 1928. The weakly rooted party had always been dependent on extremist outside pressure groups (e.g., the Pan-German League, the Agrarian League, and other groups) for electoral mobilization and fundraising. Now, facing electoral defeat, it was quickly swallowed up by these groups, and in particular by the founder of the radical right-wing Pan-German League, Alfred Hugenberg (also a major media mogul), leading to the near-disintegration of the party.[58] Without a strong constitutional party of the right,

[53] On this early period of the DNVP's history, see Hertzman (1958). [54] See Feldman (1971).
[55] See Mergel (2003). [56] See Mergel (2003).
[57] On this "golden age" period, see Mommsen (1996).
[58] See Jackisch (2012) and Jones (2009).

political instability ensued. Government coalitions could not survive, and the radical right in the form of the Nazi Party made inroads to former DNVP strongholds. Ultimately, with an opening on the right, the political regime disintegrated between 1930 and 1933, paving the way for Hitler's rise to power in January 1933.

In short, a strong old regime conservative party in Britain had helped ease a democratic transition before 1918 and helped the resulting political regime overcome its own barriers to democratic consolidation after 1918. In Germany, the converse dynamic was at work: the party most closely aligned with old regime interests had resisted even the most modest moves to democracy before 1914. Only when democracy was imposed from outside at the end of World War was a democratic transition possible. But even then, with an electorally and organizationally weak old regime conservative party as the pivot of the political system, democratic consolidation remained out of reach.

10.3 BROADENING THE VIEW: CROSS-NATIONAL PATTERNS IN DEMOCRACY'S FIRST WAVE

How generalizable are these contrasting trajectories? Did old regime conservative parties play such a dominant role in other cases during democracy's first wave? This section will first provide an overview of general cross-national patterns, which suggest confirming evidence and offer illustrative discussion of some additional cases. The focus here is on the revealing interwar years (1919–1939), the period that E. H. Carr (1946) called Europe's "twenty years' crisis," in which the diversity of political regimes is revealing of broader trends.

Scholars have long emphasized a variety of determinants of regime outcomes in the interwar years, including different war experiences, economic crises, political institutions, political cultures, ideas, and the role of effective political leadership.[59] Some have centered their analyses on the idea that enduringly powerful landed elites were the primary barriers to democracy, or the notion that if Liberals were not electorally "dominant" in a political system before 1914, the possibilities of democratic survival were dramatically narrowed.[60]

As useful as this scholarship is in framing the debate, a comparative perspective shows that anomalies remain.[61] For example, while landed elites in Germany and Italy were no great friends of post-1918 democracy, the locations in both countries where fascism found its greatest electoral support were typically not the areas of powerful landed elites and large landed estates,

---

[59] The relevant literature includes Berman (1998); Bernhard (2005); Capoccia (2005); and Møller, Schmotz, and Skaaning (2015).
[60] On the former idea, see Rueschemeyer, Stephens, and Stephens (1992). On the latter, see Luebbert (1991).
[61] See Ertman (1998), Kitschelt (1992), and Mahoney (2003).

but rather regions dominated by small family farms, such as northwestern Germany and north-central Italy.[62] Also, contra Gregory Luebbert's (1991) expectation that liberalism's pre-1914 success was a precondition of liberal democratic success in the interwar years, in neither Belgium nor the Netherlands was liberalism dominant before 1914, yet neither social democracy nor fascism triumphed in these countries in the interwar years.[63] Similarly, since proportional representation as an electoral system is sometimes blamed for having dangerously fractured political systems in these years, it is worth noting that while democracy collapsed in some countries with proportional representation (e.g., Italy and Germany), it also survived in others with this electoral system in place (e.g., Belgium and Sweden).[64] To untangle these anomalies, a focus on the role of old regime conservative parties and their varying organizational endowments provides a more comprehensive explanation. Old regime conservative parties with long pre-1914 political histories were a key factor in shaping interwar democratic experiences *beyond* Britain and Germany.

To illustrate, consider Table 10.2, which shows how an electorally consolidated or cohesive right end of the political spectrum was correlated with democratic survival in the interwar years. A legacy of conservative party organizational strength before 1914 translated into a *cohesive* electoral right after 1918. Table 10.2 provides a list of the major parties of the electoral right after 1918. It notes the name of the party of the electoral right (some self-identified as conservatives and others not) that had the greatest number of votes in the first post-1918 democratic elections, and whether or not the country experienced democratic breakdown during the interwar period.

In the group of countries at the top of list (Sweden, Britain, Denmark, the Netherlands, and Belgium), old regime conservative parties that predated 1918 survived (even if renamed) and predominated. In all of these cases, the result of a well-institutionalized pre-1918 conservative party was that one single party largely dominated the right end of the party spectrum afterwards. The sole exception was the Netherlands, where two closely allied Calvinist parties founded before 1918 dominated.[65] With a legacy of conservative party organization and electoral success in these countries, old regime conservative parties performed well electorally in the first democratic elections. And, despite the presence of proportional representation in nearly all of these countries, the right end of the party spectrum remained

---

[62] See Luebbert (1991: 308–309) and Mahoney (2003: 142).
[63] See Kitschelt (1992: 1029). See also Ertman (1998: 495–496), who observes that in Denmark and Norway, liberals were dominant before World War I, yet social democracy was the interwar outcome.
[64] This argument about the negative impact of proportional electoral systems on democratic stability was originally formulated by Hermens (1936).
[65] The older party was the Anti-Revolutionary Party (ARP). The second party, which emerged in the late nineteenth century, was the Christian Historical Union (CHU). On the ARP, see Boer (2008). On the history of the CHU in this period, see Hooven and Jong (2008: 145–180).

TABLE 10.2 *Fragmentation of the right in interwar Europe and democratic breakdown*

Country (1)	Largest right party at first post-1918 democratic election (2)	Index of fragmentation of all right parties (average of period) [i] (3)	Democratic breakdown? (4)
Sweden	Allmänna valmansförbundet	1.04	No
Great Britain	British Conservative Party	1.05	No
Denmark	Conservative Folkeparti	1.05	No
Belgium	Union Catholique Belge	1.47	No
Netherlands	Anti-Revolutionaire Partij	1.76	No
France	Fédération républicaine (Republican Union)	1.84	No[ii]
Portugal	Partido Republicano Evolucionista	1.86	1926
Spain	Partido Republicano Radical	2.13	1936
Italy	Partido Popolare Italiano [iii]	2.47	1922
Germany	Deutschnationale Volkspartei	2.81	1933

Notes:
(i) I code which political parties are "right" parties and then measure the average "fragmentation of the right." For this, I use a common measure of "effective number of parties" for right parties for each democratic election between 1918 and 1939 in a country calculated as $N = \frac{1}{\sum_{i=1}^{n} p_i^2}$, where n is the number of parties with at least one vote and p_i^2 the square of each party's portion of all votes. The measure is from Laakso and Taagepera (1979). Data on Spanish parties are from López Villaverde (1997: 231, 253, 270). Data on Italian parties are from Seton-Watson (1981: 588). All remaining data are from Nohlen and Stöver (2010).
(ii) France is coded as a case of democratic survival though its survival, in the words of one analyst, was "ambiguous" (Dobry 2000). For more discussion, see below.
(iii) Coding Italy's complex party system in 1919–1920 and identifying what "counts" as the right in this context is difficult, bolstering claims about the disarray of the Italian right in this period. Nonetheless, of the parties present in 1919, I report the score if the Partido Popolare Italiano (PPI) is coded as a center-right party, following Kalyvas (1996). If the PPI is not included, Italy's fragmentation score is higher.

cohesive. Here prewar conservative parties were also frequently in power during the interwar years, despite their elitist origins, and were viable parties shaping politics.[66] Finally, democracy survived the interwar years in these countries.

---

[66] In all five of these countries, the electoral right inherited a robust party organization from the pre–World War I era; electoral fragmentation of the right was lower; and the right was more

But what role did a cohesive right play exactly in the stabilization of democracy? To be sure, we must note that the character of the electoral right varied in significant ways across even "successful" cases. These ranged from explicitly confessional or proto-Christian Democratic parties of religious self-defense in Belgium and Netherlands, which had emerged out of a fusion of conservative and confessional groups, to more traditional parties of the secular conservative variety in Britain, Sweden, Denmark, and France. Yet in all of these otherwise diverse cases, the stabilizing effect of a cohesive right on democracy operated through two mechanisms. First, by blocking fissures at the right end of the political spectrum, strong parties of the center-right helped provide a bulwark against a more radical right. Consider the Christian Democratic right in Belgium, where, as the economy collapsed in the early 1930s, the anti-system radical right Rexist party emerged as a genuine threat to democracy. However, the Rex was effectively sidelined by the mass organization of the conservative Catholic Union Party (Union Catholique Belge) between 1934 and 1936, which carried out sophisticated strategies of exclusion and co-optation from a position of strength within the government.[67] The Catholic Union Party leadership resisted calls by some of its own to enter a coalition with the Rex in place of its coalition with the Belgian Socialist Party and took control of candidate lists that distanced the party from extremism.[68]

Sweden is another case of a democracy whose consolidation was aided by a strong old regime conservative party. In Sweden's case, though, it was the secular General Electoral League (Allmänna Valmansförbundet, AVF) that developed as a strong old regime conservative party after 1904 and helped Swedish democracy stabilize in the interwar years.[69] The positive impact of the strong Swedish right was already visible in 1907–1909 (expanded suffrage) when, under Arvid Lindman, the party defeated its own hard-liners and secured the passage of Sweden's most important prewar democratizing reform.[70] But the direct impact of party organization was most visible after 1918. Like in Belgium during the same period, Sweden faced an economic crisis, which triggered several extreme right movements in the 1920s and 1930s. However, critically for the stability of democracy, the top leadership of the conservative AVF had developed over the past twenty years the organizational capacity to distance itself from these allied movements. In 1933, the party's own "youth" association (Sveriges Nationella Ungdomförbund, SNU), with 40,000

---

typically part of governing cabinets during the Great Depression (Belgium, Netherlands, Britain) or had been in power (Sweden, Denmark) during the mid-1920s. The nonsocialist confessional right served in *every* cabinet between 1918 and the onset of World War II in the Netherlands and Belgium. In France, Sweden, Britain, and Denmark, the electoral right was in power at least once. For election data, see Nohlen and Stöver (2010).

[67] See Capoccia (2005: 116–125).   [68] See Capoccia (2005: 116–125).
[69] On the history of the Swedish right in its foundational years, see many sources, including Thermænius (1935).
[70] See Rustow (1955).

members, experienced an upsurge and embraced authoritarianism.[71] The SNU pushed for a strengthening of monarchy and was inspired by Hitler's rise to power, pushing for greater opposition to social democracy. Yet, unlike in Spain during the same period, as we see below, the strong organization of Sweden's AVF gave it the "distancing capacity" needed to make the costly decision to break its ties with the massive youth group in the critical year of 1933.[72] Ultimately, the SNU was simply expelled from the party. This demonstrated the importance of a hierarchical party's ability to distance itself from its own radical grassroots, effectively shutting down any political space for challenges on the radical right during the troubled 1930s.

In addition to sidelining the radical right, there was a second mechanism by which a cohesive electoral right could help democratic consolidation in the interwar years: electoral success. This helped turn essentially "semi-loyal" or ambivalent democrats into actors who complied with democratic institutions, with party organization in effect "lowering the costs of toleration."[73] This mechanism was also visible in the case of Swedish conservatives, who not only defeated hard-liners but also experienced an *ideological conversion* of its own party leaders in this period.[74] In Sweden, the right's orientation toward democracy is sometimes naively thought, in retrospect, to have been unproblematic. This is not correct. Recent scholarship makes plain that there was continued ambivalence about, if not outright opposition to, democracy as late as the early 1920s among elite circles of the Swedish right.[75] But access to viable party organization altered the ideological predispositions of party leaders.

In the critical month of December 1918, the stance of the AVF party leadership toward democracy remained divided between Arvid Lindman in the lower chamber and the more conservative Ernst Trygger in the upper chamber. Trygger viewed reform of the undemocratic upper chamber with intense skepticism.[76] But Lindman provided the impetus for reform, convincing his upper-chamber party colleagues to support reform with the argument that they ought not "despair" in the face of reform.[77] In the words of one historian, Lindman could point to the party's successful electoral record to make the case that "the right would do well within the new democratic system, and there was indeed no reason for despair" (Olsson 2000: 178). Likewise, conservative party newspapers argued that "there was much the right could do to win new voters" (Olsson 2000: 176). Party organization for the electoral right had become its own safeguard. And this assessment of the party's electoral fortunes proved correct: between 1920 and 1936, the AVF

---

[71] See Berggren (2002).   [72] See Olsson (2000: 43–54).
[73] On the concept of the "semi-loyal" opposition, see Linz (1978).
[74] This fact illustrates the more general argument in Mainwaring and Pérez-Liñán (2013).
[75] See Olsson (2000).   [76] For an analysis of internal fights, see Olsson (2000: 153).
[77] See Olsson (2000: 155).

always remained the second strongest party in the Swedish parliament, ahead of the agrarian Farmers' League and the Liberals, and only behind the Social Democratic Party. The result was that, while old regime conservatives had in the past consistently opposed democratic reform, by the 1930s, they thrived under democracy and were converted into fully loyal democratic actors.

If these two mechanisms helped secure democracy, the cases where party fragmentation was high – where the right was split across *multiple* political parties – demonstrate the opposite logic. In this set of cases (Italy, Portugal, Spain, and Germany), the absence of a strongly organized old regime conservative party meant that the new post-1918 electoral right did not have organizational resources upon which to draw. In these cases, the organized center-right was forming for the first time after 1918, while simultaneously facing the threat of socialist mobilization and mass democracy. This provoked a spiraling polarization among political elites and ultimately democratic breakdown in all four cases.

An illustration of this logic is plainly visible in Spain after 1931, with the abrupt end of the Spanish monarchy and the subsequent formation of the Second Spanish Republic – a hopeful but transitory moment of democratic opening. Unlike in Sweden and Britain, where a single old regime conservative party had been in place before the transition to full mass democracy, in Spain no significant party had made the shift to the new republic with its party organization intact. This meant that non-loyal (i.e., non-republican), more extreme and mobilized right-wing groups began to fill this space, dominating politics throughout the 1930s. Even the most noteworthy Tory-like group suffered from a "basic lack of organizational infrastructure" (Vincent 1996: 142). The Republican Right (Derecha Republicana), which was founded by two prominent elites, Niceto Alacalá-Zamora and Miguel Maura, was conceived as a conservative republican "defender of order and conservative classes."[78] However, it won only 27 out of 427 parliamentary seats in the inaugural elections of 1931 and fell from there, superseded by other forces.[79]

The group that emerged to fill this vacuum on the right came in the form of National Action (Acción Nacional), later renamed Popular Action (Acción Popular), finally forming the umbrella Spanish Confederation of Autonomous Rights (Confederación Española de Derechas Autónomas, CEDA) in 1933. However, even under CEDA, the right remained weak and riven by the factionalism of competing groups. CEDA was constrained by a vibrant and ever-changing collection of right-wing pressure groups, press, associations, and proto-parties. These not only made party-building more difficult but also made the party more vulnerable to radicalization. First, CEDA's leadership was quickly pressured into taking more extreme stances on the regime from its own paramilitary youth group, Popular Action Youths (Juventudes de Acción Popular, JAP). Even CEDA's leader Gil Robles admitted that JAP "succeeded in imposing some of its identity

---

[78] See Ben-Ami (1978: 56). [79] See Payne (1993: 50–51).

upon CEDA."⁸⁰ Unlike in Sweden, party leaders could not manage to extricate themselves from this critical group.⁸¹ The push toward radicalization and civil war was the result. The reason for the pull of JAP on CEDA was simple: as one *cedista* former minister, Manuel Giménez Fernández, wrote in retrospect, "The great defect of the CEDA was that in reality it was never a party."⁸²

Similarly, with its massive electoral defeat in 1936, at the first sign of electoral weakness, CEDA's radical and ideological base radicalized further still, pushing the fragile party to shed any republican inclinations entirely. Facing the threat of disintegration, it backed a failed coup d'état; began to associate itself officially with the fascist Falange; promoted right-wing violence in the streets; and, finally, participated in the planning of the military uprising that would spark civil war in July 1936 and lead to the collapse of democratic institutions.⁸³ Electoral failure, rooted in organizational failure, made the threat of the new regime even greater.⁸⁴ In short, without a cohesive and electorally viable party organization, the costs of toleration for the Spanish right had become too great for democracy to survive.

10.4 CONCLUSION

This chapter's contribution to the study of authoritarian successor parties is twofold. First, it places the concept into historical perspective, showing that, with some refinement, it can travel not only across space (as the chapters in this volume clearly illustrate) but also across time. Although Loxton (Introduction, this volume) confines his operationalization of authoritarian successor parties to those that emerged from the second and third waves of democratization, this chapter has shown that this logic began in democracy's first wave. As parties that emerged from Europe's pre-democratic "old regime," old regime conservative parties are, at the very least, close conceptual cousins of modern-day authoritarian successor parties.

The chapter's second contribution is to demonstrate the critical importance – and at times *positive* effects – of old regime conservative parties on the first wave of democratization. These parties did not passively respond to the wave of democratization that transformed European politics between the 1830s and 1930s. Instead, like authoritarian successor parties today, they played an active and critical role in shaping the divergent trajectories of new democratic regimes. Since what Arend Lijphart (1977: 30) once termed the "permanent exclusion of the minority" always shapes the stability of democracy and the *future* prospect of democratic transitions, how old regime elites cope with mass democracy is critical.

---

[80] As summarized by Lowe (2010: 66).   [81] See Lowe (2010: 66, 81).
[82] Quoted in Lowe (2010: 69).   [83] See Preston (1994: 256–259, 274).
[84] For a compatible interpretation of the Spanish case, see Alexander (2002).

In democracy's first wave, in cases as diverse as Spain, Germany, Britain, and Sweden, as in subsequent periods of democratization, a general logic holds: where strong old regime conservative parties were present, they provided a vehicle for democratic stabilization. Where they were absent, democracy was both hard to build and fragile.

Like in East Asia (Slater and Wong, Chapter 9, this volume), if the defenders of the old regime and property had access to strong party organizations, this normalized party competition in a way that helped both democratic transition and consolidation. One important issue remains: What are the implications for democracy of arguing that old regime elites must win elections much of the time for democracy to be stable? In some respects, one can imagine that the continued domination of an old regime conservative party might very well undermine the "quality of democracy" (see Flores-Macías, Chapter 8, this volume). Indeed, at first glance there appears to be a trade-off: democratic stability is bought at the price of a "compromised" version of democracy in which old regime elites continue to dominate. However, a key assumption of this chapter is that old regime forces typically resurrect themselves no matter what; the only question is *how this happens*. Do old regime elites protect themselves via hard-to-reform anti-majoritarian institutions such as a House of Lords, or do they do so via old regime conservative parties? This chapter has made the case that the latter is a preferable mode of achieving democratic stability.

In short, in democracy's first wave, the presence of robust conservative parties representing old regime elites may have been a precondition for democracy. While other collective actors, such as labor, liberals, and working-class movements, were critical in pushing for democratization at key points, a hinge of history shaping the stability of democracy was the strength and character of Europe's old regime conservative parties. Just as strong authoritarian successor parties appear to have helped stabilize new democracies in the contemporary period, this chapter has argued that strong old regime conservative parties were a crucial and underappreciated factor for successful democratization during Europe's first wave.

Conclusion

Life after Dictatorship

James Loxton

Is there life after dictatorship? The answer, as the chapters in this volume have shown, is an unequivocal "yes." Authoritarian successor parties are extraordinarily common. They have been prominent actors in nearly *three-quarters* of all third-wave democracies, and have been voted back into office in over *one-half* of all third-wave democracies (Loxton, Introduction). They are major actors in Africa (Riedl; LeBas), Asia (Cheng and Huang; Slater and Wong), Europe (Kitschelt and Singer; Grzymala-Busse), and Latin America (Power; Flores-Macías), as well as the one case of successful democratization of the Arab Spring, Tunisia. They have emerged from various types of authoritarian regime, including party-based, military, and even personalistic regimes (Loxton and Levitsky). And they are not just creatures of the third wave; there are prominent examples from the second wave, and analogues can be found from the first wave, as well (Ziblatt). In short, authoritarian successor parties are not outliers. They are part and parcel of the democratization experience – a fact that, to date, has been largely overlooked. The aim of this volume is to increase awareness of, and to launch a new research agenda on, authoritarian successor parties as a worldwide phenomenon.

In this conclusion, I highlight some of the major themes of the volume and consider the broader implications that authoritarian successor parties raise. In the first section, I discuss the surprising benefits of an authoritarian past and underscore the utility of the "authoritarian inheritance-versus-authoritarian baggage" framework. In the second section, I discuss the concept of "authoritarianism with adjectives," and ask whether authoritarian successor parties should be placed in this category. I argue that they should *not* because, despite their links to authoritarianism in the past, they operate in democracy in the present, and I highlight the empirical and theoretical payoffs of conceptualizing authoritarian successor parties in this way. In the third section, I go beyond authoritarian successor parties to discuss two related but conceptually distinct phenomena: former dictators elected back into office and "authoritarian diasporas." In the fourth section, I discuss how authoritarian successor parties can contribute to the understanding of political parties more broadly, particularly party adaptation and party-building. In the fifth section, I discuss the future of authoritarian successor parties, asking when (if ever) they become "normal" parties and speculating about where new ones might emerge in the future. In the final section, I show that while authoritarian successor parties emerge in most new democracies, there are many paths from authoritarian regime to authoritarian successor party, and highlight five in particular: the "Taiwan model," the "Poland model," the "Indonesia model," the "Benin model," and (possibly) the "Montenegro model."

BENEFITS OF AN AUTHORITARIAN PAST

One of the recurring themes of the volume is that for parties operating in democratic regimes, there can be surprising benefits to an authoritarian past. In the Introduction (Loxton, this volume), I presented this idea through the concept of *authoritarian inheritance*. This refers to the resources that authoritarian successor parties may inherit from dictatorships that, paradoxically, help them to win votes under democracy. Several of the chapters explored how authoritarian successor parties have benefited from authoritarian inheritance. In their chapter on Taiwan's Kuomintang (KMT) and South Korea's Democratic Justice Party (DJP)/Saenuri, Cheng and Huang (Chapter 2, this volume) discuss how these parties inherited organizational and financial resources, and, perhaps most importantly, strong party brands based on the achievements of the authoritarian regimes from which they emerged. In their chapter, Kitschelt and Singer (Chapter 1, this volume) show that authoritarian successor parties often inherit large territorial organizations and informal networks that help them to maintain clientelistic linkages with voters under democracy. And in his chapter on Mexico's Institutional Revolutionary Party (PRI), Flores-Macías (Chapter 8, this volume) examines how the party inherited the support of authoritarian-era labor unions, crony capitalist ties to business, and the control of state resources through its continuing control of subnational governments, all of which helped it to survive the transition to democracy in 2000 and to return to power barely a decade later.

While few will have trouble with the idea of authoritarian successor parties inheriting organizations, sources of party finance, or clientelistic networks, the idea that they can inherit popular *brands* from dictatorships may be more controversial. Authoritarian regimes, by definition, do not hold onto power through free and fair elections, and all employ coercion to varying degrees. Nevertheless, a growing literature on "popular autocrats" (Dimitrov 2009) has shown that some authoritarian regimes do, in fact, enjoy considerable popular support.[1] Indeed, as Chang, Chu, and Welsh (2013: 161) note, "the observed level of regime legitimacy

---

[1] See, for example, Chang, Chu, and Welsh (2013); Rose and Mishler (2002); Rose, Mishler, and Munro (2006, 2011); and Treisman (2011).

in nondemocratic regimes is sometimes considerably higher than in emerging democracies." While violence is an important part of the authoritarian repertoire, it is not the only part. Many authoritarian regimes go to great lengths, through propaganda and policymaking, to cultivate popular support. The reason they do this rather than rely on force alone is straightforward: "Extreme measures of coercion, involving surveillance of the private lives of individuals, arrests or terror, require the regime to invest substantial resources. Moreover, the more brutal the degree of repression, the greater the risk that this stimulates more dissent" (Rose, Mishler, and Munro 2011: 12).[2] While it can be difficult for outsiders to measure public opinion in highly repressive regimes,[3] multiple forms of evidence indicate that some dictatorships have considerable popular backing.

One source of evidence is polling. Data from the Asian Barometer Survey from 2005 to 2012, for example, show that Southeast Asia's authoritarian regimes (e.g., Singapore, Vietnam) enjoyed greater regime support than its democracies (e.g., Indonesia, Philippines) (Chang, Chu, and Welsh 2013). Polls have likewise indicated extremely high approval for Russian autocrat Vladimir Putin, which has never fallen below 60 percent, and in some years has been closer to 90 percent (Rose, Mishler, and Munro 2011: 125).[4] Another source of evidence is the results of undemocratic elections. While little can be inferred from electoral results in extremely coercive regimes (e.g., Central Asia), those in competitive authoritarian regimes can provide more information. Elections in countries such as Malaysia, Mozambique, and Venezuela take place on an uneven playing field, but they are not Soviet-style farces either (Levitsky and Way 2010). In such settings, repeated victories by incumbents may be taken as evidence of significant – albeit exaggerated – regime support. Finally, there is considerable anecdotal evidence that the overthrow of democratically elected leaders has sometimes been met with relief, or even elation, by large segments of the population in cases such as Salvador Allende in Chile in 1973; Thaksin Shinawatra and Yingluck Shinawatra in Thailand in 2006 and 2014, respectively; and Mohamed Morsi in Egypt in 2013.[5]

---

[2] Another reason is that a heavy reliance on repression may empower the armed forces to such a degree that they end up becoming a challenge to authoritarian leaders (Svolik 2012: 9–10, 123–161).

[3] In such settings, citizens have an incentive to hide their true sentiments and engage in what Kuran (1991) called "preference falsification." Interestingly, some authoritarian regimes have been mindful of this problem and have sought to get around it by actively encouraging citizens to issue complaints in order to gauge the amount of "latent discontent" in society (Dimitrov 2016).

[4] See also Treisman (2011) and Joshua Tucker, "Why We Should Be Confident that Putin Is Genuinely Popular in Russia," Monkey Cage, *Washington Post* blog, November 24, 2015.

[5] On Chile, see Power (2002). On Thailand, see Pye and Schaffar (2008) and Pepinsky (2017: 124–126). On Egypt, see Patrick Kingsley and Marwa Awad, "Egypt's Army Chief Rides Wave of Popularity towards Presidency," *The Guardian*, October 21, 2013.

Conclusion 339

While popular support for authoritarian regimes may be normatively discomfiting, it is not mysterious. As data from the World Values Survey and the Asian Barometer Survey indicate, regime support is a function not just of whether the regime is democratic or authoritarian but also of a host of factors orthogonal to regime type. These include the rule of law (Rose and Mishler 2002: 14) and performance in key areas such as the economy, public safety, and the provision of public services (Chang, Chu, and Welsh 2013: 153–155).[6] In short, people care not just about regime *type*, but also about what regimes *do*. And some dictatorships do quite a lot.[7] As Cheng and Huang discuss (Chapter 2, this volume), the KMT regime in Taiwan and the Park Chung-hee regime in South Korea oversaw two of the most dramatic instances of economic development in history, while protecting their countries from serious military threats. In Mexico, though less successful than its Taiwanese and South Korean counterparts, the PRI could claim to be "the heir to the Mexican Revolution's ideals and successes," including the incorporation of the popular sectors, substantial economic development, and the establishment of political stability after a brutal civil war (Flores-Macías, Chapter 8, this volume). Even autocrats who do not govern particularly well, such as Omar Torrijos in Panama or Hugo Chávez in Venezuela, can earn considerable good will by providing symbolic representation and enacting social policies favorable to marginalized groups (Loxton and Levitsky, Chapter 3, this volume).

In short, some dictatorships enjoy significant popular support. Popular dictatorships, in turn, generate popular brands – the "KMT brand," the "Park brand," the "PRI brand," the "Torrijos brand," etc. – which can be a source of votes for authoritarian successor parties under democracy.[8] To be sure, there are also downsides to an authoritarian past. While parties may benefit from *authoritarian inheritance*, they will also no doubt be weighed down by *authoritarian baggage*. In cases of large-scale human rights violations, this baggage is likely to be especially heavy. Yet this has not proven to be as much of a barrier to electoral success as one might expect. Even a history of literal genocide did not prevent Efraín Ríos Montt's Guatemalan Republican Front (FRG) from winning votes; indeed, his party won the presidency in 1999 with over 68 percent of the vote.[9] One reason that authoritarian baggage has not

---

[6] See also Rose, Mishler, and Munro (2011: 22–26).
[7] In a provocative article titled "Is Democracy Good for the Poor?," Ross (2006) found that authoritarian regimes were often more effective at reducing infant mortality than democracies. Anticipating my argument here, this led him to muse: "Perhaps this helps explain why people in newly democratized countries often vote for candidates and parties associated with former dictators" (Ross 2006: 860).
[8] In some cases, those brands may become even *more* attractive over time. As Flores-Macías (Chapter 8, this volume) shows in the case of Mexico, when new democratic governments perform poorly, this may make some voters nostalgic for the old days. On "authoritarian nostalgia," see Chang, Chu, and Park (2007) and Kim (2014).
[9] See Loxton and Levitsky (Chapter 3, this volume).

proven fatal is that parties have developed various strategies to offload it, including *contrition, obfuscation,* and *scapegoating* (Loxton, Introduction). In other cases, however, they have simply embraced the past, calculating – correctly – that their inheritance would outweigh their baggage.

This framework of *authoritarian inheritance*-versus-*authoritarian baggage* is a powerful tool for analyzing authoritarian successor parties, and can be applied to a range of potential research questions. To answer the question of "Why are some authoritarian successor parties more successful than others?," for example, a good starting point is to try to determine the balance of inheritance to baggage – a balance that varies widely from party to party. This, in turn, leads one to consider some of the factors affecting this balance, such as the level of popular support for the former regime (a source of inheritance) or the regime's history of human rights abuses (a source of baggage). The framework can also be applied to the question of "Why do authoritarian successor parties position themselves in different ways toward the former regime?," since parties with large amounts of authoritarian baggage have an incentive to try to offload it through strategies such as contrition, obfuscation, or scapegoating. Given the simplicity, utility, and versatility of this framework, scholars who take up the study of authoritarian successor parties may find it useful to employ it in their own work.

AUTHORITARIANISM WITH ADJECTIVES?

Authoritarian successor parties are *parties that emerge from authoritarian regimes, but that operate after a transition to democracy* (Loxton 2015; also Introduction, this volume). Given that they have a foot in both authoritarianism and democracy, they bear a superficial resemblance to a group of phenomena that we might describe as "authoritarianism with adjectives."[10] In the post–Cold War period, it was common for authoritarian regimes to open up to multiparty elections, but to leave in place institutions and/or practices that impeded – or even precluded – the full functioning of democracy. The clearest example is hybrid regimes, such as "competitive authoritarianism" (Levitsky and Way 2010) or "electoral authoritarianism" (Schedler 2013), in which competitive elections are held, but the playing field is unfairly tilted against the opposition. Such regimes are often the product of a partial opening of closed authoritarian regimes, and thus are holdovers from a more fully authoritarian past.[11] Another example is "subnational authoritarianism," or the existence of authoritarian practices at the subnational level in nationally democratic regimes, as in some states in Mexico following the transition to democracy in

---

[10] This is a reference to Collier and Levitsky's (1997) seminal essay on "democracy with adjectives." For earlier uses of the phrase "authoritarianism with adjectives," see Linz (2000: 34), Schedler (2000), and Gilbert and Mohseni (2011).

[11] See Levitsky and Way (2010: 16–20).

Conclusion

2000.[12] A final example is "authoritarian enclaves" (technically, a case of authoritarianism with a noun), or undemocratic institutions that limit the ability of elected governments to govern,[13] such as appointed senators and tutelary powers for the military after the end of the Pinochet dictatorship in Chile.[14]

Like these instances of authoritarianism with adjectives, authoritarian successor parties are holdovers from authoritarian regimes; however, they differ from them in a fundamental way. These other phenomena are all, by definition, antidemocratic: to say that a regime is competitive authoritarian is to say that it is not a democracy; to say that a province is a case of subnational authoritarianism is to say that it is not democratic. Authoritarian successor parties' relationship to authoritarianism is different: it is historical, not current. These parties have *origins* in authoritarian regimes, but they operate in the *present* under democracy. This two-part definition of authoritarian successor parties – parties that (1) emerge from authoritarian regimes, but that (2) operate *after* a transition to democracy – is one of the core conceptual contributions of this volume. While this might seem like an overly elaborate exercise in concept formation, adopting this definition has two major payoffs.

The first is empirical. In his famous essay on delegative democracy, Guillermo O'Donnell (1994) announced his discovery of a "new species" of democracy. This volume has done something similar. To date, scholars have failed to take note of how widespread authoritarian successor parties are and how common it is for them to return to power.[15] By systematically documenting the worldwide prevalence of authoritarian successor parties for the first time, this volume has helped to discover a "new species" of political party. Yet it is an odd sort of discovery, since these parties are *not*, in fact, new. They have existed since at least the second wave,[16] and they have been prevalent in virtually every major world region since the third wave. To the extent that they were hiding, they were hiding in plain sight. This volume's empirical contribution would not have been possible without first developing the concept. Concept formation and measurement go hand in hand – and alternative conceptualizations of authoritarian successor parties have serious shortcomings. If one were to look only at former authoritarian ruling parties, for example, and not reactive authoritarian successor parties (see Loxton, Introduction, for this distinction), one would have the misleading impression that it is less common for parties

---

[12] See Gibson (2012), Giraudy (2015), and Flores-Macías (Chapter 8, this volume).
[13] See Garretón (2003), Valenzuela (1992), and Stepan (1988).
[14] See Siavelis (2008: 191–192).
[15] As discussed in the Introduction (Loxton, this volume), scholars were, of course, aware of these parties in their own countries or regions of expertise. Their worldwide prevalence, however, was not adequately noted.
[16] For examples of authoritarian successor parties from the second wave, see Loxton and Levitsky (Chapter 3, this volume). According to Ziblatt (Chapter 10, this volume), analogues from the first wave can also be found, which he calls "old regime conservative parties."

with roots in dictatorship to exist in democracy than it actually is.[17] Or, if one were to lump together both authoritarian successor parties and the ruling parties of existing authoritarian regimes,[18] this would distract from what is so interesting about authoritarian successor parties in the first place: that they manage to win votes without access to the "menu of manipulation" (Schedler 2002).

The second payoff of this definition of authoritarian successor parties is theoretical. Specifying that these are parties that operate *in democracy* raises questions that would not arise otherwise. The most obvious is, "Why do so many people vote for these parties?" Authoritarian ruling parties can use dirty tricks to win votes; authoritarian successor parties cannot. To understand authoritarian *successor* parties, therefore, it is necessary to develop theories distinct from those used to understand authoritarian *ruling* parties. Another question is, "What are their effects on democracy?" Unlike the other authoritarian holdovers mentioned earlier, authoritarian successor parties' relationship to democracy is not inherently negative. To be sure, as the Introduction (Loxton, this volume) and Flores-Macías' chapter (Chapter 8, this volume) make clear, these parties *can* be harmful to democracy. However, they can also have surprisingly salutary effects. In their chapter, Slater and Wong (Chapter 9, this volume) show that authoritarian successor parties in Taiwan, South Korea, and Indonesia helped to stabilize new democratic regimes by making former authoritarian regime officials "game for democracy." And in his chapter on "old regime conservative parties" in Europe – the first wave's equivalent of authoritarian successor parties – Ziblatt (Chapter 10, this volume) finds that when they were strong, they helped make former opponents of democracy into "reluctant democrats."

Given these empirical and theoretical payoffs, there are strong reasons to adopt the definition of authoritarian successor parties used here. In addition, scholars may find it useful to draw on the broader set of terms developed in the volume – most obviously, "authoritarian successor party" itself, but also terms such as "authoritarian inheritance" and "authoritarian baggage." In the past, the absence of a shared vocabulary to discuss authoritarian successor parties impeded the accumulation of knowledge and meant that many region-specific works did not reach a broad audience. This volume, by developing a common language and shared analytical framework that can travel across regions, aims to correct this problem and lay the groundwork for a new, more cohesive literature on authoritarian successor parties worldwide.

---

[17] For example, one would miss parties such as Spain's People's Party (PP), Brazil's Liberal Front Party (PFL)/Democrats (DEM), Chile's Independent Democratic Union (UDI), and Tunisia's Nidaa Tounes.

[18] See, for example, Hicken and Kuhonta (2015).

BEYOND AUTHORITARIAN SUCCESSOR PARTIES

This volume has shown that authoritarian successor parties are commonly used by former authoritarian officials to remain influential under democracy. They are not, however, the only way. Two other phenomena that are related to, but conceptually distinct from, authoritarian successor parties are especially noteworthy. The first is *former dictators elected back into office*. In at least six third-wave democracies, former dictators have returned to the presidency as the candidates of authoritarian successor parties: Joaquín Balaguer of the Social Christian Reformist Party (PRSC) in the Dominican Republic in 1986; Didier Ratsiraka of the Association for the Rebirth of Madagascar (AREMA) in 1996; Hugo Banzer of Nationalist Democratic Action (ADN) in Bolivia in 1997; Pedro Pires of the African Party for the Independence of Cape Verde (PAICV) in 2001; Daniel Ortega of the Sandinista National Liberation Front (FSLN) in Nicaragua in 2007; and Dési Bouterse of the National Democratic Party (NDP) in Suriname in 2010.[19] In other cases, close family members of former dictators have led authoritarian successor parties to victory, such as Khaleda Zia, widow of General Zia, who became prime minister after leading the Bangladesh Nationalist Party (BNP) to victory in 1991 and 2001; Martín Torrijos, son of Omar Torrijos, who was elected president of Panama in 2004 as the candidate of the Democratic Revolutionary Party (PRD); and Park Geun-hye, daughter of Park Chung-hee, who was elected president of South Korea in 2012 as the Saenuri candidate.[20]

In these cases, there was overlap between authoritarian successor parties and the former dictators elected back into office. In other cases, however, former dictators have returned to power as *independents* or as candidates of *non-authoritarian successor parties*. In Benin, the former authoritarian ruling party, the People's Revolutionary Party of Benin (PRPB), collapsed with the transition to democracy, but former dictator Mathieu Kérékou returned to the presidency as an independent in 1996. In São Tomé and Príncipe, former dictator Manuel Pinto da Costa broke with the country's authoritarian successor party, the Movement for the Liberation of São Tomé and Príncipe/Social Democratic Party (MLSTP/PSD), but was elected president as an independent in 2011. And in Nigeria, two former military dictators – Olusegun Obasanjo and Muhammadu Buhari – were voted back into office in 1999 and 2015, respectively, as candidates of non-authoritarian successor parties.[21]

---

[19] Two cases from the second wave are Juan Perón in Argentina and Getúlio Vargas in Brazil.
[20] In Peru, Keiko Fujimori, daughter of former autocrat Alberto Fujimori, nearly won the presidency in 2011 and in 2016, losing the latter election by a mere 0.2 percent (Dargent and Muñoz 2016).
[21] A case from the second wave is Carlos Ibáñez del Campo in Chile, a former dictator who returned to the presidency democratically, but not as the candidate of an authoritarian successor party.

The second phenomenon is *authoritarian diasporas*. In an important book on Brazil, Power (2000) followed the trajectories of former members of the 1964–1985 military regime's official ruling party, the National Renovating Alliance (ARENA)/Social Democratic Party (PDS), after the transition to democracy. As Power discusses in his chapter (Chapter 7, this volume), the PDS continued to exist (eventually taking the name Progressive Party, PP), becoming, together with the Liberal Front Party (PFL)/Democrats (DEM), one of Brazil's two major authoritarian successor parties. However, the broader authoritarian "diaspora" was not limited to these two parties. Former authoritarian officials migrated to a host of other parties, including, bizarrely, the main opposition party to military rule, the Brazilian Democratic Movement Party (PMDB). As LeBas notes (Chapter 6, this volume), some countries in Africa have experienced something similar. In Kenya, for example, the Kenyan African National Union (KANU), the authoritarian ruling party, suffered mass defections in the lead-up to democratization, with KANU members forming or migrating to a multitude of other parties. The result was that virtually every major party after 2002 had roots in KANU, including the Liberal Democratic Party (LDP)/Orange Democratic Movement (ODM), founded by former minister and KANU general secretary, Raila Odinga; the Party of National Unity (PNU), founded by former vice president and minister in the KANU regime, Mwai Kibaki; and The National Alliance (TNA), which launched Uhuru Kenyatta, the son of former dictator Jomo Kenyatta and KANU's 2002 presidential candidate, to the presidency in 2013.[22]

Like former dictators elected back into office, there is some overlap between authoritarian diasporas and authoritarian successor parties. Conceptually, however, they are distinct. Following Power (2000; Chapter 7, this volume), authoritarian diasporas are the "cohort" of former authoritarian officials in democratic regimes. The particular shape that this cohort takes, however, varies on at least two dimensions.[23] The first is *degree of dispersion*. While in some countries, it is mostly concentrated in a single party, in others, it is more scattered. A dramatic example is Romania, where authoritarian officials spread to several parties, and where *both* of the country's major parties – one on the center-left, the other on the center-right – were authoritarian successor parties (Pop-Eleches 2008). Ukraine likewise saw its authoritarian diaspora spread to a multiplicity of parties (Zimmer and Haran 2008). The second is the *vehicle of political participation*. Authoritarian successor parties are obviously one vehicle, but others, as discussed above, include independent candidacies (e.g., Kérékou in Benin) and the colonization of non-authoritarian successor parties (e.g., PMDB in Brazil). Based on these dimensions, it should be possible to develop a typology of authoritarian diasporas. The question in need

---

[22] Kibaki was president from 2002 to 2013 and Odinga was prime minister from 2008 to 2013. For more, see Long, Kanyinga, Ferree, and Gibson (2013).
[23] This paragraph draws on my conversations with Timothy Power on this topic.

of further research is *why* diasporas vary in these ways. Two possible factors are: (1) preexisting tensions in the authoritarian ruling coalition that come to the fore after a transition to democracy, and (2) whether former regime officials believe that an association with the authoritarian past is an asset or a liability.

The existence of the two phenomena discussed in this section has important implications. First, the election of former dictators back into office illustrates, unambiguously, that conspicuous links to a dictatorship need not be an impediment to democratic success; there is no more conspicuous link than actually being the former dictator. The election of spouses and children of former dictators provides additional support for this conclusion. The PRD in Panama and Saenuri in South Korea, for example, did not just make Martín Torrijos and Park Geun-hye their presidential candidates; they made nostalgia for these candidates' fathers – former dictators Omar Torrijos and Park Chung-hee, respectively – central to their campaigns.[24] Second, former dictators elected back into office and authoritarian diasporas demonstrate that the prospects for former authoritarian officials under democracy are even better than the figures on authoritarian successor parties – already high – suggest.[25] In Benin and Nigeria, for example, no strong authoritarian successor parties emerged, but former dictators *were* elected back into office. In Ukraine, no authoritarian successor party was elected back into office, yet "[t]he bulk of the former Communist elite remained in power after independence" (Zimmer and Haran 2008: 557). If knowledge that they stand a good chance of remaining influential under democracy through authoritarian successor parties should bring comfort to current authoritarian incumbents, the existence of these other phenomena should ease their minds even more – and perhaps give them the courage necessary to initiate transitions to democracy.

PARTY ADAPTATION AND PARTY-BUILDING

By highlighting how common it is for parties with roots in dictatorship to thrive under democracy, this volume not only has clear implications for the study of political regimes, but also for the study of political parties. First, authoritarian successor parties can provide insights into the issue of *party adaptation*. Political scientists have long been interested in how parties do, or do not, adapt

---

[24] On the PRD's embrace of the memory of Omar Torrijos, see Loxton and Levitsky (Chapter 3, this volume). In South Korea, Park Geun-hye similarly embraced her father's legacy in the 2012 presidential election: "Park [Geun-hye] made deliberate and repeated references to her father's rule ... For instance, Park used the slogan, 'Try to Live Well, Again.' This phrase was adapted from 'Try to Live Well,' the most famous campaign slogan during her father's *saemaeul undong* (new village movement) ... Park's Geun-hye's slight tweak of this campaign slogan reminded people of her father's time" (Kim 2014: 59).

[25] For figures on authoritarian successor parties, see Appendix I.1 in the Introduction (Loxton, this volume).

to changing circumstances in order to remain viable. In his study of labor-based parties in Latin America, for example, Levitsky (2003) examines why some parties adapted to the exigencies of deindustrialization and market liberalization more successfully than others. He argues that parties with lower levels of institutionalization were better able to adapt because their less developed internal bureaucratic structures made it easier for them to respond to social and economic changes by shifting from a programmatic party–voter linkage to a clientelistic one. Like all parties, authoritarian successor parties must adapt if they wish to survive. However, the challenge of party adaptation for them is particularly demanding, since they must not just find new ways to link to voters, but also learn to operate in a totally different regime context.

Party adaptation represents a twofold challenge for authoritarian successor parties. The first is what Friedman and Wong (2008) call "learning to lose." For former authoritarian officials, this can be a difficult lesson. To be sure, some authoritarian successor parties win founding elections and one or more subsequent elections, leading Slater and Wong to lament political scientists' "collective failure to appreciate the empirical fact that *ruling parties can concede democracy without conceding defeat*" (2013: 731; emphases added). However, this is not actually true. Eventually, authoritarian successor parties *do* lose power. As discussed below, there is only one case of an authoritarian successor party that has never lost an election – the Democratic Party of Socialists of Montenegro (DPS) – and this is almost certainly an artifact of the country's short history: Montenegro only became independent in 2006.[26] With this one possible exception, then, all authoritarian successor parties must learn to lose. This means, first, learning to concede defeat rather than respond to an electoral loss by calling out the tanks, and second, maintaining party cohesion. While remaining cohesive in the face of electoral defeat is difficult for all parties, it is especially so when the "glue" holding the party together up until that point was access to power.

This volume's two chapters on Africa offer compelling – and contrasting – arguments about why some authoritarian successor parties were better at maintaining cohesion than others. In her chapter, Riedl (Chapter 5, this volume) emphasizes the different strategies that ruling parties pursued toward local brokers under authoritarianism: in countries where they *incorporated* those brokers, parties were less likely to suffer post-defeat defections than in countries where they attempted to *substitute* them with outside party agents.[27] LeBas (Chapter 6, this volume) emphasizes a different factor: *the competitive landscape*. While facing a weak or divided opposition might seem desirable, LeBas argues that it was actually in the interests of authoritarian successor parties to face strong, cohesive opposition parties, since the existence of such parties exacerbated "us-versus-them"

---

[26] Despite its lack of turnover, Montenegro is a democracy. Freedom House has scored it as "free" since 2010, and Geddes, Wright, and Frantz (2014a) score it as a democracy from 2007 onward.
[27] For more, see Riedl (2014).

Conclusion 347

tensions and raised the cost of defection.[28] Thus, Ghana's National Democratic Congress (NDC), facing strong opposition from the New Patriotic Party (NPP), remained united after its losses in 2000 and 2004, while Kenya's KANU, which did not face a similarly cohesive opposition, disintegrated following its defeat in 2002. Both chapters have broad implications for the study of parties. Riedl's chapter supports arguments in the literature that emphasize parties' origins – their "genetic model," to use Panebianco's (1988: 50) phrase – albeit with an important twist regarding territorial expansion.[29] LeBas' chapter, by contrast, suggests that we cannot understand the fates of individual parties without studying the broader party *systems* in which they operate – and that a powerful opposition can, paradoxically, be a blessing.

If the first challenge of party adaptation is "learning to lose," the second is "learning to win."[30] Because they operate in democratic regimes, authoritarian successor parties cannot rely on the kinds of dirty tricks used by authoritarian regimes, and thus must learn to do something for which they were not originally designed: win elections fair and square. In countries that previously had electoral authoritarian regimes, authoritarian successor parties may already have considerable experience with electoral mobilization and therefore be able to adapt relatively easily. A clear example is Mexico's PRI. As Flores-Macías (Chapter 8, this volume) discusses, the PRI lost the presidency in 2000, but continued to dominate at the subnational level, remained a major force in Congress, and returned to the presidency in 2012. Much of the PRI's electoral success, Flores-Macías argues, owed to its inheritance of organizational resources already well suited to electoral mobilization, such as the support of corporatist labor unions. The PRI also benefited from its continued access to state resources, thanks to the remarkable fact that, until 2016, it never controlled less than 50 percent of Mexico's state governments.

In his chapter, Power (Chapter 7, this volume) examines another case, Brazil, where party adaptation was a relatively smooth affair. Though not an electoral authoritarian regime like Mexico's, Brazil's 1964–1985 military regime

---

[28] For more, see LeBas (2006, 2011).
[29] The "genetic model," as Panebianco explains, holds that a "party's organizational characteristics depend more upon its history, i.e. on how the organization originated and how it consolidated, than upon any other factor. The characteristics of a party's origin are in fact capable of exerting a weight on its organizational structure even decades later" (1988: 50). For Panebianco, a specific application of this model concerned differences between parties that developed through territorial "penetration," with the center penetrating outward into the periphery (similar to Riedl's "substitution"), and parties that developed through territorial "diffusion," with local elites constructing their own party branches (similar to Riedl's "incorporation") (1988: 50–51). According to Panebianco, penetration tends to produce strong parties, while diffusion results in weaker parties "because of many competing elites controlling conspicuous organizational resources" (1988: 63). Riedl's argument, by emphasizing parties' *origins*, is broadly consistent with Panebianco's genetic model. However, it contradicts the specifics of Panebianco's argument by finding that incorporating local elites leads to stronger parties rather than vice versa.
[30] For an earlier use of this phrase, see chapters in Friedman and Wong (2008).

nevertheless carried out regular elections for Congress and subnational governments. To win these undemocratic elections, the military turned to traditional civilian political elites for help, who drummed up support for the regime through clientelism (Hagopian 1996). After democratization, the PFL/DEM was able to maintain these clientelistic linkages, thanks to its continued access to state resources as part of various coalition governments, as well as its control of subnational governments in the country's poor Northeast. Yet the eventual decline of the PFL/DEM shows that a smooth adaptation to democracy is no guarantee of long-term success and offers some broader lessons. First, it suggests that a heavy focus on clientelism is a risky strategy, as it becomes difficult to sustain once the party loses access to state resources. For this reason, parties that *do* rely on clientelism should do everything in their power to maintain access to those state resources. According to Power, the fact that the PFL/DEM left the governing coalition after 2002, while the PDS/PP remained part of it, helps to explain why they ended up "trading places" in terms of electoral performance. At the same time, the case of the PFL/DEM shows that while clientelism without access to state resources is hard to sustain, it is also hard to switch from one party–voter linkage to another. Thus, as Power discusses, the PFL/DEM's attempt to reinvent itself as a more ideological liberal party did nothing to halt its decline.

If party adaptation is challenging for all authoritarian successor parties, it is especially difficult for those that emerge from *non*-electoral authoritarian regimes. Parties in such contexts were originally designed for radically different purposes, and thus "learning to win" means mastering an entirely new skillset. The clearest examples are the communist successor parties, which Grzymala-Busse (2002) discussed in her classic book. Under communism, there were no competitive elections, and communist regimes were "widely despised by their own citizens" (Grzymala-Busse 2002: 2). As such, the parties that emerged from them had no experience with electoral competition and were massively burdened with authoritarian baggage. Under such circumstances, Grzymala-Busse (2002) argued that it was necessary for them to reinvent themselves if they wished to remain viable. This meant, first, centralizing and streamlining their organizations, and, second, "symbolically breaking with the past" (Grzymala-Busse 2002: 6). In short, because of the extreme nature of the regime transition – from fully closed authoritarianism to democracy – an equally extreme form of party adaptation was also needed. This, she argued, explained why reinvented parties, such as the Social Democracy of the Republic of Poland (SdRP)/Democratic Left Alliance (SLD) and the Hungarian Socialist Party (MSzP), were able to quickly return to power, while unreconstructed ones, such as the Communist Party of Bohemia and Moravia (KSČM) in the Czech Republic, remained relatively marginal actors.

In her chapter in this volume (Chapter 4), Grzymala-Busse uses the benefit of hindsight to reevaluate this earlier argument. As of 2018, the stars of her 2002 book – Poland's SdRP/SLD and Hungary's MSzP – have all but disappeared from the political map, while the KSČM, the least successful of her cases in 2002, remains "a durable fixture of Czech politics." According to Grzymala-Busse, *both* the initial success *and* the eventual collapse of the SdRP/SLD and MSzP were rooted in their strategies of party adaptation. By downplaying ideology and emphasizing managerial competence and probity, they were able to get elected back into office. Once there, however, they were harshly punished by voters when they failed to live up to the standards of good governance that they had set for themselves. The KSČM, by contrast, was not judged by the same metric, since it never came close to winning power again and essentially existed as a protest party. These parties' varying trajectories illustrate the risk of building a "party brand" (Lupu 2016) on *valence issues* rather than ideology. While doing so helped the Polish and Hungarian communist successor parties to get elected, it also led to their demise, making them, in Grzymala-Busse's words, "victims of their own success."

In addition to providing insights into party adaptation, the study of authoritarian successor parties can shed light on a second major issue: *party-building*. If party adaptation refers to the challenge that established parties face in adapting to new circumstances, party-building refers to the challenge of becoming an established party in the first place. Recent decades have been hard on parties in much of the world: not only have party systems collapsed in several countries (e.g., Venezuela, Bolivia, Peru),[31] but attempts to build new parties have often ended in failure.[32] While some new parties have managed to go against the grain and succeed, the overall record of party-building has been bleak. In a study of party-building in Latin America, for example, Levitsky, Loxton, and Van Dyck (2016) counted 307 new parties formed between 1978 and 2005. Of the 255 that could be definitively scored, only 11 (or 4 percent) took root.[33]

What is remarkable for the purposes of this volume is that of those eleven cases of successful party-building, *six* were authoritarian successor parties.[34] Further research is needed to see whether this pattern holds elsewhere, but the striking overrepresentation of authoritarian successor parties among the success cases has broad implications. First, it lends support to one of the

---

[31] See, for example, Morgan (2011) and Lupu (2016).

[32] One reason is that the rise of new forms of mass media – especially television – has made parties less essential for ambitious politicians to win office than they once were (Mainwaring and Zoco 2007).

[33] Levitsky, Loxton, and Van Dyck (2016) look at all parties formed in Latin America between 1978 and 2005 that won at least 1 percent in a national election. They operationalize successful party-building as winning at least 10 percent in five consecutive national legislative elections. Fifty-two parties were scored as "incomplete," either because they had not yet competed in five elections, or because they had competed in five elections but only recently crossed the 10-percent threshold.

[34] These are Brazil's PFL/DEM; Chile's UDI and National Renewal (RN); El Salvador's Nationalist Republican Alliance (ARENA); Nicaragua's FSLN; and Panama's PRD.

classic arguments in the parties literature: namely, that a crucial ingredient for party-building is the inheritance of preexisting resources, such as a territorial organization.[35] However, it also shows that parties scholars have been inattentive to one of the most common sources of such resources: *authoritarian regimes*. Authoritarian inheritance deserves to be added to the canon of preexisting resources for party-building, together with better-known ones such as religious organizations and labor unions. Second, it highlights the role of polarization and conflict in bringing about strong parties.[36] As mentioned, six of eleven cases of successful party-building in Latin America in recent decades were authoritarian successor parties. Four of the remaining five were also born in the context of authoritarian regimes – but in *opposition* to those regimes.[37] The fact that ten out of eleven successful new parties in Latin America were born under authoritarianism suggests that while strong parties may be essential for democracy,[38] democracy is not essential for strong parties. Indeed, something closer to the opposite appears to be true: the intense polarization and conflict that sometimes emerges around the "regime divide" is particularly conducive to the emergence of strong parties (e.g., Chile, El Salvador).

If some of the most successful new parties in recent decades have been authoritarian successor parties, Ziblatt's chapter (Chapter 10, this volume) on "old regime conservative parties" suggests that this is nothing new. In his view, parties such as the Conservative Party in Great Britain and the General Electoral League (AVF) in Sweden are the first wave's equivalent of authoritarian successor parties. They grew out of their countries' "old regime," or a "nexus of landed elites, bureaucratic and military officials, and defenders of monarchy and establishment church institutions." These regimes were clearly undemocratic, and the elites associated with them were initially unabashed enemies of democracy. In cases where old regime conservative parties proved electorally viable, those elites eventually became more supportive of democracy – much as would later occur in Taiwan with the KMT and in South Korea with the DJP/Saenuri (Slater and Wong, Chapter 9, this volume). The fact remains, though, that if one accepts Ziblatt's argument, it means that some of the most important democratic actors in Western Europe over the past century are undemocratic in origin.

---

[35] See, for example, Kalyvas (1996) and LeBas (2011).
[36] See LeBas (2006, 2011) and Levitsky, Loxton, and Van Dyck (2016).
[37] These are the Workers' Party (PT) in Brazil; Party for Democracy (PPD) in Chile; Farabundo Martí National Liberation Front (FMLN) in El Salvador; and Party of the Democratic Revolution (PRD) in Mexico. Only one of the eleven cases of successful party-building was born under conditions of "normal" democracy: the Brazilian Social Democracy Party (PSDB).
[38] As Schattschneider (2004[1942]: 1) famously asserted, democracy is "unthinkable" without parties. See also Aldrich (1995) and Mainwaring and Scully (1995: 2–4).

Conclusion

THE FUTURE OF AUTHORITARIAN SUCCESSOR PARTIES

This volume has had a broad geographical and historical sweep, examining authoritarian successor parties in Africa, Asia, Europe, and Latin America, as well as in different time periods. While it has focused on parties that emerged during the third wave, it has also examined parties from the second wave (Loxton and Levitsky, Chapter 3, this volume), as well as analogues from the first wave (Ziblatt, Chapter 10, this volume). This section expands the historical sweep further still, asking, "What is the *future* of authoritarian successor parties?" There are two dimensions to this question. The first concerns *existing authoritarian successor parties*. At what point, if ever, do they cease to be authoritarian successor parties? In some cases, the answer is clear: when the party is elected back into office and then reestablishes authoritarian rule, it ceases to be an authoritarian successor party. Thus, Nicaragua's FSLN, which returned to power in 2007 and then installed an authoritarian regime (Thaler 2017), has lost its status as an authoritarian successor party. The same was true after the PRSC returned to power in the Dominican Republic in 1986 and AREMA returned to power in Madagascar in 1996, and then installed competitive authoritarian regimes.[39] In these cases of democratic breakdown, parties reverted from authoritarian *successor* parties to authoritarian *ruling* parties, given that a core part of the definition of authoritarian successor parties is that they operate under democracy.

In the more common scenario in which the party does *not* trigger an authoritarian regression, the question of whether at some point it ceases to be an authoritarian successor party is more debatable. Does it ever become a "normal" party? In his chapter on Brazil, Power (Chapter 7, this volume) suggests one possible answer. Although he shows that the PDS/PP and the PFL/DEM were more likely to support military prerogatives than other parties, he argues that in their reliance on state resources and use of patronage to win votes, both were from the start similar to other parties in Brazil. As such, he asserts that "we should put a bit less emphasis on 'authoritarian' and on 'successor,' and quite a lot more on 'parties.'" In their chapter, Kitschelt and Singer (Chapter 1, this volume) make a similar argument, using a thirty-year cutoff point for inclusion in their universe of cases. This is defensible, they claim, because "after a thirty-year window, parties will have gone through an all but complete generational turnover," and because the resources that they inherit from authoritarian regimes are "perishable" assets. Thus, both chapters argue that at some point authoritarian successor parties become parties like any other – most likely within a generation.

But authoritarian successor parties' origins may leave a more lasting impact than these authors acknowledge. In Chile, for example, the Independent Democratic Union (UDI) continued to make ostentatious displays of loyalty to

---

[39] See Levitsky and Way (2010: 132–137, 276–282).

the memory of Augusto Pinochet well into the 2010s, over three decades after the party was formed.[40] Panama's PRD is even more explicit: its party logo, almost thirty years after the transition to democracy (and nearly four decades since the party was formed), continues to be an "O" with an "11" inside it – a reference to October 11, 1968, the day of the coup that brought Omar Torrijos to power.[41] In South Korea, the Saenuri government of Park Geun-hye introduced new history textbooks in 2015 that critics alleged were designed to whitewash the legacy of her father, former military dictator Park Chung-hee, who died in 1979.[42] And in Suriname in 2016, President Dési Bouterse of the NDP tried to use his powers to block efforts by the justice system to try him for the summary execution of fifteen prominent political opponents during his 1980–1987 dictatorship.[43]

For most of the third-wave cases, we will not know for some time whether authoritarian successor parties will ever become completely "normal." A promising research project, however, would be to examine parties from the second wave to see if they continue to exhibit distinctive characteristics. One could explore, for example, whether the "movementist" tendencies of Peronism – that is, its "hegemonic vocation" and "anything goes" approach to governing (McGuire 1995: 200–201) – are connected to its undemocratic origins.[44] Another option would be to examine authoritarian successor parties that emerged at the very beginning of the third wave, such as the People's Party (PP) in Spain, which was founded (as the People's Alliance, AP) in 1976, to see whether they still possess marks of their origins.

The second question concerns *potential future authoritarian successor parties*. Where might new ones emerge? While prediction is always a risky business, the existence of regime liberalization and/or crisis in some countries, together with the potential for authoritarian inheritance, allows for some informed speculation.[45] As Slater and Wong (2013) have argued, some of the

---

[40] See, for example, "Parlamentarios de la UDI pidieron un minuto de silencio en el Congreso en honor a Pinochet," *El Mostrador*, December 10, 2014. Available from: http://www.elmostrador.cl/noticias/pais/2014/12/10/parlamentarios-de-la-udi-pidieron-un-minuto-de-silencio-en-el-congreso-en-honor-a-pinochet/ [Accessed on May 3, 2018]. See also Loxton (2014a).

[41] See Loxton and Levitsky (Chapter 3, this volume).

[42] See Simon Mundy, "South Korea Set to Rewrite History Books," *Financial Times*, October 12, 2015.

[43] See Pieter Van Maele, "Suriname President Acts to Again Avoid Trial in 1982 Deaths," *The Washington Post*, June 29, 2016.

[44] As discussed by Loxton and Levitsky (Chapter 3, this volume), Juan Perón began his political career as a high-level official in Argentina's 1943–1946 military dictatorship. He was democratically elected president in 1946, but then established a competitive authoritarian regime.

[45] In some cases not discussed here, such as China, Russia, and Angola, a hypothetical authoritarian successor party would likely benefit from significant authoritarian inheritance. However, authoritarian regimes in these countries appear so stable that a transition to democracy in the foreseeable future is highly unlikely. In another case, Myanmar, democratization is more plausible, given significant regime liberalization in recent years. However, the probability of

strongest candidates are in Southeast Asia. Perhaps the best bet is the People's Action Party (PAP) in Singapore, which, like the KMT in Taiwan and the DJP/Saenuri in South Korea, has overseen extraordinary economic development. In recent years, the regime has shown signs of opening up (Ortmann 2011, 2015); if this process continues and Singapore democratizes, the PAP would almost certainly thrive as an authoritarian successor party. Another promising candidate is the United Malays National Organisation (UMNO) in Malaysia, which also has a strong record in office, albeit not as strong as the PAP's. UMNO's declining electoral fortunes – it lost the popular vote in 2013, but won the most seats through gerrymandering – combined with a rise in party infighting,[46] have led some to wonder whether Malaysia could follow the democratizing path of countries like Mexico and Taiwan (Nelson 2014). If this were to occur, UMNO would very likely remain highly competitive.

In Latin America, two candidates are the United Socialist Party of Venezuela (PSUV) and the Communist Party of Cuba (PCC). While Venezuela has turned increasingly autocratic since the death of Hugo Chávez in 2013 and his replacement by Nicolás Maduro,[47] a severe economic crisis, extremely low levels of support for Maduro, and increasing international pressure raise the possibility of eventual regime collapse.[48] If the regime were to suffer a crisis-fueled collapse, this would burden the PSUV with considerable authoritarian baggage. However, the party could offload much of this baggage by following a scapegoating strategy as the PRD did in Panama, blaming Maduro for the regime's failures (as the PRD did with Manuel Noriega), while embracing the popular memory of Chávez (as the PRD did with Omar Torrijos).[49] Another possible case is Cuba's PCC. While Cuba is still a full-blown authoritarian regime, it has engaged in some economic liberalization

---

a viable authoritarian successor party emerging is low, as evidenced by the results of the semi-free 2015 election, in which the military's Union Solidarity and Development Party (USDP) won barely one-tenth as many seats as the opposition National League for Democracy (NLD). See Thomas Fuller, "Final Vote Tally Confirms Rout by Myanmar Opposition," *The New York Times*, November 20, 2015. See also Blaževiè (2016).

[46] See Thomas Fuller and Louise Story, "Power Struggle in Malaysia Pits Former Premier Against a Protégé," *The New York Times*, June 17, 2015, and "Mahathir Mohamed's Return Shows the Sorry State of Malaysian Politics," *The Economist*, July 1, 2017.

[47] Freedom House, for example, downgraded Venezuela from "Partly Free" to "Not Free" in 2017. See "Venezuela: A Dictatorship Emerges after Flawed Elections," *Freedom House*, August 1, 2017. Available from: https://freedomhouse.org/article/venezuela-maduro-dictatorship-emerges-after-flawed-elections [Accessed on October 11, 2017].

[48] See, for example, Nicholas Casey and Patricia Torres, "Venezuela Drifts into New Territory: Hunger, Blackouts and Government Shutdown," *The New York Times*, May 28, 2016; Alexandra Ulmer, "Venezuelan President Approval Slips to Minimum, under 20 Percent: Poll," *Reuters*, November 18, 2016; and Sibylla Brodzinsky and Daniel Boffey, "40 Countries Protest Venezuela's New Assembly Amid Fraud Accusations," *The Guardian*, August 3, 2017.

[49] See James Loxton and Javier Corrales, "Venezuelans Are Still Demonstrating. What Happens Next for the Dictatorship of Nicolás Maduro?" Monkey Cage, *Washington Post* blog, April 20, 2017.

and political decompression since the replacement of Fidel Castro by his brother Raúl in 2006 (LeoGrande 2015). Following the resumption of diplomatic relations with the United States in 2015, growing economic problems related to the crisis in Venezuela, the death of Fidel Castro in 2016, and Raúl Castro's retirement as president in 2018, an eventual transition to democracy in Cuba, while not exactly likely, is at least more conceivable than in past decades.[50] Given the success of authoritarian successor parties in postcommunist Europe and the FSLN in Nicaragua – the PCC's closest equivalent in Latin America – there is good reason to think that the PCC could thrive in a hypothetical democratic future. The party would enter democracy with considerable authoritarian inheritance, in the form of a massive territorial organization and an attractive brand based on social policy and nationalism.

Finally, in Africa, possible candidates include the Alliance for Patriotic Reorientation and Construction (APRC) in The Gambia, Chama Cha Mapinduzi (CCM) in Tanzania, and the Mozambique Liberation Front (FRELIMO). In The Gambia, long-serving dictator Yahya Jammeh lost the 2016 presidential election and, under intense international pressure, was forced from office in early 2017 (Kora and Darboe 2017). While it is too soon to know whether democracy will take hold,[51] the APRC, Jammeh's former authoritarian ruling party, won 16 percent in the post-transition 2017 parliamentary elections, suggesting its potential to survive as an authoritarian successor party.[52] In Tanzania and Mozambique, authoritarian regimes remain firmly in place, but have held relatively competitive elections in recent years, raising the possibility of eventual democratization. The 2015 general election in Tanzania, despite flaws, was widely viewed as the country's most competitive to date.[53] Given the CCM's large territorial organization and the broad support shown for it in Afrobarometer

---

[50] On the role of linkage to the West in encouraging transitions to democracy, see Levitsky and Way (2010). On Cuba's economic problems, see Victoria Burnett, "Amid Grim Economic Forecasts, Cubans Fear a Return to Darker Times," *The New York Times*, July 12, 2016. On the prospects for democratization in Cuba, see Javier Corrales and James Loxton, "What Comes After the Castros?," *The New York Times*, February 28, 2018.

[51] Early signs, however, have been promising. In January 2017, the victor of the 2016 presidential election, Adama Barrow, took office, and in April 2017, parliamentary elections were given the blessing of election observers from the European Union. See Dionne Searcey, "Why Democracy Prevailed in Gambia," *The New York Times*, January 30, 2017, and the Preliminary Statement of the European Union Electoral Observation Mission to the Gambia, April 8, 2017: https://eeas.europa.eu/sites/eeas/files/eu_eom_the_gambia_preliminary_statement_3.pdf [Accessed on August 9, 2017].

[52] On lingering pockets of support for Jammeh, see Jon Rosen, "The Gambia's brutal strongman has been forced from power. What will happen to his staunchest supporters?," *Slate*, August 7, 2017. www.slate.com/articles/news_and_politics/roads/2017/08/the_gambia_s_brutal_strongman_has_been_forced_from_power_what_will_happen.html [Accessed on August 10, 2017].

[53] See Jeffrey Gettleman, "Election in Tanzania to Challenge Half a Century of One-Party Rule," *The New York Times*, October 23, 2015, and "Tanzania's Elections Go Off Well, Except on Zanzibar," *The Economist*, October 30, 2015.

polls (Hoffman and Robinson 2009: 125), it would most likely perform well under democracy. Similarly, Mozambique held a relatively competitive election in 2014 (Azevedo-Harman 2015). Given its revolutionary ancestry and role in winning independence from Portugal, FRELIMO would benefit from a strong brand in a hypothetical democratic future. In addition, because of powerful opposition from the Mozambican National Resistance (RENAMO), it would most likely avoid schisms, given LeBas' argument (Chapter 6, this volume) about the role of strong opposition parties for maintaining cohesion.

In sum, in considering the future of authoritarian successor parties, two different questions must be asked: When, if ever, do they become "normal" parties? And where might new ones emerge? The first question is ripe for further research, with scholars examining authoritarian successor parties that emerged during the second wave and the beginning of the third wave. The second question cannot be answered definitively, but it is highly likely that new cases will emerge in the future. Authoritarian successor parties exist in most new democracies and, as such, to the extent that there are new cases of democratization, we should also expect to see new examples of such parties.

PATHS OUT OF DICTATORSHIP

There is a strong likelihood that new authoritarian successor parties will emerge in the future. But *how* might they emerge? What paths might democratizing countries traverse from authoritarian *regimes* to authoritarian *successor parties*? The two most thoughtful considerations of this question to date come from previous works by contributors to this volume. In her study of African party systems, Riedl (2014) charts two broad paths: in one, the authoritarian ruling party, with the support of local elites, retains control during the transition; uses this control to impose electoral rules to its advantage; and thrives under democracy as an authoritarian successor party (e.g., Ghana). In the other, the authoritarian ruling party, lacking the support of local elites, loses control of the transition and collapses (e.g., Benin).[54] In the context of Asia, Slater and Wong (2013) likewise chart two broad paths. The first is what they call "conceding to thrive." In response to ominous signals, authoritarian incumbents initiate a transition to democracy, on the calculation that they will be rewarded for doing so and thrive in the new regime as authoritarian successor parties. The authors present Taiwan, South Korea, and Indonesia – all of whose ruling parties initiated transitions to democracy from a position of strength (albeit at different points within the "bittersweet spot") rather than wait for the regime to fall into terminal crisis – as illustrations. Implicit in their argument is a second

---

[54] According to Riedl (2014), whether these parties are able to control the transition is itself rooted in authoritarian incumbents' earlier decision about whether to follow a strategy of "incorporation" or "substitution."

path: ruling parties that do *not* respond to ominous signals and concede democracy in time are unlikely to do well under democracy. Thus, despite differences in their arguments, both Riedl (2014) and Slater and Wong (2013) posit two broad paths from authoritarian regime to authoritarian successor party: a "success" path, in which the party maintains the upper hand during the transition and thrives; and a "failure" path, in which it does not and suffers the consequences.

While these studies offer important insights into the paths followed by the countries on which they focus, an examination of the broader universe of cases indicates that there are in fact multiple pathways.[55] The first is the "Taiwan model." In this model, the party wins the founding election, and possibly one or more subsequent elections, but eventually loses power in the normal alternation of democratic politics. As Cheng and Huang (Chapter 2, this volume) and Slater and Wong (Chapter 9, this volume) discuss, this was the path followed by Taiwan's KMT.[56] Other countries that followed this path include Lithuania, Macedonia, Paraguay, Romania, and South Korea. In all of these cases, the path from authoritarian regime to authoritarian successor party was a smooth one. While they eventually lost power, they remained among their countries' most important political actors – and were typically voted back into office once again at a later point. This is the pathway that most closely adheres to Riedl (2014) and Slater and Wong's (2013) success scenarios.

The second path is the "Poland model." In this model, the party loses the founding election – sometimes badly, as in Poland in 1989 – but recovers and returns to power in subsequent elections. In addition to Poland, this was the path followed in countries such as Albania, Bulgaria, Cape Verde, Croatia, the Dominican Republic, Ghana, Guyana, Hungary, Madagascar, Mexico, Moldova, Mongolia, Nicaragua, Panama, Serbia, and Slovenia. While authoritarian successor parties in all of these countries eventually returned to office, they did so only after spending time in opposition. These cases do not fit the scenarios laid out by Riedl (2014) and Slater and Wong (2013). Because they lost founding elections, they could *not* tailor-make electoral institutions to their advantage (Riedl), nor could they expect to benefit from an abundance of good will from the electorate (Slater and Wong). Indeed, in some cases they lost under the worst possible circumstances, including

---

[55] For details on individual countries, see Appendix I.1 and Appendix I.2 of the Introduction (Loxton, this volume).
[56] Here I follow Cheng and Huang (Chapter 2, this volume) and Slater and Wong (Chapter 9, this volume) and treat Taiwan as democratic during the 1990s. According to Slater and Wong (Chapter 9, this volume), Taiwan's 1992 legislative election was its "first full and free electoral contest," and they suggest that the 1996 presidential election, which the KMT won, was also fully democratic. In treating Taiwan in the 1990s as democratic, I depart from Geddes, Wright, and Frantz (2014a) and Levitsky and Way (2010: 309–318), who characterize the 2000 presidential election as Taiwan's first fully democratic election. For all other countries in this section, however, I use Geddes, Wright, and Frantz's (2014a) dates for transitions to democracy.

a military invasion by the United States in 1989–1990 in the case of Panama and the loss of every single seat up for election but one in 1989 in the case of Poland. The fact that authoritarian successor parties were able to rebound – and quickly: in both Panama and Poland, they were voted back into office in the next election – suggests that history is not destiny. While it is almost certainly an advantage to hold the reins during the transition to democracy, success does not depend on it. In countries that followed the "Poland model," post-transition factors, such as the performance of the new democracy and whether or not parties crafted effective strategies to offload their authoritarian baggage (Loxton, Introduction), seemed to play a critical role.

The third path is the "Indonesia model." In this model, the party loses the founding election and never returns to the presidency or prime minister's office, but remains a significant actor either as a junior coalition partner or as a powerful opposition party. As Slater and Wong (Chapter 9, this volume) show, this was the case of Indonesia's Golkar, which has held cabinet positions in multiple governments since the 1999 transition to democracy, but has never returned to the top job. Other countries that have followed this path include Brazil, the Czech Republic, Germany, Lesotho, Malawi, Peru, São Tomé and Príncipe, and Slovakia. Although Slater and Wong (2013; Chapter 9, this volume) place Golkar together with Taiwan's KMT and South Korea's DJP/Saenuri as an example of "conceding to thrive," it has not been nearly as successful as these other parties – nor is it a case of unambiguous failure like Benin's PRPB. These middling cases require their own category. (Conceivably, they could actually be split into two categories: the "Indonesia model," in which the party holds cabinet positions, and the "Czech model," in which it remains an important opposition party but never participates in government.)[57]

The fourth path is the "Benin model." In this model, the authoritarian successor party is stillborn. As Riedl and LeBas discuss in their chapters in this volume, this was the fate of Benin's authoritarian ruling party, the PRPB, which collapsed during the transition to democracy. Other countries that followed this path include Estonia, Latvia, Kenya, and the Philippines.[58] To be sure, former authoritarian officials often found other ways to remain influential. In Benin, former dictator Mathieu Kérékou was elected president as an independent in 1996. In Kenya, KANU collapsed, but former KANU officials migrated to other parties and were elected to office as

---

[57] These two categories correspond to Sartori's (1976) distinction between "coalition potential" and "blackmail potential," the two criteria that he used to count the number of "relevant" parties.

[58] In the 1992 election, Kilusang Bagong Lipunan (KBL) presidential candidate Imelda Marcos won 10.3 percent of the vote, and thus the KBL technically meets the criteria to be considered a "prominent" authoritarian successor party, as operationalized in Appendix I.1 of the Introduction (Loxton, this volume). However, the KBL never again replicated this feat, and, for all intents and purposes, disappeared after the transition to democracy.

part of a broader authoritarian diaspora. And in the Philippines, several close family members of former dictator Ferdinand Marcos were elected to positions of influence under democracy, including his widow Imelda Marcos and his son Ferdinand "Bongbong" Marcos, despite the collapse of his former ruling party.[59] None of these countries, however, produced viable authoritarian successor parties.

A final (hypothetical) path is the "Montenegro model." In this model, the party wins the founding election – and all subsequent elections. As mentioned above, this has been the case in Montenegro, with the DPS winning all elections since democratization (Komar and Živković 2016; Vuković 2015). This is the only case, however, of an authoritarian successor party that has never lost power. Because Montenegro only became independent in 2006, there is good reason to be skeptical about whether such a thing as the "Montenegro model" really exists. The party's unbroken winning streak is almost certainly an artifact of Montenegro's short history, and in time, the DPS will likely lose, since, as Przeworski (1991: 10) reminds us, "Democracy is a system in which parties lose elections." In fact there are already signs that support for the DPS is beginning to slip.[60] Thus, while the "Montenegro model" theoretically exists, it is likely that Montenegro will eventually move into the column of the "Taiwan model."

The existence of these multiple paths out of dictatorship, in addition to providing a more complete account of the origins of authoritarian successor parties, has normative and policy implications. As discussed in the Introduction (Loxton, this volume), one of the potential salutary effects of authoritarian successor parties is that they can encourage new transitions to democracy – an argument made eloquently by Slater and Wong (2013). Given the role of timing in their argument, the implication is clear: authoritarian incumbents should get out while the getting is good so that they can thrive as authoritarian successor parties. The discussion in this section both supports and challenges this view. On the one hand, parties that followed the "Taiwan model" and thus adhered most closely to the "conceding to thrive" scenario *do* seem to have had the easiest time under democracy. If democratization is normatively desirable, then policymakers should advocate this scenario to current authoritarian incumbents. However, doing so also has the potential to backfire: if the message to authoritarian incumbents is "You could thrive under democracy, but only if you don't wait too long" – and then they *do* wait too long, what then? This section has shown, however, that this message is too emphatic. A more

---

[59] See Norimitsu Onishi, "Imelda Marcos Seeks to Restore Philippine Dynasty," *The New York Times*, May 8, 2010, and Floyd Whaley, "30 Years After Revolution, Some Filipinos Yearn for 'Golden Age' of Marcos," *The New York Times*, February 23, 2016.

[60] See Aleksandar Vasovic, "Muddy Vote Result Weakens Djukanovic's 25-Year Grip on Montenegro," *Reuters*, October 16, 2016, and Andrew MacDowall, "Montenegro's Prime Minister Resigns, Perhaps Bolstering Country's E.U. Hopes," *The New York Times*, October 26, 2016.

accurate, if less pithy, message would be something like: "You could thrive under democracy. It is better for you if you don't wait too long – but even if you do, there is still a pretty good chance that you will be fine." Clearly, the different pathways discussed in this section are not equally desirable for authoritarian incumbents. (The order of desirability would be the Montenegro model, the Taiwan model, the Poland model, the Indonesia model, and finally the Benin model.) None of them, however, is categorically *un*desirable. Even in cases where no significant authoritarian successor party emerged – the "Benin model" – former authoritarian officials often remained influential.

CONCLUSION

This volume has demonstrated, for the first time, that authoritarian successor parties are a standard feature of democratization. They have been prominent actors in nearly three-quarters of all third-wave democracies, and have been elected back into office in over one-half of all third-wave democracies. They have been major actors in Africa, Asia, Europe, and Latin America. For better or worse, authoritarian successor parties are a normal part of democracy: it is normal for them to exist, it is normal for them to win large numbers of votes, and it is normal for them to return to power. While media accounts often treat the election of an authoritarian successor party as a freak occurrence, this book has shown that the opposite is true: the unusual cases are those in which an authoritarian successor party is not elected back into office, and the truly weird cases are those in which there is no authoritarian successor party at all.

In addition to making an empirical contribution by systematically documenting the global prevalence of authoritarian successor parties, the volume has made conceptual and theoretical contributions. It has developed an original set of terms, concepts, and definitions to facilitate a new research agenda on authoritarian successor parties worldwide. These have been designed to serve as a common language that can travel across regions – something that, to date, has not existed. Theoretically, it has introduced a new set of research questions that can and should be pursued further: What explains the prevalence of authoritarian successor parties? Why are some more successful than others? What strategies can they employ to deal with the past? And what are their effects on democracy? While the chapters in this volume have provided tentative answers to all of these questions, the study of authoritarian successor parties is still at an early stage. More research needs to be done. For such a widespread phenomenon, there is much about these parties that we simply do not know. One thing, however, is clear: there is life after dictatorship.

Bibliography

Abegaz, Berhanu. 2013. "Political Parties in Business: Rent-seekers, Developmentalists, or Both?" *The Journal of Development Studies* 49(11): 1467–1483.
Abente-Brun, Diego. 2009. "Paraguay: The Unraveling of One-Party Rule." *Journal of Democracy* 20(1): 143–156.
Acemoglu, Daron and James Robinson. 2006. *Economic Origins of Dictatorship and Democracy*. New York, NY: Cambridge University Press.
Ackerman, John M. 2012. "The Return of the Mexican Dinosaur." *Foreign Policy*, July 2.
Adrogué, Gerardo. 1993. "Los ex militares en política. Bases sociales y cambios en los patrones de representación política." *Desarrollo Económico* 33(131): 425–442.
Ágh, Attila. 1995. "Partial Consolidation of the East-Central European Parties: The Case of the Hungarian Socialist Party." *Party Politics* 1(4): 491–514.
Agosto, Gabriela and Francisco Cueto Villamán. 2001. "República Dominicana." In Manuel Alcántara Sáez and Flavia Freidenberg, eds., *Partidos Políticos de América Latina: Centroamérica, México y República Dominicana*, pp. 615–698. Salamanca: Ediciones Universidad de Salamanca.
Aguayo, Sergio and Alberto Serdán. 2009. "Es Gordillo maestra del presupuesto." *Reforma*, December 13, p. 6
Aibar, Julio. 2005. "El retorno del general. El bussismo, la otra cara de la democracia argentina." *Perfiles Latinoamericanos* 26: 199–226.
Alba Vega, Carlos. 2006. "Los empresarios y la democracia en México." *Foro Internacional* 46(1): 122–149.
Albertus, Michael. 2015. *Autocracy and Redistribution: The Politics of Land Reform*. New York, NY: Cambridge University Press.
Albertus, Michael and Victor Menaldo. 2014. "Gaming Democracy: Elite Domination during Transition and the Prospects for Redistribution." *British Journal of Political Science* 44(3): 575–603.
  2017. *Authoritarianism and the Elite Origins of Democracy*. New York, NY: Cambridge University Press.
Aldrich, John. 1995. *Why Parties? The Origin and Transformation of Political Parties in America*. Chicago, IL: University of Chicago Press.

Alexander, Gerard. 2002. *The Sources of Democratic Consolidation*. Ithaca, NY: Cornell University Press.
Alidu, Seidu. 2010. "The National Reconciliation Commission and Reconciliation in Ghana." *Review of International Affairs (Belgrade)* 61: 153–177.
Almeida, Ludmila Chaves. 2004. "PPB: origem e trajetória de um partido de direita no Brasil." MA thesis, Department of Political Science, University of São Paulo.
Amsden, Alice. 1989. *Asia's Next Giant: South Korea and Late Industrialization*. New York: Oxford University Press.
Ansell, Ben and David Samuels. 2014. *Inequality and Democratization: A Contractarian Approach*. New York, NY: Cambridge University Press.
Ansell, Christopher K. and M. Steven Fish. 1999. "The Art of Being Indispensable: Noncharismatic Personalism in Contemporary Political Parties." *Comparative Political Studies* 32(3): 283–312.
Arriola, Leonardo. 2012. *Multi-Ethnic Coalitions in Africa: Business Financing of Opposition Election Campaigns*. New York, NY: Cambridge University Press.
Aspinall, Edward. 2010. "Indonesia: The Irony of Success." *Journal of Democracy* 21 (2): 20–34.
  2014. "Popular Agency and Interests in Indonesia's Democratic Transition and Consolidation." In Michele Ford and Thomas Pepinsky, eds., *Beyond Oligarchy: Wealth, Power, and Contemporary Indonesian Politics*, pp. 117–138. Ithaca, NY: Cornell Southeast Asia Program.
Auyero, Javier. 2001. *Poor People's Politics: Peronist Survival Networks and the Legacy of Evita*. Durham: Duke University Press.
  2007. *Routine Politics and Collective Violence in Argentina. The Gray Zone of State Power*. New York, NY: Cambridge University Press.
Avilés, Karla. 2012. "Al descubierto, plan del SNTE para captar 5 millones de votos." *La Jornada*, June 25.
Ayee, Joseph. 2004. "Ghana: A Top-Down Initiative." In Dele Olowu and James Wunsch, eds., *Local Governance in Africa: The Challenges of Democratic Decentralization*, pp. 125–154. Boulder, CO: Lynne Rienner Publishers.
  2009. "The Evolution and Development of the New Patriotic Party in Ghana." South African Institute of International Affairs, Political Party Systems in Africa Project. Occasional Paper #19.
Azevedo-Harman, Elisabete. 2015. "Patching Things Up in Mozambique." *Journal of Democracy* 26(2): 139–150.
Azpuru, Dinorah. 2003. "Democracy at Risk: Citizens' Support for Undemocratic Options." PhD dissertation, University of Pittsburgh.
Babireski, Flávia Roberta. 2013. "As diferenças entre a direita do Brasil, Chile e Uruguai: análise dos programas e manifestos partidários." *Revista Paraná Eleitoral* 3(1): 171–198.
Bajrovic, Ivana Cvetkovic and Janet Rabin Satter. 2014. "Albania: From Bunkers to Ballots." *Journal of Democracy* 25(1): 142–153.
Baker, Andy. 2009. "Regionalized Voting Behavior and Political Discussion in Mexico." In Jorge Domínguez, Chappell Lawson, and Alejandro Moreno, eds., *Consolidating Mexico's Democracy: The 2006 Presidential Campaign in Comparative Perspective*, pp. 71–88. Baltimore, MD: Johns Hopkins University Press.
Bako-Arifari, Nassirou. 1998. "La Démocratie à Founougo (Borgou): Paysans et 'Déscolarisés' en Compétition Pour le Pouvoir Local." In Thomas Bierschenk and

Jean-Pierre Olivier de Sardan, eds., *Les Pouvoirs au Village: le Bénin Rural entre Démocratisation et Décentralisation*, pp. 57–100. Paris: Editions Karthala.
Balfour, Sebastian. 2005. "The Reinvention of Spanish Conservatism: The Popular Party since 1989." In Sebastian Balfour, ed., *The Politics of Contemporary Spain*, pp. 146–168. New York, NY: Routledge.
Banda, Darlington Amos. 1997. *The Trade Union Situation in Zambia: An Overview of the Law, Practice and the Way Forward; a Monogram*. Lusaka: Friedrich Ebert Stiftung.
Banegas, Richard. 2003. *La Démocratie à Pas de Caméléon : Transition et Imaginaires Politiques au Bénin*. Paris: Karthala.
Baral, Lok Raj. 1995. "The 1994 Nepal Elections: Emerging Trends in Party Politics." *Asian Survey* 35(5): 426–440.
Barkan, Joel. 2008. "Legislatures on the Rise?" *Journal of Democracy* 19(2): 124–137.
  ed. 2009. *Legislative Power in Emerging African Democracies*. Boulder, CO: Lynne Rienner Publishers.
Barkan, Joel and John Okumu. 1978. "'Semi-Competitive' Elections, Clientelism, and Political Recruitment in a No-Party State: The Kenyan Experience." In Guy Hermet, Richard Rose, and Alain Rouquié, eds., *Elections without Choice*, pp. 88–107. London: Macmillan.
Bates, Robert. 1971. *Unions, Parties, and Political Development: A Study of Mineworkers in Zambia*. New Haven, CT: Yale University Press.
Béjar Alagazi, Luisa. 2014. "Cuando el ejecutivo es débil, ¿quién legisla en México?" *Política y Gobierno* 21(2): 327–349.
Ben-Ami, Shlomo. 1978. *The Origins of the Second Republic in Spain*. Oxford: Oxford University Press.
Benoit, Kenneth. 2004. "Models of Electoral System Change." *Electoral Studies* 23(3): 363–389.
Bensusán, Graciela and Kevin Middlebrook. 2013. *Sindicatos y política en México: Cambios, continuidades y contradicciones*. Mexico: UAM, FLACSO, and CLACSO.
Bensusán, Graciela and Luis Arturo Tapia. 2011. "El SNTE: Una experiencia singular en el sindicalismo mexicano." *El Cotidiano* 168: 17–32.
Berggren, Lena. 2002. "Swedish Fascism: Why Bother?" *Journal of Contemporary History* 37(3): 395–417.
Berman, Sheri. 1998. *The Social Democratic Moment: Ideas and Politics in the Making of Interwar Europe*. Cambridge, MA: Harvard University Press.
Bermeo, Nancy. 2003. *Ordinary People in Extraordinary Times: The Citizenry and the Breakdown of Democracy*. Princeton, NJ: Princeton University Press.
Bernhard, Michael H. 2005. *Institutions and the Fate of Democracy: Germany and Poland in the Twentieth Century*. Pitt Series in Russian and East European Studies. Pittsburgh: University of Pittsburgh Press.
Besley, Tim and Torsten Persson. 2012. *Pillars of Prosperity: The Political Economics of Development Clusters*. Princeton, NJ: Princeton University Press.
Bierschenk, Thomas and Jean-Pierre Olivier de Sardan, eds. 1998. *Les Pouvoirs au Village: le Bénin Rural entre Démocratisation et Décentralisation*. Paris: Editions Karthala.
Bíró-Nagy, András. 2013. "Hungary." In Jean-Michael de Waele, Fabien Escalona, and Mathieu Vieira, eds., *The Palgrave Handbook of Social Democracy in the European Union*, pp. 452–269. London: Palgrave Macmillan.

Blackbourn, David and Geoff Eley. 1984. *The Peculiarities of German History: Bourgeois Society and Politics in Nineteenth-Century Germany*. New York: Oxford University Press.

Blaževiè, Igor. 2016. "Burma Votes for Change: The Challenges Ahead." *Journal of Democracy* 27(2): 101–115.

Bleck, Jaimie and Nicolas van de Walle. 2013. "Valence Issues in African Elections: Navigating Uncertainty and the Weight of the Past." *Comparative Political Studies* 46(11): 1394–1421.

Boafo-Arthur, Kwame. 2003. "Political Parties and Democratic Sustainability in Ghana, 1992–2000." In M.A. Mohamed Salih, ed., *African Political Parties: Evolution, Institutionalisation and Governance*, pp. 207–238. London: Pluto Press.

Bob-Milliar, George. 2012. "Political Party Activism in Ghana: Factors Influencing the Decision of the Politically Active to Join a Political Party." *Democratization* 19(4): 668–689.

Bochsler, Daniel. 2010. "The Party System of Serbia." In Vera Stojarová and Peter Emerson, eds., *Party Politics in the Western Balkans*, pp. 99–118. New York, NY: Routledge.

Boer, Remco. 2008. "The Anti-Revolutionary Vanguard: The Party Cadre of the Anti-Revolutionary Party in the Netherlands, 1869–1888." MPhil, Leiden University.

Borges, André. 2011. "The Political Consequences of Center-Led Redistribution in Brazilian Federalism: The Fall of Subnational Party Machines." *Latin American Research Review* 46(3): 21–45.

Bormann, Nils-Christian and Matt Golder. 2013. "Democratic Electoral Systems around the World, 1946–2011." *Electoral Studies* 32(2): 360–369.

Bozóki, András. 1997. "The Ideology of Modernization and the Policy of Materialism: The Day after the Socialists." *Journal of Communist Studies and Transition Politics* 13(3): 56–102.

Bozóki, András and John T. Ishiyama, eds. 2002. *The Communist Successor Parties of Central and Eastern Europe*. Armonk: M. E. Sharpe.

Brancati, Dawn. 2017. "Global Elections Database" [computer file]. New York: Global Elections Database. Available from: www.globalelectionsdatabase.com [Accessed January 20, 2017].

Bratton, Michael. 1980. *The Local Politics of Rural Development: Peasant and Party-State in Zambia*. Hanover, NH: University Press of New England.

1992. "Zambia Starts Over." *Journal of Democracy* 3(2): 81–94.

Bratton, Michael and Nicolas van de Walle. 1997. *Democratic Experiments in Africa: Regime Transitions in Comparative Perspective*. Cambridge: Cambridge University Press.

Briggs, Ryan C. 2012. "Electrifying the Base? Aid and Incumbent Advantage in Ghana." *The Journal of Modern African Studies* 50(4): 603–624.

Brownlee, Jason. 2007a. *Authoritarianism in an Age of Democratization*. New York, NY: Cambridge University Press.

2007b. "Hereditary Succession in Modern Autocracies." *World Politics* 59(4): 595–628.

Bruce, Raphael and Rudi Rocha. 2014. "A reação da elite política incumbente na abertura democrática brasileira." Department of Economics, University of São Paulo. Working Paper # 9.

Burdette, Marcia M. 1988. *Zambia: Between Two Worlds*. Boulder, CO: Westview Press.
Camp, Roderic Ai. 2005. *Mexico's Military on the Democratic Stage*. Washington, DC: Center for Strategic and International Studies.
Cannadine, David. 1999. *The Decline and Fall of the British Aristocracy*. New York: Vintage.
Cantanhêde, Eliane. 2001. *O PFL*. São Paulo: Publifolha.
Cantú, Francisco and Desposato, Scott. 2012. "The New Federalism of Mexico's Party System." *Journal of Politics in Latin America* 4(2): 3–38.
Cantú, Jesús. 2009. "Los brazos del SNTE." *Proceso* 1719, October 11.
Capoccia, Giovanni. 2005. *Defending Democracy: Reactions to Extremism in Interwar Europe*. Baltimore, MD: Johns Hopkins University Press.
Carey, John and Matthew Soberg Shugart. 1995. "Incentives to Cultivate a Personal Vote: A Rank Ordering of Electoral Formulas." *Electoral Studies* 14(4): 417–439.
Carlin, Ryan, Gregory Love, and Cecilia Martinez-Gallardo. 2014. "Cushioning the Fall: Scandals, Economic Conditions, and Executive Approval." *Political Behavior* 37(1): 109–130.
Carr, Edward Hallett. 1946. *The Twenty Years' Crisis, 1919–1939: An Introduction to the Study of International Relations*. London: Macmillan & co. ltd.
Carrión, Julio F. 2006. "Public Opinion, Market Reforms, and Democracy in Fujimori's Peru." In Julio F. Carrión, ed., *The Fujimori Legacy: The Rise of Electoral Authoritarianism in Peru*, pp. 126–149. University Park, PA: Pennsylvania State University Press.
Carvalho, Alessandra. 2008. "Elites políticas durante o regime militar: um estudo sobre os parlamentares da ARENA e do MDB." PhD dissertation, Graduate Program in Sociology and Anthropology, Federal University of Rio de Janeiro.
Castañeda, Jorge and Héctor Aguilar Camín. 2009. "Un futuro para México." *Nexos*, November 1.
Chabal, Patrick and Jean-Pascal Daloz. 1999. *Africa Works: Disorder as Political Instrument*. Bloomington, IN: Indiana University Press.
Chang, Alex, Yun-han Chu, and Bridget Welsh. 2013. "Southeast Asia: Sources of Regime Support." *Journal of Democracy* 24(2): 150–164.
Chang, Yu-tzung, Yun-han Chu, and Chong-Min Park. 2007. "Authoritarian Nostalgia in Asia." *Journal of Democracy* 18(3): 66–80.
Chao, Linda and Ramon Myers. 1998. *The First Chinese Democracy: Political Life in the Republic of China on Taiwan*. Baltimore, MD: Johns Hopkins University Press.
Cheibub, José Antonio, Jennifer Gandhi, and James Raymond Vreeland. 2010. "Democracy and Dictatorship Revisited." *Public Choice* 143(1/2): 67–101.
Cheng, Tun-jen. 1989. "Democratizing the Quasi-Leninist Regime in Taiwan." *World Politics* 41(4): 471–499.
1990a. "Is The Dog Barking? The Middle Class and Democratization in the East Asian NICs." *International Studies Notes* 15(1): 10–16.
1990b. "Political Regimes and Development Strategies: South Korea and Taiwan." In Gary Gereffi and Donald Wyman, eds., *Manufacturing Miracles: Patterns of Development in Latin American and East Asia*, pp. 139–178. Princeton, NJ: Princeton University Press.
2006. "Strategizing Party Adaptation: The Case of the Kuomintang." *Party Politics* 12(3): 367–394.

2008. "Embracing Defeat: the KMT and the PRI after 2000." In Edward Friedman and Joseph Wong, eds., *Political Transitions in Dominant Party Systems: Learning to Lose*, pp. 127–147. New York, NY: Routledge.

Cheng, Tun-jen and Eun Mee Kim. 1994. "Making Democracy: Generalizing the South Korean Case." In Edward Friedman, ed., *The Politics of Democratization: Generalizing East Asian Experiences*, pp. 125–147. Boulder, CO: Westview Press.

Cheng, Tun-jen and Yung-ming Hsu. 2015. "Long in the Making: Taiwan's Institutionalized Party System." In Allen Hicken and Erik Martinez Kuhonta, eds., *Party System Institutionalization in Asia*, pp. 260–279. New York, NY: Cambridge University Press.

Chirambo, Reuben. 2004. "'Operation Bwezani': The Army, Political Change, and Dr. Banda's Hegemony in Malawi." *Nordic Journal of African Studies* 13(2): 146–163.

Chu, Yun-han. 2012. "The Taiwan Factor." *Journal of Democracy* 23(1): 42–56.

CIDE and COFETEL. 2011. *Condiciones del mercado de televisión abierta en México*. Mexico: CIDE.

Ciria, Alberto. 1983. *Política y cultura popular: la Argentina peronista, 1946–1955*. Buenos Aires: Ediciones de la Flor.

Clark, John. 1997. "Petro-Politics in Congo." *Journal of Democracy* 8(3): 62–76.

Clark, Terry D. and Jovita Praneviciute. 2008. "Perspectives on Communist Successor Parties: The Case of Lithuania." *Communist and Post-Communist Studies* 41: 443–464.

Collier, David and Ruth Berins Collier. 1991. *Shaping the Political Arena: Critical Junctures, the Labor Movement, and Regime Dynamics in Latin America*. Princeton, NJ: Princeton University Press.

Collier, David and Steven Levitsky. 1997. "Democracy with Adjectives: Conceptual Innovation in Comparative Research." *World Politics* 49(3): 430–451.

Collier, Ruth Berins. 1982. *Regimes in Tropical Africa: Changing Forms of Supremacy, 1945–1975*. Berkeley, CA: University of California Press.

Conaghan, Catherine M. 2005. *Fujimori's Peru: Deception in the Public Sphere*. Pittsburgh: University of Pittsburgh Press.

Conaghan, Catherine M., James M. Malloy, and Luis A. Abugattas. 1990. "Business and the 'Boys': The Politics of Neoliberalism in the Central Andes." *Latin American Research Review* 25(2): 3–33.

Cook, Maria. 1996. *Organizing Dissent: Unions, the State, and the Democratic Teachers' Movement in Mexico*. University Park, PA: Pennsylvania State University Press.

2007. *The Politics of Labor Reform in Latin America: Between Flexibility and Rights*. University Park, PA: Pennsylvania State University Press.

Copeland, Nicholas Matthew. 2007. "Bitter Earth: Counterinsurgency Strategy and Roots of Mayan Neo-Authoritarianism in Guatemala." PhD dissertation, University of Texas at Austin.

Copper, John F. 2013. *The KMT Returns to Power: Elections in Taiwan 2008 to 2012*. Lanham, MD: Lexington Books.

Corbellini, Juliano. 2005. "O poder como vocação: o PFL na política brasileira (1984–2002)." PhD dissertation, Department of Political Science, Federal University of Rio Grande do Sul.

Cornelius, Wayne. 1999. "Subnational Politics and Democratization: Tensions between Center and Periphery in the Mexican Political System." In Wayne Cornelius, Todd Eisenstadt, and Jane Hindley, eds., *Subnational Politics and Democratization in Mexico*, pp. 3–18. La Jolla, CA: Center for U.S.-Mexican Studies and University of California, San Diego.
  2000. "Blind Spots in Democratization: Sub-national Politics as a Constraint on Mexico's Transition." *Democratization* 7(3): 117–132.
  2002. "Mobilized Voting in the 2000 Elections: The Changing Efficacy of Vote Buying and Coercion in Mexican Electoral Politics." In Jorge Domínguez and Chappell Lawson, eds., *Mexico's Pivotal Election: Candidates Voters and the Presidential Campaign of 2000*, pp. 47–65. Palo Alto, CA: Stanford University Press.
Corrales, Javier. 2013. "Venezuela's Succession Crisis." *Current History* 112(251): 56–63.
Craig, Fred W. S. 1976. *Electoral Facts, 1885–1975*. London: Macmillan Press.
Creevey, Lucy, Paul Ngomo, and Richard Vengroff. 2005. "Party Politics and Different Paths to Democratic Transitions: A Comparison of Benin and Senegal." *Party Politics* 11(4): 471–493.
Crenzel, Emilio. 1999. "Memorias de la dictadura: Los desaparecidos y el voto al general Bussi en Tucumán, Argentina." *Revista Internacional de Filosofía* 14: 15–29.
Croissant, Aurel. 2002. "Electoral Politics in South Korea." In Aurel Croissant, Gabriele Bruns, and Marei John, eds., *Electoral Politics in Southeast and East Asia*, pp. 233–276. Friedrich-Ebert-Stiftung Press.
Crouch, Harold. 2010. *Political Reform in Indonesia after Soeharto*. Singapore: Singapore Institute of Southeast Asian Studies.
Cuenca, Alberto. 2010. "Investigan pagos a miembros del SNTE." *El Universal*, March 31.
Dahl, Robert. 1971. *Polyarchy: Participation and Opposition*. New Haven, CT: Yale University Press.
Dahou, Tarik and Vincent Foucher. 2004. "Le Sénégal, entre Changement Politique et Révolution Passive." *Politique Africaine* 96: 5–21.
Darden, Keith and Anna Grzymala-Busse. 2006. "The Great Divide: Literacy, Nationalism, and the Communist Collapse." *World Politics* 59(1): 83–115.
Dargent, Eduardo and Paula Muñoz. 2016. "Peru: A Close Win for Continuity." *Journal of Democracy* 27(4): 145–158.
Dauderstädt, Michael. 2005. "The Communist Successor Parties of Eastern and Central Europe and European Integration." *Journal of Communist Studies and Transition Politics* 21(1): 48–66.
Davidson, John Colin C. 1969. *Memoirs of a Conservative: J. C. C. Davidson's Memoirs and Papers, 1910–37*. London: Weidenfeld and Nicolson.
De Córdoba, José. 2015. "Mexico Investigating Opposition Governor of Sonora." *Wall Street Journal*, March 5.
De la Garza, Paul. 1998. "Banking Scandal Could Cost Mexico $65 Million." *Chicago Tribune*, September 1.
Deming, Jonathan Mark. 2013. "Hewing to the Past: Why Unrepentant Authoritarian Parties Succeed in Democracy, Peru 2000–2011." MA thesis, University of Chicago.
Democratic Accountability and Linkages Project (DALP). Available from: http://sites.duke.edu/democracylinkage [Accessed November 2017].

de Silva, Kingsley M. 1997. "Sri Lanka: Surviving Ethnic Strife." *Journal of Democracy* 8(1): 97–111.
DeVotta, Neil. 2002. "Illiberalism and Ethnic Conflict in Sri Lanka." *Journal of Democracy* 13(1): 84–98.
Diamond, Larry and Marc F. Plattner, eds. 2010. *Democratization in Africa: Progress and Retreat*, 2nd edn. Baltimore, MD: Johns Hopkins University Press.
Díaz-Cayeros, Alberto. 2006. *Federalism, Fiscal Authority, and Centralization in Latin America*. New York, NY: Cambridge University Press.
Díaz-Cayeros, Alberto, Federico Estévez, and Beatriz Magaloni. 2016. *The Political Logic of Poverty Relief: Electoral Strategies and Social Policy in Mexico*. New York, NY: Cambridge University Press.
Díaz Domínguez, Alejandro. 2015. "Confianza en las elecciones: México y América." *Nexos*, June 4.
Díaz Jiménez, Oniel Francisco. 2014. "Party System Change in a New Democracy: The Case of Mexico." *The Copernicus Journal* 1(5): 11–34.
Dickson, Bruce. 1997. *Democratization in China and Taiwan: The Adaptability of Leninist Parties*. Oxford: Clarendon Press.
Dimitrov, Martin K. 2009. "Popular Autocrats." *Journal of Democracy* 20(1): 78–81.
  2016. "Building Anticipatory Governance by Collecting Information on Levels of Popular Discontent in Autocracies." Paper presented at the APSA Annual Meeting. Philadelphia, PA, September 1–4.
Diop, Momar-Coumba and Mamadou Diouf. 2002a. "Léopold Ségar Senghor, Abdou Diouf, Abdoulaye Wade, et Après?" In Donal Cruise O'Brien, Momar-Coumba Diop, and Mamadou Diouf, eds., *La Construction de l'État au Sénégal*, pp. 101–141. Paris: Karthala.
  2002b. "L'administration, les Confréries Religieuses et les Paysanneries. " In Donal Cruise O'Brien, Momar-Coumba Diop, and Mamadou Diouf, eds., *La Construction de l'État au Sénégal*, pp. 29–47. Paris: Karthala.
Di Tella, Guido. 1983. *Perón-Perón, 1973–1976*. Buenos Aires: Hyspamérica.
Di Tella, Torcuato S. 1971/1972. "La búsqueda de la fórmula política argentina." *Desarrollo Económico* 11(42/44): 317–325.
Dix, Robert H. 1978. "The Varieties of Populism: The Case of Colombia." *The Western Political Quarterly* 31(3): 334–351.
Dobry, Michel. 2000. "France: An Ambiguous Survival." In Dirk Berg-Schlosser and Jeremy Mitchell, eds., *Conditions of Democracy in Europe: Systematic Case Studies*, pp. 157–183. Basingstone, Great Britain: Palgrave Macmillan.
Doerschler, Peter and Lee Ann Banaszak. 2007. "Voter Support for the German PDS over Time: Dissatisfaction, Ideology, Losers and East Identity." *Electoral Studies* 26 (2): 359–370.
Domínguez, Jorge I. and James A. McCann. 1996. *Democratizing Mexico: Public Opinion and Electoral Choices*. Baltimore, MD: Johns Hopkins University Press.
Doner, Richard, Brian K. Ritchie, and Dan Slater. 2005. "Systemic Vulnerability and the Origins of Developmental States: Northeast and Southeast Asia in Comparative Perspective." *International Organization* 59(2): 327–361.
Doorenspleet, Renske and Lia Nijzink, eds. 2013. *One-Party Dominance in African Democracies*. Boulder, CO: Lynne Rienner Publishers, Inc.

eds. 2014. *Party Systems and Democracy in Africa*. New York: Palgrave Macmillan.
Dossou, Robert. 2000. "L'Expérience Béninoise de la Conférence Nationale." Paper presented at the *Conférence sur le Bilan des Conférences Nationales et Autres Processus de Transitions Démocratiques*. Cotonou, Benin, February 19–23.
Do Vale, Helder Ferreira. 2016. "Federal Political Fragmentation in Mexico's 2015 Election." *Regional and Federal Studies* 26(2): 121–138.
Downs, Anthony. 1957. *An Economic Theory of Democracy*. New York: Harper and Row.
Dunkerley, James. 1984. *Rebellion in the Veins: Political Struggle in Bolivia, 1952–82*. London: Verso.
Durazo Herrmann, Julián. 2014. "Reflections on Regime Change and Democracy in Bahia, Brazil." *Latin American Research Review* 49(3): 23–44.
Eley, Geoff. 2002. *Forging Democracy: The History of the Left in Europe, 1850–2000*. New York: Oxford University Press.
Elischer, Sebastian. 2008. "Do African Parties Contribute to Democracy? Some Findings from Kenya, Ghana and Nigeria." *Afrika Spectrum* 43(2): 175–201.
Encarnación, Omar G. 2008. "Reconciliation after Democratization: Coping with the Past in Spain." *Political Science Quarterly* 123(3): 435–459.
Englebert, Pierre and James Ron. 2004. "Primary Commodities and War: Congo-Brazzaville's Ambivalent Resource Curse." *Comparative Politics* 37(1): 61–81.
Enyedi, Zsolt. 2006. "The Survival of the Fittest: Party System Concentration in Hungary." In Susanne Jungerstam-Mulders, ed., *Post-Communist EU Member States: Parties and Party Systems*, pp. 177–202. Aldershot: Ashgate.
Ertman, Thomas. 1998. "Democracy and Dictatorship in Interwar Western Europe Revisited." *World Politics* 50(3): 475–505.
Estévez, Federico, Alberto Díaz-Cayeros, and Beatriz Magaloni. 2008. "A House Divided Against itself: The PRI's Survival Strategy after Hegemony." In Edward Friedman and Joseph Wong, eds., *Political Transitions in Dominant Party Systems: Learning to Lose*, pp. 42–56. London: Routledge.
Evans, Geoffrey and Stephen Whitefield. 1995. "Economic Ideology and Political Success: Communist-Successor Parties in the Czech Republic, Slovakia and Hungary Compared." *Party Politics* 1(4): 565–578.
Evans, Peter. 1995. *Embedded Autonomy. States and Industrial Transformations*. Princeton, NJ: Princeton University Press.
Fanthorpe, Richard. 2006. "On the Limits of Liberal Peace: Chiefs and Democratic Decentralization in Post-War Sierra Leone." *African Affairs* 105(418): 27–49.
Fatton, Robert. 1987. *The Making of a Liberal Democracy: Senegal's Passive Revolution, 1975–1985*. Boulder, CO: L. Rienner Publishers.
Feldman, Gerald D. 1971. "Big Business and the Kapp Putsch." *Central European History* 4(2): 99–130.
Fernández Jilberto, Alex and Barbara Hogenbooom. 2007. "Latin American Conglomerates in the Neoliberal Era: The Politics of Economic Concentration in Chile and Mexico." In Alex Fernández Jilberto and Barbara Hogenboom, eds., *Big Business and Economic Development*, pp. 135–166. London: Routledge.
Ferree, Karen and Jeremy Horowitz. 2010. "Ties That Bind? The Rise and Decline of Ethno-Regional Partisanship in Malawi, 1994–2009." *Democratization* 17(3): 534–563.

Fink-Hafner, Danica. 2006. "Slovenia: Between Bipolarity and Broad Coalition-Building." In Susanne Jungerstam-Mulders, ed., *Post-Communist EU Member States: Parties and Party Systems*, pp. 203–232. Farnham: Ashgate Publishing Limited.
Fish, M. Steven. 1998a. "Mongolia: Democracy without Prerequisites." *Journal of Democracy* 9(3): 127–141.
  1998b. "Democratization's Requisites: The Postcommunist Experience." *Post-Soviet Affairs* 14(3): 212–247.
Flores-Macías, Gustavo. 2013. "Mexico's 2012 Elections: The Return of the PRI." *Journal of Democracy* 24(1): 128–141.
  2016. "Mexico's Stalled Reforms." *Journal of Democracy* 27(2): 66–78.
Ford, Michele and Teri Caraway. 2014. "Labor and Politics under Oligarchy." In Michele Ford and Thomas Pepinsky, eds., *Beyond Oligarchy: Wealth, Power, and Contemporary Indonesian Politics*, pp. 139–155. Ithaca, NY: Cornell Southeast Asia Program.
Ford González, Jaime. 2009. *Un hombre, un partido*. Panama: Imprenta Articsa.
Fowler, Brigid. 2003. "The Parliamentary Elections in Hungary, April 2002." *Electoral Studies* 22: 765–807.
Franck, Raphael and Ilia Rainer. 2012. "Does the Leader's Ethnicity Matter? Ethnic Favoritism, Education, and Health in Sub-Saharan Africa." *American Political Science Review* 106(2): 294–325.
Friedman, Edward and Joseph Wong, eds. 2008. *Political Transitions in Dominant Party Systems: Learning to Lose*. New York, NY: Routledge.
Fritz, Verena. 2008. "Mongolia: The Rise and Travails of a Deviant Democracy." *Democratization* 15(4): 766–788.
Gamarra, Eduardo A. and James M. Malloy. 1995. "The Patrimonial Dynamics of Party Politics in Bolivia." In Scott Mainwaring and Timothy R. Scully, eds., *Building Democratic Institutions: Party Systems in Latin America*, pp. 399–433. Stanford, CA: Stanford University Press.
Gandhi, Jennifer. 2008. *Political Institutions under Dictatorship*. New York, NY: Cambridge University Press.
García Díez, Fátima. 2001. "Panamá." In Manuel Alcántara Sáez and Flavia Freidenberg, eds., *Partidos Políticos de América Latina: Centroamérica, México y República Dominicana*, pp. 527–614. Salamanca: Ediciones Universidad de Salamanca.
Garrard-Burnett, Virginia. 2010. *Terror in the Land of the Holy Spirit: Guatemala under General Efraín Ríos Montt, 1982–1983*. New York: Oxford University Press.
Garretón, Manuel Antonio. 2003. *Incomplete Democracy: Political Democratization in Chile and Latin America*. Chapel Hill: University of North Carolina Press.
Garst, J. Daniel. 1998. "From Factor Endowments to Class Struggle: Pre-World War I Germany and Rogowski's Theory of Trade and Political Cleavages." *Comparative Political Studies* 31(1): 22–44.
Gay, Robert. 1994. *Popular Organization and Democracy in Rio de Janeiro: A Tale of Two Favelas*. Philadelphia: Temple University Press.
Geddes, Barbara. 1999. "What Do We Know about Democratization after Twenty Years?" *Annual Review of Political Science* 2: 115–144.

Geddes, Barbara, Joseph Wright, and Erica Frantz. 2014a. "Autocratic Breakdown and Regime Transitions: A New Data Set." *Perspectives on Politics* 12(2): 313–331.
  2014b. *Autocratic Regimes Code Book*. Version 1.2. Available from: https://journals.cambridge.org/action/displaySuppMaterial?cupCode=1&type=4&jid=PPS&volumeId=12&issueId=02&aid=9297187 [Accessed November 12, 2015].
Gerring, John, Philip Bond, William Barndt, and Carola Moreno. 2005. "Democracy and Growth: A Historical Perspective." *World Politics* 57(3): 323–364.
Gerschenkron, Alexander. 1948. *Bread and Democracy in Germany*. Berkeley, CA: University of California Press.
GfK. 2013. "Evaluación de la gestión pública. Indulto a Fujimori." *National Urban Survey*, June. Available from: http://gfk.pe/wp-content/uploads/2013/06/GfK_Pulso_Peru_Junio_2013-Evaluacion_del_gobierno5.pdf [Accessed September 22, 2016].
Gibson, Edward. 1996. *Class and Conservative Parties: Argentina in Comparative Perspective*. Baltimore, MD: Johns Hopkins University Press.
  2012. *Boundary Control: Subnational Authoritarianism in Federal Democracies*. New York, NY: Cambridge University Press.
Gilbert, Leah and Payam Mohseni. 2011. "Beyond Authoritarianism: The Conceptualization of Hybrid Regimes." *Studies in Comparative International Development* 46: 270–297.
Giraudy, Agustina. 2015. *Democrats and Autocrats: Pathways of Subnational Undemocratic Regime Continuity within Democratic Countries*. Oxford: Oxford University Press.
Glennerster, Rachel, Edward Miguel, and Alexander D. Rothenberg. 2013. "Collective Action in Diverse Sierra Leone Communities." *The Economic Journal* 123(568): 285–316.
Godoy, Angelina Snodgrass. 2006. *Popular Injustice: Violence, Community and Law in Latin America*. Palo Alto, CA: Stanford University Press.
Goemans, H. E. 2000. *War and Punishment: The Causes of War Termination and the First World War*. Princeton, NJ: Princeton University Press.
González, Francisco. 2008. *Dual Transitions in Authoritarian Rule: Institutionalized Regimes in Chile and Mexico, 1970–2000*. Baltimore, MD: Johns Hopkins University Press.
  2015. "The Role of Shocks and Social Pressures in the Development of Citizenship Rights: Great Britain and Mexico's Divergent Paths." *Mexican Law Review* 7(2): 37–61.
González Amador, Roberto. 1998. "El exbanquero y su familia llevan por lo menos tres lustros envueltos en escándalos." *La Jornada*, June 6.
  2004. "El fraude de Cabal con sus bancos costo 28 mil millones en dos años." *La Jornada*, May 20.
González-Enríquez, Carmen. 2001. "De-Communization and Political Justice in Central and Eastern Europe." In Alexandra Barahona de Brito, Carmen González-Enríquez, and Paloma Aguilar, eds., *The Politics of Memory: Transitional Justice in Democratizing Societies*, pp. 218–247. New York: Oxford University Press.
González Oropeza, Manuel. 1983. *La intervención federal en la desaparición de poderes*. Mexico: UNAM.

Bibliography

Gould, Andrew. 1999. *Origins of Liberal Dominance: State, Church, and Party in Nineteenth Century Europe*. Ann Arbor: University of Michigan Press.

Gourevitch, Peter Alexis. 1986. *Politics in Hard Times: Comparative Responses to International Economic Crises*. Cornell Studies in Political Economy. Ithaca, NY: Cornell University Press.

Greene, Kenneth. 2007. *Why Dominant Parties Lose: Mexico's Democratization in Comparative Perspective*. New York, NY: Cambridge University Press.

  2015. "Campaign Effects since Mexico's Democratization." In Jorge Domínguez, Kenneth Greene, Chappell Lawson, and Alejandro Moreno, eds., *Mexico's Evolving Democracy: A Comparative Study of the 2012 Elections*, pp. 128–152. Baltimore, MD: Johns Hopkins University Press.

Grinberg, Lucia. 2009. *Partido político ou bode expiatório: um estudo sobre a Aliança Renovadora Nacional (ARENA), 1965–1979*. Rio de Janeiro: Editora Mauad X.

Grugel, Jean. 1992. "Populism and the Political System in Chile: Ibañismo (1952–1958)." *Bulletin of Latin American Research* 11(2): 169–186.

Grzymala-Busse, Anna M. 1998. "Reform Efforts in the Czech and Slovak Communist Parties and Their Successors, 1988–1993." *East European Politics and Societies* 12(3): 442–471.

  2002. *Redeeming the Communist Past: The Regeneration of Communist Parties in East Central Europe*. Cambridge, NY: Cambridge University Press.

  2006. "Authoritarian Determinants of Democratic Party Competition: The Communist Successor Parties in East Central Europe." *Party Politics* 12: 415–436.

  2007. *Rebuilding Leviathan: Party Competition and State Exploitation in Post-Communist Democracies*. New York, NY: Cambridge University Press.

Guevara Mann, Carlos. 1996. *Panamanian Militarism: A Historical Interpretation*. Athens, OH: Ohio University Center for International Studies.

Gulhati, Ravi. 1989. *Impasse in Zambia: The Economics and Politics of Reform*. Washington, DC: World Bank.

Guzmán, Jaime. 2008. *Escritos Personales*, 4th edn. Santiago: Fundación Jaime Guzmán.

Gwiazda, Anna. 2008. "Party Patronage in Poland: The Democratic Left Alliance and Law and Justice Compared." *East European Politics and Societies* 22(4): 802–827.

Gyimah-Boadi, Emmanuel. 1993. *Ghana under PNDC Rule*. Dakar: Codesria.

Haggard, Stephan. 1990. *Pathways from the Periphery: The Politics of Growth in the Newly Industrializing Countries*. Ithaca, NY: Cornell University Press.

Haggard, Stephan and Robert R. Kaufman. 1995. *The Political Economy of Democratic Transitions*. Princeton, NJ: Princeton University Press.

  2008. *Development, Democracy, and Welfare States: Latin America, East Asia, and Eastern Europe*. Princeton, NJ: Princeton University Press.

Hagopian, Frances. 1990. "'Democracy by Undemocratic Means'? Elites, Political Pacts, and Regime Transition in Brazil." *Comparative Political Studies* 23(2): 147–170.

  1996. *Traditional Politics and Regime Change in Brazil*. New York, NY: Cambridge University Press.

Hagopian, Frances, Carlos Gervasoni, and Juan Andrés Moraes. 2008. "From Patronage to Program. The Emergence of Party-Oriented Legislatures in Brazil." *Comparative Political Studies* 42(3): 360–391.
Hale, Henry E. 2004. "Yabloko and the Challenge of Building a Liberal Party in Russia." *Europe-Asia Studies* 56(7): 993–1020.
Handy, Jim. 1984. *Gift of the Devil: A History of Guatemala*. Boston: South End Press.
Hanson, Stephen. 2010. *Post-Imperial Democracies: Ideology and Party Formation in Third Republic France, Weimar Germany, and Post-Soviet Russia*. New York, NY: Cambridge University Press.
Harbers, Imke. 2014. "States and Strategy in New Federal Democracies: Competitiveness and Intra-Party Resource Allocation in Mexico." *Party Politics* 20(6): 823–835.
Harding, Robert Claude. 2001. *Military Foundations of Panamanian Politics*. New Brunswick: Transaction Publishers.
Harmel, Robert and Kenneth Janda. 1982. *Parties and Their Environments: The Limits to Reform*. London: Longman.
Hartlyn, Jonathan. 1998. *The Struggle for Democratic Politics in the Dominican Republic*. Chapel Hill: University of North Carolina Press.
Hartmann, Christof. 2010. "Senegal's Party System: The Limits of Formal Regulation." *Democratization* 17(4): 769–786.
Haughton, Tim. 2004. "Explaining the Limited Success of the Communist-Successor Left in Slovakia: The Case of the Party of the Democratic Left (SDL)." *Party Politics* 10(2): 177–191.
Haughton, Tim and Marek Rybar. 2008. "A Change of Direction: The 2006 Parliamentary Elections and Party Politics in Slovakia." *Journal of Communist Studies and Transition Politics* 24(2): 232–255.
Hayes, William. 1982. *The Background and Passage of the Third Reform Act*. New York: Garland Publishing.
Hayward, Fred M. and Siba N. Grovogui. 1987. "Persistence and Change in Senegalese Electoral Processes." In Fred M. Hayward, ed., *Elections in Independent Africa*, pp. 239–270. Boulder, CO: Westview Press.
Hellmann, Olli. 2011. *Political Parties and Electoral Strategy: The Development of Party Organization in East Asia*. Basingstoke: Palgrave-Macmillan.
Helmke, Gretchen. 2005. *Courts under Constraints: Judges, Generals, and Presidents in Argentina*. New York, NY: Cambridge University Press.
Herbst, Jeffrey. 1993. *The Politics of Reform in Ghana, 1982–1991*. Berkeley, CA: University of California Press.
Hermens, Ferdinand A. 1936. "Proportional Representation and the Breakdown of German Democracy." *Social Research* 3(4): 411–433.
Hernández-Rodríguez, Rogelio. 2003. "The Renovation of Old Institutions: State Governors and the Political Transition in Mexico." *Latin American Politics and Society* 45(4): 97–127.
Hertzman, Lewis. 1958. "The Founding of the German National People's Party (DNVP), November 1918–January 1919." *The Journal of Modern History* 30(1): 24–36.
Hicken, Allen. 2011. "Clientelism." *Annual Review of Political Science* 14: 289–310.
  2015. "Party and Party System Institutionalization in the Philippines." In Allen Hicken and Erik Martinez Kuhonta, eds., *Party System Institutionalization in Asia:*

Democracies, Autocracies, and the Shadows of the Past, pp. 307–327. New York, NY: Cambridge University Press.

Hicken, Allen and Erik Martinez Kuhonta. 2011. "Shadows from the Past: Party System Institutionalization in Asia." *Comparative Political Studies* 44(5): 572–597.

eds. 2015. *Party System Institutionalization in Asia: Democracies, Autocracies, and the Shadows of the Past*. New York, NY: Cambridge University Press.

Higley, John, Judith Kullberg, and Jan Pakulski. 1996. "The Persistence of Postcommunist Elites." *Journal of Democracy* 7(2): 133–147.

Hoffman, Barak and Lindsay Robinson. 2009. "Tanzania's Missing Opposition." *Journal of Democracy* 20(4): 123–136.

Holland, Alisha. 2013. "Right on Crime? Conservative Party Politics and *Mano Dura* Policies in El Salvador." *Latin American Research Review* 48(1): 44–67.

Holland, Alisha and Brian Palmer-Rubin. 2015. "Beyond the Machine: Clientelist Brokers and Interest Organizations in Latin America." *Comparative Political Studies* 48(9): 1186–1223.

Hooven, Marcel ten and Ron de Jong. 2008. *Geschiedenis Van De Christelijk-Historische Unie 1908–1980*. Meppel: Boom Distributie Centrum.

Hopkin, Jonathan. 1999. *Party Formation and Democratic Transition in Spain: The Creation and Collapse of the Union of the Democratic Centre*. Basingstoke: Macmillan.

Horowitz, Donald L. 2013. *Constitutional Change and Democracy in Indonesia*. New York, NY: Cambridge University Press.

Hossain, Golam. 2004. "Bangladesh Nationalist Party: From Military Rule to the Champion of Democracy." In Subrata K. Mitra, Mike Enskat, and Clemens Spiess, eds., *Political Parties in South Asia*, pp. 196–215. Westport: Praeger.

Hough, Dan and Michael Koß. 2009. "Populism Personified or Reinvigorated Reformers? The German Left Party in 2009 and Beyond." *German Politics and Society* 27(2): 76–91.

Houngnikpo, Mathurin C. and Samuel Decalo. 2013. *Historical Dictionary of Benin*, 4th edn. Lanham, MD: Scarecrow Press.

Howard, Marc Morjé and Philip G. Roessler. 2006. "Liberalizing Electoral Outcomes in Competitive Authoritarian Regimes." *American Political Science Review* 50(2): 365–381.

Hsu, Nai-fu. 1992. "Na hsieh shih yi shih Kuomintang te chin mu chi ?" [What are the golden hens of Kuomintang's business?] *Ch'ai-hsun* [Wealth Magazine], November.

Hu, Fu. 1993. "The Electoral Mechanism and Political Change in Taiwan." In Steve Tsang, ed., *In the Shadow of China: Political Developments in Taiwan Since 1949*, pp. 134–168. Honolulu: University of Hawaii Press.

Huang, Teh-fu. 1996. "Elections and the Evolution of the Kuomintang." In Hung-mao Tien, ed., *Taiwan's Electoral Politics and Democratic Transition*, pp. 105–136. Armonk, New York: M. E. Sharpe.

Huerta-Wong, Juan Enrique and Rodrigo Gómez García. 2013. "Concentración y diversidad de los medios de comunicación y las telecomunicaciones en México." *Comunicación y Sociedad* 19: 113–152.

Hughes, Sally and Chappell Lawson. 2004. "Propaganda and Crony Capitalism: Partisan Bias in Mexican Television News." *Latin American Research Review* 39 (3): 81–105.

Human Rights Watch. 2017. *World Report 2017*. New York: Human Rights Watch.
Hunter, Wendy. 2010. *The Transformation of the Brazilian Workers' Party, 1989–2009*. New York, NY: Cambridge University Press.
Hunter, Wendy and Timothy J. Power. 2007. "Rewarding Lula: Executive Power, Social Policy, and the Brazilian Elections of 2006." *Latin American Politics and Society* 49(1): 1–30.
Huntington, Samuel P. 1991. *The Third Wave: Democratization in the Late Twentieth Century*. Norman: University of Oklahoma Press.
  1996. "Democracy for the Long Haul." *Journal of Democracy* 7(2): 3–13.
Ibrahim, Jibrin and Abdoulaye Niandou Souley. 1998. "The Rise to Power of an Opposition Party: The MNSD in Niger Republic." In Adebayo O. Olukoshi, ed., *The Politics of Opposition in Contemporary Africa*, pp. 144–170. Uppsala: Nordiska Afrikainstitutet.
Ichino, Nahomi and Noah L. Nathan. 2012. "Primaries on Demand? Intra-Party Politics and Nominations in Ghana." *British Journal of Political Science* 42(4): 769–791.
  2013. "Do Primaries Improve Electoral Performance? Clientelism and Intra-Party Conflict in Ghana." *American Journal of Political Science* 57(2): 428–441.
Im, Hyug Baeg. 1987. "The Rise of Bureaucratic Authoritarianism in South Korea." *World Politics* 39(2): 231–257.
Instituto de Defensa Legal. 2015. "Balance del gobierno de Ollanta Humala: Un quinquenio sin cambios sustanciales." Seguridad Ciudadana, Informe Anual. Lima, Peru.
Instituto Nacional de Estadística, Geografía, e Informática (INEGI). 2016. *Estadística de defunciones* [online resource]. Mexico: Instituto Nacional de Estadística, Geografía, e Informática.
Instituto Nacional de Estadística, Geografía, e Informática (INEGI). 2017. *Serie histórica censal e intercensal*. Mexico: Instituto Nacional de Estadística, Geografía, e Informática.
Instituto Nacional Electoral (INE). 2016. *Atlas de Resultados de las Elecciones Federales 1991–2015*. Mexico: INE.
Ipsos, Apoyo. 2006. "La elección se polariza." *Resumen de Encuestas a la Opinión Pública* 6(65). Lima: Ipsos Perú.
  2011. "Avanza Keiko." *Resumen de Encuestas a la Opinión Pública* 11(140). Lima: Ipsos Perú.
Ishiyama, John T. 1995. "Communist Parties in Transition: Structures, Leaders and Processes of Democratization in Eastern Europe." *Comparative Politics* 27(2): 147–166.
  1997. "The Sickle or the Rose? Previous Regime Types and the Evolution of the Ex-Communist Parties in Post-Communist Politics." *Comparative Political Studies* 30(3): 299–330.
  1998. "Strange Bedfellows: Explaining Political Cooperation between Communist Successor Parties and Nationalists in Eastern Europe." *Nations and Nationalism* 4(1): 61–85.
  ed. 1999a. *Communist Successor Parties in Post-Communist Politics*. Carmack, NY: Nova Science Publishers.
  1999b. "The Communist Successor Parties and Organizational Development in Post-Communist Politics." *Political Research Quarterly* 52(1): 87–112.

1999c. "Sickles into Roses: The Communist Successor Parties and Democratic Consolidation in Comparative Perspective." *Democratization* 6(4): 52–73.

2000. "Candidate Recruitment, Party Organisation and the Communist Successor Parties: The Case of the MSzP, the KPRF, and the LDDP." *Europe-Asia Studies* 52 (5): 875–896.

2001a. "Party Organization and the Political Success of the Communist Successor Parties." *Political Science Quarterly* 82(4): 844–864.

2001b. "Sickles into Roses: Successor Parties and Democratic Consolidation in Post-Communist Politics." In Paul Lewis, ed., *Party Development and Democratic Change in Post-Communist Europe*, pp. 32–54. London: Frank Cass.

2006. "Europeanization and the Communist Successor Parties in Post-Communist Politics." *Politics and Society* 34(1): 3–29.

2008 "Learning to Lose (and Sometimes Win): The Neocommunist Parties in Post-Soviet Politics." In Edward Friedman and Joseph Wong, eds., *Political Transitions in Dominant Party Systems: Learning to Lose*, Ch. 9. London: Routledge.

Ishiyama, John T. and András Bozóki. 2001. "Adaptation and Change: Characterizing the Survival Strategies of the Communist Successor Parties." *Journal of Communist Studies and Transition Politics* 17(3): 32–51.

Ishiyama, John T. and John James Quinn. 2006. "African Phoenix? Explaining the Electoral Performance of the Formerly Dominant Parties in Africa." *Party Politics* 12(3): 317–340.

Ishiyama, John T. and Sahar Shafqat. 2000. "Party Identity Change in Post-Communist Politics: The Cases of the Successor Parties in Hungary, Poland and Russia." *Communist and Post-Communist Studies* 33: 439–455.

Jackisch, Barry A. 2012. *The Pan-German League and Radical Nationalist Politics in Interwar Germany, 1918–39*. Farnham: Ashgate Publishing Limited.

James, Daniel. 1988. *Resistance and Integration: Peronism and the Argentine Working Class, 1946–1976*. New York, NY: Cambridge University Press.

Janda, Kenneth. 1980. *Political Parties. A Cross-National Survey*. New York: Free Press.

2009. "Laws against Party Switching, Defecting, or Floor-Crossing in National Parliaments." Paper presented at the World Congress of the International Political Science Association. Santiago, Chile, July 12–16.

Janicki, Mariusz. 2002. "Duża partia, duży kłopot." *Polityka*, September 14: 24–26.

Jenks, Margaret Sarles. 1979. "Political Parties in Authoritarian Brazil." PhD dissertation, Department of Political Science, Duke University.

Jetté, Christian, Carmiña Foronda, and Miriam López. 1997. "La renovación de Acción Democrática Nacionalista: ¿hasta dónde se puede ser liberal y fiel al jefe?" In Isabel Arauco, ed., *Gobernabilidad y partidos políticos*, pp. 45–63. La Paz: CIDES-PNUD.

Jhee, Byong-Kuen. 2008. "Economic Origins of Electoral Support for Authoritarian Successors: A Cross-National Analysis of Economic Voting in New Democracies." *Comparative Political Studies* 41(3): 362–388.

Johnson, Chalmers. 1982. *MITI and the Japanese Miracle: The Growth of Industrial Policy, 1925–1975*. Stanford, CA: Stanford University Press.

Joignant, Alfredo and Patricio Navia. 2003. "De la política de individuos a los hombres del partido: Socialización, competencia política y penetración electoral de la UDI (1989–2001)." *Estudios Públicos* 89: 129–171.

Jones, Larry Eugene. 2009. "German Conservatism at the Crossroads: Count Kuno Von Westarp and the Struggle for Control of the DNVP, 1928–30." *Contemporary European History* 18(2): 147–177.

Kalaycioglu, Ersin. 2002. "The Motherland Party: The Challenge of Institutionalization in a Charismatic Leader Party." *Turkish Studies* 3(1): 41–61.

Kalyvas, Stathis N. 1996. *The Rise of Christian Democracy in Europe*. Ithaca, NY: Cornell University Press.

Kamwenda, Gregory. 1997. "Language Rights in the Dictatorship: The Case of Malawi During Dr Banda's Rule." *Language Matters* 28(1): 36–50.

Kandeh, Jimmy D. 2003. "Sierra Leone's Post-Conflict Elections of 2002." *The Journal of Modern African Studies* 41(2): 189–216.

Kanté, Babacar. 1994. "Senegal's Empty Elections." *Journal of Democracy* 5(1): 96–108.

Karl, Terry Lynn. 1990. "Dilemmas of Democratization in Latin America." *Comparative Politics* 23(1): 1–21.

Kasfir, Nelson. 1974. "Departicipation and Political Development in Black African Politics." *Studies in Comparative International Development* 9(3): 3–25.

Kaspin, Deborah. 1995. "The Politics of Ethnicity in Malawi's Democratic Transition." *The Journal of Modern African Studies* 33(4): 595–620.

Keefer, Philip. 2007. "Clientelism, Credibility and the Policy Choices of Young Democracies." *American Journal of Political Science* 51(4): 804–821.

Kelly, Catherine Lena. 2013. "The 2012 Legislative Election in Senegal." *Electoral Studies* 32(4): 905–908.

  2014. "Why (So Many) Parties? The Logic of Party Formation in Senegal." PhD dissertation, Department of Government, Harvard University.

Kim, Byung-kook. 2008. "Defeat in Victory, Victory in Defeat: The Korean Conservative in Democratic Defeat." In Edward Friedman and Joseph Wong, eds., *Political Transitions in Dominant Party Systems: Learning to Lose*, pp. 169–187. New York, NY: Routledge.

Kim, Hyejin. 2014. "A Link to the Authoritarian Past? Older Voters as a Force in the 2012 South Korean Presidential Election." *Taiwan Journal of Democracy* 10(2): 49–71.

Kim, Youngmi. 2011. *The Politics of Coalition in Korea: Between Institutions and Culture*. New York, NY: Routledge.

Kimmo, Elo. 2008. "The Left Party and the Long-Term Developments of the German Party System." *German Politics and Society* 26(3): 50–68.

Kinnear, Michael. 1968. *The British Voter: An Atlas and Survey since 1885*. London: Batsford.

  1973. *The Fall of Lloyd George: The Political Crisis of 1922*. London: Macmillan.

Kinzo, Maria D'Alva Gil. 1988. *Legal Opposition Politics under Authoritarian Rule in Brazil*. New York: St. Martin's.

Kirchick, James. 2012. "Return of the Czech Communists." *Foreign Policy*, October 12.

Kitschelt, Herbert. 1992. "Political Regime Change: Structure and Process-Driven Explanations." *American Political Science Review* 86(4): 1028–1034.

  2000. "Linkages between Citizens and Politicians in Democratic Polities." *Comparative Political Studies* 33(6–7): 845–879.

  2007. "The Demise of Clientelism in Affluent Capitalist Democracies." In Herbert Kitschelt and Steven I. Wilkinson, eds., *Patrons, Clients, and Policies:*

Patterns of Democratic Accountability and Political Competition. Patterns of Democratic Accountability and Competition, pp. 298–321. Cambridge: Cambridge University Press.
   2011a. "Do Institutions Matter for Parties' Political Linkage Strategies?" Paper presented at the APSA Annual Meeting. Seattle, September 1–4.
   2011b. "Clientelistic Linkage Strategies. A Descriptive Exploration." Paper presented at the Workshop on Democratic Accountability Strategies. Duke University, May 18–19.
   2012. "Research and Dialogue on Programmatic Parties and Party Systems. Main Report." January 8. Stockholm: International Institute for Democracy and Electoral Assistance (IDEA).
   2013. "Research and Dialogue on Programmatic Parties and Party Systems. Case Study Report." Stockholm: International Institute for Democracy and Electoral Assistance (IDEA).
Kitschelt, Herbert and Kent Freeze. 2010. "Programmatic Party System Structuration: Developing and Comparing Cross-National and Cross-Party Measures with a New Global Data Set." Paper presented at the APSA Annual Meeting. Washington, DC.
Kitschelt, Herbert and Daniel M. Kselman. 2013. "Economic Development, Democratic Experience, and Political Linkage Strategies." *Comparative Political Studies* 46(11): 1453–1484.
   2014. "Clientelistic Party Organization. Brokerage and Centralization." Paper presented at the Annual Meeting of the European Political Science Association (EPSA). Edinburgh, Scotland, June 19–21.
   2015. *Programmatic Partisan Accountability and Organizational Design. A Comparative Analysis.* Unpublished manuscript. Duke University and IE Madrid.
Kitschelt, Herbert and Matthew Singer. 2016. "Diversified Partisan Linkage Strategies. Comparative Argument and Post-Communist Evidence." Paper presented at the 23rd Meeting of the Council for European Studies. Philadelphia, April 14–16.
Kitschelt, Herbert and Yi-Ting Wang. 2014. "Programmatic Parties and Party Systems. Opportunities and Constraints." In International Institute for Democracy and Electoral Assistance, ed., *Politics Meets Policies. The Emergence of Programmatic Political Parties*, pp. 43–76. Stockholm: IDEA.
Kitschelt, Herbert, Zdenka Mansfeldova, Radoslow Markowski, and Gábor Tóka. 1999. *Post-Communist Party Systems: Competition, Representation, and Inter-Party Competition.* New York, NY: Cambridge University Press.
Klein, Herbert S. 2011. *A Concise History of Bolivia.* 2nd edn. New York, NY: Cambridge University Press.
Klein, Marcus. 2004. "The Unión Demócrata Independiente and the Poor (1983–1992): The Survival of Clientelistic Traditions in Chilean Politics." *Jahrbuch für Geschichte Lateinamerikas* 41: 301–324.
Klesner, Joseph. 1993. "Modernization, Economic Crisis, and Electoral Alignment in Mexico." *Mexican Studies/Estudios Mexicanos* 9(2): 187–223.
   2005. "Electoral Competition and the New Party System in Mexico." *Latin American Politics and Society* 47(2): 103–142.
Kohli, Atul. 2004. *State-Directed Development: Political Power and Industrialization in the Global Periphery.* New York, NY: Cambridge University Press.
Koivumaeki, Riita-Ilona. 2010. "Business, Economic Experts, and Conservative Party Building in Latin America: The Case of El Salvador." *Journal of Politics in Latin America* 2(1): 79–106.

2014. "El Salvador: Societal Cleavages, Strategic Elites, and the Success of the Right." In Juan Pablo Luna and Cristóbal Rovira Kaltwasser, eds., *The Resilience of the Latin American Right*, pp. 268–293. Baltimore, MD: Johns Hopkins University Press.
Kolev, Kiril and Yiting Wang. 2010. "Ethnic Group Divisions and Clientelism." Paper presented at the APSA Annual Meeting. Washington, DC.
Komar, Olivera and Slaven Živković. 2016. "Montenegro: A Democracy without Alternations." *East European Politics and Societies* 30(4): 785–804.
Kopeček, Michal. 2013. "The Stigma of the Past and the Bond of Belonging: Czech Communists in the First Decade after 1989." *Czech Journal of Contemporary History* 1: 101–130.
Kopeček, Lubomír and Pavel Pseja. 2008. "Czech Social Democracy and Its 'Cohabitation' with the Communist Party: The Story of a Neglected Affair." *Communist and Post-Communist Studies* 41: 317–338.
Kora, Sheriff and Momodou N. Darboe. 2017. "The Gambia's Electoral Earthquake." *Journal of Democracy* 28(2): 147–156.
Kostadinova, Tatiana and Barry Levitt. 2014. "Toward a Theory of Personalist Parties: Concept Formation and Theory Building." *Politics & Policy* 42(4): 490–512.
Koter, Dominika. 2013. "King Makers: Local Leaders and Ethnic Politics in Africa." *World Politics* 65(2): 187–232.
Ku, Jae H. 2017. "Public Opinion, Regionalism and Foreign Policy Evaluation in South Korea." In Tun-jen Cheng and Wei-chin Lee, ed., *National Security, Public Opinion and Regime Asymmetry: A Six-Country Study*, pp. 49–77. Singapore: World Scientific Publishing.
Kuran, Timur. 1987a. "Preference Falsification, Policy Continuity, and Collective Conservatism." *The Economic Journal* 97(387): 642–665.
  1987b. *Private Truths, Public Lies: The Social Consequences of Preference Falsification*. Cambridge, MA: Harvard University Press.
  1991. "Now Out of Never: The Element of Surprise in the East European Revolution of 1989." *World Politics* 44(1): 7–48.
Kuzio, Taras. 2008. "Comparative Perspectives on Communist Successor Parties in Central-Eastern Europe and Eurasia." *Communist and Post-Communist Studies* 41(4): 397–419.
  2015. *Ukraine: Democratization, Corruption, and the New Russian Imperialism*. Santa Barbara: Praeger Security International.
Kyle, Brett J. 2016. *Recycling Dictators in Latin American Elections: Legacies of Military Rule*. Boulder, CO: Lynne Rienner Publishers.
Laakso, Markku and Rein Taagepera. 1979. "'Effective' Number of Parties: A Measure with Application to West Europe." *Comparative Political Studies* 12(1): 3–27.
Langston, Joy. 2006a. "The Changing Party of the Institutional Revolution." *Party Politics* 12(3): 395–413.
  2006b. "The Birth and Transformation of the *Dedazo* in Mexico." In Gretchen Helmke and Steven Levitsky, eds., *Informal Institutions and Democracy: Lessons from Latin America*, pp. 143–159. Baltimore, MD: Johns Hopkins University Press.
  2017. *Democratization and Authoritarian Party Survival: Mexico's PRI*. New York: Oxford University Press.

Larmer, Miles. 2009. "Zambia since 1990: Paradoxes of Democratic Transition." In Abdul Raufu Mustapha and Lindsay Whitfield, eds., *Turning Points in African Democracy*, pp. 114–133. Suffolk, Rochester, NY: James Currey Press.
Larreguy, Horacio, César Montiel, and Pablo Querubín. 2016. "Political Brokers: Partisans or Agents? Evidence from the Mexican Teacher's Union." Department of Government, Harvard University, Working paper.
Latinobarómetro. 2016. *Informe 2015*. Chile: Corporación Latinobarómetro.
Lavareda, Antonio. 1985. "O Partido da Frente Liberal: o dissenso dos governadores pedessistas nordestinos e a busca de uma nova imagem." In Joaquim Falcão and Constança Pereira de Sá, eds., *Nordeste: Eleições*, pp. 39–60. Recife: Fundação Joaquim Nabuco.
Lawson, Chappell. 2000. "Mexico's Unfinished Transition: Democratization and Authoritarian Enclaves." *Mexican Studies/Estudios Mexicanos* 16(2): 267–287.
  2002. *Building the Fourth Estate: Democratization and the Rise of a Free Press in Mexico*. Berkeley, CA: University of California Press.
  2008. "Election Coverage in Mexico: Regulation Meets Crony Capitalism." In Jesper Stromback and Lynda Lee Kaid, eds., *Handbook of Election News Coverage around the World*, pp. 370–384. New York, NY: Routledge.
Leal, Victor Nunes. 1977. *Coronelismo: The Municipality and Representative Government in Brazil* (trans. June Henfrey). New York, NY: Cambridge University Press.
LeBas, Adrienne. 2006. "Polarization as Craft: Party Formation and State Violence in Zimbabwe" *Comparative Politics* 38(4): 419–438.
  2011. *From Protest to Parties: Party-Building and Democratization in Africa*. New York: Oxford University Press.
Lee, Namhee. 2007. *The Making of Minjung: Democracy and the Politics of Representation in South Korea*. Ithaca, NY: Cornell University Press.
Lefèvre, Raphaël. 2015. "Tunisia: A Fragile Political Transition." *The Journal of North African Studies* 20(2): 307–311.
LeoGrande, William M. 2015. "Cuba's Perilous Political Transition to the Post-Castro Era." *Journal of Latin American Studies* 47(2): 377–405.
Levine, Robert M. 1998. *Father of the Poor? Vargas and His Era*. New York, NY: Cambridge University Press.
Levitsky, Steven. 2003. *Transforming Labor-Based Parties in Latin America: Argentine Peronism in Comparative Perspective*. New York, NY: Cambridge University Press.
  2018. "Peru: The Institutionalization of Politics without Parties." In Scott Mainwaring, ed., *Party Systems in Latin America: Institutionalization, Decay, and Collapse*, pp. 326–355. New York, NY: Cambridge University Press.
Levitsky, Steven, James Loxton, and Brandon Van Dyck. 2016. "Introduction: Challenges of Party-Building in Latin America." In Steven Levitsky, James Loxton, Brandon Van Dyck, and Jorge I. Domínguez, eds., *Challenges of Party-Building in Latin America*, pp. 1–48. New York, NY: Cambridge University Press.
Levitsky, Steven and Lucan A. Way. 2010. *Competitive Authoritarianism: Hybrid Regimes after the Cold War*. New York, NY: Cambridge University Press.
  2012. "Beyond Patronage: Violent Struggle, Ruling Party Cohesion, and Authoritarian Durability." *Perspectives on Politics* 10(4): 869–889.
Levitsky, Steven and Mauricio Zavaleta. 2016. "Why No Party-Building in Peru?" In Steven Levitsky, James Loxton, Brandon Van Dyck, and Jorge I. Domínguez,

eds., *Challenges of Party-Building in Latin America*, pp. 412–439. New York, NY: Cambridge University Press.
Lewin, Leif. 1988. *Ideology and Strategy: A Century of Swedish Politics.* Cambridge: Cambridge University Press.
Lewis, Paul G., ed. 2001. *Party Development and Democratic Change in Post-Communist Europe: The First Decade.* Portland, OR: Frank Cass.
Lijphart, Arend. 1977. *Democracy in Plural Society: A Comparative Exploration.* New Haven, CT: Yale University Press.
Limongi, Fernando and Rafael Cortez. 2010. "As eleições de 2010 e o quadro partidário." *Novos Estudos Cebrap* 88: 21–37.
Lin, Teh-Rui. 2014. "Zhong-guo guomindang dang-chan bao-gau" [Report on KMT Party-Owned Assets]. By vice secretary-general and chair of administrative management committee, December 31.
Lin, Tse-min and Yen-pin Su. 2015. "Taiwan kwai-shan zhengzhi" [Flash-Mob Politics in Taiwan]. *Taiwan Democracy Quarterly* 12(2): 123–147.
Lindberg, Staffan. 2003. "'It's Our Time to "Chop"': Do Elections in Africa Feed Neo-Patrimonialism rather than Counter-Act It?" *Democratization* 10(2): 121–140.
Lindberg, Staffan and Minion K. C. Morrison. 2005. "Exploring Voter Alignments in Africa: Core and Swing Voters in Ghana." *The Journal of Modern African Studies* 43(4): 565–586.
Linz, Juan J., 1978. *The Breakdown of Democratic Regimes: Crisis, Breakdown, and Reequilibration.* Baltimore, MD: Johns Hopkins University Press.
　2000. *Totalitarianism and Authoritarian Regimes.* Boulder, CO: Lynne Rienner Publishers.
Lipset, Seymour Martin and Stein Rokkan. 1967. *Party Systems and Voter Alignments: Cross-National Perspectives.* International Yearbook of Political Behavior Research. New York: Free Press.
Loaeza, Soledad. 1999. *El Partido Acción Nacional: la larga marcha, 1939–1994.* México, DF: Fondo de Cultura Económica.
Long, James D., Karuti Kanyinga, Karen E. Ferree, and Clark Gibson. 2013. "Kenya's 2013 Elections: Choosing Peace over Democracy." *Journal of Democracy* 24(3): 140–155.
López Nieto, Lourdes. 1998. "The Organizational Dynamics of AP/PP." In Piero Ignazi and Colette Ysmal, eds., *The Organization of Political Parties in Southern Europe*, pp. 254–269. London: Praeger.
López Villaverde, Ángel Luis. 1997. *Cuenca durante la II República: Elecciones, partidos y vida política, 1931–1936.* Cuenca: Universidad de Castilla-La Mancha.
Lowe, Sid. 2010. *Catholicism, War and the Foundation of Francoism: The Juventud de Acción Popular in Spain, 1931–1939.* Portland: Sussex Academic Press.
Loxton, James. 2014a. "Authoritarian Inheritance and Conservative Party-Building in Latin America." PhD dissertation, Department of Government, Harvard University.
　2014b. "The Authoritarian Roots of New Right Party Success in Latin America." In Juan Pablo Luna and Cristóbal Rovira Kaltwasser, eds., *The Resilience of the Latin American Right*, pp. 117–140. Baltimore, MD: Johns Hopkins University Press.
　2015. "Authoritarian Successor Parties." *Journal of Democracy* 26(3): 157–170.
　2016. "Authoritarian Successor Parties and the Right in Latin America." In Steven Levitsky, James Loxton, Brandon Van Dyck, and Jorge I. Domínguez, eds., *Challenges of Party-Building in Latin America*, pp. 245–272. New York, NY: Cambridge University Press.

Luebbert, Gregory M. 1991. *Liberalism, Fascism, or Social Democracy: Social Classes and the Political Origins of Regimes in Interwar Europe.* New York: Oxford University Press.

Luna, Juan Pablo. 2010. "Segmented Party–Voter Linkages in Latin America: The Case of the UDI." *Journal of Latin American Studies* 42: 325–356.

2014. *Segmented Representation: Political Party Strategies in Unequal Democracies.* Oxford: Oxford University Press.

Lupu, Noam. 2014. "Brand Dilution and the Breakdown of Political Parties in Latin America." *World Politics* 66(4): 561–602.

2016. *Party Brands in Crisis: Partisanship, Brand Dilution, and the Breakdown of Political Parties in Latin America.* New York, NY: Cambridge University Press.

Lupu, Noam and Rachel Beatty Riedl. 2013. "Political Parties and Uncertainty in Developing Democracies." *Comparative Political Studies* 46(11): 1339–1365.

Lwanda, John. 2006. "Kwacha: The Violence of Money in Malawi's Politics, 1954–2004." *Journal of Southern African Studies* 32(3): 525–544.

Lyne, Mona. 2007. "Rethinking Economics and Institutions: The Voter's Dilemma and Democratic Accountability." In Herbert Kitschelt and Steven I. Wilkinson, eds., *Patrons, Clients and Policies: Patterns of Democratic Accountability and Political Competition*, pp. 159–182. Cambridge: Cambridge University Press.

2008. *The Voter's Dilemma and Democratic Accountability: Latin America and Beyond.* University Park, PA: Pennsylvania State University Press.

Madrid, Raúl L. 2003. "Labouring against Neoliberalism: Unions and Patterns of Reform in Latin America." *Journal of Latin American Studies* 35(1): 53–88.

Magalhães Ferreira, Patrícia. 2004. "Guinea-Bissau: Between Conflict and Democracy." *African Security Review* 13(4): 45–56.

Magaloni, Beatriz. 2005. "The Demise of Mexico's One-Party Dominant Regime: Elite Choices and the Masses in the Establishment of Democracy." In Frances Hagopian and Scott Mainwaring, eds., *The Third Wave of Democratization in Latin America: Advances and Setbacks*, pp. 121–146. New York, NY: Cambridge University Press.

2006. *Voting For Autocracy: Hegemonic Party Survival and Its Demise in Mexico.* New York, NY: Cambridge University Press.

Magaloni, Beatriz, Alberto Díaz-Cayeros, and Federico Estévez. 2007. "Clientelism and Portfolio Diversification. A Model of Electoral Investment with Applications to Mexico." In Herbert Kitschelt and Steven I. Wilkinson, eds., *Patrons, Clients and Policies: Patterns of Democratic Accountability and Political Competition*, pp. 182–205. Cambridge: Cambridge University Press.

Magar, Edgar. 2012. "Gubernatorial Coattails in Mexican Congressional Elections." *Journal of Politics* 74(2): 383–399.

Magnusson, Bruce A. 2001. "Democratization and Domestic Insecurity: Navigating the Transition in Benin." *Comparative Politics* 33(2): 211–230.

Mahoney, James. 2003. "Knowledge Accumulation in Comparative Historical Research: The Case of Democracy and Authoritarianism." In James Mahoney and Dietrich Rueschemeyer, eds., *Comparative Historical Analysis in the Social Sciences*, pp. 131–176. New York, NY: Cambridge University Press.

Mahr, Alison and John Nagle. 1995. "Resurrection of the Successor Parties and Democratization in East-Central Europe." *Communist and Post-Communist Studies* 28(4): 393–409.

Mainwaring, Scott, ed. 2018. *Party Systems in Latin America: Institutionalization, Decay, and Collapse.* New York, NY: Cambridge University Press.

Mainwaring, Scott and Aníbal Pérez-Liñán. 2013. *Democracies and Dictatorships in Latin America: Emergence, Survival, and Fall.* New York, NY: Cambridge University Press.

Mainwaring, Scott and Edurne Zoco. 2007. "Political Sequences and the Stabilization of Interparty Competition: Electoral Volatility in Old and New Democracies." *Party Politics* 13(2): 155–178.

Mainwaring, Scott, Rachel Meneguello, and Timothy J. Power. 2000. *Partidos conservadores no Brasil contemporâneo: quais são, o que defendem, quais são suas bases.* São Paulo: Editora Paz e Terra.

Mainwaring, Scott, Timothy J. Power, and Fernando Bizzarro. 2018. "The Uneven Institutionalization of a Party System: Brazil." In Scott Mainwaring, ed., *Party Systems in Latin America: Institutionalization, Decay, and Collapse,* pp. 164–200. New York, NY: Cambridge University Press.

Mainwaring, Scott and Timothy R. Scully. 1995. "Introduction: Party Systems in Latin America." In Scott Mainwaring and Timothy R. Scully, eds., *Building Democratic Institutions: Party Systems in Latin America,* pp. 1–34. Stanford, CA: Stanford University Press.

Makoa, Francis K. 1996. "Political Instability in Post-Military Lesotho: The Crisis of the Basotho Nation-State?" *African Security Review* 5(3): 13–20.

2004. "Electoral Reform and Political Stability in Lesotho." *African Journal on Conflict Resolution* 4(2): 79–96.

Malloy, James M. and Eduardo A. Gamarra. 1988. *Revolution and Reaction: Bolivia, 1964–1985.* New Brunswick, NJ: Transaction Books.

Marcelino, Daniel, Sérgio Braga, and Luiz Domingos. 2009. "Parlamentares na Constituinte de 1987/88: uma contribuição à solução do 'enigma do Centrão'." *Revista Política Hoje* 18(2): 239–279.

March, Luke. 2005. "The Moldovan Communists: From Leninism to Democracy?" *Eurojournal.org – Journal of Foreign Policy of Moldova* 9(September): 1–25.

2006. "Power and Opposition in the Former Soviet Union: The Communist Parties of Moldova and Russia." *Party Politics* 12(3): 341–365.

Marchand, Iris. 2014. "Dogla Politics? Questioning Ethnic Consociationalism in Suriname's National Elections of 25 May 2010." *Ethnic and Racial Studies* 37(2): 342–362.

Marcus, Richard R. 2001. "Madagascar: Legitimizing Autocracy." *Current History* 100 (646): 226–231.

Marcus, Richard R. and Adrien M. Ratsimbaharison. 2005. "Political Parties in Madagascar: Neopatrimonial Tools or Democratic Instruments?" *Party Politics* 11(4): 495–512.

Marshall, Monty, Ted Gurr, and Keith Jaggers. 2014. "Political Regime Characteristics and Transitions, 1800–2013." Polity IV Project, Center for Systemic Peace. Available from: www.systemicpeace.org/inscrdata.html [Accessed January 20, 2017].

Martí i Puig, Salvador. 2010. "The Adaptation of the FSLN: Daniel Ortega's Leadership and Democracy in Nicaragua." *Latin American Politics and Society* 52(4): 79–106.

2013. "Nicaragua: La consolidación de un régimen híbrido." *Revista de Ciencia Política* 33(1): 269–286.

Martz, John D. and Enrique A. Baloyra. 1976. *Electoral Mobilization and Public Opinion: The Venezuelan Campaign of 1973.* Chapel Hill: University of North Carolina Press.

Masoud, Tarek. 2011. "The Upheavals in Egypt and Tunisia: The Road to (and from) Liberation Square." *Journal of Democracy* 22(3): 20–34.

2013. "How Morsy Could Have Saved Himself." *Foreign Policy*, July 19.

Maurer, Noel and Carlos Yu. 2011. *The Big Ditch: How America Took, Built, Ran, and Ultimately Gave Away the Panama Canal*. Princeton, NJ: Princeton University Press.

Mayer, Arno J. 1981. *The Persistence of the Old Regime: Europe to the Great War*. New York: Pantheon Books.

Mbodji, Mohamed. 1991. "The Politics of Independence: 1960–1986." In Christopher L. Delgado and Sidi C. Jammeh, eds., *The Political Economy of Senegal Under Structural Adjustment*, pp. 119–126. New York: Praeger.

McCann, James A. 2015. "Time to Turn Back the Clock? Retrospective Judgments of the Single-Party Era and Support for the Institutional Revolutionary Party in 2012." In Jorge I. Domínguez, Kenneth F. Greene, Chappell H. Lawson, and Alejandro Moreno, eds., *Mexico's Evolving Democracy: A Comparative Study of the 2012 Elections*, pp. 86–106. Baltimore, MD: Johns Hopkins University Press.

McCargo, Duncan. 1997. "Thailand's Political Parties: Real, Authentic and Actual." In Kevin Hewison, ed., *Political Change in Thailand: Democracy and Participation*, pp. 114–131. London and New York: Routledge.

McCracken, John. 1998. "Democracy and Nationalism in Historical Perspective: The Case of Malawi." *African Affairs* 97(387): 231–249.

McGuire, James W. 1995. "Political Parties and Democracy in Argentina." In Scott Mainwaring and Timothy R. Scully, eds., *Building Democratic Institutions: Party Systems in Latin America*, pp. 200–246. Stanford, CA: Stanford University Press.

1997. *Peronism without Perón: Unions, Parties, and Democracy in Argentina*. Stanford, CA: Stanford University Press.

McKibbin, Ross. 2010. *Parties and People, England, 1914–1951*. Oxford: Oxford University Press.

Medina Vidal, D. Xavier, Antonio Ugues Jr., Shaun Bowler, and Jonathan Hiskey. 2010. "Partisan Attachment and Democracy in Mexico: Some Cautionary Observations." *Latin American Politics and Society* 52(1): 63–87.

Mehler, Andreas. 2005. "The Shaky Foundations, Adverse Circumstances, and Limited Achievements of Democratic Transition in the Central African Republic." In Leonardo A. Villalón and Peter VonDoepp, eds., *The Fate of Africa's Democratic Experiments: Elites and Institutions*, pp. 126–152. Bloomington, IN: Indiana University Press.

Meléndez, Carlos. 2012. *La soledad de la política: Transformaciones estructurales, intermediación política y conflictos sociales en el Perú (2000–2012)*. Lima: Mitin.

2014. "Is There a Right Track in Post-Party System Collapse Scenarios? Comparing the Andean Countries." In Juan Pablo Luna and Cristóbal Rovira Kaltwasser, eds., *The Resilience of the Latin American Right*, pp. 167–193. Baltimore, MD: Johns Hopkins University Press.

Mercado Gasca, Lauro. 2013. "Clientelismo electoral: Compra, coacción y otros mecanismos que limitan el voto libre y secreto en México." In Luis Carlos Ugalde and Gustavo Rivera Loret de Mola, eds., *Fortalezas y Debilidades del Sistema Electoral Mexicano (2000–2012)*, pp. 236–275. Mexico, DF: Centro de Estudios Espinosa Yglesias.

Mergel, Thomas. 2003. "Das Scheitern Des Deutschen Tory-Konservatismus. Die Umformung Der DNVP Zu Einer Rechtsradikalen Partei 1928–1932." *Historische Zeitschrift* 276: 323–368.
Merino, Gustavo. 2001. "Federalismo fiscal: diagnóstico y propuestas." *Gaceta de Economía (ITAM)* Special Issue: 145–185.
Meyns, Peter. 2002. "Cape Verde: An African Exception." *Journal of Democracy* 13(3): 153–165.
Middlebrook, Kevin. 1995. *The Paradox of Revolution: Labor, the State, and Authoritarianism in Mexico*. Baltimore, MD: Johns Hopkins University Press.
Mietzner, Marcus. 2012. "Indonesia's Democratic Stagnation: Anti-Reformist Elites and Resilient Civil Society." *Democratization* 19(2): 209–229.
  2015. "State Capacity in Post-Authoritarian Indonesia: Securing Democracy's Survival, Entrenching its Low Quality." Working paper, Australia National University.
Mitchell, B. R. 2003. *International Historical Statistics: Europe, 1750–2000*. 5th edn. New York: Palgrave Macmillan.
Møller, Jørgen, Alexander Schmotz, and Svend-Erik Skaaning. 2015. "Economic Crisis and Democratic Breakdown in the Interwar Years: A Reassessment." *Historical Social Research* 40(2): 301–318.
Momba, Jotham C. 2005. *Political Parties and the Quest for Democratic Consolidation in Zambia*. Johannesburg: EISA.
Mommsen, Hans. 1996. *The Rise and Fall of Weimar Democracy*. Chapel Hill: University of North Carolina Press.
Montero, José Ramón. 1987. "Los fracasos políticos y electorales de la derecha española: Alianza Popular, 1976–1986." *Revista Española de Investigaciones Sociológicas* 39: 7–43.
Montero, Alfred P. 2012. "A Reversal of Political Fortune: The Transitional Dynamics of Conservative Rule in the Brazilian Northeast." *Latin American Politics and Society* 54(1): 1–36.
Moody, Peter. 1992. *Political Change on Taiwan: A Study of Ruling Party Adaptability*. New York: Praeger.
Moore, Barrington. 1966. *Social Origins of Dictatorship and Democracy: Lord and Peasant in the Making of the Modern World*. Boston: Beacon Press.
Moreno, Alejandro. 2015. "El elector mexicano frente al 2015." ITAM keynote address, April 10, Mexico City.
Morgan, Jana. 2011. *Bankrupt Representation and Party System Collapse*. University Park, PA: Pennsylvania State University Press.
Morrison, Minion K. C. and Jae Woo Hong. 2006. "Ghana's Political Parties: How Ethno/Regional Variations Sustain the National Two-Party System." *The Journal of Modern African Studies* 44(4): 623–647.
Murillo, Maria Victoria. 2001. *Labor Unions, Partisan Coalitions, and Market Reforms in Latin America*. New York, NY: Cambridge University Press.
Muyard, Frank. 2008. "Taiwan Elections 2008: Ma Ying-jeou's Victory and the KMT's Return to Power." *China Perspectives* 1: 79–94.
Mwanakatwe, John M. 1994. *End of Kaunda Era*. Lusaka, Zambia: Multimedia Publishers.
  2003. *John M. Mwanakatwe: Teacher, Politician, Lawyer: My Autobiography*. Lusaka, Zambia: Bookworld Publishers.

Nalepa, Monika. 2010. *Skeletons in the Closet: Transitional Justice in Post-Communist Europe*. New York, NY: Cambridge University Press.
Navarro, Melissa. 2011. "La organización partidaria fujimorista a 20 años de su origen." BA thesis, Department of Social Science, Pontificia Universidad Católica del Perú.
Nelson, Joan M. 2014. "Will Malaysia Follow the Path of Taiwan and Mexico?" *Journal of Democracy* 25(3): 105–119.
Nichter, Simeon. 2014. "Conceptualizing Vote Buying." *Electoral Studies* 35(3): 315–327.
Nikolenyi, Csaba. 2011. "Constitutional Sources of Party Cohesion: Anti-Defection Laws Around the World." Paper presented at the Oslo-Rome International Workshop on Democracy. Rome, Italy, November 7–9.
Ninsin, Kwame Akon and F. K. Drah, eds. 1987. *The Search for Democracy in Ghana: A Case Study of Political Instability in Africa*. Accra, Ghana: Asempa Publishers.
  1991. "Ghana's Transition to Constitutional Rule." Proceedings of a Seminar Organised by the Department of Political Science, University of Ghana, Legon. Accra, Ghana: Ghana Universities Press.
Nohlen, Dieter and Philip Stöver. 2010. *Elections in Europe: A Data Handbook*. Baden-Baden, Germany: Nomos.
Nordsieck, Wolfram. "Parties and Elections in Europe." Available from: parties-and-elections.eu [Accessed January 20, 2017].
O'Donnell, Guillermo. 1992. "Transitions, Continuities, and Paradoxes." In Scott Mainwaring, Guillermo O'Donnell, and J. Samuel Valenzuela, eds., *Issues in Democratic Consolidation: The New South American Democracies in Comparative Perspective*, pp. 17–56. Notre Dame: Notre Dame University Press.
  1994. "Delegative Democracy." *Journal of Democracy* 5(1): 55–69.
O'Donnell, Guillermo and Philippe C. Schmitter. 1986. *Transitions from Authoritarian Rule: Tentative Conclusions about Uncertain Democracies*. Baltimore, MD: Johns Hopkins University Press.
Oh, Chang Hun and Celeste Arrington. 2007. "Democratization and Changing Anti-American Sentiments in South Korea." *Asian Survey* 47(2): 327–350.
Ohnezeit, Maik. 2011. *Zwischen "Schärfster Opposition" Und Dem "Willen Zur Macht": Die Deutschnationale Volkspartei (DNVP) in Der Weimarer Republik 1918–1928*. Düsseldorf: Droste Verlag.
Olmeda, Juan C. and María Alejandra Armesto. 2013. "México: El regreso del PRI a la presidencia." *Revista de Ciencia Política* 33(1): 247–267.
Olsen, Jonathan. 2007. "The Merger of the PDS and WASG: From Eastern German Regional Party to National Radical Left Party?" *German Politics* 16(2): 205–221.
Olsson, Stefan. 2000. "Den Svenska Hoegerns Anpassning Till Demokratin." PhD dissertation, Uppsala University.
O'Neill, Kathleen. 2003. "Decentralization as an Electoral Strategy." *Comparative Political Studies* 36(9): 1068–1091.
Oquaye, Mike. 2004. *Politics in Ghana, 1982–1992: Rawlings, Revolution, and Populist Democracy*. Osu, Accra, Ghana: Tornado Publications.
O'Regan, Davin. 2015. "Cycles of Regime Change in Guinea-Bissau." In Claire Metelits and Stephanie Matti, eds., *Democratic Contestation on the Margins: Regimes in Small African Countries*, pp. 123–148. Lanham, MD: Lexington Books.

Orenstein, Michael. 1998. "A Genealogy of Communist Successor Parties in East Central Europe and the Determinants of Their Success." *East European Politics and Societies* 12(3): 472–499.

Orogváni, Andrej. 2006. "Strana Smer–pokus o novú definíciu slovenskej ľavice" [Smer Party – An Attempt to Reinvent the Slovak Left]. In Grigorij Mesežnikov, Oľga Gyárfášová, and Kollár, Miroslav, eds., *Slovenské voľby '06. Výsledky, príčiny, súvislosti*, pp. 95–109. Bratislava: Inštitút pre verejné otázky.

Ortega Hegg, Manuel. 2007. "Nicaragua 2006: El regreso del FSLN al poder." *Revista de Ciencia Política* 27: 205–219.

Ortmann, Stephan. 2011. "Singapore: Authoritarian but Newly Competitive." *Journal of Democracy* 22(4): 153–164.

2015. "Singapore: From Hegemonic to Competitive Authoritarianism." In William Case, ed., *Routledge Handbook of Southeast Asian Democratization*, pp. 384–398. New York, NY: Routledge.

Ossou, François Gomlan. 1993. "Les Forces Armées dans la Vie Politique Béninoise sous le Régime de Mathieu Kérékou: 1972–1990." Paper presented at the CODESRIA workshop Militaires et le Militarisme en Afrique. Accra, Ghana, April 21–23.

Ostiguy, Pierre. 2009a. "The High and Low in Politics: A Two-Dimensional Space for Comparative Analysis and Electoral Studies." *Kellogg Institute for International Studies*. Working Paper #360.

2009b. "Argentina's Double Political Spectrum: Party System, Political Identities, and Strategies, 1944–2007." *Kellogg Institute for International Studies*. Working Paper #361.

Owusu, Maxwell. 1996. "Tradition and Transformation: Democracy and the Politics of Popular Power in Ghana." *The Journal of Modern African Studies* 34(2): 307–343.

Page, Joseph A. 1983. *Perón: A Biography*. New York: Random House.

Paiva, Denise Ferreira. 2002. *PFL x PMDB: marchas e contramarchas (1982–2000)*. Goiânia: Editora Alternativa.

Panebianco, Angelo. 1988. *Political Parties: Organization and Power*. Cambridge: Cambridge University Press.

Paoli Bolio, Francisco. 2012. "Tiempo de coaliciones: cinco lustros de elecciones en México." *Revista IUS* 6(30): 136–148.

Paradowska, Janina. 2002. "Aparat na części." *Polityka*, December 14: 28–30.

Park, Kyungmee. 2010. "Party Mergers and Splits in New Democracies: The Case of South Korea (1987–2007)." *Government and Opposition* 45(4): 531–552.

Pastor, Manuel and Carol Wise. 2005. "The Lost Sexenio: Vicente Fox and the New Politics of Economic Reform in Mexico." *Latin American Politics and Society* 47(4): 135–160.

Patton, David F. 1998. "Germany's Party of Democratic Socialism in Comparative Perspective." *East European Politics and Societies* 12(3): 500–526.

2011. *Out of the East: From PDS to Left Party in Unified Germany*. Albany: State University of New York Press.

Payne, Stanley G. 1993. *Spain's First Democracy: The Second Republic, 1931–1936*. Madison: University of Wisconsin Press.

Peng, Ito and Joseph Wong. 2008. "Institutions and Institutional Purpose: Continuity and Change in East Asian Social Policy." *Politics and Society* 36(1): 61–88.

Peñaranda Bojanic, Martha. 2004. *Vida, tiempos y ritmos de ADN (Acción Democrática Nacionalista): Historia de un partido*. La Paz: Facultad de Derecho y Ciencias Políticas (UMSA).

Pepinsky, Thomas. 2017. "Southeast Asia: Voting Against Disorder." *Journal of Democracy* 28(2): 120–131.
Pérez, Andrés. 1992. "The FSLN after the Debacle: The Struggle for the Definition of Sandinismo." *Journal of Interamerican Studies and World Affairs* 34(1): 111–139.
Pérez, Orlando J. 2000. "The Past as Prologue? Political Parties in Post-Invasion Panama." In Pérez, Orlando J., ed., *Post-Invasion Panama: The Challenges of Democratization in the New World Order*, pp. 125–145. Lanham, MD: Lexington Books.
  2011. *Political Culture in Panama: Democracy after Invasion*. New York: Palgrave Macmillan.
Phillips, Ann L. 1994. "Socialism with a New Face? The PDS in Search of Reform." *East European Politics and Societies* 8(3): 495–530.
Piattoni, Simona, ed. 2001. *Clientelism, Interests, and Democratic Representation: The European Experience in Historical and Comparative Perspective*. Cambridge: Cambridge University Press.
Pollack, Marcelo. 1999. *The New Right in Chile, 1973–97*. Basingstoke: Palgrave Macmillan.
Pop-Eleches, Grigore. 1999. "Separated at Birth or Separated by Birth? The Communist Successor Parties in Romania and Hungary." *East European Politics and Societies* 13(1): 117–147.
  2007. "Historical Legacies and Post-Communist Regime Change." *The Journal of Politics* 69(4): 908–926.
  2008. "A Party for All Seasons: Electoral Adaptation of Romanian Communist Successor Parties." *Communist and Post-Communist Studies* 41(4): 465–479.
  2010. "Throwing Out the Bums: Protest Voting and Anti-Establishment Parties after Communism." *World Politics* 62(2): 221–260.
Posner, Daniel N. 1995. "Malawi's New Dawn." *Journal of Democracy* 6(1): 131–145.
  2005. *Institutions and Ethnic Politics in Africa*. Cambridge; New York: Cambridge University Press.
Power, Margaret. 2002. *Right-Wing Women in Chile: Feminine Power and the Struggle Against Allende, 1964–1973*. University Park, PA: Pennsylvania State University Press.
Power, Timothy J. 2000. *The Political Right in Postauthoritarian Brazil: Elites, Institutions, and Democratization*. University Park, PA: Pennsylvania State University Press.
  2010. "Optimism, Pessimism, and Coalitional Presidentialism: Debating the Institutional Design of Brazilian Democracy." *Bulletin of Latin American Research* 29(1): 18–33.
  2016. "The Reduction of Poverty and Inequality in Brazil: Political Causes, Political Consequences." In Ben Ross Schneider, ed., *New Order and Progress: Development and Democracy in Brazil*, pp. 212–237. New York: Oxford University Press.
Power, Timothy J. and Cesar Zucco Jr. 2009. "Estimating Ideology of Brazilian Legislative Parties, 1990–2005." *Latin American Research Review* 44(1): 218–245.
Power, Timothy and Cesar Zucco. 2014. "Brazilian Legislative Surveys (1990–2013)." Available from: hdl:1902.1/14970, Harvard Dataverse [Accessed July 31, 2017].
Preston, Paul. 1994. *The Coming of the Spanish Civil War: Reform, Reaction and Revolution in the Second Republic*. 2nd edn. London: Routledge.
Pryce, Paul and Raphael Oidtmann. 2014. "The 2012 General Election in Ghana." *Electoral Studies* 34: 330–334.

Przeworski, Adam. 1991. *Democracy and the Market: Political and Economic Reforms in Eastern Europe and Latin America*. New York, NY: Cambridge University Press.

Putzel, James. 1995. "Democratization and Clan Politics: The 1992 Philippine Elections." *South East Asia Research* 3(1): 18–45.

Pye, Oliver and Wolfram Schaffar. 2008. "The 2006 Anti-Thaksin Movement in Thailand: An Analysis." *Journal of Contemporary Asia* 38(1): 38–61.

Racz, Barnabas. 1993. "The Socialist Left Opposition in Post-Communist Hungary." *Europe-Asia Studies* 45(4): 647–670.

Raile, Eric, Carlos Pereira, and Timothy J. Power. 2011. "The Executive Toolbox: Building Legislative Support in a Multiparty Presidential Regime." *Political Research Quarterly* 64(2): 323–334.

Rakner, Lise, Lars Svåsand, and Nixon S. Khembo. 2007. "Fissions and Fusions, Foes and Friends: Party System Restructuring in Malawi in the 2004 General Elections." *Comparative Political Studies* 40(9): 1112–1137.

Ramos, Jorge. 2009. "Seis de cada 10 no cree en elecciones limpias." *El Universal*, April 18.

Raphael, Ricardo. 2007. *Los socios de Elba Esther*. Mexico: Editorial Planeta.

Remmer, Karen L. 1989. *Military Rule in Latin America*. Boston: Unwin Hyman.

Resnick, Danielle. 2013. "Continuity and Change in Senegalese Party Politics: Lessons from the 2012 Elections." *African Affairs* 112(449): 623–645.

Ribeiro, Pedro Floriano. 2013. "Organização e poder nos partidos brasileiros; uma análise dos estatutos." *Revista Brasileira de Ciência Política* 10(January): 225–265.

Ribeiro, Ricardo. 2014. "Decadência longe do poder: Refundação e crise do PFL." *Revista de Sociologia e Política* 22(49): 5–37.

Riedl, Rachel. 2014. *Authoritarian Origins of Democratic Party Systems in Africa*. New York, NY: Cambridge University Press.

Riedl, Rachel Beatty and J. Tyler Dickovick. 2014. "Party Systems and Decentralization in Africa." *Studies in Comparative International Development* 49(3): 321–342.

Rizova, Tatiana Petrova. 2008. "The Party Is Dead, Long Live the Party! Successor Party Adaptation to Democracy." PhD dissertation, University of California at Los Angeles.

  2012. "Communist Successor Party Adaptation in Candidate-Centered Systems: The Communist Party of Bohemia and Moravia and the Czech Social Democratic Party in the Czech Republic." *Journal of Politics and Law* 5(2): 145–161.

Roberts, Kenneth M. 2006. "Latin America's Conservative Party Deficit." Paper presented at the annual conference of the Latin American Studies Association. San Juan, Puerto Rico, March 15–18.

  2012. "Historical Timing, Political Cleavages, and Party Building in 'Third Wave' Democracies." Paper presented at the conference Challenges of Party Building in Latin America. Harvard University, November 16–17.

  2015. *Changing Course in Latin America: Party Systems in the Neoliberal Era*. New York, NY: Cambridge University Press.

  2016. "Historical Timing, Political Cleavages, and Party-Building in Latin America." In Steven Levitsky, James Loxton, Brandon Van Dyck, and Jorge I. Domínguez, eds., *Challenges of Party-Building in Latin America*, pp. 51–75. New York, NY: Cambridge University Press.

Roberts, Matthew. 2006. "'Villa Toryism' and Popular Conservatism in Leeds, 1885–1902." *The Historical Journal* 49(1): 217–246.

Rock, David. 1985. *Argentina, 1516–1982: From Spanish Colonization to the Falklands War*. Berkeley, CA: University of California Press.
Rodrigues, Leôncio Martins. 2002. *Partidos, ideologia e composição social: um estudo das bancadas partidárias na Câmara dos Deputados*. São Paulo: Edusp.
  2014. *Pobres e ricos na luta pelo poder: novas elites na política brasileira*. Rio de Janeiro: Topbooks.
Rodríguez Castañeda, Rafael. 1993. *Prensa vendida*. Mexico: Grijalbo.
Rodrik, Dani. 2011. *The Globalization Paradox: Democracy and the Future of the World Economy*. New York: Norton.
Rogowski, Ronald. 1989. *Commerce and Coalitions: How Trade Affects Domestic Political Alignments*. Princeton, NJ: Princeton University Press.
Rokkan, Stein. 1999. *State Formation, Nation-Building, and Mass Politics in Europe: The Theory of Stein Rokkan Based on His Collected Works*. Edited by Peter Flora, Stein Kuhnle, and Derek W. Urwin. New York: Oxford University Press.
Romdhani, Oussama. 2014. "Embracing Enemies in Tunisia." *Foreign Policy*, June 4.
Romero, Vidal, Beatriz Magaloni, and Alberto Díaz-Cayeros. 2016. "Presidential Approval and Public Security in Mexico's War on Crime." *Latin American Politics and Society* 58(2): 100–123.
Ropp, Steve C. 1982. *Panamanian Politics: From Guarded Nation to National Guard*. New York: Praeger.
Rosas, Guillermo and Joy Langston. 2011. "Gubernatorial Effects on the Voting Behavior of National Legislators." *Journal of Politics* 73(2): 477–493.
Rose, Richard and William Mishler. 2002. "Comparing Regime Support in Non-Democratic and Democratic Countries." *Democratization* 9(2): 1–20.
Rose, Richard, William Mishler, and Neil Munro. 2006. *Russia Transformed: Developing Popular Support for a New Regime*. New York, NY: Cambridge University Press.
  2011. *Popular Support for an Undemocratic Regime: The Changing Views of Russians*. New York, NY: Cambridge University Press.
Ross, Michael. 2006. "Is Democracy Good for the Poor?" *American Journal of Political Science* 50(4): 860–874.
Rothchild, Donald and Michael Foley. 1988. "African States and the Politics of Inclusive Coalitions." In Naomi Chazan and Donald Rothchild, eds., *The Precarious Balance: State and Society in Africa*, pp. 149–171. Boulder, CO: Westview Press.
Rueschemeyer, Dietrich, Evelyne Huber Stephens, and John D. Stephens. 1992. *Capitalist Development and Democracy*. Chicago, IL: University of Chicago Press.
Ruiz, José. 2015. "El impacto de los medios de comunicación sobre la definición del voto de los ciudadanos de Monterrey en las elecciones presidenciales del 2012." *Revista Mexicana de Ciencias Políticas y Sociales* 60(225): 203–226.
Rustow, Dankwart A. 1955. *The Politics of Compromise: A Study of Parties and Cabinet Government in Sweden*. Princeton, NJ: Princeton University Press.
Rybar, Marek and Kevin Deegan-Krause. 2008. "Slovakia's Communist Successor Parties in Comparative Perspective." *Communist and Post-Communist Studies* 41: 497–519.
Samuels, David J. 2004. "From Socialism to Social Democracy. Party Organization and the Transformation of the Workers' Party in Brazil." *Comparative Political Studies* 37(9): 999–1024.

Samuels, David J. and Matthew S. Shugart. 2010. *Presidents, Parties, and Prime Ministers: How the Separation of Powers Affects Party Organization and Behavior*. New York, NY: Cambridge University Press.

Sánchez, Omar. 2008. "Guatemala's Party Universe: A Case Study in Underinstitutionalization." *Latin American Politics and Society* 50(1): 123–151.

Sanders, Robert. 1984. *Real Old Tory Politics: The Political Diaries of Sir Robert Sanders, Lord Bayford, 1910–35*. Edited by John Ramsden. London: The Historians' Press.

Sarti, Roland. 1990. "Italian Fascism: Radical Politics and Conservative Goals." Martin Blinkhorn, ed., *Fascists and Conservatives: The Radical Right and the Establishment in Twentieth Century Europe*, pp. 14–30. Abingdon: Routledge.

Sartori, Giovanni. 1970. "Concept Misformation in Comparative Politics." *The American Political Science Review* 64(4): 1033–1053.

 1976. *Parties and Party Systems: A Framework for Analysis*. Cambridge: Cambridge University Press.

Schatzl, Ludwig, Karin Wessell, and Yong-woo Lee. 2007. *Regional Development and Decentralization Policy in South Korea*. Singapore: Institute of Southeast Asian Studies.

Schattschneider, Elmer Eric. 2004[1942]. *Party Government: American Government in Action*. New Brunswick, NJ: Transaction Publishers.

Schedler, Andreas. 2000. "The Democratic Revelation." *Journal of Democracy* 11(4): 5–19.

 2002. "The Menu of Manipulation." *Journal of Democracy* 13(2): 36–50.

 2013. *The Politics of Uncertainty: Sustaining and Subverting Electoral Authoritarianism*. New York: Oxford University Press.

Schirmer, Jennifer. 1998. *The Guatemalan Military Project: A Violence Called Democracy*. Philadelphia: University of Philadelphia Press.

Schmidt, Elizabeth. 2005. "Top Down or Bottom Up? Nationalist Mobilization Reconsidered, with Special Reference to Guinea (French West Africa)." *The American Historical Review* 110(4): 975–1014.

Schmidt, Steffen W., Laura Guasti, Carl H. Landé, and James C. Scott, eds. 1977. *Friends, Followers, and Factions. A Reader in Political Clientelism*. Berkeley, CA: University of California Press.

Schneider, Ben Ross. 2002. "Why Is Mexican Business So Organized?" *Latin American Research Review* 37(1): 77–118.

Scott, Ian. 1980. "Party and Administration under the One-Party State." In William Tordoff, ed., *Administration in Zambia*, pp. 139–161. Madison: University of Wisconsin Press.

Scranton, Margaret E. 1995. "Panama's First Post-Transition Election." *Journal of Interamerican Studies and World Affairs* 37(1): 69–100.

Šedo, Jakub. 2010a. "The Party System of Croatia." In Vera Stojarová and Peter Emerson, eds., *Party Politics in the Western Balkans*, pp. 73–84. New York, NY: Routledge.

 2010b. "The Party System of Macedonia." In Vera Stojarová and Peter Emerson, eds., *Party Politics in the Western Balkans*, pp. 167–179. New York, NY: Routledge.

Seibert, Gerhard. 2006. *Comrades, Clients and Cousins: Colonialism, Socialism and Democratization in São Tomé and Príncipe*. Leiden: Brill Academic Publishers.

Serra, Gilles. 2013. "Research Note: Demise and Resurrection of a Dominant Party: Understanding the PRI's Comeback in Mexico." *Journal of Politics in Latin America* 5(3): 133–154.

Seton-Watson, Christopher. 1981. *Italy from Liberalism to Fascism, 1870–1925.* London: Methuen.

Shafquat, Sahar. 1999. "Adaptation and Change in Formerly Dominant Political Parties: Comparing Experiences in Hungary, Taiwan, and Tanzania." In John T. Ishiyama, ed., *Communist Successor Parties in Post-Communist Politics*, pp. 19–41. Carmack, NY: Nova Science Publishers.

Share, Donald and Scott Mainwaring. 1986. "Transitions through Transaction: Democratization in Brazil and Spain." In Wayne Selcher, ed., *Political Liberalization in Brazil: Dynamics, Dilemmas, and Future Prospects*, pp. 175–215. Boulder: Westview.

Sharma, Bishnu, Bronwyn Stevens, and Patrick Weller. 2008. "Nepal – A Revolution through the Ballot Box." *Australian Journal of International Affairs* 62(4): 513–528.

Shefter, Martin. 1977. "Party and Patronage: Germany, England, and Italy." *Politics & Society* 7(3): 403–451.

Shin, Doh Chull and Jason Wells. 2005. "Is Democracy the Only Game in Town?" *Journal of Democracy* 16(2): 88–101.

Shin, Gi-Wook and Rennie J. Moon. 2017. "South Korea after Impeachment." *Journal of Democracy* 28(4): 117–131.

Siavelis, Peter. 2006. "Accommodating Informal Institutions and Chilean Democracy." In Gretchen Helmke and Stephen Levitsky, eds., *Informal Institutions and Democracy: Lessons from Latin America*, pp. 33–55. Baltimore, MD: Johns Hopkins University Press.

  2008. "Chile: The End of the Unfinished Transition." In Jorge I. Domínguez and Michael Shifter, eds., *Constructing Democratic Governance in Latin America*, 3rd edn., pp. 177–208. Baltimore, MD: Johns Hopkins University Press.

Sikkink, Kathryn. 2011. *The Justice Cascade: How Human Rights Prosecutions Are Changing World Politics.* New York: W.W. Norton & Co.

Simmance, Alan J. 1973. *Urbanization in Zambia.* New York: Ford Foundation.

Simutanyi, Neo R. and Njekwa Mate. 2006. "One-Party Dominance and Democracy in Zambia." Paper prepared within the framework of the Fredriech Ebert Stiftung Mozambique Regional Study on Dominant Parties and Southern Africa.

Singer, Matthew. 2009. "Defendamos lo que hemos logrado: Economic Voting in the 2006 Mexican Presidential Election." *Política y gobierno* 15: 199–233.

  2011. "Buying Voters with Dirty Money: The Relationship between Clientelism and Corruption." Workshop on Democratic Accountability Strategies, Duke University. May 18–19, 2011.

Singh, Chaitram. 2008. "Re-democratization in Guyana and Suriname: Critical Comparisons." *European Review of Latin American and Caribbean Studies* 84: 71–85.

Sivak, Martín. 2001. *El dictador elegido: Biografía no autorizada de Hugo Banzer Suárez.* La Paz: Plural Editores.

Slater, Dan. 2004. "Indonesia's Accountability Trap: Party Cartels and Presidential Power after Democratic Transition." *Indonesia* 78(October): 61–92.

  2010. *Ordering Power: Contentious Politics and Authoritarian Leviathans in Southeast Asia.* New York, NY: Cambridge University Press.

2012. "Strong-State Democratization in Malaysia and Singapore." *Journal of Democracy* 23(2): 19–33.
2013. "Democratic Careening." *World Politics* 65(4): 729–763.
2014a. "The Elements of Surprise: Assessing Burma's Double-Edged Détente." *South East Asia Research* 22(2): 171–182.
2014b. "Unbuilding Blocs: Indonesia's Accountability Deficit in Historical Perspective." *Critical Asian Studies* 46(2): 287–315.
Slater, Dan and Erica Simmons. 2013. "Coping by Colluding: Political Uncertainty and Promiscuous Powersharing in Indonesia and Bolivia." *Comparative Political Studies* 46(11): 1366–1393.
Slater, Dan and Joseph Wong. 2013. "The Strength to Concede: Ruling Parties and Democratization in Developmental Asia." *Perspectives on Politics* 11(3): 717–733.
Slater, Dan and Nicholas Rush Smith. 2016. "The Power of Counterrevolution: Elitist Origins of Political Order in Postcolonial Asia and Africa." *American Journal of Sociology* 121(5): 1472–1516.
Smith, Benjamin. 2005. "Life of the Party: The Origins of Regime Breakdown and Persistence under Single-Party Rule." *World Politics* 57(3): 421–451.
  2007. *Hard Times in the Lands of Plenty: Oil Politics in Iran and Indonesia*. Ithaca, NY: Cornell University Press.
Snyder, Richard. 1999. "After the State Withdraws: Neoliberalism and Subnational Authoritarian Regimes in Mexico." In Wayne Cornelius, Todd Eisenstadt, and Jane Hindley, eds., *Subnational Politics and Democratization in Mexico*, pp. 295–341. La Jolla, CA: Center for US Mexican Studies, University of California, San Diego.
Somfalvi, Attila. 2007. "Labor Party to Liquidate All of Its Assets." *Israel News*, August 28.
Sosa Villagarcia, Paolo. 2016. "¿El despertar de la Fuerza Popular? Keiko Fujimori y el partido de las paradojas." In Carlos Meléndez, ed., *Anti-candidatos. El thriller político de las elecciones 2016*, pp. 15–42. Lima: Editorial Planeta.
Souza, Celina. 2016. "The Rise and Fall of Illiberal Politics in the Brazilian State of Bahia." In Jacqueline Behrend and Laurence Whitehead, eds., *Illiberal Practices: Territorial Variance within Large Federal Democracies*, pp. 197–230. Baltimore, MD: Johns Hopkins University Press.
Spirova, Maria. 2008. "The Bulgarian Socialist Party: The Long Road to Europe." *Communist and Post-Communist Studies* 41: 481–495.
Steenbergen, Marco R. and Bradford S. Jones. 2002. "Modeling Multilevel Data Structures." *American Journal of Political Science* 46(1): 218–237.
Steinberg, David I. 1998. "Korea: Triumph and Turmoil." *Journal of Democracy* 9(2): 76–90.
Stepan, Alfred. 1988. *Rethinking Military Politics: Brazil and the Southern Cone*. Princeton, NJ: Princeton University Press.
Stojarová, Vera and Peter Emerson, eds. 2010. *Party Politics in the Western Balkans*. New York, NY: Routledge.
Stokes, Donald E. 1963. "Spatial Models of Party Competition." *The American Political Science Review* 57(2): 368–377.
Stokes, Susan C. 2005. "Perverse Accountability: A Formal Model of Machine Politics with Evidence from Argentina." *American Political Science Review* 99(3): 315–325.

Stokes, Susan C., Thad Dunning, Marcelo Nazareno, and Valeria Brusco. 2013. *Brokers, Voters, and Clientelism: The Puzzle of Distributive Politics*. New York, NY: Cambridge University Press.
Stoll, David. 1990/1991. "Guatemala: Why They Like Ríos Montt." *NACLA Report on the Americas* 24(4): 4–7.
Suh, Doowon. 2015. "Democracy Disenchanted and Autocracy Glamorized in Korea." *International Journal of Social Science Studies* 3(6): 9–19.
Svolik, Milan W. 2012. *The Politics of Authoritarian Rule*. New York, NY: Cambridge University Press.
Szwarcberg, Mariela. 2012. "Uncertainty, Political Clientelism, and Voter Turnout in Latin America: Why Parties Conduct Rallies in Argentina." *Comparative Politics* 45(1): 88–106.
  2013. "The Microfoundations of Political Clientelism: Lessons from the Argentine Case." *Latin American Research Review* 48(2): 32–54.
  2014. "Political Parties and Rallies in Latin America." *Party Politics* 20(3): 456–466.
Tarouco, Gabriela da Silva. 1999. "O Partido da Frente Liberal: trajetória e papel no sistema político." MA thesis, Department of Political Science, University of Campinas.
Tarouco, Gabriela da Silva and Rafael Machado Madeira. 2013. "Partidos, programas e o debate sobre esquerda e direita no Brasil." *Revista de Sociologia e Política* 21 (45): 149–165.
Tavits, Margit. 2013. *Post-Communist Democracies and Party Organization*. New York, NY: Cambridge University Press.
Tavits, Margit and Natalia Letki. 2009. "When Left is Right: Party Ideology and Policy in Post-Communist Europe." *American Political Science Review* 104(4): 555–569.
Taylor, Matthew M. 2017. "Corruption and Accountability in Brazil." In Peter Kingstone and Timothy J. Power, eds., *Democratic Brazil Divided*, pp. 77–96. Pittsburgh: University of Pittsburgh Press.
Thaler, Kai M. 2017. "Nicaragua: A Return to Caudillismo." *Journal of Democracy* 28 (2): 157–169.
Thermænius, Edvard. 1935. *Riksdagspartierna*, Vol. 17. Stockholm: Sveriges Riksdag.
Thompson, Wayne C. 1996. "The Party of Democratic Socialism in the New Germany." *Communist and Post-Communist Studies* 29(4): 435–452.
Tomsa, Dirk. 2008. *Party Politics and Democratization in Indonesia: Golkar in the Post-Suharto Era*. London: Routledge.
  2012. "Still the Natural Government Party? Challenges and Opportunities for Golkar ahead of the 2014 Election." *South East Asia Research* 20(4): 491–509.
Toole, James. 2003. "Straddling the East-West Divide: Party Organisation and Communist Legacies in East Central Europe." *Europe-Asia Studies* 55(1): 101–118.
Torre, Juan Carlos. 1990. *La vieja guardia sindical y Perón: sobre los orígenes del peronismo*. Buenos Aires: Editorial Sudamericana-Instituto Torcuato Di Tella.
Treisman, Daniel. 2011. "Presidential Popularity in a Hybrid Regime: Russia under Yeltsin and Putin." *American Journal of Political Science* 55(3): 590–609.
Trejo, Raúl, ed. 1988. *Las redes de Televisa*. Mexico: Claves Latinoamericanas.
Treviño-Rangel, Javier. 2012. "Policing the Past: Transitional Justice and the Special Prosecutor's Office in Mexico, 2000–2006." PhD dissertation, Department of Sociology, London School of Economics and Political Science.

Trudeau, Robert H. 1993. *Guatemalan Politics: The Popular Struggle for Democracy.* Boulder: Lynne Rienner.

Tsebelis, George. 1990. *Nested Games: Rational Choice in Comparative Politics.* Berkeley, CA: University of California Press.

Tucker, Joshua A. 2006. *Regional Economic Voting: Russia, Poland, Hungary, Slovakia and the Czech Republic, 1990–1999.* New York, NY: Cambridge University Press.

Tucker, Joshua and Eleanor Neff Powell. 2014. "Revisiting Electoral Volatility in Post-Communist Countries: New Data, New Results and New Approaches." *British Journal of Political Science* 44(1): 123–147.

Tuckman, Jo. 2011. "Scandal Erupts Around Union Chief in Mexico." *The Guardian*, July 8.

2012. "Mexican Media Scandal: Secretive Televisa Unit Promoted PRI Candidate." *The Guardian*, June 26.

Turner, Brian. 2014. "Paraguay: La vuelta del Partido Colorado al poder." *Revista de Ciencia Política* 34(1): 249–266.

Urrutia, Adriana. 2011a. "Que la Fuerza (2011) esté con Keiko: El nuevo baile del fujimorismo." In Carlos Meléndez, ed., *Post-candidatos: Guía analítica de supervivencia hasta las próximas elecciones*, pp. 93–120. Lima: Aerolíneas Editoriales.

2011b. "Hacer campaña y construir partido: Fuerza 2011 y su estrategia para (re)legitimar al fujimorismo a través de su organización." *Argumentos* 5(2), http://revistaargumentos.iep.org.pe/articulos/hacer-campana-y-construir-partido-fuerza-2011-y-su-estrategia-para-relegitimar-al-fujimorismo-a-traves-de-su-organizacion/ [Accessed March 21, 2018].

Valenzuela, J. Samuel. 1992. "Democratic Consolidation in Post-Transitional Settings: Notion, Process and Facilitating Conditions." In Scott Mainwaring, Guillermo O'Donnell, and J. Samuel Valenzuela, eds., *Issues in Democratic Consolidation: The New South American Democracies in Comparative Perspective*, pp. 353–375. Notre Dame: Notre Dame University Press.

van Biezen, Ingrid, Peter Mair, and Thomas Poguntke. 2012. "Going, Going ... Gone? The Decline of Party Membership in Contemporary Europe." *European Journal of Political Research* 51: 24–56.

van de Walle, Nicolas. 2001. *African Economies and the Politics of Permanent Crisis, 1979–1999.* New York, NY: Cambridge University Press.

2003. "Presidentialism and Clientelism in Africa's Emerging Party Systems." *The Journal of Modern African Studies* 41(2): 297–321.

2007. "Meet the New Boss, Same as the Old Boss? The Evolution of Political Clientelism in Africa." In Herbert Kitschelt and Steven I. Wilkinson, eds., *Patrons, Clients and Policies: Patterns of Democratic Accountability and Political Competition*, pp. 50–67. Cambridge: Cambridge University Press.

van Donge, Jan Kees. 1995. "Kamuzu's Legacy: The Democratization of Malawi: Or Searching for the Rules of the Game in African Politics." *African Affairs* 94(375): 227–257.

Van Dyck, Brandon. 2018. "External Appeal, Internal Dominance: How Party Leaders Contribute to Successful Party Building." *Latin American Politics and Society* 60 (1): 1–26.

Vázquez Rosas, Fernando. 2012. "En Tabasco el petróleo es tricolor." *Revista Nueva Era Online* 1(6): 29.

Vengroff, Richard and Lucy Creevey. 1997 "Senegal: The Evolution of a Quasi Democracy." In John F. Clark and David E. Gardinier, eds., *Political Reform in Francophone Africa*, pp. 204–222. Boulder, CO: Westview Press.

Villalón, Leonardo. 2006. *Islamic Society and State Power in Senegal: Disciples and Citizens in Fatick*. New York, NY: Cambridge University Press.

Villalón, Leonardo A. and Peter VonDoepp, eds. 2005. *The Fate of Africa's Democratic Experiments: Elites and Institutions*. Bloomington, IN: Indiana University Press.

Vincent, Mary. 1996. *Catholicism in the Second Spanish Republic: Religion and Politics in Salamanca, 1930–1936*. New York: Clarendon Press.

von Beyme, Klaus. 1984. *Parteien Im Westlichen Demokratien*. Munich: Piper.

von Gerlach, Hellmut. 1925. *Errinerungen Eines Junkers* [Memoir of a Junker]. Berlin: Die Welt am Montag.

Vuković, Ivan. 2015. "Political Dynamics of the Post-Communist Montenegro: One-Party Show." *Democratization* 22(1): 73–91.

Wade, Robert. 1990. *Governing the Market: Economic Theory and the Role of Government in East Asian Industrialization*. Princeton, NJ: Princeton University Press.

Wald, Kenneth D. 1983. *Crosses on the Ballot: Patterns of British Voter Alignment since 1885*. Princeton, NJ: Princeton University Press.

Waller, Michael. 1995. "Adaptation of the Former Communist Parties of East Central Europe: A Case of Social-Democratization?" *Party Politics* 1(4): 473–490.

Wang, Yi-Ting. 2013. "A Case Study of Parties' Programmatic and Clientelistic Electoral Appeals in South Korea." In Herbert Kitschelt, ed., *Research and Dialogue on Programmatic Parties and Party Systems. Case Study Report*, pp. 158–188. Stockholm: International Institute for Democracy and Electoral Assistance (IDEA).

Way, Lucan. 2015. *Pluralism by Default: Weak Autocrats and the Rise of Competitive Politics*. Baltimore, MD: Johns Hopkins University Press.

Weitz-Shapiro, Rebecca. 2014. *Curbing Clientelism in Argentina: Politics, Poverty, and Social Policy*. New York, NY: Cambridge University Press.

Weyden, Patrick Vander. 2006. "The Comeback of Désiré Bouterse? General Elections in Suriname 2005." *Representation* 42(3): 235–242.

Weyland, Kurt. 1996. "Neo-Populism and Neo-Liberalism in Latin America: Unexpected Affinities." *Studies in Comparative International Development* 32 (3): 3–31.

 1999. "Neoliberal Populism in Latin America and Eastern Europe." *Comparative Politics* 31(4): 379–401.

Whitehead, Laurence. 1986. "Bolivia's Failed Democratization, 1977–1980." In Guillermo O'Donnell, Philippe C. Schmitter, and Laurence Whitehead, eds., *Transitions from Authoritarian Rule, Vol. 2: Latin America*, pp. 49–71. Baltimore, MD: Johns Hopkins University Press.

Whitfield, Lindsay. 2009. "'Change for a Better Ghana': Party Competition, Institutionalization, and Alternation in Ghana's 2008 Elections." *African Affairs* 108(433): 621–641.

Widner, Jennifer A. 1992. *The Rise of a Party-State in Kenya: From Harambee! to Nyayo!*. Berkeley, CA: University of California Press.

Winckler, Edwin. 1984. "Institutionalization and Participation on Taiwan: From Hard to Soft Authoritarianism?" *The China Quarterly* 99: 481–499.

Wolf, Anne. 2014. *Can Secular Parties Lead the New Tunisia?* Washington, DC: Carnegie Endowment for International Peace.

Wong, Joseph. 2004. *Healthy Democracies: Welfare Politics in Taiwan and South Korea.* Ithaca, NY: Cornell University Press.

2008. "Maintaining KMT Dominance: Party Adaptation in Authoritarian and Democratic Taiwan." In Edward Friedman and Joseph Wong, eds., *Political Transitions in Dominant Party Systems: Learning to Lose,* pp. 57–74. New York, NY: Routledge.

2011. *Betting on Biotech: Innovation and the Limits of Asia's Developmental State.* Ithaca, NY: Cornell University Press.

Woo-Cumings, Meredith, ed. 1999. *The Developmental State.* Ithaca, NY: Cornell University Press.

World Bank. 2014. *World Bank Development Indicators.* Available from: http://databank.worldbank.org/data/views/variableSelection/selectvariables.aspx?source=world-development-indicators [Accessed January 20, 2017].

2016. *World Development Indicators,* Online. Washington, DC: World Bank.

Wu, Jieh-min and Mei Liao. 2015. "Chong tung-du dau zhong-guo in-sou" [National Identity and the China Factor]. *Taiwan Shihui Xue [Taiwan Sociology]* 29: 87–130.

Wu, Yu-Shan. 2011. "Power Shift, Strategic Triangle, and Alliances in East Asia." *Issues & Studies* 47(4): 1–42.

Wyrod, Christopher. 2008. "Sierra Leone: A Vote for Better Governance." *Journal of Democracy* 19(1): 70–83.

Young, Crawford. 2012. *The Postcolonial State in Africa: Fifty Years of Independence, 1960–2010.* Madison: University of Wisconsin Press.

Zechmeister, Elizabeth J. and Daniel Zizumbo-Colunga. 2013. "The Varying Political Toll of Concerns about Corruption in Good versus Bad Economic Times." *Comparative Political Studies* 46(10): 1190–1218.

Zederman, Mathilde. 2016. "The Hegemonic Bourguibist Discourse on Modernity in Post-Revolutionary Tunisia." *Middle East Law and Governance* 8(2–3): 179–200.

Ziblatt, Daniel. 1998a. "The Adaptation of Ex-Communist Parties to Post-Communist East Central Europe: A Comparative Study of the East German and Hungarian Ex-Communist Parties." *Communist and Post-Communist Studies* 31(2): 119–137.

1998b. "Putting Humpty Dumpty Back Together Again: Communism's Collapse and the Reconstruction of the East German Ex-Communist Party." *German Politics and Society* 16(1): 1–29.

2006. "How Did Europe Democratize?" *World Politics* 58(2): 311–338.

2008. "Does Landholding Inequality Block Democratization?" *World Politics* 60(4): 610–641.

2017. *Conservative Parties and the Birth of Democracy.* New York, NY: Cambridge University Press.

Zimmer, Kerstin and Olexiy Haran. 2008. "Unfriendly Takeover: Successor Parties in Ukraine." *Communist and Post-Communist Studies.* 41: 541–561.

Zolberg, Aristide R. 1966. *Creating Political Order: The Party-States of West Africa.* Chicago: Rand McNally.

Zubek, Voytek. 1994. "The Reassertion of the Left in Post-Communist Poland." *Europe-Asia Studies* 46(5): 801–837.

1995. "The Phoenix Out of the Ashes: The Rise to Power of Poland's Post-Communist SdRP." *Communist and Post-Communist Studies* 28(3): 275–306.

Zucco Jr., Cesar. 2007. "Where's the Bias? A Reassessment of the Chilean Electoral System." *Electoral Studies* 26: 303–314.
　2008. "The President's 'New' Constituency: Lula and the Pragmatic Vote in Brazil's 2006 Presidential Elections." *Journal of Latin American Studies* 40: 29–49.
Zucco Jr., Cesar and Timothy J. Power. 2012. "Elite Preferences in a Consolidating Democracy: The Brazilian Legislative Surveys, 1990–2009." *Latin American Politics and Society* 54(4): 1–27.

Index

ADN. *See* Nationalist Democratic Action (Bolivia)
Africa, patronage structures in, 211
African Party for the Independence of Cape Verde, 1, 3, 13, 48, 178, 212, 218, 343
All People's Congress (Sierra Leone), 24, 45, 178, 217
ANAPO. *See* National Popular Alliance (Colombia)
APC. *See* All People's Congress (Sierra Leone)
AREMA. *See* Association for the Rebirth of Madagascar
ARENA (Brazil). *See* National Renovating Alliance (Brazil)
ARENA (El Salvador). *See* Nationalist Republican Alliance (El Salvador)
Association for the Rebirth of Madagascar, 28, 41, 343, 351
authoritarian baggage, 2, 14–15, 58, 339–340
authoritarian diasporas, 33, 212, 234, 336, 344–345, 358
authoritarian enclaves, 26, 27, 235, 281, 341
authoritarian inheritance, xix, 1, 14, 209, 266, 285, 337, 350
  and source of party finance, 10, 12–13
  clientelistic networks, 12
  concept of, 9–10
  party brands, 10–11
  source of cohesion, 13
  territorial organization, 11–12
authoritarian regimes
  popular support for, 10, 12, 337–339
  ruling parties of, 209–211, 259, 285, 288–290
  types of, 23–24, 115, 340–341

authoritarian successor parties. *See also* authoritarian baggage; authoritarian inheritance; communist successor parties
  and authoritarian preferences, 351–352
  and authoritarian regime type, 23–24
  and authoritarian regression, 27–28
  and authoritarian vestiges, 26–27
  and competitive landscape, 24
  and electoral institutions, 22–23, 204
  and party adaptation, 345–346
  and party brands, 10–11
  and party system institutionalization, 28–29
  and performance of the authoritarian regime, 19–20, 122, 204
  and performance of the new democracy, 20–21
  and the disloyal opposition, 29–30
  and transitional justice, 25–26
  and transitions to democracy, 21–22, 30–31, 98, 217
  and usable pasts, xviii, 290
  causes of existence, xix, 9
  clientelistic networks of, 12
  definition of, xvii, 2–4, 5, 36, 213, 340–342
  effects on democracy of, xx, 25, 279, 342
  funding of, 12–13
  future of, 351, 352–353
  operationalization of, 36, 47, 172, 213, 334
  party cohesion in, 13
  pathways of, 355–359
  performance of, xix, 18–19, 24, 121–122, 146
  prevalence of, xvii, 1, 6–9, 336, 341
  reinvention of, 158

398

Index

strategies of, 14–18, 114, 118–119, 121, 209, 340
study of, xviii, 4–5, 340
territorial organization of, 11–12
types of, xvii, 53, 58
authoritarian successor parties in developmental Asia
  and democratic stabilization, xx, 285, 286–288, 313
  and transitions to democracy, 286, 311–312
  coalitional strength of, 290–291
  democratic moderation of, 285–286, 292–295, 312
authoritarian successor parties in Sub-Saharan Africa, 213
  and authoritarian inheritance, 176, 182–183, 185, 210, 216–217
  and charismatic leadership, 228
  and competitive landscape, 208, 211–212, 346–347
  and economic performance, 187–188, 203–204
  and electoral institutions, 183–184, 185, 228
  and elite defection, 207, 212
  and new ruling party cohesion, 184, 186–187
  and party system fragmentation, 217–219
  and party-switching, 179–181
  and patronage structures, 207–208, 211
  as opposition parties, 176–178, 181–182, 203, 205
  performance of, 216
  strategies of, 183, 346
  success of, 176, 178, 179, 184–185
  survival of, 203, 207, 219–220, 227–228
AVF. *See* General Electoral League (Sweden)

Balaguer, Joaquín, 13, 28, 114, 116, 343
Banda, Hastings Kamuzu, 224, 228
  regime of, 226
Banzer, Hugo, 3, 13, 114, 115, 120, 121, 343
  dictatorship and human rights violations of, 122–123, 124
Basotho National Party, 218
Ben Ali, Zine El Abidine, 16, 18, 49
Benin
  electoral rules, 202
  party system of, 218
BNP. *See* Basotho National Party
Bourguiba, Habib, 17, 18, 49
Bouterse, Dési, 17, 26, 49, 343, 352
Brazil
  authoritarian diaspora in, 234, 344
  authoritarian regime, 229–230, 250, 253
  authoritarian successor parties. *See* Liberal Front Party/Democrats (Brazil); Social Democratic Party/Progressive Party (Brazil)
  coalitional presidentialism in, 243–245
  transition to democracy in, 229–230, 235, 250, 252
Brazilian Labor Party, 114, 130, 139, 234, 244
Brazilian Social Democracy Party, 233, 243, 246, 247, 249, 251
Britain
  democratization in, 323–324
  economic modernization in, 319–320
British Conservative Party
  and democracy, 322, 326–327, 350
  strategy of, 324–326

Calderón, Felipe, 21, 266, 268, 276
Cárdenas, Cuauhtémoc, 260, 261
Cárdenas, Lázaro, 258
Cardoso, Fernando Henrique, 233, 236
CCN. *See* Nationalist Civic Crusade (Venezuela)
Chávez, Hugo, 119, 131, 138, 339, 353
Chiang Ching-kuo, 90, 106, 108, 297
Chiang Kai-shek, 296, 297
Chile
  authoritarian elites in, 234
  authoritarian preferences in, 10
  authoritarian regime in, 252–253
  electoral rules in, 22
  party system, 252
  transition to democracy in, 252
Chun Doo-hwan, 302, 304
  regime of, 301
clientelism, 12
  and type of polity, 62
  dimensions of, 59–60
  types of, 60–61
Collor de Mello, Fernando, 232, 246
Communist Party of Bohemia and Moravia (Czech Republic), 3, 17, 39, 149, 153, 158, 159, 160, 163, 348, 349
Communist Party of Cuba, 9, 353–354
communist successor parties, 145, 173–174
  and brand dilution, 160–162, 171
  and democratic transition, 145
  and electoral success, 163
  and incumbent punishment, 158–160, 171
  and organizational strength, 160–161

communist successor parties (cont.)
    and reinvention, 145–147, 155–156, 158, 162–163, 170–171, 348
    failure of, 153, 348–349
    orthodox, 146, 147–148, 155–156, 163–164
    strategies of, 15, 148–150
competitive authoritarianism, 2, 122, 206, 340, *See also* electoral authoritarianism
competitive landscape, 24, 32, 176, 179, 196, 208, 209, 211, 218, 227, 346

D'Aubuisson, Roberto, 16, 39
da Silva, Luiz Inácio Lula, 233, 238, 247–248, 249, 251
DEM. *See* Liberal Front Party/Democrats (Brazil)
Democratic Accountability and Linkage Project (DALP), 65–66
    indicators, 66–68
Democratic Justice Party. *See* South Korea, authoritarian successor party of
Democratic Labor Party of Lithuania, 41, 63, 155, 159
Democratic Left Alliance (Poland), 82, 151–152, 159, 162, 166–167
    collapse and corruption scandals of, 154, 166, 168
Democratic Liberal Party. *See* South Korea, authoritarian successor party
Democratic Party of Socialists (Montenegro), 42, 346, 358
Democratic Progressive Party (Taiwan), 88, 90, 94, 95, 101, 102, 103, 111, 298
    agenda of, 106, 107, 297
    performance of, 100, 107–108, 109, 111, 299, 300
Democratic Republican Party. *See* South Korea, authoritarian successor party of
Democratic Revolutionary Party (Panama), 3, 43, 134–135, 140, 352
    and *Torrijismo*, 136
    de-personalization of, 135
    strategies of, 16, 119, 126–127
    survival and success of, 114, 135, 136–137
democratic stability, 291–292
developmental Asia, authoritarian ruling parties in
    and state capacity, 289–290
    and transitions to democracy, 288–289, 291
    strength of, 285, 290

Direction-Social Democracy (Slovakia), 7, 37, 63, 153
    success of, 165
DJP. *See* South Korea, authoritarian successor party of
DKP. *See* German Conservative Party
DNVP. *See* German National People's Party
DPP. *See* Democratic Progressive Party (Taiwan)
DPS. *See* Democratic Party of Socialists (Montenegro)

electoral authoritarianism, 2, 340, *See also* competitive authoritarianism
Essebsi, Beji Caid, 4, 17, 49
Europe
    cohesion of the right in, 331–333
    democratization of, 314–316
    interwar years in, 328–329
    party fragmentation in, 333–334

Federal Electoral Institute (Mexico), 261, 274, 275
Fico, Robert, 153, 164, 165
Fidesz (Hungary), 153, 154, 159
former authoritarian ruling parties
    clientelistic linkage strategies of, 53, 56, 59, 61, 72–78
    definition of, 3, 59
    in Sub-Saharan Africa, 175–176, 178–179, 206, 207
    linkage capabilities of, 58
    network extensiveness of, 68–72
    operationalization of, 62–65
    organizational stock and advantages of, 59, 81–82
    programmatic profile and strategies of, 53–54, 58, 78–80
former dictators elected back into office, 343, 345
Fox, Vicente, 261, 266, 267, 268, 269, 276, 279
FRG. *See* Guatemalan Republican Front
FSLN. *See* Sandinista National Liberation Front (Nicaragua)
Fujimori, Alberto
    and political parties, 120
    government of, 113, 127, 131
    popularity of, 127
Fujimori, Keiko, 113, 116, 127, 128, 130, 138
Fujimorismo
    and leadership succession, 130
    strategy of, 127–128
    success of, 113, 114, 127, 137–138

Index

General Electoral League (Sweden), 331–333, 350
German Conservative Party. *See also* German National People's Party
  and democracy, 321, 322–323
German National People's Party, 323, 327–328, *See also* German Conservative Party
Germany
  democracy in, 320–321
  economic modernization in, 319–320
  labor in, 320
  Weimar republic, 320, 327
Ghana
  party system in, 218–219, 224
  transition to democracy in, 220
Golkar (Indonesia), 36, 40, 357
  and transition to democracy, xx, 307
  authoritarian inheritance of, 285
  democratic reforms of, 309
  policy positions of, 310
  strategies of, 310
  success of, 3, 22, 307–309
Grand National Party. *See* South Korea, authoritarian successor party
Guatemalan Republican Front, 17, 40, 116, 140
  and transitional justice, 26
  performance of, 22–23, 339
  strategy of, 125–126
Guzmán, Jaime, 27, 252
Gyurcsány, Ferenc, 154, 169, 170

Habibie, B. J., 307, 308, 309, 310
Hungarian Socialist Party, 1, 3, 40, 82
  collapse of, 154–155, 170
  ideological position, 168
  organizational structure of, 169–170
  performance of, 152–153, 159, 168–169
  reinvention of, 152, 348

IFE. *See* Federal Electoral Institute (Mexico)
Independent Democratic Union (Chile), 3, 13, 22, 38, 234
  and authoritarianism, 27, 352
Indonesia
  authoritarian diaspora in, 310–311
  democracy in, 292, 311
  economic crisis in, 309
  New Order regime, 306–307
  transition to democracy in, 307, 309

Institutional Revolutionary Party (Mexico), 3, 41, 339
  and big business, 272
  and democratic governability, 279–280
  and labor unions, 266–267, 271
  and party system institutionalization, 280
  and Pemex, 270–271
  and performance of opponents, 278–279
  and subnational authoritarianism, 27, 341
  and subnational resources, 263, 264–266, 347
  and the judiciary, 275
  and the media, 273–275
  and transitional justice, 26
  as authoritarian ruling party, 259
  corruption scandals, 281–282
  effects on democracy of, xx, 281–282
  ideological shift of, 260
  origins of, 258
  resilience of, 1, 262–263, 283

Justicialista Party. *See* Peronist Party (Argentina)

KANU. *See* Kenya African National Union
Kenya African National Union, 24, 179, 358
  and polarization, 223–224
  authoritarian diaspora in, 344
  authoritarian inheritance of, 222–223
  internal governance of, 223
  performance of, 220–221
  strategies of, 222
Kérékou, Mathieu, 36, 202, 343, 357
Kim Dae-jung, 98, 104, 302, 305
Kim Young-sam, 98, 104, 105, 302, 304
KMT. *See* Kuomintang (Taiwan)
KSČM. *See* Communist Party of Bohemia and Moravia (Czech Republic)
Kuomintang (Taiwan), xvii, xx, 1, 3, 13, 46, 84, 90, 296, 356
  and issue dynamics, 103–104, 106–107
  and national security, 94
  and transition to democracy, 98, 296–298
  authoritarian inheritance of, 93–94, 285
  business holdings of, 95–96, 103, 111
  crisis of, 100, 110–111, 300
  economic reform, 299
  electoral performance of, 86, 88, 108, 109–110, 297, 299–300
  endurance of, 111–112
  ideological position of, 90
  party brand of, 94–95, 110–111

Kuomintang (Taiwan) (cont.)
  reform strategy of, 100–101, 298–299, 300
  success of, 19, 84–85, 86, 88–89, 108, 300
  territorial organization of, 11, 95, 101–103, 111

Labour Party (UK), 323, 324, 325, 326
LDDP. *See* Democratic Labor Party of Lithuania
LDP. *See* Liberal Democratic Party (Japan)
Lee Teng-hui, 106, 298, 300
Left, The. *See* Party of Democratic Socialism/The Left (Germany)
Liberal Democratic Party (Japan), 82, 99, 304
Liberal Front Party/Democrats (Brazil), 344, 351
  as authoritarian successor party, 38, 231–232
  decline of, 232–233, 243, 247, 248, 251, 347–348
  history of, 113, 230
  ideological position of, 238–239
  internal organization of, 241–242
  participation in coalitions, 242
  party elites of, 241
  performance of, 19, 245–246, 251
  policy positions of, 235–237
  resources, 246–247
  strategies of, 15–16, 242, 250, 251, 347–348
  territorial penetration of, 239–241
Liberia, 216
Liberty Korea Party. *See* South Korea, authoritarian successor party

Ma Ying-jeou, 108, 109, 300
Maduro, Nicolás, 119, 138, 353
Malawi, 225–226
Malawi Congress Party, 18, 41, 179, 182, 228
  performance of, 224–225, 228
  survival and success of, 226–227
Mali, 178, 187, 216
Maluf, Paolo, 230, 239, 245, 249, 252
Martínez de Perón, Isabel, 116, 129, 130, 133
MCP. *See* Malawi Congress Party
Medgyessy, Péter, 168, 170
Mexico
  authoritarian preferences in, 10
  authoritarian regime in, 257, 258–260, 271–272
  labor unions in, 267
  party identification in, 277–278
  party system in, 278

  perception of democracy, 281
  political system of, 263–265
  retrospective voting in, 276–277
  the media in, 258, 261, 266, 275, 282
  transition to democracy in, 21, 26, 257, 260–261
Miller, Leszek, 165, 166, 168
minjung movement, 301–302, 304
MLSTP. *See* Movement for the Liberation of São Tomé and Príncipe
MMD. *See* Movement for Multiparty Democracy (Zambia)
Mongolian People's Party, 3, 42
Montesinos, Vladimiro, 127
Movement for Multiparty Democracy (Zambia), 199–200
  weak cohesion of, 200–201
Movement for the Liberation of São Tomé and Príncipe, 3, 48, 178, 343
MPP. *See* Mongolian People's Party
MSzP. *See* Hungarian Socialist Party

National Action Party (Mexico)
  administrations, 266, 276
  and labor unions, 267–268
  internal rifts in, 279
  performance of, 259
National Democratic Congress (Ghana), 1, 4, 40, 217, 347
  and polarization, 224
  authoritarian inheritance of, 222–223
  cohesion of, 192–193
  internal governance, 223
  strategies of, 190–192, 221–222
  success of, 24, 178, 190, 192, 217, 220–221
National Democratic Party (Suriname), 49, 343, 352
  strategies of, 17
National Party (South Africa), 121, 179, 187
National Popular Alliance (Colombia), 116, 118, 130, 131, 139
National Renovating Alliance (Brazil), 230, 231, 234, 235, 236, 248, 250, 252
National Union of Education Workers (Mexico), 268–270
Nationalist Civic Crusade (Venezuela), 22, 140
Nationalist Democratic Action (Bolivia), 1, 3, 13, 17, 38, 139, 343
  electoral performance of, 120
  strategy of, 123–123
Nationalist Democratic Organization (El Salvador), 11–12

Index

Nationalist Republican Alliance (El Salvador), 40
  cohesion of, 13
  history of, 11
  strategies of, 16
NDC. *See* National Democratic Congress (Ghana)
NDP. *See* National Democratic Party (Suriname)
negative legitimacy, 20
Neves, Tancredo, 230, 235
New Alliance Party (Mexico), 262, 270, 279
New Party (Taiwan), 112, 290, 299
New Patriotic Party (Ghana), 347
  cohesion of, 192–193
  performance of, 220
Nidaa Tounes (Tunisia), xvii, 1, 4, 49
  and democracy, 30
  strategies of, 16–17
Noriega, Manuel, 16
  ousting of, 26
  regime of, 126, 135
NP (South Africa). *See* National Party (South Africa)
NP (Taiwan). *See* New Party (Taiwan)
NPP. *See* New Patriotic Party (Ghana)

old regime conservative parties
  and democratization, 30, 314–315, 317–319, 329–330, 334–335, 342
  features of, 5, 316–317
  opposition parties, 3, 13, 213
  and party cohesion, 24, 32
  challenges of, 177, 181–182, 203
ORDEN. *See* Nationalist Democratic Organization (El Salvador)

PAICV. *See* African Party for the Independence of Cape Verde
PAN. *See* National Action Party (Mexico)
PANAL. *See* New Alliance Party (Mexico)
PAP. *See* People's Action Party (Singapore)
Park Chung-hee, 10, 45, 106, 339, 345, 352
  regime of, 301
Park Geun-hye, 106, 306, 313, 343
  impeachment of, 112
party brands, 5, 10, 128, 130, 349
Party of Democratic Socialism/The Left (Germany), 48, 159
Party of the Brazilian Democratic Movement, 233, 234, 243, 246, 248, 251, 344

Party of the Democratic Left (Slovakia), 37, 45, 63
  collapse of, 153–154, 164–165
  performance of, 150–151
  strategy of, 149–150
Party of the Democratic Revolution (Mexico), 7, 260–261
  corruption scandals, 276
  party system institutionalization, 28, 184, 279, 280
party-building, 10, 349
  and authoritarian inheritance, 349–350
  and personalism, 119, 120, 137
PCC. *See* Communist Party of Cuba
PDS (Germany). *See* Party of Democratic Socialism/The Left (Germany)
PDS (Senegal). *See* Senegalese Democratic Party
PDS/PP. *See* Social Democratic Party/Progressive Party (Brazil)
Peña Nieto, Enrique, 21, 262, 271, 277, 282
People's Action Party (Singapore), 31, 353
People's Party (Spain), xvii, 1, 3, 18, 46, 352
People's Revolutionary Party of Benin, 23, 24, 343
  collapse of, 201, 202, 357
  policies of, 201–202
Pérez Balladares, Ernesto, 16, 26, 136
Pérez Jiménez, Marcos, 22
Perón, Juan, 120, 132–133
Peronism. *See* Peronist Party (Argentina)
Peronist Party (Argentina), 139, 352
  survival and success of, 133–134
personalistic authoritarian successor parties
  and leadership succession, 129–130
  and partisan identities, 130–131
  and personalistic leaders, 119–121, 137
  definition of, 115
  de-personalization of, 114–115, 128–129, 132, 137
  electoral performance of, 114, 132, 137
  features of, 113, 115–116
  in Latin America, 113, 116, 118, 122, 137
  organizational strength of, 118
  strategies of, 119, 121, 137
PFL. *See* Liberal Front Party/Democrats (Brazil)
Pinochet, Augusto, 10, 12, 22, 253
PJ. *See* Peronist Party (Argentina)
PMDB. *See* Party of the Brazilian Democratic Movement
Polish Peasants' Party, 44, 152
political parties. *See also* party-building
  and polarization, 131

political parties (cont.)
  career development model of, 54–55
  clientelistic strategies of, 55–56, 60–61
  geographical extensiveness of, 66
  programmatic appeal of, 67
  programmatic linkage strategies of, 56–57
popular autocrats, 10, 122, 337
portable skills, 9, 10, 148, 207, 209, 280
Portillo, Alfonso, 116, 126
PP (Brazil). *See* Social Democratic Party/Progressive Party (Brazil)
PP (Spain). *See* People's Party (Spain)
PRD (Mexico). *See* Party of the Democratic Revolution (Mexico)
PRD (Panama). *See* Democratic Revolutionary Party (Panama)
PRI. *See* Institutional Revolutionary Party (Mexico)
Progressive Party. *See* Social Democratic Party/Progressive Party (Brazil)
PRPB. *See* People's Revolutionary Party of Benin
PRSC. *See* Social Christian Reformist Party (Dominican Republic)
PS. *See* Socialist Party of Senegal
PSD. *See* Social Democratic Party (São Tomé and Príncipe)
PSDB. *See* Brazilian Social Democracy Party
PSL. *See* Polish Peasants' Party
PSUV. *See* United Socialist Party of Venezuela
PT. *See* Workers' Party (Brazil)
PTB. *See* Brazilian Labor Party

Ratsiraka, Didier, 28, 343
Rawlings, Jerry John, 4, 23, 40, 178, 220, 221, 223, 228
RB. *See* Renaissance Party of Benin
reactive authoritarian successor parties, 3–4, 53, 82, 233, *See also* Liberal Front Party/Democrats (Brazil)
Renaissance Party of Benin, 202–203
Ríos Montt, Efraín, 22, 26, 116, 119, 124
  human rights violations, 124
  popularity of, 124–124
Roh Tae-woo, 302, 303–304
Rojas Pinilla, Gustavo, 118, 122, 129
Rousseff, Dilma, 238, 242, 249

Saenuri. *See* South Korea, authoritarian successor party of
Salinas de Gortari, Carlos, 261, 271
Sandinista National Liberation Front (Nicaragua), 28, 42, 343, 351, 354
Sarney, José, 36, 230, 235, 241, 245, 246
SBY. *See* Yudhoyono, Susilo Bambang
SDL'. *See* Party of the Democratic Left (Slovakia)
SdRP. *See* Social Democracy of the Republic of Poland
Senegalese Democratic Party, 194, 196–197
Sierra Leone, 218–219
SLD. *See* Democratic Left Alliance (Poland)
Smer-SD. *See* Direction-Social Democracy (Slovakia)
SNTE. *See* National Union of Education Workers (Mexico)
Social Christian Reformist Party (Dominican Republic), 13, 28, 39, 116, 139, 343, 351
Social Democracy of the Republic of Poland, xvii, 3, 44
  organizational structure, 165–166
  performance of, 151–152
  strategy of, 151, 348
Social Democratic Party (São Tomé and Príncipe), 3, 48
Social Democratic Party/Progressive Party (Brazil), 3, 38, 231–232, 241–242, 344, 351
  ideological position of, 239
  participation in coalitions, 242
  party elites, 241
  performance of, 19, 245, 251
  policy positions of, 235–237
  scandals involving, 248–249
  strategies of, 242, 250
  territorial penetration of, 239–241
Socialist Party of Senegal
  and electoral rules, 194–195, 196
  and new ruling party cohesion, 196
  as opposition party, 194
  performance of, 196, 197, 217
  strategies of, 193–194
  success of, 179, 193
Solidarity (Poland), xvii, 159
South Korea
  authoritarian preferences in, 10
  democracy in, 84, 292
  economic crisis in, 105, 301, 305
  political landscape of, 89–90
  transition to democracy in, 98–99, 301–302
South Korea, authoritarian successor party of, 3, 45, 84, 94, 112
  and big business, 97, 103

Index

and democracy, 104–105, 304–305
and issue dynamics, 103–104, 105–106
and transition to democracy, xx, 98, 302–303
authoritarian inheritance of, 93–94, 285
clientelist networks of, 96–97, 102
democratic reform of, 303–304
economic reform of, 304
endurance of, 305–306
organizational development of, 99, 101–103
success of, 84–85, 86–89, 108, 303, 305
Spain, democratic breakdown in, 333–334
subnational authoritarianism, 26, 275, 281, 341
Sub-Saharan Africa
  authoritarian ruling parties in, 210–211
  transitions to democracy in, 206–207, 213–216
Suharto, 306, 308, 309, 310
Sweden, democratization in, 320, 331–333

Taiwan
  democracy in, 84, 292
  party identification in, 90–92
  political landscape of, 90
  relations with China, 94
Temer, Michel, 242, 249
Torrijos, Martín, 126, 127, 343, 345
Torrijos, Omar, 16, 339, 352
  regime of, 126, 134–136

UCD. *See* Union of the Democratic Center (Spain)
UDF. *See* United Democratic Front (Malawi)
UDI. *See* Independent Democratic Union (Chile)
UMNO. *See* United Malays National Organisation
Union of the Democratic Center (Spain), 18, 23, 45
UNIP. *See* United National Independence Party (Zambia)
United Democratic Front (Malawi), 225, 226–227
United Malays National Organisation, 9, 353
United National Independence Party (Zambia), 179
  and electoral rules, 199–200
  failure of, 197–198, 200, 201
  performance of, 218
  strategies of, 198–199
United Socialist Party of Venezuela, 114, 119, 138, 353
usable pasts, 9, 15, 148, 210, 253

Vargas, Getúlio, 114, 122, 139

Workers' Party (Brazil), 233, 238, 241, 243, 244, 246, 251, 252

Yudhoyono, Susilo Bambang, 308

Zedillo, Ernesto, 261, 263, 272